INSTRUCTOR'S MANUAL

C++ HOW TO PROGRAM

Second Edition

H.M. DEITEL
DEITEL & ASSOCIATES

P.J. DEITEL
DEITEL & ASSOCIATES

with T.R. NIETO
DEITEL & ASSOCIATES

PRENTICE HALL, Upper Saddle River, NJ 07458

Acquisitions Editor: Laura Steele
Special Projects Manager: Barbara A. Murray
Production Editor: Mindy DePalma
Supplement Cover Manager: Paul Gourhan
Supplement Cover Designer: Liz Nemeth
Manufacturing Buyer: Donna Sullivan
Editorial Assistant: Kate Kaibni

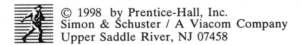

© 1998 by Prentice-Hall, Inc.
Simon & Schuster / A Viacom Company
Upper Saddle River, NJ 07458

Printed in the United States of America

10 9 8 7 6 5 4 3 2 1

ISBN 0-13-565912-4

Prentice-Hall International (UK) Limited, *London*
Prentice-Hall of Australia Pty. Limited, *Sydney*
Prentice-Hall Canada, Inc., *London*
Prentice-Hall Hispanoamericana, S.A., *Mexico*
Prentice-Hall of India Private Limited, *New Delhi*
Prentice-Hall of Japan, Inc., *Tokyo*
Simon & Schuster Asia Pte. Ltd., *Singapore*
Editora Prentice-Hall do Brazil, Ltda., *Rio de Janeiro*

Preface

The old guy (H.M.D) and the young guy (P.J.D) would like to thank you for considering and/or adopting our text *C++ How to Program: Second Edition.* We have worked hard to produce a textbook and ancillaries that we hope you and your students will find valuable.

Before designing this ancillary package, we spoke with college professors and professional seminar instructors who offer C++ courses worldwide. We asked what ancillaries would be most valuable to them. The most frequent request was for a PC-format disk containing all the C++ source code for the programs in the text. Instructors indicate this would help them prepare lectures faster and with the assurance that the programs really work. Many instructors said they would also like to make the programs available to their students. The second most frequent request was for disks with answers to the exercises in the book. Instructors indicated this would be helpful for assigning homework problems and distributing selected solutions in machine-readable format to students.

The enclosed PC-format disk contains 248 programs from the text and 290 program solutions to the exercises. The disk includes two PC-format ZIP compressed files: `example.zip` contains the text examples and `solution.zip` contains the programming exercise solutions. The programs are separated into directories by chapter and by example or solution. All these materials have been tested in our classes and professional seminars. When extracting the source code from these ZIP files, you must use a ZIP-file reader that understands directories such as WinZip (`http://www.winzip.com`) or PKZIP (`http://www.pkware.com`). Each file should be extracted into a separate directory (e.g., examples and solutions).

A key feature of the text is the substantial term project introduced in Chapters 1 through 7—an object-oriented elevator simulator. We carefully guide the student through the object-oriented design and programming of an elevator simulator. We have thoroughly class tested this problem with positive results. The students enjoy the substantial challenge, reinforce their knowledge of C++ and OOP, and compete amongst themselves to develop the best implementations. We have grouped the solutions for the elevator simulator problems at the end of this instructor's manual into a 36 page appendix,

A word of caution: C++ is in transition to the new ANSI/ISO version. Some compilers support the new features and some do not. In this second edition, we have concentrated the new features in Chapters 19–21. The programs in Chapters 1–18 should generally run on older and newer compilers. The programs in Chapters 19–21 will require the newer compilers.

We would sincerely appreciate your comments, criticisms and corrections. Please send them to:

`deitel@deitel.com`

We will respond immediately. Watch our Deitel & Associates, Inc. web site and our Prentice Hall web site for book and product updates

`http://www.deitel.com`
`http://www.prenhall.com/deitel`

We would like to thank the extraordinary team of publishing professionals at Prentice Hall who made *C++ How to Program: Second Edition* and its ancillaries possible. Our Computer Science editor, Laura Steele, worked closely with us to ensure the timely availability and professional quality of these ancillaries. We would also like to extend a special note of thanks to our Deitel & Associates, Inc. colleague, Temujin Nieto, who put many months of effort into writing a major portion of the solutions that appear in this instructor's manual.

Harvey M. Deitel
Paul J. Deitel

Contents

Chapter 1 Solutions

Introduction to Computers and C++ Programming

Solutions

1.10 Categorize each of the following items as either hardware or software:

    a) CPU
    ANS: hardware.
    b) C++ compiler
    ANS: software.
    c) ALU
    ANS: hardware.
    d) C++ preprocessor
    ANS: software.
    e) input unit
    ANS: hardware.
    f) an editor program
    ANS: software.

1.11 Why might you want to write a program in a machine-independent language instead of a machine-dependent language? Why might a machine-dependent language be more appropriate for writing certain types of programs?

    ANS: Machine independent languages are useful for writing programs to be executed on multiple computer platforms. Machine dependent languages are appropriate for writing programs to be executed on a single platform. Machine dependent languages tend to exploit the efficiencies of a particular machine.

1.12 Fill in the blanks in each of the following statements:

    a) Which logical unit of the computer receives information from outside the computer for use by the computer? _____.
    ANS: input unit.
    b) The process of instructing the computer to solve specific problems is called _____.
    ANS: computer programming.
    c) What type of computer language uses English-like abbreviations for machine language instructions? _____.
    ANS: high-level language.
    d) Which logical unit of the computer sends information that has already been processed by the computer to various devices so that the information may be used outside the computer? _____.
    ANS: output unit.
    e) Which logical unit of the computer retains information? _____.
    ANS: memory unit and secondary storage unit.
    f) Which logical unit of the computer performs calculations? _____.
    ANS: arithmetic and logical unit.
    g) Which logical unit of the computer makes logical decisions? _____.
    ANS: arithmetic and logical unit.
    h) The level of computer language most convenient to the programmer for writing programs quickly and easily is _____.
    ANS: high-level language.
    i) The only language that a computer can directly understand is called that computer's _____.
    ANS: machine language.
    j) Which logical unit of the computer coordinates the activities of all the other logical units? _____.
    ANS: central processing unit.

1.13   Discuss the meaning of each of the following objects:

a) **cin**

ANS: This object refers to the standard input device that is normally connected to the keyboard.

b) **cout**

ANS: This object refers to the standard output device that is normally connected to the computer screen.

c) **cerr**

ANS: This object refers to the standard error device that is normally connected to the computer screen.

1.14   Why is so much attention today focused on object-oriented programming in general and C++ in particular?

ANS: Object-oriented programming enables the programmer to build reusable software components that model items in the real world. Building software quickly, correctly, and economically has been an elusive goal in the software industry. The modular, object-oriented design and implementation approach has been found to increase productivity 10 to 100 times over conventional programming languages while reducing development time, errors, and cost. C++ is extremely popular because it is a superset of the widely used C programming language. Programmers already framilar with C have an easier time learing C++.

1.15   Fill in the blanks in each of the following:

a) _____ are used to document a program and improve its readability.

ANS: comments

b) The object used to print information on the screen is _____.

ANS: cout

c) A C++ statement that makes a decision is _____.

ANS: if

d) Calculations are normally performed by _____ statements.

ANS: assignment

e) The _____ object inputs values from the keyboard.

ANS: cin

1.16   Write a single C++ statement or line that accomplishes each of the following:

a) Print the message **"Enter two numbers"**.

ANS: cout << "Enter two numbers";

b) Assign the product of variables **b** and **c** to variable **a**.

ANS: a = b * c;

c) State that a program performs a sample payroll calculation (i.e., use text that helps to document a program).

ANS: // Sample Payroll Calculation Program

d) Input three integer values from the keyboard and into integer variables **a**, **b**, and **c**.

ANS: cin >> a >> b >> c;

1.17   State which of the following are true and which are false. Explain your answers.

a) C++ operators are evaluated from left to right.

ANS: False. Some operators are evaluated from left to right, while other operators are evaluated right to left.

b) The following are all valid variable names: **_under_bar_**, **m928134**, **t5**, **j7**, **her_sales**, **his_account_total**, **a**, **b**, **c**, **z**, **z2**.

ANS: True. All variables begin with an underscore or letter.

c) The statement **cout << "a = 5;";** is a typical example of an assignment statement.

ANS: False. The statement is an output statement. **a = 5;** is output to the screen.

d) A valid C++ arithmetic expression with no parentheses is evaluated from left to right.

ANS: False. Arithmetic operators can appear in any order in an expression. Since multiplication, division, and modulus have higher precendence than addition and subtraction the statement cannot be true.

e) The following are all invalid variable names: **3g**, **87**, **67h2**, **h22**, **2h**.

ANS: False. **h22** is a valid variable name.

1.18   Fill in the blanks in each of the following:

a) What arithmetic operations are on the same level of precedence as multiplication? _____.

ANS: division and modulus.

b) When parentheses are nested, which set of parentheses is evaluated first in an arithmetic expression? _____.

ANS: innermost.

c) A location in the computer's memory that may contain different values at various times throughout the execution of a program is called a _____.

ANS: variable.

1.19 What, if anything, prints when each of the following C++ statements is performed? If nothing prints, then answer "nothing." Assume `x = 2` and `y = 3`.

    a) `cout << x;`
    ANS: 2
    b) `cout << x + x;`
    ANS: 4
    c) `cout << "x=";`
    ANS: x=
    d) `cout << "x = " << x;`
    ANS: x = 2
    e) `cout << x + y << " = " << y + x;`
    ANS: 5 = 5
    f) `z = x + y;`
    ANS: nothing.
    g) `cin >> x >> y;`
    ANS: 23
    h) `// cout << "x + y = " << x + y;`
    ANS: nothing.
    i) `cout << "\n";`
    ANS: A newline is output which positions the cursor at the beginning of the next line on the screen.

1.20 Which of the following C++ statements contain variables whose values are destroyed?

    a) `cin >> b >> c >> d >> e >> f;`
    b) `p = i + j + k + 7;`
    c) `cout << "variables whose values are destroyed";`
    d) `cout << "a = 5";`
    ANS: Parts (a) and (b).

1.21 Given the algebraic equation $y = ax^3 + 7$, which of the following, if any, are correct C++ statements for this equation?

    a) `y = a * x * x * x + 7;`
    b) `y = a * x * x * (x + 7);`
    c) `y = (a * x) * x * (x + 7);`
    d) `y = (a * x) * x * x + 7;`
    e) `y = a * (x * x * x) + 7;`
    f) `y = a * x * (x * x + 7);`
    ANS: Parts (a), (d), and (e).

1.22 State the order of evaluation of the operators in each of the following C++ statements, and show the value of `x` after each statement is performed.

    a) `x = 7 + 3 * 6 / 2 - 1;`
    ANS: *, /, +, -, =, *15*
    b) `x = 2 % 2 + 2 * 2 - 2 / 2;`
    ANS: %, *, /, +, -, =, *3*
    c) `x = (3 * 9 * (3 + (9 * 3/ (3))));`
    ANS: 5 6   4   2 3 1, *324*

1.23 Write a program that asks the user to enter two numbers, obtains the two numbers from the user, and prints the sum, product, difference, and quotient of the two numbers.

    ANS:

```
1   // Exercise 1.23 Solution
2   #include <iostream.h>
3
4   int main()
5   {
6      int num1, num2;  // declare variables
7
8      cout << "Enter two integers: ";  // prompt user
9      cin >> num1 >> num2;             // read values from keyboard
10
```

```
11        // output the results
12        cout << "The sum is " << num1 + num2 << endl
13             << "The product is " << num1 * num2 << endl
14             << "The difference is " << num1 - num2 << endl
15             << "The quotient is " << num1 / num2 << endl;
16
17        return 0;  // indicate successful termination
18    }
```

```
Enter two integers: 8 22
The sum is 30
The product is 176
The difference is -14
The quotient is 0
```

1.24   Write a program that prints the numbers 1 to 4 on the same line with each pair of adjacent numbers separated by one space. Write the program using the following methods:

    a) Using one output statement with one stream insertion operator.

    b) Using one output statement with four stream insertion operators.

    c) Using four output statements.

    ANS:

```
1    // Exercise 1.24 Solution
2    #include <iostream.h>
3
4    int main ()
5    {
6       // Part A
7       cout << "1 2 3 4\n";
8
9       // Part B
10      cout << "1 " << "2 " << "3 " << "4\n";
11
12      // Part C
13      cout << "1 ";
14      cout << "2 ";
15      cout << "3 ";
16      cout << "4" << endl;
17
18      return 0;
19   }
```

```
1 2 3 4
1 2 3 4
1 2 3 4
```

1.25   Write a program that asks the user to enter two integers, obtains the numbers from the user, then prints the larger number followed by the words "**is larger.**" If the numbers are equal, print the message "**These numbers are equal.**"

    ANS:

```
1    // Exercise 1.25 Solution
2    #include <iostream.h>
3
4    int main()
5    {
6       int num1, num2;    // declaration
7
8       cout << "Enter two integers: ";  // prompt
9       cin >> num1 >> num2;             // input to numbers
```

```
10
11      if ( num1 == num2 )
12         cout << "These numbers are equal." << endl;
13
14      if ( num1 > num2 )
15         cout << num1 << " is larger." << endl;
16
17      if ( num2 > num1 )
18         cout << num2 << " is larger." << endl;
19
20      return 0;
21   }
```

```
     Enter two integers: 22 8
     22 is larger.
```

1.26   Write a program that inputs three integers from the keyboard, and prints the sum, average, product, smallest, and largest of these numbers. The screen dialogue should appear as follows:

```
     Input three different integers: 13 27 14
     Sum is 54
     Average is 18
     Product is 4914
     Smallest is 13
     Largest is 27
```

ANS:

```
1    // Exercise 1.26 Solution
2    #include <iostream.h>
3
4    int main()
5    {
6       int num1, num2, num3, smallest, largest;  // declaration
7
8       cout << "Input three different integers: ";  // prompt
9       cin >> num1 >> num2 >> num3;                 // input
10
11      largest = num1;  // assume first number is largest
12
13      if ( num2 > largest )  // is num2 larger?
14         largest = num2;
15
16      if ( num3 > largest )  // is num3 larger?
17         largest = num3;
18
19      smallest = num1;  // assume first number is smallest
20
21      if ( num2 < smallest )
22         smallest = num2;
23
24      if ( num3 < smallest )
25         smallest = num3;
26
27      cout << "Sum is " << num1 + num2 + num3
28           << "\nAverage is " << (num1 + num2 + num3) / 3
29           << "\nProduct is " << num1 * num2 * num3
30           << "\nSmallest is " << smallest
31           << "\nLargest is " << largest << endl;
32
33      return 0;
34   }
```

1.27   Write a program that reads in the radius of a circle and prints the circle's diameter, circumference, and area. Use the constant value 3.14159 for π. Do these calculations in output statements. (Note: In this chapter, we have discussed only integer constants and variables. In Chapter 3 we will discuss floating point numbers, i.e., values that can have decimal points.)

        ANS:

```
1   // Exercise 1.27 Solution
2   #include <iostream.h>
3
4   int main()
5   {
6      int radius;  // declaration
7
8      cout << "Enter the circle radius: ";  // prompt
9      cin >> radius;                        // input
10
11     cout << "Diameter is " << radius * 2.0
12          << "\nCircumference is " << 2 * 3.14159 * radius
13          << "\nArea is " << 3.14159 * radius * radius << endl;
14
15     return 0;
16  }
```

```
Enter the circle radius: 8
Diameter is 16
Circumference is 50.2654
Area is 201.062
```

1.28   Write a program that prints a box, an oval, an arrow, and a diamond as follows:

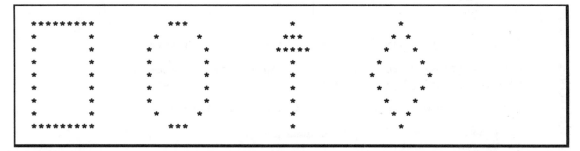

        ANS:

```
1   // Exercise 1.28 Solution
2   #include <iostream.h>
3
4   main()
5   {
6      cout << "*********    ***       *         *\n"
7           << "*       *   *   *     ***       * *\n"
8           << "*       *  *     *   *****      *   *\n"
9           << "*       *  *     *     *       *     *\n"
10          << "*       *  *     *     *      *       *\n"
11          << "*       *  *     *     *       *     *\n"
12          << "*       *  *     *     *        *   *\n"
13          << "*       *   *   *     *          * *\n"
14          << "*********    ***       *           *" << endl;
15
16     return 0;
17  }
```

1.29 What does the following code print?

```
cout << "*\n**\n***\n****\n*****\n";
```

ANS:

```
*
**
***
****
*****
```

1.30 Write a program that reads in five integers and determines and prints the largest and the smallest integers in the group. Use only the programming techniques you learned in this chapter.

ANS:

```cpp
// Exercise 1.30 Solution
#include <iostream.h>

int main()
{
   int num1, num2, num3, num4, num5, largest, smallest;

   cout << "Enter five integers: ";
   cin >> num1 >> num2 >> num3 >> num4 >> num5;

   largest = num1;

   if ( num1 > largest )
      largest = num1;

   if ( num2 > largest )
      largest = num2;

   if ( num3 > largest )
      largest = num3;

   if ( num4 > largest )
      largest = num4;

   if ( num5 > largest )
      largest = num5;

   if ( num1 < smallest )
      smallest = num1;

   if ( num2 < smallest )
      smallest = num2;

   if ( num3 < smallest )
      smallest = num3;

   if ( num4 < smallest )
      smallest = num4;

   if ( num5 < smallest )
      smallest = num5;

   cout << "Largest is " << largest
        << "\nSmallest is " << smallest << endl;

   return 0;
}
```

```
Enter five integers: 88 22 8 78 21
Largest is 88
Smallest is 8
```

1.31   Write a program that reads an integer and determines and prints whether it is odd or even. (Hint: Use the modulus operator. An even number is a multiple of two. Any multiple of two leaves a remainder of zero when divided by 2.)

ANS:

```
1   // Exercise 1.31 Solution
2   #include <iostream.h>
3
4   int main()
5   {
6      int num;
7
8      cout << "Enter a number: ";
9      cin >> num;
10
11     if ( num % 2 == 0 )
12        cout << "The number " << num << " is even." << endl;
13
14     if ( num % 2 != 0 )
15        cout << "The number " << num << " is odd." << endl;
16
17     return 0;
18  }
```

```
Enter a number: 73
The number 73 is odd.
```

1.32   Write a program that reads in two integers and determines and prints if the first is a multiple of the second. (Hint: Use the modulus operator.)

ANS:

```
1   // Exercise 1.32 Solution
2   #include <iostream.h>
3
4   int main()
5   {
6      int num1, num2;
7
8      cout << "Enter two integers: ";
9      cin >> num1 >> num2;
10
11     if ( num1 % num2 == 0 )
12        cout << num1 << " is a multiple of " << num2 << endl;
13
14     if ( num1 % num2 != 0 )
15        cout << num1 << " is not a multiple of " << num2 << endl;
16
17     return 0;
18  }
```

```
Enter two integers: 22 8
22 is not a multiple of 8
```

1.33   Display a checkerboard pattern with eight output statements, then display the same pattern with as few output statements as possible.

```
    * * * * * * * *
     * * * * * * * *
    * * * * * * * *
     * * * * * * * *
    * * * * * * * *
     * * * * * * * *
    * * * * * * * *
     * * * * * * * *
```

ANS:

```
1   // Exercise 1.33 Solution
2   #include <iostream.h>
3
4   int main()
5   {
6      // Eight output statements
7      cout << "* * * * * * *\n";
8      cout << " * * * * * * * *\n";
9      cout << "* * * * * * * *\n";
10     cout << " * * * * * * * *\n";
11     cout << "* * * * * * * *\n";
12     cout << " * * * * * * * *\n";
13     cout << "* * * * * * * *\n";
14     cout << " * * * * * * * *\n\n";
15
16     // One output statement; 3 parts
17     cout << "* * * * * * * *\n * * * * * * * *\n* * * * * * * *\n"
18          << " * * * * * * * *\n* * * * * * * *\n * * * * * * * *\n"
19          << "* * * * * * * *\n * * * * * * * *\n";
20
21     cout << endl;    // ensure everything is displayed
22     return 0;
23  }
```

1.34 Distinguish between the terms fatal error and non–fatal error. Why might you prefer to experience a fatal error rather than a non–fatal error?

> **ANS:** A fatal error causes a program to terminate prematurely. A nonfatal error occurs when the logic of the program is incorrect, and the program does not work properly. A fatal error is preferred for debugging purposes. A fatal error immediately lets you know there is a problem with the program, whereas a nonfatal error can be subtle and possibly go undetected.

1.35 Here's a peek ahead. In this chapter you learned about integers and the type **int**. C++ can also represent uppercase letters, lowercase letters, and a considerable variety of special symbols. C++ uses small integers internally to represent each different character. The set of characters a computer uses and the corresponding integer representations for those characters is called that computer's *character set*. You can print a character by simply enclosing that character in single quotes as with

```
cout << 'A';
```

You can print the integer equivalent of a character by preceding that character with **(int)**—this is called a *cast* (we will say more about casts in Chapter 2):

```
cout << (int) 'A';
```

When the preceding statement executes, it prints the value 65 (on systems that use the so-called *ASCII character set*). Write a program that prints the integer equivalents of some uppercase letters, lowercase letters, digits and special symbols. At a minimum, determine the integer equivalents of the following: **A B C a b c 0 1 2 $ * + /** and the blank character.

> **ANS:** NOTE: This problem statement incorrectly uses the C-style cast operator. Draft Standard ANSI C++ introduces the **static_cast** operator for casting. This operator is introduced in Chapter 2. The solution presented here uses **static_cast**.

```
1   // Exercise 1.35 Solution
2   #include <iostream.h>
3
4   int main()
5   {
6      char symbol;
7
8      cout << "Enter a character: ";
9      cin >> symbol;
10
11     cout << symbol << "'s integer equivalent is "
12          << static_cast< int >( symbol ) << endl;
13
14     return 0;
15  }
```

```
Enter a character: A
A's integer equivalent is 65
```

1.36 Write a program that inputs a five-digit number, separates the number into its individual digits and prints the digits separated from one another by three spaces each. (Hint: Use the integer division and modulus operators.) For example, if the user types in **42339** the program should print

```
4   2   3   3   9
```

ANS:

```
1   // Exercise 1.36 Solution
2   #include <iostream.h>
3
4   int main()
5   {
6      int num;
7
8      cout << "Enter a five-digit number: ";
9      cin >> num;
10
11     cout << num / 10000 << "    ";
12     num = num % 10000;
13     cout << num / 1000 << "   ";
14     num = num % 1000;
15     cout << num / 100 << "   ";
16     num = num % 100;
17     cout << num / 10 << "   ";
18     num = num % 10;
19     cout << num << endl;
20
21     return 0;
22  }
```

```
Enter a five-digit number: 23456
2   3   4   5   6
```

1.37 Using only the techniques you learned in this chapter, write a program that calculates the squares and cubes of the numbers from 0 to 10 and uses tabs to print the following table of values:

```
number   square   cube
  0         0        0
  1         1        1
  2         4        8
  3         9       27
  4        16       64
  5        25      125
  6        36      216
  7        49      343
  8        64      512
  9        81      729
 10       100     1000
```

ANS:

```
1   // Exercise 1.37 Solution
2   #include <iostream.h>
3
4   int main()
5   {
6      int num;
7
8      num = 0;
9      cout << "\nnumber\tsquare\tcube\n"
10          << num << '\t' << num * num << '\t' << num * num * num << "\n";
11
12     num = num + 1;
13     cout << num << '\t' << num * num << '\t' << num * num * num << "\n";
14
15     num = num + 1;
16     cout << num << '\t' << num * num << '\t' << num * num * num << "\n";
17
18     num = num + 1;
19     cout << num << '\t' << num * num << '\t' << num * num * num << "\n";
20
21     num = num + 1;
22     cout << num << '\t' << num * num << '\t' << num * num * num << "\n";
23
24     num = num + 1;
25     cout << num << '\t' << num * num << '\t' << num * num * num << "\n";
26
27     num = num + 1;
28     cout << num << '\t' << num * num << '\t' << num * num * num << "\n";
29
30     num = num + 1;
31     cout << num << '\t' << num * num << '\t' << num * num * num << "\n";
32
33     num = num + 1;
34     cout << num << '\t' << num * num << '\t' << num * num * num << "\n";
35
36     num = num + 1;
37     cout << num << '\t' << num * num << '\t' << num * num * num << "\n";
38
39     num = num + 1;
40     cout << num << '\t' << num * num << '\t' << num * num * num << endl;
41
42     return 0;
43  }
```

1.38 Give a brief answer to each of the following "object think" questions:

   a) Why does this text choose to discuss structured programming in detail before proceeding with an in-depth treatment of object-oriented programming?

ANS: Objects are composed in part by structured program pieces.

b) What are the typical steps (mentioned in the text) of an object-oriented design process?

ANS: (1) Determine which objects are needed to implement the system. (2) Determine's each object's attributes. (3) Determine each object's behaviors. (4) Determine the interaction between the objects.

c) How is multiple inheritance exhibited by human beings?

ANS: Children. A child receives genes from both parents.

d) What kinds of messages do people send to one another?

ANS: People send messages through body language, speech, writings, email, telephones, etc.

e) Objects send messages to one another across well-defined interfaces. What interfaces does a car radio (object) present to its user (a person object)?

ANS: Dials and buttons that allow the user to select a station, adjust the volume, adjust bass and treble, play a CD or tape, etc.

1.39   You are probably wearing on your wrist one of the world's most common types of objects—a watch. Discuss how each of the following terms and concepts applies to the notion of a watch: object, attributes, behaviors, class, inheritance (consider, for example, an alarm clock), abstraction, modeling, messages, encapsulation, interface, information hiding, data members, and member functions.

ANS: The entire watch is an object that is composed of many other objects (such as the moving parts, the band, the face, etc.) Watch attributes are time, color, band, style (digital or analog), etc. The behaviors of the watch include setting the time and getting the time. A watch can be considered a specific type of clock (as can an alarm clock). With that in mind, it is possible that a class called **Clock** could exist from which other classes such as watch and alarm clock can inherit the basic features in the clock. The watch is an abstraction of the mechanics needed to keep track of the time. The user of the watch does not need to know the mechanics of the watch in order to use it; the user only needs to know that the watch keeps the proper time. In this sense, the mechanics of the watch are encapsulated (hidden) inside the watch. The interface to the watch (its face and controls for setting the time) allows the user to set and get the time. The user is not allowed to directly touch the internal mechanics of the watch. All interaction with the internal mechanics is controlled by the interface to the watch. The data members stored in the watch are hidden inside the watch and the member functions (looking at the face to get the time and setting the time) provide the interface to the data.

Chapter 2 Solutions

Control Structures

Solutions

2.14 Identify and correct the errors in each of the following (Note: There may be more than one error in each piece of code):

a)
```
if ( age >= 65 );
    cout << "Age is greater than or equal to 65" << endl;
else
    cout << "Age is less than 65 << endl";
```
ANS: The semicolon at the end of the **if** should be removed. The closing double quote after the second **endl** should be placed after **65**.

b)
```
if ( age >= 65 )
    cout << "Age is greater than or equal to 65" << endl;
else;
    cout << "Age is less than 65 << endl";
```
ANS: The semicolon after the **else** should be removed. The closing double quote after the second **endl** should be placed after **65**.

c)
```
int x = 1, total;
while ( x <= 10 ) {
    total += x;
    ++x;
}
```
ANS: Variable **total** should be initialized to **0**.

d)
```
While ( x <= 100 )
    total += x;
    ++x;
```
ANS: The **W** in **while** should be lowercase. The **while**'s body should be enclosed in braces **{ }**.

e)
```
while ( y > 0 ) {
    cout << y << endl;
    ++y;
}
```
ANS: The variable **y** should be decremented (i.e., **--y;**) not incremented (**++y;**).

2.15 What does the following program print?
```
#include <iostream.h>
int main()
{
    int y, x = 1, total = 0;
    while ( x <= 10 ) {
        y = x * x;
        cout << y << endl;
        total += y;
        ++x;
    }
    cout << "Total is " << total << endl;
    return 0;
}
```

ANS:

```
1
4
9
16
25
36
49
64
81
100
Total is 385
```

For Exercises 2.16 to 2.19 perform each of these steps:
 a) Read the problem statement.
 b) Formulate the algorithm using pseudocode and top-down, stepwise refinement.
 c) Write a C++ program.
 d) Test, debug, and execute the C++ program.

2.16   Drivers are concerned with the mileage obtained by their automobiles. One driver has kept track of several tankfuls of gasoline by recording miles driven and gallons used for each tankful. Develop a C++ program that will input the miles driven and gallons used for each tankful. The program should calculate and display the miles per gallon obtained for each tankful. After processing all input information, the program should calculate and print the combined miles per gallon obtained for all tankfuls.

```
Enter the gallons used (-1 to end): 12.8
Enter the miles driven: 287
The miles / gallon for this tank was 22.421875

Enter the gallons used (-1 to end): 10.3
Enter the miles driven: 200
The miles / gallon for this tank was 19.417475

Enter the gallons used (-1 to end): 5
Enter the miles driven: 120
The miles / gallon for this tank was 24.000000

Enter the gallons used (-1 to end): -1

The overall average miles/gallon was 21.601423
```

ANS:
 Top:
 Determine the average miles/gallon for each tank of gas, and the overall miles/gallons for an arbitrary
   number of tanks of gas.

 First refinement:
 Initialize variables.
 Input the gallons used and the miles driven, and calculate and print the miles/gallon for each tank of gas.
   Keep track of the total miles and total gallons.
 Calculate and print the overall average miles/gallon.

 Second refinement:
 Initialize totalGallons to zero
 Initialize totalMiles to zero

 Input the gallons used for the first tank

While the sentinel value (-1) has not been entered for the gallons
    Add gallons to the running total in totalGallons
    Input the miles driven for the current tank
    Add miles to the running total in totalMiles
    Calculate and print the miles/gallon
    Input the gallons used for thenext tank

Print the average miles/gallon

```
1   // Exercise 2.16 Solution
2   #include <iostream.h>
3
4   int main()
5   {
6      float gallons, miles, totalGallons = 0.0,
7            totalMiles = 0.0, average;
8
9      cout << "Enter the gallons used (-1 to end): ";
10     cin >> gallons;
11
12     while ( gallons != -1.0 ) {
13        totalGallons += gallons;
14
15        cout << "Enter the miles driven: ";
16        cin >> miles;
17        totalMiles += miles;
18
19        cout << "The Miles / Gallon for this tank was "
20             << miles / gallons
21             << "\n\nEnter the gallons used (-1 to end): ";
22        cin >> gallons;
23     }
24
25     average = totalMiles / totalGallons;
26     cout << "\nThe overall average Miles/Gallon was "
27          << average << endl;
28
29     return 0;
30  }
```

```
Enter the gallons used (-1 to end): 16
Enter the miles driven: 220
The Miles / Gallon for this tank was 13.75

Enter the gallons used (-1 to end): 16.5
Enter the miles driven: 272
The Miles / Gallon for this tank was 16.4848

Enter the gallons used (-1 to end): -1

The overall average Miles/Gallon was 15.1385
```

2.17   Develop a C++ program that will determine if a department store customer has exceeded the credit limit on a charge account. For each customer, the following facts are available:
  a) Account number (an integer)
  b) Balance at the beginning of the month
  c) Total of all items charged by this customer this month
  d) Total of all credits applied to this customer's account this month
  e) Allowed credit limit

The program should input each of these facts, calculate the new balance (= beginning balance + charges - credits), and determine if the new balance exceeds the customer's credit limit. For those customers whose credit limit is exceeded, the program should display the customer's account number, credit limit, new balance, and the message "Credit limit exceeded."

```
Enter account number (-1 to end): 100
Enter beginning balance: 5394.78
Enter total charges: 1000.00
Enter total credits: 500.00
Enter credit limit: 5500.00
Account:       100
Credit limit: 5500.00
Balance:       5894.78
Credit Limit Exceeded.

Enter account number (-1 to end): 200
Enter beginning balance: 1000.00
Enter total charges: 123.45
Enter total credits: 321.00
Enter credit limit: 1500.00

Enter account number (-1 to end): 300
Enter beginning balance: 500.00
Enter total charges: 274.73
Enter total credits: 100.00
Enter credit limit: 800.00

Enter account number (-1 to end): -1
```

ANS:

Top:

Determine if each of an arbitrary number of department store customers has exceeded the credit limit on a charge account.

First refinement:

Input the account number, beginning balance, total charges, total credits, and credit limit for a customer, calculate the customer's new balance and determine if the balance exceeds the credit limit. Then process the next customer.

Second refinement:

Input the first customer's account number

While the sentinel value (-1) has not been entered for the account number
    Input the customer's beginning balance
    Input the customer's total charges
    Input the customer's total credits
    Input the customer's credit limit
    Calculate the customer's new balance

    If the balance exceeds the credit limit
        Print the account number
        Print the credit limit
        Print the balance
        Print "Credit Limit Exceeded"

    Input the next customer's account number

```
1   // Exercise 2.17 Solution
2   #include <iostream.h>
3   #include <iomanip.h>
4
5   int main()
6   {
7       int accountNumber;
8       float balance, charges, credits, limit;
9
10      cout << "Enter account number (-1 to end): "
11           << setiosflags(ios::fixed | ios::showpoint);
12      cin >> accountNumber;
13
14      while ( accountNumber != -1 ) {
15         cout << "Enter beginning balance: ";
16         cin >> balance;
17         cout << "Enter total charges: ";
18         cin >> charges;
19         cout << "Enter total credits: ";
20         cin >> credits;
21         cout << "Enter credit limit: ";
22         cin >> limit;
23         balance += charges - credits;
24
25         if ( balance > limit )
26            cout << "Account:        " << accountNumber
27                 << "\nCredit limit: " << setprecision( 2 ) << limit
28                 << "\nBalance:        " << setprecision( 2 ) << balance
29                 << "\nCredit Limit Exceeded.\n";
30
31         cout << "\nEnter account number (-1 to end): ";
32         cin >> accountNumber;
33      }
34
35      cout << endl;  // ensure all output is displayed
36      return 0;
37  }
```

```
Enter account number (-1 to end): 88
Enter beginning balance: 900.57
Enter total charges: 324.78
Enter total credits: 100
Enter credit limit: 1500

Enter account number (-1 to end): 89
Enter beginning balance: 2789.65
Enter total charges: 1540.55
Enter total credits: 25
Enter credit limit: 1500
Account:      89
Credit limit: 1500.00
Balance:      4305.20
Credit Limit Exceeded.

Enter account number (-1 to end): -1
```

2.18   One large chemical company pays its salespeople on a commission basis. The salespeople receive $200 per week plus 9 percent of their gross sales for that week. For example, a salesperson who sells $5000 worth of chemicals in a week receives $200 plus 9 percent of $5000, or a total of $650. Develop a C++ program that will input each salesperson's gross sales for last week and calculate and display that salesperson's earnings. Process one salesperson's figures at a time.

```
Enter sales in dollars (-1 to end): 5000.00
Salary is: $650.00

Enter sales in dollars (-1 to end): 6000.00
Salary is: $740.00

Enter sales in dollars (-1 to end): 7000.00
Salary is: $830.00

Enter sales in dollars (-1 to end): -1
```

ANS:

Top:

For an arbitrary number of salespeople, determine each salesperson's earnings for the last week.

First refinement:

Initialize variables

Input the salesperson's sales for the week, calculate and print the salesperson's wages for the week then process the next salesperson.

Second refinement:

Input the first salesperson's sales in dollars

While the sentinel value (-1) has not been entered for the sales
    Calculate the salesperson's wages for the week
    Print the salesperson's wages for the week
    Input the next salesperson's sales in dollars

```cpp
1   // Exercise 2.18 Solution
2   #include <iostream.h>
3   #include <iomanip.h>
4
5   int main()
6   {
7      float sales, wage;
8
9      cout << "Enter sales in dollars (-1 to end): "
10            << setiosflags( ios::fixed | ios::showpoir' );
11     cin >> sales;
12
13     while ( sales != -1.0 ) {
14        wage = 200.0 + 0.09 * sales;
15        cout << "Salary is: $" << setprecision( 2 ) << wage
16              << "\n\nEnter sales in dollars (-1 to end): ";
17        cin >> sales;
18     }
19
20     return 0;
21  }
```

```
Enter sales in dollars (-1 to end): 7000
Salary is: $830.00

Enter sales in dollars (-1 to end): 500
Salary is: $245.00

Enter sales in dollars (-1 to end): -1
```

2.19 Develop a C++ program that will determine the gross pay for each of several employees. The company pays "straight-time" for the first 40 hours worked by each employee and pays "time-and-a-half" for all hours worked in excess of 40 hours. You are given a list of the employees of the company, the number of hours each employee worked last week, and the hourly rate of each employee. Your program should input this information for each employee, and should determine and display the employee's gross pay.

```
Enter hours worked (-1 to end): 39
Enter hourly rate of the worker ($00.00): 10.00
Salary is $390.00

Enter hours worked (-1 to end): 40
Enter hourly rate of the worker ($00.00): 10.00
Salary is $400.00

Enter hours worked (-1 to end): 41
Enter hourly rate of the worker ($00.00): 10.00
Salary is $415.00

Enter hours worked (-1 to end): -1
```

ANS:
Top:
Determine the gross pay for an arbitrary number of employees

Second refinement:
Input the hours worked for the first employee

While the sentinel value (-1) has not been entered for the hours
    Input the employee's hourly rate

    If the hours input is less than or equal to 40
        Calculate gross pay by multiplying hours worked by hourly rate
    Else
        Calculate gross pay by multiplying hours worked above forty by 1.5 times the hourly rate and adding 40 hours worked by the hourly rate.
    Display the employee's gross pay.
    Input the hours worked for thenext employee

    Print the average miles/gallon

```
1  // Exercise 2.19 Solution
2  #include <iostream.h>
3  #include <iomanip.h>
4
5  int main()
6  {
7     float hours, rate, salary;
8
```

```
9      cout << "Enter hours worked (-1 to end): "
10          << setiosflags( ios::fixed | ios::showpoint );
11     cin >> hours;
12
13     while ( hours != -1.0 ) {
14        cout << "Enter hourly rate of the worker ($00.00): ";
15        cin >> rate;
16
17        if ( hours <= 40 )
18           salary = hours * rate;
19        else
20           salary = 40.0 * rate + ( hours - 40.0 ) * rate * 1.5;
21
22        cout << "Salary is $" << setprecision( 2 ) << salary
23             << "\n\nEnter hours worked (-1 to end): ";
24        cin >> hours;
25     }
26
27     return 0;
28  }
```

```
Enter hours worked (-1 to end): 40
Enter hourly rate of the worker ($00.00): 10
Salary is $400.00

Enter hours worked (-1 to end): 50
Enter hourly rate of the worker ($00.00): 10
Salary is $550.00

Enter hours worked (-1 to end): -1
```

2.20   The process of finding the largest number (i.e., the maximum of a group of numbers) is used frequently in computer applications. For example, a program that determines the winner of a sales contest would input the number of units sold by each salesperson. The salesperson who sells the most units wins the contest. Write a pseudocode program and then a C++ program that inputs a series of 10 numbers, and determines and prints the largest of the numbers. Hint: Your program should use three variables as follows:

counter: A counter to count to 10 (i.e., to keep track of how many numbers have been input, and to determine when all 10 numbers have been processed).
number: The current number input to the program.
largest: The largest number found so far.

ANS:

```
1   // Exercise 2.20 solution
2   #include <iostream.h>
3
4   int main()
5   {
6      int counter = 0, number, largest;
7
8      cout << "Enter the first number: ";
9      cin >> largest;
10
11     while ( ++counter < 10 ) {
12        cout << "Enter the next number : ";
13        cin >> number;
14
15        if ( number > largest )
16           largest = number;
17     }
18
```

```
19    cout << "Largest is " << largest << endl;
20    return 0;
21  }
```

```
Enter the first number: 78
Enter the next number : 19
Enter the next number : 99
Enter the next number : 33
Enter the next number : 22
Enter the next number : 10
Enter the next number : 8
Enter the next number : 88
Enter the next number : 22
Enter the next number : 34
Largest is 99
```

2.21   Write a C++ program that utilizes looping and the tab escape sequence \t to print the following table of values:

```
N       10*N    100*N   1000*N

1       10      100     1000
2       20      200     2000
3       30      300     3000
4       40      400     4000
5       50      500     5000
```

ANS:

```
1   // Exercise 2.21 Solution
2   #include <iostream.h>
3
4   int main()
5   {
6      int n = 0;
7
8      cout << "N\t10 * N\t100 * N\t1000 * N\n\n";
9
10     while ( ++n <= 5 )
11        cout << n << '\t' << 10 * n << '\t' << 100 * n
12            << '\t' << 1000 * n << '\n';
13
14     cout << endl;
15     return 0;
16  }
```

```
N       10 * N  100 * N 1000 * N

1       10      100     1000
2       20      200     2000
3       30      300     3000
4       40      400     4000
5       50      500     5000
```

2.22   Using an approach similar to Exercise 2.20, find the *two* largest values of the 10 numbers. Note: You may input each number only once.

ANS:

```
1   // Exercise 2.22 Solution
2   #include <iostream.h>
```

```
3
4   int main()
5   {
6      int counter = 0, number, largest, secondLargest = 0;
7
8      cout << "Enter the first number: ";
9      cin >> largest;
10
11     while ( ++counter < 10 ) {
12        cout << "Enter next number: ";
13        cin >> number;
14
15        if ( number > largest ) {
16           secondLargest = largest;
17           largest = number;
18        }
19        else if ( number > secondLargest )
20           secondLargest = number;
21     }
22
23     cout << "\nLargest is " <<  largest
24          << "\nSecond largest is " << secondLargest << endl;
25
26     return 0;
27  }
```

```
Enter the first number: 77
Enter next number: 33
Enter next number: 44
Enter next number: 73
Enter next number: 79
Enter next number: 45
Enter next number: 3
Enter next number: 22
Enter next number: 21
Enter next number: 8

Largest is 79
Second largest is 77
```

2.23   Modify the program in Fig. 2.11 to validate its inputs. On any input, if the value entered is other than 1 or 2, keep looping until the user enters a correct value.

ANS:

```
1   // Exercise 2.23 Solution
2   #include <iostream.h>
3
4   int main()
5   {
6      int passes = 0, failures = 0, student = 0, result;
7
8      while ( ++student <= 10 ) {
9         cout << "Enter result (1=pass, 2=fail): ";
10        cin >> result;
11
12        while ( result != 1 && result != 2 ) {
13           cout << "Invalid result"
14                << "\nEnter result (1=pass, 2=fail): ";
15           cin >> result;
16        }
17
```

```
18          if ( result == 1 )
19              ++passes;
20          else
21              ++failures;
22      }
23
24      cout << "Passed: " << passes
25          << "\nFailed: " << failures;
26
27      if ( passes >= 8 )
28          cout << "\nRaise tuition\n";
29
30      cout << endl;
31      return 0;
32  }
```

```
  Enter result (1=pass, 2=fail): 1
  Enter result (1=pass, 2=fail): 4
  Invalid result
  Enter result (1=pass, 2=fail): 1
  Enter result (1=pass, 2=fail): 1
  Enter result (1=pass, 2=fail): 5
  Invalid result
  Enter result (1=pass, 2=fail): 2
  Enter result (1=pass, 2=fail): 1
  Enter result (1=pass, 2=fail): 1
  Enter result (1=pass, 2=fail): 1
  Enter result (1=pass, 2=fail): 2
  Enter result (1=pass, 2=fail): 2
  Enter result (1=pass, 2=fail): 2
  Passed: 6
  Failed: 4
```

2.24   What does the following program print?

```
#include <iostream.h>
int main()
{
   int count = 1;
   while ( count <= 10 ) {
      cout << ( count % 2 ? "****" : "++++++++" )
           << endl;
      ++count;
   }
   return 0;
}
```

ANS:

```
****
++++++++
****
++++++++
****
++++++++
****
++++++++
****
++++++++
```

2.25   What does the following program print?

```cpp
#include <iostream.h>
int main()
{
   int row = 10, column;
   while ( row >= 1 ) {
      column = 1;
      while ( column <= 10 ) {
         cout << ( row % 2 ? "<" : ">" );
         ++column;
      }
      --row;
      cout << endl;
   }
   return 0;
}
```

ANS:

```
>>>>>>>>>>
<<<<<<<<<<
>>>>>>>>>>
<<<<<<<<<<
>>>>>>>>>>
<<<<<<<<<<
>>>>>>>>>>
<<<<<<<<<<
>>>>>>>>>>
<<<<<<<<<<
```

2.26   *(Dangling Else Problem)* Determine the output for each of the following when **x** is **9** and **y** is **11** and when **x** is **11** and **y** is **9**. Note that the compiler ignores the indentation in a C++ program. Also, the C++ compiler always associates an **else** with the previous **if** unless told to do otherwise by the placement of braces **{ }**. Because, on first glance, the programmer may not be sure which **if** an **else** matches, this is referred to as the "dangling else" problem. We have eliminated the indentation from the following code to make the problem more challenging. (Hint: Apply indentation conventions you have learned.)

a)
```cpp
if ( x < 10 )
if ( y > 10 )
cout << "*****" << endl;
else
cout << "#####" << endl;
cout << "$$$$$" << endl;
```
ANS: x = 9, y = 11

```
*****
$$$$$
```

ANS: x = 11, y = 9

```
$$$$$
```

b)
```cpp
if ( x < 10 ) {
if ( y > 10 )
cout << "*****" << endl;
}
else {
cout << "#####" << endl;
cout << "$$$$$" << endl;
}
```

ANS: x = 9, y = 11

```
*****
```

ANS: x = 11, y = 9

```
#####
$$$$$
```

2.27 *(Another Dangling Else Problem)* Modify the following code to produce the output shown. Use proper indentation techniques. You may not make any changes other than inserting braces. The compiler ignores indentation in a C++ program. We have eliminated the indentation from the following code to make the problem more challenging. Note: It is possible that no modification is necessary.

```
if ( y == 8 )
if ( x == 5 )
cout << "@@@@@" << endl;
else
cout << "#####" << endl;
cout << "$$$$$" << endl;
cout << "&&&&&" << endl;
```

a) Assuming **x = 5** and **y = 8**, the following output is produced.

```
@@@@@
$$$$$
&&&&&
```

ANS:

```
1  if ( y == 8 )
2     if ( x == 5 )
3        cout << "@@@@@\n";
4     else
5        cout << "#####\n";
6
7  cout << "$$$$$\n";
8  cout << "&&&&&\n";
```

b) Assuming **x = 5** and **y = 8**, the following output is produced.

```
@@@@@
```

ANS:

```
1  if ( y == 8 )
2     if ( x == 5 )
3        cout << "@@@@@\n";
4     else {
5        cout << "#####\n";
6        cout << "$$$$$\n";
7        cout << "&&&&&\n";
8     }
```

c) Assuming **x = 5** and **y = 8**, the following output is produced.

```
@@@@@
&&&&&
```

ANS:
```
1   if ( y == 8 )
2      if ( x == 5 )
3         cout << "@@@@@\n";
4      else {
5         cout << "#####\n";
6         cout << "$$$$$\n";
7      }
8
9   cout << "&&&&&\n";
```

d) Assuming **x = 5** and **y = 7**, the following output is produced. Note: The last three output statements after the **else** are all part of a compound statement.

```
#####
$$$$$
&&&&&
```

ANS:
```
1   if ( y == 8 ) {
2      if ( x == 5 )
3         cout << "@@@@@\n";
4   }
5   else {
6      cout << "#####\n";
7      cout << "$$$$$\n";
8      cout << "&&&&&\n";
9   }
```

2.28 Write a program that reads in the size of the side of a square and then prints a hollow square of that size out of asterisks and blanks. Your program should work for squares of all side sizes between 1 and 20. For example, if your program reads a size of 5, it should print

```
*****
*   *
*   *
*   *
*****
```

ANS:

```
1   // Exercise 2.28 Solution
2   #include <iostream.h>
3
4   int main()
5   {
6      int side, rowPosition, size;
7
8      cout << "Enter the square side: ";
9      cin >> side;
10
11     size = side;
12
13     while ( side > 0 ) {
14        rowPosition = size;
15
16        while ( rowPosition > 0 ) {
17
18           if ( size == side || side == 1 || rowPosition == 1 ||
19                rowPosition == size )
```

```
20              cout << '*';
21            else
22              cout << ' ';
23
24            --rowPosition;
25         }
26
27         cout << '\n';
28         --side;
29      }
30
31      cout << endl;
32      return 0;
33   }
```

```
Enter the square side: 8
********
*      *
*      *
*      *
*      *
*      *
*      *
********
```

2.29   A palindrome is a number or a text phrase that reads the same backwards as forwards. For example, each of the following five-digit integers are palindromes: 12321, 55555, 45554 and 11611. Write a program that reads in a five-digit integer and determines whether or not it is a palindrome. (Hint: Use the division and modulus operators to separate the number into its individual digits.)

ANS:

```
1    // Exercise 2.29 Solution
2    #include <iostream.h>
3
4    int main()
5    {
6       int number, firstDigit, secondDigit, fourthDigit, fifthDigit;
7
8       cout << "Enter a five-digit number: ";
9       cin >> number;
10
11      firstDigit = number / 10000;
12      secondDigit = number % 10000 / 1000;
13      fourthDigit = number % 10000 % 1000 % 100 / 10;
14      fifthDigit = number % 10000 % 1000 % 10;
15
16      if ( firstDigit == fifthDigit && secondDigit == fourthDigit )
17         cout << number << " is a palindrome" << endl;
18      else
19         cout << number << " is not a palindrome" << endl;
20
21      return 0;
22   }
```

```
Enter a five-digit number: 57475
57475 is a palindrome
```

2.30   Input an integer containing only 0s and 1s (i.e., a "binary" integer) and print its decimal equivalent. (Hint: Use the modulus and division operators to pick off the "binary" number's digits one at a time from right to left. Just as in the decimal number system where the rightmost digit has a positional value of 1, and the next digit left has a positional value of 10, then

100, then 1000, etc., in the binary number system the rightmost digit has a positional value of 1, the next digit left has a positional value of 2, then 4, then 8, etc. Thus the decimal number 234 can be interpreted as 4 * 1 + 3 * 10 + 2 * 100. The decimal equivalent of binary 1101 is 1 * 1 + 0 * 2 + 1 * 4 + 1 * 8 or 1 + 0 + 4 + 8 or 13.)

ANS:

```
1   // Exercise 2.30 Solution
2   #include <iostream.h>
3
4   int main()
5   {
6      int binary, number, decimal = 0, highBit = 16, factor = 10000;
7
8      cout << "Enter a binary number (5 digits maximum): ";
9      cin >> binary;
10
11     number = binary;
12
13     while ( highBit >= 1 ) {
14        decimal += binary / factor * highBit;
15        highBit /= 2;
16        binary %= factor;
17        factor /= 10;
18     }
19
20     cout << "The decimal equivalent of "
21          << number << " is " << decimal << endl;
22
23     return 0;
24  }
```

```
Enter a binary number (5 digits maximum): 10010
The decimal equivalent of 10010 is 18
```

2.31   Write a program that displays the following checkerboard pattern

```
* * * * * * * *
 * * * * * * * *
* * * * * * * *
 * * * * * * * *
* * * * * * * *
 * * * * * * * *
* * * * * * * *
 * * * * * * * *
```

Your program may use only three output statements, one of each of the following forms:

```
cout << "* ";
cout << ' ';
cout << endl;
```

ANS:

```
1   // Exercise 2.31 Solution
2   #include <iostream.h>
3
4   int main()
5   {
6      int side = 8, row;
7
8      while ( side-- > 0 ) {
```

```
9          row = 8;
10
11         if ( side % 2 == 0 )
12            cout << ' ';
13
14         while ( row-- > 0 )
15            cout << "* ";
16
17         cout << '\n';
18      }
19
20      cout << endl;
21      return 0;
22   }
```

2.32   Write a program that keeps printing the multiples of the integer 2, namely 2, 4, 8, 16, 32, 64, etc. Your loop should not terminate (i.e., you should create an infinite loop). What happens when you run this program?

ANS:

```
1   // Exercise 2.32 Solution
2   #include <iostream.h>
3
4   int main()
5   {
6      int multiple = 1;
7
8      while ( multiple *= 2 )
9         cout << multiple << "\n";
10
11      cout << endl;
12      return 0;
13   }
```

```
2
4
...
32768
65536
131072
262144
524288
1048576
2097152
4194304
8388608
16777216
33554432
67108864
134217728
268435456
536870912
1073741824
-2147483648
```

2.33   Write a program that reads the radius of a circle (as a **float** value) and computes and prints the diameter, the circumference, and the area. Use the value 3.14159 for π.

ANS:

```
1   // Exercise 2.33 Solution
2   #include <iostream.h>
3
```

```
4   int main()
5   {
6      float radius, pi = 3.14159;
7
8      cout << "Enter the radius: ";
9      cin >> radius;
10
11     cout << "The diameter is " << radius * 2.0
12          << "\nThe circumference is " << 2.0 * pi * radius
13          << "\nThe area is " << pi * radius * radius << endl;
14
15     return 0;
16  }
```

```
Enter the radius: 5
The diameter is 10
The circumference is 31.4159
The area is 78.5397
```

2.34   What's wrong with the following statement? Provide the correct statement to accomplish what the programmer was probably trying to do.

```
cout << ++( x + y );
```

ANS: The **++** operator must be used in conjuction with variables. The programmer probably intended to write the statement: **cout << x + y + 1;**.

2.35   Write a program that reads three nonzero **float** values and determines and prints if they could represent the sides of a triangle.

ANS:

```
1   // Exercise 2.35 Solution
2   #include <iostream.h>
3
4   int main()
5   {
6      float a, b, c;
7
8      cout << "Enter three floating point numbers: ";
9      cin >> a >> b >> c;
10
11     if ( c * c == a * a + b * b )
12        cout << "The three numbers could"
13             << " be sides of a right triangle" << endl;
14     else
15        cout << "The three numbers probably"
16             << " are not the sides of a right triangle" << endl;
17
18     return 0;
19  }
```

```
Enter three floating point numbers: 4.5 7.7 6.6
The three numbers probably are not the sides of a right triangle
```

2.36   Write a program that reads three nonzero integers and determines and prints if they could be the sides of a right triangle.

ANS:

```
1   // Exercise 2.36 Solution
2   #include <iostream.h>
3
4   int main()
5   {
6      int a, b, c;
7
8      do {
9         cout << "Enter three integers: ";
10        cin >> a >> b >> c;
11     } while ( a <= 0 || b <= 0 || c <= 0 );
12
13     if ( c * c == a * a + b * b )
14        cout << "The three integers are the"
15             << " sides of a right triangle\n";
16     else
17        cout << "The three integers are not the"
18             << " sides of a right triangle\n";
19
20     cout << endl;
21     return 0;
22  }
```

```
Enter three integers: 3 4 5
The three integers are the sides of a right triangle
```

2.37   A company wants to transmit data over the telephone, but they are concerned that their phones may be tapped. All of their data is transmitted as four-digit integers. They have asked you to write a program that encrypts their data so that it may be transmitted more securely. Your program should read a four-digit integer and encrypt it as follows: Replace each digit by *(the sum of that digit plus 7) modulus 10*. Then, swap the first digit with the third, swap the second digit with the fourth, and print the encrypted integer. Write a separate program that inputs an encrypted four-digit integer, and decrypts it to form the original number.

ANS:

```
1   // Exercise 2.37 Part A Solution
2   #include <iostream.h>
3
4   int main()
5   {
6      int first, second, third, fourth, digit, temp;
7      int encryptedNumber;
8
9      cout << "Enter a four digit number to be encrypted: ";
10     cin >> digit;
11
12     first = ( digit / 1000 + 7 ) % 10;
13     second = ( digit % 1000 / 100 + 7 ) % 10;
14     third = ( digit % 1000 % 100 / 10 + 7 ) % 10;
15     fourth = ( digit % 1000 % 100 % 10 + 7 ) % 10;
16
17     temp = first;
18     first = third * 1000;
19     third = temp * 10;
20
21     temp = second;
22     second = fourth * 100;
23     fourth = temp * 1;
24
25     encryptedNumber = first + second + third + fourth;
26     cout << "Encrypted number is " << encryptedNumber << endl;
27     return 0;
28  }
```

```
Enter a four digit number to be encrypted: 1009
Encrypted number is 7687
```

ANS:

```cpp
1   // Exercise 2.37 Part B Solution
2   #include <iostream.h>
3
4   int main()
5   {
6       int first, second, third, fourth, decrypted, temp, num;
7
8       cout << "Enter a four digit encrypted number: ";
9       cin >> num;
10
11      first = num / 1000;
12      second = num % 1000 / 100;
13      third = num % 1000 % 100 / 10;
14      fourth = num % 1000 % 100 % 10;
15
16      temp = ( first + 3 ) % 10;
17      first = ( third + 3 ) % 10;
18      third = temp;
19
20      temp = ( second + 3 ) % 10;
21      second = ( fourth + 3 ) % 10;
22      fourth = temp;
23
24      decrypted = first * 1000 + second * 100 + third * 10 + fourth;
25      cout << "Decrypted number is " << decrypted << endl;
26      return 0;
27  }
```

```
Enter a four digit encrypted number: 7687
Decrypted number is 1009
```

2.38   The factorial of a nonnegative integer n is written $n!$ (pronounced "n factorial") and is defined as follows:
$n! = n \cdot (n - 1) \cdot (n - 2) \cdot ... \cdot 1$ (for values of n greater than or equal to 1)
and
$n! = 1$ (for $n = 0$).
For example, $5! = 5 \cdot 4 \cdot 3 \cdot 2 \cdot 1$ which is 120.

a) Write a program that reads a nonnegative integer and computes and prints its factorial.
b) Write a program that estimates the value of the mathematical constant e by using the formula:

$$e = 1 + \frac{1}{1!} + \frac{1}{2!} + \frac{1}{3!} + ...$$

c) Write a program that computes the value of e^x by using the formula

$$e^x = 1 + \frac{x}{1!} + \frac{x^2}{2!} + \frac{x^3}{3!} + ...$$

ANS:

```cpp
1   // Exercise 2.38 Part A Solution
2   #include <iostream.h>
3
4   int main()
5   {
6       int n = 0, number;
7       unsigned factorial = 1;
```

```
 8
 9      do {
10         cout << "Enter a positive integer: ";
11         cin >> number;
12      } while ( number < 0 );
13
14      while ( n++ < number )
15         factorial *= n == 0 ? 1 : n;
16
17      cout << number << "! is " << factorial << endl;
18      return 0;
19   }
```

```
   Enter a positive integer: 8
   8! is 40320
```

ANS:

```
 1   // Exercise 2.38 Part B Solution
 2   #include <iostream.h>
 3
 4   int main()
 5   {
 6      int n = 0, fact = 1, accuracy = 10;
 7      float e = 1;
 8
 9      while ( ++n < accuracy ) {
10         fact *= n;
11         e += 1.0 / fact;
12      }
13
14      cout << "e is " << e << endl;
15      return 0;
16   }
```

```
   e is 2.71828
```

ANS:

```
 1   // Exercise 2.38 Part C Solution
 2   #include <iostream.h>
 3   #include <iomanip.h>
 4
 5   int main()
 6   {
 7      int n = 0, accuracy = 15, x = 3.0, times = 0, count;
 8      float e = 1.0, exp = 0.0, fact = 1.0;
 9
10      while ( n++ <= accuracy ) {
11         count = n;
12         fact *= n == 0 ? 1.0 : n;
13
14         while ( times < count ) {
15
16            if ( times == 0 )
17               exp = 1.0;
18
19            exp *= x;
20            ++times;
21         }
```

```
22
23          e += exp / fact;
24      }
25
26      cout << setiosflags( ios::fixed | ios::showpoint )
27           << "e raised to the " << x << " power is "
28           << setprecision( 4 ) << e << endl;
29
30      return 0;
31  }
```

```
e raised to the 3 power is 20.0855
```

2.39   Find the error in each of the following (Note: There may be more than one error):

a) `For ( x = 100, x >= 1, x++ )`
   `    cout << x << endl;`

ANS: **For** should be **for**. The commas should be semicolons. The **++** should be a decrement such as **--**.

b) The following code should print whether integer **value** is odd or even:

```
switch ( value % 2 ) {
   case 0:
      cout << "Even integer" << endl;
   case 1:
      cout << "Odd integer" << endl;
}
```

ANS: **case** 0 needs a **break** statement.

c) The following code should output the odd integers from 19 to 1:

```
for ( x = 19; x >= 1; x += 2 )
   cout << x << endl;
```

ANS: **+=** should be **-=**.

d) The following code should output the even integers from 2 to 100:

```
counter = 2;
do {
   cout << counter << endl;
   counter += 2;
} While ( counter < 100 );
```

ANS: **While** should be **while**. Operator **<** should be **<=**.

2.40   Write a program that sums a sequence of integers. Assume that the first integer read specifies the number of values remaining to be entered. Your program should read only one value per input statement. A typical input sequence might be

   5 100 200 300 400 500

where the **5** indicates that the subsequent **5** values are to be summed.

   ANS:

```
1   // Exercise 2.40 Solution
2   #include <iostream.h>
3
4   int main()
5   {
6      int sum = 0, number, value;
7
8      cout << "Enter the number of values to be processed: ";
9      cin >> number;
10
11     for ( int i = 1; i <= number; i++ ) {
12        cout << "Enter a value: ";
13        cin >> value;
14        sum += value;
15     }
```

```
16
17        cout << "Sum of the " << number << " values is "
18            << sum << endl;
19
20        return 0;
21    }
```

```
    Enter the number of values to be processed: 3
    Enter a value: 7
    Enter a value: 8
    Enter a value: 9
    Sum of the 3 values is 24
```

2.41 Write a program that calculates and prints the average of several integers. Assume the last value read is the sentinel **9999**. A typical input sequence might be

        10 8 11 7 9 9999

indicating that the average of all the values preceding **9999** is to be calculated.

ANS:

```
1    // Exercise 2.41 Solution
2    #include <iostream.h>
3
4    int main()
5    {
6        int value, count = 0, total = 0;
7
8        cout << "Enter an integer (9999 to end): ";
9        cin >> value;
10
11       while ( value != 9999 ) {
12           total += value;
13           ++count;
14           cout << "Enter next integer (9999 to end): ";
15           cin >> value;
16       }
17
18       if ( count != 0 )
19           cout << "\nThe average is: "
20                << static_cast< float > ( total ) / count << endl;
21       else
22           cout << "\nNo values were entered." << endl;
23
24       return 0;
25   }
```

```
    Enter an integer (9999 to end): 88
    Enter next integer (9999 to end): 65
    Enter next integer (9999 to end): 77
    Enter next integer (9999 to end): 43
    Enter next integer (9999 to end): 90
    Enter next integer (9999 to end): 45
    Enter next integer (9999 to end): 76
    Enter next integer (9999 to end): 2
    Enter next integer (9999 to end): 9999

    The average is: 60.75
```

2.42   What does the following program do?

```
#include <iostream.h>
int main()
{
    int x, y;
    cout << "Enter two integers in the range 1-20: ";
    cin >> x >> y;
    for ( int i = 1; i <= y; i++ ) {
        for ( int j = 1; j <= x; j++ )
            cout << '@';
        cout << endl;
    }
    return 0;
}
```

ANS:

```
Enter two integers in the range 1-20: 3 4
@@@
@@@
@@@
@@@
```

2.43   Write a program that finds the smallest of several integers. Assume that the first value read specifies the number of values remaining.

ANS:

```
1   // Exercise 2.43 Solution
2   #include <iostream.h>
3
4   int main()
5   {
6       int number, value, smallest;
7
8       cout << "Enter the number of integers to be processed: ";
9       cin >> number;
10      cout << "Enter an integer: ";
11      cin >> smallest;
12
13      for ( int i = 2; i <= number; i++ ) {
14          cout << "Enter next integer: ";
15          cin >> value;
16
17          if ( value < smallest )
18              smallest = value;
19      }
20
21      cout << "\nThe smallest integer is: " << smallest << endl;
22
23      return 0;
24  }
```

```
Enter the number of integers to be processed: 5
Enter an integer: 5
Enter next integer: 4
Enter next integer: 3
Enter next integer: 1
Enter next integer: 8

The smallest integer is: 1
```

2.44   Write a program that calculates and prints the product of the odd integers from 1 to 15.
ANS:

```
1    // Exercise 2.44 Solution
2    #include <iostream.h>
3
4    int main()
5    {
6       long product = 1;
7
8       for ( long i = 3; i <= 15; i += 2 )
9          product *= i;
10
11      cout << "Product of the odd integers from 1 to 15 is: "
12           << product << endl;
13
14      return 0;
15   }
```

```
Product of the odd integers from 1 to 15 is: 2027025
```

2.45   The *factorial* function is used frequently in probability problems. The factorial of a positive integer *n* (written *n!* and pronounced "n factorial") is equal to the product of the positive integers from 1 to *n*. Write a program that evaluates the factorials of the integers from 1 to 5. Print the results in tabular format. What difficulty might prevent you from calculating the factorial of 20?
ANS:

```
1    // Exercise 2.45 Solution
2    #include <iostream.h>
3
4    int main()
5    {
6       int factorial;
7
8       cout << "X\tFactorial of X\n";
9
10      for ( int i = 1; i <= 5; ++i ) {
11         factorial = 1;
12
13         for ( int j = 1; j <= i; ++j )
14            factorial *= j;
15
16         cout << i << '\t' << factorial << '\n';
17      }
18
19      cout << endl;
20      return 0;
21   }
```

```
X        Factorial of X
1        1
2        2
3        6
4        24
5        120
```

2.46   Modify the compound interest program of Section 2.15 to repeat its steps for interest rates of 5 percent, 6 percent, 7 percent, 8 percent, 9 percent, and 10 percent. Use a **for** loop to vary the interest rate.

ANS:

```
1   // Exercise 2.46 Solution
2   #include <iostream.h>
3   #include <iomanip.h>
4   #include <math.h>
5
6   int main()
7   {
8      double amount, principal = 1000.00;
9
10     cout << setiosflags( ios::fixed | ios::showpoint );
11
12     for ( int rate = 5; rate <= 10; rate++ ) {
13        cout << "Interest Rate: " << setprecision( 2 ) << rate / 100.0
14             << "\nYear\tAmount on deposit\n";
15
16        for ( int year = 1; year <= 10; year++ ) {
17           amount = principal * pow( 1 + ( rate / 100.0 ), year );
18           cout << year << '\t' << setprecision( 2 ) << amount << '\n';
19        }
20
21        cout << '\n';
22     }
23
24     cout << endl;
25     return 0;
26  }
```

```
...
Interest Rate: 0.10
Year    Amount on deposit
1       1100.00
2       1210.00
3       1331.00
4       1464.10
5       1610.51
6       1771.56
7       1948.72
8       2143.59
9       2357.95
10      2593.74
```

2.47   Write a program that prints the following patterns separately one below the other. Use **for** loops to generate the patterns. All asterisks (*) should be printed by a single statement of the form **cout << '*';** (this causes the asterisks to print side by side). Hint: The last two patterns require that each line begin with an appropriate number of blanks. Extra credit: Combine your code from the four separate problems into a single program that prints all four patterns side by side making clever use of nested **for** loops.

```
(A)              (B)               (C)               (D)
*                *********         *********                 *
**               ********          ********                 **
***              *******           *******                 ***
****             ******            ******                 ****
*****            *****             *****                  *****
******           ****              ****                  ******
*******          ***               ***                  *******
********          **                **                  ********
*********          *                 *                 *********
**********                                            **********
```

ANS:

```
1   // Exercise 2.47 Solution
2   #include <iostream.h>
3
4   int main()
5   {
6      // Pattern A
7      for ( int row = 1; row <= 10; ++row ) {
8
9         for ( int col = 1; col <= row; ++col )
10           cout << '*';
11
12        cout << '\n';
13     }
14
15     cout << '\n';
16
17     // Pattern B
18     for ( row = 10; row >= 1; --row ) {
19
20        for ( int col = 1; col <= row; ++col )
21           cout << '*';
22
23        cout << '\n';
24     }
25
26     cout << '\n';
27
28     // Pattern C
29     for ( row = 10; row >= 1; --row ) {
30
31        for ( int space = 1; space <= 10 - row; ++space )
32           cout << ' ';
33
34        for ( int col = 1; col <= row; ++col )
35           cout << '*';
36
37        cout << '\n';
38     }
39
40     cout << '\n';
41
42     // Pattern D
43     for ( row = 1; row <= 10; ++row ) {
44
45        for ( int space = 1; space <= 10 - row; ++space )
46           cout << ' ';
47
48        for ( int col = 1; col <= row; ++col )
49           cout << '*';
50
51        cout << '\n';
52     }
53
54     cout << endl;
55
56     return 0;
57  }
```

ANS:

```
1   // Exercise 2.47 Extra Credit Solution
2   #include <iostream.h>
3
```

```
4   int main()
5   {
6      int row, column, space;
7
8      for ( row = 1; row <= 10; ++row ) {
9
10        // part a
11        for ( column = 1; column <= row; ++column )
12           cout << '*';
13
14        for ( space = 1; space <= 10 - row; ++space )
15           cout << ' ';
16
17        cout << '\t';
18
19        // part b
20        for ( column = 10; column >= row; --column )
21           cout << '*';
22
23        for ( space = 1; space < row; ++space )
24           cout << ' ';
25
26        cout << '\t';
27
28        // part c
29        for ( space = 10; space > row; --space )
30           cout << ' ';
31
32        for ( column = 1; column <= row; ++column )
33           cout << '*';
34
35        cout << '\t';
36
37        // part d
38        for ( space = 1; space < row; ++space )
39           cout << ' ';
40
41        for ( column = 10; column >= row; --column )
42           cout << '*';
43
44        cout << endl;
45     }
46  }
```

```
*               *********              *        *********
**              ********               **       ********
***             *******                ***      *******
****            ******                 ****     ******
*****           *****                   *****     *****
******          ****                   ******     ****
*******         ***                    *******      ***
********        **                     ********      **
*********       *                      *********      *
**********      *                      **********      *
```

2.48   One interesting application of computers is drawing graphs and bar charts (sometimes called "histograms"). Write a program that reads five numbers (each between 1 and 30). For each number read, your program should print a line containing that number of adjacent asterisks. For example, if your program reads the number seven, it should print *******.

ANS:

```
1   // Exercise 2.48 Solution
2   #include <iostream.h>
```

```
3
4    int main()
5    {
6       int number;
7
8       cout << "Enter 5 numbers between 1 and 30: ";
9
10      for ( int i = 1; i <= 5; ++i ) {
11         cin >> number;
12
13         for ( int j = 1; j <= number; ++j )
14            cout << '*';
15
16         cout << '\n';
17      }
18
19      cout << endl;
20      return 0;
21   }
```

```
Enter 5 numbers between 1 and 30: 16 12 8 27 9
****************
************
********
***************************
*********
```

2.49   A mail order house sells five different products whose retail prices are product 1 — $2.98, product 2—$4.50, product 3—$9.98, product 4—$4.49, and product 5—$6.87. Write a program that reads a series of pairs of numbers as follows:

   a) Product number
   b) Quantity sold for one day

Your program should use a **switch** statement to help determine the retail price for each product. Your program should calculate and display the total retail value of all products sold last week.

   ANS:

```
1    // Exercise 2.49 Solution
2    #include <iostream.h>
3    #include <iomanip.h>
4
5    int main()
6    {
7       int product, quantity;
8       float total = 0.0;
9
10      cout << "Enter pairs of item numbers and quantities."
11           << "\nEnter -1 for the item number to end input: ";
12      cin >> product;
13
14      while ( product != -1 ) {
15         cin >> quantity;
16
17         switch ( product ) {
18            case 1:
19               total += quantity * 2.98;
20               break;
21            case 2:
22               total += quantity * 4.50;
23               break;
24            case 3:
25               total += quantity * 9.98;
26               break;
```

```
27                case 4:
28                   total += quantity * 4.49;
29                   break;
30                case 5:
31                   total += quantity * 6.87;
32                   break;
33                default:
34                   cout << "Invalid product code: " << product
35                        << "\n                 Quantity: " << quantity << '\n';
36                   break;
37             }
38
39             cout << "Enter pairs of item numbers and quantities.\n"
40                  << "Enter -1 for the item number to end input: ";
41             cin >> product;
42          }
43
44          cout << setiosflags( ios::fixed | ios::showpoint )
45               << "The total retail value was: " << setprecision( 2 )
46               << total << endl;
47
48          return 0;
49       }
```

```
Enter pairs of item numbers and quantities.
Enter -1 for the item number to end input: 2 10
Enter pairs of item numbers and quantities.
Enter -1 for the item number to end input: 1 5
Enter pairs of item numbers and quantities.
Enter -1 for the item number to end input: -1
The total retail value was: 59.90
```

2.50 Modify the program of Fig. 2.22 so that it calculates the grade point average for the class. A grade of 'A' is worth 4 points, 'B' is worth 3 points, etc.

ANS:

```
1    // Exercise 2.50 Solution
2    #include <iostream.h>
3    #include <iomanip.h>
4
5    int main()
6    {
7       int grade, gradeTotal = 0, gradeCount, aCount = 0,
8           bCount = 0, cCount = 0, dCount = 0, fCount = 0;
9
10      cout << "Enter the letter grades."
11           << "\nEnter the EOF character to end input.\n"
12           << setiosflags(ios::fixed | ios::showpoint);
13
14      while ( ( grade = cin.get() ) != EOF ) {
15
16         switch ( grade ) {
17            case 'A': case 'a':
18               gradeTotal += 4;
19               ++aCount;
20               break;
21            case 'B': case 'b':
22               gradeTotal += 3;
23               ++bCount;
24               break;
```

```
25              case 'C': case 'c':
26                 gradeTotal += 2;
27                 ++cCount;
28                 break;
29              case 'D': case 'd':
30                 ++gradeTotal;
31                 ++dCount;
32                 break;
33              case 'F': case 'f':
34                 ++fCount;
35                 break;
36              case ' ': case '\n':
37                 break;
38              default:
39                 cout << "Incorrect letter grade entered."
40                      << " Enter a new grade.\n";
41                 break;
42          }
43       }
44
45       gradeCount = aCount + bCount + cCount + dCount + fCount;
46
47       if ( gradeCount != 0 )
48          cout << "\nThe class average is: " << setprecision( 1 )
49               << static_cast< float > ( gradeTotal ) / gradeCount
50               << endl;
51
52       return 0;
53    }
```

```
Enter the letter grades.
Enter the EOF character to end input.
aABcccBbDf
E
Incorrect letter grade entered. Enter a new grade.
F
The class average is: 2.2
```

2.51 Modify the program in Fig. 2.21 so it uses only integers to calculate the compound interest. (Hint: Treat all monetary amounts as integral numbers of pennies. Then "break" the result into its dollar portion and cents portion by using the division and modulus operations. Insert a period.)

ANS:

```
1   // Exercise 2.51 Solution
2   #include <iostream.h>
3   #include <iomanip.h>
4   #include <math.h>
5
6   int main()
7   {
8      int amount, principal = 1000, dollars, cents;
9      double rate = .05;
10
11     cout << "Year" << setw( 24 ) << "Amount on deposit\n";
12
13     for ( int year = 1; year <= 10; ++year ) {
14        amount = principal * pow( 1.0 + rate, year );
15        cents = amount % 100;
16        dollars = amount;  // assignment truncates decimal places
17        cout << setw( 4 ) << year << setw( 21 ) << dollars << '.';
18
```

```
19          if ( cents < 10 )
20              cout << '0' << cents << endl;
21          else
22              cout << cents << endl;
23      }
24
25      return 0;
26  }
```

```
Year        Amount on deposit
   1              1050.50
   2              1102.02
   3              1157.57
   4              1215.15
   5              1276.76
   6              1340.40
   7              1407.07
   8              1477.77
   9              1551.51
  10              1628.28
```

2.52 Assume **i = 1, j = 2, k = 3**, and **m = 2**. What does each of the following statements print? Are the parentheses necessary in each case?

a) `cout << ( i == 1 ) << endl;`
ANS: 1, no.
b) `cout << ( j == 3 ) << endl;`
ANS: 1, no.
c) `cout << ( i >= 1 && j < 4 ) << endl;`
ANS: 1, no.
d) `cout << ( m <= 99 && k < m ) << endl;`
ANS: 0, no.
e) `cout << ( j >= i || k == m ) << endl;`
ANS: 1, no.
f) `cout << ( k + m < j || 3 - j >= k ) << endl;`
ANS: 0, no.
g) `cout << ( !m ) << endl;`
ANS: 0, no.
h) `cout << ( !( j - m ) ) << endl;`
ANS: 1, yes. The inner pair of parenthesis are required.
i) `cout << ( !( k > m ) ) << endl;`
ANS: 0, yes. The inner pair of parenthesis are required.

2.53 Write a program that prints a table of the binary, octal, and hexadecimal equivalents of the decimal numbers in the range 1 through 256. If you are not familiar with these number systems, read Appendix E first.
ANS:

```
1   // Exercise 2.53 Solution
2   // The oct, hex, and dec identifiers are stream manipulators
3   // like endl that are defined in Chapter 11. The manipulator
4   // oct causes integers to be output in octal, the manipulator
5   // hex causes integers to be output in hexadecimal, and the manipulator
6   // dec causes integers to be output in decimal.
7   #include <iostream.h>
8
9   int main()
10  {
11      cout << "Decimal\t\tBinary\t\t\tOctal\tHexadecimal\n";
12
13      for ( int loop = 1; loop <= 256; ++loop ) {
14          cout << dec << loop << "\t\t";
```

```
15
16          // Output binary number
17          int number = loop;
18          cout << ( number == 256 ? '1' : '0' );
19          int factor = 256;
20
21          do {
22             cout << ( number < factor && number >= ( factor / 2 ) ? '1' : '0' );
23             factor /= 2;
24             number %= factor;
25          } while ( factor > 2 );
26
27          // Output octal and hexadecimal numbers
28          cout << '\t' << oct << loop << '\t' << hex << loop << endl;
29       }
30
31       return 0;
32    }
```

Decimal	Binary	Octal	Hexadecimal
1	00000001	1	1
2	00000010	2	2
...			
245	01111010	365	f5
246	01111011	366	f6
247	01111011	367	f7
248	01111100	370	f8
249	01111100	371	f9
250	01111101	372	fa
251	01111101	373	fb
252	01111110	374	fc
253	01111110	375	fd
254	01111111	376	fe
255	01111111	377	ff
256	10000000	400	100

2.54   Calculate the value of π from the infinite series

$$\pi = 4 - \frac{4}{3} + \frac{4}{5} - \frac{4}{7} + \frac{4}{9} - \frac{4}{11} + \cdots$$

Print a table that shows the value of π approximated by 1 term of this series, by two terms, by three terms, etc. How many terms of this series do you have to use before you first get 3.14? 3.141? 3.1415? 3.14159?

   ANS:

```
1    // Exercise 2.54 Solution
2    #include <iostream.h>
3    #include <iomanip.h>
4
5    int main()
6    {
7       long double pi = 0.0, num = 4.0, denom = 1.0;
8       long accuracy = 400000;      // set decimal accuracy
9
10      cout << setiosflags( ios::fixed | ios::showpoint )
11           << "Accuracy set at: " << accuracy
12           << "\nterm\t\t   pi\n";
13
14      for ( long loop = 1; loop <= accuracy; ++loop ) {
15
16         if ( loop % 2 != 0 )
17            pi += num / denom;
```

```
18            else
19               pi -= num / denom;
20
21            cout << loop << "\t\t" << setprecision( 8 ) << pi << '\n';
22            denom += 2.0;
23         }
24
25      cout << endl;
26      return 0;
27   }
```

```
Accuracy set at: 400000
term       pi
1          4.00000000
2          2.66666667
3          3.46666667
4          2.89523810
...
376138     3.14158999
376139     3.14159531
376140     3.14159000
...
```

2.55 *(Pythagorean Triples)* A right triangle can have sides that are all integers. The set of three integer values for the sides of a right triangle is called a Pythagorean triple. These three sides must satisfy the relationship that the sum of the squares of two of the sides is equal to the square of the hypotenuse. Find all Pythagorean triples for **side1**, **side2**, and the **hypotenuse** all no larger than 500. Use a triple-nested **for**-loop that tries all possibilities. This is an example of "brute force" computing. You will learn in more advanced computer science courses that there are many interesting problems for which there is no known algorithmic approach other than using sheer brute force.

ANS:

```
1   // Exercise 2.55 Solution
2   #include<iostream.h>
3
4   int main()
5   {
6      int count = 0;
7      long int hyptSquared, sidesSquared;
8
9      for ( long side1 = 1; side1 <= 500; ++side1 ) {
10
11         for ( long side2 = 1; side2 <= 500; ++side2 ) {
12
13            for ( long hypt = 1; hypt <= 500; ++hypt ) {
14               hyptSquared = hypt * hypt;
15               sidesSquared = side1 * side1 + side2 * side2;
16
17               if ( hyptSquared == sidesSquared ) {
18                  cout << side1 << '\t' << side2 << '\t'
19                       << hypt << '\n';
20                  ++count;
21               }
22            }
23         }
24      }
25
26      cout << "A total of " << count << " triples were found." << endl;
27
28      return 0;
29   }
```

```
3        4        5
4        3        5
5        12       13
6        8        10
7        24       25
8        6        10
8        15       17
9        12       15
...
475      132      493
476      93       485
...
483      44       485
A total of 772 triples were found.
```

2.56   A company pays its employees as managers (who receive a fixed weekly salary), hourly workers (who receive a fixed hourly wage for up to the first 40 hours they work and "time-and-a-half," i.e., 1.5 times their hourly wage, for overtime hours worked), commission workers (who receive $250 plus 5.7% of their gross weekly sales), or pieceworkers (who receive a fixed amount of money per item for each of the items they produce—each pieceworker in this company works on only one type of item). Write a program to compute the weekly pay for each employee. You do not know the number of employees in advance. Each type of employee has its own pay code: Managers have paycode 1, hourly workers have code 2, commission workers have code 3 and pieceworkers have code 4. Use a **switch** to compute each employee's pay based on that employee's paycode. Within the **switch**, prompt the user (i.e., the payroll clerk) to enter the appropriate facts your program needs to calculate each employee's pay based on that employee's paycode.

ANS:

```cpp
1   // Exercise 2.56 Solution
2   #include<iostream.h>
3   #include<iomanip.h>
4
5   int main()
6   {
7       int payCode, managers = 0, hWorkers = 0, cWorkers = 0;
8       int pWorkers = 0, pieces;
9       float mSalary, hSalary, cSalary, pSalary, hours;
10      float pay;
11
12      cout << "Enter paycode (-1 to end): "
13           << setiosflags( ios::fixed | ios::showpoint );
14      cin >> payCode;
15
16      while ( payCode != -1 ) {
17         switch ( payCode ) {
18            case 1:
19               cout << "Manager selected."
20                    << "\nEnter weekly salary: ";
21               cin >> mSalary;
22               cout << "The manager's pay is $ "
23                    << setprecision( 2 ) << mSalary;
24               ++managers;
25               break;
26            case 2:
27               cout << "Hourly worker selected.\n"
28                    << "Enter the hourly salary: ";
29               cin >> hSalary;
30               cout << "Enter the total hours worked: ";
31               cin >> hours;
32
33               pay = hours > 40.0 ? ( hours - 40 ) * 1.5 * hSalary + hSalary * 40.0:
34                                    hSalary * hours;
35               cout << "Worker's pay is $ " << setprecision( 2 ) << pay << '\n';
```

```
36                    ++hWorkers;
37                    break;
38                 case 3:
39                    cout << "Commission worker selected.\n"
40                         << "Enter gross weekly sales: ";
41                    cin >> cSalary;
42                    pay = 250.0 + 0.057 * cSalary;
43                    cout << "Commission Worker's pay is $ " << setprecision( 2 )
44                         << pay << '\n';
45                    ++cWorkers;
46                    break;
47                 case 4:
48                    cout << "Piece worker selected.\n"
49                         << "Enter number of pieces: ";
50                    cin >> pieces;
51                    cout << "Enter wage per piece: ";
52                    cin >> pSalary;
53                    pay = pieces * pSalary;
54                    cout << "Piece Worker's pay is $ " << setprecision( 2 )
55                         << pay << '\n';
56                    ++pWorkers;
57                    break;
58                 default:
59                    cout << "Invalid pay code.\n";
60                    break;
61           }
62
63        cout << "\nEnter paycode (-1 to end): ";
64        cin >> payCode;
65     }
66
67     cout << "\n\nTotal number of managers paid          : "
68          << managers
69          << "\nTotal number of hourly workers paid    : "
70          << hWorkers
71          << "\nTotal number of commission workers paid: "
72          << cWorkers
73          << "\nTotal number of piece workers paid     : "
74          << pWorkers << endl;
75
76     return 0;
77  }
```

```
Enter paycode (-1 to end): 3
Commission worker selected.
Enter gross weekly sales: 4000
Commission Worker's pay is $ 478.00
Enter paycode (-1 to end): 2
Hourly worker selected.
Enter the hourly salary: 4.50
Enter the total hours worked: 20
Worker's pay is $ 90.00
Enter paycode (-1 to end): 4
Piece worker selected.
Enter number of pieces: 50
Enter wage per piece: 3
Piece Worker's pay is $ 150.00
Enter paycode (-1 to end): -1

Total number of managers paid          : 0
Total number of hourly workers paid    : 1
Total number of commission workers paid: 1
Total number of piece workers paid     : 1
```

2.57   *(De Morgan's Laws)* In this chapter, we discussed the logical operators **&&**, **||**, and **!**. De Morgan's Laws can some-times make it more convenient for us to express a logical expression. These laws state that the expression **!**(*condition1* **&&** *condition2*) is logically equivalent to the expression (**!***condition1* **||** **!***condition2*). Also, the expression **!**(*condition1* **||** *condition2*) is logically equivalent to the expression (**!***condition1* **&&** **!***condition2*). Use De Morgan's Laws to write equiv-alent expressions for each of the following, and then write a program to show that both the original expression and the new expression in each case are equivalent:

```
a) !( x < 5 ) && !( y >= 7 )
b) !( a == b ) || !( g != 5 )
c) !( ( x <= 8 ) && ( y > 4 ) )
d) !( ( i > 4 ) || ( j <= 6 ) )
```

ANS:

```
1   // Exercise 2.57 Solution
2   #include<iostream.h>
3
4   int main()
5   {
6      int x = 10, y = 1, a = 3, b = 3,
7          g = 5, Y = 1, i = 2, j = 9;
8
9      cout << "current variable values are:" << endl
10        << "x = " << x << ", y = " << y << ", a = " << a
11        << ", b = " << b << endl << "g = " << g << ", Y = "
12        << Y << ", i = " << i << ", j = " << j << "\n\n";
13
14     if ((!(x < 5) && !(y >= 7)) && (!((x < 5) || (y >= 7))))
15        cout << "!(x < 5) && !(y >= 7) is equivalent to"
16              << " !((x < 5) || (y >= 7))" << endl;
17     else
18        cout << "!(x < 5) && !(y >= 7) is not equivalent to"
19              << " !((x < 5) || (y >= 7))" << endl;
20
21     if ((!(a == b) || !(g != 5)) && (!((a == b) && (g != 5))))
22        cout << "!(a == b) || !(g != 5) is equivalent to"
23              << " !((a == b) && (g != 5))" << endl;
24     else
25        cout << "!(a == b) || !(g != 5) is not equivalent to"
26              << " !((a == b) && (g != 5))" << endl;
27
28     if (!((x <= 8) && (Y > 4)) && (!((x <= 8) || (Y > 4))))
29        cout << "!((x <= 8) && (Y > 4)) is equivalent to"
30              << " !((x <= 8) || (Y > 4))" << endl;
31     else
32        cout << "!((x <= 8) && (Y > 4)) is not equivalent to"
33              << " !((x <= 8) || (Y > 4))" << endl;
34
35     if (!((i > 4) || (j <= 6)) && !((i > 4) && (j <= 6)))
36        cout << "!((i > 4) || (j <= 6)) is equivalent to"
37              << " !((i > 4) && (j <= 6))" << endl;
38     else
39        cout << "!((i > 4) || (j <= 6)) is not equivalent to"
40              << " !((i > 4) && (j <= 6))" << endl;
41     return 0;
42  }
```

```
current variable values are:
x = 10, y = 1, a = 3, b = 3
g = 5, Y = 1, i = 2, j = 9
!(x < 5) && !(y >= 7) is equivalent to !((x < 5) || (y >= 7))
!(a == b) || !(g != 5) is equivalent to !((a == b) && (g != 5))
!((x <= 8) && (Y > 4)) is equivalent to !((x <= 8) || (Y > 4))
!((i > 4) || (j <= 6)) is equivalent to !((i > 4) && (j <= 6))
```

2.58   Write a program that prints the following diamond shape. You may use output statements that print either a single asterisk (*) or a single blank. Maximize your use of repetition (with nested **for** structures) and minimize the number of output statements.

```
        *
       ***
      *****
     *******
    *********
     *******
      *****
       ***
        *
```

ANS:

```
1   // Exercise 2.58 Solution
2   #include <iostream.h>
3
4   int main()
5   {
6      // top half
7      for ( int row = 1; row <= 5; ++row ) {
8
9         for ( int space = 1; space <= 5 - row; ++space )
10           cout << ' ';
11
12        for ( int asterisk = 1; asterisk <= 2 * row - 1; ++asterisk )
13           cout << '*';
14
15        cout << '\n';
16     }
17
18     // bottom half
19     for ( row = 4; row >= 1; --row ) {
20
21        for ( int space = 1; space <= 5 - row; ++space )
22           cout << ' ';
23
24        for ( int asterisk = 1; asterisk <= 2 * row - 1; ++asterisk )
25           cout << '*';
26
27        cout << '\n';
28     }
29
30     cout << endl;
31     return 0;
32  }
```

2.59   Modify the program you wrote in Exercise 2.58 to read an odd number in the range 1 to 19 to specify the number of rows in the diamond. Your program should then display a diamond of the appropriate size.

ANS:

```
1   // Exercise 2.59 Solution
2   #include <iostream.h>
3
4   int main()
5   {
6      int size;
7
8      cout << "Enter an odd number for the diamond size (1-19): \n";
9      cin >> size;
10
11     // top half
12     for ( int rows = 1; rows <= size -  2; rows += 2 ) {
13
14        for ( int space = ( size - rows ) / 2; space > 0; --space )
15           cout << ' ';
16
17        for ( int asterisk = 1; asterisk <= rows; ++asterisk )
18           cout << '*';
19
20        cout << '\n';
21     }
22
23     // bottom half
24     for ( rows = size; rows >= 0; rows -= 2 ) {
25
26        for ( int space = ( size - rows ) / 2; space > 0; --space )
27           cout << ' ';
28
29        for ( int asterisk = 1; asterisk <= rows; ++asterisk )
30           cout << '*';
31
32        cout << '\n';
33     }
34
35     cout << endl;
36     return 0;
37  }
```

```
Enter an odd number for the diamond size (1-19):
15
       *
      ***
     *****
    *******
   *********
  ***********
 *************
***************
 *************
  ***********
   *********
    *******
     *****
      ***
       *
```

2.60   A criticism of the **break** statement and the **continue** statement is that each is unstructured. Actually **break** statements and **continue** statements can always be replaced by structured statements, although doing so can be awkward. Describe in general how you would remove any **break** statement from a loop in a program and replace that statement with some structured equivalent. (Hint: The **break** statement leaves a loop from within the body of the loop. The other way to leave is by failing the loop-continuation test. Consider using in the loop-continuation test a second test that indicates "early exit because of a 'break' condition.") Use the technique you developed here to remove the break statement from the program of Fig. 2.26.

ANS:

```
1   // Exercise 2.0 Solution
2   #include <iostream.h>
3
4   int main()
5   {
6      bool breakOut = false;
7      int x;
8
9      for ( x = 1; x <= 10 && !breakOut; ++x ) {
10
11        if ( x == 4 )
12           breakOut = true;
13
14        cout << x << ' ';
15     }
16
17     cout << "\nBroke out of loop at x = " << x << endl;
18     return 0;
19  }
```

```
1 2 3 4
Broke out of loop at x = 5
```

2.61   What does the following program segment do?

```
for ( i = 1; i <= 5; i++ ) {
    for ( j = 1; j <= 3; j++ ) {
        for ( k = 1; k <= 4; k++ )
            cout << '*';
        cout << endl;
    }
    cout << endl;
}
```

```
****
****
****

****
****
****

****
****
****

****
****
****

****
****
****
```

2.62   Describe in general how you would remove any **continue** statement from a loop in a program and replace that statement with some structured equivalent. Use the technique you developed here to remove the **continue** statement from the program of Fig. 2.27.

       ANS:

```
1   // Exercise 2.62 Solution
2   #include <iostream.h>
3
```

```
4   int main()
5   {
6      for ( int x = 1; x <= 10; ++x ) {
7
8         if ( x == 5 )
9            ++x;
10
11        cout << x << ' ';
12     }
13
14     cout << "\nUsed ++x to skip printing the value 5" << endl;
15
16     return 0;
17  }
```

```
1 2 3 4 6 7 8 9 10
Used ++x to skip printing the value 5
```

2.63   *("The Twelve Days of Christmas" Song)* Write a program that uses repetition and **switch** structures to print the song "The Twelve Days of Christmas." One **switch** structure should be used to print the day (i.e., "First," "Second," etc.). A separate **switch** structure should be used to print the remainder of each verse.

ANS:

```
1   // Exercise 2.63 Solution
2   #include <iostream.h>
3
4   int main()
5   {
6      for ( int day = 1; day < 13; day++ ) {
7         cout << "On the ";
8
9         switch ( day ) {          // switch for current day
10           case 1:
11              cout << "first";
12              break;
13           case 2:
14              cout << "second";
15              break;
16           case 3:
17              cout << "third";
18              break;
19           case 4:
20              cout << "fourth";
21              break;
22           case 5:
23              cout << "fifth";
24              break;
25           case 6:
26              cout << "sixth";
27              break;
28           case 7:
29              cout << "seventh";
30              break;
31           case 8:
32              cout << "eighth";
33              break;
34           case 9:
35              cout << "nineth";
36              break;
37           case 10:
38              cout << "tenth";
39              break;
```

```
40              case 11:
41                 cout << "eleventh";
42                 break;
43              case 12:
44                 cout << "twelfth";
45                 break;
46           }
47
48           cout << " day of Christmas,\nMy true love sent to me:\n";
49
50           switch ( day ) {        // switch for gifts
51              case 12:
52                 cout << "\tTwelve drummers drumming,\n";
53              case 11:
54                 cout << "\tEleven pipers piping,\n";
55              case 10:
56                 cout << "\tTen lords a-leaping,\n";
57              case 9:
58                 cout << "\tNine ladies dancing,\n";
59              case 8:
60                 cout << "\tEight maids a-milking,\n";
61              case 7:
62                 cout << "\tSeven swans a-swimming,\n";
63              case 6:
64                 cout << "\tSix geese a-laying,\n";
65              case 5:
66                 cout << "\tFive golden rings,\n";
67              case 4:
68                 cout << "\tFour calling birds,\n";
69              case 3:
70                 cout << "\tThree French hens,\n";
71              case 2:
72                 cout << "\tTwo turtle doves, and\n";
73              case 1:
74                 cout << "A partridge in a pear tree.\n\n\n";
75           }
76        }
77
78        cout << endl;
79        return 0;
80     }
```

```
On the twelfth day of Christmas,
My true love sent to me:
A partridge in a pear tree.
...
On the twelfth day of Christmas,
My true love sent to me:
        Twelve drummers drumming,
        Eleven pipers piping,
        Ten lords a-leaping,
        Nine ladies dancing,
        Eight maids a-milking,
        Seven swans a-swimming,
        Six geese a-laying,
        Five golden rings,
        Four calling birds,
        Three French hens,
        Two turtle doves, and
A partridge in a pear tree.
```

Exercise 2.64 corresponds to Section 2.22, "Thinking About Objects."

2.64 Describe in 200 words or less what an automobile is and does. List the nouns and verbs separately. In the text, we stated that each noun may correspond to an object that will need to be built to implement a system, in this case a car. Pick five of the objects you listed and for each list several attributes and several behaviors. Describe briefly how these objects interact with one another and other objects in your description. You have just performed several of the key steps in a typical object-oriented design.

> **ANS:**
>
> A specific type of vehicle containing 4 wheels, doors, seats, windows, steering wheel, brakes, radio, engine, exhaust system, transmission, axels, windshield, mirrors, etc.
>
> A car can accelerate, decelerate, turn, move forward, move backward, stop, etc.
>
> Wheels:
> > Attributes: size, type, tread depth.
> > Behaviors: rotate forward, rotate backward.
>
> Doors:
> > Attributes: type (passenger, trunk, etc.), open or closed.
> > Behaviors: open, close, lock, unlock.
>
> Steering Wheel:
> > Attributes: adjustible.
> > Behaviors: turn left, turn right, adjust up, adjust down.
>
> Brakes:
> > Attributes: pressed or not pressed, pressure of press.
> > Behaviors: press, antilock.
>
> Engine:
> > Attributes: cylinders, radiator, timing belts, spark plugs, etc.
> > Behaviors: accelerate, decelerate, turn on, turn off.
>
> Interactions:
> > Person turns the steering wheel which causes the wheels to turn in the appropriate direction.
> > Person presses the accelerator pedal which causes the engine revolutions per minute to increase, resulting in a faster rotation of the wheels.
> > Person opens door. Person closes door.
> > Person releases accelerator pedal which causes engine RPMs to decrease, resulting in a slower rotation of the wheels.
> > Person presses brake pedal which causes brakes to be applied to wheels slows the rotation of the-wheels.

2.65 *(Peter Minuet Problem)* Legend has it that in 1626 Peter Minuet purchased Manhattan for $24.00 in barter. Did he make a good investment? To answer this question, modify the compound interest program of Fig. 2.21 to begin with a principal of $24.00 and to calculate the amount of interest on deposit if that money had been kept on deposit until this year (372 years through 1998). Run the program with interest rates of 5%, 6%, 7%, 8%, 9% and 10% to observe the wonders of compound interest.

Chapter 3 Solutions

Functions

Solutions

3.11 Show the value of **x** after each of the following statements is performed:

a) `x = fabs( 7.5 )`
ANS: 7.5
b) `x = floor( 7.5 )`
ANS: 7.0
c) `x = fabs( 0.0 )`
ANS: 0.0
d) `x = ceil( 0.0 )`
ANS: 0.0
e) `x = fabs( -6.4 )`
ANS: 6.4
f) `x = ceil( -6.4 )`
ANS: -6.0
g) `x = ceil( -fabs( -8 + floor( -5.5 ) ) )`
ANS: -14.0

3.12 A parking garage charges a $2.00 minimum fee to park for up to three hours. The garage charges an additional $0.50 per hour for each hour *or part thereof* in excess of three hours. The maximum charge for any given 24-hour period is $10.00. Assume that no car parks for longer than 24 hours at a time. Write a program that will calculate and print the parking charges for each of 3 customers who parked their cars in this garage yesterday. You should enter the hours parked for each customer. Your program should print the results in a neat tabular format, and should calculate and print the total of yesterday's receipts. The program should use the function **calculateCharges** to determine the charge for each customer. Your outputs should appear in the following format:

```
Car         Hours        Charge
1            1.5          2.00
2            4.0          2.50
3           24.0         10.00
TOTAL       29.5         14.50
```

ANS:

```
1    // Exercise 3.12 Solution
2    #include <iostream.h>
3    #include <iomanip.h>
4    #include <math.h>
5
6    float calculateCharges( float );
7
8    main()
9    {
10       float hour, currentCharge, totalCharges = 0.0, totalHours = 0.0;
11       int first = 1;
12
```

```
13        cout << "Enter the hours parked for 3 cars: ";
14
15        for ( int i = 1; i <= 3; i++ ) {
16           cin >> hour;
17           totalHours += hour;
18
19           if ( first ) {
20              cout << setw( 5 ) << "Car" << setw( 15 ) << "Hours"
21                   << setw( 15 ) << "Charge\n";
22              first = 0;    // prevents this from printing again
23           }
24
25           totalCharges += ( currentCharge = calculateCharges( hour ) );
26           cout << setiosflags( ios::fixed | ios::showpoint )
27                << setw( 3 ) << i << setw( 17 ) << setprecision( 1 ) << hour
28                << setw( 15 ) << setprecision( 2 ) << currentCharge << "\n";
29        }
30
31        cout << setw( 7 ) << "TOTAL" << setw( 13 ) << setprecision( 1 )
32             << totalHours << setw( 15 ) << setprecision( 2 )
33             << totalCharges << endl;
34
35        return 0;
36  }
37
38  float calculateCharges( float hours )
39  {
40     float charge;
41
42     if ( hours < 3.0 )
43        charge = 2.0;
44     else if ( hours < 19.0 )
45        charge = 2.0 + .5 * ceil( hours - 3.0 );
46     else
47        charge = 10.0;
48
49     return charge;
50  }
```

```
Enter the hours parked for 3 cars: 1 2 3
   Car           Hours          Charge
   1             1.0            2.00
   2             2.0            2.00
   3             3.0            2.00
   TOTAL         6.0            6.00
```

3.13   An application of function **floor** is rounding a value to the nearest integer. The statement

```
y = floor( x + .5 );
```

will round the number **x** to the nearest integer and assign the result to **y**. Write a program that reads several numbers and uses the preceding statement to round each of these numbers to the nearest integer. For each number processed, print both the original number and the rounded number.

ANS:

```
1  // Exercise 3.13 Solution
2  #include <iostream.h>
3  #include <iomanip.h>
4  #include <math.h>
5
6  void roundToIntegers( void );
7
```

```
 8   int main()
 9   {
10      roundToIntegers();
11      return 0;
12   }
13
14   void roundToIntegers( void )
15   {
16      double x, y;
17
18      cout << setiosflags( ios::fixed | ios::showpoint );
19
20      for ( int loop = 1; loop <= 5; loop++ ) {
21         cout << "Enter a floating point value: ";
22         cin >> x;
23         y = floor( x + .5 );
24         cout << x << " rounded is " << setprecision( 1 ) << y << endl;
25      }
26   }
```

```
Enter a floating point value: 8.22
8.220000 rounded is 8.0
Enter a floating point value: 7.98
8.0 rounded is 8.0
Enter a floating point value: 4.52
4.5 rounded is 5.0
Enter a floating point value: 6.9999
7.0 rounded is 7.0
Enter a floating point value: 3.345
3.3 rounded is 3.0
```

3.14   Function **floor** may be used to round a number to a specific decimal place. The statement

```
y = floor( x * 10 + .5 ) / 10;
```

rounds **x** to the tenths position (the first position to the right of the decimal point). The statement

```
y = floor( x * 100 + .5 ) / 100;
```

rounds **x** to the hundredths position (i.e., the second position to the right of the decimal point). Write a program that defines four functions to round a number **x** in various ways:

   a) **roundToInteger(number)**
   b) **roundToTenths(number)**
   c) **roundToHundredths(number)**
   d) **roundToThousandths(number)**

For each value read, your program should print the original value, the number rounded to the nearest integer, the number rounded to the nearest tenth, the number rounded to the nearest hundredth, and the number rounded to the nearest thousandth.

   ANS:

```
 1   // Exercise 3.14 Solution
 2   #include <iostream.h>
 3   #include <iomanip.h>
 4   #include <math.h>
 5
 6   double roundToInteger( double );
 7   double roundToTenths( double );
 8   double roundToHundreths( double );
 9   double roundToThousandths( double );
10
```

```
11  int main()
12  {
13     int count;
14     double number;
15
16     cout << "How many numbers do you want to process? "
17          << setiosflags( ios::fixed );
18     cin >> count;
19
20     for ( int i = 0; i < count; ++i ) {
21        cout << "\nEnter number: ";
22        cin >> number;
23        cout << number << " rounded to the nearest integer is:     "
24             << setprecision( 0 ) << roundToInteger( number ) << '\n'
25             << setiosflags( ios::showpoint )
26             << number << " rounded to the nearest tenth is:       "
27             << setprecision( 1 ) << roundToTenths( number ) << '\n'
28             << number << " rounded to the nearest hundredth is:   "
29             << setprecision( 2 ) << roundToHundreths( number ) << '\n'
30             << number << " rounded to the nearest thousandth is: "
31             << setprecision( 3 ) << roundToThousandths( number ) << '\n'
32             << resetiosflags( ios::showpoint );
33     }
34
35     return 0;
36  }
37
38  double roundToInteger( double n )
39  {
40     return floor( n + .5 );
41  }
42
43  double roundToTenths( double n )
44  {
45     return floor( n * 10 + .5 ) / 10;
46  }
47
48  double roundToHundreths( double n )
49  {
50     return floor( n * 100 + .5 ) / 100;
51  }
52
53  double roundToThousandths( double n )
54  {
55     return floor( n * 1000 + .5 ) / 1000.0;
56  }
```

```
How many numbers do you want to process? 1
Enter number: 2.564
2.564000 rounded to the nearest integer is:     3
3. rounded to the nearest tenth is:       2.6
2.6 rounded to the nearest hundredth is:  2.56
2.56 rounded to the nearest thousandth is: 2.564
```

3.15   Answer each of the following questions.

a) What does it mean to choose numbers "at random?"

ANS: Every number has an equal chance of being chosen at any time.

b) Why is the **rand** function useful for simulating games of chance?

ANS: Because it produces a sequence of pseudo-random numbers that when scaled appear to be random.

c) Why would you randomize a program using **srand**? Under what circumstances is it desirable not to randomize?

ANS: The sequence of numbers produced by the random number generator differ each time function **srand** is called. Not randomizing is useful for debugging purposes—the programmer knows the sequence of numbers.

d) Why is it often necessary to scale and/or shift the values produced by **rand**?

ANS: To produce random values in a specific range.

e) Why is computerized simulation of real-world situations a useful technique?

ANS: It enables more accurate predictions of random events such as cars arriving at a toll booth, people arriving in lines, birds arriving at a tree, etc. The results of a simulation can help determine how many toll booths to have open or how many cashiers to have open at specified times.

3.16 Write statements that assign random integers to the variable n in the following ranges:

a) $1 \leq n \leq 2$

ANS: **n = 1 + rand() % 2;**

b) $1 \leq n \leq 100$

ANS: **n = 1 + rand() % 100;**

c) $0 \leq n \leq 9$

ANS: **n = rand() % 10;**

d) $1000 \leq n \leq 1112$

ANS: **n = 1000 + rand() % 13;**

e) $-1 \leq n \leq 1$

ANS: **n = rand() % 3 - 1;**

f) $-3 \leq n \leq 11$

ANS: **n = rand() % 15 - 3;**

3.17 For each of the following sets of integers, write a single statement that will print a number at random from the set.

a) 2, 4, 6, 8, 10.

ANS: **cout << 2 * (1 + rand() % 5)) << '\n';**

b) 3, 5, 7, 9, 11.

ANS: **cout << 1 + 2 * (1 + rand() % 5)) << '\n';**

c) 6, 10, 14, 18, 22.

ANS: **cout << 6 + 4 * (rand() % 5) << '\n';**

3.18 Write a function **integerPower(base, exponent)** that returns the value of

$$base^{\,exponent}$$

For example, **integerPower(3,4) = 3 * 3 * 3 * 3**. Assume that **exponent** is a positive, nonzero integer, and **base** is an integer. The function **integerPower** should use **for** or **while** to control the calculation. Do not use any math library functions.

ANS:

```
1   // Exercise 3.18 Solution
2   #include <iostream.h>
3
4   int integerPower( int, int );
5
6   int main()
7   {
8      int exp, base;
9
10     cout << "Enter base and exponent: ";
11     cin >> base >> exp;
12     cout << base << " to the power " << exp << " is: "
13          << integerPower( base, exp ) << endl;
14
15     return 0;
16  }
17
18  int integerPower( int b, int e )
19  {
20     int product = 1;
21
22     for ( int i = 1; i <= e; ++i )
23        product *= b;
```

```
24
25      return product;
26   }
```

```
Enter base and exponent: 5 2
5 to the power 2 is: 25
```

3.19   Define a function **hypotenuse** that calculates the length of the hypotenuse of a right triangle when the other two sides are given. Use this function in a program to determine the length of the hypotenuse for each of the following triangles. The function should take two arguments of type **double** and return the hypotenuse as a **double**.

Triangle	Side 1	Side 2
1	3.0	4.0
2	5.0	12.0
3	8.0	15.0

ANS:

```
1    // Exercise 3.19 Solution
2    #include <iostream.h>
3    #include <iomanip.h>
4    #include <math.h>
5
6    double hypotenuse( double, double );
7
8    int main()
9    {
10       double side1, side2;
11
12       cout << setiosflags( ios::fixed | ios::showpoint );
13
14       for ( int i = 1; i <= 3; ++i ) {
15          cout << "\nEnter 2 sides of right triangle: ";
16          cin >> side1 >> side2;
17          cout << "Hypotenuse:  " << setprecision( 1 )
18               << hypotenuse( side1, side2 ) << endl;
19       }
20
21       return 0;
22    }
23
24    double hypotenuse( double s1, double s2 )
25    {
26       return sqrt( s1 * s1 + s2 * s2 );
27    }
```

```
Enter 2 sides of right triangle: 4 5
Hypotenuse:  6.4

Enter 2 sides of right triangle: 3 4
Hypotenuse:  5.0

Enter 2 sides of right triangle: 12 7
Hypotenuse:  13.9
```

3.20   Write a function **multiple** that determines for a pair of integers whether the second integer is a multiple of the first. The function should take two integer arguments and return **true** if the second is a multiple of the first, and **false** otherwise. Use this function in a program that inputs a series of pairs of integers.

  ANS:

```
1   // Exercise 3.20 Solution
2   #include <iostream.h>
3
4   bool multiple( int, int );
5
6   int main()
7   {
8      int x, y;
9
10     for ( int i = 1; i <= 3; ++i ) {
11        cout << "Enter two integers: ";
12        cin >> x >> y;
13
14        if ( multiple( x, y ) )
15           cout << y << " is a multiple of " << x << "\n\n";
16        else
17           cout << y << " is not a multiple of " << x << "\n\n";
18     }
19
20     cout << endl;
21     return 0;
22  }
23
24  bool multiple( int a, int b )
25  {
26     return !( b % a );
27  }
```

```
Enter two integers: 3 4
4 is not a multiple of 3

Enter two integers: 12 3
3 is not a multiple of 12

Enter two integers: 3 12
12 is a multiple of 3
```

3.21   Write a program that inputs a series of integers and passes them one at a time to function **even** which uses the modulus operator to determine if an integer is even. The function should take an integer argument and return **true** if the integer is even and **false** otherwise.

  ANS:

```
1   // Exercise 3.21 Solution
2   #include <iostream.h>
3
4   bool even( int );
5
6   int main()
7   {
8      int x;
9
10     for ( int i = 1; i <= 3; ++i ) {
11        cout << "Enter an integer: ";
12        cin >> x;
13
```

```
14              if ( even( x ) )
15                  cout << x << " is an even integer\n\n";
16              else
17                  cout << x << " is an odd integer\n\n";
18          }
19
20          cout << endl;
21          return 0;
22      }
23
24      bool even( int a )
25      {
26          return !( a % 2 );
27      }
```

```
Enter an integer: 8
8 is an even integer

Enter an integer: 3
3 is an odd integer

Enter an integer: 99
99 is an odd integer
```

3.22   Write a function that displays at the left margin of the screen a solid square of asterisks whose side is specified in integer parameter **side**. For example, if **side** is **4**, the function displays

```
****
****
****
****
```

ANS:

```
1   // Exercise 3.22 Solution
2   #include <iostream.h>
3
4   void square( int );
5
6   int main()
7   {
8       int side;
9
10      cout << "Enter side: ";
11      cin >> side;
12      cout << '\n';
13
14      square( side );
15
16      cout << endl;
17      return 0;
18  }
19
20  void square( int s )
21  {
22      for ( int row = 1; row <= s; ++row ) {
23
24          for ( int col = 1; col <= s; ++col )
25              cout << '*';
26
27          cout << '\n';
28      }
29  }
```

```
Enter side: 8

*******
*******
*******
*******
*******
*******
*******
*******
```

3.23   Modify the function created in Exercise 3.22 to form the square out of whatever character is contained in character parameter **fillCharacter**. Thus if **side** is **5** and **fillCharacter** is "**#**" then this function should print

```
#####
#####
#####
#####
#####
```

ANS:

```
1   // Exercise 3.23 Solution
2   #include <iostream.h>
3
4   void square( int, char );
5
6   int main()
7   {
8      int s;
9      char c;
10
11     cout << "Enter a character and the side length: ";
12     cin >> c >> s;
13     cout << '\n';
14
15     square( s, c );
16
17     cout << endl;
18     return 0;
19  }
20
21  void square( int side, char fillCharacter )
22  {
23     for ( int row = 1; row <= side; ++row ) {
24
25        for ( int col = 1; col <= side; ++col )
26           cout << fillCharacter;
27
28        cout << '\n';
29     }
30  }
```

```
Enter a character and the side length: H 5

HHHHH
HHHHH
HHHHH
HHHHH
HHHHH
```

3.24   Use techniques similar to those developed in Exercises 3.22 and 3.23 to produce a program that graphs a wide range of shapes.

3.25   Write program segments that accomplish each of the following:
  a) Calculate the integer part of the quotient when integer **a** is divided by integer **b**.
  b) Calculate the integer remainder when integer **a** is divided by integer **b**.
  c) Use the program pieces developed in a) and b) to write a function that inputs an integer between **1** and **32767** and prints it as a series of digits, each pair of which is separated by two spaces. For example, the integer **4562** should be printed as

```
    4   5   6   2
```

ANS:

```
1   // Exercise 3.25 Solution
2   #include <iostream.h>
3   #include <iomanip.h>
4
5   int quotient( int, int );
6   int remainder( int, int );
7
8   int main()
9   {
10     int number, divisor = 10000;
11
12     cout << "Enter an integer between 1 and 32767: ";
13     cin >> number;
14
15     cout << "The digits in the number are:\n";
16
17     while ( number >= 1 ) {
18
19       if ( number >= divisor ) {
20         cout << setw( 3 ) << quotient( number, divisor );
21         number = remainder( number, divisor );
22         divisor = quotient( divisor, 10 );
23       }
24       else
25         divisor = quotient( divisor, 10 );
26     }
27
28     cout << endl;
29     return 0;
30   }
31
32   // Part A: determine quotient using integer division
33   int quotient( int a, int b )
34   {
35     return a / b;
36   }
37
38   // Part B: determine remainder using the modulus operator
39   int remainder( int a, int b )
40   {
41     return a % b;
42   }
```

```
Enter an integer between 1 and 32767: 6758

The digits in the number are:
   6   7   5   8
```

3.26 Write a function that takes the time as three integer arguments (for hours, minutes, and seconds), and returns the number of seconds since the last time the clock "struck 12." Use this function to calculate the amount of time in seconds between two times, both of which are within one 12-hour cycle of the clock.

ANS:

```
1   // Exercise 3.26 Solution
2   #include <iostream.h>
3
4   unsigned seconds( unsigned, unsigned, unsigned );
5
6   int main()
7   {
8      unsigned hours, minutes, secs, temp;
9
10     cout << "Enter the first time as three integers: ";
11     cin >> hours >> minutes >> secs;
12
13     temp = seconds( hours, minutes, secs );
14
15     cout << "Enter the second time as three integers: ";
16     cin >> hours >> minutes >> secs;
17
18     cout << "The difference between the times is "
19          << seconds( hours, minutes, secs ) - temp
20          << " seconds" << endl;
21
22     return 0;
23  }
24
25  unsigned seconds( unsigned h, unsigned m, unsigned s )
26  {
27     return 3600 * ( h >= 12 ? h - 12 : h ) + 60 * m + s;
28  }
```

```
Enter the first time as three integers: 5 33 45
Enter the second time as three integers: 9 22 8
The difference between the times is 13703 seconds
```

3.27 Implement the following integer functions:
  a) Function **celsius** returns the Celsius equivalent of a Fahrenheit temperature.
  b) Function **fahrenheit** returns the Fahrenheit equivalent of a Celsius temperature.
  c) Use these functions to write a program that prints charts showing the Fahrenheit equivalents of all Celsius temperatures from 0 to 100 degrees, and the Celsius equivalents of all Fahrenheit temperatures from 32 to 212 degrees. Print the outputs in a neat tabular format that minimizes the number of lines of output while remaining readable.

ANS:

```
1   // Exercise 3.27 Solution
2   #include <iostream.h>
3
4   int celcius( int );
5   int fahrenheit( int );
6
```

```
7   int main()
8   {
9      cout << "Fahrenheit equivalents of Celcius temperatures:\n"
10          << "Celcius\t\tFahrenheit\n";
11
12      for ( int i = 0; i <= 100; ++i )
13         cout << i << "\t\t" << fahrenheit( i ) << '\n';
14
15      cout << "\nCelcius equivalents of Fahrenheit temperatures:"
16          << "\nFahrenheit\tCelcius\n";
17
18      for ( int j = 32; j <= 212; ++j )
19         cout << j << "\t\t" << celcius( j ) << '\n';
20
21      cout << endl;
22      return 0;
23   }
24
25   int celcius( int fTemp )
26   {
27      return static_cast< int > ( 5.0 / 9.0 * ( fTemp - 32 ) );
28   }
29
30   int fahrenheit( int cTemp )
31   {
32      return static_cast< int > ( 9.0 / 5.0 * cTemp + 32 );
33   }
```

```
Fahrenheit equivalents of Celcius temperatures:
Celcius        Fahrenheit
0              32
1              33
2              35
...
Celcius equivalents of Fahrenheit temperatures:
32             0
33             0
34             1
...
```

3.28   Write a function that returns the smallest of three floating-point numbers.
            ANS:

```
1   // Exercise 3.28 Solution
2   #include <iostream.h>
3   #include <iomanip.h>
4
5   float smallest3( float, float, float );
6
7   int main()
8   {
9      float x, y, z;
10
11      cout << "Enter three floating point values: ";
12      cin >> x >> y >> z;
13      cout << "The smallest value is " << smallest3( x, y, z ) << endl;
14      return 0;
15   }
16
17   float smallest3( float smallest, float b, float c )
18   {
19      if ( b < smallest && c > smallest )
20         return b;
```

```
21        else if ( c < smallest )
22           return c;
23        else
24           return smallest;
25     }
```

```
Enter three floating point values: 4.3 6.77 9.76
The smallest value is 4.3
```

3.29   An integer number is said to be a *perfect number* if its factors, including 1 (but not the number itself), sum to the number. For example, 6 is a perfect number because $6 = 1 + 2 + 3$. Write a function **perfect** that determines if parameter **number** is a perfect number. Use this function in a program that determines and prints all the perfect numbers between 1 and 1000. Print the factors of each perfect number to confirm that the number is indeed perfect. Challenge the power of your computer by testing numbers much larger than 1000.

ANS:

```
1     // Exercise 3.29 Solution
2     #include <iostream.h>
3
4     bool perfect( int );
5
6     int main()
7     {
8        cout << "For the integers from 1 to 1000:\n";
9
10       for ( int j = 2; j <= 1000; ++j )
11          if ( perfect( j ) )
12             cout << j << " is perfect\n";
13
14       cout << endl;
15       return 0;
16    }
17
18    bool perfect( int value )
19    {
20       int factorSum = 1;
21
22       for ( int i = 2; i <= value / 2; ++i )
23          if ( value % i == 0 )
24             factorSum += i;
25
26       return factorSum == value ? true : false;
27    }
```

```
For the integers from 1 to 1000:
6 is perfect
28 is perfect
496 is perfect
```

3.30   An integer is said to be *prime* if it is divisible only by 1 and itself. For example, 2, 3, 5, and 7 are prime, but 4, 6, 8, and 9 are not.

    a) Write a function that determines if a number is prime.

    b) Use this function in a program that determines and prints all the prime numbers between 1 and 10,000. How many of these 10,000 numbers do you really have to test before being sure that you have found all the primes?

    c) Initially you might think that $n/2$ is the upper limit for which you must test to see if a number is prime, but you need only go as high as the square root of n. Why? Rewrite the program, and run it both ways. Estimate the performance improvement.

ANS:

```
1   // Exercise 3.30 Part A Solution
2   #include <iostream.h>
3   #include <iomanip.h>
4
5   bool prime( int );
6
7   int main()
8   {
9      int count = 0;
10
11     cout << "The prime numbers from 1 to 10000 are:\n";
12
13     for ( int loop = 2; loop <= 10000; ++loop )
14        if ( prime( loop ) ) {
15           ++count;
16           cout << setw( 6 ) << loop;
17
18           if ( count % 10 == 0 )
19              cout << '\n';
20        }
21
22     return 0;
23  }
24
25  bool prime( int n )
26  {
27     for ( int loop2 = 2; loop2 <= n / 2; loop2++ )
28        if ( n % loop2 == 0 )
29           return false;
30
31     return true;
32  }
```

```
The prime numbers from 1 to 10000 are:
     2     3     5     7    11    13    17    19    23    29
    31    37    41    43    47    53    59    61    67    71
    73    79    83    89    97   101   103   107   109   113
   127   131   137   139   149   151   157   163   167   173
   179   181   191   193   197   199   211   223   227   229
   233   239   241   251   257   263   269   271   277   281
   283   293   307   311   313   317   331   337   347   349
   353   359   367   373   379   383   389   397   401   409
   419   421   431   433   439   443   449   457   461   463
...
  9739  9743  9749  9767  9769  9781  9787  9791  9803  9811
  9817  9829  9833  9839  9851  9857  9859  9871  9883  9887
  9901  9907  9923  9929  9931  9941  9949  9967  9973
```

```
1   // Exercise 3.30 Part C Solution
2   #include <iostream.h>
3   #include <iomanip.h>
4   #include <math.h>
5
6   bool prime( int n );
7
8   int main()
9   {
10     int count = 0;
11
12     cout << "The prime numbers from 1 to 10000 are:\n";
13
```

```
14        for ( int j = 2; j <= 10000; ++j )
15           if ( prime( j ) ) {
16              ++count;
17              cout << setw( 5 ) << j;
18
19              if ( count % 10 == 0 )
20                 cout << '\n';
21           }
22
23        return 0;
24     }
25
26     bool prime( int n )
27     {
28        for ( int i = 2; i <= static_cast< int > ( sqrt( n ) ); ++i )
29           if ( n % i == 0 )
30              return false;
31
32        return true;
33     }
```

```
The prime numbers from 1 to 10000 are:
    2     3     5     7    11    13    17    19    23    29
   31    37    41    43    47    53    59    61    67    71
   73    79    83    89    97   101   103   107   109   113
  127   131   137   139   149   151   157   163   167   173
  179   181   191   193   197   199   211   223   227   229
  233   239   241   251   257   263   269   271   277   281
  283   293   307   311   313   317   331   337   347   349
  353   359   367   373   379   383   389   397   401   409
  419   421   431   433   439   443   449   457   461   463
...
 9739  9743  9749  9767  9769  9781  9787  9791  9803  9811
 9817  9829  9833  9839  9851  9857  9859  9871  9883  9887
 9901  9907  9923  9929  9931  9941  9949  9967  9973
```

3.31   Write a function that takes an integer value and returns the number with its digits reversed. For example, given the number 7631, the function should return 1367.

ANS:

```
1    // Exercise 3.31 Solution
2    #include <iostream.h>
3    #include <iomanip.h>
4
5    int reverseDigits( int );
6    int width( int );
7
8    int main()
9    {
10       int number;
11
12       cout << "Enter a number between 1 and 9999: ";
13       cin >> number;
14
15       cout << "The number with its digits reversed is: "
16            << setw( ( width( number ) ) ) << setfill( '0' )
17            << reverseDigits( number )
18            << endl;
19
20       return 0;
21    }
22
```

```
23   int reverseDigits( int n )
24   {
25      int reverse = 0, divisor = 1000, multiplier = 1;
26
27      while ( n > 10 ) {
28
29         if ( n >= divisor ) {
30            reverse += n / divisor * multiplier;
31            n %= divisor;
32            divisor /= 10;
33            multiplier *= 10;
34         }
35         else
36            divisor /= 10;
37      }
38
39      reverse += n * multiplier;
40      return reverse;
41   }
42
43   int width( int n )
44   {
45      if ( n /= 1000 )
46         return 4;
47      else if ( n /= 100 )
48         return 3;
49      else if ( n /= 10 )
50         return 2;
51      else
52         return 1;
53   }
```

```
Enter a number between 1 and 9999: 8765
The number with its digits reversed is: 5678
```

3.32   The *greatest common divisor (GCD)* of two integers is the largest integer that evenly divides each of the numbers.
Write a function **gcd** that returns the greatest common divisor of two integers.
   ANS:

```
1    // Exercise 3.32 Solution
2    #include <iostream.h>
3
4    int gcd( int, int );
5
6    int main()
7    {
8       int a, b;
9
10      for ( int j = 1; j <= 5; ++j ) {
11         cout << "Enter two integers: ";
12         cin >> a >> b;
13         cout << "The greatest common divisor of " << a << " and "
14              << b << " is " <<  gcd( a, b ) << "\n\n";
15      }
16
17      return 0;
18   }
19
20   int gcd( int x, int y )
21   {
22      int greatest = 1;
23
```

```
24        for ( int i = 2; i <= ( ( x < y ) ? x: y ); ++i )
25          if ( x % i == 0 && y % i == 0 )
26             greatest = i;
27
28        return greatest;
29   }
```

```
    Enter two integers: 6 8
    The greatest common divisor of 6 and 8 is 2

    Enter two integers: 789 4
    The greatest common divisor of 789 and 4 is 1

    Enter two integers: 9999 27
    The greatest common divisor of 9999 and 27 is 9

    Enter two integers: 73652 8
    The greatest common divisor of 73652 and 8 is 4

    Enter two integers: 99 11
    The greatest common divisor of 99 and 11 is 11
```

3.33   Write a function **qualityPoints** that inputs a student's average and returns 4 if a student's average is 90-100, 3 if the average is 80-89, 2 if the average is 70-79, 1 if the average is 60-69, and 0 if the average is lower than 60.

ANS:

```
 1   // Exercise 3.33 Solution
 2   #include <iostream.h>
 3
 4   int qualityPoints( int );
 5
 6   int main()
 7   {
 8      int average;
 9
10      for ( int loop = 1; loop <= 5; ++loop ) {
11         cout << "\nEnter the student's average: ";
12         cin >> average;
13         cout << average << " on a 4 point scale is "
14              << qualityPoints( average ) << '\n';
15      }
16
17      cout << endl;
18      return 0;
19   }
20
21   int qualityPoints( int average )
22   {
23      if ( average >= 90 )
24         return 4;
25      else if ( average >= 80 )
26         return 3;
27      else if ( average >= 70 )
28         return 2;
29      else if ( average >= 60 )
30         return 1;
31      else
32         return 0;
33   }
```

```
Enter the student's average: 99
99 on a 4 point scale is 4

Enter the student's average: 72
72 on a 4 point scale is 2

Enter the student's average: 88
88 on a 4 point scale is 3

Enter the student's average: 65
65 on a 4 point scale is 1

Enter the student's average: 33
33 on a 4 point scale is 0
```

3.34   Write a program that simulates coin tossing. For each toss of the coin the program should print **Heads** or **Tails**. Let the program toss the coin 100 times, and count the number of times each side of the coin appears. Print the results. The program should call a separate function **flip** that takes no arguments and returns **0** for tails and **1** for heads. *Note:* If the program realistically simulates the coin tossing, then each side of the coin should appear approximately half the time.

       ANS:

```
1   // Exercise 3.34 Solution
2   #include <iostream.h>
3   #include <stdlib.h>
4   #include <time.h>
5
6   int flip( void );
7
8   int main()
9   {
10      int headCount = 0, tailCount = 0;
11
12      srand( time( 0 ) );
13
14      for ( int loop = 1; loop <= 100; loop++ ) {
15
16         if ( flip() == 0 ) {
17            tailCount++;
18            cout << "Tails ";
19         }
20         else {
21            headCount++;
22            cout << "Heads ";
23         }
24
25         if ( loop % 10 == 0 )
26            cout << '\n';
27      }
28
29      cout << "\nThe total number of Heads was "
30           << headCount << "\nThe total number of Tails was "
31           << tailCount << endl;
32
33      return 0;
34   }
35
36   int flip( void )
37   {
38      return rand() % 2;
39   }
```

```
Tails Tails Heads Tails Tails Tails Tails Tails Tails Heads
Tails Tails Tails Tails Tails Heads Tails Tails Tails Heads
Tails Heads Heads Tails Heads Tails Tails Heads Tails Heads
Tails Tails Heads Tails Heads Heads Tails Tails Heads Heads
Heads Heads Heads Heads Tails Heads Heads Heads Heads Heads
Tails Heads Heads Tails Tails Tails Tails Tails Heads Tails
Tails Heads Heads Heads Tails Heads Heads Tails Tails Tails
Heads Heads Tails Heads Tails Heads Heads Tails Heads Tails
Heads Heads Heads Tails Tails Tails Heads Tails Heads Tails
Tails Heads Heads Heads Heads Tails Tails Tails Tails Heads

The total number of Heads was 47
The total number of Tails was 53
```

3.35 Computers are playing an increasing role in education. Write a program that will help an elementary school student learn multiplication. Use **rand** to produce two positive one-digit integers. It should then type a question such as:

```
How much is 6 times 7?
```

The student then types the answer. Your program checks the student's answer. If it is correct, print **"Very good!"** and then ask another multiplication question. If the answer is wrong, print **"No. Please try again."** and then let the student try the same question again repeatedly until the student finally gets it right.

ANS:

```cpp
1   // Exercise 3.35 Solution
2   #include <iostream.h>
3   #include <stdlib.h>
4   #include <time.h>
5
6   void multiplication( void );
7
8   int main()
9   {
10     srand( time( 0 ) );
11     multiplication();
12     return 0;
13  }
14
15  void multiplication( void )
16  {
17     int x, y, response = 0;
18
19     cout << "Enter -1 to End.\n";
20
21     while ( response != -1 ) {
22        x = rand() % 10;
23        y = rand() % 10;
24
25        cout << "How much is " << x << " times " << y << " (-1 to End)? ";
26        cin >> response;
27
28        while ( response != -1 && response != x * y ) {
29           cout << "No. Please try again.\n? ";
30           cin >> response;
31        }
32
33        if ( response != -1 )
34           cout << "Very good!\n\n";
35     }
36
37     cout << "That's all for now. Bye." << endl;
38  }
```

```
Enter -1 to End.
How much is 8 times 1 (-1 to End)? 8
Very good!

How much is 5 times 2 (-1 to End)? 9
No. Please try again.
? 7
No. Please try again.
? 10
Very good!

How much is 1 times 5 (-1 to End)? -1
That's all for now. Bye.
```

3.36 The use of computers in education is referred to as *computer-assisted instruction* (CAI). One problem that develops in CAI environments is student fatigue. This can be eliminated by varying the computer's dialogue to hold the student's attention. Modify the program of Exercise 3.35 so the various comments are printed for each correct answer and each incorrect answer as follows:

Responses to a correct answer

```
Very good!
Excellent!
Nice work!
Keep up the good work!
```

Responses to an incorrect answer

```
No. Please try again.
Wrong. Try once more.
Don't give up!
No. Keep trying.
```

Use the random number generator to choose a number from 1 to 4 to select an appropriate response to each answer. Use a **switch** structure to issue the responses.

ANS:

```
1   // Exercise 3.36 Solution
2   #include <iostream.h>
3   #include <stdlib.h>
4   #include <time.h>
5
6   void correctMessage( void );
7   void incorrectMessage( void );
8   void multiplication( void );
9
10  int main()
11  {
12     srand( time( 0 ) );
13     multiplication();
14     return 0;
15  }
16
17  void correctMessage( void )
18  {
19     switch ( rand() % 4 ) {
20        case 0:
21           cout << "Very good!";
22           break;
```

```
23              case 1:
24                 cout << "Excellent!";
25                 break;
26              case 2:
27                 cout << "Nice work!";
28                 break;
29              case 3:
30                 cout << "Keep up the good work!";
31                 break;
32          }
33
34          cout << "\n\n";
35     }
36
37     void incorrectMessage( void )
38     {
39          switch ( rand() % 4 ) {
40              case 0:
41                 cout << "No. Please try again.";
42                 break;
43              case 1:
44                 cout << "Wrong. Try once more.";
45                 break;
46              case 2:
47                 cout << "Don't give up!";
48                 break;
49              case 3:
50                 cout << "No. Keep trying.";
51                 break;
52          }
53
54          cout << "\n? ";
55     }
56
57     void multiplication( void )
58     {
59          int x, y, response = 0;
60
61          while ( response != -1 ) {
62              x = rand() % 10;
63              y = rand() % 10;
64
65              cout << "How much is " << x << " times " << y
66                  << " (-1 to End)? ";
67              cin >> response;
68
69              while ( response != -1 && response != x * y ) {
70                  incorrectMessage();
71                  cin >> response;
72              }
73
74              if ( response != -1 ) {
75                  correctMessage();
76              }
77          }
78
79          cout << "That's all for now. Bye." << endl;
80     }
```

```
How much is 1 times 7 (-1 to End)? 8
No. Keep trying.
? 0
No. Please try again.
? 5
No. Keep trying.
? 6
Don't give up!
? 3
No. Please try again.
? 1
No. Keep trying.
? 3
No. Please try again.
? 9
Don't give up!
? 6
Don't give up!
? 7
Nice work!

How much is 0 times 4 (-1 to End)? -1
That's all for now. Bye.
```

3.37 More sophisticated computer-aided instruction systems monitor the student's performance over a period of time. The decision to begin a new topic is often based on the student's success with previous topics. Modify the program of Exercise 3.36 to count the number of correct and incorrect responses typed by the student. After the student types 10 answers, your program should calculate the percentage of correct responses. If the percentage is lower than 75 percent, your program should print **"Please ask your instructor for extra help"** and then terminate.

ANS:

```
1  // Exercise 3.37 Solution
2  #include <iostream.h>
3  #include <stdlib.h>
4  #include <time.h>
5
6  void multiplication( void );
7  void correctMessage( void );
8  void incorrectMessage( void );
9
10 int main()
11 {
12    srand( time( 0 ) );
13    multiplication();
14    return 0;
15 }
16
17 void multiplication( void )
18 {
19    int x, y, response, right = 0, wrong = 0;
20
21    for ( int i = 1; i <= 10; ++i ) {
22       x = rand() % 10;
23       y = rand() % 10;
24
25       cout << "How much is " << x << " times " << y << "? ";
26       cin >> response;
27
```

```
28          while ( response != x * y ) {
29             ++wrong;
30             incorrectMessage();
31             cin >> response;
32          }
33
34          ++right;
35          correctMessage();
36       }
37
38       if ( static_cast< float > ( right ) / ( right + wrong ) < .75 )
39          cout << "Please ask your instructor for extra help.\n";
40
41       cout << "That's all for now. Bye." << endl;
42    }
43
44    void correctMessage( void )
45    {
46       switch ( rand() % 4 ) {
47          case 0:
48             cout << "Very good!";
49             break;
50          case 1:
51             cout << "Excellent!";
52             break;
53          case 2:
54             cout << "Nice work!";
55             break;
56          case 3:
57             cout << "Keep up the good work!";
58             break;
59       }
60
61       cout << "\n\n";
62    }
63
64    void incorrectMessage( void )
65    {
66       switch ( rand() % 4 ) {
67          case 0:
68             cout << "No. Please try again.";
69             break;
70          case 1:
71             cout << "Wrong. Try once more.";
72             break;
73          case 2:
74             cout << "Don't give up!";
75             break;
76          case 3:
77             cout << "No. Keep trying.";
78             break;
79       }
80
81       cout << "\n? ";
82    }
```

```
...
How much is 8 times 4? 32
Excellent!

How much is 9 times 0? 0
Nice work!

How much is 6 times 3? 18
Very good!

How much is 8 times 0? 0
Nice work!

That's all for now. Bye.
```

3.38   Write a program that plays the game of "guess the number" as follows: Your program chooses the number to be guessed by selecting an integer at random in the range 1 to 1000. The program then types:

```
I have a number between 1 and 1000.
Can you guess my number?
Please type your first guess.
```

The player then types a first guess. The program responds with one of the following:

```
1. Excellent! You guessed the number!
   Would you like to play again (y or n)?
2. Too low. Try again.
3. Too high. Try again.
```

If the player's guess is incorrect, your program should loop until the player finally gets the number right. Your program should keep telling the player **Too high** or **Too low** to help the player "zero in" on the correct answer. Note: The searching technique employed in this problem is called *binary search*. We will say more about this in the next problem.

ANS:

```cpp
1   // Exercise 3.38 Solution
2   #include <iostream.h>
3   #include <stdlib.h>
4   #include <time.h>
5
6   void guessGame( void );
7   bool isCorrect( int, int );
8
9   int main()
10  {
11     srand( time( 0 ) );
12     guessGame();
13     return 0;
14  }
15
16  void guessGame( void )
17  {
18     int answer, guess;
19     char response;
20
21     do {
22        answer = 1 + rand() % 1000;
23        cout << "\nI have a number between 1 and 1000.\n"
24             << "Can you guess my number?\nPlease type your"
25             << " first guess.\n? ";
```

```
26          cin >> guess;
27
28          while ( !isCorrect( guess, answer ) )
29             cin >> guess;
30
31          cout << "\nExcellent! You guessed the number!\n"
32               << "Would you like to play again?\nPlease type (y/n)? ";
33          cin >> response;
34
35       } while ( response == 'y' );
36    }
37
38    bool isCorrect( int g, int a )
39    {
40       if ( g == a )
41          return true;
42
43       if ( g < a )
44          cout << "Too low. Try again.\n? ";
45       else
46          cout << "Too high. Try again.\n? ";
47
48       return false;
49    }
```

```
I have a number between 1 and 1000.
Can you guess my number?
Please type your first guess.
? 500
Too low. Try again.
? 750
Too low. Try again.
? 875
Too high. Try again.
? 812
Too high. Try again.
? 781
Too high. Try again.
? 765
Too high. Try again.
? 757
Too high. Try again.
? 753
Too low. Try again.
? 756

Excellent! You guessed the number!
Would you like to play again?
Please type (y/n)? n
```

3.39   Modify the program of Exercise 3.38 to count the number of guesses the player makes. If the number is 10 or fewer, print **Either you know the secret or you got lucky!** If the player guesses the number in 10 tries, then print **Ahah! You know the secret!** If the player makes more than 10 guesses, then print **You should be able to do better!** Why should it take no more than 10 guesses? Well with each "good guess" the player should be able to eliminate half of the numbers. Now show why any number 1 to 1000 can be guessed in 10 or fewer tries.

ANS:

```
1    // Exercise 3.39 Solution
2    #include <iostream.h>
3    #include <stdlib.h>
4    #include <time.h>
5
```

```
 6   void guessGame( void );
 7   bool isCorrect( int, int );
 8   void display( int );
 9
10   int main()
11   {
12      srand( time( 0 ) );
13      guessGame();
14      return 0;
15   }
16
17   void guessGame( void )
18   {
19      int answer, guess, total = 1;
20      char response;
21
22      do {
23         answer = 1 + rand() % 1000;
24         cout << "I have a number between 1 and 1000."
25              << "\nCan you guess my number?\nPlease type"
26              << " your first guess.\n? ";
27         cin >> guess;
28
29         while ( !isCorrect( guess, answer ) ) {
30            cin >> guess;
31            ++total;
32         }
33
34         cout << "\nExcellent! You guessed the number!\n";
35
36         display( total );
37
38         cout << "Would you like to play again?\nPlease type (y/n)? ";
39         cin >> response;
40
41      } while ( response == 'y' );
42   }
43
44   bool isCorrect( int g, int a )
45   {
46      if ( g == a )
47         return true;
48
49      if ( g < a )
50         cout << "Too low. Try again.\n? ";
51      else
52         cout << "Too high. Try again.\n? ";
53
54      return false;
55   }
56
57   void display( int t )
58   {
59      if ( t < 10 )
60         cout << "Either you know the secret or you got lucky!\n";
61      else if ( t == 10 )
62         cout << "Ahah! You know the secret!\n";
63      else
64         cout << "You should be able to do better!\n\n";
65   }
```

```
I have a number between 1 and 1000.
Can you guess my number?
Please type your first guess.
? 800
Too high. Try again.
? 300
Too high. Try again.
? 220
Too low. Try again.
? 280
Too high. Try again.
? 255
Too high. Try again.
? 238
Too low. Try again.
? 247
Too high. Try again.
? 243

Excellent! You guessed the number!
Either you know the secret or you got lucky!
Would you like to play again?
Please type (y/n)? n
```

3.40 Write a recursive function **power (base, exponent)** that when invoked returns

$$base^{exponent}$$

For example, **power(3, 4)** = 3 * 3 * 3 * 3. Assume that **exponent** is an integer greater than or equal to 1. *Hint:* The recursion step would use the relationship

$$base^{exponent} = base \cdot base^{exponent - 1}$$

and the terminating condition occurs when **exponent** is equal to **1** because

$$base^{1} = base$$

ANS:

```
1   // Exercise 3.40 Solution
2   #include <iostream.h>
3
4   long power( long, long );
5
6   int main()
7   {
8      long b, e;
9
10     cout << "Enter a base and an exponent: ";
11     cin >> b >> e;
12     cout << b << " raised to the " << e << " is "
13          << power( b, e ) << endl;
14
15     return 0;
16  }
17
18  long power( long base, long exponent )
19  {
20     return exponent == 1 ? base : base * power( base, exponent - 1 );
21  }
```

```
Enter a base and an exponent: 7 2
7 raised to the 2 is 49
```

3.41   The Fibonacci series

  0, 1, 1, 2, 3, 5, 8, 13, 21, ...

begins with the terms 0 and 1 and has the property that each succeeding term is the sum of the two preceding terms. a) Write a *nonrecursive* function **fibonacci(n)** that calculates the *n*th Fibonacci number. b) Determine the largest Fibonacci number that can be printed on your system. Modify the program of part a) to use **double** instead of **int** to calculate and return Fibonacci numbers, and use this modified program to repeat part b).

  ANS:

```
1   // Exercise 3.41 Part A Solution
2   // NOTE: This exercise was accidently placed in this
3   // chapter. The solution utilizes ARRAYS which are
4   // introduced in the next chapter.
5   #include <iostream.h>
6
7   int MAX = 23;    // the maximum number for which the
8                    // fibonacci value can be calculated
9                    // on 2-byte integer systems
10
11  int fibonacci( int );
12
13  int main()
14  {
15     for ( int loop = 0; loop <= MAX; ++loop )
16        cout << "fibonacci(" << loop << ") = " << fibonacci( loop )
17             << "\n";
18
19     cout << endl;
20     return 0;
21  }
22
23  int fibonacci( int n )
24  {
25     int fib[ 23 ];
26
27     fib[ 0 ] = 0;
28     fib[ 1 ] = 1;
29
30     for ( int j = 2; j <= n; ++j )
31        fib[ j ] = fib[ j - 1 ] + fib[ j - 2 ];
32
33     return fib[ n ];
34  }
```

```
fibonacci(1) = 1
fibonacci(2) = 1
fibonacci(3) = 2
fibonacci(4) = 3
fibonacci(5) = 5
fibonacci(6) = 8
fibonacci(7) = 13
fibonacci(8) = 21
fibonacci(9) = 34
fibonacci(10) = 55
fibonacci(11) = 89
fibonacci(12) = 144
```

```
fibonacci(13)  =  233
fibonacci(14)  =  377
fibonacci(15)  =  610
fibonacci(16)  =  987
fibonacci(17)  =  1597
fibonacci(18)  =  2584
fibonacci(19)  =  4181
fibonacci(20)  =  6765
fibonacci(21)  =  10946
fibonacci(22)  =  17711
fibonacci(23)  =  28658
```

```cpp
1    // Exercise 3.41 Part B Solution
2    // NOTE: This exercise was accidently placed in this
3    // chapter. The solution utiliizes ARRAYS which are
4    // introduced in the next chapter.
5    #include <iostream.h>
6    #include <iomanip.h>
7
8    double fibonacci( int );
9
10   int main()
11   {
12      cout << setiosflags( ios::fixed | ios::showpoint );
13
14      for ( int loop = 0; loop < 100; ++loop )
15         cout << setprecision( 1 ) << "fibonacci(" << loop << ") = "
16              << fibonacci( loop ) << endl;
17
18      return 0;
19   }
20
21   double fibonacci( int n )
22   {
23      double fib[ 100 ];
24
25      fib[ 0 ] = 0.0;
26      fib[ 1 ] = 1.0;
27
28      for ( int j = 2; j <= n; j++ )
29         fib[ j ] = fib[ j - 1 ] + fib[ j - 2 ];
30
31      return fib[ n ];
32   }
```

```
fibonacci(0)  =  0.0
fibonacci(1)  =  1.0
fibonacci(2)  =  1.0
fibonacci(3)  =  2.0
fibonacci(4)  =  3.0
fibonacci(5)  =  5.0
fibonacci(6)  =  8.0
fibonacci(7)  =  13.0

...
fibonacci(96)  =  51680708854858326000.0
fibonacci(97)  =  83621143489848426000.0
fibonacci(98)  =  135301852344706760000.0
fibonacci(99)  =  218922995834555200000.0
```

3.42   *(Towers of Hanoi)* Every budding computer scientist must grapple with certain classic problems. The Towers of Hanoi (see Fig. 3.28) is one of the most famous of these. Legend has it that in a temple in the Far East, priests are attempting to move a stack of disks from one peg to another. The initial stack had 64 disks threaded onto one peg and arranged from bottom to top by decreasing size. The priests are attempting to move the stack from this peg to a second peg under the constraints that exactly one disk is moved at a time, and at no time may a larger disk be placed above a smaller disk. A third peg is available for temporarily holding disks. Supposedly the world will end when the priests complete their task, so there is little incentive for us to facilitate their efforts.

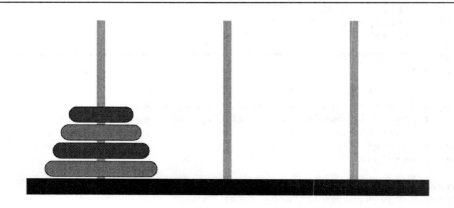

Fig. 3.28   The Towers of Hanoi for the case with four disks.

Let us assume that the priests are attempting to move the disks from peg 1 to peg 3. We wish to develop an algorithm that will print the precise sequence of peg-to-peg disk transfers.

If we were to approach this problem with conventional methods, we would rapidly find ourselves hopelessly knotted up in managing the disks. Instead, if we attack the problem with recursion in mind, it immediately becomes tractable. Moving n disks can be viewed in terms of moving only $n - 1$ disks (and hence the recursion) as follows:

a)   Move $n - 1$ disks from peg 1 to peg 2, using peg 3 as a temporary holding area.
b)   Move the last disk (the largest) from peg 1 to peg 3.
c)   Move the $n - 1$ disks from peg 2 to peg 3, using peg 1 as a temporary holding area.

The process ends when the last task involves moving $n = 1$ disk, i.e., the base case. This is accomplished by trivially moving the disk without the need for a temporary holding area.

Write a program to solve the Towers of Hanoi problem. Use a recursive function with four parameters:

a)   The number of disks to be moved
b)   The peg on which these disks are initially threaded
c)   The peg to which this stack of disks is to be moved
d)   The peg to be used as a temporary holding area

Your program should print the precise instructions it will take to move the disks from the starting peg to the destination peg. For example, to move a stack of three disks from peg 1 to peg 3, your program should print the following series of moves:

1 → 3 (This means move one disk from peg 1 to peg 3.)
1 → 2
3 → 2
1 → 3
2 → 1
2 → 3
1 → 3
ANS:

```
1   // Exercise 3.42 Solution
2   #include <iostream.h>
3
4   void towers( int, int, int, int );
5
```

```
6    int main()
7    {
8        int nDisks;
9
10       cout << "Enter the starting number of disks: ";
11       cin >> nDisks;
12       towers( nDisks, 1, 3, 2 );
13       return 0;
14   }
15
16   void towers( int disks, int start, int end, int temp )
17   {
18       if ( disks == 1 ) {
19           cout << start << " --> " << end << '\n';
20           return;
21       }
22
23       // move disks - 1 disks from start to temp
24       towers( disks - 1, start, temp, end );
25
26       // move last disk from start to end
27       cout << start << " --> " << end << '\n';
28
29       // move disks - 1 disks from temp to end
30       towers( disks - 1, temp, end, start );
31   }
```

```
Enter the starting number of disks: 4
1 --> 2
1 --> 3
2 --> 3
1 --> 2
3 --> 1
3 --> 2
1 --> 2
1 --> 3
2 --> 3
2 --> 1
3 --> 1
2 --> 3
1 --> 2
1 --> 3
2 --> 3
```

3.43   Any program that can be implemented recursively can be implemented iteratively, although sometimes with more difficulty and less clarity. Try writing an iterative version of the Towers of Hanoi. If you succeed, compare your iterative version with the recursive version you developed in Exercise 3.42. Investigate issues of performance, clarity, and your ability to demonstrate the correctness of the programs.

3.44   (Visualizing Recursion) It is interesting to watch recursion "in action." Modify the factorial function of Fig. 3.14 to print its local variable and recursive call parameter. For each recursive call, display the outputs on a separate line and add a level of indentation. Do your utmost to make the outputs clear, interesting, and meaningful. Your goal here is to design and implement an output format that helps a person understand recursion better. You may want to add such display capabilities to the many other recursion examples and exercises throughout the text.

   ANS:

```
1    // Exercise 3.44 Solution
2    #include <iostream.h>
3    #include <iomanip.h>
4
5    long factorial( long );
6    void printRecursion( int );
```

```
7
8   int main()
9   {
10      for ( int i = 0; i <= 10; ++i )
11          cout << setw( 3 ) << i << "! = " << factorial( i ) << endl;
12
13      return 0;
14  }
15
16  long factorial( long number )
17  {
18      if ( number <= 1 )
19          return 1;
20      else {
21          printRecursion( number );
22          return ( number * factorial( number - 1 ) );
23      }
24  }
25
26  void printRecursion( int n )
27  {
28      cout << "number =" << setw( n ) << n << '\n';
29  }
```

```
   0! = 1
   1! = 1
 number = 2
   2! = 2
 number =  3
 number = 2
   3! = 6
 number =   4
 number =  3
 number = 2
   4! = 24
 number =    5
 number =   4
 number =  3
 number = 2
   5! = 120
 ...
 number =          10
 number =         9
 number =        8
 number =       7
 number =      6
 number =     5
 number =    4
 number =  3
 number = 2
  10! = 3628800
```

3.45 The greatest common divisor of integers **x** and **y** is the largest integer that evenly divides both **x** and **y**. Write a recursive function **gcd** that returns the greatest common divisor of **x** and **y**. The **gcd** of **x** and **y** is defined recursively as follows: If **y** is equal to **0**, then **gcd(x, y)** is **x**; otherwise **gcd(x, y)** is **gcd(y, x % y)** where **%** is the modulus operator.
        ANS:

```
1   // Exercise 3.45 Solution
2   #include <iostream.h>
3
4   unsigned gcd( unsigned int, unsigned int );
5
```

```
6   int main()
7   {
8      unsigned x, y, gcDiv;
9
10     cout << "Enter two integers: ";
11     cin >> x >> y;
12
13     gcDiv = gcd( x, y );
14     cout << "Greatest common divisor of " << x << " and "
15          << y << " is " << gcDiv << endl;
16
17     return 0;
18  }
19
20  unsigned gcd( unsigned xMatch, unsigned yMatch )
21  {
22     return yMatch == 0 ? xMatch : gcd( yMatch, xMatch % yMatch );
23  }
```

```
Enter two integers: 32727 9
Greatest common divisor of 32727 and 9 is 3
```

3.46 Can **main** be called recursively? Write a program containing a function **main**. Include **static** local variable **count** initialized to 1. Postincrement and print the value of **count** each time **main** is called. Run your program. What happens?

3.47 Exercises 3.35 through 3.37 developed a computer-assisted instruction program to teach an elementary school student multiplication. This exercise suggests enhancements to that program.
   a) Modify the program to allow the user to enter a grade-level capability. A grade level of 1 means to use only single-digit numbers in the problems, a grade level of two means to use numbers as large as two-digits, etc.
   b) Modify the program to allow the user to pick the type of arithmetic problems he or she wishes to study. An option of 1 means addition problems only, 2 means subtraction problems only, 3 means multiplication problems only, 4 means division problems only, and 5 means to randomly intermix problems of all these types.
   ANS:

```
1   // Exercise 3.47 Part A Solution
2   #include <iostream.h>
3   #include <stdlib.h>
4   #include <time.h>
5
6   int randValue( int );
7   void multiplication( void );
8   void correctMessage( void );
9   void incorrectMessage( void );
10
11  int main()
12  {
13     srand( time( 0 ) );
14     multiplication();
15     return 0;
16  }
17
18  int randValue( int level )
19  {
20     switch ( level ) {
21        case 1:
22           return rand() % 10;
23        case 2:
24           return rand() % 100;
25        case 3:
26           return rand() % 1000;
```

```
27          default:
28             return rand() % 10;
29       }
30  }
31
32  void multiplication( void )
33  {
34     int x, y, gradeLevel, right = 0, wrong = 0;
35     unsigned int response;
36
37     cout << "Enter the grade-level (1 to 3): ";
38     cin >> gradeLevel;
39
40     for ( int i = 1; i <= 10; i++ ) {
41        x = randValue( gradeLevel );
42        y = randValue( gradeLevel );
43
44        cout << "How much is " << x << " times " << y << "? ";
45        cin >> response;
46
47        while ( response != x * y ) {
48           ++wrong;
49           incorrectMessage();
50           cin >> response;
51        }
52
53        ++right;
54        correctMessage();
55     }
56
57     if ( static_cast< float > ( right ) / ( right + wrong ) < .75 )
58        cout << "Please ask your instructor for extra help.\n";
59
60     cout << "That's all for now. Bye." << endl;
61  }
62
63  void correctMessage( void )
64  {
65     switch ( rand() % 4 ) {
66        case 0:
67           cout << "Very good!";
68           break;
69        case 1:
70           cout << "Excellent!";
71           break;
72        case 2:
73           cout << "Nice work!";
74           break;
75        case 3:
76           cout << "Keep up the good work!";
77           break;
78     }
79
80     cout << "\n\n";
81  }
82
83  void incorrectMessage( void )
84  {
85     switch ( rand() % 4 ) {
86        case 0:
87           cout << "No. Please try again.";
88           break;
```

```
89          case 1:
90             cout << "Wrong. Try once more.";
91             break;
92          case 2:
93             cout << "Don't give up!";
94             break;
95          case 3:
96             cout << "No. Keep trying.";
97             break;
98       }
99
100    cout << "\n? ";
101 }
```

```
Enter the grade-level (1 to 3): 3
How much is 260 times 123? 31980
Excellent!

How much is 776 times 21? 16299
No. Keep Trying.
? 16296
Keep up the good work!
...
```

```
1  // Exercise 3.47 Part B Solution
2  #include <iostream.h>
3  #include <stdlib.h>
4  #include <time.h>
5
6  int menu( void );
7  void arithmetic( void );
8  void correctMessage( void );
9  void incorrectMessage( void );
10
11 int main()
12 {
13    srand( time( 0 ) );
14    arithmetic();
15    return 0;
16 }
17
18 int menu( void )
19 {
20    int choice;
21
22    do {
23       cout << "Choose type of problem to study."
24            << "\nEnter: 1 for addition, 2 for subtraction"
25            << "\nEnter: 3 for multiplication, 4 for division"
26            << "\nEnter: 5 for a combination of 1 through 4\n? ";
27       cin >> choice;
28
29    } while ( choice < 1 || choice > 5 );
30
31    return choice;
32 }
33
```

```
34   void incorrectMessage( void )
35   {
36      switch ( rand() % 4 ) {
37         case 0:
38            cout << "No. Please try again.";
39            break;
40         case 1:
41            cout << "Wrong. Try once more.";
42            break;
43         case 2:
44            cout << "Don't give up!";
45            break;
46         case 3:
47            cout << "No. Keep trying.";
48            break;
49      }
50
51      cout << "\n? ";
52   }
53
54   void correctMessage( void )
55   {
56      switch ( rand() % 4 ) {
57         case 0:
58            cout << "Very good!";
59            break;
60         case 1:
61            cout << "Excellent!";
62            break;
63         case 2:
64            cout << "Nice work!";
65            break;
66         case 3:
67            cout << "Keep up the good work!";
68            break;
69      }
70
71      cout << "\n\n";
72   }
73
74   void arithmetic( void )
75   {
76      int x, y, response, answer, selection, right = 0, wrong = 0;
77      int type, problemMix;
78      char op;
79
80      selection = menu();
81      type = selection;
82
83      for ( int i = 1; i <= 10; ++i ) {
84         x = rand() % 10;
85         y = rand() % 10;
86
87         if ( selection == 5 ) {
88            problemMix = 1 + rand() % 4;
89            type = problemMix;
90         }
91
92         switch ( type ) {
93            case 1:
94               op = '+';
95               answer = x + y;
96               break;
```

```
97              case 2:                 // note negative answers can exist
98                 op = '-';
99                 answer = x - y;
100                break;
101             case 3:
102                op = '*';
103                answer = x * y;
104                break;
105             case 4:                 // note this is integer division
106                op = '/';
107
108                if ( y == 0 ) {
109                   y = 1;             // eliminate divide by zero error
110                   answer = x / y;
111                }
112                else {
113                   x *= y;            // create "nice" division
114                   answer = x / y;
115                }
116
117                break;
118          }
119
120          cout << "How much is " << x << " " << op << " " << y << "? ";
121          cin >> response;
122
123          while ( response != answer ) {
124             ++wrong;
125             incorrectMessage();
126             cin >> response;
127          }
128
129          ++right;
130          correctMessage();
131       }
132
133       if ( static_cast< float > ( right ) / ( right + wrong ) < .75 )
134          cout << "Please ask your instructor for extra help.\n";
135
136       cout << "That's all for now. Bye." << endl;
137    }
```

```
Choose type of problem to study.
Enter: 1 for addition, 2 for subtraction
Enter: 3 for multiplication, 4 for division
Enter: 5 for a combination of 1 through 4
? 5

How much is 0 * 9? 0
Nice work!

How much is 7 / 1? 7
Nice work!

How much is 8 * 9? 72
Keep up the good work!

How much is 0 - 1? -1
...
```

3.48   Write function **distance** that calculates the distance between two points (x1, y1) and (x2, y2). All numbers and return values should be of type **float**.

ANS:

```
1   // Exercise 3.48 Solution
2   #include <iostream.h>
3   #include <iomanip.h>
4   #include <math.h>
5
6   float distance( float, float, float, float );
7
8   int main()
9   {
10      float x1, y1, x2, y2, dist;
11
12      cout << "Enter the first point: ";
13      cin >> x1 >> y1;
14
15      cout << "Enter the second point: ";
16      cin >> x2 >> y2;
17
18      dist = distance( x1, y1, x2, y2 );
19
20      cout << setiosflags( ios::fixed | ios::showpoint )
21           << "Distance between (" << setprecision( 1 ) << x1 << ", "
22           << y1 << ") and (" << x2 << ", " << y2 << ") is "
23           << dist << endl;
24
25      return 0;
26   }
27
28   float distance( float xOne, float yOne, float xTwo, float yTwo )
29   {
30      return sqrt( pow( xOne - xTwo, 2 ) + pow( yOne - yTwo, 2 ) );
31   }
```

```
Enter the first point: 8 9
Enter the second point: 0 1
Distance between (8.0, 9.0) and (0.0, 1.0) is 11.3
```

3.49   What does the following program do?

```
1   // ex3.49.cpp
2   #include <iostream.h>
3
4   int main()
5   {
6      int c;
7
8      if ( ( c = cin.get() ) != EOF ) {
9         main();
10        cout << c;
11     }
12
13     return 0;
14   }
```

3.50   What does the following program do?

```
1   // ex03_50.cpp
2   #include <iostream.h>
3
4   int mystery( int, int );
5
```

```
6   int main()
7   {
8      int x, y;
9
10     cout << "Enter two integers: ";
11     cin >> x >> y;
12     cout << "The result is " << mystery( x, y ) << endl;
13     return 0;
14  }
15
16  // Parameter b must be a positive
17  // integer to prevent infinite recursion
18  int mystery( int a, int b )
19  {
20     if ( b == 1 )
21        return a;
22     else
23        return a + mystery( a, b - 1 );
24  }
```

ANS: Calculates **x** times **y**.

```
Enter two integers: 8 2
The result is 16
```

3.51   After you determine what the program of Exercise 3.50 does, modify the program to function properly after removing the restriction of the second argument being nonnegative.
    ANS:

```
1   // Exercise 3.51 Solution
2   #include <iostream.h>
3
4   int mystery( int, int );
5
6   int main()
7   {
8      int x, y;
9
10     cout << "Enter two integers: ";
11     cin >> x >> y;
12     cout << "The result is " << mystery( x, y ) << endl;
13     return 0;
14  }
15
16  int mystery( int a, int b )
17  {
18     if ( ( a < 0 && b < 0 ) || b < 0 ) {
19        a *= -1;
20        b *= -1;
21     }
22
23     return b == 1 ? a : a + mystery( a, b - 1 );
24  }
```

```
Enter two integers: -8 8
The result is -64
```

3.52   Write a program that tests as many of the math library functions in Fig. 3.2 as you can. Exercise each of these functions by having your program print out tables of return values for a diversity of argument values.
    ANS:

```
1    // Exercise 3.52 Solution
2    #include <iostream.h>
3    #include <iomanip.h>
4    #include <math.h>
5
6    int main()
7    {
8       cout << "function";          // header
9
10      for ( int a = 1; a < 6; ++a )
11         cout << setw( 12 ) << a << ' ';
12
13      cout << setiosflags( ios::fixed | ios::showpoint ) << "\n\nsqrt()   ";
14
15      for ( int b = 1; b < 6; ++b )
16         cout << setw( 12 ) << setprecision( 2 ) << sqrt( b ) << ' ';
17
18      cout << "\nexp()    ";
19
20      for ( int c = 1; c < 6; ++c )
21         cout << setw( 12 ) << setprecision( 2 ) << exp( c ) << ' ';
22
23      cout << "\nlog()    ";
24
25      for ( int d = 1; d < 6; ++d )
26         cout << setw( 12 ) << setprecision( 2 ) << log( d ) << ' ';
27
28      cout << "\nlog10() ";
29
30      for ( int e = 1; e < 6; ++e )
31         cout << setw( 12 ) << setprecision( 2 ) << log10( e ) << ' ';
32
33      cout << "\npow(2,x)";
34
35      for ( int f = 1; f < 6; ++f )
36         cout << setw( 12 ) << setprecision( 2 ) << pow( 2, f ) << ' ';
37
38      cout << "\n\n\nfunction";          // header
39
40      for ( double g = -1.5; g < 3.0; g += 1.1 )
41         cout << setw( 12 ) << setprecision( 2 ) << g << ' ';
42
43      cout << "\n\n\nfabs()   ";
44
45      for ( double h = -1.5; h < 3.0; h += 1.1 )
46         cout << setw( 12 ) << setprecision( 2 ) << fabs( h ) << ' ';
47
48      cout << "\nceil()   ";
49
50      for ( double i = -1.5; i < 3.0; i += 1.1 )
51         cout << setw( 12 ) << setprecision( 2 ) << ceil( i ) << ' ';
52
53      cout << "\nfloor() ";
54
55      for ( double j = -1.5; j < 3.0; j += 1.1 )
56         cout << setw( 12 ) << setprecision( 2 ) << floor( j ) << ' ';
57
58      cout << "\nsin()    ";
59
60      for ( double k = -1.5; k < 3.0; k += 1.1 )
61         cout << setw( 12 ) << setprecision( 2 ) << sin( k ) << ' ';
62
63      cout << "\ncos()    ";
64
```

```
65      for ( double l = -1.5; l < 3.0; l += 1.1 )
66          cout << setw( 12 ) << setprecision( 2 ) << cos( l ) << ' ';
67
68      cout << "\ntan()    ";
69
70      for ( double m = -1.5; m < 3.0; m += 1.1 )
71          cout << setw( 12 ) << setprecision( 2 ) << tan( m ) << ' ';
72
73      cout << endl;
74      return 0;
75   }
```

function	1	2	3	4	5
sqrt()	1.00	1.41	1.73	2.00	2.24
exp()	2.72	7.39	20.09	54.60	148.41
log()	0.00	0.69	1.10	1.39	1.61
log10()	0.00	0.30	0.48	0.60	0.70
pow(2,x)	2.00	4.00	8.00	16.00	32.00
function	-1.50	-0.40	0.70	1.80	2.90
fabs()	1.50	0.40	0.70	1.80	2.90
ceil()	-1.00	0.00	1.00	2.00	3.00
floor()	-2.00	-1.00	0.00	1.00	2.00
sin()	-1.00	-0.39	0.64	0.97	0.24
cos()	0.07	0.92	0.76	-0.23	-0.97
tan()	-14.10	-0.42	0.84	-4.29	-0.25

3.53   Find the error in each of the following program segments and explain how to correct it:

a) `float cube( float );    /* function prototype */`

   `...`

   `cube( float number )    /* function definition */`

   `{`

   `    return number * number * number;`

   `}`

   ANS: The function definition defaults to a return type of **int**. Specify a return type of **float** for the definition.

b) `register auto int x = 7;`

   ANS: Only one storage class specifier can be used. Either **register** or **auto** must be removed.

c) `int randomNumber = srand();`

   ANS: Function **srand** takes an **unsigned** argument and does not return a value. Use **rand** instead of **srand**.

d) `float y = 123.45678;`

   `int x;`

   `x = y;`

   `cout << static_cast< float>( x ) << endl;`

   ANS: The assignment of **y** to **x** truncates decimal places.

e) `double square( double number )`

   `{`

   `    double number;`

   `    return number * number;`

   `}`

   ANS: Variable **number** is declared twice. Remove the declaration within the **{}**.

f) `int sum( int n )`

   `{`

   `    if ( n == 0 )`

   `        return 0;`

   `    else`

   `        return n + sum( n );`

   `}`

   ANS: Infinite recursion. Change operator **+** to operator **-**.

3.54 Modify the craps program of Fig. 3.10 to allow wagering. Package as a function the portion of the program that runs one game of craps. Initialize variable **bankBalance** to 1000 dollars. Prompt the player to enter a **wager**. Use a **while** loop to check that **wager** is less than or equal to **bankBalance** and if not prompt the user to reenter **wager** until a valid **wager** is entered. After a correct **wager** is entered, run one game of craps. If the player wins, increase **bankBalance** by **wager** and print the new **bankBalance**. If the player loses, decrease **bankBalance** by **wager**, print the new **bankBalance**, check if **bankBalance** has become zero, and if so print the message **"Sorry. You busted!"** As the game progresses, print various messages to create some "chatter" such as **"Oh, you're going for broke, huh?"**, or **"Aw cmon, take a chance!"**, or **"You're up big. Now's the time to cash in your chips!"**.

ANS:

```
1   // Exercise 3.54 Solution
2   #include <iostream.h>
3   #include <stdlib.h>
4   #include <time.h>
5
6   enum Status { WON, LOST, CONTINUE };
7
8   int rollDice( void );
9   int craps( void );
10  void chatter( void );
11
12  int main()
13  {
14     int result, wager = 0, bankBalance = 1000;
15     char playAgain;
16
17     srand( time( 0 ) );
18
19     do {
20        cout << "You have $" << bankBalance
21            << " in the bank.\nPlace your wager: ";
22        cin >> wager;
23
24        while ( wager <= 0 || wager > bankBalance ) {
25           cout << "Please bet a valid amount.\n";
26           cin >> wager;
27        }
28
29        result = craps();
30
31        if ( result == LOST ) {
32           bankBalance -= wager;
33           cout << "Your new bank balance is $" << bankBalance << "\n";
34
35           if ( bankBalance == 0 ) {
36              cout << "Sorry. You Busted! Thank You For Playing.\n";
37              break;
38           }
39        }
40        else {
41           bankBalance += wager;
42           cout << "Your new bank balance is $" << bankBalance << "\n";
43        }
44
45        cout << "Would you like to try your luck again (y/n)? ";
46        cin >> playAgain;
47     } while ( playAgain == 'y' || playAgain == 'Y' );
48
49     cout << endl;
50     return 0;
51  }
52
```

```
53   int rollDice( void )
54   {
55      int die1, die2, workSum;
56
57      die1 = 1 + rand() % 6;
58      die2 = 1 + rand() % 6;
59      workSum = die1 + die2;
60      cout << "Player rolled " << die1 << " + " << die2 << " = "
61           << workSum << '\n';
62
63      return workSum;
64   }
65
66   int craps( void )
67   {
68      int gameStatus, sum, myPoint;
69
70      sum = rollDice();
71
72      switch ( sum ) {
73         case 7: case 11:
74            gameStatus = WON;
75            chatter();
76            break;
77         case 2: case 3: case 12:
78            gameStatus = LOST;
79            chatter();
80            break;
81         default:
82            gameStatus = CONTINUE;
83            myPoint = sum;
84            cout << "Point is " << myPoint << '\n';
85            chatter();
86            break;
87      }
88
89      while ( gameStatus == CONTINUE ) {
90         chatter();
91         sum = rollDice();
92
93         if ( sum == myPoint )
94            gameStatus = WON;
95         else if ( sum == 7 )
96            gameStatus = LOST;
97      }
98
99      if ( gameStatus == WON ) {
100        cout << "Player wins\n";
101        return WON;
102     }
103     else {
104        cout << "Player loses\n";
105        return LOST;
106     }
107  }
108
109  void chatter( void )
110  {
111     switch ( 1 + rand() % 9 ) {
112        case 1:
113           cout << "Oh, you're going for broke, huh?";
114           break;
```

```
115       case 2:
116          cout << "Aw cmon, take a chance!";
117          break;
118       case 3:
119          cout << "Hey, I think this guy is going to break the bank!!";
120          break;
121       case 4:
122          cout << "You're up big. Now's the time to cash in your chips!";
123          break;
124       case 5:
125          cout << "Way too lucky! Those dice have to be loaded!";
126          break;
127       case 6:
128          cout << "Bet it all! Bet it all!";
129          break;
130       case 7:
131          cout << "Can I borrow a chip?";
132          break;
133       case 8:
134          cout << "Let's try our luck at another table.";
135          break;
136       case 9:
137          cout << "You're a cheat! It is just a matter of time"
138               << "\nbefore I catch you!!!";
139          break;
140    }
141
142    cout << endl;
143 }
```

```
You have $1000 in the bank.
Place your wager: 1000
Player rolled 5 + 1 = 6
Point is 6
Bet it all! Bet it all!
Oh, you're going for broke, huh?
Player rolled 3 + 6 = 9
Aw cmon, take a chance!
Player rolled 3 + 4 = 7
Player loses
Your new bank balance is $0
Sorry. You Busted! Thank You For Playing.
```

3.55 Write a C++ program that uses an **inline** function **circleArea** to prompt the user for the radius of a circle, and to calculate and print the area of that circle.

ANS:

```
1  // Exercise 3.55 Solution
2  #include <iostream.h>
3
4  double pi = 3.14159;   // global variable
5
6  inline double circleArea( double r ) { return pi * r * r; }
7
8  int main()
9  {
10    double radius;
11
12    cout << "Enter the radius of the circle: ";
13    cin >> radius;
14    cout << "The area of the circle is " << circleArea( radius ) << endl;
15    return 0;
16 }
```

```
Enter the radius of the circle: 10
The area of the circle is 314.159
```

3.56   Write a complete C++ program with the two alternate functions specified below that each simply triple the variable **count** defined in **main**. Then compare and contrast the two approaches. These two functions are

    a)   Function **tripleCallByValue** that passes a copy of **count** call-by-value, triples the copy, and returns the new value.

    b)   Function **tripleByReference** that passes **count** with true call-by-reference via a reference parameter, and triples the original copy of **count** through its alias (i.e., the reference parameter).

ANS:

```
1   // Exercise 3.56 Solution
2   #include <iostream.h>
3
4   int tripleCallByValue( int );
5   void tripleByReference( int & );
6
7   int main()
8   {
9      int value, &valueRef = value;
10
11     cout << "Enter an integer: ";
12     cin >> value;
13
14     cout << "\nValue before call to tripleCallByValue() is: "
15          << value << "\nValue returned from tripleCallByValue() is: "
16          << tripleCallByValue( value )
17          << "\nValue (in main) after tripleCallByValue() is: " << value
18          << "\n\nValue before call to tripleByReference() is: "
19          << value << '\n';
20
21     tripleByReference( valueRef );
22
23     cout << "Value (in main) after call to tripleByReference() is: "
24          << value << endl;
25
26     return 0;
27  }
28
29  int tripleCallByValue( int valueCopy )
30  {
31     return valueCopy *= 3;
32  }
33
34  void tripleByReference( int &aliasRef )
35  {
36     aliasRef *= 3;
37  }
```

```
Enter an integer: 8

Value before call to tripleCallByValue() is: 8
Value returned from tripleCallByValue() is: 24
Value (in main) after tripleCallByValue() is: 8

Value before call to tripleByReference() is: 8
Value (in main) after call to tripleByReference() is: 24
```

3.57   What is the purpose of the unary scope resolution operator?

       ANS: The unary scope resolution operator is used to access a global variable. In particular, the unary scope resolution operator is useful when a global variable needs to be accessed and a local varible has the same name.

3.58   Write a program that uses a function template called **min** to determine the smaller of two arguments. Test the program using integer, character, and floating-point number pairs.

       ANS:

```cpp
1   // Exercise 3.58 Solution
2   #include <iostream.h>
3
4   template < class T >
5   void min( T value1, T value2 )    // find the smallest value
6   {
7      if ( value1 > value2 )
8         cout << value2 << " is smaller than " << value1;
9      else
10        cout << value1 << " is smaller than " << value2;
11
12     cout << endl;
13  }
14
15  int main()
16  {
17     min( 7, 54 );        // integers
18     min( 4.35, 8.46 ); // doubles
19     min( 'g', 'T' );    // characters
20     return 0;
21  }
```

```
7 is smaller than 54
4.35 is smaller than 8.46
T is smaller than g
```

3.59   Write a program that uses a function template called **max** to determine the largest of three arguments. Test the program using integer, character, and floating-point number pairs.

       ANS:

```cpp
1   // Exercise 3.59 Solution
2   #include <iostream.h>
3
4   template < class T >
5   void max( T value1, T value2, T value3 )  // find the largest value
6   {
7      if ( value1 > value2 && value1 > value3 )
8         cout << value1 << " is greater than " << value2
9              << " and " << value3;
10     else if ( value2 > value1 && value2 > value3 )
11        cout << value2 << " is greater than " << value1
12             << " and " << value3;
13     else
14        cout << value3 << " is greater than " << value1
15             << " and " << value2;
16
17     cout << endl;
18  }
19
20  int main()
21  {
22     max( 7, 5, 2 );                 // integers
23     max( 9.35, 8.461, 94.3 );  // doubles
```

```
24      max( '!', 'T', '$' );          // characters
25      return 0;
26  }
```

```
7 is greater than 5 and 2
94.3 is greater than 9.35 and 8.461
T is greater than ! and $
```

3.60 Determine if the following program segments contain errors. For each error, explain how it can be corrected. Note: For a particular program segment, it is possible that no errors are present in the segment.

a)
```
template < class A >
int sum( int num1, int num2, int num3 )
{
    return num1 + num2 + num3;
}
```
ANS: The function return type and parameter types should be **A**.

b)
```
void printResults( int x, int y )
{
    cout << "The sum is " << x + y << '\n';
    return x + y;
}
```
ANS: The function specifies a **void** return type and attempts to return a value. Two possible solutions: (1) change **void** to **int**. or (2) remove the line **return x + y;**.

c)
```
template < A >
A product( A num1, A num2, A num3 )
{
    return num1 * num2 * num3;
}
```
ANS: The keyword class is needed in the template declaration **template <class A>**.

d)
```
double cube( int );
int cube( int );
```
ANS: The signatures are not different. Overloaded functions must have different signatures meaning that the name and parameter list must be different. If only the returns types differ, the compiler generates an error message.

Chapter 4 Solutions

Arrays

Solutions

4.6 Fill in the blanks in each of the following:

a) C++ stores lists of values in _____.

ANS: arrays.

b) The elements of an array are related by the fact that they _____.

ANS: have the same name and type.

c) When referring to an array element, the position number contained within parentheses is called a _____.

ANS: subscript.

d) The names of the four elements of array **p** are _____, _____, _____, and _____.

ANS: p[0], p[1], p[2], p[3]

e) Naming an array, stating its type, and specifying the number of elements in the array is called _____ the array.

ANS: declaring.

f) The process of placing the elements of an array into either ascending or descending order is called _____.

ANS: sorting.

g) In a double-subscripted array, the first subscript (by convention) identifies the _____ of an element, and the second subscript (by convention) identifies the _____ of an element.

ANS: row, column.

h) An m-by-n array contains _____ rows, _____ columns, and _____ elements.

ANS: m, n, m x n.

i) The name of the element in row 3 and column 5 of array **d** is _____.

ANS: d[2][4].

4.7 State which of the following are true and which are false; for those that are false, explain why they are false.

a) To refer to a particular location or element within an array, we specify the name of the array and the value of the particular element.

ANS: False. The name of the array and the subscript of the array are specified.

b) An array declaration reserves space for the array.

ANS: True.

c) To indicate that 100 locations should be reserved for integer array **p**, the programmer writes the declaration

```
p[ 100 ];
```

ANS: False. A data type must be specified. An example of a correct definition would be: **unsigned p[100];**.

d) A C++ program that initializes the elements of a 15-element array to zero must contain at least one **for** statement.

ANS: False. The array can be initialized in a declaration with a member initializer list.

e) A C++ program that totals the elements of a double-subscripted array must contain nested **for** statements.

ANS: False. The sum of the elements can be obtained without **for** loops, with one **for** loop, three **for** loops, etc.

4.8 Write C++ statements to accomplish each of the following:

a) Display the value of the seventh element of character array **f**.

ANS: cout << f[6] << '\n';

b) Input a value into element 4 of single-subscripted floating-point array **b**.

ANS: cin >> b[4];

c) Initialize each of the 5 elements of single-subscripted integer array **g** to **8**.
ANS:
```
    int g[ 5 ] = { 8, 8, 8, 8, 8 };
```
or
```
    for ( int j = 0; j < 5; ++j )
       g[ j ] = 8;
```
d) Total and print the elements of floating-point array **c** of 100 elements.
ANS:
```
    for ( int k = 0; k < 5; ++k ) {
       total += c[ k ];   // assume total declared and initalized
       cout << c[ k ] << '\n'
    }
```
e) Copy array **a** into the first portion of array **b**. Assume **float a[11], b[34];**
ANS:
```
    for ( int i = 0; i < 11; ++i )
       b[ i ] = a[ i ];
```
f) Determine and print the smallest and largest values contained in 99-element floating-point array **w**.
ANS:
```
    // assume all variables declared and initialized
    for ( int j = 0; j < 99; ++j )
       if ( w[ j ] < smallest )
          smallest = w[ j ];
       else if ( w[ j ] > largest )
          largest = w[ j ];
```

4.9   Consider a 2-by-3 integer array **t**.
a) Write a declaration for **t**.
ANS: `int t[ 2 ][ 3 ];`
b) How many rows does **t** have?
ANS: 2
c) How many columns does **t** have?
ANS: 3
d) How many elements does **t** have?
ANS: 6
e) Write the names of all the elements in the second row of **t**.
ANS: `t[ 1 ][ 0 ],t[ 1 ][ 1 ],t[ 1 ][ 2 ]`
f) Write the names of all the elements in the third column of **t**.
ANS: `t[ 0 ][ 2 ],t[ 1 ][ 2 ]`
g) Write a single statement that sets the element of **t** in row 1 and column 2 to zero.
ANS: `t[ 0 ][ 1 ] = 0;`
h) Write a series of statements that initializes each element of **t** to zero. Do not use a repetition structure.
ANS:
```
    t[ 0 ][ 0 ] = 0;
    t[ 0 ][ 1 ] = 0;
    t[ 0 ][ 2 ] = 0;
    t[ 1 ][ 0 ] = 0;
    t[ 1 ][ 1 ] = 0;
    t[ 1 ][ 2 ] = 0;
```
i) Write a nested **for** structure that initializes each element of **t** to zero.
ANS:
```
    for ( int i = 0; i < 2; ++i )
       for ( int j = 0; j < 3; ++j )
          t[ i ][ j ] = 0;
```
j) Write a statement that inputs the values for the elements of **t** from the terminal.
ANS:
```
    for ( int r = 0; r < 2; ++r )
       for ( int c = 0; c < 3; ++c )
          t[ r ][ c ] = 0;
```

k) Write a series of statements that determines and prints the smallest value in array **t**.

ANS:

```
int smallest = t[ 0 ][ 0 ];
for ( int r = 1; r < 2; ++r )
   for ( int c = 1; c < 3; ++c )
      if ( t[ r ][ c ] < smallest )
         smallest = t[ r ][ c ];
cout << smallest;
```

l) Write a statement that displays the elements of the first row of **t**.

ANS: cout << t[0][0] << ' ' << t[0][1] << ' ' << t[0][2] << '\n';

m) Write a statement that totals the elements of the fourth column of **t**.

ANS: t does not contain a fourth column.

n) Write a series of statements that prints the array **t** in neat, tabular format. List the column subscripts as headings across the top and list the row subscripts at the left of each row.

ANS:

```
cout << "  0     1    2\n";
for ( int r = 0; r < 2; ++r ) {
   cout << r << ' ';

   for ( int c = 0; c < 3; ++c )
      cout << t[ r ][ c ] << "    ";

   cout << '\n';
}
```

4.10   Use a single-subscripted array to solve the following problem. A company pays its salespeople on a commission basis. The salespeople receive $200 per week plus 9 percent of their gross sales for that week. For example, a salesperson who grosses $5000 in sales in a week receives $200 plus 9 percent of $5000, or a total of $650. Write a program (using an array of counters) that determines how many of the salespeople earned salaries in each of the following ranges (assume that each salesperson's salary is truncated to an integer amount):

    a) $200-$299
    b) $300-$399
    c) $400-$499
    d) $500-$599
    e) $600-$699
    f) $700-$799
    g) $800-$899
    h) $900-$999
    i) $1000 and over

ANS:

```
1   // Exercise 4.10 Solution
2   #include <iostream.h>
3   #include <iomanip.h>
4
5   void wages( int [] );
6   void display( const int [] );
7
8   int main()
9   {
10     int salaries[ 11 ] = { 0 };
11
12     cout << setiosflags( ios::fixed | ios::showpoint );
13     wages( salaries );
14     display( salaries );
15
16     return 0;
17  }
18
```

```
19   void wages( int money[] )
20   {
21      double sales, i = 0.09;
22
23      cout << "Enter employee gross sales (-1 to end): ";
24      cin >> sales;
25
26      while ( sales != -1 ) {
27         double salary = 200.0 + sales * i;
28         cout << setprecision( 2 ) << "Employee Commission is $"
29              << salary << '\n';
30
31         int x = static_cast< int > ( salary ) / 100;
32         ++money[ ( x < 10 ? x : 10 ) ];
33
34         cout << "\nEnter employee gross sales (-1 to end): ";
35         cin >> sales;
36      }
37   }
38
39   void display( const int dollars[] )
40   {
41      cout << "Employees in the range:";
42      for ( int i = 2; i < 10; ++i )
43         cout << "\n$" << i << "00-$" << i << "99 : " << dollars[ i ];
44
45      cout << "\nOver $1000: " << dollars[ 10 ] << endl;
46   }
```

```
Enter employee gross sales (-1 to end): 10000
Employee Commission is $1100.00

Enter employee gross sales (-1 to end): 4235
Employee Commission is $581.15

Enter employee gross sales (-1 to end): 600
Employee Commission is $254.00

Enter employee gross sales (-1 to end): 12500
Employee Commission is $1325.00

Enter employee gross sales (-1 to end): -1

Employees in the range:
$200-$299 : 1
$300-$399 : 0
$400-$499 : 0
$500-$599 : 1
$600-$699 : 0
$700-$799 : 0
$800-$899 : 0
$900-$999 : 0
Over $1000: 2
```

4.11   The bubble sort presented in Fig. 4.16 is inefficient for large arrays. Make the following simple modifications to improve the performance of the bubble sort.

    a) After the first pass, the largest number is guaranteed to be in the highest-numbered element of the array; after the second pass, the two highest numbers are "in place," and so on. Instead of making nine comparisons on every pass, modify the bubble sort to make eight comparisons on the second pass, seven on the third pass, and so on.

b) The data in the array may already be in the proper order or near-proper order, so why make nine passes if fewer will suffice? Modify the sort to check at the end of each pass if any swaps have been made. If none has been made, then the data must already be in the proper order, so the program should terminate. If swaps have been made, then at least one more pass is needed.

ANS:

```
1   // Exercise 4.11 Part A Solution
2   #include <iostream.h>
3   #include <iomanip.h>
4
5   int main()
6   {
7      const int SIZE = 10;
8      int a[ SIZE ] = { 2, 6, 4, 8, 10, 12, 89, 68, 45, 37 };
9      int hold, numberOfComp = 0, comp;
10
11     cout << "Data items in original order\n";
12     for ( int i = 0; i < SIZE; ++i )
13        cout << setw( 4 ) << a[ i ];
14
15     cout << "\n\n";
16
17     for ( int pass = 1; pass < SIZE; ++pass ) {
18        cout << "After pass " << pass - 1 << ": ";
19
20        for ( comp = 0; comp < SIZE - pass; ++comp ) {
21           ++numberOfComp;
22
23           if ( a[ comp ] > a[ comp + 1 ] ) {
24              hold = a[ comp ];
25              a[ comp ] = a[ comp + 1 ];
26              a[ comp + 1 ] = hold;
27           }
28
29           cout << setw( 3 ) << a[ comp ];
30        }
31
32        cout << setw( 3 ) << a[ comp ] << '\n';   // print last array value
33     }
34
35     cout << "\nData items in ascending order\n";
36
37     for ( int j = 0; j < SIZE; ++j )
38        cout << setw( 4 ) << a[ j ];
39
40     cout << "\nNumber of comparisons = " << numberOfComp << endl;
41     return 0;
42  }
```

```
Data items in original order
    2   6   4   8  10  12  89  68  45  37

After pass 0:   2   4   6   8  10  12  68  45  37  89
After pass 1:   2   4   6   8  10  12  45  37  68
After pass 2:   2   4   6   8  10  12  37  45
After pass 3:   2   4   6   8  10  12  37
After pass 4:   2   4   6   8  10  12
After pass 5:   2   4   6   8  10
After pass 6:   2   4   6   8
After pass 7:   2   4   6
After pass 8:   2   4                        continued...
```

```
Data items in ascending order
    2    4    6    8   10   12   37   45   68   89
Number of comparisons = 45
```

```
1    // Exercise 4.11 Part B Solution
2    #include <iostream.h>
3    #include <iomanip.h>
4
5    int main()
6    {
7       const int SIZE = 10;
8       int a[ SIZE ] = { 6, 4, 2, 8, 10, 12, 37, 45, 68, 89 };
9       int hold, numberOfComp = 0, comp;
10      bool swapCheck = true;
11
12      cout << "Data items in original order\n";
13      for ( int i = 0; i < SIZE; ++i )
14         cout << setw( 4 ) << a[ i ];
15
16      cout << "\n\n";
17
18      for ( int pass = 1; pass < SIZE - 1 && swapCheck == true; ++pass ) {
19         cout << "After pass " << pass - 1 << ": ";
20         swapCheck = false;   // assume no swaps will be made
21
22         for ( comp = 0; comp < SIZE - pass; ++comp ) {
23            ++numberOfComp;
24
25            if ( a[ comp ] > a[ comp + 1 ] ) {
26               hold = a[ comp ];
27               a[ comp ] = a[ comp + 1 ];
28               a[ comp + 1 ] = hold;
29               swapCheck = true;   // a swap has been made
30            }
31
32            cout << setw( 3 ) << a[ comp ];
33         }
34
35         cout << setw( 3 ) << a[ comp ] << '\n';    // print last array value
36      }
37
38      cout << "\nData items in ascending order\n";
39
40      for ( int q = 0; q < SIZE; ++q )
41         cout << setw( 4 ) << a[ q ];
42
43      cout << "\nNumber of comparisons = " << numberOfComp << endl;
44      return 0;
45   }
```

```
Data items in original order
    6    4    2    8   10   12   37   45   68   89

After pass 0:    4  2  6  8 10 12 37 45 68 89
After pass 1:    2  4  6  8 10 12 37 45 68
After pass 2:    2  4  6  8 10 12 37 45

Data items in ascending order
    2    4    6    8   10   12   37   45   68   89
Number of comparisons = 24
```

4.12   Write single statements that perform the following single-subscripted array operations:
a) Initialize the 10 elements of integer array **counts** to zeros.
ANS: `int counts[ 10 ] = { 0 };`
b) Add 1 to each of the 15 elements of integer array **bonus**.
ANS:
```
for ( int i = 0; i < 15; ++i )
    ++bonus[ i ];
```
c) Read 12 values for **float** array **monthlyTemperatures** from the keyboard.
ANS:
```
for ( int p = 0; p < 12; ++p )
    cin >> monthlyTemperatures[ p ];
```
d) Print the 5 values of integer array **bestScores** in column format.
ANS:
```
for ( int u = 0; u < 5; ++u )
    cout << bestScores[ u ] << '\t';
```

4.13   Find the error(s) in each of the following statements:
a) Assume: `char str[ 5 ];`
`cin >> str;      // User types hello`
ANS: Inadequate length. The string input exceeds the valid subscript range.
b) Assume: `int a[ 3 ];`
`cout << a[ 1 ] << " " << a[ 2 ] << " " << a[ 3 ] << endl;`
ANS: `a[ 3 ]` is not a valid location in the array. `a[ 2 ]` is the last valid location.
c) `float f[ 3 ] = { 1.1, 10.01, 100.001, 1000.0001 };`
ANS: Too many initializers in the initializer list. Only 1, 2, or 3 values may be provided in the initializer list.
d) Assume: `double d[ 2 ][ 10 ];`
`d[ 1, 9 ] = 2.345;`
ANS: Incorrect syntax array element access. `d[ 1 ][ 9 ]` is the correct syntax.

4.14   Modify the program of Fig. 4.17 so function **mode** is capable of handling a tie for the mode value. Also modify function **median** so the two middle elements are averaged in an array with an even number of elements.
ANS:

```
1   // Exercise 4.14 Solution
2   #include <iostream.h>
3   #include <iomanip.h>
4
5   void mean( int [], int );
6   void median( int [], int );
7   void mode( int [], int [], int, int );
8
9   int main()
10  {
11      const int SIZE = 100, MAXFREQUENCY = 10;
12      int response[ SIZE ] = { 6, 7, 8, 9, 8, 7, 8, 9, 8, 9,
13                               7, 8, 9, 5, 9, 8, 7, 8, 7, 1,
14                               6, 7, 8, 9, 3, 9, 8, 7, 1, 7,
15                               7, 8, 9, 8, 9, 8, 9, 7, 1, 9,
16                               6, 7, 8, 7, 8, 7, 9, 8, 9, 2,
17                               7, 8, 9, 8, 9, 8, 9, 7, 5, 3,
18                               5, 6, 7, 2, 5, 3, 9, 4, 6, 4,
19                               7, 8, 9, 6, 8, 7, 8, 9, 7, 1,
20                               7, 4, 4, 2, 5, 3, 8, 7, 5, 6,
21                               4, 5, 6, 1, 6, 5, 7, 8, 7, 9 };
22      int frequency[ MAXFREQUENCY ] = { 0 };
23
24      mean( response, SIZE );
25      median( response, SIZE );
26      mode( frequency, response, SIZE, MAXFREQUENCY );
27      return 0;
28  }
29
```

```
30   void mean( int answer[], int size )         // mean
31   {
32      int total = 0;
33
34      cout << "******\nMean\n******\n";
35
36      for ( int j = 0; j < size; ++j )
37         total += answer[ j ];
38
39      cout << setiosflags( ios::fixed | ios::showpoint )
40           << "The mean is the average value of the data items.\n"
41           << "The mean is equal to the total of all the data\n"
42           << "items divided by the number of data items (" << size << ")."
43           << "\nThe mean value for this run is: " << total
44           << " / " << size << " = " << setprecision( 2 )
45           << static_cast< float > ( total ) / size << "\n\n";
46   }
47
48   void median( int answer[], int size )                    // median
49   {
50      int hold;
51      bool firstRow = true;
52
53      cout << "\n******\nMedian\n******\n"
54           << "The unsorted array of responses is\n";
55
56      for ( int loop = 0; loop < size; loop++ ) {
57         if ( loop % 20 == 0 && !firstRow )
58            cout << '\n';
59
60         cout << setw( 2 ) << answer[ loop ];
61         firstRow = false;
62      }
63
64      cout << "\n\n";
65
66      for ( int pass = 0; pass <= size - 2; ++pass )
67         for ( int k = 0; k <= size - 2; ++k )
68            if ( answer[ k ] > answer[ k + 1 ] ) {
69               hold = answer[ k ];
70               answer[ k ] = answer[ k + 1 ];
71               answer[ k + 1 ] = hold;
72            }
73
74      cout << "The sorted array is\n";
75
76      firstRow = true;
77      for ( int j = 0; j < size; ++j ) {
78         if ( j % 20 == 0 && !firstRow )
79            cout << '\n';
80
81         cout << setw( 2 ) << answer[ j ];
82         firstRow = false;
83      }
84
85      cout << "\n\n";
86
87      if ( size % 2 == 0 )      // even number of elements
88         cout << "The median is the average of elements " << ( size + 1 ) / 2
89              << " and " << 1 + ( size + 1 ) / 2 << " of the sorted "
90              << size << " element array.\nFor this run the median is "
91              << setprecision( 1 )
```

```
92                << static_cast< float >( answer[ ( size + 1 ) / 2 ] +
93                                   answer[ ( size + 1 ) / 2 + 1 ] ) / 2
94           << "\n\n";
95      else                    // odd number of elements
96         cout << "The median is element " << ( size + 1 ) / 2  << " of "
97              << "the sorted " << size << " element array.\n"
98              << "For this run the median is " << answer[ ( size + 1 ) / 2 - 1 ]
99              << "\n\n";
100 }
101
102 void mode( int freq[], int answer[], int aSize, int fSize )
103 {
104     const int SIZE2 = 10;
105     int largest = 0, array[ SIZE2 ] = { 0 }, count = 0;
106
107     cout << "\n******\nMode\n******\n";
108
109     for ( int rating = 1; rating < fSize; ++rating )
110        freq[ rating ] = 0;
111
112     for ( int loop = 0; loop < aSize; ++loop )
113        ++freq[ answer[ loop ] ];
114
115     cout << setw( 13 ) << "Response" << setw( 11 ) << "Frequency" << setw( 19 )
116          << "Histogram\n\n" << setw( 55 ) << "1    1    2    2\n"
117          << setw( 56 ) << "5    0    5    0    5\n\n";
118
119     for ( int r = 1; r < fSize; ++r ) {
120        cout << setw( 8 ) << rating << setw( 11 ) << freq[ r ] << "          ";
121
122        if ( freq[ r ] > largest ) {
123           largest = freq[ r ];
124
125           for ( int v = 0; v < SIZE2; ++v )
126              array[ v ] = 0;
127
128           array[ r ] = largest;
129           ++count;
130        }
131        else if ( freq[ r ] == largest ) {
132           array[ r ] = largest;
133           ++count;
134        }
135
136        for ( int b = 1; b <= freq[ r ]; b++ )
137           cout << '*';
138
139        cout << '\n';
140     }
141
142     cout << ( count > 1 ? "\nThe modes are:  " : "\nThe mode is: " );
143
144     for ( int m = 1; m < SIZE2; ++m )
145        if ( array[ m ] != 0 )
146           cout << m << " with a frequency of " << array[ m ] << "\n\t\t";
147
148     cout << endl;
149 }
```

```
******
Mean
******
The mean is the average value of the data items.
The mean is equal to the total of all the data
items divided by the number of data items (100).
The mean value for this run is: 662 / 100 = 6.62


******
Median
******
The unsorted array of responses is
  6 7 8 9 8 7 8 9 8 9 7 8 9 5 9 8 7 8 7 1
  6 7 8 9 3 9 8 7 1 7 7 8 9 8 9 8 9 7 1 9
  6 7 8 7 8 7 9 8 9 2 7 8 9 8 9 8 9 7 5 3
  5 6 7 2 5 3 9 4 6 4 7 8 9 6 8 7 8 9 7 1
  7 4 4 2 5 3 8 7 5 6 4 5 6 1 6 5 7 8 7 9

The sorted array is
  1 1 1 1 2 2 2 3 3 3 4 4 4 4 4 5 5 5
  5 5 5 5 5 6 6 6 6 6 6 6 6 7 7 7 7 7
  7 7 7 7 7 7 7 7 7 7 7 7 7 7 7 7 8 8
  8 8 8 8 8 8 8 8 8 8 8 8 8 8 8 8 8 8
  9 9 9 9 9 9 9 9 9 9 9 9 9 9 9 9 9 9

The median is the average of elements 50 and 51 of the sorted 100 element
array.
For this run the median is 7.0


******
Mode
******
     Response   Frequency       Histogram

                                    1     1     2     2
                              5     0     5     0     5

        10          5        *****
        10          3        ***
        10          4        ****
        10          5        *****
        10          8        ********
        10          9        *********
        10         23        ***********************
        10         23        ***********************
        10         20        ********************

The modes are:  7 with a frequency of 23
                8 with a frequency of 23
```

4.15 Use a single-subscripted array to solve the following problem. Read in 20 numbers, each of which is between 10 and 100, inclusive. As each number is read, print it only if it is not a duplicate of a number already read. Provide for the "worst case" in which all 20 numbers are different. Use the smallest possible array to solve this problem.

ANS:

```
1  // Exercise 4.15 Solution
2  #include <iostream.h>
3  #include <iomanip.h>
4
```

```
5   int main()
6   {
7      const int SIZE = 20;
8      int a[ SIZE ] = { 0 }, subscript = 0, duplicate, value;
9
10     cout << "Enter 20 integers between 10 and 100:\n";
11
12     for ( int i = 0; i < SIZE; ++i ) {
13        duplicate = 0;
14        cin >> value;
15
16        for ( int j = 0; j < subscript; ++j )
17           if ( value == a[ j ] ) {
18              duplicate = 1;
19              break;
20           }
21
22        if ( !duplicate )
23           a[ subscript++ ] = value;
24     }
25
26     cout << "\nThe nonduplicate values are:\n";
27
28     for ( i = 0; a[ i ] != 0; ++i )
29        cout << setw( 4 ) << a[ i ];
30
31     cout << endl;
32     return 0;
33  }
```

```
Enter 20 integers between 10 and 100:
22 56 78 94 22 94 38 10 11 12 22 12 13 14 15 16 17 88 88 77

The nonduplicate values are:
  22   56   78   94   38   10   11   12   13   14   15   16   17   88   77
```

4.16 Label the elements of 3-by-5 double-subscripted array **sales** to indicate the order in which they are set to zero by the following program segment:

```
for ( row = 0; row < 3; row++ )
   for ( column = 0; column < 5; column++ )
      sales[ row ][ column ] = 0;
```

ANS:
```
sales[ 0 ][ 0 ], sales[ 0 ][ 1 ], sales[ 0 ][ 2 ], sales[ 0 ][ 3 ],
sales[ 0 ][ 4 ], sales[ 1 ][ 0 ], sales[ 1 ][ 1 ], sales[ 1 ][ 2 ],
sales[ 1 ][ 3 ], sales[ 1 ][ 4 ], sales[ 2 ][ 0 ], sales[ 2 ][ 1 ],
sales[ 2 ][ 2 ], sales[ 2 ][ 3 ], sales[ 2 ][ 4 ]
```

4.17 Write a program that simulates the rolling of two dice. The program should use **rand** to roll the first die, and should use **rand** again to roll the second die. The sum of the two values should then be calculated. *Note:* Since each die can show an integer value from 1 to 6, then the sum of the two values will vary from 2 to 12 with 7 being the most frequent sum and 2 and 12 being the least frequent sums. Figure 4.24 shows the 36 possible combinations of the two dice. Your program should roll the two dice 36,000 times. Use a single-subscripted array to tally the numbers of times each possible sum appears. Print the results in a tabular format. Also, determine if the totals are reasonable, i.e., there are six ways to roll a 7, so approximately one sixth of all the rolls should be 7.

	1	2	3	4	5	6
1	2	3	4	5	6	7
2	3	4	5	6	7	8
3	4	5	6	7	8	9
4	5	6	7	8	9	10
5	6	7	8	9	10	11
6	7	8	9	10	11	12

Fig. 4.24   The 36 possible outcomes of rolling two dice.

ANS:

```
1   // Exercise 4.17 Solution
2   #include <iostream.h>
3   #include <iomanip.h>
4   #include <stdlib.h>
5   #include <time.h>
6
7   int main()
8   {
9      const long ROLLS = 36000;
10     const int SIZE = 13;
11     // array expected contains counts for the expected
12     // number of times each sum occurs in 36 rolls of the dice
13     int expected[ SIZE ] = { 0, 0, 1, 2, 3, 4, 5, 6, 5, 4, 3, 2, 1 };
14     int x, y, sum[ SIZE ] = { 0 };
15
16     srand( time( 0 ) );
17
18     for ( long i = 1; i <= ROLLS; ++i ) {
19        x = 1 + rand() % 6;
20        y = 1 + rand() % 6;
21        ++sum[ x + y ];
22     }
23
24     cout << setw( 10 ) << "Sum" << setw( 10 ) << "Total" << setw( 10 )
25          << "Expected" << setw( 10 ) << "Actual\n"
26          << setiosflags( ios::fixed | ios::showpoint );
27
28     for ( int j = 2; j < SIZE; ++j )
29        cout << setw( 10 ) << j << setw( 10 ) << sum[ j ] << setprecision( 3 )
30             << setw( 9 ) << 100.0 * expected[ j ] / 36 << "%" << setprecision( 3 )
31             << setw( 9 ) << 100.0 * sum[ j ] / 36000 << "%\n";
32
33     return 0;
34  }
```

Sum	Total	Expected	Actual
2	1000	2.778%	2.778%
3	1958	5.556%	5.439%
4	3048	8.333%	8.467%
5	3979	11.111%	11.053%
6	5007	13.889%	13.908%
7	6087	16.667%	16.908%
8	4996	13.889%	13.878%
9	3971	11.111%	11.031%
10	2996	8.333%	8.322%
11	2008	5.556%	5.578%
12	950	2.778%	2.639%

4.18   What does the following program do?

```
1   // ex04_18.cpp
2   #include <iostream.h>
3
4   int whatIsThis( int [], int );
5
6   int main()
7   {
8      const int arraySize = 10;
9      int a[ arraySize ] = { 1, 2, 3, 4, 5, 6, 7, 8, 9, 10 };
10
11     int result = whatIsThis( a, arraySize );
12
13     cout << "Result is " << result << endl;
14     return 0;
15  }
16
17  int whatIsThis( int b[], int size )
18  {
19     if ( size == 1 )
20        return b[ 0 ];
21     else
22        return b[ size - 1 ] + whatIsThis( b, size - 1 );
23  }
```

ANS: Recursively sums the elements of **a**.

```
Result is 55
```

4.19   Write a program that runs 1000 games of craps and answers the following questions:
   a) How many games are won on the first roll, second roll, ..., twentieth roll, and after the twentieth roll?
   b) How many games are lost on the first roll, second roll, ..., twentieth roll, and after the twentieth roll?
   c) What are the chances of winning at craps? (*Note:* You should discover that craps is one of the fairest casino games. What do you suppose this means?)
   d) What is the average length of a game of craps?
   e) Do the chances of winning improve with the length of the game?
   ANS:

```
1   // Exercise 4.19 Solution
2   #include <iostream.h>
3   #include <iomanip.h>
4   #include <stdlib.h>
5   #include <time.h>
6
7   int rollDice( void );
8
```

```
 9  int main()
10  {
11      enum Outcome { CONTINUE, WIN, LOSE };
12      const int SIZE = 22, ROLLS = 1000;
13      int gameStatus, sum, myPoint, roll, length = 0, wins[ SIZE ] = { 0 },
14          losses[ SIZE ] = { 0 }, winSum = 0, loseSum = 0;
15
16      srand( time( 0 ) );
17
18      for ( int i = 1; i <= ROLLS; ++i ) {
19          sum = rollDice();
20          roll = 1;
21
22          switch ( sum ) {
23             case 7: case 11:
24                gameStatus = WIN;
25                break;
26             case 2: case 3: case 12:
27                gameStatus = LOSE;
28                break;
29             default:
30                gameStatus = CONTINUE;
31                myPoint = sum;
32                break;
33          }
34
35          while ( gameStatus == CONTINUE ) {
36             sum = rollDice();
37             ++roll;
38
39             if ( sum == myPoint )
40                gameStatus = WIN;
41             else if ( sum == 7 )
42                gameStatus = LOSE;
43          }
44
45          if ( roll > 21 )
46             roll = 21;
47
48          if ( gameStatus == WIN ) {
49             ++wins[ roll ];
50             ++winSum;
51          }
52          else {
53             ++losses[ roll ];
54             ++loseSum;
55          }
56      }
57
58      cout << "Games won or lost after the 20th roll"
59          << "\nare displayed as the 21st roll.\n\n";
60
61      for ( int z = 1; z <= 21; ++z )
62         cout << setw( 3 ) << wins[ z ] << " games won and " << setw( 3 )
63             << losses[ z ] << " games lost on roll " << z << '\n';
64
65      // calculate chances of winning
66      cout << setiosflags( ios::fixed | ios::showpoint )
67          << "\nThe chances of winning are " << winSum << " / "
68          << winSum + loseSum << " = " << setprecision( 2 )
69          << 100.0 * winSum / ( winSum + loseSum ) << "%\n";
70
```

```
71        // calculate average length of game
72        for ( int k = 1; k <= 21; ++k )
73           length += wins[ k ] * k + losses[ k ] * k;
74
75        cout << "The average game length is " << setprecision( 2 )
76             << length / 1000.0 << " rolls." << endl;
77
78        return 0;
79   }
80
81   int rollDice( void )
82   {
83        int die1, die2, workSum;
84
85        die1 = 1 + rand() % 6;
86        die2 = 1 + rand() % 6;
87        workSum = die1 + die2;
88
89        return workSum;
90   }
```

```
Games won or lost after the 20th roll
are displayed as the 21st roll.

217 games won and 113 games lost on roll 1
 84 games won and 125 games lost on roll 2
 62 games won and  74 games lost on roll 3
 44 games won and  43 games lost on roll 4
 31 games won and  37 games lost on roll 5
 17 games won and  26 games lost on roll 6
 12 games won and  26 games lost on roll 7
 11 games won and  13 games lost on roll 8
 11 games won and  10 games lost on roll 9
  4 games won and   6 games lost on roll 10
  4 games won and   6 games lost on roll 11
  1 games won and   6 games lost on roll 12
  2 games won and   4 games lost on roll 13
  0 games won and   1 games lost on roll 14
  1 games won and   3 games lost on roll 15
  0 games won and   0 games lost on roll 16
  0 games won and   0 games lost on roll 17
  2 games won and   0 games lost on roll 18
  0 games won and   0 games lost on roll 19
  1 games won and   1 games lost on roll 20
  1 games won and   1 games lost on roll 21

The chances of winning are 505 / 1000 = 50.50%
The average game length is 3.31 rolls.
```

4.20   (*Airline Reservations System*) A small airline has just purchased a computer for its new automated reservations system. You have been asked to program the new system. You are to write a program to assign seats on each flight of the airline's only plane (capacity: 10 seats).

Your program should display the following menu of alternatives—**Please type 1 for "smoking"** and **Please type 2 for "nonsmoking"**. If the person types 1, your program should assign a seat in the smoking section (seats 1-5). If the person types 2, your program should assign a seat in the nonsmoking section (seats 6-10). Your program should print a boarding pass indicating the person's seat number and whether it is in the smoking or nonsmoking section of the plane.

Use a single-subscripted array to represent the seating chart of the plane. Initialize all the elements of the array to 0 to indicate that all seats are empty. As each seat is assigned, set the corresponding elements of the array to 1 to indicate that the seat is no longer available.

Your program should, of course, never assign a seat that has already been assigned. When the smoking section is full, your program should ask the person if it is acceptable to be placed in the nonsmoking section (and vice versa). If yes, then make the appropriate seat assignment. If no, then print the message **"Next flight leaves in 3 hours."**

ANS:

```
1   // Exercise 4.20 Solution
2   #include <iostream.h>
3   #include <ctype.h>
4
5   int main()
6   {
7      const int SEATS = 11;
8      int plane[ SEATS ] = { 0 }, people = 0, nonSmoking = 1, smoking = 6,
9         choice;
10     char response;
11
12     while ( people < 10 ) {
13        cout << "\nPlease type 1 for \"smoking\"\n"
14           << "Please type 2 for \"non-smoking\"\n";
15        cin >> choice;
16
17        if ( choice == 1 ) {
18           if ( !plane[ smoking ] && smoking <= 10 ) {
19              cout << "Your seat assignment is " << smoking << ' ';
20              plane[ smoking++ ] = 1;
21              ++people;
22           }
23           else if ( smoking > 10 && nonSmoking <= 5 ) {
24              cout << "The smoking section is full.\n"
25                 << "Would you like to sit in the non-smoking"
26                 << " section (Y or N)? ";
27              cin >> response;
28
29              if ( toupper( response ) == 'Y' ) {
30                 cout << "Your seat assignment is " << nonSmoking << ' ';
31                 plane[ nonSmoking++ ] = 1;
32                 ++people;
33              }
34              else
35                 cout << "Next flight leaves in 3 hours.\n";
36           }
37           else
38              cout << "Next flight leaves in 3 hours.\n";
39        }
40        else {
41           if ( !plane[ nonSmoking ] && nonSmoking <= 5 ) {
42              cout << "Your seat assignment is " << nonSmoking << '\n';
43              plane[ nonSmoking++ ] = 1;
44              ++people;
45           }
46           else if ( nonSmoking > 5 && smoking <= 10 ) {
47              cout << "The non-smoking section is full.\n"
48                 << "Would you like to sit in the smoking"
49                 << " section (Y or N)? ";
50              cin >> response;
51
52              if ( toupper( response ) == 'Y' ) {
53                 cout << "Your seat assignment is " << smoking << '\n';
54                 plane[ smoking++ ] = 1;
55                 ++people;
56              }
```

```
57                    else
58                        cout << "Next flight leaves in 3 hours.\n";
59                }
60            else
61                cout << "Next flight leaves in 3 hours.\n";
62        }
63    }
64
65    cout << "All seats for this flight are sold." << endl;
66    return 0;
67 }
```

```
   Please type 1 for "smoking"
   Please type 2 for "non-smoking"
   1
   Your seat assignment is 6

   Please type 1 for "smoking"
   Please type 2 for "non-smoking"
   1

   Your seat assignment is 7
   Please type 1 for "smoking"
   Please type 2 for "non-smoking"
   2

   Your seat assignment is 1
   Please type 1 for "smoking"
   Please type 2 for "non-smoking"
   ...
   Please type 1 for "smoking"
   Please type 2 for "non-smoking"
   1
   Your seat assignment is 10

   All seats for the flight are sold.
```

4.21   What does the following program do?

```
1   // ex04_21.cpp
2   #include <iostream.h>
3
4   void someFunction( int [], int );
5
6   int main()
7   {
8       const int arraySize = 10;
9       int a[ arraySize ] = { 32, 27, 64, 18, 95, 14, 90, 70, 60, 37 };
10
11      cout << "The values in the array are:" << endl;
12      someFunction( a, arraySize );
13      cout << endl;
14      return 0;
15  }
16
17  void someFunction( int b[], int size )
18  {
19      if ( size > 0 ) {
20          someFunction( &b[ 1 ], size - 1 );
21          cout << b[ 0 ] << "  ";
22      }
23  }
```

ANS: Recursively outputs an array in reverse order.

```
The values in the array are:
37   60   70   90   14   95   18   64   27   32
```

4.22   Use a double-subscripted array to solve the following problem. A company has four salespeople (1 to 4) who sell five different products (1 to 5). Once a day, each salesperson passes in a slip for each different type of product sold. Each slip contains:

a) The salesperson number

b) The product number

c) The total dollar value of that product sold that day

Thus, each salesperson passes in between 0 and 5 sales slips per day. Assume that the information from all of the slips for last month is available. Write a program that will read all this information for last month's sales, and summarize the total sales by salesperson by product. All totals should be stored in the double-subscripted array **sales**. After processing all the information for last month, print the results in tabular format with each of the columns representing a particular salesperson and each of the rows representing a particular product. Cross total each row to get the total sales of each product for last month; cross total each column to get the total sales by salesperson for last month. Your tabular printout should include these cross totals to the right of the totaled rows and to the bottom of the totaled columns.

ANS:

```cpp
1   // Exercise 4.22 Solution
2   #include <iostream.h>
3   #include <iomanip.h>
4
5   int main()
6   {
7      const int PEOPLE = 5, PRODUCTS = 6;
8      float sales[ PEOPLE ][ PRODUCTS ] = { 0.0 }, value, totalSales,
9         productSales[ PRODUCTS ] = { 0.0 };
10     int salesPerson, product;
11
12     cout << "Enter the salesperson (1 - 4), product number (1 - 5), "
13        << "and total sales.\nEnter -1 for the salesperson"
14        << " to end input.\n";
15     cin >> salesPerson;
16
17     while ( salesPerson != -1 ) {
18        cin >> product >> value;
19        sales[ salesPerson ][ product ] += value;
20        cin >> salesPerson;
21     }
22
23     cout << "\nThe total sales for each salesperson are displayed"
24        << " at the end of each row,\n" << "and the total sales for"
25        << " each product are displayed at the bottom of each\n"
26        << "column.\n " << setw( 12 ) << 1 << setw( 12 ) << 2
27        << setw( 12 ) << 3 << setw( 12 ) << 4 << setw( 12 ) << 5 << setw( 13 )
28        << "Total\n" << setiosflags( ios::fixed | ios::showpoint );
29
30     for ( int i = 1; i < PEOPLE; ++i ) {
31        totalSales = 0.0;
32        cout << i;
33
34        for ( int j = 1; j < PRODUCTS; ++j ) {
35           totalSales += sales[ i ][ j ];
36           cout << setw( 12 ) << setprecision( 2 ) << sales[ i ][ j ];
37           productSales[ j ] += sales[ i ][ j ];
38        }
39
40        cout << setw( 12 ) << setprecision( 2 ) << totalSales << '\n';
41     }
```

```
42
43        cout << "\nTotal" << setw( 8 ) << setprecision( 2 ) << productSales[ 1 ];
44
45        for ( int j = 2; j < PRODUCTS; ++j )
46           cout << setw( 12 ) << setprecision( 2 ) << productSales[ j ];
47
48        cout << endl;
49        return 0;
50   }
```

```
Enter the salesperson (1 - 4), product number (1 - 5), and total sales.
Enter -1 for the salesperson to end input.
1 1 9.99
3 3 5.99
2 2 4.99
-1

The total sales for each salesperson are displayed at the end of each row,
and the total sales for each product are displayed at the bottom of each
column.
             1          2          3          4          5      Total
1          9.99       0.00       0.00       0.00       0.00       9.99
2          0.00       4.99       0.00       0.00       0.00       4.99
3          0.00       0.00       5.99       0.00       0.00       5.99
4          0.00       0.00       0.00       0.00       0.00       0.00

Total      9.99       4.99       5.99       0.00       0.00
```

4.23   (*Turtle Graphics*) The Logo language, which is particularly popular among personal computer users, made the concept of *turtle graphics* famous. Imagine a mechanical turtle that walks around the room under the control of a C++ program. The turtle holds a pen in one of two positions, up or down. While the pen is down, the turtle traces out shapes as it moves; while the pen is up, the turtle moves about freely without writing anything. In this problem you will simulate the operation of the turtle and create a computerized sketchpad as well.

Use a 20-by-20 array **floor** which is initialized to zeros. Read commands from an array that contains them. Keep track of the current position of the turtle at all times and whether the pen is currently up or down. Assume that the turtle always starts at position 0,0 of the floor with its pen up. The set of turtle commands your program must process are as follows:

Command	Meaning
1	Pen up
2	Pen down
3	Turn right
4	Turn left
5,10	Move forward 10 spaces (or a number other than 10)
6	Print the 20-by-20 array
9	End of data (sentinel)

Suppose that the turtle is somewhere near the center of the floor. The following "program" would draw and print a 12-by 12-square leaving the pen in the up position:

```
        2
        5,12
        3
        5,12
        3
        5,12
        3
        5,12
        1
        6
        9
```

As the turtle moves with the pen down, set the appropriate elements of array **floor** to **1**s. When the **6** command (print) is given, wherever there is a **1** in the array, display an asterisk, or some other character you choose. Wherever there is a zero display a blank. Write a program to implement the turtle graphics capabilities discussed here. Write several turtle graphics programs to draw interesting shapes. Add other commands to increase the power of your turtle graphics language.

       ANS:

```
1   // Exercise 4.23 Solution
2   #include <iostream.h>
3
4   const int MAXCOMMANDS = 100, SIZE = 20;
5
6   int turnRight( int );
7   int turnLeft( int );
8   void getCommands( int [][ 2 ] );
9   void movePen( int, int [][ SIZE ], int, int );
10  void printArray( const int [][ SIZE ] );
11
12  int main()
13  {
14     int floor[ SIZE ][ SIZE ] = { 0 }, command, direction = 0,
15        commandArray[ MAXCOMMANDS ][ 2 ] = { 0 }, distance, count = 0;
16     bool penDown = false;
17
18     getCommands( commandArray );
19     command = commandArray[ count ][ 0 ];
20
21     while ( command != 9 ) {
22        switch ( command ) {
23           case 1:
24              penDown = false;
25              break;
26           case 2:
27              penDown = true;
28              break;
29           case 3:
30              direction = turnRight( direction );
31              break;
32           case 4:
33              direction = turnLeft( direction );
34              break;
35           case 5:
36              distance = commandArray[ count ][ 1 ];
37              movePen( penDown, floor, direction, distance );
38              break;
39           case 6:
40              cout << "\nThe drawing is:\n\n";
41              printArray( floor );
42              break;
43        }
44
45        command = commandArray[ ++count ][ 0 ];
46     }
```

```
47
48      return 0;
49   }
50
51   void getCommands( int commands[][ 2 ] )
52   {
53      int tempCommand;
54
55      cout << "Enter command (9 to end input): ";
56      cin >> tempCommand;
57
58      for ( int i = 0; tempCommand != 9 && i < MAXCOMMANDS; ++i ) {
59         commands[ i ][ 0 ] = tempCommand;
60
61         if ( tempCommand == 5 ) {
62            cin.ignore();    // skip comma
63            cin >> commands[ i ][ 1 ];
64         }
65
66         cout << "Enter command (9 to end input): ";
67         cin >> tempCommand;
68      }
69
70      commands[ i ][ 0 ] = 9;   // last command
71   }
72
73   int turnRight( int d )
74   {
75      return ++d > 3 ? 0 : d;
76   }
77
78   int turnLeft( int d )
79   {
80      return --d < 0 ? 3 : d;
81   }
82
83   void movePen( int down, int a[][ SIZE ], int dir, int dist )
84   {
85      static int xPos = 0, yPos = 0;
86      int j;  // looping variable
87
88      switch ( dir ) {
89         case 0:   // move to the right
90            for ( j = 1; j <= dist && yPos + j < SIZE; ++j )
91               if ( down )
92                  a[ xPos ][ yPos + j ] = 1;
93
94            yPos += j - 1;
95            break;
96         case 1:    // move down
97            for ( j = 1; j <= dist && xPos + j < SIZE; ++j )
98               if ( down )
99                  a[ xPos + j ][ yPos ] = 1;
100
101           xPos += j - 1;
102           break;
103        case 2:    // move to the left
104           for ( j = 1; j <= dist && yPos - j >= 0; ++j )
105              if ( down )
106                 a[ xPos ][ yPos - j ] = 1;
107
108           yPos -= j - 1;
109           break;
```

```
110        case 3:    // move up
111           for ( j = 1; j <= dist && xPos - j >= 0; ++j )
112              if ( down )
113                 a[ xPos - j ][ yPos ] = 1;
114
115           xPos -= j - 1;
116           break;
117        }
118 }
119
120 void printArray( const int a[][ SIZE ] )
121 {
122    for ( int i = 0; i < SIZE; ++i ) {
123       for ( int j = 0; j < SIZE; ++j )
124          cout << ( a[ i ][ j ] ? '*' : ' ' );
125
126       cout << endl;
127    }
128 }
```

```
Enter command (9 to end input): 2
Enter command (9 to end input): 5,6
Enter command (9 to end input): 3
Enter command (9 to end input): 5,12
Enter command (9 to end input): 3
Enter command (9 to end input): 5,12
Enter command (9 to end input): 3
Enter command (9 to end input): 5,12
Enter command (9 to end input): 1
Enter command (9 to end input): 6
Enter command (9 to end input): 9

The drawing is:

******
*    *
*    *
*    *
*    *
*    *
*    *
*    *
*    *
*    *
*    *
*    *
******
```

4.24   (*Knight's Tour*) One of the more interesting puzzlers for chess buffs is the Knight's Tour problem, originally proposed by the mathematician Euler. The question is this: Can the chess piece called the knight move around an empty chessboard and touch each of the 64 squares once and only once? We study this intriguing problem in depth here.

The knight makes L-shaped moves (over two in one direction and then over one in a perpendicular direction). Thus, from a square in the middle of an empty chessboard, the knight can make eight different moves (numbered 0 through 7) as shown in Fig. 4.25.

a) Draw an 8-by-8 chessboard on a sheet of paper and attempt a Knight's Tour by hand. Put a **1** in the first square you move to, a **2** in the second square, a **3** in the third, etc. Before starting the tour, estimate how far you think you will get, remembering that a full tour consists of 64 moves. How far did you get? Was this close to your estimate?

Fig. 4.25   The eight possible moves of the knight.

b) Now let us develop a program that will move the knight around a chessboard. The board is represented by an 8-by-8 double-subscripted array **board**. Each of the squares is initialized to zero. We describe each of the eight possible moves in terms of both their horizontal and vertical components. For example, a move of type 0 as shown in Fig. 4.25 consists of moving two squares horizontally to the right and one square vertically upward. Move 2 consists of moving one square horizontally to the left and two squares vertically upward. Horizontal moves to the left and vertical moves upward are indicated with negative numbers. The eight moves may be described by two single-subscripted arrays, **horizontal** and **vertical**, as follows:

```
horizontal[ 0 ] = 2
horizontal[ 1 ] = 1
horizontal[ 2 ] = -1
horizontal[ 3 ] = -2
horizontal[ 4 ] = -2
horizontal[ 5 ] = -1
horizontal[ 6 ] = 1
horizontal[ 7 ] = 2

vertical[ 0 ] = -1
vertical[ 1 ] = -2
vertical[ 2 ] = -2
vertical[ 3 ] = -1
vertical[ 4 ] = 1
vertical[ 5 ] = 2
vertical[ 6 ] = 2
vertical[ 7 ] = 1
```

c) Let the variables **currentRow** and **currentColumn** indicate the row and column of the knight's current position. To make a move of type **moveNumber**, where **moveNumber** is between 0 and 7, your program uses the statements

```
currentRow += vertical[ moveNumber ];
currentColumn += horizontal[ moveNumber ];
```

d) Keep a counter that varies from **1** to **64**. Record the latest count in each square the knight moves to. Remember to test each potential move to see if the knight has already visited that square. And, of course, test every potential move to make sure that the knight does not land off the chessboard. Now write a program to move the knight around the chessboard. Run the program. How many moves did the knight make?

e) After attempting to write and run a Knight's Tour program, you have probably developed some valuable insights. We will use these to develop a *heuristic* (or strategy) for moving the knight. Heuristics do not guarantee success, but a carefully developed heuristic greatly improves the chance of success. You may have observed that the outer squares are more troublesome than the squares nearer the center of the board. In fact, the most troublesome, or inaccessible, squares are the four corners.

f) Intuition may suggest that you should attempt to move the knight to the most troublesome squares first and leave open those that are easiest to get to so when the board gets congested near the end of the tour there will be a greater chance of success.

g) We may develop an "accessibility heuristic" by classifying each of the squares according to how accessible they are, and then always moving the knight to the square (within the knight's L-shaped moves, of course) that is most inaccessible. We label a double-subscripted array **accessibility** with numbers indicating from how many squares each particular square is accessible. On a blank chessboard, each center square is rated as **8**, each corner square is rated as **2**, and the other squares have accessibility numbers of **3**, **4**, or **6** as follows:

```
2   3   4   4   4   4   3   2
3   4   6   6   6   6   4   3
4   6   8   8   8   8   6   4
4   6   8   8   8   8   6   4
4   6   8   8   8   8   6   4
4   6   8   8   8   8   6   4
3   4   6   6   6   6   4   3
2   3   4   4   4   4   3   2
```

h) Now write a version of the Knight's Tour program using the accessibility heuristic. At any time, the knight should move to the square with the lowest accessibility number. In case of a tie, the knight may move to any of the tied squares. Therefore, the tour may begin in any of the four corners. (*Note:* As the knight moves around the chessboard, your program should reduce the accessibility numbers as more and more squares become occupied. In this way, at any given time during the tour, each available square's accessibility number will remain equal to precisely the number of squares from which that square may be reached.) Run this version of your program. Did you get a full tour? Now modify the program to run 64 tours, one starting from each square of the chessboard. How many full tours did you get?

i) Write a version of the Knight's Tour program which, when encountering a tie between two or more squares, decides what square to choose by looking ahead to those squares reachable from the "tied" squares. Your program should move to the square for which the next move would arrive at a square with the lowest accessibility number.

ANS:

```
1   // Exercise 4.24 Part C Solution
2   // Knight's Tour - access version
3   // runs one tour
4   #include <iostream.h>
5   #include <iomanip.h>
6   #include <stdlib.h>
7   #include <time.h>
8
9   const int SIZE = 8;
10
11  void clearBoard( int [][ SIZE ] );
12  void printBoard( const int [][ SIZE ] );
13  bool validMove( int, int, const int [][ SIZE ] );
14
15  int main()
16  {
17     int board[ SIZE ][ SIZE ], currentRow, currentColumn, moveNumber = 0,
18        access[ SIZE ][ SIZE ] = { 2, 3, 4, 4, 4, 4, 3, 2,
19                                   3, 4, 6, 6, 6, 6, 4, 3,
20                                   4, 6, 8, 8, 8, 8, 6, 4,
21                                   4, 6, 8, 8, 8, 8, 6, 4,
22                                   4, 6, 8, 8, 8, 8, 6, 4,
23                                   4, 6, 8, 8, 8, 8, 6, 4,
24                                   3, 4, 6, 6, 6, 6, 4, 3,
25                                   2, 3, 4, 4, 4, 4, 3, 2 },
26
27        testRow, testColumn, count, minRow, minColumn,
28        minAccess = 9, accessNumber,
```

```
29              horizontal[ SIZE ] = { 2, 1, -1, -2, -2, -1, 1, 2 },
30              vertical[ SIZE ] = { -1, -2, -2, -1, 1, 2, 2, 1 };
31       bool done;
32
33       srand( time( 0 ) );
34
35       clearBoard( board );    // initialize array board
36       currentRow = rand() % 8;
37       currentColumn = rand() % 8;
38       board[ currentRow ][ currentColumn ] = ++moveNumber;
39       done = false;
40
41       while ( !done ) {
42          accessNumber = minAccess;
43
44          for ( int moveType = 0; moveType < SIZE; ++moveType ) {
45             testRow = currentRow + vertical[ moveType ];
46             testColumn = currentColumn + horizontal[ moveType ];
47
48             if ( validMove( testRow, testColumn, board ) ) {
49
50                if ( access[ testRow ][ testColumn ] < accessNumber ) {
51                   accessNumber = access[ testRow ][ testColumn ];
52                   minRow = testRow;
53                   minColumn = testColumn;
54                }
55
56                --access[ testRow ][ testColumn ];
57             }
58          }
59
60          if ( accessNumber == minAccess )
61             done = true;
62          else {
63             currentRow = minRow;
64             currentColumn = minColumn;
65             board[ currentRow ][ currentColumn ] = ++moveNumber;
66          }
67       }
68
69       cout << "The tour ended with " << moveNumber << " moves.\n";
70
71       if ( moveNumber == 64 )
72          cout << "This was a full tour!\n\n";
73       else
74          cout << "This was not a full tour.\n\n";
75
76       cout << "The board for this test is:\n\n";
77       printBoard( board );
78       return 0;
79    }
80
81    void clearBoard( int workBoard[][ SIZE ] )
82    {
83       for ( int row = 0; row < SIZE; ++row )
84          for ( int col = 0; col < SIZE; ++col )
85             workBoard[ row ][ col ] = 0;
86    }
87
88    void printBoard( const int workBoard[][ SIZE ] )
89    {
90       cout << "   0 1 2 3 4 5 6 7\n";
91
```

```
92      for ( int row = 0; row < SIZE; ++row ) {
93         cout << row;
94
95         for ( int col = 0; col < SIZE; ++col )
96            cout << setw( 3 ) << workBoard[ row ][ col ];
97
98         cout << '\n';
99      }
100
101     cout << endl;
102  }
103
104  bool validMove( int row, int column, const int workBoard[][ SIZE ] )
105  {
106     // NOTE: This test stops as soon as it becomes false
107     return ( row >= 0 && row < SIZE && column >= 0 && column < SIZE
108             && workBoard[ row ][ column ] == 0 );
109  }
```

```
The tour ended with 64 moves.
This was a full tour!

The board for this test is:

    0   1   2   3   4   5   6   7
0  33   8  47  38  31  10  49  14
1  46  39  32   9  48  13  30  11
2   7  34  45  52  37  60  15  50
3  40  53  36  59  62  51  12  29
4  35   6  63  44  57  28  61  16
5  54  41  58  27  64  19  22   1
6   5  26  43  56   3  24  17  20
7  42  55   4  25  18  21   2  23
```

4.25   (*Knight's Tour: Brute Force Approaches*) In Exercise 4.24 we developed a solution to the Knight's Tour problem. The approach used, called the "accessibility heuristic," generates many solutions and executes efficiently.

As computers continue increasing in power, we will be able to solve more problems with sheer computer power and relatively unsophisticated algorithms. Let us call this approach "brute force" problem solving.

   a) Use random number generation to enable the knight to walk around the chess board (in its legitimate L-shaped moves, of course) at random. Your program should run one tour and print the final chessboard. How far did the knight get?

   b) Most likely, the preceding program produced a relatively short tour. Now modify your program to attempt 1000 tours. Use a single-subscripted array to keep track of the number of tours of each length. When your program finishes attempting the 1000 tours, it should print this information in neat tabular format. What was the best result?

   c) Most likely, the preceding program gave you some "respectable" tours but no full tours. Now "pull all the stops out" and simply let your program run until it produces a full tour. (*Caution:* This version of the program could run for hours on a powerful computer.) Once again, keep a table of the number of tours of each length, and print this table when the first full tour is found. How many tours did your program attempt before producing a full tour? How much time did it take?

   d) Compare the brute force version of the Knight's Tour with the accessibility heuristic version. Which required a more careful study of the problem? Which algorithm was more difficult to develop? Which required more computer power? Could we be certain (in advance) of obtaining a full tour with the accessibility heuristic approach? Could we be certain (in advance) of obtaining a full tour with the brute force approach? Argue the pros and cons of brute force problem solving in general.

   ANS:

```
1   // Exercise 4.25 Part A Solution
2   #include <iostream.h>
3   #include <iomanip.h>
4   #include <stdlib.h>
5   #include <time.h>
```

```
 6
 7    const int SIZE = 8;
 8
 9    bool validMove( int, int, const int [][ SIZE ] );
10    void printBoard( const int [][ SIZE ] );
11
12    int main()
13    {
14       int currentRow, currentColumn, moveType, moveNumber = 0,
15          testRow, testColumn, board[ SIZE ][ SIZE ] = { 0 },
16          horizontal[ SIZE ] = { 2, 1, -1, -2, -2, -1, 1, 2 },
17          vertical[ SIZE ] = { -1, -2, -2, -1, 1, 2, 2, 1 };
18       bool done, goodMove;
19
20       srand( time( 0 ) );
21
22       currentRow = rand() % SIZE;
23       currentColumn = rand() % SIZE;
24       board[ currentRow ][ currentColumn ] = ++moveNumber;
25       done = false;
26
27       while ( !done ) {
28          moveType = rand() % SIZE;
29          testRow = currentRow + vertical[ moveType ];
30          testColumn = currentColumn + horizontal[ moveType ];
31          goodMove = validMove( testRow, testColumn, board );
32
33          if ( goodMove ) {
34             currentRow = testRow;
35             currentColumn = testColumn;
36             board[ currentRow ][ currentColumn ] = ++moveNumber;
37          }
38          else {
39
40             for ( int count = 0; count < SIZE - 1 && !goodMove; ++count ) {
41                moveType = ++moveType % SIZE;
42                testRow = currentRow + vertical[ moveType ];
43                testColumn = currentColumn + horizontal[ moveType ];
44                goodMove = validMove( testRow, testColumn, board );
45
46                if ( goodMove ) {
47                   currentRow = testRow;
48                   currentColumn = testColumn;
49                   board[ currentRow ][ currentColumn ] = ++moveNumber;
50                }
51             }
52
53             if ( !goodMove )
54                done = true;
55          }
56
57          if ( moveNumber == 64 )
58             done = true;
59       }
60
61       cout << "The tour has ended with " << moveNumber << " moves.\n";
62
63       if ( moveNumber == 64 )
64          cout << "This was a full tour!\n";
65       else
66          cout << "This was not a full tour.\n";
67
68       cout << "The board for this random test was:\n\n";
69       printBoard( board );
```

```
70      return 0;
71   }
72
73   bool validMove( int row, int column, const int workBoard[][ SIZE ] )
74   {
75      // NOTE: This test stops as soon as it becomes false
76      return ( row >= 0 && row < SIZE && column >= 0 && column < SIZE
77              && workBoard[ row ][ column ] == 0 );
78   }
79
80   void printBoard( const int board[][ SIZE ] )
81   {
82      cout << "   0  1  2  3  4  5  6  7\n";
83
84      for ( int row = 0; row < SIZE; ++row ) {
85         cout << row;
86
87         for ( int col = 0; col < SIZE; ++col )
88            cout << setw( 3 ) << board[ row ][ col ];
89
90         cout << '\n';
91      }
92
93      cout << endl;
94   }
```

```
The tour has ended with 44 moves.
This was not a full tour.

The board for this random test was:

    0  1  2  3  4  5  6  7
0   1  0  0 36  0 14 17 34
1   0 37  2 13 22 35  0 15
2   3  0 21  0 11 16 33 18
3  38 25 12 23 20  0  0  0
4   0  4  0 40  0 10 19 32
5  26 39 24  0 30 43  0  9
6   5  0 41 28  7  0 31 44
7   0 27  6  0 42 29  8  0
```

```
1    // Exercise 4.25 Part B Solution
2    #include <iostream.h>
3    #include <iomanip.h>
4    #include <stdlib.h>
5    #include <time.h>
6
7    const int SIZE = 8, TOURS = 1000, MAXMOVES = 65;
8
9    bool validMove( int, int, int, const int [][ SIZE ] );
10
11   int main()
12   {
13      int currentRow, currentColumn, moveType, moveNumber, testRow, testColumn,
14         moveTotal[ MAXMOVES ] = { 0 }, goodMove, board[ SIZE ][ SIZE ],
15         horizontal[ SIZE ] = { 2, 1, -1, -2, -2, -1, 1, 2 },
16         vertical[ SIZE ] = { -1, -2, -2, -1, 1, 2, 2, 1 };
17      bool done;
18
19      srand( time( 0 ) );
20
```

```
21      for ( int i = 0; i < TOURS; ++i ) {
22         for ( int row = 0; row < SIZE; ++row )
23            for ( int col = 0; col < SIZE; ++col )
24               board[ row ][ col ] = 0;
25
26         moveNumber = 0;
27
28         currentRow = rand() % SIZE;
29         currentColumn = rand() % SIZE;
30         board[ currentRow ][ currentColumn ] = ++moveNumber;
31         done = false;
32
33         while ( !done ) {
34            moveType = rand() % SIZE;
35            testRow = currentRow + vertical[ moveType ];
36            testColumn = currentColumn + horizontal[ moveType ];
37            goodMove = validMove( testRow, testColumn, moveType, board );
38
39            if ( goodMove ) {
40               currentRow = testRow;
41               currentColumn = testColumn;
42               board[ currentRow ][ currentColumn ] = ++moveNumber;
43            }
44            else {
45
46               for ( int count = 0; count < SIZE - 1 && !goodMove; ++count ) {
47                  moveType = ++moveType % SIZE;
48                  testRow = currentRow + vertical[ moveType ];
49                  testColumn = currentColumn + horizontal[ moveType ];
50                  goodMove = validMove( testRow, testColumn, moveType, board );
51
52                  if ( goodMove ) {
53                     currentRow = testRow;
54                     currentColumn = testColumn;
55                     board[ currentRow ][ currentColumn ] = ++moveNumber;
56                  }
57
58               }
59
60               if ( !goodMove )
61                  done = true;
62            }
63
64            if ( moveNumber == 64 )
65               done = true;
66         }
67
68         ++moveTotal[ moveNumber ];
69      }
70
71      for ( int j = 1; j < MAXMOVES; ++j )
72         if ( moveTotal[ j ] )
73            cout << "There were " << moveTotal[ j ] << " tours of " << j
74                 << " moves." << endl;
75
76      return 0;
77   }
78
79   bool validMove( int testRow, int testColumn, int moveType,
80                   const int board[][ SIZE ] )
81   {
82      if ( testRow >= 0 && testRow < SIZE && testColumn >= 0 &&
83           testColumn < SIZE )
84         return board[ testRow ][ testColumn ] != 0 ? false : true;
```

```
85      else
86          return false;
87  }
```

```
There were 1 tours of 4 moves.
There were 2 tours of 6 moves.
There were 5 tours of 7 moves.
There were 1 tours of 9 moves.
There were 2 tours of 10 moves.
There were 3 tours of 11 moves.
There were 9 tours of 12 moves.
There were 3 tours of 13 moves.
There were 5 tours of 14 moves.
There were 8 tours of 15 moves.
There were 8 tours of 16 moves.
There were 3 tours of 17 moves.
There were 16 tours of 18 moves.
There were 9 tours of 19 moves.
There were 20 tours of 20 moves.
There were 10 tours of 21 moves.
There were 15 tours of 22 moves.
There were 8 tours of 23 moves.
There were 20 tours of 24 moves.
There were 12 tours of 25 moves.
There were 22 tours of 26 moves.
There were 26 tours of 27 moves.
There were 20 tours of 28 moves.
There were 20 tours of 29 moves.
There were 26 tours of 30 moves.
There were 24 tours of 31 moves.
There were 33 tours of 32 moves.
There were 17 tours of 33 moves.
There were 33 tours of 34 moves.
There were 20 tours of 35 moves.
There were 25 tours of 36 moves.
There were 40 tours of 37 moves.
There were 42 tours of 38 moves.
There were 33 tours of 39 moves.
There were 35 tours of 40 moves.
There were 40 tours of 41 moves.
There were 45 tours of 42 moves.
There were 39 tours of 43 moves.
There were 35 tours of 44 moves.
There were 22 tours of 45 moves.
There were 31 tours of 46 moves.
There were 22 tours of 47 moves.
There were 32 tours of 48 moves.
There were 28 tours of 49 moves.
There were 27 tours of 50 moves.
There were 23 tours of 51 moves.
There were 23 tours of 52 moves.
There were 15 tours of 53 moves.
There were 14 tours of 54 moves.
There were 5 tours of 55 moves.
There were 11 tours of 56 moves.
There were 1 tours of 57 moves.
There were 6 tours of 58 moves.
There were 2 tours of 59 moves.
There were 2 tours of 60 moves.
There were 1 tours of 61 moves.
```

4.26   (*Eight Queens*) Another puzzler for chess buffs is the Eight Queens problem. Simply stated: Is it possible to place eight queens on an empty chessboard so that no queen is "attacking" any other, i.e., no two queens are in the same row, the same column, or along the same diagonal? Use the thinking developed in Exercise 4.24 to formulate a heuristic for solving the Eight Queens problem. Run your program. (*Hint:* It is possible to assign a value to each square of the chessboard indicating how many squares of an empty chessboard are "eliminated" if a queen is placed in that square. Each of the corners would be assigned the value 22, as in Fig. 4.26.) Once these "elimination numbers" are placed in all 64 squares, an appropriate heuristic might be: Place the next queen in the square with the smallest elimination number. Why is this strategy intuitively appealing?

```
* * * * * * * *
* *
*   *
*     *
*       *
*         *
*           *
*             *
```

Fig. 4.26   The 22 squares eliminated by placing a queen in the upper-left corner.

4.27   (*Eight Queens: Brute Force Approaches*) In this exercise you will develop several brute force approaches to solving the Eight Queens problem introduced in Exercise 4.26.

    a) Solve the Eight Queens exercise, using the random brute force technique developed in Exercise 4.25.

    b) Use an exhaustive technique, i.e., try all possible combinations of eight queens on the chessboard.

    c) Why do you suppose the exhaustive brute force approach may not be appropriate for solving the Knight's Tour problem?

    d) Compare and contrast the random brute force and exhaustive brute force approaches in general.

    ANS:

```
1   // Exercise 4.27 Part A Solution
2   #include <iostream.h>
3   #include <iomanip.h>
4   #include <time.h>
5   #include <stdlib.h>
6
7   bool queenCheck( const char [][ 8 ], int, int );
8   void placeQueens( char [][ 8 ] );
9   void printBoard( const char [][ 8 ] );
10  void xConflictSquares( char [][ 8 ], int, int );
11  void xDiagonals( char [][ 8 ], int, int );
12  bool availableSquare( const char [][ 8 ] );
13  inline int validMove( const char board[][ 8 ], int row, int col )
14     { return ( row >= 0 && row < 8 && col >= 0 && col < 8 ); }
15
16  int main()
17  {
18     char board [ 8 ][ 8 ] = { '\0' };
19
20     srand( time( 0 ) );
21
22     placeQueens( board );
23     printBoard( board );
24     return 0;
25  }
26
27  bool availableSquare( const char board[][ 8 ] )
28  {
29     for ( int row = 0; row < 8; ++row )
30        for ( int col = 0; col < 8; ++col )
31           if ( board[ row ][ col ] == '\0' )
32              return false;  // at least one open square is available
33
```

```
34      return true;   // no available squares
35   }
36
37   void placeQueens( char board[][ 8 ] )
38   {
39      const char QUEEN = 'Q';
40      int rowMove, colMove, queens = 0;
41      bool done = false;
42
43      while ( queens < 8 && !done ) {
44         rowMove = rand() % 8;
45         colMove = rand() % 8;
46
47         if ( queenCheck( board, rowMove, colMove ) ) {
48            board[ rowMove ][ colMove ] = QUEEN;
49            xConflictSquares( board, rowMove, colMove );
50            ++queens;
51         }
52
53         done = availableSquare( board );
54      }
55   }
56
57   void xConflictSquares( char board[][ 8 ], int row, int col )
58   {
59      for ( int loop = 0; loop < 8; ++loop ) {
60         // place an '*' in the row occupied by the queen
61         if ( board[ row ][ loop ] == '\0' )
62            board[ row ][ loop ] = '*';
63
64         // place an '*' in the col occupied by the queen
65         if ( board[ loop ][ col ] == '\0' )
66            board[ loop ][ col ] = '*';
67      }
68
69      // place an '*' in the diagonals occupied by the queen
70      xDiagonals( board, row, col );
71   }
72
73   bool queenCheck( const char board[][ 8 ], int row, int col )
74   {
75      int r = row, c = col;
76
77      // check row and column for a queen
78      for ( int d = 0; d < 8; ++d )
79         if ( board[ row ][ d ] == 'Q' || board[ d ][ col ] == 'Q' )
80            return false;
81
82      // check upper left diagonal for a queen
83      for ( int e = 0; e < 8 && validMove( board, --r, --c ); ++e )
84         if ( board[ r ][ c ] == 'Q' )
85            return false;
86
87      r = row;
88      c = col;
89      // check upper right diagonal for a queen
90      for ( int f = 0; f < 8 && validMove( board, --r, ++c ); ++f )
91         if ( board[ r ][ c ] == 'Q' )
92            return false;
93
94      r = row;
95      c = col;
```

```
96         // check lower left diagonal for a queen
97         for ( int g = 0; g < 8 && validMove( board, ++r, --c ); ++g )
98            if (board[ r ][ c ] == 'Q' )
99               return false;
100
101        r = row;
102        c = col;
103        // check lower right diagonal for a queen
104        for ( int h = 0; h < 8 && validMove( board, ++r, ++c ); ++h )
105           if ( board[ r ][ c ] == 'Q' )
106              return false;
107
108        return true;   // no queen in conflict
109   }
110
111   void xDiagonals( char board[][ 8 ], int row, int col )
112   {
113        int r = row, c = col;
114
115        // upper left diagonal
116        for ( int a = 0; a < 8 && validMove( board, --r, --c ); ++a )
117           board[ r ][ c ] = '*';
118
119        r = row;
120        c = col;
121        // upper right diagonal
122        for ( int b = 0; b < 8 && validMove( board, --r, ++c ); ++b )
123           board[ r ][ c ] = '*';
124
125        r = row;
126        c = col;
127        // lower left diagonal
128        for ( int d = 0; d < 8 && validMove( board, ++r, --c ); ++d )
129           board[ r ][ c ] = '*';
130
131        r = row;
132        c = col;
133        // lower right diagonal
134        for ( int e = 0; e < 8 && validMove( board, ++r, ++c ); ++e )
135           board[ r ][ c ] = '*';
136   }
137
138   void printBoard( const char board[][ 8 ] )
139   {
140        int queens = 0;
141
142        // header for columns
143        cout << "   0 1 2 3 4 5 6 7\n";
144
145        for ( int r = 0; r < 8; ++r ) {
146           cout << setw( 2 ) << r << ' ';
147
148           for ( int c = 0; c < 8; ++c ) {
149              cout << board[ r ][ c ] << ' ';
150
151              if ( board[ r ][ c ] == 'Q' )
152                 ++queens;
153           }
154
155           cout << '\n';
156        }
157
158        if ( queens == 8 )
159           cout << "\nEight Queens were placed on the board!" << endl;
```

```
160     else
161         cout << '\n' << queens << " Queens were placed on the board." << endl;
162 }
```

```
      0 1 2 3 4 5 6 7
    0 * * * * * * * Q
    1 * Q * * * * * *
    2 * * * * * * * *
    3 * * * * * Q * *
    4 Q * * * * * * *
    5 * * * * * * Q *
    6 * * * * Q * * *
    7 * * Q * * * * *
    7 Queens were placed on the board.
```

4.28   (*Knight's Tour: Closed Tour Test*) In the Knight's Tour, a full tour occurs when the knight makes 64 moves touching each square of the chess board once and only once. A closed tour occurs when the 64th move is one move away from the location in which the knight started the tour. Modify the Knight's Tour program you wrote in Exercise 4.24 to test for a closed tour if a full tour has occurred.

ANS:

```
1   // Exercise 4.28 Solution
2   #include <iostream.h>
3   #include <iomanip.h>
4   #include <stdlib.h>
5   #include <time.h>
6
7   const int SIZE = 8;
8
9   void clearBoard( int [][ SIZE ] );
10  void printBoard( const int [][ SIZE ] );
11  bool validMove( int, int, const int [][ SIZE ] );
12
13  int main()
14  {
15     int board[ SIZE ][ SIZE ], firstMoveRow, firstMoveCol,
16        access[ SIZE ][ SIZE ] = { 2, 3, 4, 4, 4, 4, 3, 2,
17                                   3, 4, 6, 6, 6, 6, 4, 3,
18                                   4, 6, 8, 8, 8, 8, 6, 4,
19                                   4, 6, 8, 8, 8, 8, 6, 4,
20                                   4, 6, 8, 8, 8, 8, 6, 4,
21                                   4, 6, 8, 8, 8, 8, 6, 4,
22                                   3, 4, 6, 6, 6, 6, 4, 3,
23                                   2, 3, 4, 4, 4, 4, 3, 2 },
24        currentRow, currentColumn, moveNumber = 0, testRow, testColumn,
25        minRow, minColumn, minAccess = 9, accessNumber,
26        horizontal[ SIZE ] = { 2, 1, -1, -2, -2, -1, 1, 2 },
27        vertical[ SIZE ] = { -1, -2, -2, -1, 1, 2, 2, 1 };
28     bool done, closedTour = false;
29
30     srand( time( 0 ) );
31
32     clearBoard( board );   // initialize array board
33     currentRow = rand() % SIZE;
34     currentColumn = rand() % SIZE;
35     firstMoveRow = currentRow;        // store first moves row
36     firstMoveCol = currentColumn;     // store first moves col
37
38     board[ currentRow ][ currentColumn ] = ++moveNumber;
39     done = false;
40
```

```
41     while ( !done ) {
42        accessNumber = minAccess;
43
44        for ( int moveType = 0; moveType < SIZE; ++moveType ) {
45           testRow = currentRow + vertical[ moveType ];
46           testColumn = currentColumn + horizontal[ moveType ];
47
48           if ( validMove( testRow, testColumn, board ) ) {
49              if ( access[ testRow ][ testColumn ] < accessNumber ) {
50                 accessNumber = access[ testRow ][ testColumn ];
51                 minRow = testRow;
52                 minColumn = testColumn;
53              }
54
55              --access[ testRow ][ testColumn ];
56           }
57        }
58
59        if ( accessNumber == minAccess )
60           done = true;
61        else {
62           currentRow = minRow;
63           currentColumn = minColumn;
64           board[ currentRow ][ currentColumn ] = ++moveNumber;
65
66           // check for closed tour
67           if ( moveNumber == 64 )
68              for ( int m = 0; m < SIZE; ++m ) {
69                 testRow = currentRow + vertical[ m ];
70                 testColumn = currentColumn + horizontal[ m ];
71
72                 if ( testRow == firstMoveRow && testColumn == firstMoveCol )
73                    closedTour = true;
74              }
75        }
76     }
77
78     cout << "The tour ended with " << moveNumber << " moves.\n";
79
80     if ( moveNumber == 64 && closedTour == true )
81        cout << "This was a CLOSED tour!\n\n";
82     else if ( moveNumber == 64 )
83        cout << "This was a full tour!\n\n";
84     else
85        cout << "This was not a full tour.\n\n";
86
87     cout << "The board for this test is:\n\n";
88     printBoard( board );
89     return 0;
90  }
91
92  void clearBoard( int workBoard[][ SIZE ] )
93  {
94     for ( int row = 0; row < SIZE; ++row )
95        for ( int col = 0; col < SIZE; ++col )
96           workBoard[ row ][ col ] = 0;
97  }
98
99  void printBoard( const int workBoard[][ SIZE ] )
100 {
101    cout << "    0  1  2  3  4  5  6  7\n";
102
103    for ( int row = 0; row < SIZE; ++row ) {
104       cout << row;
```

```
105
106            for ( int col = 0; col < SIZE; ++col )
107               cout << setw( 3 ) << workBoard[ row ][ col ];
108
109            cout << '\n';
110         }
111
112         cout << endl;
113      }
114
115      bool validMove( int row, int column, const int workBoard[][ SIZE ] )
116      {
117         // NOTE: This test stops as soon as it becomes false
118         return ( row >= 0 && row < SIZE && column >= 0 && column < SIZE
119                  && workBoard[ row ][ column ] == 0 );
120      }
```

```
The tour ended with 64 moves.
This was a CLOSED tour!

The board for this test is:

     0  1  2  3  4  5  6  7
0    4 23 38 49  6 21 28 61
1   39 48  5 22 37 60  7 20
2   24  3 50 45 52 27 62 29
3   47 40 53 26 59 36 19  8
4    2 25 46 51 44 63 30 35
5   41 54 13 64 33 58  9 18
6   14  1 56 43 16 11 34 31
7   55 42 15 12 57 32 17 10
```

4.29 (*The Sieve of Eratosthenes*) A prime integer is any integer that is evenly divisible only by itself and 1. The Sieve of Eratosthenes is a method of finding prime numbers. It operates as follows:

a) Create an array with all elements initialized to 1 (true). Array elements with prime subscripts will remain 1. All other array elements will eventually be set to zero.

b) Starting with array subscript 2 (subscript 1 must be prime), every time an array element is found whose value is 1, loop through the remainder of the array and set to zero every element whose subscript is a multiple of the subscript for the element with value 1. For array subscript 2, all elements beyond 2 in the array that are multiples of 2 will be set to zero (subscripts 4, 6, 8, 10, etc.); for array subscript 3, all elements beyond 3 in the array that are multiples of 3 will be set to zero (subscripts 6, 9, 12, 15, etc.); and so on.

When this process is complete, the array elements that are still set to one indicate that the subscript is a prime number. These subscripts can then be printed. Write a program that uses an array of 1000 elements to determine and print the prime numbers between 1 and 999. Ignore element 0 of the array.

ANS:

```
1    // Exercise 4.29 Solution
2    #include <iostream.h>
3    #include <iomanip.h>
4
5    int main()
6    {
7       const int SIZE = 1000;
8       int array[ SIZE ], count = 0;
9
10      for ( int k = 0; k < SIZE; ++k )
11         array[ k ] = 1;
12
13      for ( int i = 1; i < SIZE; ++i )
14         if ( array[ i ] == 1 && i != 1 )
15            for ( int j = i; j <= SIZE; ++j )
```

```
16                    if ( j % i == 0 && j != i )
17                        array[ j ] = 0;
18
19      // range 2 - 197
20      for ( int q = 2; q < SIZE; ++q )
21         if ( array[ q ] == 1 ) {
22            cout << setw( 3 ) << q << " is a prime number.\n";
23            ++count;
24         }
25
26      cout << "A total of " << count << " prime numbers were found." << endl;
27      return 0;
28   }
```

```
There were 1 tours of 4 moves.
There were 2 tours of 6 moves.
There were 5 tours of 7 moves.
There were 1 tours of 9 moves.
There were 2 tours of 10 moves.
There were 3 tours of 11 moves.
There were 9 tours of 12 moves.
There were 3 tours of 13 moves.
There were 5 tours of 14 moves.
There were 8 tours of 15 moves.
There were 8 tours of 16 moves.
There were 3 tours of 17 moves.
There were 16 tours of 18 moves.
There were 9 tours of 19 moves.
There were 20 tours of 20 moves.
There were 10 tours of 21 moves.
There were 15 tours of 22 moves.
There were 8 tours of 23 moves.
There were 20 tours of 24 moves.
There were 12 tours of 25 moves.
There were 22 tours of 26 moves.
There were 26 tours of 27 moves.
There were 20 tours of 28 moves.
There were 20 tours of 29 moves.
There were 26 tours of 30 moves.
There were 24 tours of 31 moves.
There were 33 tours of 32 moves.
There were 17 tours of 33 moves.
There were 33 tours of 34 moves.
There were 20 tours of 35 moves.
There were 25 tours of 36 moves.
There were 40 tours of 37 moves.
There were 42 tours of 38 moves.
There were 33 tours of 39 moves.
There were 35 tours of 40 moves.
There were 40 tours of 41 moves.
There were 45 tours of 42 moves.
There were 39 tours of 43 moves.
There were 35 tours of 44 moves.
There were 22 tours of 45 moves.
There were 31 tours of 46 moves.
There were 22 tours of 47 moves.
There were 32 tours of 48 moves.
There were 28 tours of 49 moves.
There were 27 tours of 50 moves.
There were 23 tours of 51 moves.
There were 23 tours of 52 moves.
There were 15 tours of 53 moves.
There were 14 tours of 54 moves.
There were 5 tours of 55 moves.
There were 11 tours of 56 moves.
There were 1 tours of 57 moves.
There were 6 tours of 58 moves.
There were 2 tours of 59 moves.
There were 2 tours of 60 moves.
There were 1 tours of 61 moves.
```

4.30   (*Bucket Sort*) A bucket sort begins with a single-subscripted array of positive integers to be sorted, and a double-subscripted array of integers with rows subscripted from 0 to 9 and columns subscripted from 0 to *n* - 1 where *n* is the number of values in the array to be sorted. Each row of the double-subscripted array is referred to as a bucket. Write a function **bucketSort** that takes an integer array and the array size as arguments and performs as follows:

- a) Place each value of the single-subscripted array into a row of the bucket array based on the value's ones digit. For example, 97 is placed in row 7, 3 is placed in row 3, and 100 is placed in row 0. This is called a "distribution pass."
- b) Loop through the bucket array row-by-row and copy the values back to the original array. This is called a "gathering pass." The new order of the preceding values in the single-subscripted array is 100, 3, and 97.
- c) Repeat this process for each subsequent digit position (tens, hundreds, thousands, etc.).

On the second pass, 100 is placed in row 0, 3 is placed in row 0 (because 3 has no tens digit), and 97 is placed in row 9. After the gathering pass, the order of the values in the single-subscripted array is 100, 3, and 97. On the third pass, 100 is placed in row 1, 3 is placed in row zero and 97 is placed in row zero (after the 3). After the last gathering pass, the original array is now in sorted order.

Note that the double-subscripted array of buckets is ten times the size of the integer array being sorted. This sorting technique provides better performance than a bubble sort, but requires much more memory. The bubble sort requires space for only one additional element of data. This is an example of the space-time tradeoff: The bucket sort uses more memory than the bubble sort, but performs better. This version of the bucket sort requires copying all the data back to the original array on each pass. Another possibility is to create a second double-subscripted bucket array and repeatedly swap the data between the two bucket arrays.

ANS:

```
1   // Exercise 4.30 Solution
2   #include <iostream.h>
3   #include <iomanip.h>
4
5   // constant size must be defined as the array size for bucketSort to work
6   const int SIZE = 12;
7
8   void bucketSort( int [] );
9   void distributeElements( int [], int [][ SIZE ], int );
10  void collectElements( int [], int [][ SIZE ] );
11  int numberOfDigits( int [], int );
12  void zeroBucket( int [][ SIZE ] );
13
14  int main()
15  {
16     int array[ SIZE ] = { 19, 13, 5, 27, 1, 26, 31, 16, 2, 9, 11, 21 };
17
18     cout << "Array elements in original order:\n";
19
20     for ( int i = 0; i < SIZE; ++i )
21        cout << setw( 3 ) << array[ i ];
22
23     cout << '\n';
24     bucketSort( array );
25
26     cout << "\nArray elements in sorted order:\n";
27
28     for ( int j = 0; j < SIZE; ++j )
29        cout << setw( 3 ) << array[ j ];
30
31     cout << endl;
32     return 0;
33  }
34
35  // Perform the bucket sort algorithm
36  void bucketSort( int a[] )
37  {
38     int totalDigits, bucket[ 10 ][ SIZE ] = { 0 };
39
40     totalDigits = numberOfDigits( a, SIZE );
```

```
41
42      for ( int i = 1; i <= totalDigits; ++i ) {
43         distributeElements( a, bucket, i );
44         collectElements( a, bucket );
45
46         if ( i != totalDigits )
47            zeroBucket( bucket );   // set all bucket contents to zero
48      }
49   }
50
51   // Determine the number of digits in the largest number
52   int numberOfDigits( int b[], int arraySize )
53   {
54      int largest = b[ 0 ], digits = 0;
55
56      for ( int i = 1; i < arraySize; ++i )
57         if ( b[ i ] > largest )
58            largest = b[ i ];
59
60      while ( largest != 0 ) {
61         ++digits;
62         largest /= 10;
63      }
64      return digits;
65   }
66
67   // Distribute elements into buckets based on specified digit
68   void distributeElements( int a[], int buckets[][ SIZE ], int digit )
69   {
70      int divisor = 10, bucketNumber, elementNumber;
71
72      for ( int i = 1; i < digit; ++i )    // determine the divisor
73         divisor *= 10;                    // used to get specific digit
74
75      for ( int k = 0; k < SIZE; ++k ) {
76         // bucketNumber example for hundreds digit:
77         // (1234 % 1000 - 1234 % 100) / 100 --> 2
78         bucketNumber = ( a[ k ] % divisor - a[ k ] %
79                         ( divisor / 10 ) ) / ( divisor / 10 );
80
81         // retrieve value in buckets[bucketNumber][0] to determine
82         // which element of the row to store a[i] in.
83         elementNumber = ++buckets[ bucketNumber ][ 0 ];
84         buckets[ bucketNumber ][ elementNumber ] = a[ k ];
85      }
86   }
87
88   // Return elements to original array
89   void collectElements( int a[], int buckets[][ SIZE ] )
90   {
91      int subscript = 0;
92
93      for ( int i = 0; i < 10; ++i )
94         for ( int j = 1; j <= buckets[ i ][ 0 ]; ++j )
95            a[ subscript++ ] = buckets[ i ][ j ];
96   }
97
98   // Set all buckets to zero
99   void zeroBucket( int buckets[][ SIZE ] )
100  {
101     for ( int i = 0; i < 10; ++i )
102        for ( int j = 0; j < SIZE; ++j )
103           buckets[ i ][ j ] = 0;
104  }
```

```
Array elements in original order:
  19 13   5 27   1 26 31 16   2   9 11 21
Array elements in sorted order:
   1   2   5   9 11 13 16 19 21 26 27 31
```

Recursion Exercises

4.31   (*Selection Sort*) A selection sort searches an array looking for the smallest element in the array. Then, the smallest element is swapped with the first element of the array. The process is repeated for the subarray beginning with the second element of the array. Each pass of the array results in one element being placed in its proper location. This sort performs comparably to the bubble sort—for an array of *n* elements, *n* - 1 passes must be made, and for each subarray, *n* - 1 comparisons must be made to find the smallest value. When the subarray being processed contains one element, the array is sorted. Write recursive function **selectionSort** to perform this algorithm.

ANS:

```
1   // Exercise 4.31 Solution
2   #include <iostream.h>
3   #include <iomanip.h>
4   #include <stdlib.h>
5   #include <time.h>
6
7   void selectionSort( int [], int );
8
9   int main()
10  {
11     const int SIZE = 10, MAXRANGE = 1000;
12     int sortThisArray[ SIZE ] = { 0 };
13
14     srand( time( 0 ) );
15
16     for ( int i = 0; i < SIZE; ++i )
17        sortThisArray[ i ] = 1 + rand() % MAXRANGE;
18
19     cout << "\nUnsorted array is:\n";
20     for ( int j = 0; j < SIZE; ++j )
21        cout << ' ' << sortThisArray[ j ] << ' ';
22
23     selectionSort( sortThisArray, SIZE );
24
25     cout << "\n\nSorted array is:\n";
26     for ( int k = 0; k < SIZE; ++k )
27        cout << ' ' << sortThisArray[ k ] << ' ';
28
29     cout << '\n' << endl;
30     return 0;
31  }
32
33  void selectionSort( int array[], int size )
34  {
35     int temp;
36
37     if ( size >= 1 ) {
38        for ( int loop = 0; loop < size; ++loop )
39           if ( array[ loop ] < array[ 0 ] ) {
40              temp = array[ loop ];
41              array[ loop ] = array[ 0 ];
42              array[ 0 ] = temp;
43           }
44
45        selectionSort( &array[ 1 ], size - 1 );
46     }
47  }
```

```
Unsorted array is:
224   775   967   110   374   883   779   986   259   114

Sorted array is:
110   114   224   259   374   775   779   883   967   986
```

4.32   (*Palindromes*) A palindrome is a string that is spelled the same way forwards and backwards. Some examples of palindromes are: "radar," "able was i ere i saw elba," and (if blanks are ignored) "a man a plan a canal panama." Write a recursive function **testPalindrome** that returns **true** if the string stored in the array is a palindrome, and **false** otherwise. The function should ignore spaces and punctuation in the string.

ANS:

```
1    // Exercise 4.32 Solution
2    #include <iostream.h>
3
4    bool testPalindrome( const char [], int, int );
5
6    int main()
7    {
8       const int SIZE = 80;
9       char c, string[ SIZE ], copy[ SIZE ];
10      int count = 0, copyCount, i;
11
12      cout << "Enter a sentence:\n";
13
14      while ( ( c = cin.get() ) != '\n' && count < SIZE )
15         string[ count++ ] = c;
16
17      string[ count ] = '\0';    // terminate string
18
19      // make a copy of string without spaces
20      for ( copyCount = 0, i = 0; string[ i ] != '\0'; ++i )
21         if ( string[ i ] != ' ' )
22            copy[ copyCount++ ] = string[ i ];
23
24      if ( testPalindrome( copy, 0, copyCount - 1 ) )
25         cout << '\"' << string << "\" is a palindrome" << endl;
26      else
27         cout << '\"' << string << "\" is not a palindrome" << endl;
28
29      return 0;
30   }
31
32   bool testPalindrome( const char array[], int left, int right )
33   {
34      if ( left == right || left > right )
35         return true;
36      else if ( array[ left ] != array[ right ] )
37         return false;
38      else
39         return testPalindrome( array, left + 1, right - 1 );
40   }
```

```
Enter a sentence:
alucard e dracula
"alucard e dracula" is a palindrome
```

4.33   (*Linear Search*) Modify Fig. 4.19 to use recursive function **linearSearch** to perform a linear search of the array. The function should receive an integer array and the size of the array as arguments. If the search key is found, return the array subscript; otherwise, return –1.

ANS:

```
1   // Exercise 4.33 Solution
2   #include <iostream.h>
3
4   int linearSearch( const int [], int, int, int );
5
6   int main()
7   {
8      const int SIZE = 100;
9      int array[ SIZE ], searchKey, element;
10
11     for ( int loop = 0; loop < SIZE; ++loop )
12        array[ loop ] = 2 * loop;
13
14     cout << "Enter the integer search key: ";
15     cin >> searchKey;
16
17     element = linearSearch( array, searchKey, 0, SIZE - 1 );
18
19     if ( element != -1 )
20        cout << "Found value in element " << element << endl;
21     else
22        cout << "Value not found" << endl;
23
24     return 0;
25  }
26
27  int linearSearch( const int array[], int key, int low, int high )
28  {
29     if ( array[low] == key )
30        return low;
31     else if ( low == high )
32        return -1;
33     else
34        return linearSearch( array, key, low + 1, high );
35  }
```

```
Enter the integer search key: 22
Found value in element 11
```

4.34   (*Binary Search*) Modify the program of Fig. 4.20 to use a recursive function **binarySearch** to perform the binary search of the array. The function should receive an integer array and the starting subscript and ending subscript as arguments. If the search key is found, return the array subscript; otherwise, return –1.

ANS:

```
1   // Exercise 4.34 Solution
2   #include <iostream.h>
3   #include <iomanip.h>
4
5   const int SIZE = 15;
6
7   int binarySearch( const int [], int, int, int );
8   void printRow( const int [], int, int, int );
9   void printHeader( void );
10
11  int main()
12  {
13     int a[ SIZE ], key, result;
14
15     for ( int i = 0; i < SIZE; ++i )
16        a[ i ] = 2 * i;
```

```
17
18        cout << "Enter a number between 0 and 28: ";
19        cin >> key;
20
21        printHeader();
22        result = binarySearch( a, key, 0, SIZE - 1 );
23
24        if ( result != -1 )
25           cout << '\n' << key << " found in array element " << result << endl;
26        else
27           cout << '\n' << key << " not found" << endl;
28
29        return 0;
30    }
31
32    int binarySearch( const int b[], int searchKey, int low, int high )
33    {
34        int middle;
35
36        if ( low <= high ) {
37           middle = ( low + high ) / 2;
38           printRow( b, low, middle, high );
39
40           if ( searchKey == b[ middle ] )
41              return middle;
42           else if ( searchKey < b[ middle ] )
43              return binarySearch( b, searchKey, low, middle - 1 );
44           else
45              return binarySearch( b, searchKey, middle + 1, high );
46        }
47
48        return -1;    // searchKey not found
49    }
50
51    // Print a header for the output
52    void printHeader( void )
53    {
54        cout << "Subscripts:\n";
55
56        for ( int i = 0; i < SIZE; ++i )
57           cout << setw( 3 ) << i << ' ';
58
59        cout << '\n';
60
61        for ( int k = 1; k <= 4 * SIZE; ++k )
62           cout << '-';
63
64        cout << '\n';
65    }
66
67    // print one row of output showing the current
68    // part of the array being processed.
69    void printRow( const int b[], int low, int mid, int high )
70    {
71        for ( int i = 0; i < SIZE; ++i )
72           if ( i < low || i > high )
73              cout << "    ";
74           else if ( i == mid )
75              cout << setw( 3 ) << b[ i ] << '*';     // mark middle value
76           else
77              cout << setw( 3 ) << b[ i ] << ' ';
78
79        cout << '\n';
80    }
```

```
Enter a number between 0 and 28: 17
Subscripts:
 0   1   2   3   4   5   6   7   8   9  10  11  12  13  14
------------------------------------------------------------
 0   2   4   6   8  10  12  14* 16  18  20  22  24  26  28
                            16  18  20  22* 24  26  28
                            16  18* 20
                            16*
17 not found
```

4.35   (*Eight Queens*) Modify the Eight Queens program you created in Exercise 4.26 to solve the problem recursively.

4.36   (*Print an array*) Write a recursive function **printArray** that takes an array and the size of the array as arguments and returns nothing. The function should stop processing and return when it receives an array of size zero.

ANS:

```
1   // Exercise 4.36 Solution
2   #include <iostream.h>
3   #include <iomanip.h>
4   #include <stdlib.h>
5   #include <time.h>
6
7   void printArray( const int [], int, int );
8
9   int main()
10  {
11     const int SIZE = 10, MAXNUMBER = 500;
12     int array[ SIZE ];
13
14     srand( time( 0 ) );
15
16     for ( int loop = 0; loop < SIZE; ++loop )
17        array[ loop ] = 1 + rand() % MAXNUMBER;
18
19     cout << "Array values printed in main:\n";
20
21     for ( int j = 0; j < SIZE; ++j )
22        cout << setw( 5 ) << array[ j ];
23
24     cout << "\n\nArray values printed in printArray:\n";
25     printArray( array, 0, SIZE - 1 );
26     cout << endl;
27     return 0;
28  }
29
30  void printArray( const int array[], int low, int high )
31  {
32     cout << setw( 5 ) << array[ low ];
33
34     if ( low == high )
35        return;
36     else
37        printArray( array, low + 1, high );
38  }
```

```
Array values printed in main:
  156   496   122   427    49    74   118   491    37   409
Array values printed in printArray:
  156   496   122   427    49    74   118   491    37   409
```

4.37   (*Print a string backwards*) Write a recursive function **stringReverse** that takes a character array containing a string as an argument, prints the string backwards, and returns nothing. The function should stop processing and return when the terminating null character is encountered.

ANS:

```
1    // Exercise 4.37 Solution
2    #include <iostream.h>
3
4    void stringReverse( const char [] );
5
6    int main()
7    {
8       const int SIZE = 30;
9       char strArray[ SIZE ] = "Print this string backwards.";
10
11       for ( int loop = 0; loop < SIZE; ++loop )
12          cout << strArray[ loop ];
13
14       cout << '\n';
15       stringReverse( strArray );
16       cout << endl;
17       return 0;
18    }
19
20    void stringReverse( const char strArray[] )
21    {
22       if ( strArray[ 0 ] == '\0' )
23          return;
24
25       stringReverse( &strArray[ 1 ] );
26       cout << strArray[ 0 ];
27    }
```

```
    Print this string backwards.
    .sdrawkcab gnirts siht tnirP
```

4.38   (*Find the minimum value in an array*) Write a recursive function **recursiveMinimum** that takes an integer array and the array size as arguments and returns the smallest element of the array. The function should stop processing and return when it receives an array of 1 element.

ANS:

```
1    // Exercise 4.38 Solution
2    #include <iostream.h>
3    #include <iomanip.h>
4    #include <stdlib.h>
5    #include <time.h>
6
7    const int MAXRANGE = 1000;
8    int recursiveMinimum( const int [], int, int );
9
10   int main()
11   {
12      const int SIZE = 10;
13      int array[ SIZE ], smallest;
14
15      srand( time( 0 ) );
16
17      for ( int loop = 0; loop < SIZE; ++loop )
18         array[ loop ] = 1 + rand() % MAXRANGE;
19
20      cout << "Array members are:\n";
```

```
21      for ( int k = 0; k < SIZE; ++k )
22         cout << setw( 5 ) << array[ k ];
23
24      cout << '\n';
25      smallest = recursiveMinimum( array, 0, SIZE - 1 );
26      cout << "\nSmallest element is: " << smallest << endl;
27      return 0;
28   }
29
30   int recursiveMinimum( const int array[], int low, int high )
31   {
32      static int smallest = MAXRANGE;
33
34      if ( array[ low ] < smallest )
35         smallest = array[ low ];
36
37      return low == high ? smallest : recursiveMinimum( array, low + 1, high );
38   }
```

```
Array members are:
  243    4  615  119  162  955  488  748  373  486
Smallest element is: 4
```

Chapter 5 Solutions
Pointers and Strings

Solutions

5.8   State whether the following are true or false. If false, explain why.

a) Two pointers that point to different arrays cannot be compared meaningfully.

ANS: True.

b) Because the name of an array is a pointer to the first element of the array, array names may be manipulated in precisely the same manner as pointers.

ANS: False. An array name cannot be used to refer to another location in memory.

5.9   Answer each of the following. Assume that unsigned integers are stored in 2 bytes, and that the starting address of the array is at location 1002500 in memory.

a) Declare an array of type **unsigned int** called **values** with 5 elements, and initialize the elements to the even integers from 2 to 10. Assume the symbolic constant **SIZE** has been defined as **5**.

ANS: unsigned values[SIZE] = { 2, 4, 6, 8, 10 };

b) Declare a pointer **vPtr** that points to an object of type **unsigned int**.

ANS: unsigned *vPtr;

c) Print the elements of array **values** using array subscript notation. Use a **for** structure and assume integer control variable **i** has been declared.

ANS:
```
for ( i = 0; i < SIZE; ++i )
    cout << setw( 4 ) << values[ i ];
```

d) Give two separate statements that assign the starting address of array **values** to pointer variable **vPtr**.

ANS: vPtr = values; and **vPtr = &values[0];**

e) Print the elements of array **values** using pointer/offset notation.

ANS:
```
for ( i = 0; i < SIZE; ++i )
    cout << setw( 4 ) << *( vPtr + i );
```

f) Print the elements of array **values** using pointer/offset notation with the array name as the pointer.

ANS:
```
for ( i = 0; i < SIZE; ++i )
    cout << setw( 4 ) << *( values + i );
```

g) Print the elements of array **values** by subscripting the pointer to the array.

ANS:
```
for ( i = 0; i < SIZE; ++i )
    cout << setw( 4 ) << vPtr[ i ];
```

h) Refer to element 5 of **values** using array subscript notation, pointer/offset notation with the array name as the pointer, pointer subscript notation, and pointer/offset notation.

ANS: values[4], *(values + 4), vPtr[4], *(vPtr + 4)

i) What address is referenced by **vPtr + 3**? What value is stored at that location?

ANS: The address of the location pertaining to **values[3]** (i.e., 1002506). 8.

j) Assuming **vPtr** points to **values[4]**, what address is referenced by **vPtr -= 4**? What value is stored at that location?

ANS: The address of where **values** begins in memory (i.e., 1002500). 2.

5.10　For each of the following, write a single statement that performs the indicated task. Assume that long integer variables **value1** and **value2** have been declared, and that **value1** has been initialized to **200000**.

　　a) Declare the variable **lPtr** to be a pointer to an object of type **long**.

　　ANS: `long *lPtr;`

　　b) Assign the address of variable **value1** to pointer variable **lPtr**.

　　ANS: `lPtr = &value1;`

　　c) Print the value of the object pointed to by **lPtr**.

　　ANS: `cout << *lPtr << '\n';`

　　d) Assign the value of the object pointed to by **lPtr** to variable **value2**.

　　ANS: `value2 = *lPtr;`

　　e) Print the value of **value2**.

　　ANS: `cout << value2 << '\n';`

　　f) Print the address of **value1**.

　　ANS: `cout << &value1 << '\n';`

　　g) Print the address stored in **lPtr**. Is the value printed the same as the address of **value1**?

　　ANS: `cout << lPtr << '\n';` yes.

5.11　Do each of the following.

　　a) Write the function header for function **zero** which takes a long integer array parameter **bigIntegers** and does not return a value.

　　ANS: `void zero( long bigIntegers[] )` or
　　　　`void zero( long *bigIntegers )`

　　b) Write the function prototype for the function in part **(a)**.

　　ANS: `void zero( long [] );` or `void zero( long * );`

　　c) Write the function header for function **add1AndSum** which takes an integer array parameter **oneTooSmall** and returns an integer.

　　ANS: `int add1AndSum( int oneTooSmall[] )` or
　　　　`int add1AndSum( int *oneTooSmall )`

　　d) Write the function prototype for the function described in part **(c)**.

　　ANS: `int add1AndSum( int [] );` or `int add1AndSum( int * );`

Note: Exercises 5.12 through 5.15 are reasonably challenging. Once you have done these problems, you ought to be able to implement most popular card games easily.

5.12　Modify the program in Fig. 5.24 so that the card dealing function deals a five-card poker hand. Then write functions to accomplish each of the following:

　　a) Determine if the hand contains a pair.

　　b) Determine if the hand contains two pairs.

　　c) Determine if the hand contains three of a kind (e.g., three jacks).

　　d) Determine if the hand contains four of a kind (e.g., four aces).

　　e) Determine if the hand contains a flush (i.e., all five cards of the same suit).

　　f) Determine if the hand contains a straight (i.e., five cards of consecutive face values).

　　ANS:

```
1   // Exercise 5.12 Solution
2   #include <iostream.h>
3   #include <iomanip.h>
4   #include <stdlib.h>
5   #include <time.h>
6
7   void shuffle( int [][ 13 ] );
8   void deal( const int [][ 13 ], const char *[], const char *[], int [][ 2 ] );
9   void pair( const int [][ 13 ], const int [][ 2 ], const char *[] );
10  void threeOfKind( const int [][ 13 ], const int [][ 2 ], const char *[] );
11  void fourOfKind( const int [][ 13 ], const int [][ 2 ], const char *[] );
12  void flushHand( const int [][ 13 ], const int [][ 2 ], const char *[] );
13  void straightHand( const int [][ 13 ], const int [][ 2 ], const char *[],
14                     const char *[] );
15
```

```
16  int main()
17  {
18      const char *suit[] = { "Hearts", "Diamonds", "Clubs", "Spades" },
19                  *face[] = { "Ace", "Deuce", "Three", "Four", "Five", "Six",
20                              "Seven", "Eight", "Nine", "Ten", "Jack", "Queen",
21                              "King" };
22      int deck[ 4 ][ 13 ] = { 0 }, hand[ 5 ][ 2 ] = { 0 };
23
24      srand( time( 0 ) );
25
26      shuffle( deck );
27      deal( deck, face, suit, hand );
28      pair( deck, hand, face );
29      threeOfKind( deck, hand, face );
30      fourOfKind( deck, hand, face );
31      flushHand( deck, hand, suit );
32      straightHand( deck, hand, suit, face );
33      return 0;
34  }
35
36  void shuffle( int wDeck[][ 13 ] )
37  {
38      int row, column;
39
40      for ( int card = 1; card <= 52; ++card ) {
41          do {
42              row = rand() % 4;
43              column = rand() % 13;
44          } while ( wDeck[ row ][ column ] != 0 );
45
46          wDeck[ row ][ column ] = card;
47      }
48  }
49
50  // deal a five card poker hand
51  void deal( const int wDeck[][ 13 ], const char *wFace[],
52             const char *wSuit[], int wHand[][ 2 ] )
53  {
54      int r = 0;
55
56      cout << "The hand is:\n";
57
58      for ( int card = 1; card < 6; ++card )
59          for ( int row = 0; row <= 3; ++row )
60              for ( int column = 0; column <= 12; ++column )
61                  if ( wDeck[ row ][ column ] == card ) {
62                      wHand[ r ][ 0 ] = row;
63                      wHand[ r ][ 1 ] = column;
64                      cout << setw( 5 ) << wFace[ column ]
65                           << " of " << setw( 8 ) << setiosflags( ios::left )
66                           << wSuit[ row ] << ( card % 2 == 0 ? '\n' : '\t' )
67                           << resetiosflags( ios::left );
68                      ++r;
69                  }
70
71      cout << '\n';
72  }
73
74  // pair determines if the hand contains one or two pair
75  void pair( const int wDeck[][ 13 ], const int wHand[][ 2 ],
76             const char *wFace[] )
77  {
78      int counter[ 13 ] = { 0 };
79
```

```
80       for ( int r = 0; r < 5; ++r )
81          ++counter[ wHand[ r ][ 1 ] ];
82
83       cout << '\n';
84
85       for ( int p = 0; p < 13; ++p )
86          if ( counter[ p ] == 2 )
87             cout << "The hand contains a pair of " << wFace[ p ] << "'s.\n";
88    }
89
90    void threeOfKind( const int wDeck[][ 13 ], const int wHand[][ 2 ],
91                     const char *wFace[] )
92    {
93       int counter[ 13 ] = { 0 };
94
95       for ( int r = 0; r < 5; ++r )
96          ++counter[ wHand[ r ][ 1 ] ];
97
98       for ( int t = 0; t < 13; t++ )
99          if ( counter[ t ] == 3 )
100            cout << "The hand contains three " << wFace[ t ] << "'s.\n";
101   }
102
103   void fourOfKind( const int wDeck[][ 13 ], const int wHand[][ 2 ],
104                    const char *wFace[] )
105   {
106      int counter[ 13 ] = { 0 };
107
108      for ( int r = 0; r < 5; ++r )
109         ++counter[ wHand[ r ][ 1 ] ];
110
111      for ( int k = 0; k < 13; ++k )
112         if ( counter[ k ] == 4 )
113            cout << "The hand contains four " << wFace[ k ] << "'s.\n";
114   }
115
116   void flushHand( const int wDeck[][ 13 ], const int wHand[][ 2 ],
117                   const char *wSuit[] )
118   {
119      int count[ 4 ] = { 0 };
120
121      for ( int r = 0; r < 5; ++r )
122         ++count[ wHand[ r ][ 0 ] ];
123
124      for ( int f = 0; f < 4; ++f )
125         if ( count[ f ] == 5 )
126            cout << "The hand contains a flush of " << wSuit[ f ] << "'s.\n";
127   }
128
129   void straightHand( const int wDeck[][ 13 ], const int wHand[][ 2 ],
130                      const char *wSuit[], const char *wFace[] )
131   {
132      int s[ 5 ] = { 0 }, temp;
133
134      // copy column locations to sort
135      for ( int r = 0; r < 5; ++r )
136         s[ r ] = wHand[ r ][ 1 ];
137
138      // bubble sort column locations
139      for ( int pass = 1; pass < 5; ++pass )
140         for ( int comp = 0; comp < 4; ++comp )
```

```
141                 if ( s[ comp ] > s[ comp + 1 ] ) {
142                     temp = s[ comp ];
143                     s[ comp ] = s[ comp + 1 ];
144                     s[ comp + 1 ] = temp;
145                 }
146
147     // check if sorted columns are a straight
148     if ( s[ 4 ] - 1 == s[ 3 ] && s[ 3 ] - 1 == s[ 2 ]
149         && s[ 2 ] - 1 == s[ 1 ] && s[ 1 ] - 1 == s[ 0 ] ) {
150       cout << "The hand contains a straight consisting of\n";
151
152       for ( int j = 0; j < 5; ++j )
153         cout << wFace[ wHand[ j ][ 1 ] ] << " of " << wSuit[ wHand[ j ][ 0 ] ]
154             << '\n';
155     }
156 }
```

```
The hand is:
Queen of Spades        King of Diamonds
 Nine of Diamonds      Jack of Spades
  Ten of Hearts

The hand contains a straight consisting of
Queen of Spades
King of Diamonds
Nine of Diamonds
Jack of Spades
Ten of Hearts
```

5.13   Use the functions developed in Exercise 5.12 to write a program that deals two five-card poker hands, evaluates each hand, and determines which is the better hand.

5.14   Modify the program developed in Exercise 5.13 so that it can simulate the dealer. The dealer's five-card hand is dealt "face down" so the player cannot see it. The program should then evaluate the dealer's hand and, based on the quality of the hand, the dealer should draw one, two, or three more cards to replace the corresponding number of unneeded cards in the original hand. The program should then reevaluate the dealer's hand. (*Caution:* This is a difficult problem!)

5.15   Modify the program developed in Exercise 5.14 so that it can handle the dealer's hand automatically, but the player is allowed to decide which cards of the player's hand to replace. The program should then evaluate both hands and determine who wins. Now use this new program to play 20 games against the computer. Who wins more games, you or the computer? Have one of your friends play 20 games against the computer. Who wins more games? Based on the results of these games, make appropriate modifications to refine your poker playing program (this, too, is a difficult problem). Play 20 more games. Does your modified program play a better game?

5.16   In the card shuffling and dealing program of Fig. 5.24, we intentionally used an inefficient shuffling algorithm that introduced the possibility of indefinite postponement. In this problem, you will create a high-performance shuffling algorithm that avoids indefinite postponement.

Modify Fig. 5.24 as follows. Initialize the **deck** array as shown in Fig. 5.35. Modify the **shuffle** function to loop row-by-row and column-by-column through the array touching every element once. Each element should be swapped with a randomly selected element of the array. Print the resulting array to determine if the deck is satisfactorily shuffled (as in Fig. 5.36, for example). You may want your program to call the **shuffle** function several times to ensure a satisfactory shuffle.

Note that although the approach in this problem improves the shuffling algorithm, the dealing algorithm still requires searching the **deck** array for card 1, then card 2, then card 3, and so on. Worse yet, even after the dealing algorithm locates and deals the card, the algorithm continues searching through the remainder of the deck. Modify the program of Fig. 5.24 so that once a card is dealt, no further attempts are made to match that card number, and the program immediately proceeds with dealing the next card.

Unshuffled **deck** array												
	0	1	2	3	4	5	6	7	8	9	10	11	12
0	1	2	3	4	5	6	7	8	9	10	11	12	13
1	14	15	16	17	18	19	20	21	22	23	24	25	26
2	27	28	29	30	31	32	33	34	35	36	37	38	39
3	40	41	42	43	44	45	46	47	48	49	50	51	52

Fig. 5.35 Unshuffled **deck** array.

Sample shuffled **deck** array												
	0	1	2	3	4	5	6	7	8	9	10	11	12
0	19	40	27	25	36	46	10	34	35	41	18	2	44
1	13	28	14	16	21	30	8	11	31	17	24	7	1
2	12	33	15	42	43	23	45	3	29	32	4	47	26
3	50	38	52	39	48	51	9	5	37	49	22	6	20

Fig. 5.36 Sample shuffled **deck** array.

ANS:

```
1   // Exercise 5.16 Solution
2   #include <iostream.h>
3   #include <iomanip.h>
4   #include <stdlib.h>
5   #include <time.h>
6
7   void shuffle( int [][ 13 ] );
8   void deal( const int [][ 13 ], const char *[], const char *[] );
9
10  int main()
11  {
12     int card = 1, deck[ 4 ][ 13 ] = { 0 };
13     const char *suit[ 4 ] = { "Hearts", "Diamonds", "Clubs", "Spades" };
14     const char *face[ 13 ] = { "Ace", "Deuce", "Three", "Four", "Five", "Six",
15                                "Seven", "Eight", "Nine", "Ten", "Jack", "Queen",
16                                "King" };
17
18     srand( time( 0 ) );
19
20     // initialize deck
21     for ( int row = 0; row <= 3; ++row )
22        for ( int column = 0; column <= 12; ++column )
23           deck[ row ][ column ] = card++;
24
25     shuffle( deck );
26     deal( deck, face, suit );
27     return 0;
28  }
29
30  void shuffle( int workDeck[][ 13 ] )
31  {
32     int temp, randRow, randColumn;
33
```

```
34     for ( int row = 0; row <= 3; ++row )
35        for ( int column = 0; column <= 12; ++column ) {
36           randRow = rand() % 4;
37           randColumn = rand() % 13;
38           temp = workDeck[ row ][ column ];
39           workDeck[ row][ column ] = workDeck[ randRow ][ randColumn ];
40           workDeck[ randRow ][ randColumn ] = temp;
41        }
42  }
43
44  void deal( const int workDeck2[][ 13 ], const char *workFace[],
45             const char *workSuit[] )
46  {
47     for ( int card = 1; card <= 52; ++card )
48        for ( int row = 0; row <= 3; ++row )
49           for ( int column = 0; column <= 12; ++column )
50              if ( workDeck2[ row ][ column ] == card ) {
51                 cout << setw( 8 ) << workFace[ column ] << " of "
52                      << setiosflags( ios::left ) << setw( 8 )
53                      << workSuit[ row ]
54                      << ( card % 2 == 0 ? '\n' : '\t' )
55                      << resetiosflags( ios::left );
56                 break;
57              }
58  }
```

```
   Deuce of Hearts      Seven of Hearts
     Six of Clubs       Eight of Spades
    Nine of Clubs         Ten of Hearts
   Deuce of Clubs        Jack of Diamonds
   Three of Hearts      Queen of Diamonds
    King of Hearts      Eight of Diamonds
    Jack of Spades       Four of Hearts
     Ace of Clubs       Deuce of Diamonds
   Seven of Clubs       Three of Spades
   Seven of Diamonds      Ace of Spades
    Five of Diamonds     Four of Clubs
   Queen of Hearts       King of Spades
    Nine of Hearts       Nine of Diamonds
    Five of Hearts        Ace of Hearts
    Five of Spades      Three of Diamonds
     Ten of Diamonds    Deuce of Spades
    Five of Clubs         Ace of Diamonds
    King of Diamonds      Six of Spades
     Ten of Clubs        Jack of Hearts
    Four of Diamonds      Six of Diamonds
    Nine of Spades        Six of Hearts
    King of Clubs       Queen of Clubs
   Eight of Hearts        Ten of Spades
   Queen of Spades      Seven of Spades
    Four of Spades      Eight of Clubs
    Jack of Clubs       Three of Clubs
```

5.17 (*Simulation: The Tortoise and the Hare*) In this problem you will recreate the classic race of the tortoise and the hare. You will use random number generation to develop a simulation of this memorable event.

Our contenders begin the race at "square 1" of 70 squares. Each square represents a possible position along the race course. The finish line is at square 70. The first contender to reach or pass square 70 is rewarded with a pail of fresh carrots and lettuce. The course weaves its way up the side of a slippery mountain, so occasionally the contenders lose ground.

There is a clock that ticks once per second. With each tick of the clock, your program should adjust the position of the animals according to the following rules:

Animal	Move type	Percentage of the time	Actual move
Tortoise	Fast plod	50%	3 squares to the right
	Slip	20%	6 squares to the left
	Slow plod	30%	1 square to the right
Hare	Sleep	20%	No move at all
	Big hop	20%	9 squares to the right
	Big slip	10%	12 squares to the left
	Small hop	30%	1 square to the right
	Small slip	20%	2 squares to the left

Use variables to keep track of the positions of the animals (i.e., position numbers are 1-70). Start each animal at position 1 (i.e., the "starting gate"). If an animal slips left before square 1, move the animal back to square 1.

Generate the percentages in the preceding table by producing a random integer, i, in the range $1 \leq i \leq 10$. For the tortoise, perform a "fast plod" when $1 \leq i \leq 5$, a "slip" when $6 \leq i \leq 7$, or a "slow plod" when $8 \leq i \leq 10$. Use a similar technique to move the hare.

Begin the race by printing

```
BANG !!!!!
AND THEY'RE OFF !!!!!
```

For each tick of the clock (i.e., each repetition of a loop), print a 70-position line showing the letter **T** in the tortoise's position and the letter **H** in the hare's position. Occasionally, the contenders land on the same square. In this case, the tortoise bites the hare and your program should print **OUCH!!!** beginning at that position. All print positions other than the **T**, the **H**, or the **OUCH!!!** (in case of a tie) should be blank.

After printing each line, test if either animal has reached or passed square 70. If so, print the winner and terminate the simulation. If the tortoise wins, print **TORTOISE WINS!!! YAY!!!** If the hare wins, print **Hare wins. Yuch.** If both animals win on the same clock tick, you may want to favor the turtle (the "underdog"), or you may want to print **It's a tie**. If neither animal wins, perform the loop again to simulate the next tick of the clock. When you are ready to run your program, assemble a group of fans to watch the race. You'll be amazed how involved the audience gets!

ANS:

```cpp
// Exercise 5.17 Solution
#include <iostream.h>
#include <stdlib.h>
#include <time.h>
#include <iomanip.h>

const int RACE_END = 70;

void moveTortoise( int * const );
void moveHare( int * const );
void printCurrentPositions( const int * const, const int * const );

int main()
{
   int tortoise = 1, hare = 1, timer = 0;

   srand( time( 0 ) );

   cout << "ON YOUR MARK, GET SET\nBANG                  !!!!"
        << "\nAND THEY'RE OFF    !!!!\n";

   while ( tortoise != RACE_END && hare != RACE_END ) {
      moveTortoise( &tortoise );
      moveHare( &hare );
```

```
25              printCurrentPositions( &tortoise, &hare );
26              ++timer;
27          }
28
29      if ( tortoise >= hare )
30          cout << "\nTORTOISE WINS!!! YAY!!!\n";
31      else
32          cout << "Hare wins. Yuch.\n";
33
34      cout << "TIME ELAPSED = " << timer << " seconds" << endl;
35      return 0;
36  }
37
38  void moveTortoise( int * const turtlePtr )
39  {
40      int x = 1 + rand() % 10;
41
42      if ( x >= 1 && x <= 5 )          // fast plod
43          *turtlePtr += 3;
44      else if ( x == 6 || x == 7 )     // slip
45          *turtlePtr -= 6;
46      else                             // slow plod
47          ++( *turtlePtr );
48
49      if ( *turtlePtr < 1 )
50          *turtlePtr = 1;
51      else if ( *turtlePtr > RACE_END )
52          *turtlePtr = RACE_END;
53  }
54
55  void moveHare( int * const rabbitPtr )
56  {
57      int y = 1 + rand() % 10;
58
59      if ( y == 3 || y == 4 )          // big hop
60          *rabbitPtr += 9;
61      else if ( y == 5 )               // big slip
62          *rabbitPtr -= 12;
63      else if ( y >= 6 && y <= 8 )     // small hop
64          ++( *rabbitPtr );
65      else if ( y > 8 )                // small slip
66          *rabbitPtr -= 2;
67
68      if ( *rabbitPtr < 1 )
69          *rabbitPtr = 1;
70      else if ( *rabbitPtr > RACE_END )
71          *rabbitPtr = RACE_END;
72  }
73
74  void printCurrentPositions( const int * const snapperPtr,
75                              const int * const bunnyPtr )
76  {
77      if ( *bunnyPtr == *snapperPtr )
78          cout << setw( *bunnyPtr ) << "OUCH!!!";
79      else if ( *bunnyPtr < *snapperPtr )
80          cout << setw( *bunnyPtr ) << 'H'
81              << setw( *snapperPtr - *bunnyPtr ) << 'T';
82      else
83          cout << setw( *snapperPtr ) << 'T'
84              << setw( *bunnyPtr - *snapperPtr ) << 'H';
85
86      cout << '\n';
87  }
```

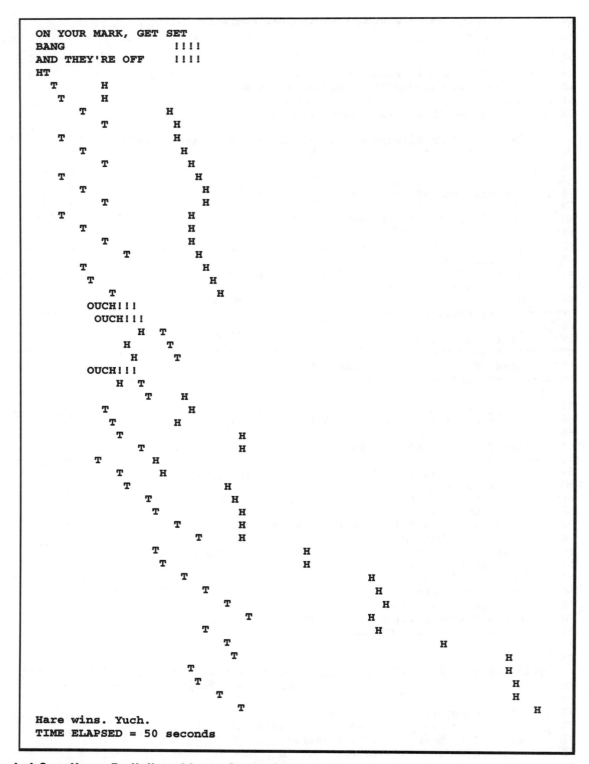

Special Section: Building Your Own Computer

In the next several problems, we take a temporary diversion away from the world of high-level language programming. We "peel open" a computer and look at its internal structure. We introduce machine language programming and write several machine language programs. To make this an especially valuable experience, we then build a computer (through the technique of software-based *simulation*) on which you can execute your machine language programs!

5.18   (*Machine Language Programming*) Let us create a computer we will call the Simpletron. As its name implies, it is a simple machine, but, as we will soon see, a powerful one as well. The Simpletron runs programs written in the only language it directly understands; that is, Simpletron Machine Language, or SML for short.

The Simpletron contains an *accumulator*—a "special register" in which information is put before the Simpletron uses that information in calculations or examines it in various ways. All information in the Simpletron is handled in terms of *words*. A word is a signed four-digit decimal number such as **+3364**, **-1293**, **+0007**, **-0001**, etc. The Simpletron is equipped with a 100-word memory, and these words are referenced by their location numbers **00**, **01**, ..., **99**.

Before running an SML program, we must *load* or place the program into memory. The first instruction (or statement) of every SML program is always placed in location **00**. The simulator will start executing at this location.

Each instruction written in SML occupies one word of the Simpletron's memory (thus, instructions are signed four-digit decimal numbers). We shall assume that the sign of an SML instruction is always plus, but the sign of a data word may be either plus or minus. Each location in the Simpletron's memory may contain an instruction, a data value used by a program, or an unused (and hence undefined) area of memory. The first two digits of each SML instruction are the *operation code,* that specifies the operation to be performed. SML operation codes are shown in Fig. 5.37.

The last two digits of an SML instruction are the *operand*—the address of the memory location containing the word to which the operation applies.

Operation code	Meaning
Input/output operations:	
`const int READ = 10`	Read a word from the keyboard into a specific location in memory.
`const int WRITE = 11;`	Write a word from a specific location in memory to the screen.
Load/store operations:	
`const int LOAD = 20;`	Load a word from a specific location in memory into the accumulator.
`const int STORE = 21;`	Store a word from the accumulator into a specific location in memory.
Arithmetic operations:	
`const int ADD = 30;`	Add a word from a specific location in memory to the word in the accumulator (leave result in accumulator).
`const int SUBTRACT = 31;`	Subtract a word from a specific location in memory from the word in the accumulator (leave result in accumulator).
`const int DIVIDE = 32;`	Divide a word from a specific location in memory into the word in the accumulator (leave result in accumulator).
`const int MULTIPLY = 33;`	Multiply a word from a specific location in memory by the word in the accumulator (leave result in accumulator).
Transfer of control operations:	
`const int BRANCH = 40;`	Branch to a specific location in memory.
`const int BRANCHNEG = 41;`	Branch to a specific location in memory if the accumulator is negative.
`const int BRANCHZERO = 42;`	Branch to a specific location in memory if the accumulator is zero.
`const int HALT = 43;`	Halt—the program has completed its task.

Fig. 5.37   Simpletron Machine Language (SML) operation codes .

Now let us consider several simple SML programs. The first SML program (Example 1) reads two numbers from the keyboard and computes and prints their sum. The instruction **+1007** reads the first number from the keyboard and places it into location **07** (which has been initialized to zero). Then instruction **+1008** reads the next number into location **08**. The *load* instruction, **+2007**, puts (copies) the first number into the accumulator, and the *add* instruction, **+3008**, adds the second number to the number in the accumulator. *All SML arithmetic instructions leave their results in the accumulator*. The *store* instruction, **+2109**, places (copies) the result back into memory location **09** from which the *write* instruction, **+1109**, takes the number and prints it (as a signed four-digit decimal number). The *halt* instruction, **+4300**, terminates execution.

Example 1 Location	Number	Instruction
00	+1007	(Read A)
01	+1008	(Read B)
02	+2007	(Load A)
03	+3008	(Add B)
04	+2109	(Store C)
05	+1109	(Write C)
06	+4300	(Halt)
07	+0000	(Variable A)
08	+0000	(Variable B)
09	+0000	(Result C)

The SML program in Example 2 reads two numbers from the keyboard and determines and prints the larger value. Note the use of the instruction **+4107** as a conditional transfer of control, much the same as C++'s **if** statement.

Example 2 Location	Number	Instruction
00	+1009	(Read A)
01	+1010	(Read B)
02	+2009	(Load A)
03	+3110	(Subtract B)
04	+4107	(Branch negative to 07)
05	+1109	(Write A)
06	+4300	(Halt)
07	+1110	(Write B)
08	+4300	(Halt)
09	+0000	(Variable A)
10	+0000	(Variable B)

Now write SML programs to accomplish each of the following tasks.

a) Use a sentinel-controlled loop to read 10 positive numbers and compute and print their sum.

ANS: NOTE: This program terminates when a negative number is input. The problem statement should state that only positive numbers should be input.

```
00  +1009        (Read Value)
01  +2009        (Load Value)
02  +4106        (Branch negative to 06)
03  +3008        (Add Sum)
04  +2108        (Store Sum)
05  +4000        (Branch 00)
06  +1108        (Write Sum)
07  +4300        (Halt)
08  +0000        (Storage for Sum)
09  +0000        (Storage for Value)
```

b) Use a counter-controlled loop to read seven numbers, some positive and some negative, and compute and print
    their average.

ANS:

```
00  +2018        (Load Counter)
01  +3121        (Subtract Termination)
02  +4211        (Branch zero to 11)
03  +2018        (Load Counter)
04  +3019        (Add Increment)
05  +2118        (Store Counter)
06  +1017        (Read Value)
07  +2016        (Load Sum)
08  +3017        (Add Value)
09  +2116        (Store Sum)
10  +4000        (Branch 00)
11  +2016        (Load Sum)
12  +3218        (Divide Counter)
13  +2120        (Store Result)
14  +1120        (Write Result)
15  +4300        (Halt)
16  +0000        (Variable Sum)
17  +0000        (Variable Value)
18  +0000        (Variable Counter)
19  +0001        (Variable Increment)
20  +0000        (Variable Result)
21  +0007        (Variable Termination)
```

c) Read a series of numbers and determine and print the largest number. The first number read indicates how many
    numbers should be processed.

ANS:

```
00  +1017        (Read Endvalue)
01  +2018        (Load Counter)
02  +3117        (Subtract Endvalue)
03  +4215        (Branch zero to 15)
04  +2018        (Load Counter)
05  +3021        (Add Increment)
06  +2118        (Store Counter)
07  +1019        (Read Value)
08  +2020        (Load Largest)
09  +3119        (Subtract Value)
10  +4112        (Branch negative to 12)
11  +4001        (Branch 01)
12  +2019        (Load Value)
13  +2120        (Store Largest)
14  +4001        (Branch 01)
15  +1120        (Write Largest)
16  +4300        (Halt)
17  +0000        (Variable EndValue)
18  +0000        (Variable Counter)
19  +0000        (Variable Value)
20  +0000        (Variable Largest)
21  +0001        (Variable Increment)
```

5.19   (*A Computer Simulator*) It may at first seem outrageous, but in this problem you are going to build your own computer.
No, you will not be soldering components together. Rather, you will use the powerful technique of *software-based simulation*
to create a *software model* of the Simpletron. You will not be disappointed. Your Simpletron simulator will turn the computer
you are using into a Simpletron, and you will actually be able to run, test, and debug the SML programs you wrote in Exercise
5.18.

When you run your Simpletron simulator, it should begin by printing:

```
*** Welcome to Simpletron! ***
```

```
*** Please enter your program one instruction ***
*** (or data word) at a time. I will type the ***
*** location number and a question mark (?).  ***
*** You then type the word for that location. ***
*** Type the sentinel -99999 to stop entering ***
*** your program. ***
```

Simulate the memory of the Simpletron with a single-subscripted array **memory** that has 100 elements. Now assume that the simulator is running, and let us examine the dialog as we enter the program of Example 2 of Exercise 5.18:

```
00 ? +1009
01 ? +1010
02 ? +2009
03 ? +3110
04 ? +4107
05 ? +1109
06 ? +4300
07 ? +1110
08 ? +4300
09 ? +0000
10 ? +0000
11 ? -99999

*** Program loading completed ***
*** Program execution begins  ***
```

The SML program has now been placed (or loaded) in array **memory**. Now the Simpletron executes your SML program. Execution begins with the instruction in location **00** and, like C++, continues sequentially, unless directed to some other part of the program by a transfer of control.

Use the variable **accumulator** to represent the accumulator register. Use the variable **counter** to keep track of the location in memory that contains the instruction being performed. Use variable **operationCode** to indicate the operation currently being performed, i.e., the left two digits of the instruction word. Use variable **operand** to indicate the memory location on which the current instruction operates. Thus, **operand** is the rightmost two digits of the instruction currently being performed. Do not execute instructions directly from memory. Rather, transfer the next instruction to be performed from memory to a variable called **instructionRegister**. Then "pick off" the left two digits and place them in **operationCode**, and "pick off" the right two digits and place them in **operand**. When Simpletron begins execution, the special registers are all initialized to 0

Now let us "walk through" the execution of the first SML instruction, **+1009** in memory location **00**. This is called an *instruction execution cycle*.

The **counter** tells us the location of the next instruction to be performed. We *fetch* the contents of that location from **memory** by using the C++ statement

```
instructionRegister = memory[ counter ];
```

The operation code and operand are extracted from the instruction register by the statements

```
operationCode = instructionRegister / 100;
operand = instructionRegister % 100;
```

Now the Simpletron must determine that the operation code is actually a *read* (versus a *write*, a *load*, etc.). A **switch** differentiates among the twelve operations of SML.

In the **switch** structure, the behavior of various SML instructions is simulated as follows (we leave the others to the reader):

read: `cin >> memory[ operand ];`

load: `accumulator = memory[ operand ];`

add: `accumulator += memory[ operand ];`

branch: We will discuss the branch instructions shortly.

halt: This instruction prints the message
               `*** Simpletron execution terminated ***`

and then prints the name and contents of each register as well as the complete contents of memory. Such a printout is often called a *computer dump* (and, no, a computer dump is not a place where old computers go). To help you program your dump function, a sample dump format is shown in Fig. 5.38. Note that a dump after executing a Simpletron program would show the actual values of instructions and data values at the moment execution terminated.

Let us proceed with the execution of our program's first instruction—**+1009** in location **00**. As we have indicated, the **switch** statement simulates this by performing the C++ statement

```
cin >> memory[ operand ];
```

A question mark (**?**) should be displayed on the screen before the **cin** is executed to prompt the user for input. The Simpletron waits for the user to type a value and then press the *Return key*. The value is then read into location **09**.

At this point, simulation of the first instruction is completed. All that remains is to prepare the Simpletron to execute the next instruction. Since the instruction just performed was not a transfer of control, we need merely increment the instruction counter register as follows:

```
++counter;
```

This completes the simulated execution of the first instruction. The entire process (i.e., the instruction execution cycle) begins anew with the fetch of the next instruction to be executed.

Now let us consider how the branching instructions—the transfers of control—are simulated. All we need to do is adjust the value in the instruction counter appropriately. Therefore, the unconditional branch instruction (**40**) is simulated within the **switch** as

```
counter = operand;
```

The conditional "branch if accumulator is zero" instruction is simulated as

```
if ( accumulator == 0 )
    counter = operand;
```

At this point you should implement your Simpletron simulator and run each of the SML programs you wrote in Exercise 5.18. You may embellish SML with additional features and provide for these in your simulator.

Your simulator should check for various types of errors. During the program loading phase, for example, each number the user types into the Simpletron's **memory** must be in the range **-9999** to **+9999**. Your simulator should use a **while** loop to test that each number entered is in this range, and, if not, keep prompting the user to reenter the number until the user enters a correct number.

```
REGISTERS:
accumulator              +0000
counter                     00
instructionRegister      +0000
operationCode               00
operand                     00

MEMORY:
         0       1       2       3       4       5       6       7       8       9
 0  +0000   +0000   +0000   +0000   +0000   +0000   +0000   +0000   +0000   +0000
10  +0000   +0000   +0000   +0000   +0000   +0000   +0000   +0000   +0000   +0000
20  +0000   +0000   +0000   +0000   +0000   +0000   +0000   +0000   +0000   +0000
30  +0000   +0000   +0000   +0000   +0000   +0000   +0000   +0000   +0000   +0000
40  +0000   +0000   +0000   +0000   +0000   +0000   +0000   +0000   +0000   +0000
50  +0000   +0000   +0000   +0000   +0000   +0000   +0000   +0000   +0000   +0000
60  +0000   +0000   +0000   +0000   +0000   +0000   +0000   +0000   +0000   +0000
70  +0000   +0000   +0000   +0000   +0000   +0000   +0000   +0000   +0000   +0000
80  +0000   +0000   +0000   +0000   +0000   +0000   +0000   +0000   +0000   +0000
90  +0000   +0000   +0000   +0000   +0000   +0000   +0000   +0000   +0000   +0000
```

Fig. 5.38 A sample dump.

During the execution phase, your simulator should check for various serious errors, such as attempts to divide by zero, attempts to execute invalid operation codes, accumulator overflows (i.e., arithmetic operations resulting in values larger than **+9999** or smaller than **-9999**), and the like. Such serious errors are called *fatal errors*. When a fatal error is detected, your simulator should print an error message such as:

```
*** Attempt to divide by zero ***
*** Simpletron execution abnormally terminated ***
```

and should print a full computer dump in the format we have discussed previously. This will help the user locate the error in the program.

ANS:

```cpp
1   // Exercise 5.19 Solution
2   #include <iostream.h>
3   #include <iomanip.h>
4
5   const int SIZE = 100, MAX_WORD = 9999, MIN_WORD = -9999;
6   const long SENTINEL = -99999;
7   enum Commands { READ = 10, WRITE, LOAD = 20, STORE, ADD = 30, SUBTRACT,
8                   DIVIDE, MULTIPLY, BRANCH = 40, BRANCHNEG, BRANCHZERO, HALT };
9
10  void load( int * const );
11  void execute( int * const, int * const, int * const, int * const,
12                int * const, int * const);
13  void dump( const int * const, int, int, int, int, int );
14  bool validWord( int );
15
16  int main()
17  {
18     int memory[ SIZE ] = { 0 }, accumulator = 0, instructionCounter = 0,
19         opCode = 0, operand = 0, instructionRegister = 0;
20
21     load( memory );
22     execute( memory, &accumulator, &instructionCounter, &instructionRegister,
23              &opCode, &operand );
24     dump( memory, accumulator, instructionCounter, instructionRegister,
25           opCode, operand );
26
27     return 0;
28  }
29
30  void load( int * const loadMemory )
31  {
32     long instruction;
33     int i = 0;
34
35     cout << "***              Welcome to Simpletron              ***\n"
36          << "*** Please enter your program one instruction ***\n"
37          << "*** (or data word) at a time. I will type the ***\n"
38          << "*** location number and a question mark (?).  ***\n"
39          << "*** You then type the word for that location. ***\n"
40          << "*** Type the sentinel -99999 to stop entering ***\n"
41          << "*** your program.                             ***\n" << "00 ? ";
42     cin >> instruction;
43
44     while ( instruction != SENTINEL ) {
45
46        if ( !validWord( instruction ) )
47           cout << "Number out of range. Please enter again.\n";
48        else
49           loadMemory[ i++ ] = instruction;
50
```

```
51              // function setfill sets the padding character for unused
52              // field widths.
53              cout << setw( 2 ) << setfill( '0' ) << i << " ? ";
54              cin >> instruction;
55      }
56  }
57
58  void execute( int * const memory, int * const acPtr, int * const icPtr,
59                int * const irPtr, int * const opCodePtr, int * const opPtr )
60  {
61      bool fatal = false;
62      int temp;
63      const char *messages[] = { "Accumulator overflow        ***",
64                                 "Attempt to divide by zero   ***",
65                                 "Invalid opcode detected     *** },
66          *termString = "\n*** Simpletron execution abnormally terminated ***",
67          *fatalString = "*** FATAL ERROR: ";
68
69      cout << "\n***********START SIMPLETRON EXECUTION***********\n\n";
70
71      do {
72          *irPtr = memory[ *icPtr ];
73          *opCodePtr = *irPtr / 100;
74          *opPtr = *irPtr % 100;
75
76          switch ( *opCodePtr ) {
77              case READ:
78                  cout << "Enter an integer: ";
79                  cin >> temp;
80
81                  while ( !validWord( temp ) ) {
82                      cout << "Number out of range. Please enter again: ";
83                      cin >> temp;
84                  }
85
86                  memory[ *opPtr ] = temp;
87                  ++( *icPtr );
88                  break;
89              case WRITE:
90                  cout << "Contents of " << setw( 2 ) << setfill( '0' ) << *opPtr
91                       << ": " << memory[ *opPtr ] << '\n';
92                  ++( *icPtr );
93                  break;
94              case LOAD:
95                  *acPtr = memory[ *opPtr ];
96                  ++( *icPtr );
97                  break;
98              case STORE:
99                  memory[ *opPtr ] = *acPtr;
100                 ++( *icPtr );
101                 break;
102             case ADD:
103                 temp = *acPtr + memory[ *opPtr ];
104
105                 if ( !validWord( temp ) ) {
106                     cout << fatalString << messages[ 0 ] << termString << '\n';
107                     fatal = true;
108                 }
109                 else {
110                     *acPtr = temp;
111                     ++( *icPtr );
112                 }
113
114                 break;
```

```
115          case SUBTRACT:
116             temp = *acPtr - memory[ *opPtr ];
117
118             if ( !validWord( temp ) ) {
119                cout << fatalString << messages[ 0 ] << termString << '\n';
120                fatal = true;
121             }
122             else {
123                *acPtr = temp;
124                ++( *icPtr );
125             }
126
127             break;
128          case DIVIDE:
129             if ( memory[ *opPtr ] == 0 ) {
130                cout << fatalString << messages[ 1 ] << termString << '\n';
131                fatal = true;
132             }
133             else {
134                *acPtr /= memory[ *opPtr ];
135                ++( *icPtr );
136             }
137
138             break;
139          case MULTIPLY:
140             temp = *acPtr * memory[ *opPtr ];
141
142             if ( !validWord( temp ) ) {
143                cout << fatalString << messages[ 0 ] << termString << '\n';
144                fatal = true;
145             }
146             else {
147                *acPtr = temp;
148                ++( *icPtr );
149             }
150             break;
151          case BRANCH:
152             *icPtr = *opPtr;
153             break;
154          case BRANCHNEG:
155             *acPtr < 0 ? *icPtr = *opPtr : ++( *icPtr );
156             break;
157          case BRANCHZERO:
158             *acPtr == 0 ? *icPtr = *opPtr : ++( *icPtr );
159             break;
160          case HALT:
161             cout << "*** Simpletron execution terminated ***\n";
162             break;
163          default:
164             cout << fatalString << messages[ 2 ] << termString << '\n';
165             fatal = true;
166             break;
167       }
168    } while ( *opCodePtr != HALT && !fatal );
169
170    cout << "\n*************END SIMPLETRON EXECUTION*************\n";
171 }
172
173 void dump( const int * const memory, int accumulator, int instructionCounter,
174           int instructionRegister, int operationCode, int operand )
175 {
176    void output( const char * const, int, int, bool );   // prototype
177
```

```
178        cout << "\nREGISTERS:\n";
179        output( "accumulator", 5, accumulator, true );
180        output( "instructionCounter", 2, instructionCounter, false );
181        output( "instructionRegister", 5, instructionRegister, true );
182        output( "operationCode", 2, operationCode, false );
183        output( "operand", 2, operand, false );
184        cout << "\n\nMEMORY:\n";
185
186        int i = 0;
187        cout << setfill( ' ' ) << setw( 3 ) << ' ';
188
189        // print header
190        for ( ; i <= 9; ++i )
191           cout << setw( 5 ) << i << ' ';
192
193        for ( i = 0; i < SIZE; ++i ) {
194           if ( i % 10 == 0 )
195              cout << '\n' << setw( 2 ) << i << ' ';
196
197           cout << setiosflags( ios::internal | ios::showpos )
198                 << setw( 5 ) << setfill( '0' ) << memory[ i ] << ' '
199                 << resetiosflags( ios::internal | ios::showpos );
200        }
201
202     cout << endl;
203  }
204
205  bool validWord( int word )
206  {
207     return word >= MIN_WORD && word <= MAX_WORD;
208  }
209
210  void output( const char * const sPtr, int width, int value, bool sign )
211  {
212     // format of "accumulator", etc.
213     cout << setfill( ' ' ) << setiosflags( ios::left ) << setw( 20 )
214           << sPtr << ' ';
215
216     // is a +/- sign needed?
217     if ( sign )
218        cout << setiosflags( ios::showpos | ios::internal );
219
220     // setup for displaying accumulator value, etc.
221     cout << resetiosflags( ios::left ) << setfill( '0' );
222
223     // determine the field widths and display value
224     if ( width == 5 )
225        cout << setw( width ) << value << '\n';
226     else  // width is 2
227        cout << setfill( ' ' ) << setw( 3 ) << ' ' << setw( width )
228              << setfill( '0' ) << value << '\n';
229
230     // disable sign if it was set
231     if ( sign )
232        cout << resetiosflags( ios::showpos | ios::internal );
233  }
```

```
***                Welcome to Simpletron          ***
*** Please enter your program one instruction ***
*** (or data word) at a time. I will type the ***
*** location number and a question mark (?).  ***
*** You then type the word for that location. ***
*** Type the sentinel -99999 to stop entering ***
*** your program.                             ***
00 ? 1099
01 ? 1098
02 ? 2099
03 ? 3398
04 ? 2150
05 ? 1150
06 ? 1199
07 ? 1198
08 ? 4300
09 ? -99999
************START SIMPLETRON EXECUTION************

Enter an integer: 4
Enter an integer: 9
Contents of 50: 36
Contents of 99: 4
Contents of 98: 9
*** Simpletron execution terminated ***

*************END SIMPLETRON EXECUTION*************

REGISTERS:
accumulator             +0036
instructionCounter        08
instructionRegister     +4300
operationCode             43
operand                   00


MEMORY:
        0      1      2      3      4      5      6      7      8      9
 0  +1099  +1098  +2099  +3398  +2150  +1150  +1199  +1198  +4300  00000
10  00000  00000  00000  00000  00000  00000  00000  00000  00000  00000
20  00000  00000  00000  00000  00000  00000  00000  00000  00000  00000
30  00000  00000  00000  00000  00000  00000  00000  00000  00000  00000
40  00000  00000  00000  00000  00000  00000  00000  00000  00000  00000
50  +0036  00000  00000  00000  00000  00000  00000  00000  00000  00000
60  00000  00000  00000  00000  00000  00000  00000  00000  00000  00000
70  00000  00000  00000  00000  00000  00000  00000  00000  00000  00000
80  00000  00000  00000  00000  00000  00000  00000  00000  00000  00000
90  00000  00000  00000  00000  00000  00000  00000  00000  +0009  +0004
```

More Pointer Exercises

5.20   Modify the card shuffling and dealing program of Fig. 5.24 so the shuffling and dealing operations are performed by the same function (**shuffleAndDeal**). The function should contain one nested looping structure that is similar to function **shuffle** in Fig. 5.24.

ANS:

```
1   // Exercise 5.20 Solution
2   #include <iostream.h>
3   #include <iomanip.h>
4   #include <stdlib.h>
5   #include <time.h>
```

```
6
7   void shuffleAndDeal( int [][ 13 ], const char *[], const char *[] );
8
9   int main()
10  {
11     const char *suit[ 4 ] = { "Hearts", "Diamonds", "Clubs", "Spades" };
12     const char *face[ 13 ] = { "Ace", "Deuce", "Three", "Four", "Five",
13                                "Six", "Seven", "Eight", "Nine", "Ten",
14                                "Jack", "Queen", "King" };
15     int deck[ 4 ][ 13 ] = { 0 };
16
17     srand( time( 0 ) );
18     shuffleAndDeal( deck, face, suit );
19     return 0;
20  }
21
22  void shuffleAndDeal( int workDeck[][ 13 ], const char *workFace[],
23                       const char *workSuit[] )
24  {
25     int row, column;
26
27     for ( int card = 1; card <= 52; ++card ) {
28
29        do {
30           row = rand() % 4;
31           column = rand() % 13;
32        } while ( workDeck[ row ][ column ] != 0 );
33
34        workDeck[ row ][ column ] = card;
35        cout << setw( 8 ) << workFace[ column ] << " of "
36             << setiosflags( ios::left ) << setw( 8 )
37             << workSuit[ row ] << resetiosflags( ios::left )
38             << ( card % 2 == 0 ? '\n' : '\t' );
39     }
40  }
```

```
        Jack of Diamonds      Ace of Hearts
       Eight of Hearts       Four of Spades
         Ten of Clubs       Deuce of Spades
       Eight of Spades       Jack of Hearts
        Five of Hearts       Jack of Spades
        Nine of Diamonds      Six of Clubs
       Three of Spades       King of Hearts
       Queen of Spades       King of Spades
       Queen of Diamonds    Three of Clubs
       Eight of Diamonds    Queen of Hearts
       Queen of Clubs        Four of Clubs
       Seven of Clubs        Jack of Clubs
         Ace of Spades        Ten of Hearts
       Three of Diamonds      Ace of Diamonds
        King of Clubs       Seven of Diamonds
       Three of Hearts      Eight of Clubs
         Six of Diamonds     Four of Diamonds
        Five of Clubs        Four of Hearts
        Five of Spades      Seven of Hearts
        Nine of Spades       King of Diamonds
         Ace of Clubs        Five of Diamonds
        Nine of Clubs         Six of Hearts
         Six of Spades       Nine of Hearts
       Deuce of Clubs       Deuce of Diamonds
       Seven of Spades        Ten of Spades
         Ten of Diamonds    Deuce of Hearts
```

5.21   What does this program do?

```
1   // ex05_21.cpp
2   #include <iostream.h>
3
4   void mystery1( char *, const char * );
5
6   int main()
7   {
8      char string1[ 80 ], string2[ 80 ];
9
10     cout << "Enter two strings: ";
11     cin >> string1 >> string2;
12
13     mystery1( string1, string2 );
13     cout << string1 << endl;
14     return 0;
15  }
16
17  void mystery1( char *s1, const char *s2 )
18  {
19     while ( *s1 != '\0' )
20        ++s1;
21
22     for ( ; *s1 = *s2; s1++, s2++ )
23        ;   // empty statement
24  }
```

ANS: Function **mystery** concatenates **s2** onto the end of **s1**.

5.22   What does this program do?

```
1   // ex05_22.cpp
2   #include <iostream.h>
3
4   int mystery2( const char * );
5
6   int main()
7   {
8      char string[ 80 ];
9
10     cout << "Enter a string: ";
11     cin >> string;
12     cout << mystery2( string ) << endl;
13     return 0;
14  }
15
16  int mystery2( const char *s )
17  {
18     for ( int x = 0; *s != '\0'; s++ )
19        ++x;
20
21     return x;
22  }
```

ANS: Function **mystery2** determines and returns the length of a string.

5.23   Find the error in each of the following program segments. If the error can be corrected, explain how.

a) **int *number;**
   cout << number << endl;

ANS: Pointer **number** does not "point" to a valid address. Assigning **number** to an address would correct the problem.

b) ```
float *realPtr;
long *integerPtr;
integerPtr = realPtr;
```
ANS:  A pointer of type **float** cannot be directly assigned to a pointer of type **long**.

c) ```
int * x, y;
x = y;
```
ANS: Variable **y** is not a pointer, and therefore cannot be assigned to **x**. Change the assignment statement to **x = &y;**.

d) ```
char s[] = "this is a character array";
for (; *s != '\0'; s++)
    cout << *s << ' ';
```
ANS:  **s** is not a modifiable value. Attempting to use operator **++** is a syntax error. Changing to **[]** notation corrects the problem as in:
```
for (int t = 0; s[t] != '\0'; ++t)
    cout << s[t] << ' ';
```

e) ```
short *numPtr, result;
void *genericPtr = numPtr;
result = *genericPtr + 7;
```
ANS: A **void *** pointer cannot be dereferenced.

f) ```
float x = 19.34;
float xPtr = &x;
cout << xPtr << endl;
```
ANS:  **xPtr** is not a pointer and therefore cannot be assigned an address. Place a **\*** before **xPtr** (in the declaration) to correct the problem. The **cout** statement display's the address to which **xPtr** points (once the previous correction is made)—this is not an error.

g) ```
char *s;
cout << s << endl;
```
ANS: **s** does not "point" to anything. **s** should be provided with an address.

5.24 (*Quicksort*) In the examples and exercises of Chapter 4, we discussed the sorting techniques of bubble sort, bucket sort, and selection sort. We now present the recursive sorting technique called Quicksort. The basic algorithm for a single-subscripted array of values is as follows:

a) *Partitioning Step:* Take the first element of the unsorted array and determine its final location in the sorted array, i.e., all values to the left of the element in the array are less than the element, and all values to the right of the element in the array are greater than the element. We now have one element in its proper location and two unsorted subarrays.

b) *Recursive Step:* Perform step 1 on each unsorted subarray.

Each time step 1 is performed on a subarray, another element is placed in its final location of the sorted array, and two unsorted subarrays are created. When a subarray consists of one element, it must be sorted, therefore that element is in its final location.

The basic algorithm seems simple enough, but how do we determine the final position of the first element of each subarray. As an example, consider the following set of values (the element in bold is the partitioning element—it will be placed in its final location in the sorted array):

37 2 6 4 89 8 10 12 68 45

a) Starting from the rightmost element of the array, compare each element to **37** until an element less than **37** is found, then swap **37** and that element. The first element less than **37** is 12, so **37** and 12 are swapped. The new array is:

12 2 6 4 89 8 10 **37** 68 45

Element 12 is in italic to indicate that it was just swapped with **37**.

b) Starting from the left of the array, but beginning with the element after 12, compare each element to **37** until an element greater than **37** is found, then swap **37** and that element. The first element greater than **37** is 89, so **37** and 89 are swapped. The new array is:

12 2 6 4 **37** 8 10 *89* 68 45

c) Starting from the right, but beginning with the element before 89, compare each element to **37** until an element less than **37** is found, then swap **37** and that element. The first element less than **37** is 10, so **37** and 10 are swapped. The new array is:

12 2 6 4 *10* 8 **37** 89 68 45

d) Starting from the left, but beginning with the element after 10, compare each element to **37** until an element greater than **37** is found, then swap **37** and that element. There are no more elements greater than **37**, so when we compare **37** to itself we know that **37** has been placed in its final location of the sorted array.

Once the partition has been applied on the above array, there are two unsorted subarrays. The subarray with values less than 37 contains 12, 2, 6, 4, 10, and 8. The subarray with values greater than 37 contains 89, 68, and 45. The sort continues with both subarrays being partitioned in the same manner as the original array.

Based on the preceding discussion, write recursive function **quickSort** to sort a single-subscripted integer array. The function should receive as arguments an integer array, a starting subscript, and an ending subscript. Function **partition** should be called by **quickSort** to perform the partitioning step.

ANS:

```
1   // Exercise 5.24 Solution
2   #include <iostream.h>
3   #include <iomanip.h>
4   #include <stdlib.h>
5   #include <time.h>
6
7   const int SIZE = 10, MAX_NUMBER = 1000;
8
9   void quicksort( int * const, int, int );
10  void swap( int * const, int * const );
11
12  int main()
13  {
14     int arrayToBeSorted[ SIZE ] = { 0 };
15     int loop;
16
17     srand( time( 0 ) );
18
19     for ( loop = 0; loop < SIZE; ++loop )
20        arrayToBeSorted[ loop ] = rand() % MAX_NUMBER;
21
22     cout << "Initial array values are:\n";
23
24     for ( loop = 0; loop < SIZE; ++loop )
25        cout << setw( 4 ) << arrayToBeSorted[ loop ];
26
27     cout << "\n\n";
28
29     if ( SIZE == 1 )
30        cout << "Array is sorted: " << arrayToBeSorted[ 0 ] << '\n';
31     else {
32        quicksort( arrayToBeSorted, 0, SIZE - 1 );
33        cout << "The sorted array values are:\n";
34
35        for ( loop = 0; loop < SIZE; ++loop )
36           cout << setw( 4 ) << arrayToBeSorted[ loop ];
37
38        cout << endl;
39     }
40
41     return 0;
42  }
43
44  void quicksort( int * const array, int first, int last )
45  {
46     int partition( int * const, int, int );
47     int currentLocation;
48
49     if ( first >= last )
50        return;
51
```

```
52      currentLocation = partition( array, first, last );   // place an element
53      quicksort( array, first, currentLocation - 1 );      // sort left side
54      quicksort( array, currentLocation + 1, last );       // sort right side
55   }
56
57   int partition( int * const array, int left, int right )
58   {
59      int position = left;
60
61      while ( true ) {
62         while ( array[ position ] <= array[ right ] && position != right )
63            --right;
64
65         if ( position == right )
66            return position;
67
68         if ( array[ position ] > array[ right ]) {
69            swap( &array[ position ], &array[ right ] );
70            position = right;
71         }
72
73         while ( array[ left ] <= array[ position ] && left != position )
74            ++left;
75
76         if ( position == left )
77            return position;
78
79         if ( array[ left ] > array[ position ] ) {
80            swap( &array[ position ], &array[ left ] );
81            position = left;
82         }
83      }
84   }
85
86   void swap( int * const ptr1, int * const ptr2 )
87   {
88      int temp;
89
90      temp = *ptr1;
91      *ptr1 = *ptr2;
92      *ptr2 = temp;
93   }
```

```
Initial array values are:
 603 612 103 202 279 721 808 562 966 343

The sorted array values are:
 103 202 279 343 562 603 612 721 808 966
```

5.25   (*Maze Traversal*) The following grid of #s and dots (.) is a double-subscripted array representation of a maze.

```
# # # # # # # # # # # #
# . . . # . . . . . . #
. . # . # . # # # # . #
# # # . # . . . . # . #
# . . . . # # # . # . .
# # # # . # . # . # . #
# . . # . # . # . # . #
# # . # . # . # . # . #
# . . . . . . . . # . #
# # # # # . # # # . # #
# . . . . . # . . . # #
# # # # # # # # # # # #
```

In the preceding double-subscripted array, the #s represent the walls of the maze and the dots represent squares in the possible paths through the maze. Moves can only be made to a location in the array that contains a dot.

There is a simple algorithm for walking through a maze that guarantees finding the exit (assuming there is an exit). If there is not an exit, you will arrive at the starting location again. Place your right hand on the wall to your right and begin walking forward. Never remove your hand from the wall. If the maze turns to the right, you follow the wall to the right. As long as you do not remove your hand from the wall, eventually you will arrive at the exit of the maze. There may be a shorter path than the one you have taken, but you are guaranteed to get out of the maze if you follow the algorithm.

Write recursive function **mazeTraverse** to walk through the maze. The function should receive as arguments a 12-by-12 character array representing the maze, and the starting location of the maze. As **mazeTraverse** attempts to locate the exit from the maze, it should place the character **X** in each square in the path. The function should display the maze after each move so the user can watch as the maze is solved.

ANS:

```
1   // Exercise 5.25 Solution
2   // This solution assumes that there is only one
3   // entrance and one exit for a given maze, and
4   // these are the only two zeroes on the borders.
5   #include <iostream.h>
6   #include <stdlib.h>
7
8   enum Direction { DOWN, RIGHT, UP, LEFT };
9   const int X_START = 2, Y_START = 0;    // starting coordinate for maze
10
11  void mazeTraversal( char [][ 12 ], int, int, int );
12  void printMaze( const char[][ 12 ] );
13  bool validMove( const char [][ 12 ], int, int );
14  bool coordsAreEdge( int, int );
15
16  int main()
17  {
18     char maze[ 12 ][ 12 ] =
19        { {'#', '#', '#', '#', '#', '#', '#', '#', '#', '#', '#', '#'},
20          {'#', '.', '.', '.', '#', '.', '.', '.', '.', '.', '.', '#'},
21          {'.', '.', '#', '.', '#', '.', '#', '#', '#', '#', '.', '#'},
22          {'#', '#', '#', '.', '#', '.', '.', '.', '.', '#', '.', '#'},
23          {'#', '.', '.', '.', '.', '#', '#', '#', '.', '#', '.', '.'},
24          {'#', '#', '#', '#', '.', '#', '.', '#', '.', '#', '.', '#'},
25          {'#', '.', '.', '#', '.', '#', '.', '#', '.', '#', '.', '#'},
26          {'#', '#', '.', '#', '.', '#', '.', '#', '.', '#', '.', '#'},
27          {'#', '.', '.', '.', '.', '.', '.', '.', '.', '#', '.', '#'},
28          {'#', '#', '#', '#', '#', '#', '.', '#', '#', '#', '.', '#'},
29          {'#', '.', '.', '.', '.', '.', '.', '#', '.', '.', '.', '#'},
30          {'#', '#', '#', '#', '#', '#', '#', '#', '#', '#', '#', '#'} };
31
32     mazeTraversal( maze, X_START, Y_START, RIGHT );
33     return 0;
34  }
35
36  // Assume that there is exactly 1 entrance and exactly 1 exit to the maze.
37  void mazeTraversal( char maze[][ 12 ], int xCoord, int yCoord, int direction )
38  {
39     static bool flag = false;
40
41     maze[ xCoord ][ yCoord ] = 'x';
42     printMaze( maze );
43
44     if ( coordsAreEdge(xCoord, yCoord) && xCoord != X_START &&
45          yCoord != Y_START ) {
46        cout << "\nMaze successfully exited!\n\n";
47        return;    // maze is complete
48     }
```

```
49         else if ( xCoord == X_START && yCoord == X_START && flag ) {
50            cout << "\nArrived back at the starting location.\n\n";
51            return;
52         }
53         else {
54            flag = true;
55
56            for ( int move = direction, count = 0; count < 4; ++count,
57                  ++move, move %= 4 )
58               switch( move ) {
59                  case DOWN:
60                     if ( validMove( maze, xCoord + 1, yCoord ) ) { // move down
61                        mazeTraversal( maze, xCoord + 1, yCoord, LEFT );
62                        return;
63                     }
64                     break;
65                  case RIGHT:
66                     if ( validMove( maze, xCoord, yCoord + 1 ) ) { // move right
67                        mazeTraversal( maze, xCoord, yCoord + 1, DOWN );
68                        return;
69                     }
70                     break;
71                  case UP:
72                     if ( validMove( maze, xCoord - 1, yCoord ) ) { // move up
73                        mazeTraversal( maze, xCoord - 1, yCoord, RIGHT );
74                        return;
75                     }
76                     break;
77                  case LEFT:
78                     if ( validMove( maze, xCoord, yCoord - 1 ) ) { // move left
79                        mazeTraversal( maze, xCoord, yCoord - 1, UP );
80                        return;
81                     }
82                     break;
83               }
84         }
85 }
86
87 bool validMove( const char maze[][ 12 ], int r, int c )
88 {
89    return ( r >= 0 && r <= 11 && c >= 0 && c <= 11 && maze[ r ][ c ] != '#' );
90 }
91
92 bool coordsAreEdge( int x, int y )
93 {
94    if ( ( x == 0 || x == 11 ) && ( y >= 0 && y <= 11 ) )
95       return true;
96    else if ( ( y == 0 || y == 11 ) && ( x >= 0 && x <= 11 ) )
97       return true;
98    else
99       return false;
100 }
101
102 void printMaze( const char maze[][ 12 ] )
103 {
104    for ( int x = 0; x < 12; ++x ) {
105
106       for ( int y = 0; y < 12; ++y )
107          cout << maze[ x ][ y ] << ' ';
108
109       cout << '\n';
110    }
111
112    cout << "\nHit return to see next move\n";
```

```
113     cin.get();
114 }
```

```
# # # # # # # # # # #
# . . . # . . . . . #
x . # . # . # # # # . #
# # # . # . . . . # . #
# . . . . # # # . # . .
# # # # . # . # . # . #
# . . # . # . # . # . #
# # . # . # . # . # . #
# . . . . . . . . # . #
# # # # # . # # # . #
# . . . . . # . . . #
# # # # # # # # # # #
Hit return to see next move
...
# # # # # # # # # # #
# x x x # x x x x x #
x x # x # x # # # # x #
# # # x # x x x x # x #
# x x x x # # # x # x x
# # # # x # . # x # x #
# x x # x # . # x # x #
# # x # x # . # x # x #
# x x x x x x x x # x #
# # # # # # x # # # x #
# x x x x x x # x x x #
# # # # # # # # # # # #


Hit return to see next move


Maze successfully exited!
```

5.26   (*Generating Mazes Randomly*) Write a function **mazeGenerator** that takes as an argument a double-subscripted 12-by-12 character array and randomly produces a maze. The function should also provide the starting and ending locations of the maze. Try your function **mazeTraverse** from Exercise 5.25 using several randomly generated mazes.

ANS:

```
1   // Exercise 5.26 Solution
2   #include <iostream.h>
3   #include <stdlib.h>
4   #include <time.h>
5
6   enum Direction { DOWN, RIGHT, UP, LEFT };
7   const int MAX_DOTS = 100;   // maximum possible dots for maze
8
9   void mazeTraversal( char [][ 12 ], const int, const int, int, int, int );
10  void mazeGenerator( char [][ 12 ], int *, int * );
11  void printMaze( const char[][ 12 ] );
12  bool validMove( const char [][ 12 ], int, int );
13  bool coordsAreEdge( int, int );
14
15  int main()
16  {
17     char maze[ 12 ][ 12 ];
18     int xStart, yStart, x, y;
19
20     srand( time( 0 ) );
21
```

```
22       for ( int loop = 0; loop < 12; ++loop )
23          for ( int loop2 = 0; loop2 < 12; ++loop2 )
24             maze[ loop ][ loop2 ] = '#';
25
26       mazeGenerator( maze, &xStart, &yStart );
27
28       x = xStart;  // starting row
29       y = yStart;  // starting col
30
31       mazeTraversal( maze, xStart, yStart, x, y, RIGHT );
32       return 0;
33   }
34
35   // Assume that there is exactly 1 entrance and exactly 1 exit to the maze.
36   void mazeTraversal( char maze[][ 12 ], const int xCoord, const int yCoord,
37                       int row, int col, int direction )
38   {
39       static bool flag = false;    // starting position flag
40
41       maze[ row ][ col ] = 'x';  // insert X at current location
42       printMaze( maze );
43
44       if ( coordsAreEdge( row, col ) && row != xCoord && col != yCoord ) {
45          cout << "Maze successfully exited!\n\n";
46          return;    // maze is complete
47       }
48       else if ( row == xCoord && col == yCoord && flag ) {
49          cout << "Arrived back at the starting location.\n\n";
50          return;
51       }
52       else {
53          flag = true;
54
55          for ( int move = direction, count = 0; count < 4;
56                ++count, ++move, move %= 4 )
57
58             switch( move ) {
59                case DOWN:
60                   if ( validMove( maze, row + 1, col ) ) { // move down
61                      mazeTraversal( maze, xCoord, yCoord, row + 1, col, LEFT );
62                      return;
63                   }
64                   break;
65                case RIGHT:
66                   if ( validMove( maze, row, col + 1 ) ) { // move right
67                      mazeTraversal( maze, xCoord, yCoord, row, col + 1, DOWN );
68                      return;
69                   }
70                   break;
71                case UP:
72                   if ( validMove( maze, row - 1, col ) ) { // move up
73                      mazeTraversal( maze, xCoord, yCoord, row - 1, col, RIGHT );
74                      return;
75                   }
76                   break;
77                case LEFT:
78                   if ( validMove( maze, row, col - 1 ) ) { // move left
79                      mazeTraversal( maze, xCoord, yCoord, row, col - 1, UP );
80                      return;
81                   }
82                   break;
83             }
84       }
85   }
```

```
86
87    bool validMove( const char maze[][ 12 ], int r, int c )
88    {
89       return ( r >= 0 && r <= 11 && c >= 0 && c <= 11 && maze[ r ][ c ] != '#' );
90    }
91
92    bool coordsAreEdge( int x, int y )
93    {
94       if ( ( x == 0 || x == 11 ) && ( y >= 0 && y <= 11 ) )
95          return true;
96       else if ( ( y == 0 || y == 11 ) && ( x >= 0 && x <= 11 ) )
97          return true;
98       else
99          return false;
100   }
101
102   void printMaze( const char maze[][ 12 ] )
103   {
104      for ( int x = 0; x < 12; ++x ) {
105
106         for ( int y = 0; y < 12; ++y )
107            cout << maze[ x ][ y ] << ' ';
108
109         cout << '\n';
110      }
111
112      cout << "Hit return to see next move";
113      cin.get();
114   }
115
116   void mazeGenerator(char maze[][ 12 ], int *xPtr, int *yPtr )
117   {
118      int a, x, y, entry, exit;
119
120      do {
121         entry = rand() % 4;
122         exit = rand() % 4;
123      } while ( entry == exit );
124
125      // Determine entry position
126
127      if ( entry == 0 ) {
128         *xPtr = 1 + rand() % 10;       // avoid corners
129         *yPtr = 0;
130         maze[ *xPtr ][ 0 ] = '.';
131      }
132      else if ( entry == 1 ) {
133         *xPtr = 0;
134         *yPtr = 1 + rand() % 10;
135         maze[ 0 ][ *yPtr ] = '.';
136      }
137      else if ( entry == 2 ) {
138         *xPtr = 1 + rand() % 10;
139         *yPtr = 11;
140         maze[ *xPtr ][ 11 ] = '.';
141      }
142      else {
143         *xPtr = 11;
144         *yPtr = 1 + rand() % 10;
145         maze[ 11 ][ *yPtr ] = '.';
146      }
147
148      // Determine exit location
149
```

```
150    if ( exit == 0 ) {
151        a = 1 + rand() % 10;
152        maze[ a ][ 0 ] = '.';
153    }
154    else if ( exit == 1 ) {
155        a = 1 + rand() % 10;
156        maze[ 0 ][ a ] = '.';
157    }
158    else if ( exit == 2 ) {
159        a = 1 + rand() % 10;
160        maze[ a ][ 11 ] = '.';
161    }
162    else {
163        a = 1 + rand() % 10;
164        maze[ 11 ][ a ] = '.';
165    }
166
167    for ( int loop = 1; loop < MAX_DOTS; ++loop ) {    // add dots randomly
168        x = 1 + rand() % 10;
169        y = 1 + rand() % 10;
170        maze[ x ][ y ] = '.';
171    }
172 }
```

```
# # # # # # # # # # # #
# . # # # . . . # . . #
# # . . . . . . . . . #
# . # . . . # # . . . #
# . . . . . # # . # # #
# # # # # # . # # # . #
# . . # # . . # # . . #
x . . # . . # . . . . #
# . # . . . # . . . . #
# . # # . # . . # . . .
# # . . # . . . . . # #
# # # # # # # # # # # #
Hit return to see next move
...
# # # # # # # # # # # #
# . # # # . . . # . . #
# # . . . . . . . . . #
# . # . . . # # . . . #
# . . . . . # # . # # #
# # # # # # . # # # . #
# x x # # . . # # . . #
x x x # . . # . . . . #
# x # . . . . # . . . #
# x # # . # . . # . . .
# # . . # . . . . . # #
# # # # # # # # # # # #
Hit return to see next move
Arrived back at the starting location.
```

5.27   (*Mazes of Any Size*) Generalize functions **mazeTraverse** and **mazeGenerator** of Exercises 5.25 and 5.26 to process mazes of any width and height.

    ANS:

```
1    // Exercise 5.27 Solution
2    #include <iostream.h>
3    #include <stdlib.h>
4    #include <time.h>
5
```

```
6    enum Direction { DOWN, RIGHT, UP, LEFT };
7    const int ROWS = 15, COLS = 30;
8
9    void mazeTraversal( char [][ COLS ], const int, const int, int, int, int );
10   void mazeGenerator( char [][ COLS ], int *, int * );
11   void printMaze( const char[][ COLS ] );
12   bool validMove( const char [][ COLS ], int, int );
13   bool coordsAreEdge( int, int );
14
15   int main()
16   {
17      char maze[ ROWS ][ COLS ];
18      int xStart, yStart, x, y;
19
20      srand( time( 0 ) );
21
22      for ( int loop = 0; loop < ROWS; ++loop )
23         for ( int loop2 = 0; loop2 < COLS; ++loop2 )
24            maze[ loop ][ loop2 ] = '#';
25
26      mazeGenerator( maze, &xStart, &yStart );
27
28      x = xStart;   // starting row
29      y = yStart;   // starting col
30
31      mazeTraversal( maze, xStart, yStart, x, y, RIGHT );
32      return 0;
33   }
34
35   // Assume that there is exactly 1 entrance and exactly 1 exit to the maze.
36   void mazeTraversal( char maze[][ COLS ], const int xCoord, const int yCoord,
37                       int row, int col, int direction )
38   {
39      static bool flag = false;    // starting position flag
40
41      maze[ row ][ col ] = 'x';   // insert x at current location
42      printMaze( maze );
43
44      if ( coordsAreEdge( row, col ) && row != xCoord && col != yCoord ) {
45         cout << endl << "Maze successfully exited!\n\n";
46         return;    // maze is complete
47      }
48      else if ( row == xCoord && col == yCoord && flag ) {
49         cout << "\nArrived back at the starting location.\n\n";
50         return;
51      }
52      else {
53         flag = true;
54
55         for ( int move = direction, count = 0; count < 4;
56               ++count, ++move, move %= 4 )
57            switch( move ) {
58               case DOWN:
59                  if ( validMove( maze, row + 1, col ) ) { // move down
60                     mazeTraversal( maze, xCoord, yCoord, row + 1, col, LEFT );
61                     return;
62                  }
63                  break;
64               case RIGHT:
65                  if ( validMove( maze, row, col + 1 ) ) { // move right
66                     mazeTraversal( maze, xCoord, yCoord, row, col + 1, DOWN );
67                     return;
68                  }
69                  break;
```

```
70                      case UP:
71                         if ( validMove( maze, row - 1, col ) ) { // move up
72                            mazeTraversal( maze, xCoord, yCoord, row - 1, col, RIGHT );
73                            return;
74                         }
75                         break;
76                      case LEFT:
77                         if ( validMove( maze, row, col - 1 ) ) { // move left
78                            mazeTraversal( maze, xCoord, yCoord, row, col - 1, UP );
79                            return;
80                         }
81                         break;
82                   }
83          }
84   }
85
86   bool validMove( const char maze[][ COLS ], int r, int c )
87   {
88      return ( r >= 0 && r <= ROWS - 1 && c >= 0 && c <= COLS - 1 &&
89               maze[ r ][ c ] != '#' );   // a valid move
90   }
91
92   bool coordsAreEdge( int x, int y )
93   {
94      if ( ( x == 0 || x == ROWS - 1 ) && ( y >= 0 && y <= COLS - 1 ) )
95         return true;
96      else if ( ( y == 0 || y == COLS - 1 ) && ( x >= 0 && x <= ROWS - 1 ) )
97         return true;
98      else
99         return false;
100  }
101
102  void printMaze( const char maze[][ COLS ] )
103  {
104     for ( int x = 0; x < ROWS; ++x ) {
105
106        for ( int y = 0; y < COLS; ++y )
107           cout << maze[ x ][ y ] << ' ';
108
109        cout << '\n';
110     }
111
112     cout << "\nHit return to see next move";
113     cin.get();
114  }
115
116  void mazeGenerator( char maze[][ COLS ], int *xPtr, int *yPtr )
117  {
118     int a, x, y, entry, exit;
119
120     do {
121        entry = rand() % 4;
122        exit = rand() % 4;
123     } while ( entry == exit );
124
125     // Determine entry position
126     if ( entry == 0 ) {
127        *xPtr = 1 + rand() % ( ROWS - 2 );     // avoid corners
128        *yPtr = 0;
129        maze[ *xPtr ][ *yPtr ] = '.';
130     }
```

```
131        else if ( entry == 1 ) {
132           *xPtr = 0;
133           *yPtr = 1 + rand() % ( COLS - 2 );
134           maze[ *xPtr ][ *yPtr ] = '.';
135        }
136        else if ( entry == 2 ) {
137           *xPtr = 1 + rand() % ( ROWS - 2 );
138           *yPtr = COLS - 1;
139           maze[ *xPtr ][ *yPtr ] = '.';
140        }
141        else {
142           *xPtr = ROWS - 1;
143           *yPtr = 1 + rand() % ( COLS - 2 );
144           maze[ *xPtr ][ *yPtr ] = '.';
145        }
146
147        // Determine exit location
148        if ( exit == 0 ) {
149           a = 1 + rand() % ( ROWS - 2 );
150           maze[ a ][ 0 ] = '.';
151        }
152        else if ( exit == 1 ) {
153           a = 1 + rand() % ( COLS - 2 );
154           maze[ 0 ][ a ] = '.';
155        }
156        else if ( exit == 2 ) {
157           a = 1 + rand() % ( ROWS - 2 );
158           maze[ a ][ COLS - 1 ] = '.';
159        }
160        else {
161           a = 1 + rand() % ( COLS - 2 );
162           maze[ ROWS - 1 ][ a ] = '.';
163        }
164
165        for ( int loop = 1; loop < ( ROWS - 2 ) * ( COLS - 2 ); ++loop ) {
166           x = 1 + rand() % ( ROWS - 2 );    // add dots to maze
167           y = 1 + rand() % ( COLS - 2 );
168           maze[ x ][ y ] = '.';
169        }
170 }
```

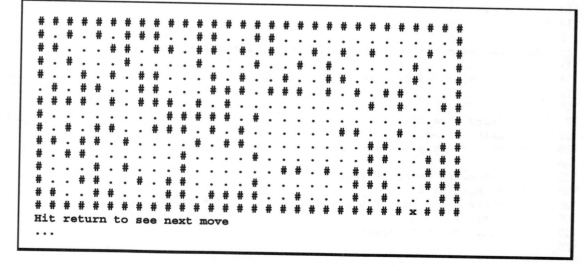

```
# # # # # # # # # # # # # # # # # # # # # # # # # # # #
# . # . # . # # # . . # # . . # # x x x x x x x x x x #
# # . . . # # . # # . # # . # . # x . # . # . # . . . # x #
# . # . . . # . . . . # . . . # x x # . # . . . . . # . x #
# . . # . # . # # . . . # . # x x # . . # # . . . . # . x #
. # . # # . . . # # . . . . # # # x # # # . # . # . # # . x x x #
# # # # . # . # # # . # . # x x x . . . . . . # . # . x # #
# . . . . . . . . # # # # # x # x . . . x x x x x x x x x #
# . # . # # . . # # # . # . # x x . . . x # # x x # x x x #
# # . # # . # . . . . # x # # x x . . . x x x # # x x x # #
# . # # . . . . . . # x x x x # x . . . . x x # # x x x # # #
# . . . # . # . . . . # x . . x x x # # . # x # # x x x # # #
# . . # # . # . . # . # # x x x x # x x x x . x # # # x x x # # #
# # . . # # . . . # # x x x # x x x x # . x # # . # x x x # #
# # # # # # # # # # # # # # # # # # # # # # # # # x # # #

Hit return to see next move

Arrived back at the starting location.
```

5.28   *(Arrays of Pointers to Functions)* Rewrite the program of Fig. 4.23 to use a menu-driven interface. The program should offer the user 5 options as follows (these should be displayed on the screen):

```
Enter a choice:
   0  Print the array of grades
   1  Find the minimum grade
   2  Find the maximum grade
   3  Print the average on all tests for each student
   4  End program
```

One restriction on using arrays of pointers to functions is that all the pointers must have the same type. The pointers must be to functions of the same return type that receive arguments of the same type. For this reason, the functions in Fig. 4.23 must be modified so they each return the same type and take the same parameters. Modify functions **minimum** and **maximum** to print the minimum or maximum value and return nothing. For option 3, modify function **average** of Fig. 4.23 to output the average for each student (not a specific student). Function **average** should return nothing and take the same parameters as **printArray**, **minimum**, and **maximum**. Store the pointers to the four functions in array **processGrades** and use the choice made by the user as the subscript into the array for calling each function.

       ANS:

```
1   // Exercise 5.28 Solution
2   #include <iostream.h>
3   #include <iomanip.h>
4
5   const int STUDENTS = 3, EXAMS = 4;
6
7   void minimum( const int [][ EXAMS ], int, int );
8   void maximum( const int [][ EXAMS ], int, int );
9   void average( const int [][ EXAMS ], int, int );
10  void printArray( const int [][ EXAMS ], int, int );
11  void printMenu( void );
12  int test( bool ( * )( int, int ), int, int, int, const int [][ EXAMS ] );
13
14  int main()
15  {
16      void ( *processGrades[ 4 ] )( const int [][ EXAMS ], int, int )
17                    = { printArray, minimum, maximum, average };
18
19      int choice = 0,
20          studentGrades[ STUDENTS ][ EXAMS ] = { { 77, 68, 86, 73 },
21                                                 { 96, 87, 89, 78 },
22                                                 { 70, 90, 86, 81 } };
```

```
23
24      while ( choice != 4 ) {
25
26         do {
27            printMenu();
28            cin >> choice;
29         } while ( choice < 0 || choice > 4 );
30
31         if ( choice != 4 )
32            ( *processGrades[ choice ] )( studentGrades, STUDENTS, EXAMS );
33         else
34            cout << "Program Ended.\n";
35      }
36
37      return 0;
38   }
39
40   void minimum( const int grades[][ EXAMS ], int pupils, int tests )
41   {
42      bool smaller( int, int );
43
44      cout << "\n\tThe lowest grade is "
45           << test( smaller, pupils, tests, 100, grades ) << '\n';
46   }
47
48   void maximum( const int grades[][ EXAMS ], int pupils, int tests )
49   {
50      bool greater( int, int );
51
52      cout << "\n\tThe highest grade is "
53           << test( greater, pupils, tests, 0, grades ) << '\n';
54   }
55
56   int test( bool ( *ptr )( int, int ), int p, int t, int value,
57             const int g[][ EXAMS ] )
58   {
59      for ( int i = 0; i < p; ++i )
60        for ( int j = 0; j < t; ++j )
61           if ( ( *ptr )( g[ i ][ j ], value ) )
62              value = g[ i ][ j ];
63
64      return value;    // return max/min value
65   }
66
67   void average( const int grades[][ EXAMS ], int pupils, int tests )
68   {
69      int total;
70
71      cout << setiosflags( ios::fixed | ios::showpoint ) << '\n';
72
73      for ( int i = 0; i < pupils; ++i ) {
74         total = 0;   // reset total
75
76         for ( int j = 0; j < tests; ++j )
77            total += grades[ i ][ j ];
78
79         cout << "\tThe average for student " << pupils + 1 << " is "
80              << setprecision( 1 )
81              << static_cast< float > ( total ) / tests << '\n';
82      }
83
84      cout << resetiosflags( ios::fixed | ios::showpoint );
85   }
86
```

```
87  void printArray( const int grades[][ EXAMS ], int pupils, int tests )
88  {
89      cout << "\n                        [0]  [1]  [2]  [3]";
90
91      for ( int i = 0; i < pupils; ++i ) {
92          cout << "\nstudentGrades[" << i << ']';
93
94          for ( int j = 0; j < tests; ++j )
95              cout << setw( 5 ) << grades[ i ][ j ];
96      }
97
98      cout << '\n';
99  }
100
101 void printMenu( void )
102 {
103     cout << "\nEnter a choice:\n"
104          << "  0  Print the array of grades\n"
105          << "  1  Find the minimum grade\n"
106          << "  2  Find the maximum grade\n"
107          << "  3  Print the average on all tests for each student\n"
108          << "  4  End program\n? ";
109 }
110
111 bool greater( int a, int b )
112 {
113     return a > b;
114 }
115
116 bool smaller( int a, int b )
117 {
118     return a < b;
119 }
```

```
Enter a choice:
   0  Print the array of grades
   1  Find the minimum grade
   2  Find the maximum grade
   3  Print the average on all tests for each student
   4  End program
? 0
                    [0]  [1]  [2]  [3]
studentGrades[0]    77   68   86   73
studentGrades[1]    96   87   89   78
studentGrades[2]    70   90   86   81

Enter a choice:
   0  Print the array of grades
   1  Find the minimum grade
   2  Find the maximum grade
   3  Print the average on all tests for each student
   4  End program
? 1

        The lowest grade is 68

Enter a choice:
   0  Print the array of grades
   1  Find the minimum grade
   2  Find the maximum grade
   3  Print the average on all tests for each student
   4  End program
? 2
```
continued...

```
        The highest grade is 96

Enter a choice:
   0  Print the array of grades
   1  Find the minimum grade
   2  Find the maximum grade
   3  Print the average on all tests for each student
   4  End program
? 3


        The average for student 4 is 76.0
        The average for student 4 is 87.5
        The average for student 4 is 81.8

Enter a choice:
   0  Print the array of grades
   1  Find the minimum grade
   2  Find the maximum grade
   3  Print the average on all tests for each student
   4  End program
? 4
Program Ended.
```

5.29   (*Modifications to the Simpletron Simulator*) In Exercise 5.19, you wrote a software simulation of a computer that executes programs written in Simpletron Machine Language (SML). In this exercise, we propose several modifications and enhancements to the Simpletron Simulator. In Exercises 15.26 and 15.27, we propose building a compiler that converts programs written in a high-level programming language (a variation of BASIC) to SML. Some of the following modifications and enhancements may be required to execute the programs produced by the compiler.

a)   Extend the Simpletron Simulator's memory to contain 1000 memory locations to enable the Simpletron to handle larger programs.

b)   Allow the simulator to perform modulus calculations. This requires an additional Simpletron Machine Language instruction.

c)   Allow the simulator to perform exponentiation calculations. This requires an additional Simpletron Machine Language instruction.

d)   Modify the simulator to use hexadecimal values rather than integer values to represent Simpletron Machine Language instructions.

e)   Modify the simulator to allow output of a newline. This requires an additional Simpletron Machine Language instruction.

f)   Modify the simulator to process floating-point values in addition to integer values.

g)   Modify the simulator to handle string input. Hint: Each Simpletron word can be divided into two groups, each holding a two-digit integer. Each two-digit integer represents the ASCII decimal equivalent of a character. Add a machine language instruction that will input a string and store the string beginning at a specific Simpletron memory location. The first half of the word at that location will be a count of the number of characters in the string (i.e., the length of the string). Each succeeding half-word contains one ASCII character expressed as two decimal digits. The machine language instruction converts each character into its ASCII equivalent and assigns it to a half-word.

h)   Modify the simulator to handle output of strings stored in the format of part (g). Hint: Add a machine language instruction that will print a string beginning at a certain Simpletron memory location. The first half of the word at that location is a count of the number of characters in the string (i.e., the length of the string). Each succeeding half-word contains one ASCII character expressed as two decimal digits. The machine language instruction checks the length and prints the string by translating each two-digit number into its equivalent character.

5.30   What does this program do?

```
1  // ex05_30.cpp
2  #include <iostream.h>
3
4  int mystery3( const char *, const char * );
5
```

```
 6   int main()
 7   {
 8      char string1[ 80 ], string2[ 80 ];
 9
10      cout << "Enter two strings: ";
11      cin >> string1 >> string2;
12      cout << "The result is "
13          << mystery3( string1, string2 ) << endl;
14
15      return 0;
16   }
17
18   int mystery3( const char *s1, const char *s2 )
19   {
20      for ( ; *s1 != '\0' && *s2 != '\0'; s1++, s2++ )
21
22         if ( *s1 != *s2 )
23            return 0;
24
25      return 1;
26   }
```

ANS: Function **mystery3** compares two strings for equality.

String Manipulation Exercises

5.31   Write a program that uses function **strcmp** to compare two strings input by the user. The program should state whether the first string is less than, equal to, or greater than the second string.

ANS:

```
 1   // Exercise 5.31 Solution
 2   #include <iostream.h>
 3   #include <string.h>
 4
 5   const int SIZE = 20;
 6
 7   int main()
 8   {
 9      char string1[ SIZE ], string2[ SIZE ];
10      int result;
11
12      cout << "Enter two strings: ";
13      cin >> string1 >> string2;
14
15      result = strcmp( string1, string2 );
16
17      if ( result > 0 )
18         cout << '\"' << string1 << '\"' << " is greater than \""
19             << string2 << '\"' << endl;
20      else if ( result == 0 )
21         cout << '\"' << string1 << '\"' << " is equal to \"" << string2
22             << '\"' << endl;
23      else
24         cout << '\"' << string1 << '\"' << " is less than \"" << string2
25             << '\"' << endl;
26
27      return 0;
28   }
```

```
    Enter two strings: green leaf
    "green" is less than "leaf"
```

5.32   Write a program that uses function **strncmp** to compare two strings input by the user. The program should input the number of characters to be compared. The program should state whether the first string is less than, equal to, or greater than the second string.

ANS:

```
1   // Exercise 5.32 Solution
2   #include <iostream.h>
3   #include <string.h>
4
5   const int SIZE = 20;
6
7   int main()
8   {
9      char string1[ SIZE ], string2[ SIZE ];
10     int result, compareCount;
11
12     cout << "Enter two strings: ";
13     cin >> string1 >> string2;
14     cout << "How many characters should be compared: ";
15     cin >> compareCount;
16
17     result = strncmp( string1, string2, compareCount );
18
19     if ( result > 0 )
20        cout << '\"' << string1 << "\" is greater than \"" << string2
21             << "\" up to " << compareCount << " characters\n";
22     else if ( result == 0 )
23        cout << '\"' << string1 << "\" is equal to \"" << string2
24             << "\" up to " << compareCount << " characters\n";
25     else
26        cout << '\"' << string1 << "\" is less than \"" << string2
27             << "\" up to " << compareCount << " characters\n";
28
29     cout << endl;
30     return 0;
31  }
```

```
Enter two strings: sand sandpiper
How many characters should be compared: 4
"sand" is equal to "sandpiper" up to 4 characters
```

5.33   Write a program that uses random number generation to create sentences. The program should use four arrays of pointers to **char** called **article**, **noun**, **verb**, and **preposition**. The program should create a sentence by selecting a word at random from each array in the following order: **article**, **noun**, **verb**, **preposition**, **article**, and **noun**. As each word is picked, it should be concatenated to the previous words in an array which is large enough to hold the entire sentence. The words should be separated by spaces. When the final sentence is output, it should start with a capital letter and end with a period. The program should generate 20 such sentences.

The arrays should be filled as follows: the **article** array should contain the articles **"the"**, **"a"**, **"one"**, **"some"**, and **"any"**; the **noun** array should contain the nouns **"boy"**, **"girl"**, **"dog"**, **"town"**, and **"car"**; the **verb** array should contain the verbs **"drove"**, **"jumped"**, **"ran"**, **"walked"**, and **"skipped"**; the **preposition** array should contain the prepositions **"to"**, **"from"**, **"over"**, **"under"**, and **"on"**.

After the preceding program is written and working, modify the program to produce a short story consisting of several of these sentences. (How about the possibility of a random term paper writer!)

ANS:

```
1   // Exercise 5.33 Solution
2   #include <iostream.h>
3   #include <stdlib.h>
4   #include <time.h>
```

```
5   #include <string.h>
6   #include <ctype.h>
7
8   const int SIZE = 100;
9
10  int main()
11  {
12     const char *article[] = { "the", "a", "one", "some", "any" },
13            *noun[] = { "boy", "girl", "dog", "town", "car" },
14            *verb[] = { "drove", "jumped", "ran", "walked", "skipped" },
15            *preposition[] = { "to", "from", "over", "under", "on" };
16     char sentence[ SIZE ] = "";
17
18     for ( int i = 1; i <= 20; ++i ) {
19        strcat( sentence, article[ rand() % 5 ] );
20        strcat( sentence, " " );
21        strcat( sentence, noun[ rand() % 5 ] );
22        strcat( sentence, " " );
23        strcat( sentence, verb[ rand() % 5 ] );
24        strcat( sentence, " " );
25        strcat( sentence, preposition[ rand() % 5 ] );
26        strcat( sentence, " " );
27        strcat( sentence, article[ rand() % 5 ] );
28        strcat( sentence, " " );
29        strcat( sentence, noun[ rand() % 5 ] );
30        cout << static_cast< char > ( toupper( sentence[ 0 ] ) )
31             << &sentence[ 1 ] << ".\n";
32        sentence[ 0 ] = '\0';
33     }
34
35     cout << endl;
36     return 0;
37  }
```

```
A dog skipped to any car.
Some town ran on the boy.
A dog jumped from the dog.
One girl jumped on one town.
One dog jumped from some boy.
One girl jumped under any dog.
One car drove on some girl.
One town walked on a girl.
Some town ran on one dog.
One car walked from any town.
A boy drove over some girl.
The dog skipped under a boy.
The car drove to a girl.
Some town skipped under any car.
A boy jumped from a town.
Any car jumped under one town.
Some dog skipped from some boy.
Any town skipped to one girl.
Some girl jumped to any dog.
The car ran under one dog.
```

5.34   *(Limericks)* A limerick is a humorous five-line verse in which the first and second lines rhyme with the fifth, and the third line rhymes with the fourth. Using techniques similar to those developed in Exercise 5.33, write a C++ program that produces random limericks. Polishing this program to produce good limericks is a challenging problem, but the result will be worth the effort!

5.35   Write a program that encodes English language phrases into pig Latin. Pig Latin is a form of coded language often used for amusement. Many variations exist in the methods used to form pig Latin phrases. For simplicity, use the following algorithm:

To form a pig Latin phrase from an English language phrase, tokenize the phrase into words with function **strtok**. To translate each English word into a pig Latin word, place the first letter of the English word at the end of the English word, and add the letters "**ay**." Thus the word "**jump**" becomes "**umpjay**," the word "**the**" becomes "**hetay**," and the word "**computer**" becomes "**omputercay**." Blanks between words remain as blanks. Assume the following: The English phrase consists of words separated by blanks, there are no punctuation marks, and all words have two or more letters. Function **printLatinWord** should display each word. Hint: Each time a token is found in a call to **strtok**, pass the token pointer to function **printLatinWord**, and print the pig Latin word.

ANS:

```
1    // Exercise 5.35 Solution
2    #include <iostream.h>
3    #include <string.h>
4
5    const int SIZE = 80;
6
7    void printLatinWord( char const * const );
8
9    int main()
10   {
11      char sentence[ SIZE ], *tokenPtr;
12
13      cout << "Enter a sentence:\n";
14      cin.getline( sentence, SIZE );
15
16      cout << "\nThe sentence in Pig Latin is:\n";
17      tokenPtr = strtok( sentence, " .,;" );
18
19      while ( tokenPtr ) {
20         printLatinWord( tokenPtr );
21         tokenPtr = strtok( 0, " .,;" );
22
23         if ( tokenPtr )
24            cout << ' ';
25      }
26
27      cout << '.' << endl;
28      return 0;
29   }
30
31   void printLatinWord( char const * const wordPtr )
32   {
33      int len = strlen( wordPtr );
34      for (int i = 1; i < len; ++i )
35         cout << *( wordPtr + i );
36
37      cout << *wordPtr << "ay";
38   }
```

```
Enter a sentence:
mirror mirror on the wall

The sentence in Pig Latin is:
irrormay irrormay noay hetay allway.
```

5.36 Write a program that inputs a telephone number as a string in the form **(555) 555-5555**. The program should use function **strtok** to extract the area code as a token, the first three digits of the phone number as a token, and the last four digits of the phone number as a token. The seven digits of the phone number should be concatenated into one string. The program should convert the area code string to **int** and convert the phone number string to **long**. Both the area code and the phone number should be printed.

ANS:

```
1   // Exercise 5.36 Solution
2   #include <iostream.h>
3   #include <string.h>
4   #include <stdlib.h>
5
6   int main()
7   {
8      const int SIZE1 = 20, SIZE2 = 10;
9      char p[ SIZE1 ],
10          phoneNumber[ SIZE2 ] = { '\0' }, *tokenPtr;
11     int  areaCode;
12     long phone;
13
14     cout << "Enter a phone number in the form (555) 555-5555:\n";
15     cin.getline( p, SIZE1 );
16
17     areaCode = atoi( strtok( p, "()" ) );
18
19     tokenPtr = strtok( 0, "-" );
20     strcpy( phoneNumber, tokenPtr );
21     tokenPtr = strtok( 0, "" );
22     strcat( phoneNumber, tokenPtr );
23     phone = atol( phoneNumber );
24
25     cout << "\nThe integer area code is " << areaCode
26          << "\nThe long integer phone number is " << phone << endl;
27
28     return 0;
29  }
```

```
Enter a phone number in the form (555) 555-5555:
(555) 492-4195

The integer area code is 555
The long integer phone number is 4924195
```

5.37   Write a program that inputs a line of text, tokenizes the line with function **strtok**, and outputs the tokens in reverse order.

   ANS:

```
1   // Exercise 5.37 Solution
2   #include <iostream.h>
3   #include <string.h>
4
5   void reverseTokens( char * const );
6
7   int main()
8   {
9      const int SIZE = 80;
10     char text[ SIZE ];
11
12     cout << "Enter a line of text:\n";
13     cin.getline( text, SIZE );
14     reverseTokens( text );
15     cout << endl;
16     return 0;
17  }
18
19  void reverseTokens( char * const sentence )
20  {
21     char *pointers[ 50 ], *temp;
22     int count = 0;
```

```
23
24      temp = strtok( sentence, " " );
25
26      while ( temp ) {
27         pointers[ count++ ] = temp;
28         temp = strtok( 0, " " );
29      }
30
31      cout << "\nThe tokens in reverse order are:\n";
32
33      for ( int i = count - 1; i >= 0; --i )
34         cout << pointers[ i ] << ' ';
35   }
```

```
Enter a line of text:
twinkle twinkle little star

The tokens in reverse order are:
star little twinkle twinkle
```

5.38   Use the string comparison functions discussed in Section 5.12.2 and the techniques for sorting arrays developed in Chapter 4 to write a program that alphabetizes a list of strings. Use the names of 10 or 15 towns in your area as data for your program.

ANS:

```
1    // Exercise 5.38 Solution
2    #include <iostream.h>
3    #include <string.h>
4
5    const int SIZE = 50;
6    void bubbleSort( char [][ SIZE ] );
7
8    int main()
9    {
10      char array[ 10 ][ SIZE ];
11      int i;
12
13      for ( i = 0; i < 10; ++i ) {
14         cout << "Enter a string: ";
15         cin >> &array[ i ][ 0 ];
16      }
17
18      bubbleSort( array );
19      cout << "\nThe strings in sorted order are:\n";
20
21      for ( i = 0; i < 10; ++i )
22         cout << &array[ i ][ 0 ] << endl;
23
24      return 0;
25   }
26
27   void bubbleSort( char a[][ SIZE ] )
28   {
29      char temp[ SIZE ];
30
31      for ( int i = 0; i <= 8; ++i )
32         for ( int j = 0; j <= 8; ++j )
33            if ( strcmp( &a[ j ][ 0 ], &a[ j + 1 ][ 0 ] ) > 0 ) {
34               strcpy( temp, &a[ j ][ 0 ] );
35               strcpy( &a[ j ][ 0 ], &a[ j + 1 ][ 0 ] );
36               strcpy(&a[ j + 1 ][ 0 ], temp );
37            }
38   }
```

```
Enter a string: Windsor
Enter a string: Pittsford
Enter a string: Warren
Enter a string: Killington
Enter a string: Marlboro
Enter a string: Grafton
Enter a string: Middlebury
Enter a string: Barre
Enter a string: Montpelier
Enter a string: Wolcott

The strings in sorted order are:
Barre
Grafton
Killington
Marlboro
Middlebury
Montpelier
Pittsford
Warren
Windsor
Wolcott
```

5.39   Write two versions of each of the string copy and string concatenation functions in Fig. 5.29. The first version should use array subscripting, and the second version should use pointers and pointer arithmetic.

   ANS:

```
1   // Exercise 5.39 Solution
2   #include <iostream.h>
3
4   char *stringCopy1( char *, const char * );
5   char *stringCopy2( char *, const char * );
6   char *stringNCopy1( char *, const char *, unsigned );
7   char *stringNCopy2( char *, const char *, unsigned );
8   char *stringCat1( char *, const char * );
9   char *stringCat2( char *, const char * );
10  char *stringNCat1( char *, const char *, unsigned );
11  char *stringNCat2( char *, const char *, unsigned );
12
13  int main()
14  {
15     int n = 4;
16     char string1[ 100 ], string2[ 100 ];
17
18     cout << "Enter a string: ";
19     cin >> string2;
20
21     cout << "Copied string returned from stringCopy1 is "
22          << stringCopy1( string1, string2 )
23          << "\nCopied string returned from stringCopy2 is "
24          << stringCopy2( string1, string2 );
25     cout << "\nCopied " << n << " elements returned from stringNCopy1 is "
26          << stringNCopy1( string1, string2, n );
27     cout << "\nCopied " << n << " elements returned from stringNCopy2 is "
28          << stringNCopy2(string1, string2, n);
29     cout << "\nConcatenated string returned from stringCat1 is "
30          << stringCat1( string1, string2 );
31     cout << "\nConcatenated string returned from stringCat2 is "
32          << stringCat2( string1, string2 );
33     cout << "\nConcatenated string returned from stringNCat1 is "
34          << stringNCat1( string1, string2, n );
```

```
35        cout << "\nConcatenated string returned from stringNCat2 is "
36             << stringNCat2( string1, string2, n ) << endl;
37        return 0;
38   }
39
40   char *stringCopy1( char *s1, const char *s2 )
41   {
42       for ( int sub = 0; s1[ sub ] = s2[ sub ]; ++sub )
43          ; // empty body
44
45       return s1;
46   }
47
48   char *stringCopy2( char *s1, const char *s2 )
49   {
50       char *ptr = s1;
51
52       for ( ; *s1 = *s2; ++s1, ++s2 )
53          ; // empty body
54
55       return ptr;
56   }
57
58   char *stringNCopy1( char *s1, const char *s2, unsigned n )
59   {
60       unsigned c;
61
62       for ( c = 0; c < n && ( s1[ c ] = s2[ c ] ); ++c )
63          ; // empty body
64
65       s1[ c ] = '\0';
66       return s1;
67   }
68
69   char *stringNCopy2( char *s1, const char *s2, unsigned n )
70   {
71       char *ptr = s1;
72
73       for ( unsigned c = 0; c < n; ++c, ++s1, ++s2 )
74          *s1 = *s2;
75
76       *s1 = '\0';
77       return ptr;
78   }
79
80   char *stringCat1( char *s1, const char *s2 )
81   {
82       int x;
83
84       for ( x = 0; s1[ x ] != '\0'; ++x )
85          ; // empty body
86
87       for ( int y = 0; s1[ x ] = s2[ y ]; ++x, ++y )
88          ; // empty body
89
90       return s1;
91   }
92
93   char *stringCat2( char *s1, const char *s2 )
94   {
95       char *ptr = s1;
96
97       for ( ; *s1 != '\0'; ++s1 )
98          ; // empty body
```

```
99
100     for ( ; *s1 = *s2; ++s1, ++s2 )
101        ; // empty body
102
103     return ptr;
104  }
105
106  char *stringNCat1( char *s1, const char *s2, unsigned n )
107  {
108     int x;
109
110     for ( x = 0; s1[ x ] != '\0'; ++x )
111        ; // empty body
112
113     for ( unsigned y = 0; y < n && ( s1[ x ] = s2[ y ] ); ++x, ++y )
114        ; // empty body
115
116     s1[ x ] = '\0';
117     return s1;
118  }
119
120  char *stringNCat2( char *s1, const char *s2, unsigned n )
121  {
122     char *ptr = s1;
123
124     for ( ; *s1 != '\0'; ++s1 )
125        ; // empty body
126
127     for ( unsigned c = 0 ; c < n && ( *s1 = *s2 ); ++s1, ++s2 )
128        ; // empty body
129
130     *s1 = '\0';
131     return ptr;
132  }
```

```
Enter a string: coo
Copied string returned from stringCopy1 is coo
Copied string returned from stringCopy2 is coo
Copied 4 elements returned from stringNCopy1 is coo
Copied 4 elements returned from stringNCopy2 is coo
Concatenated string returned from stringCat1 is coocoo
Concatenated string returned from stringCat2 is coocoocoo
Concatenated string returned from stringNCat1 is coocoocoocoo
Concatenated string returned from stringNCat2 is coocoocoocoocoo
```

5.40 Write two versions of each string comparison function in Fig. 5.29. The first version should use array subscripting, and the second version should use pointers and pointer arithmetic.

ANS:

```
1   // Exercise 5.40 Solution
2   #include <iostream.h>
3
4   int stringCompare1( const char *, const char * );
5   int stringCompare2( const char *, const char * );
6   int stringNCompare1( const char *, const char *, unsigned );
7   int stringNCompare2( const char *, const char *, unsigned );
8
9   int main()
10  {
11     char string1[ 100 ], string2[ 100 ];
12     unsigned n = 3;  // number of characters to be compared
13
```

```
14        cout << "Enter two strings: ";
15        cin >> string1 >> string2;
16
17        cout << "The value returned from stringCompare1(\"" << string1
18             << "\", \"" << string2 << "\") is "
19             << stringCompare1(string1, string2)
20             << "\nThe value returned from stringCompare2(\"" << string1
21             << "\", \"" << string2 << "\") is "
22             << stringCompare2(string1, string2) << '\n';
23
24        cout << "\nThe value returned from stringNCompare1(\"" << string1
25             << "\", \"" << string2 << "\", " << n << ") is "
26             << stringNCompare1(string1, string2, n)
27             << "\nThe value returned from stringNCompare2(\"" << string1
28             << "\", \"" << string2 << "\", " << n << ") is "
29             << stringNCompare2( string1, string2, n ) << endl;
30
31        return 0;
32    }
33
34    int stringCompare1( const char *s1, const char *s2 )
35    {
36        int sub;
37
38        // array subscript notation
39        for ( sub = 0; s1[ sub ] == s2[ sub ]; ++sub )
40           ; // empty statement
41
42        --sub;
43
44        if ( s1[ sub ] == '\0' && s2[ sub ] == '\0')
45           return 0;
46        else if ( s1[ sub] < s2[ sub ] )
47           return -1;
48        else
49           return 1;
50    }
51
52    int stringCompare2( const char *s1, const char *s2 )
53    {
54        // pointer notation
55        for ( ; *s1 == *s2; s1++, s2++ )
56           ; // empty statement
57
58        --s1;
59        --s2;
60
61        if ( *s1 == '\0' && *s2 == '\0' )
62           return 0;
63        else if ( *s1 < *s2 )
64           return -1;
65        else
66           return 1;
67    }
68
69    int stringNCompare1( const char *s1, const char *s2, unsigned n )
70    {
71        unsigned sub;
72
73        // array subscript notation
74        for ( sub = 0; sub < n && ( s1[ sub ] == s2[ sub ] ); sub++ )
75           ; // empty body
76
77        --sub;
```

```
78
79      if ( s1[ sub ] == s2[ sub ] )
80          return 0;
81      else if ( s1[ sub ] < s2[ sub ] )
82          return -1;
83      else
84          return 1;
85   }
86
87   int stringNCompare2( const char *s1, const char *s2, unsigned n )
88   {
89      // pointer notation
90      for ( unsigned c = 0; c < n && (*s1 == *s2); c++, s1++, s2++ )
91          ; // empty statement
92
93      --s1;
94      --s2;
95
96      if ( *s1 == *s2 )
97          return 0;
98      else if ( *s1 < *s2 )
99          return -1;
100     else
101         return 1;
102  }
```

```
Enter two strings: tommy tomato
The value returned from stringCompare1("tommy", "tomato") is 1
The value returned from stringCompare2("tommy", "tomato") is 1
The value returned from stringNCompare1("tommy", "tomato", 3) is 0
The value returned from stringNCompare2("tommy", "tomato", 3) is 0
```

5.41   Write two versions of function **strlen** in Fig. 5.29. The first version should use array subscripting, and the second version should use pointers and pointer arithmetic.

ANS:

```
1    // Exercise 5.41 Solution
2    #include <iostream.h>
3
4    unsigned long stringLength1( const char * );
5    unsigned long stringLength2( const char * );
6
7    int main()
8    {
9       char string[ 100 ];
10
11      cout << "Enter a string: ";
12      cin >> string;
13
14      cout << "\nAccording to stringLength1 the string length is: "
15           << stringLength1( string )
16           << "\nAccording to stringLength2 the string length is: "
17           << stringLength2( string ) << endl;
18
19      return 0;
20   }
21
22   unsigned long stringLength1( const char *sPtr )
23   {
24      // array subscript notation
25      for ( int length = 0; sPtr[ length ] != '\0'; ++length )
26          ; // empty body
```

```
27
28     return length;
29  }
30
31  unsigned long stringLength2( const char *sPtr )
32  {
33     // pointer notation
34     for ( int length = 0; *sPtr != '\0'; ++sPtr, ++length )
35        ; // empty body
36
37     return length;
38  }
```

```
Enter a string: howLongCanThisNameWithoutQuestionPossiblyBe?

According to stringLength1 the string length is: 44
According to stringLength2 the string length is: 44
```

Special Section: Advanced String Manipulation Exercises

The preceding exercises are keyed to the text and designed to test the reader's understanding of fundamental string manipulation concepts. This section includes a collection of intermediate and advanced string manipulation exercises. The reader should find these problems challenging yet enjoyable. The problems vary considerably in difficulty. Some require an hour or two of program writing and implementation. Others are useful for lab assignments that might require two or three weeks of study and implementation. Some are challenging term projects.

5.42   *(Text Analysis)* The availability of computers with string manipulation capabilities has resulted in some rather interesting approaches to analyzing the writings of great authors. Much attention has been focused on whether William Shakespeare ever lived. Some scholars believe there is substantial evidence indicating that Christopher Marlowe or other authors actually penned the masterpieces attributed to Shakespeare. Researchers have used computers to find similarities in the writings of these two authors. This exercise examines three methods for analyzing texts with a computer.

a) Write a program that reads several lines of text from the keyboard and prints a table indicating the number of occurrences of each letter of the alphabet in the text. For example, the phrase

   To be, or not to be: that is the question:

   contains one "a," two "b's," no "c's," etc.

b) Write a program that reads several lines of text and prints a table indicating the number of one-letter words, two-letter words, three-letter words, etc. appearing in the text. For example, the phrase

   Whether 'tis nobler in the mind to suffer

   contains

Word length	Occurrences
1	0
2	2
3	2
4	2 (including 'tis)
5	0
6	2
7	1

c) Write a program that reads several lines of text and prints a table indicating the number of occurrences of each different word in the text. The first version of your program should include the words in the table in the same order in which they appear in the text. For example, the lines

```
          To be, or not to be: that is the question:
          Whether 'tis nobler in the mind to suffer
```

d) contain the words "to" three times, the word "be" two times, the word "or" once, etc. A more interesting (and use-ful) printout should then be attempted in which the words are sorted alphabetically.

ANS:

```
1    // Exercise 5.42 Part A Solution
2    #include <iostream.h>
3    #include <iomanip.h>
4    #include <ctype.h>
5
6    const int SIZE = 80;
7
8    int main()
9    {
10      char letters[ 26 ] = { 0 }, text[ 3 ][ SIZE ], i;
11
12      cout << "Enter three lines of text:\n";
13
14      for ( i = 0; i <= 2; ++i )
15         cin.getline( &text[ i ][ 0 ], SIZE );
16
17      for ( i = 0; i <= 2; ++i )
18         for ( int j = 0; text[ i ][ j ] != '\0'; ++j )
19            if ( isalpha( text[ i ][ j ] ) )
20               ++letters[ tolower( text[ i ][ j ] ) - 'a' ];
21
22      cout << "\nTotal letter counts:\n";
23
24      for ( i = 0; i <= 25; ++i )
25         cout << setw( 3 ) << static_cast< char > ( 'a' + i ) << ':' << setw( 3 )
26               << static_cast< int > ( letters[ i ] ) << endl;
27
28      return 0;
29   }
```

```
Enter three lines of text:
when the cats away the mice will play
still waters run deep
out of sight out of mind

Total letter counts:
  a:   5
  b:   0
  c:   2
  d:   2
  e:   7
  f:   2
  g:   1
  h:   4
  i:   5
  j:   0
  k:   0
  l:   5
  m:   2
  n:   3
  o:   4
  p:   2
  q:   0
  r:   2                                    continued...
```

```
s:    4
t:    8
u:    3
v:    0
w:    4
x:    0
y:    2
z:    0
```

```
1   // Exercise 5.42 Part B Solution
2   #include <iostream.h>
3   #include <string.h>
4
5   int main()
6   {
7      const int SIZE = 80;
8      char text[ 3 ][ SIZE ], *temp;
9      int lengths[ 20 ] = { 0 }, i;
10
11     cout << "Enter three lines of text:\n";
12
13     for ( i = 0; i <= 2; ++i )
14        cin.getline( &text[ i ][ 0 ], SIZE );
15
16     for ( i = 0; i <= 2; ++i ) {
17        temp = strtok( &text[ i ][ 0 ], ". \n" );
18
19        while ( temp ) {
20           ++lengths[ strlen( temp ) ];
21           temp = strtok( 0, ". \n" );
22        }
23     }
24
25     cout << '\n';
26
27     for ( i = 1; i <= 19; ++i )
28        if ( lengths[ i ] )
29           cout << lengths[ i ] << " word(s) of length " << i << endl;
30
31     return 0;
32  }
```

```
Enter three lines of text:
the five time super bowl champion dallas cowboys
americas team the dallas cowboys
the once and future champion dallas cowboys

4 word(s) of length 3
5 word(s) of length 4
1 word(s) of length 5
4 word(s) of length 6
3 word(s) of length 7
3 word(s) of length 8
```

```
1   // Exercise 5.42 Part C Solution
2   #include <iostream.h>
3   #include <string.h>
4
```

```
5   const int SIZE = 80;
6
7   int main()
8   {
9       char text[ 3 ][ SIZE ], *temp, words[ 100 ][ 20 ] = { "" };
10      int count[ 100 ] = { 0 }, i;
11
12      cout << "Enter three lines of text:\n";
13
14      for ( i = 0; i <= 2; ++i )
15          cin.getline( &text[ i ][ 0 ], SIZE );
16
17      for ( i = 0; i <= 2; ++i ) {
18          temp = strtok( &text[ i ][ 0 ], ". \n" );
19
20          while ( temp ) {
21              int j;
22
23              for ( j = 0; words[ j ][ 0 ] &&
24                          strcmp( temp, &words[ j ][ 0 ] ) != 0; ++j )
25                  ;   // empty body
26
27              ++count[ j ];
28
29              if ( !words[ j ][ 0 ] )
30                  strcpy( &words[ j ][ 0 ], temp );
31
32              temp = strtok( 0, ". \n" );
33          }
34      }
35
36      cout << '\n';
37
38      for ( int k = 0; words[ k ][ 0 ] != '\0' && k <= 99; ++k )
39          cout << "\"" << &words[ k ][ 0 ] << "\" appeared " << count[ k ]
40              << " time(s)\n";
41
42      cout << endl;
43      return 0;
44  }
```

```
Enter three lines of text:
lovebirds make great pets
the dallas cowboys are a great organization
peach faced lovebirds are small birds

"lovebirds" appeared 2 time(s)
"make" appeared 1 time(s)
"great" appeared 2 time(s)
"pets" appeared 1 time(s)
"the" appeared 1 time(s)
"dallas" appeared 1 time(s)
"cowboys" appeared 1 time(s)
"are" appeared 2 time(s)
"a" appeared 1 time(s)
"organization" appeared 1 time(s)
"peach" appeared 1 time(s)
"faced" appeared 1 time(s)
"small" appeared 1 time(s)
"birds" appeared 1 time(s)
```

5.43   *(Word Processing)* One important function in word processing systems is *type-justification*—the alignment of words to both the left and right margins of a page. This generates a professional-looking document that gives the appearance of being set in type rather than prepared on a typewriter. Type-justification can be accomplished on computer systems by inserting blank characters between each of the words in a line so that the rightmost word aligns with the right margin.

Write a program that reads several lines of text and prints this text in type-justified format. Assume that the text is to be printed on 8 1/2-inch-wide paper, and that one-inch margins are to be allowed on both the left and right sides of the printed page. Assume that the computer prints 10 characters to the horizontal inch. Therefore, your program should print 6 1/2 inches of text or 65 characters per line.

5.44   *(Printing Dates in Various Formats)* Dates are commonly printed in several different formats in business correspondence. Two of the more common formats are:

> **07/21/55 and July 21, 1955**

Write a program that reads a date in the first format and prints that date in the second format.
>   ANS:

```
1   // Exercise 5.44 Solution
2   #include <iostream.h>
3
4   int main()
5   {
6      const char *months[ 13 ] = { "", "January", "February", "March", "April",
7                                   "May", "June", "July", "August", "September",
8                                   "October", "November", "December" };
9      int m, d, y;
10
11     cout << "Enter a date in the form mm/dd/yy: \n";
12     cin >> m;
13     cin.ignore();
14     cin >> d;
15     cin.ignore();
16     cin >> y;
17
18     cout << "The date is: " << months[ m ] << ' ' << d << ' '
19          << 1900 + y << endl;
20     return 0;
21  }
```

```
Enter a date in the form mm/dd/yy:
8/1/93
The date is: August 1 1993
```

5.45   *(Check Protection)* Computers are frequently employed in check-writing systems such as payroll and accounts payable applications. Many strange stories circulate regarding weekly paychecks being printed (by mistake) for amounts in excess of $1 million. Weird amounts are printed by computerized check-writing systems because of human error and/or machine failure. Systems designers build controls into their systems to prevent such erroneous checks from being issued.

Another serious problem is the intentional alteration of a check amount by someone who intends to cash a check fraudulently. To prevent a dollar amount from being altered, most computerized check-writing systems employ a technique called *check protection.*

Checks designed for imprinting by computer contain a fixed number of spaces in which the computer may print an amount. Suppose a paycheck contains eight blank spaces in which the computer is supposed to print the amount of a weekly paycheck. If the amount is large, then all eight of those spaces will be filled, for example:

> **1,230.60**   (check amount)
> **--------**
> **12345678**   (position numbers)

On the other hand, if the amount is less than $1000, then several of the spaces would ordinarily be left blank. For example,

```
     99.87
--------
12345678
```

contains three blank spaces. If a check is printed with blank spaces, it is easier for someone to alter the amount of the check. To prevent a check from being altered, many check-writing systems insert *leading asterisks* to protect the amount as follows:

```
***99.87
--------
12345678
```

Write a program that inputs a dollar amount to be printed on a check, and then prints the amount in check-protected format with leading asterisks if necessary. Assume that nine spaces are available for printing an amount.

ANS:

```cpp
1   // Exercise 5.45 Solution
2   #include <iostream.h>
3   #include <iomanip.h>
4
5   int main()
6   {
7      double amount, base = 100000.0;
8      int i;
9
10     cout << "Enter check amount: ";
11     cin >> amount;
12     cout << "The protected amount is $";
13
14     for ( i = 0; amount < base; ++i )
15        base /= 10;
16
17     for ( int j = 1; j <= i; ++j )
18        cout << '*';
19
20     cout << setiosflags( ios::fixed | ios::showpoint )
21          << setw( 9 - i ) << setfill( '*' )
22          << setprecision( 2 ) << amount << endl;
23     return 0;
24  }
```

```
Enter check amount: 22.88
The protected amount is $****22.88
```

5.46 *(Writing the Word Equivalent of a Check Amount)* Continuing the discussion of the previous example, we reiterate the importance of designing check-writing systems to prevent alteration of check amounts. One common security method requires that the check amount be written both in numbers, and "spelled out" in words as well. Even if someone is able to alter the numerical amount of the check, it is extremely difficult to change the amount in words.

Many computerized check-writing systems do not print the amount of the check in words. Perhaps the main reason for this omission is the fact that most high-level languages used in commercial applications do not contain adequate string manipulation features. Another reason is that the logic for writing word equivalents of check amounts is somewhat involved.

Write a C++ program that inputs a numeric check amount and writes the word equivalent of the amount. For example, the amount 112.43 should be written as

ONE HUNDRED TWELVE and 43/100

ANS:

```
1   // Exercise 5.46 Solution
2   // NOTE: THAT THIS PROGRAM ONLY HANDLES VALUES UP TO $99.99
3   // The program is easily modified to process larger values
4   #include <iostream.h>
5
6   int main()
7   {
8      const char *digits[ 10 ] = { "", "ONE", "TWO", "THREE", "FOUR", "FIVE",
9                                   "SIX", "SEVEN", "EIGHT", "NINE" };
10     const char *teens[ 10 ] = { "TEN", "ELEVEN", "TWELVE", "THIRTEEN",
11                                 "FOURTEEN", "FIFTEEN", "SIXTEEN",
12                                 "SEVENTEEN", "EIGHTEEN", "NINETEEN"};
13     const char *tens[ 10 ] = { "", "TEN", "TWENTY", "THIRTY", "FORTY", "FIFTY",
14                                "SIXTY", "SEVENTY", "EIGHTY", "NINETY" };
15     int dollars, cents, digit1, digit2;
16
17     cout << "Enter the check amount (0.00 to 99.99): ";
18     cin >> dollars;
19     cin.ignore();
20     cin >> cents;
21     cout << "The check amount in words is:\n";
22
23     if ( dollars < 10 )
24        cout << digits[ dollars ] << ' ';
25     else if ( dollars < 20 )
26        cout << teens[ dollars - 10 ] << ' ';
27     else {
28        digit1 = dollars / 10;
29        digit2 = dollars % 10;
30
31        if ( !digit2 )
32           cout << tens[ digit1 ] << ' ';
33        else
34           cout << tens[ digit1 ] << "-" << digits[ digit2 ] << ' ';
35     }
36
37     cout << "Dollars and " << cents << "/100" << endl;
38     return 0;
39  }
```

```
Enter the check amount (0.00 to 99.99): 72.68
The check amount in words is:
SEVENTY-TWO Dollars and 68/100
```

5.47   (Morse Code) Perhaps the most famous of all coding schemes is the Morse code, developed by Samuel Morse in 1832 for use with the telegraph system. The Morse code assigns a series of dots and dashes to each letter of the alphabet, each digit, and a few special characters (such as period, comma, colon, and semicolon). In sound-oriented systems, the dot represents a short sound and the dash represents a long sound. Other representations of dots and dashes are used with light-oriented systems and signal-flag systems.

Separation between words is indicated by a space, or, quite simply, the absence of a dot or dash. In a sound-oriented system, a space is indicated by a short period of time during which no sound is transmitted. The international version of the Morse code appears in Fig. 5.39.

Write a program that reads an English language phrase and encodes the phrase into Morse code. Also write a program that reads a phrase in Morse code and converts the phrase into the English language equivalent. Use one blank between each Morse-coded letter and three blanks between each Morse-coded word.

Character	Code	Character	Code
A	.‒	T	‒
B	‒...	U	..‒
C	‒.‒.	V	...‒
D	‒..	W	.‒‒
E	.	X	‒..‒
F	..‒.	Y	‒.‒‒
G	‒‒.	Z	‒‒..
H	....		
I	..	Digits	
J	.‒‒‒	1	.‒‒‒‒
K	‒.‒	2	..‒‒‒
L	.‒..	3	...‒‒
M	‒‒	4	....‒
N	‒.	5	.....
O	‒‒‒	6	‒....
P	.‒‒.	7	‒‒...
Q	‒‒.‒	8	‒‒‒..
R	.‒.	9	‒‒‒‒.
S	...	0	‒‒‒‒‒

Fig. 5.39 The letters of the alphabet as expressed in international Morse code.

5.48 *(A Metric Conversion Program)* Write a program that will assist the user with metric conversions. Your program should allow the user to specify the names of the units as strings (i.e., centimeters, liters, grams, etc. for the metric system and inches, quarts, pounds, etc. for the English system) and should respond to simple questions such as

```
"How many inches are in 2 meters?"
"How many liters are in 10 quarts?"
```

Your program should recognize invalid conversions. For example, the question

```
"How many feet in 5 kilograms?"
```

is not meaningful because **"feet"** are units of length while **"kilograms"** are units of weight.

A challenging string manipulation project

5.49 *(A Crossword Puzzle Generator)* Most people have worked a crossword puzzle, but few have ever attempted to generate one. Generating a crossword puzzle is a difficult problem. It is suggested here as a string manipulation project requiring substantial sophistication and effort. There are many issues the programmer must resolve to get even the simplest crossword puzzle generator program working. For example, how does one represent the grid of a crossword puzzle inside the computer? Should one use a series of strings, or should double-subscripted arrays be used? The programmer needs a source of words (i.e., a computerized dictionary) that can be directly referenced by the program. In what form should these words be stored to facilitate the complex manipulations required by the program? The really ambitious reader will want to generate the "clues" portion of the puzzle in which the brief hints for each "across" word and each "down" word are printed for the puzzle worker. Merely printing a version of the blank puzzle itself is not a simple problem.

Chapter 6 Solutions
Classes and Data Abstraction

6.3   What is the purpose of the scope resolution operator?

ANS: The scope resolution operator is used to specify the class to which a function belongs. It also resolves the ambiguity caused by multiple classes having member functions of the same name.

6.4   Compare and contrast the notions of **struct** and **class** in C++.

ANS: In C++, the keywords **struct** and **class** are used to define types containing data members (and member functions for **class**es). The differences occur in the default access privileges for each. The default access for **class** members is **private** and the default access for **struct** members is **public**. The access privileges for **class** and **struct** can be specified explicitly.

6.5   Provide a constructor that is capable of using the current time from the **time()** function—declared in the C Standard Library header **time.h**—to initialize an object of the **Time** class.

ANS:

```
1   // P6_05.H
2   #ifndef p6_05_H
3   #define p6_05_H
4   #include <iostream.h>
5   #include <time.h>
6
7   class Time {
8   public:
9      Time();
10     void setHour( int h ) { hour = ( h >= 0 && h < 24 ) ? h : 0; }
11     void setMinute( int m ) { minute = ( m >= 0 && m < 60 ) ? m : 0; }
12     void setSecond( int s ) { second = ( s >= 0 && s < 60 ) ? s : 0; }
13     int getHour( void ) { return hour; }
14     int getMinute( void ) { return minute; }
15     int getSecond( void ) { return second; }
16     void printStandard( void );
17  private:
18     int hour;
19     int minute;
20     int second;
21  };
22
23  #endif
```

```
24  // P6_5M.cpp
25  // member function definitions for p6_05.cpp
26  #include <iostream.h>
27  #include <time.h>
28  #include "p6_05.h"
29
```

```
30  Time::Time()
31  {
32     long int totalTime;              // time in seconds since 1970
33     int currentYear = 1998 - 1970;   // current year
34     double totalYear;                // current time in years
35     double totalDay;                 // days since beginning of year
36     double day;                      // current time in days
37     double divisor;                  // conversion divisor
38     int timeShift = 7;               // time returned by time() is
39                                      // given as the number of seconds
40                                      // elapsed since 1/1/70 GMT.
41                                      // Depending on the time zone
42                                      // you are in, you must shift
43                                      // the time by a certain
44                                      // number of hours. For this
45                                      // problem, 7 hours is the
46                                      // current shift for EST.
47     double tempMinute;               // Used in conversion to seconds.
48
49     totalTime = time( 0 );
50     divisor = ( 60.0 * 60.0 * 24.0 * 365.0 );
51     totalYear = totalTime / divisor - currentYear;
52     totalDay = 365 * totalYear;      // leap years ignored
53     day = totalDay - static_cast< int >( totalDay );
54     tempMinute = totalDay * 24 * 60;
55     setHour( day * 24 + timeShift );
56     setMinute( ( day * 24 - static_cast< int >( day * 24 ) ) * 60 );
57     setSecond( ( tempMinute - static_cast< int >( tempMinute ) ) * 60 );
58  }
59
60  void Time::printStandard()
61  {
62     cout << ( ( hour % 12 == 0 ) ? 12 : hour % 12 ) << ':'
63          << ( minute < 10 ? "0" : "" ) << minute << ':'
64          << ( second < 10 ? "0" : "" ) << second << '\n';
65  }
```

```
66  // driver for p6_05.cpp
67  #include <iostream.h>
68  #include "p6_05.h"
69
70  int main()
71  {
72     Time t;
73
74     t.printStandard();
75     return 0;
76  }
```

```
1:05:43
```

6.6 Create a class called **Complex** for performing arithmetic with complex numbers. Write a driver program to test your class.

Complex numbers have the form

    `realPart + imaginaryPart * i`

where *i* is

    $\sqrt{-1}$

Use floating-point variables to represent the **private** data of the class. Provide a constructor function that enables an object of this class to be initialized when it is declared. The constructor should contain default values in case no initializers are provided. Provide **public** member functions for each of the following:

    a) Addition of two **Complex** numbers: The real parts are added together and the imaginary parts are added together.

    b) Subtraction of two **Complex** numbers: The real part of the right operand is subtracted from the real part of the left operand and the imaginary part of the right operand is subtracted from the imaginary part of the left operand.

    c) Printing **Complex** numbers in the form **(a, b)** where **a** is the real part and **b** is the imaginary part.

    ANS:

```
1   // P6_06.H
2   #ifndef p6_06_H
3   #define p6_06_H
4   #include <iostream.h>
5
6   class Complex {
7   public:
8      Complex( double = 0.0, double = 0.0 ); // default constructor
9      void addition( const Complex & );
10     void subtraction( const Complex & );
11     void printComplex( void );
12     void setComplexNumber( double, double );
13  private:
14     double realPart;
15     double imaginaryPart;
16  };
17
18  #endif
```

```
19  // p6_06M.cpp
20  // member function definitions for p6_06.cpp
21  #include <iostream.h>
22  #include "p6_06.h"
23
24  Complex::Complex( double real, double imaginary )
25    { setComplexNumber( real, imaginary ); }
26
27  void Complex::addition( const Complex &a )
28  {
29     realPart += a.realPart;
30     imaginaryPart += a.imaginaryPart;
31  }
32
33  void Complex::subtraction( const Complex &s )
34  {
35     realPart -= s.realPart;
36     imaginaryPart -= s.imaginaryPart;
37  }
38
39  void Complex::printComplex( void )
40    { cout << '(' << realPart << ", " << imaginaryPart << ')'; }
41
42  void Complex::setComplexNumber( double rp, double ip )
43  {
44     realPart = rp;
45     imaginaryPart = ip;
46  }
```

```
47  // driver for p6_06.cpp
48  #include <iostream.h>
49  #include "p6_06.h"
50
```

```
51  int main()
52  {
53     Complex b( 1, 7 ), c( 9, 2 );
54
55     b.printComplex();
56     cout << " + ";
57     c.printComplex();
58     cout << " = ";
59     b.addition( c );
60     b.printComplex();
61
62     cout << '\n';
63     b.setComplexNumber( 10, 1 );    // reset realPart and imaginaryPart
64     c.setComplexNumber( 11, 5 );
65     b.printComplex();
66     cout << " - ";
67     c.printComplex();
68     cout << " = ";
69     b.subtraction( c );
70     b.printComplex();
71     cout << endl;
72
73     return 0;
74  }
```

```
(1, 7) + (9, 2) = (10, 9)
(10, 1) - (11, 5) = (-1, -4)
```

6.7   Create a class called **Rational** for performing arithmetic with fractions. Write a driver program to test your class.

Use integer variables to represent the **private** data of the class—the numerator and the denominator. Provide a constructor function that enables an object of this class to be initialized when it is declared. The constructor should contain default values in case no initializers are provided and should store the fraction in reduced form (i.e., the fraction

$$\frac{2}{4}$$

would be stored in the object as 1 in the numerator and 2 in the denominator). Provide **public** member functions for each of the following:

a) Addition of two **Rational** numbers. The result should be stored in reduced form.
b) Subtraction of two **Rational** numbers. The result should be stored in reduced form.
c) Multiplication of two **Rational** numbers. The result should be stored in reduced form.
d) Division of two **Rational** numbers. The result should be stored in reduced form.
e) Printing **Rational** numbers in the form **a/b** where **a** is the numerator and **b** is the denominator.
f) Printing **Rational** numbers in floating-point format.

ANS:

```
1   // P6_07.H
2   #ifndef P6_07_H
3   #define P6_07_H
4   #include <iostream.h>
5
6   class Rational {
7   public:
8      Rational( int = 0, int = 1 );   // default constructor
9      Rational addition( const Rational & );
10     Rational subtraction( const Rational & );
11     Rational multiplication( const Rational & );
12     Rational division( Rational & );
13     void printRational( void );
14     void printRationalAsFloating( void );
15  private:
16     int numerator;
```

```
17      int denominator;
18      void reduction( void );    // utility function
19   };
20
21   #endif
```

```
22   // P6_07M.cpp
23   // member function definitions for p6_07.cpp
24   #include <iostream.h>
25   #include "p6_07.h"
26
27   Rational::Rational( int n, int d )
28   {
29      numerator = n;
30      denominator = d;
31   }
32
33   Rational Rational::addition( const Rational &a )
34   {
35      Rational t;
36
37      t.numerator = a.numerator * denominator + a.denominator * numerator;
38      t.denominator = a.denominator * denominator;
39      t.reduction();
40
41      return t;
42   }
43
44   Rational Rational::subtraction( const Rational &s )
45   {
46      Rational t;
47
48      t.numerator = s.denominator * numerator - denominator * s.numerator;
49      t.denominator = s.denominator * denominator;
50      t.reduction();
51
52      return t;
53   }
54
55   Rational Rational::multiplication( const Rational &m )
56   {
57      Rational t;
58
59      t.numerator = m.numerator * numerator;
60      t.denominator = m.denominator * denominator;
61      t.reduction();
62
63      return t;
64   }
65
66   Rational Rational::division( Rational &v )
67   {
68      Rational t;
69
70      t.numerator = v.denominator * numerator;
71      t.denominator = denominator * v.numerator;
72      t.reduction();
73
74      return t;
75   }
76
```

```
77   void Rational::printRational( void )
78   {
79      if ( denominator == 0 )
80         cout << "\nDIVIDE BY ZERO ERROR!!!" << '\n';
81      else if ( numerator == 0 )
82         cout << 0;
83      else
84         cout << numerator << '/' << denominator;
85   }
86
87   void Rational::printRationalAsFloating( void )
88      { cout << static_cast< double >( numerator ) / denominator; }
89
90   void Rational::reduction( void )
91   {
92      int largest = numerator > denominator ? numerator : denominator;
93      int gcd = 0;   // greatest common divisor
94
95      for ( int loop = 2; loop <= largest; ++loop )
96         if ( numerator % loop == 0 && denominator % loop == 0 )
97            gcd = loop;
98
99      if (gcd != 0) {
100        numerator /= gcd;
101        denominator /= gcd;
102     }
103  }
```

```
104  // driver for P6_07.cpp
105  #include <iostream.h>
106  #include "p6_07.h"
107
108  int main()
109  {
110     Rational c( 1, 3 ), d( 7, 8 ), x;
111
112     c.printRational();
113     cout << " + ";
114     d.printRational();
115     x = c.addition( d );
116     cout << " = ";
117     x.printRational();
118     cout << '\n';
119     x.printRational();
120     cout << " = ";
121     x.printRationalAsFloating();
122     cout << "\n\n";
123
124     c.printRational();
125     cout << " - ";
126     d.printRational();
127     x = c.subtraction( d );
128     cout << " = ";
129     x.printRational();
130     cout << '\n';
131     x.printRational();
132     cout << " = ";
133     x.printRationalAsFloating();
134     cout << "\n\n";
135
136     c.printRational();
137     cout << " x ";
138     d.printRational();
```

```
139      x = c.multiplication( d );
140      cout << " = ";
141      x.printRational();
142      cout << '\n';
143      x.printRational();
144      cout << " = ";
145      x.printRationalAsFloating();
146      cout << "\n\n";
147
148      c.printRational();
149      cout << " / ";
150      d.printRational();
151      x = c.division( d );
152      cout << " = ";
153      x.printRational();
154      cout << '\n';
155      x.printRational();
156      cout << " = ";
157      x.printRationalAsFloating();
158      cout << endl;
159
160      return 0;
161  }
```

```
1/3 + 7/8 = 29/24
29/24 = 1.20833

1/3 - 7/8 = -13/24
-13/24 = -0.541667

1/3 x 7/8 = 7/24
7/24 = 0.291667

1/3 / 7/8 = 8/21
8/21 = 0.380952
```

6.8   Modify the **Time** class of Fig. 6.10 to include a **tick** member function that increments the time stored in a **Time** object by one second. The **Time** object should always remain in a consistent state. Write a driver program that tests the **tick** member function in a loop that prints the time in standard format during each iteration of the loop to illustrate that the **tick** member function works correctly. Be sure to test the following cases:

    a) Incrementing into the next minute.
    b) Incrementing into the next hour.
    c) Incrementing into the next day (i.e., 11:59:59 PM to 12:00:00 AM).
    ANS:

```
1   // P6_08.H
2   #ifndef p6_08_H
3   #define p6_08_H
4   #include <iostream.h>
5
6   class Time {
7   public:
8      Time( int = 0, int = 0, int = 0 );
9      void setTime( int, int, int );
10     void setHour( int );
11     void setMinute( int );
12     void setSecond( int );
13     int getHour( void );
14     int getMinute( void );
15     int getSecond( void );
16     void printStandard( void );
17     void tick( void );
```

```
18  private:
19     int hour;
20     int minute;
21     int second;
22  };
23
24  #endif
```

```
25  // P6_08M.cpp
26  // member function definitions for p6_08.cpp
27  #include <iostream.h>
28  #include "p6_08.h"
29
30  Time::Time( int hr, int min, int sec ) { setTime( hr, min, sec ); }
31
32  void Time::setTime( int h, int m, int s )
33  {
34     setHour( h );
35     setMinute( m );
36     setSecond( s );
37  }
38
39  void Time::setHour( int h ) { hour = ( h >= 0 && h < 24 ) ? h : 0; }
40
41  void Time::setMinute( int m ) { minute = ( m >= 0 && m < 60 ) ? m : 0; }
42
43  void Time::setSecond( int s ) { second = ( s >= 0 && s < 60 ) ? s : 0; }
44
45  int Time::getHour( void ) { return hour; }
46
47  int Time::getMinute( void ) { return minute; }
48
49  int Time::getSecond( void ) { return second; }
50
51  void Time::printStandard( void )
52  {
53     cout << ( ( hour % 12 == 0 ) ? 12 : hour % 12 ) << ':'
54        << ( minute < 10 ? "0" : "" ) << minute << ':'
55        << ( second < 10 ? "0" : "" ) << second
56        << ( hour < 12 ? " AM" : " PM" );
57  }
58
59  void Time::tick( void )
60  {
61     setSecond( getSecond() + 1 );
62
63     if ( getSecond() == 0 ) {
64        setMinute( getMinute() + 1 );
65
66        if ( getMinute() == 0 )
67           setHour( getHour() + 1 );
68     }
69  }
```

```
70  // driver for p6_08.cpp
71  #include <iostream.h>
72  #include "p6_08.h"
73
74  const int MAX_TICKS = 3000;
75
```

```
76   main()
77   {
78      Time t;
79
80      t.setTime( 23, 59, 57 );
81
82      for ( int ticks = 1; ticks < MAX_TICKS; ++ticks ) {
83         t.printStandard();
84         cout << endl;
85         t.tick();
86      }
87
88      return 0;
89   }
```

```
11:59:57 PM
11:59:58 PM
11:59:59 PM
12:00:00 AM
12:00:01 AM
12:00:02 AM
...
12:49:52 AM
12:49:53 AM
12:49:54 AM
12:49:55 AM
```

6.9 Modify the **Date** class of Fig. 6.12 to perform error checking on the initializer values for data members **month**, **day**, and **year**. Also, provide a member function **nextDay** to increment the day by one. The **Date** object should always remain in a consistent state. Write a driver program that tests the **nextDay** function in a loop that prints the date during each iteration of the loop to illustrate that the **nextDay** function works correctly. Be sure to test the following cases:
   a) Incrementing into the next month.
   b) Incrementing into the next year.
   ANS:

```
1    // P6_09.H
2    #ifndef p6_09_H
3    #define p6_09_H
4
5    #include <iostream.h>
6
7    class Date {
8    public:
9       Date( int = 1, int = 1, int = 1900 );  // default constructor
10      void print( void );
11      void setDate( int, int, int );
12      void setMonth( int );
13      void setDay( int );
14      void setYear( int );
15      int getMonth( void );
16      int getDay( void );
17      int getYear( void );
18      bool leapYear( void );
19      int monthDays( void );
20      void nextDay( void );
21   private:
22      int month;
23      int day;
24      int year;
25   };
26
27   #endif
```

```
28  // p6_09M.cpp
29  // member function definitions for p6_09.cpp
30  #include <iostream.h>
31  #include "p6_09.h"
32
33  Date::Date( int m, int d, int y ) { setDate( m, d, y ); }
34
35  int Date::getDay() { return day; }
36
37  int Date::getMonth() { return month; }
38
39  int Date::getYear() { return year; }
40
41  void Date::setDay( int d )
42  {
43     if ( month == 2 && leapYear() )
44        day = ( d <= 29 && d >= 1 ) ? d : 1;
45     else
46        day = ( d <= monthDays() && d >= 1 ) ? d : 1;
47  }
48
49  void Date::setMonth( int m ) { month = m <= 12 && m >= 1 ? m : 1; }
50
51  void Date::setYear( int y ) { year = y <= 2000 && y >= 1900 ? y : 1900; }
52
53  void Date::setDate( int mo, int dy, int yr )
54  {
55     setMonth( mo );
56     setDay( dy );
57     setYear( yr );
58  }
59
60  void Date::print()
61     { cout << month << '-' << day << '-' << year << '\n'; }
62
63  void Date::nextDay()
64  {
65     setDay( day + 1 );
66
67     if ( day == 1 ) {
68        setMonth( month + 1 );
69
70        if ( month == 1 )
71           setYear( year + 1 );
72     }
73  }
74
75  bool Date::leapYear( void )
76  {
77     if ( year % 400 == 0 || ( year % 4 == 0 && year % 100 != 0 ) )
78           return true;
79        else
80           return false;    // not a leap year
81  }
82
83  int Date::monthDays( void )
84  {
85     const int days[ 12 ] = { 31, 28, 31, 30, 31, 30, 31, 31, 30, 31, 30, 31 };
86
87     return month == 2 && leapYear() ? 29 : days[ month - 1 ];
88  }
```

```
89  // driver for p6_09.cpp
90  #include <iostream.h>
91  #include "p6_09.h"
92
93  int main()
94  {
95      const int MAXDAYS = 160;
96      Date d( 3, 2, 1998 );
97
98      for ( int loop = 1; loop <= MAXDAYS; ++loop ) {
99          d.print();
100         d.nextDay();
101     }
102
103     cout << endl;
104     return 0;
105 }
```

```
3-2-1998
3-3-1998
3-4-1998
3-5-1998
3-6-1998
3-7-1998
3-8-1998
3-9-1998
3-10-1998
...
7-31-1998
8-1-1998
8-2-1998
8-3-1998
8-4-1998
8-5-1998
8-6-1998
8-7-1998
8-8-1998
```

6.10 Combine the modified **Time** class of Exercise 6.8 and the modified **Date** class of Exercise 6.9 into one class called **DateAndTime** (in Chapter 9 we will discuss inheritance which will enable us to accomplish this task quickly without modifying the existing class definitions). Modify the **tick** function to call the **nextDay** function if the time is incremented into the next day. Modify function **printStandard** and **printMilitary** to output the date in addition to the time. Write a driver program to test the new class **DateAndTime**. Specifically test incrementing the time into the next day.

ANS:

```
1   // P6_10.H
2   #ifndef p6_10_H
3   #define p6_10_H
4   #include <iostream.h>
5
6   class DateAndTime {
7   public:
8       DateAndTime( int = 1, int = 1, int = 1900,
9                    int = 0, int = 0, int = 0 );
10      void setDate( int, int, int );
11      void setMonth( int );
12      void setDay( int );
13      void setYear( int );
14      int getMonth( void );
15      int getDay( void );
16      int getYear( void );
17      void nextDay( void );
```

```
18        void setTime( int, int, int );
19        void setHour( int );
20        void setMinute( int );
21        void setSecond( int );
22        int getHour( void );
23        int getMinute( void );
24        int getSecond( void );
25        void printStandard( void );
26        void printMilitary( void );
27        int monthDays( void );
28        void tick( void );
29        bool leapYear( void );
30   private:
31        int month;
32        int day;
33        int year;
34        int hour;
35        int minute;
36        int second;
37   };
38
39   #endif
```

```
40   // P6_10M.cpp
41   // member function definitions for p6_10.cpp
42   #include <iostream.h>
43   #include "p6_10.h"
44
45   DateAndTime::DateAndTime( int m, int d, int y, int hr,
46                              int min, int sec )
47   {
48        setDate( m, d, y );
49        setTime( hr, min, sec );
50   }
51
52   void DateAndTime::setDate( int mo, int dy, int yr )
53   {
54        setMonth( mo );
55        setDay( dy );
56        setYear( yr );
57   }
58
59   int DateAndTime::getDay( void ) { return day; }
60
61   int DateAndTime::getMonth( void ) { return month; }
62
63   int DateAndTime::getYear( void ) { return year; }
64
65   void DateAndTime::setDay( int d )
66   {
67        if ( month == 2 && leapYear() )
68            day = ( d <= 29 && d >= 1 ) ? d : 1;
69        else
70            day = ( d <= monthDays() && d >= 1 ) ? d : 1;
71   }
72
73   void DateAndTime::setMonth( int m )
74        { month = m <= 12 && m >= 1 ? m : 1; }
75
76   void DateAndTime::setYear( int y )
77        { year = y <= 2000 && y >= 1900 ? y : 1900; }
78
```

```
79   void DateAndTime::nextDay( void )
80   {
81      setDay( day + 1 );
82
83      if ( day == 1 ) {
84         setMonth( month + 1 );
85
86         if ( month == 1 )
87            setYear( year + 1 );
88      }
89   }
90
91   void DateAndTime::setTime( int hr, int min, int sec )
92   {
93      setHour( hr );
94      setMinute( min );
95      setSecond( sec );
96   }
97
98   void DateAndTime::setHour( int h ) { hour = ( h >= 0 && h < 24 ) ? h : 0; }
99
100  void DateAndTime::setMinute( int m ) { minute = ( m >= 0 && m < 60 ) ? m : 0; }
101
102  void DateAndTime::setSecond( int s ) { second = ( s >= 0 && s < 60 ) ? s : 0; }
103
104  int DateAndTime::getHour( void ) { return hour; }
105
106  int DateAndTime::getMinute( void ) { return minute; }
107
108  int DateAndTime::getSecond( void ) { return second; }
109
110  void DateAndTime::printStandard( void )
111  {
112     cout << ( ( hour % 12 == 0 ) ? 12 : hour % 12 ) << ':'
113  << ( minute < 10 ? "0" : "" ) << minute << ':'
114  << ( second < 10 ? "0" : "" ) << second
115  << ( hour < 12 ? " AM " : " PM " )
116     << month << '-' << day << '-' << year << endl;
117  }
118
119  void DateAndTime::printMilitary( void )
120  {
121     cout << ( hour < 10 ? "0" : "" ) << hour << ':'
122  << ( minute < 10 ? "0" : "" ) << minute << ':'
123  << ( second < 10 ? "0" : "" ) << second << "     "
124     << month << '-' << day << '-' << year << endl;
125  }
126
127  void DateAndTime::tick( void )
128  {
129     setSecond( second + 1 );
130
131     if ( second == 0 ) {
132        setMinute( minute + 1 );
133
134        if ( minute == 0 ) {
135           setHour( hour + 1 );
136
137           if ( hour == 0 )
138              nextDay();
139        }
140     }
141  }
142
```

```
143  bool DateAndTime::leapYear( void )
144  {
145     if ( year % 400 == 0 || ( year % 4 == 0 && year % 100 != 0 ) )
146           return true;
147        else
148           return false;     // not a leap year
149  }
150
151  int DateAndTime::monthDays( void )
152  {
153     const int days[ 12 ] = { 31, 28, 31, 30, 31, 30, 31, 31, 30, 31, 30, 31 };
154
155     return ( month == 2 && leapYear() ) ? 29 : days[ ( month - 1 ) ];
156  }
```

```
157  // driver for p6_10.cpp
158  #include <iostream.h>
159  #include "p6_10.h"
160
161  int main()
162  {
163     const int MAXTICKS = 3000;
164
165     DateAndTime d( 3, 2, 1998, 23, 50, 0 );
166
167     for ( int ticks = 1; ticks <= MAXTICKS; ++ticks ) {
168        cout << "Military time: ";
169        d.printMilitary();
170        cout << "Standard time: ";
171        d.printStandard();
172        d.tick();
173     }
174
175     cout << endl;
176     return 0;
177  }
```

```
Military time: 23:50:00     3-2-1998
Standard time: 11:50:00 PM 3-2-1998
Military time: 23:50:01     3-2-1998
Standard time: 11:50:01 PM 3-2-1998
Military time: 23:50:02     3-2-1998
...
Military time: 00:00:00     3-3-1998
Standard time: 12:00:00 AM 3-3-1998
Military time: 00:00:01     3-3-1998
...
Military time: 00:39:58     3-3-1998
Standard time: 12:39:58 AM 3-3-1998
Military time: 00:39:59     3-3-1998
Standard time: 12:39:59 AM 3-3-1998
```

6.11   Modify the *set* functions in the program of Fig. 6.10 to return appropriate error values if an attempt is made to *set* a data member of an object of class **Time** to an invalid value.

ANS:

```
1  // P6_11.H
2  #ifndef P6_11_H
3  #define P6_11_H
4
```

```
5   class Time {
6   public:
7      Time( int = 0, int = 0, int = 0 );
8      void setTime( int, int, int );
9      void setHour( int );
10     void setMinute( int );
11     void setSecond( int );
12     void setInvalidTime( int t ) { invalidTime = t; }
13     int getHour( void ) { return hour; }
14     int getMinute( void ) { return minute; }
15     int getSecond( void ) { return second; }
16     int getInvalidTime( void ) { return invalidTime; }
17     void printMilitary( void );
18     void printStandard( void );
19  private:
20     int hour;
21     int minute;
22     int second;
23     int invalidTime;    // set if an invalid time is attempted
24  };
25
26  #endif
```

```
27  // P6_11M.cpp
28  // member function defintions for p6_11.cpp
29  #include <iostream.h>
30  #include "p6_11.h"
31
32  Time::Time( int hr, int min, int sec )
33     { setTime( hr, min, sec ); }
34
35  void Time::setTime( int h, int m, int s )
36  {
37     setHour( h );
38     setMinute( m );
39     setSecond( s );
40  }
41
42  void Time::setHour( int hr )
43  {
44     if ( hr >= 0 && hr < 24 ) {
45        hour = hr;
46        setInvalidTime( 1 );  // hour is valid
47     }
48     else {
49        hour = 0;
50        setInvalidTime( 0 );  // hour is invalid
51     }
52  }
53
54  void Time::setMinute( int min )
55  {
56     if ( min >= 0 && min < 60 ) {
57        minute = min;
58        setInvalidTime( 1 );  // minute is valid
59     }
60     else {
61        minute = 0;
62        setInvalidTime( 0 );  // minute is invalid
63     }
64  }
65
```

```
66  void Time::setSecond( int sec )
67  {
68     if ( sec >= 0 && sec < 60 ) {
69        second = sec;
70        setInvalidTime( 1 );   // second is valid
71     }
72     else {
73        second = 0;
74        setInvalidTime( 0 );   // second is invalid
75     }
76  }
77
78  void Time::printMilitary( void )
79  {
80     cout << ( hour < 10 ? "0" : "" ) << hour << ':'
81          << ( minute < 10 ? "0" : "" ) << minute << ':'
82          << ( second < 10 ? "0" : "" ) << second;
83  }
84
85  void Time::printStandard( void )
86  {
87     cout << ( ( hour % 12 == 0 ) ? 12 : hour % 12 ) << ':'
88          << ( minute < 10 ? "0": "" ) << minute << ':'
89          << ( second < 10 ? "0": "" ) << second
90          << ( hour < 12 ? " AM" : " PM" );
91  }
```

```
92   // driver for p6_11.cpp
93   #include <iostream.h>
94   #include "p6_11.h"
95
96   int main()
97   {
98      Time t1( 17, 34, 25 ), t2( 99, 345, -897 );
99
100     // all t1 object's times are valid
101     if ( !t1.getInvalidTime() )
102        cout << "Error: invalid time setting(s) attempted." << '\n'
103             << "Invalid setting(s) changed to zero." << '\n';
104
105     t1.printStandard();
106
107     // object t2 has invalid time settings
108     if ( !t2.getInvalidTime() )
109        cout << "\nError: invalid time setting(s) attempted.\n"
110             << "Invalid setting(s) changed to zero.\n";
111
112     t2.printMilitary();
113     cout << endl;
114     return 0;
115  }
```

```
5:34:25 PM
Error: invalid time setting(s) attempted.
Invalid setting(s) changed to zero.
00:00:00
```

6.12   Create a class **Rectangle**. The class has attributes **length** and **width**, each of which defaults to 1. It has member functions that calculate the **perimeter** and the **area** of the rectangle. It has *set* and *get* functions for both **length** and **width**. The *set* functions should verify that **length** and **width** are each floating-point numbers larger than 0.0 and less than 20.0.

ANS:

```
 1    // P6_12.H
 2    #ifndef P6_12_H
 3    #define P6_12_H
 4    #include <iostream.h>
 5
 6    class Rectangle {
 7    public:
 8       Rectangle( double = 1.0, double = 1.0 );
 9       double perimeter( void );
10       double area( void );
11       void setWidth( double w );
12       void setLength( double l );
13       double getWidth( void );
14       double getLength( void );
15    private:
16       double length;
17       double width;
18    };
19
20    #endif
```

```
21    // P6_12M.cpp
22    // member function definitions for p6_12.cpp
23    #include <iostream.h>
24    #include "p6_12.h"
25
26    Rectangle::Rectangle( double w, double l )
27    {
28       setWidth(w);
29       setLength(l);
30    }
31
32    double Rectangle::perimeter( void ) { return 2 * ( width + length ); }
33
34    double Rectangle::area( void ) { return width * length; }
35
36    void Rectangle::setWidth( double w ) { width = w > 0 && w < 20.0 ? w : 1.0; }
37
38    void Rectangle::setLength( double l ) { length = l > 0 && l < 20.0 ? l : 1.0; }
39
40    double Rectangle::getWidth( void ) { return width; }
41
42    double Rectangle::getLength( void ) { return length; }
```

```
43    // driver for p6_12.cpp
44    #include <iostream.h>
45    #include <iomanip.h>
46    #include "p6_12.h"
47
48    int main()
49    {
50       Rectangle a, b( 4.0, 5.0 ), c( 67.0, 888.0 );
51
52       cout << setiosflags( ios::fixed | ios::showpoint );
53       cout << setprecision( 1 );
54
55       // output Rectangle a
56       cout << "a: length = " << a.getLength() << "; width = " << a.getWidth()
57            << "; perimeter = " << a.perimeter() << "; area = "
58            << a.area() << '\n';
59
60       // output Rectangle b
61       cout << "b: length = " << b.getLength() << "; width = " << b.getWidth()
```

```
62              << "; perimeter = " << b.perimeter() << "; area = "
63              << b.area() << '\n';
64
65      // output Rectangle c; bad values attempted
66      cout << "c: length = " << c.getLength() << "; width = " << c.getWidth()
67              << "; perimeter = " << c.perimeter() << "; area = "
68              << c.area() << endl;
69
70      return 0;
71   }
```

```
a: length = 1.0; width = 1.0; perimeter = 4.0; area = 1.0
b: length = 5.0; width = 4.0; perimeter = 18.0; area = 20.0
c: length = 1.0; width = 1.0; perimeter = 4.0; area = 1.0
```

6.13   Create a more sophisticated **Rectangle** class than the one you created in Exercise 6.12. This class stores only the Cartesian coordinates of the four corners of the rectangle. The constructor calls a *set* function that accepts four sets of coordinates and verifies that each of these is in the first quadrant with no single x or y coordinate larger than 20.0. The *set* function also verifies that the supplied coordinates do, in fact, specify a rectangle. Member functions calculate the **length**, **width**, **perimeter**, and **area**. The length is the larger of the two dimensions. Include a predicate function **square** that determines if the rectangle is a square.

ANS:

```
1    // P6_13.H
2    #ifndef P6_13_H
3    #define P6_13_H
4
5    class Rectangle {
6    public:
7       Rectangle( double *, double *, double *, double * );
8       void setCoord( double *, double *, double *, double * );
9       void perimeter( void );
10      void area( void );
11      void square( void );
12   private:
13      double point1[ 2 ];
14      double point2[ 2 ];
15      double point3[ 2 ];
16      double point4[ 2 ];
17   };
18
19   #endif
```

```
20   // P6_13M.cpp
21   // member function definitions for p6_13.cpp
22   #include <iostream.h>
23   #include <iomanip.h>
24   #include <math.h>
25   #include "p6_13.h"
26
27   Rectangle::Rectangle( double *a, double *b, double *c, double *d )
28      { setCoord( a, b, c, d ); }
29
30   void Rectangle::setCoord( double *p1, double *p2, double *p3, double *p4 )
31   {
32      // Arrangement of points
33      // p4.........p3
34      //  .          .
35      //  .          .
36      // p1.........p2
37
```

```
38        const int x = 0, y = 1;   // added for clarity
39
40        // validate all points
41        point1[ x ] = ( p1[ x ] > 20.0 || p1[ x ] < 0.0 )? 0.0 : p1[ x ];
42        point1[ y ] = ( p1[ y ] > 20.0 || p1[ y ] < 0.0 )? 0.0 : p1[ y ];
43        point2[ x ] = ( p2[ x ] > 20.0 || p2[ x ] < 0.0 )? 0.0 : p2[ x ];
44        point2[ y ] = ( p2[ y ] > 20.0 || p2[ y ] < 0.0 )? 0.0 : p2[ y ];
45        point3[ x ] = ( p3[ x ] > 20.0 || p3[ x ] < 0.0 )? 0.0 : p3[ x ];
46        point3[ y ] = ( p3[ y ] > 20.0 || p3[ y ] < 0.0 )? 0.0 : p3[ y ];
47        point4[ x ] = ( p4[ x ] > 20.0 || p4[ x ] < 0.0 )? 0.0 : p4[ x ];
48        point4[ y ] = ( p4[ y ] > 20.0 || p4[ y ] < 0.0 )? 0.0 : p4[ y ];
49
50        // verify that points form a rectangle
51        if ( p1[ y ] == p2[ y ] && p1[ x ] == p4[ x ] && p2[ x ] == p3[ x ] &&
52             p3[ y ] == p4[ y ] ) {
53
54           perimeter();
55           area();
56           square();
57        }
58        else
59           cout << "Coordinates do not form a rectangle!\n";
60     }
61
62     void Rectangle::perimeter( void )
63     {
64        double l = fabs( point4[ 1 ] - point1[ 1 ] ),
65               w = fabs( point2[ 0 ] - point1[ 0 ] );
66
67        cout << setiosflags( ios::fixed | ios::showpoint )
68             << "length = " << setprecision( 1 ) << ( l > w ? l : w )
69             << '\t' << "width = " << ( l > w ? w : l )
70             << "\nThe perimeter is: " << 2 * ( w + l ) << '\n'
71             << resetiosflags( ios::fixed | ios::showpoint );
72     }
73
74     void Rectangle::area( void )
75     {
76        double l = fabs( point4[ 1 ] - point1[ 1 ] ),
77               w = fabs( point2[ 0 ] - point1[ 0 ] );
78
79        cout << setiosflags( ios::fixed | ios::showpoint )
80             << "The area is: " << setprecision( 1 ) << w * l
81             << resetiosflags( ios::fixed | ios::showpoint ) << "\n\n" ;
82     }
83
84     void Rectangle::square( void )
85     {
86        const int x = 0, y = 1;    // added for clarity
87
88        if ( fabs( point4[ y ] - point1[ y ] ) == fabs( point2[ x ] - point1[ x ] ) )
89           cout << "The rectangle is a square.\n\n";
90     }
```

```
91     // driver for p6_13.cpp
92     #include <iostream.h>
93     #include "p6_13.h"
94
95     int main()
96     {
97        double w[ 2 ] = { 1.0, 1.0 }, x[ 2 ] = { 5.0, 1.0 },
98               y[ 2 ] = { 5.0, 3.0 }, z[ 2 ] = { 1.0, 3.0 },
99               j[ 2 ] = { 0.0, 0.0 }, k[ 2 ] = { 1.0, 0.0 },
```

```
100            m[ 2 ] = { 1.0, 1.0 }, n[ 2 ] = { 0.0, 1.0 },
101            v[ 2 ] = { 99.0, -2.3 };
102       Rectangle a( z, y, x, w ), b( j, k, m, n ),
103            c( w, x, m, n ), d( v, x, y, z );
104
105       return 0;
106 }
```

```
length = 4.0     width = 2.0
The perimeter is: 12.0
The area is: 8.0

length = 1.0     width = 1.0
The perimeter is: 4.0
The area is: 1.0

The rectangle is a square.

Coordinates do not form a rectangle!
Coordinates do not form a rectangle!
```

6.14   Modify the **Rectangle** class of Exercise 6.13 to include a **draw** function that displays the rectangle inside a 25-by-25 box enclosing the portion of the first quadrant in which the rectangle resides. Include a **setFillCharacter** function to specify the character out of which the body of the rectangle will be drawn. Include a **setPerimeterCharacter** function to specify the character that will be used to draw the border of the rectangle. If you feel ambitious you might include functions to scale the size of the rectangle, rotate it, and move it around within the designated portion of the first quadrant.

ANS:

```cpp
1   // P6_14.H
2   #ifndef P6_14_H
3   #define P6_14_H
4
5   class Rectangle {
6   public:
7      Rectangle( double *, double *, double *, double *, char, char );
8      void setCoord( double *, double *, double *, double * );
9      void perimeter( void );
10     void area( void );
11     void draw( void );
12     void square( void );
13     void setFillCharacter( char c ) { fillChar = c; }
14     void setPerimeterCharacter( char c ) { periChar = c;}
15     bool isValid( void ) { return valid; }
16     void setValid( bool v ) { valid = v; }
17  private:
18     double point1[ 2 ];
19     double point2[ 2 ];
20     double point3[ 2 ];
21     double point4[ 2 ];
22     char fillChar;
23     char periChar;
24     bool valid;
25  };
26
27  #endif
```

```cpp
28  // P6_14M.cpp
29  // member function definitions for p6_14.cpp
30  #include <iostream.h>
31  #include <iomanip.h>
32  #include <math.h>
33  #include "p6_14.h"
```

```
34   Rectangle::Rectangle( double *a, double *b, double *c, double *d,
35                         char x, char y )
36   {
37      setCoord( a, b, c, d );
38      setFillCharacter( x );
39      setPerimeterCharacter( y );
40   }
41
42   void Rectangle::setCoord( double *p1, double *p2, double *p3, double *p4 )
43   {
44      // Arrangement of points
45      // p4.........p3
46      //  .         .
47      //  .         .
48      // p1.........p2
49
50      const int x = 0, y = 1;   // added for clarity
51
52      // validate all points
53      point1[ x ] = ( p1[ x ] > 20.0 || p1[ x ] < 0.0 )? 0.0 : p1[ x ];
54      point1[ y ] = ( p1[ y ] > 20.0 || p1[ y ] < 0.0 )? 0.0 : p1[ y ];
55      point2[ x ] = ( p2[ x ] > 20.0 || p2[ x ] < 0.0 )? 0.0 : p2[ x ];
56      point2[ y ] = ( p2[ y ] > 20.0 || p2[ y ] < 0.0 )? 0.0 : p2[ y ];
57      point3[ x ] = ( p3[ x ] > 20.0 || p3[ x ] < 0.0 )? 0.0 : p3[ x ];
58      point3[ y ] = ( p3[ y ] > 20.0 || p3[ y ] < 0.0 )? 0.0 : p3[ y ];
59      point4[ x ] = ( p4[ x ] > 20.0 || p4[ x ] < 0.0 )? 0.0 : p4[ x ];
60      point4[ y ] = ( p4[ y ] > 20.0 || p4[ y ] < 0.0 )? 0.0 : p4[ y ];
61
62      // verify that points form a rectangle
63      if (point1[ y ] == point2[ y ] && point1[ x ] == point4[ x ] &&
64          point2[ x ] == point3[ x ] && point3[ y ] == point4[ y ]) {
65
66         perimeter();
67         area();
68         square();
69         setValid( true );    // valid set of points
70      }
71      else {
72         cout << "Coordinates do not form a rectangle!\n";
73         setValid( false );   // invalid set of points
74      }
75   }
76
77   void Rectangle::perimeter( void )
78   {
79      double l = fabs( point4[ 1 ] - point1[ 1 ] ),
80             w = fabs( point2[ 0 ] - point1[ 0 ] );
81
82      cout << setiosflags( ios::fixed | ios::showpoint )
83           << "length = " << setprecision( 1 ) << ( l > w ? l : w )
84           << "\twidth = " << ( l > w ? w : l )
85           << "\nThe perimeter is: " << 2 * ( w + l ) << '\n'
86           << resetiosflags( ios::fixed | ios::showpoint );
87   }
88
89   void Rectangle::area( void )
90   {
91      double l = fabs( point4[ 1 ] - point1[ 1 ] ),
92             w = fabs( point2[ 0 ] - point1[ 0 ] );
93
94      cout << setiosflags( ios::fixed | ios::showpoint )
95           << "The area is: " << setprecision( 1 ) << w * l
96           << resetiosflags( ios::fixed | ios::showpoint ) << "\n\n";
97   }
```

```
98
99   void Rectangle::square( void )
100  {
101      const int x = 0, y = 1;     // added for clarity
102
103      if ( fabs( point4[ y ] - point1[ y ] ) == fabs( point2[ x ] - point1[ x ] ) )
104         cout << "The rectangle is a square.\n\n";
105  }
106
107  void Rectangle::draw( void )
108  {
109      for ( double y = 25.0; y >= 0.0; --y ) {
110         for ( double x = 0.0; x <= 25.0; ++x ) {
111            if ( ( point1[ 0 ] == x && point1[ 1 ] == y ) ||
112                 ( point4[ 0 ] == x && point4[ 1 ] == y ) ) {
113
114               // print horizontal perimeter of rectangle
115               while ( x <= point2[ 0 ] ) {
116                  cout << periChar;
117                  ++x;
118               }
119
120               // print remainder of quadrant
121               cout << '.';
122            }
123            // prints vertical perimeter of rectangle
124            else if ( ( ( x <= point4[ 0 ] && x >= point1[ 0 ] ) ) &&
125                    point4[ 1 ] >= y && point1[ 1 ] <= y ) {
126               cout << periChar;
127
128               // fill inside of rectangle
129               for ( x++; x < point2[ 0 ]; ) {
130                  cout << fillChar;
131                  ++x;
132               }
133
134               cout << periChar;
135            }
136            else
137               cout << '.';   // print quadrant background
138         }
139
140         cout << '\n';
141      }
142  }
```

```
143  // driver for p6_14.cpp
144  #include <iostream.h>
145  #include "p6_14.h"
146
147  int main()
148  {
149      double xy1[ 2 ] = { 12.0, 12.0 }, xy2[ 2 ] = { 18.0, 12.0 },
150             xy3[ 2 ] = { 18.0, 20.0 }, xy4[ 2 ] = { 12.0, 20.0 };
151      Rectangle a( xy1, xy2, xy3, xy4, '?', '*' );
152
153      if ( a.isValid() )
154         a.draw();
155
156      return 0;
157  }
```

```
length = 8.0    width = 6.0
The perimeter is: 28.0
The area is: 48.0


..............................
..............................
..............................
..............................
..............................
...............*******........
...............*?????*........
...............*?????*........
...............*?????*........
...............*?????*........
...............*?????*........
...............*?????*........
...............*?????*........
...............*******........
..............................
..............................
..............................
..............................
..............................
..............................
..............................
..............................
..............................
..............................
```

6.15 Create a class **HugeInteger** that uses a 40-element array of digits to store integers as large as 40-digits each. Provide member functions **inputHugeInteger**, **outputHugeInteger**, **addHugeIntegers**, and **substractHugeIntegers**. For comparing **HugeInteger** objects provide functions **isEqualTo**, **isNotEqualTo**, **isGreaterThan**, **isLessThan**, **IsGreaterThanOrEqualTo**, and **isLessThanOrEqualTo**—each of these is a "predicate" function that simply returns **true** if the relationship holds between the two huge integers and returns **false** if the relationship does not hold. Provide a predicate function **isZero**. If you feel ambitious, also provide member functions **multiplyHugeIntegers**, **divideHugeIntegers**, and **modulusHugeIntegers**.

6.16 Create a class **TicTacToe** that will enable you to write a complete program to play the game of tic-tac-toe. The class contains as **private** data a 3-by-3 double array of integers. The constructor should initialize the empty board to all zeros. Allow two human players. Wherever the first player moves, place a 1 in the specified square; place a 2 wherever the second player moves. Each move must be to an empty square. After each move, determine if the game has been won or if the game is a draw. If you feel ambitious, modify your program so that the computer makes the moves for one of the players automatically. Also, allow the player to specify whether he or she wants to go first or second. If you feel exceptionally ambitious, develop a program that will play three-dimensional tic-tac-toe on a 4-by-4-by-4 board (Caution: This is an extremely challenging project that could take many weeks of effort!).

   ANS:

```
1   // p6.16_H
2   #ifndef P6_16_H
3   #define P6_16_H
4
5   class TicTacToe {
6   private:
7       enum Status { WIN, DRAW, CONTINUE };
8       int board[ 3 ][ 3 ];
```

```
 9   public:
10      TicTacToe();
11      void makeMove( void );
12      void printBoard( void );
13      bool validMove( int, int );
14      bool xoMove( int );
15      Status gameStatus( void );
16   };
17
18   #endif
```

```
 1   // P6_16M.cpp
 2   // member function definitions for p6_16.cpp
 3   #include <iostream.h>
 4   #include <iomanip.h>
 5   #include "p6_16.h"
 6
 7   TicTacToe::TicTacToe()
 8   {
 9      for ( int j = 0; j < 3; ++j )      // initialize board
10         for ( int k = 0; k < 3; ++k )
11            board[ j ][ k ] = ' ';
12   }
13
14   bool TicTacToe::validMove( int r, int c )
15   {
16      return r >= 0 && r < 3 && c >= 0 && c < 3 && board[ r ][ c ] == ' ';
17   }
18
19   // must specify that type Status is part of the TicTacToe namespace.
20   // See Chapter 21 for a discussion of namespaces.
21   TicTacToe::Status TicTacToe::gameStatus( void )
22   {
23      int a;
24
25      // check for a win on diagonals
26      if ( board[ 0 ][ 0 ] != ' ' && board[ 0 ][ 0 ] == board[ 1 ][ 1 ] &&
27           board[ 0 ][ 0 ] == board[ 2 ][ 2 ] )
28         return WIN;
29      else if ( board[ 2 ][ 0 ] != ' ' && board[ 2 ][ 0 ] == board[ 1 ][ 1 ] &&
30                board[ 2 ][ 0 ] == board[ 0 ][ 2 ] )
31         return WIN;
32
33      // check for win in rows
34      for ( a = 0; a < 3; ++a )
35         if ( board[ a ][ 0 ] != ' ' && board[ a ][ 0 ] == board[ a ][ 1 ] &&
36              board[ a ][ 0 ] == board[ a ][ 2 ] )
37            return WIN;
38
39      // check for win in columns
40      for ( a = 0; a < 3; ++a )
41         if ( board[ 0 ][ a ] != ' ' && board[ 0 ][ a ] == board[ 1 ][ a ] &&
42              board[ 0 ][ a ] == board[ 2 ][ a ] )
43            return WIN;
44
45      // check for a completed game
46      for ( int r = 0; r < 3; ++r )
47         for ( int c = 0; c < 3; ++c )
48            if ( board[ r ][ c ] == ' ' )
49               return CONTINUE; // game is not finished
50
51      return DRAW; // game is a draw
52   }
```

```
53
54   void TicTacToe::printBoard( void )
55   {
56      cout << "   0   1   2\n\n";
57
58      for ( int r = 0; r < 3; ++r ) {
59         cout << r;
60
61         for ( int c = 0; c < 3; ++c ) {
62            cout << setw( 3 ) << static_cast< char > ( board[ r ][ c ] );
63
64            if ( c != 2 )
65               cout << " |";
66         }
67
68         if ( r != 2 )
69            cout << "\n ___|___|___"
70                 << "\n    |   |   \n";
71      }
72
73      cout << "\n\n";
74   }
75
76   void TicTacToe::makeMove( void )
77   {
78      printBoard();
79
80      while ( true ) {
81         if ( xoMove( 'X' ) )
82            break;
83         else if ( xoMove( 'O' ) )
84            break;
85      }
86   }
87
88   bool TicTacToe::xoMove( int symbol )
89   {
90      int x, y;
91
92      do {
93         cout << "Player " << static_cast< char >( symbol ) << " enter move: ";
94         cin >> x >> y;
95         cout << '\n';
96      } while ( !validMove( x, y ) );
97
98      board[ x ][ y ] = symbol;
99      printBoard();
100     Status xoStatus = gameStatus();
101
102     if ( xoStatus == WIN ) {
103        cout << "Player " << static_cast< char >( symbol ) << " wins!\n";
104        return true;
105     }
106     else if ( xoStatus == DRAW ) {
107        cout << "Game is a draw.\n";
108        return true;
109     }
110     else // CONTINUE
111        return false;
112  }
```

```
113  // driver for p6_16.cpp
114  #include "p6_16.h"
115
116  int main()
117  {
118      TicTacToe g;
119      g.makeMove();
120      return 0;
121  }
```

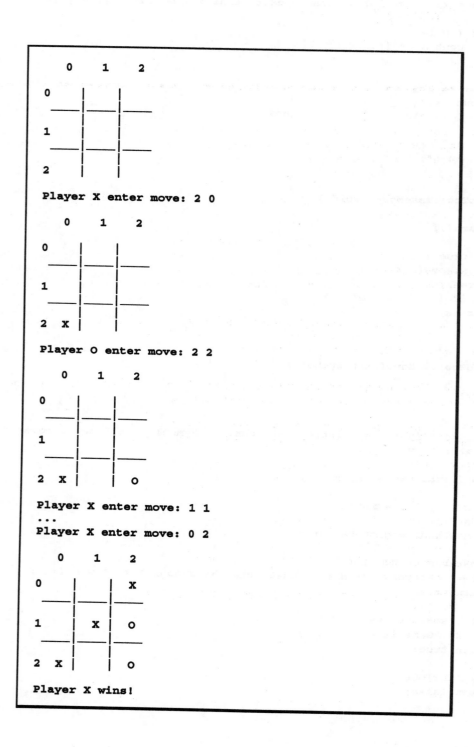

Chapter 7 Solutions
Classes: Part II

Solutions

7.3   Compare and contrast dynamic memory allocation with the C++ operators **new** and **delete**, with dynamic memory allocation with the C Standard Library functions **malloc** and **free**.

ANS: In C, dynamic memory allocation requires function calls to **malloc** and **free**. Also, **malloc** must be told the exact number of bytes to allocate (normally this is accomplished with the **sizeof** operator), then it returns a **void** pointer. C++ uses operators **new** and **delete**. The **new** operator automatically determines the number of bytes to allocate and returns a pointer to the appropriate type. The **delete** operator guarantees a call to the destructor for the object(s) being deleted.

7.4   Explain the notion of friendship in C++. Explain the negative aspects of friendship as described in the text.

ANS: Functions that are declared as **friend**s of a class have access to that class's **private** and **protected** members. Some people in the object-oriented programming community prefer not to use **friend** functions because they break the encapsulation of a class—i.e., they allow direct access to a class's impementation details that are supposed to be hidden.

7.5   Can a correct **Time** class definition include both of the following constructors? If not, explain why not.

```
Time ( int h = 0, int m = 0, int s = 0 );
Time();
```

ANS: No, because there is ambiguity between the two constructors. When a call is made to the default constructor, the compiler cannot determine which one to use because they can both be called with no arguments.

7.6   What happens when a return type, even **void**, is specified for a constructor or destructor?

ANS: A compiler syntax error occurs. No return types can be specified for constructors.

7.7   Create a **Date** class with the following capabilities:

a) Output the date in multiple formats such as

```
DDD YYYY
MM/DD/YY
June 14, 1992
```

b) Use overloaded constructors to create **Date** objects initialized with dates of the formats in part (a).

c) Create a **Date** constructor that reads the system date using the standard library functions of the **time.h** header and sets the **Date** members.

In Chapter 8, we will be able to create operators for testing the equality of two dates and for comparing dates to determine if one date is prior to, or after, another.

ANS:

```
1   // P7_07.H
2   #ifndef p7_07_H
3   #define p7_07_H
4
5   #include <iostream.h>
6   #include <time.h>
7   #include <string.h>
```

```
8
9   class Date {
10  public:
11     Date();
12     Date( int, int );
13     Date( int, int, int );
14     Date( char *, int, int );
15     void setMonth( int );
16     void setDay( int );
17     void setYear( int );
18     void printDateSlash( void ) const;
19     void printDateMonth( void ) const;
20     void printDateDay( void ) const;
21     const char *monthName( void ) const;
22     bool leapYear( void ) const;
23     int daysOfMonth( void ) const;
24     void convert1( int );
25     int convert2( void ) const;
26     void convert3( const char * const );
27     const char *monthList( int ) const;
28     int days( int ) const;
29  private:
30     int day;
31     int month;
32     int year;
33  };
34
35  #endif
```

```
36  // P7_07M.cpp
37  // member function definitions for p7_07.cpp
38  #include <iostream.h>
39  #include <string.h>
40  #include <time.h>
41  #include "p7_07.h"
42
43  // Date constructor that uses functions from time.h
44  Date::Date()
45  {
46     struct tm *ptr;              // pointer of type struct tm
47                                  // which holds calendar time components
48     time_t t = time( 0 );        // determine the current calendar time
49                                  // which is assigned to timePtr
50     ptr = localtime( &t );       // convert the current calendar time
51                                  // pointed to by timePtr into
52                                  // broken down time and assign it to ptr
53     day = ptr->tm_mday;          // broken down day of month
54     month = 1 + ptr->tm_mon;     // broken down month since January
55     year = ptr->tm_year + 1900;  // broken down year since 1900
56  }
57
58  // Date constructor that uses day of year and year
59  Date::Date( int ddd, int yyyy )
60  {
61     setYear( yyyy );
62     convert1( ddd );   // convert to month and day
63  }
64
65  // Date constructor that uses month, day and year
66  Date::Date( int mm, int dd, int yy )
67  {
68     setYear( yy + 1900 );
69     setMonth( mm );
```

```
70      setDay( dd );
71   }
72
73   // Date constructor that uses month name, day and year
74   Date::Date( char *mPtr, int dd, int yyyy )
75   {
76      setYear( yyyy );
77      convert3( mPtr );
78      setDay( dd );
79   }
80
81   // Set the day
82   void Date::setDay( int d )
83      { day = d >= 1 && d <= daysOfMonth() ? d : 1; }
84
85   // Set the month
86   void Date::setMonth( int m ) { month = m >= 1 && m <= 12 ? m : 1; }
87
88   // Set the year
89   void Date::setYear( int y ) { year = y >= 1900 && y <= 1999 ? y : 1900; }
90
91   // Print Date in the form: mm/dd/yyyy
92   void Date::printDateSlash( void ) const
93      { cout << month << '/' << day << '/' << year << '\n'; }
94
95   // Print Date in the form: monthname dd, yyyy
96   void Date::printDateMonth( void ) const
97      { cout << monthName() << ' ' << day << ", " << year << '\n'; }
98
99   // Print Date in the form: ddd yyyy
100  void Date::printDateDay( void ) const
101     { cout << convert2() << ' ' << year << '\n'; }
102
103  // Return the month name
104  const char *Date::monthName( void ) const { return monthList( month - 1 ); }
105
106  // Return the number of days in the month
107  int Date::daysOfMonth( void ) const
108     { return leapYear() && month == 2 ? 29 : days( month ); }
109
110  // Test for a leap year
111  bool Date::leapYear( void ) const
112  {
113     if ( year % 400 == 0 || ( year % 4 == 0 && year % 100 != 0 ) )
114        return true;
115     else
116        return false;
117  }
118
119  // Convert ddd to mm and dd
120  void Date::convert1( int ddd )  // convert to mm / dd / yyyy
121  {
122     int dayTotal = 0;
123
124     if ( ddd < 1 || ddd > 366 )  // check for invalid day
125        ddd = 1;
126
127     setMonth( 1 );
128
129     for ( int m = 0; m < 13 && ( dayTotal + daysOfMonth() ) < ddd; ++m ) {
130        dayTotal += daysOfMonth();
131        setMonth( m + 1 );
132     }
133
```

```
134          setDay( ddd - dayTotal );
135          setMonth( m );
136    }
137
138    // Convert mm and dd to ddd
139    int Date::convert2( void ) const     // convert to a ddd yyyy format
140    {
141        int ddd = 0;
142
143        for ( int m = 1; m < month; ++m )
144            ddd += days( m );
145
146        ddd += day;
147        return ddd;
148    }
149
150    // Convert from month name to month number
151    void Date::convert3( const char * const mPtr )   // convert to mm / dd / yyyy
152    {
153        bool flag = false;
154
155        for ( int subscript = 0; subscript < 12; ++subscript )
156            if ( !strcmp( mPtr, monthList( subscript ) ) ) {
157                setMonth( subscript + 1 );
158                flag = true; // set flag
159                break;       // stop checking for month
160            }
161
162        if ( !flag )
163            setMonth( 1 ); // invalid month default is january
164    }
165
166    // Return the name of the month
167    const char *Date::monthList( int mm ) const
168    {
169        char *months[] = { "January", "February", "March", "April", "May",
170                           "June", "July", "August", "September", "October",
171                           "November", "December" };
172        return months[ mm ];
173    }
174
175    // Return the days in the month
176    int Date::days( int m ) const
177    {
178        const int monthDays[] = { 31, 28, 31, 30, 31, 30, 31, 31, 30, 31, 30, 31 };
179
180        return monthDays[ m - 1 ];
181    }
```

```
182    // driver for p7_07.cpp
183    #include <iostream.h>
184    #include "p7_07.h"
185
186    int main()
187    {
188        Date d1( 7, 4, 98 ), d2( 86, 1999 ),
189             d3, d4( "September", 1, 1998 );
190
191        d1.printDateSlash();     // format m / dd / yy
192        d2.printDateSlash();
193        d3.printDateSlash();
194        d4.printDateSlash();
195        cout << '\n';
```

```
196
197    d1.printDateDay();         // format ddd yyyy
198    d2.printDateDay();
199    d3.printDateDay();
200    d4.printDateDay();
201    cout << '\n';
202
203    d1.printDateMonth();       // format "month" d, yyyy
204    d2.printDateMonth();
205    d3.printDateMonth();
206    d4.printDateMonth();
207    cout << endl;
208
209    return 0;
210 }
```

```
7/4/1998
2/24/1999
12/26/1997
9/1/1998

185 1998
55 1999
360 1997
244 1998

July 4, 1998
February 24, 1999
December 26, 1997
September 1, 1998
```

7.8 Create a **SavingsAccount** class. Use a **static** data member to contain the **annualInterestRate** for each of the savers. Each member of the class contains a **private** data member **savingsBalance** indicating the amount the saver currently has on deposit. Provide a **calculateMonthlyInterest** member function that calculates the monthly interest by multiplying the **balance** by **annualInterestRate** divided by 12; this interest should be added to **savingsBalance**. Provide a **static** member function **modifyInterestRate** that sets the **static annualInterestRate** to a new value. Write a driver program to test class **SavingsAccount**. Instantiate two different **savingsAccount** objects, **saver1** and **saver2**, with balances of $2000.00 and $3000.00, respectively. Set **annualInterestRate** to 3%, then calculate the monthly interest and print the new balances for each of the savers. Then set the **annualInterestRate** to 4% and calculate the next month's interest and print the new balances for each of the savers.

ANS:

```
1   // P7_08.H
2   #ifndef P7_08_H
3   #define P7_08_H
4
5   class SavingsAccount {
6   public:
7      SavingsAccount( double b ) { savingsBalance = b >= 0 ? b : 0; }
8      void calculateMonthlyInterest( void );
9      static void modifyInterestRate( double );
10     void printBalance( void ) const;
11  private:
12     double savingsBalance;
13     static double annualInterestRate;
14  };
15
16  #endif
```

```
17   // P7.08M.cpp
18   // Member function defintions for p7_08.cpp
19   #include "p7_08.h"
20   #include <iostream.h>
21   #include <iomanip.h>
22
23   // initialize static data member
24   double SavingsAccount::annualInterestRate = 0.0;
25
26   void SavingsAccount::calculateMonthlyInterest( void )
27      { savingsBalance += savingsBalance * ( annualInterestRate / 12.0 ); }
28
29   void SavingsAccount::modifyInterestRate( double i )
30      { annualInterestRate = ( i >= 0 && i <= 1.0 ) ? i : 0.03; }
31
32   void SavingsAccount::printBalance( void ) const
33   {
34      cout << setiosflags( ios::fixed | ios::showpoint )
35           << '$' << setprecision( 2 ) << savingsBalance
36           << resetiosflags( ios::fixed | ios::showpoint );
37   }
```

```
38   // driver for p7_08.cpp
39   #include <iostream.h>
40   #include <iomanip.h>
41   #include "p7_08.h"
42
43   int main()
44   {
45      SavingsAccount saver1( 2000.0 ), saver2( 3000.0 );
46
47      SavingsAccount::modifyInterestRate( .03 );
48
49      cout << "\nOutput monthly balances for one year at .03"
50           << "\nBalances: Saver 1 ";
51      saver1.printBalance();
52      cout << "\tSaver 2 ";
53      saver2.printBalance();
54
55      for ( int month = 1; month <= 12; ++month ) {
56         saver1.calculateMonthlyInterest();
57         saver2.calculateMonthlyInterest();
58
59         cout << "\nMonth" << setw( 3 ) << month << ": Saver 1 ";
60         saver1.printBalance();
61         cout << "\tSaver 2 ";
62         saver2.printBalance();
63      }
64
65      SavingsAccount::modifyInterestRate( .04 );
66      saver1.calculateMonthlyInterest();
67      saver2.calculateMonthlyInterest();
68      cout << "\nAfter setting interest rate to .04"
69           << "\nBalances: Saver 1 ";
70      saver1.printBalance();
71      cout << "\tSaver 2 ";
72      saver2.printBalance();
73      cout << endl;
74      return 0;
75   }
```

```
Output monthly balances for one year at .03
Balances: Saver 1 $2000.00      Saver 2 $3000.00
Month  1: Saver 1 $2005.00      Saver 2 $3007.50
Month  2: Saver 1 $2010.01      Saver 2 $3015.02
Month  3: Saver 1 $2015.04      Saver 2 $3022.56
Month  4: Saver 1 $2020.08      Saver 2 $3030.11
Month  5: Saver 1 $2025.13      Saver 2 $3037.69
Month  6: Saver 1 $2030.19      Saver 2 $3045.28
Month  7: Saver 1 $2035.26      Saver 2 $3052.90
Month  8: Saver 1 $2040.35      Saver 2 $3060.53
Month  9: Saver 1 $2045.45      Saver 2 $3068.18
Month 10: Saver 1 $2050.57      Saver 2 $3075.85
Month 11: Saver 1 $2055.69      Saver 2 $3083.54
Month 12: Saver 1 $2060.83      Saver 2 $3091.25
After setting interest rate to .04
Balances: Saver 1 $2067.70      Saver 2 $3101.55
```

7.9 Create a class called **IntegerSet**. Each object of class **IntegerSet** can hold integers in the range 0 through 100. A set is represented internally as an array of ones and zeros. Array element **a[i]** is 1 if integer *i* is in the set. Array element **a[j]** is 0 if integer *j* is not in the set. The default constructor initializes a set to the so-called "empty set," i.e., a set whose array representation contains all zeros.

Provide member functions for the common set operations. For example, provide a **unionOfIntegerSets** member function that creates a third set which is the set-theoretic union of two existing sets (i.e., an element of the third set's array is set to 1 if that element is 1 in either or both of the existing sets, and an element of the third set's array is set to 0 if that element is 0 in each of the existing sets).

Provide an **intersectionOfIntegerSets** member function that creates a third set which is the set-theoretic intersection of two existing sets (i.e., an element of the third set's array is set to 0 if that element is 0 in either or both of the existing sets, and an element of the third set's array is set to 1 if that element is 1 in each of the existing sets).

Provide an **insertElement** member function that inserts a new integer *k* into a set (by setting **a[k]** to 1). Provide a **deleteElement** member function that deletes integer *m* (by setting **a[m]** to 0).

Provide a **setPrint** member function that prints a set as a list of numbers separated by spaces. Print only those elements that are present in the set (i.e., their position in the array has a value of 1). Print --- for an empty set.

Provide an **isEqualTo** member function that determines if two sets are equal.

Provide an additional constructor to take five integer arguments which can be used to initialize a set object. If you want to provide fewer than five elements in the set, use default arguments of -1 for the others.

Now write a driver program to test your **IntegerSet** class. Instantiate several **IntegerSet** objects. Test that all your member functions work properly.

ANS:

```
1   // P7_09.H
2   #ifndef P7_09_H
3   #define P7_09_H
4
5   class IntegerSet {
6   public:
7      IntegerSet() { emptySet(); }
8      IntegerSet( int, int = -1, int = -1, int = -1, int = -1 );
9      IntegerSet unionOfIntegerSets( const IntegerSet& );
10     IntegerSet intersectionOfIntegerSets( const IntegerSet& );
11     void emptySet( void );
12     void inputSet( void );
13     void insertElement( int );
14     void deleteElement( int );
15     void setPrint( void ) const;
16     bool isEqualTo( const IntegerSet& ) const;
```

```
17  private:
18     int set[ 101 ];   // range of 0 - 100
19     int validEntry( int x ) const { return x >= 0 && x <= 100; }
20  };
21
22  #endif
```

```
23  //P7_09M.cpp
24  //Member function definitions for p7_09.cpp
25  #include <iostream.h>
26  #include <iomanip.h>
27  #include "p7_09.h"
28
29  IntegerSet::IntegerSet( int a, int b, int c, int d, int e )
30  {
31     emptySet();
32
33     if ( validEntry( a ) )
34        insertElement( a );
35
36     if ( validEntry( b ) )
37        insertElement( b );
38
39     if ( validEntry( c ) )
40        insertElement( c );
41
42     if ( validEntry( d ) )
43        insertElement( d );
44
45     if ( validEntry( e ) )
46        insertElement( e );
47  }
48
49  void IntegerSet::emptySet( void )
50  {
51     for ( int y = 0; y < 101; ++y )
52        set[ y ] = 0;
53  }
54
55  void IntegerSet::inputSet( void )
56  {
57     int number;
58
59     do {
60        cout << "Enter an element (-1 to end): ";
61        cin >> number;
62
63        if ( validEntry( number ) )
64           set[ number ] = 1;
65        else if ( number != -1 )
66           cerr << "Invalid Element\n";
67     } while ( number != -1 );
68
69     cout << "Entry complete\n";
70  }
71
72  void IntegerSet::setPrint( void ) const
73  {
74     int x;
75     bool empty = true;   // assume set is empty
76
77     cout << '{';
78
```

```
79      for (int u = 0; u < 101; ++u )
80         if ( set[ u ] ) {
81            cout << setw( 4 ) << u << ( x % 10 == 0 ? "\n" : "" );
82            empty = false; // set is not empty
83            ++x;
84         }
85
86         if ( empty )
87            cout << setw( 4 ) << "---";   // display an empty set
88
89         cout << setw( 4 ) << "}" << '\n';
90      }
91
92   IntegerSet IntegerSet::unionOfIntegerSets( const IntegerSet &r )
93   {
94      IntegerSet temp;
95
96      for ( int n = 0; n < 101; ++n )
97         if ( set[ n ] == 1 || r.set[ n ] == 1 )
98            temp.set[ n ] = 1;
99
100     return temp;
101  }
102
103  IntegerSet IntegerSet::intersectionOfIntegerSets( const IntegerSet &r )
104  {
105     IntegerSet temp;
106
107     for ( int w = 0; w < 101; ++w )
108        if ( set[ w ] == 1 && r.set[ w ] == 1 )
109           temp.set[ w ] = 1;
110
111     return temp;
112  }
113
114  void IntegerSet::insertElement( int k )
115  {
116     if ( validEntry( k ) )
117        set[ k ] = 1;
118     else
119        cerr << "Invalid insert attempted!\n";
120  }
121
122  void IntegerSet::deleteElement( int m )
123  {
124     if ( validEntry( m ) )
125        set[ m ] = 0;
126     else
127        cerr << "Invalid delete attempted!\n";
128  }
129
130  bool IntegerSet::isEqualTo( const IntegerSet &r ) const
131  {
132     for ( int v = 0; v < 101; ++v )
133        if ( set[ v ] != r.set[ v ] )
134           return false;    // sets are not-equal
135
136     return true;    // sets are equal
137  }

138  // driver for p7_09.cpp
139  #include <iostream.h>
140  #include "p7_09.h"
```

```
141
142  int main()
143  {
144
145      IntegerSet a, b, c, d, e( 8, 5, 7 );
146
147      cout << "Enter set A:\n";
148      a.inputSet();
149      cout << "\nEnter set B:\n";
150      b.inputSet();
151      c = a.unionOfIntegerSets( b );
152      d = a.intersectionOfIntegerSets( b );
153      cout << "\nUnion of A and B is:\n";
154      c.setPrint();
155      cout << "Intersection of A and B is:\n";
156      d.setPrint();
157
158      if ( a.isEqualTo( b ) )
159          cout << "Set A is equal to set B\n";
160      else
161          cout << "Set A is not equal to set B\n";
162
163      cout << "\nInserting 77 into set A...\n";
164      a.insertElement( 77 );
165      cout << "Set A is now:\n";
166      a.setPrint();
167
168      cout << "\nDeleting 77 from set A...\n";
169      a.deleteElement( 77 );
170      cout << "Set A is now:\n";
171      a.setPrint();
172
173      cout << "\nSet e is:\n";
174      e.setPrint();
175
176      cout << endl;
177      return 0;
178  }
```

```
Enter set A:
Enter an element (-1 to end): 1
Enter an element (-1 to end): 2
Enter an element (-1 to end): 3
Enter an element (-1 to end): 4
Enter an element (-1 to end): -1
Entry complete

Enter set B:
Enter an element (-1 to end): 3
Enter an element (-1 to end): 4
Enter an element (-1 to end): 5
Enter an element (-1 to end): 9
Enter an element (-1 to end): 22
Enter an element (-1 to end): -1
Entry complete

Union of A and B is:
{   1   2   3   4   5   9  22    }
Intersection of A and B is:
{   3   4    }
Set A is not equal to set B                    continued...
```

```
Inserting 77 into set A...
Set A is now:
{   1   2   3   4  77   }

Deleting 77 from set A...
Set A is now:
{   1   2   3   4   }

Set e is:
{   5   7   8   }
```

7.10   It would be perfectly reasonable for the **Time** class of Fig. 7.8 to represent the time internally as the number of seconds since midnight rather than the three integer values **hour, minute** and **second**. Clients could use the same **public** methods and get the same results. Modify the **Time** class of Fig. 7.8 to implement the **Time** as the number of seconds since midnight and show that there is no visible change in functionality to the clients of the class.

Chapter 8 Solutions

Operator Overloading

Solutions

8.6   Give as many examples as you can of operator overloading implicit in C++. Give a reasonable example of a situation in which you might want to overload an operator explicitly in C++.

ANS: In C, the operators +, -, *, and & are overloaded. The context of these operators determines how they are used. It can be argued that the arithmetic operators are all overloaded, because they can be used to perform operations on more than one type of data. In C++, the same operators as in C are overloaded, as well as << and >>.

8.7   The C++ operators that cannot be overloaded are _____, _____, _____, _____, and _____.
ANS: **sizeof**, **.**, **?:**, **.***, and **::**.

8.8   String concatenation requires two operands—the two strings that are to be concatenated. In the text we showed how to implement an overloaded concatenation operator that concatenates the second **String** object to the right of the first **String** object, thus modifying the first **String** object. In some applications, it is desirable to produce a concatenated **String** object without modifying the **String** arguments. Implement **operator+** to allow operations such as

```
        string1 = string2 + string3;
```

ANS:

```
1   // P8_08.H
2   #ifndef p8_08_H
3   #define p8_08_H
4
5   #include <iostream.h>
6   #include <string.h>
7   #include <assert.h>
8
9   class String {
10     friend ostream &operator<<( ostream &, const String & );
11  public:
12     String( const char * const = "" ); // conversion constructor
13     String( const String & );     // copy constructor
14     ~String();                    // destructor
15     const String &operator=( const String & );
16     String operator+( const String & );
17  private:
18     char *sPtr;
19     int length;
20  };
21
22  #endif
```

```
23  // P8_08M.cpp
24  // member function definitions for p8_08.cpp
25  // class String
26  #include <iostream.h>
27  #include <string.h>
28  #include "p8_08.h"
```

```
29
30   // Conversion constructor: Convert a char * to String
31   String::String( const char * const zPtr )
32   {
33      length = strlen( zPtr );            // compute length
34      sPtr = new char[ length + 1 ]; // allocate storage
35      assert( sPtr != 0 );   // terminate if memory not allocated
36      strcpy( sPtr, zPtr );              // copy literal to object
37   }
38
39   // Copy constructor
40   String::String( const String &copy )
41   {
42      length = copy.length;           // copy length
43      sPtr = new char[ length + 1 ]; // allocate storage
44      assert( sPtr != 0 );            // ensure memory allocated
45      strcpy( sPtr, copy.sPtr );      // copy string
46   }
47
48   // Destructor
49   String::~String() { delete [] sPtr; }  // reclaim string
50
51   // Overloaded = operator; avoids self assignment
52   const String &String::operator=( const String &right )
53   {
54      if ( &right != this ) {            // avoid self assignment
55         delete [] sPtr;                 // prevents memory leak
56         length = right.length;          // new String length
57         sPtr = new char[ length + 1 ]; // allocate memory
58         assert( sPtr != 0 );            // ensure memory allocated
59         strcpy( sPtr, right.sPtr );     // copy string
60      }
61      else
62         cout << "Attempted assignment of a String to itself\n";
63
64      return *this;    // enables concatenated assignments
65   }
66
67   // Concatenate right operand and this object and
68   // store in temp object.
69   String String::operator+( const String &right )
70   {
71      String temp;
72
73      temp.length = length + right.length;
74      temp.sPtr = new char[ temp.length + 1 ]; // create space
75      assert( sPtr != 0 );   // terminate if memory not allocated
76      strcpy( temp.sPtr, sPtr );         // left part of new String
77      strcat( temp.sPtr, right.sPtr ); // right part of new String
78      return temp;                       // enables concatenated calls
79   }
80
81   // Overloaded output operator
82   ostream &operator<<( ostream &output, const String &s )
83   {
84      output << s.sPtr;
85      return output;   // enables concatenation
86   }
```

```
87   // driver for p8_08.cpp
88   #include <iostream.h>
89   #include "p8_08.h"
90
```

```
91   int main()
92   {
93      String string1, string2( "The date is" );
94      String string3( " August 1, 1993" );
95
96      cout << "string1 = string2 + string3\n";
97      string1 = string2 + string3;
98      cout << string1 << " = " << string2 << " + "
99           << string3 << endl;
100
101     return 0;
102  }
```

```
string1 = string2 + string3
The date is August 1, 1993 = The date is +  August 1, 1993
```

8.9   *(Ultimate operator overloading exercise)* To appreciate the care that should go into selecting operators for overloading, list each of C++'s overloadable operators and for each list a possible meaning (or several, if appropriate) for each of several classes you have studied in this course. We suggest you try:

  a)   Array
  b)   Stack
  c)   String

After doing this, comment on which operators seem to have meaning for a wide variety of classes. Which operators seem to be of little value for overloading? Which operators seem ambiguous?

8.10   Now work the process described in the previous problem in reverse. List each of C++'s overloadable operators. For each, list what you feel is perhaps the "ultimate operation" the operator should be used to represent. If there are several excellent operations, list them all.

8.11   *(Project)* C++ is an evolving language, and new languages are always being developed. What additional operators would you recommend adding to C++ or to a future language like C++ that would support both procedural programming and object-oriented programming? Write a careful justification. You might consider sending your suggestions to the ANSI C++ Committee.

8.12   One nice example of overloading the function call operator **( )** is to allow the more common form of double-array subscripting. Instead of saying

        chessBoard[row][column]

for an array of objects, overload the function call operator to allow the alternate form

        chessBoard(row, column)

    ANS:

```
1   // P8_12.H
2   #ifndef P8_12_H
3   #define P8_12_H
4   #include <iostream.h>
5
6   class CallOperator {
7   public:
8      CallOperator();
9      int operator()( int, int ); // overloaded function call operator
10  private:
11     int chessBoard[ 8 ][ 8 ];
12  };
13
14  #endif
```

```
15   // P8_12M.CPP
16   // member function definitions for p8_12.cpp
17   #include "p8_12.h"
18
19   CallOperator::CallOperator()
20   {
21      for ( int loop = 0; loop < 8; ++loop )
22         for ( int loop2 = 0; loop2 < 8; ++loop2 )
23            chessBoard[ loop ][ loop2 ] = loop2;
24   }
25
26   int CallOperator::operator()( int r, int c ) { return chessBoard[ r ][ c ]; }
```

```
27   // driver for p8_12.cpp
28   #include <iostream.h>
29   #include "p8_12.h"
30
31   int main()
32   {
33      CallOperator board;
34
35      cout << "board[2][5] is " << board( 2, 5 ) << endl;
36
37      return 0;
38   }
```

```
board[2][5] is 5
```

8.13 Create a class **DoubleSubscriptedArray** that has similar features to class **Array** in Fig. 8.4. At construction time, the class should be able to create an array of any number of rows and any number of columns. The class should supply **operator()** to perform double subscripting operations. For example, in a 3-by-5 **DoubleSubscriptedArray** called **a**, the user could write **a(1, 3)** to access the element at row **1** and column **3**. Remember that **operator()** can receive any number of arguments (see class **String** in Fig. 18.5 for an example of **operator()**). The underlying representation of the double-subscripted array should be a single-subscripted array of integers with *rows* * *columns* number of elements. Function **operator()** should perform the proper pointer arithmetic to access each element of the array. There should be two versions of **operator()**—one that returns **int &** so an element of a **DoubleSubscriptedArray** can be used as an *lvalue* and one that returns **const int &** so an element of a **const DoubleSubscriptedArray** can be used as an *rvalue*. The class should also provide the following operators: **==, !=, =, <<** (for outputting the array in row and column format) and **>>** (for inputting the entire array contents).

8.14 Overload the subscript operator to return the largest element of a collection, the second largest, the third largest, etc.

8.15 Consider class **Complex** shown in Fig. 8.7. The class enables operations on so-called *complex numbers*. These are numbers of the form **realPart + imaginaryPart * i** where *i* has the value:

$$i = \sqrt{-1}$$

a) Modify the class to enable input and output of complex numbers through the overloaded **>>** and **<<** operators, respectively (you should remove the print function from the class).
b) Overload the multiplication operator to enable multiplication of two complex numbers as in algebra.
c) Overload the **==** and **!=** operators to allow comparisons of complex numbers.

```
1   // Fig. 8.7: complex1.h
2   // Definition of class Complex
3   #ifndef COMPLEX1_H
4   #define COMPLEX1_H
5
6   class Complex {
7   public:
8      Complex( double = 0.0, double = 0.0 );        // constructor
```

```
 9        Complex operator+( const Complex & ) const;  // addition
10        Complex operator-( const Complex & ) const;  // subtraction
11        const Complex &operator=( const Complex & ); // assignment
12        void print() const;                          // output
13    private:
14        double real;          // real part
15        double imaginary;  // imaginary part
16    };
17
18    #endif
```

```
19    // Fig. 8.7: complex1.cpp
20    // Member function definitions for class Complex
21    #include <iostream.h>
22    #include "complex1.h"
23
24    // Constructor
25    Complex::Complex( double r, double i )
26       : real( r ), imaginary( i ) { }
27
28    // Overloaded addition operator
29    Complex Complex::operator+( const Complex &operand2 ) const
30    {
31        return Complex( real + operand2.real,
32                        imaginary + operand2.imaginary );
33    }
34
35    // Overloaded subtraction operator
36    Complex Complex::operator-( const Complex &operand2 ) const
37    {
38        return Complex( real - operand2.real,
39                        imaginary - operand2.imaginary );
40    }
41
42    // Overloaded = operator
43    const Complex& Complex::operator=( const Complex &right )
44    {
45        real = right.real;
46        imaginary = right.imaginary;
47        return *this;    // enables cascading
48    }
49
50    // Display a Complex object in the form: (a, b)
51    void Complex::print() const
52       { cout << '(' << real << ", " << imaginary << ')'; }
```

```
53    // Fig. 8.7: fig08_07.cpp
54    // Driver for class Complex
55    #include <iostream.h>
56    #include "complex1.h"
57
58    int main()
59    {
60        Complex x, y( 4.3, 8.2 ), z( 3.3, 1.1 );
61
62        cout << "x: ";
63        x.print();
64        cout << "\ny: ";
65        y.print();
66        cout << "\nz: ";
67        z.print();
68
69        x = y + z;
```

```
70    cout << "\n\nx = y + z:\n";
71    x.print();
72    cout << " = ";
73    y.print();
74    cout << " + ";
75    z.print();
76
77    x = y - z;
78    cout << "\n\nx = y - z:\n";
79    x.print();
80    cout << " = ";
81    y.print();
82    cout << " - ";
83    z.print();
84    cout << endl;
85
86    return 0;
87 }
```

```
x: (0, 0)
y: (4.3, 8.2)
z: (3.3, 1.1)

x = y + z:
(7.6, 9.3) = (4.3, 8.2) + (3.3, 1.1)

x = y - z:
(1, 7.1) = (4.3, 8.2) - (3.3, 1.1)
```

Fig. 8.7   Demonstrating class **Complex**.

ANS:

```
1   // P8_15.H
2   #ifndef P8_15_H
3   #define P8_15_H
4   #include <iostream.h>
5
6   class Complex {
7      friend ostream &operator<<( ostream &, const Complex & );
8      friend istream &operator>>( istream &, Complex & );
9   public:
10     Complex( double = 0.0, double = 0.0 );      // constructor
11     Complex operator+( const Complex& ) const; // addition
12     Complex operator-( const Complex& ) const; // subtraction
13     Complex operator*( const Complex& ) const; // multiplication
14     Complex& operator=( const Complex& );       // assignment
15     bool operator==( const Complex& ) const;
16     bool operator!=( const Complex& ) const;
17  private:
18     double real;        // real part
19     double imaginary;   // imaginary part
20  };
21
22  #endif
```

```
23  // P8_15M.cpp
24  // member function definitions for p8_15.cpp
25  #include "p8_15.h"
26
27  // Constructor
28  Complex::Complex( double r, double i )
29  {
30     real = r;
31     imaginary = i;
32  }
33
34  // Overloaded addition operator
35  Complex Complex::operator+( const Complex &operand2 ) const
36  {
37     Complex sum;
38
39     sum.real = real + operand2.real;
40     sum.imaginary = imaginary + operand2.imaginary;
41     return sum;
42  }
43
44  // Overloaded subtraction operator
45  Complex Complex::operator-( const Complex &operand2 ) const
46  {
47     Complex diff;
48
49     diff.real = real - operand2.real;
50     diff.imaginary = imaginary - operand2.imaginary;
51     return diff;
52  }
53
54  // Overloaded multiplication operator
55  Complex Complex::operator*( const Complex &operand2 ) const
56  {
57     Complex times;
58
59     times.real = real * operand2.real + imaginary * operand2.imaginary;
60     times.imaginary = real * operand2.imaginary + imaginary * operand2.real;
61     return times;
62  }
63
64  // Overloaded = operator
65  Complex& Complex::operator=( const Complex &right )
66  {
67     real = right.real;
68     imaginary = right.imaginary;
69     return *this;    // enables concatenation
70  }
71
72  bool Complex::operator==( const Complex &right ) const
73     { return right.real == real && right.imaginary == imaginary ? true : false; }
74
75  bool Complex::operator!=( const Complex &right ) const
76     { return !( *this == right ); }
77
78  ostream& operator<<( ostream &output, const Complex &complex )
79  {
80     output << complex.real << " + " << complex.imaginary << 'i';
81     return output;
82  }
83
84  istream& operator>>( istream &input, Complex &complex )
85  {
86     input >> complex.real;
```

```
87        input.ignore( 3 );          // skip spaces and +
88        input >> complex.imaginary;
89        input.ignore( 2 );
90
91        return input;
92   }
```

```
93   // driver for p8_15.cpp
94   #include "p8_15.h"
95
96   int main()
97   {
98        Complex x, y( 4.3, 8.2 ), z( 3.3, 1.1 ), k;
99
100       cout << "Enter a complex number in the form: a + bi\n? ";
101       cin >> k;
102
103       cout << "x: " << x << "\ny: " << y << "\nz: " << z << "\nk: "
104            << k << '\n';
105
106       x = y + z;
107       cout << "\nx = y + z:\n" << x << " = " << y << " + " << z << '\n';
108
109       x = y - z;
110       cout << "\nx = y - z:\n" << x << " = " << y << " - " << z << '\n';
111
112       x = y * z;
113       cout << "\nx = y * z:\n" << x << " = " << y << " * " << z << "\n\n";
114
115       if ( x != k )
116          cout << x << " != " << k << '\n';
117
118       cout << '\n';
119
120       x = k;
121
122       if ( x == k )
123          cout << x << " == " << k << '\n';
124
125       return 0;
126   }
```

```
Enter a complex number in the form: a + bi
? 22 + 8i
x: 0 + 0i
y: 4.3 + 8.2i
z: 3.3 + 1.1i
k: 22 + 8i

x = y + z:
7.6 + 9.3i = 4.3 + 8.2i + 3.3 + 1.1i

x = y - z:
1 + 7.1i = 4.3 + 8.2i - 3.3 + 1.1i

x = y * z:
23.21 + 31.79i = 4.3 + 8.2i * 3.3 + 1.1i

23.21 + 31.79i != 22 + 8i

22 + 8i == 22 + 8i
```

8.16   A machine with 32-bit integers can represent integers in the range of approximately –2 billion to +2 billion. This fixed-size restriction is rarely troublesome. But there are applications in which we would like to be able to use a much wider range of integers. This is what C++ was built to do, namely create powerful new data types. Consider class **HugeInt** of Fig. 8.8. Study the class carefully, then

    a) Describe precisely how it operates.
    b) What restrictions does the class have?
    c) Overload the ***** multiplication operator.
    d) Overload the **/** division operator.
    e) Overload all the relational and equality operators.

```
1   // Fig. 8.8: hugeint1.h
2   // Definition of the HugeInt class
3   #ifndef HUGEINT1_H
4   #define HUGEINT1_H
5
6   #include <iostream.h>
7
8   class HugeInt {
9      friend ostream &operator<<( ostream &, HugeInt & );
10  public:
11     HugeInt( long = 0 );          // conversion/default constructor
12     HugeInt( const char * );        // conversion constructor
13     HugeInt operator+( HugeInt & );   // add another HugeInt
14     HugeInt operator+( int );        // add an int
15     HugeInt operator+( const char * ); // add an int in a char *
16  private:
17     short integer[30];
18  };
19
20  #endif
```

```
21  // Fig. 8.8: hugeint1.cpp
22  // Member and friend function definitions for class HugeInt
23  #include <string.h>
24  #include "hugeint1.h"
25
26  // Conversion constructor
27  HugeInt::HugeInt( long val )
28  {
29     int i;
30
31     for ( i = 0; i <= 29; i++ )
32        integer[ i ] = 0;    // initialize array to zero
33
34     for ( i = 29; val != 0 && i >= 0; i-- ) {
35        integer[ i ] = val % 10;
36        val /= 10;
37     }
38  }
39
40  HugeInt::HugeInt( const char *string )
41  {
42     int i, j;
43
44     for ( i = 0; i <= 29; i++ )
45        integer[ i ] = 0;
46
47     for ( i = 30 - strlen( string ), j = 0; i <= 29; i++, j++ )
48        integer[ i ] = string[ j ] - '0';
49  }
50
```

```
51   // Addition
52   HugeInt HugeInt::operator+( HugeInt &op2 )
53   {
54      HugeInt temp;
55      int carry = 0;
56
57      for ( int i = 29; i >= 0; i-- ) {
58         temp.integer[ i ] = integer[ i ] +
59                             op2.integer[ i ] + carry;
60
61         if ( temp.integer[ i ] > 9 ) {
62            temp.integer[ i ] %= 10;
63            carry = 1;
64         }
65         else
66            carry = 0;
67      }
68
69      return temp;
70   }
71
72   // Addition
73   HugeInt HugeInt::operator+( int op2 )
74      { return *this + HugeInt( op2 ); }
75
76   // Addition
77   HugeInt HugeInt::operator+( const char *op2 )
78      { return *this + HugeInt( op2 ); }
79
80   ostream& operator<<( ostream &output, HugeInt &num )
81   {
82      int i;
83
84      for ( i = 0; ( num.integer[ i ] == 0 ) && ( i <= 29 ); i++ )
85         ; // skip leading zeros
86
87      if ( i == 30 )
88         output << 0;
89      else
90         for ( ; i <= 29; i++ )
91            output << num.integer[ i ];
92
93      return output;
94   }
```

```
95    // Fig. 8.8: fig08_08.cpp
96    // Test driver for HugeInt class
97    #include <iostream.h>
98    #include "hugeint1.h"
99
100   int main()
101   {
102      HugeInt n1( 7654321 ), n2( 7891234 ),
103              n3( "99999999999999999999999999999" ),
104              n4( "1" ), n5;
105
106      cout << "n1 is " << n1 << "\nn2 is " << n2
107           << "\nn3 is " << n3 << "\nn4 is " << n4
108           << "\nn5 is " << n5 << "\n\n";
109
110      n5 = n1 + n2;
111      cout << n1 << " + " << n2 << " = " << n5 << "\n\n";
112
```

```
113        cout << n3 << " + " << n4 << "\n= " << ( n3 + n4 )
114             << "\n\n";
115
116        n5 = n1 + 9;
117        cout << n1 << " + " << 9 << " = " << n5 << "\n\n";
118
119        n5 = n2 + "10000";
120        cout << n2 << " + " << "10000" << " = " << n5 << endl;
121
122        return 0;
123    }
```

```
    n1 is 7654321
    n2 is 7891234
    n3 is 999999999999999999999999999999
    n4 is 1
    n5 is 0

    7654321 + 7891234 = 15545555

    999999999999999999999999999999 + 1
    = 1000000000000000000000000000000

    7654321 + 9 = 7654330

    7891234 + 10000 = 7901234
```

Fig. 8.8   A user-defined huge integer class.

8.17   Create a class **RationalNumber** (fractions) with the following capabilities:

   a) Create a constructor that prevents a 0 denominator in a fraction, reduces or simplifies fractions that are not in re-
      duced form, and avoids negative denominators.
   b) Overload the addition, subtraction, multiplication and division operators for this class.
   c) Overload the relational and equality operators for this class.

   ANS:

```
1    // P8_17.H
2    #ifndef P8_17_H
3    #define P8_17_H
4    #include <iostream.h>
5
6    class RationalNumber {
7    public:
8       RationalNumber( int = 0, int = 1 ); // default constructor
9       RationalNumber operator+( const RationalNumber& );
10      RationalNumber operator-( const RationalNumber& );
11      RationalNumber operator*( const RationalNumber& );
12      RationalNumber operator/( RationalNumber& );
13      bool operator>( const RationalNumber& ) const;
14      bool operator<( const RationalNumber& ) const;
15      bool operator>=( const RationalNumber& ) const;
16      bool operator<=( const RationalNumber& ) const;
17      bool operator==( const RationalNumber& ) const;
18      bool operator!=( const RationalNumber& ) const;
19      void printRational( void ) const;
20   private:
21      int numerator;
22      int denominator;
23      void reduction( void );
24   };
25
26   #endif
```

```cpp
27    // P8_17M.cpp
28    // member function definitions for p8_17.cpp
29    #include <stdlib.h>
30    #include "p8_17.h"
31
32    RationalNumber::RationalNumber( int n, int d )
33    {
34       numerator = n;
35       denominator = d;
36       reduction();
37    }
38
39    RationalNumber RationalNumber::operator+( const RationalNumber &a )
40    {
41       RationalNumber sum;
42
43       sum.numerator = numerator * a.denominator + denominator * a.numerator;
44       sum.denominator = denominator * a.denominator;
45       sum.reduction();
46       return sum;
47    }
48
49    RationalNumber RationalNumber::operator-( const RationalNumber &s )
50    {
51       RationalNumber sub;
52
53       sub.numerator = numerator * s.denominator - denominator * s.numerator;
54       sub.denominator = denominator * s.denominator;
55       sub.reduction();
56       return sub;
57    }
58
59    RationalNumber RationalNumber::operator*( const RationalNumber &m )
60    {
61       RationalNumber multiply;
62
63       multiply.numerator = numerator * m.numerator;
64       multiply.denominator = denominator * m.denominator;
65       multiply.reduction();
66       return multiply;
67    }
68
69    RationalNumber RationalNumber::operator/( RationalNumber &d )
70    {
71       RationalNumber divide;
72
73       if ( d.numerator != 0 ) {    // check for a zero in numerator
74          divide.numerator = numerator * d.denominator;
75          divide.denominator = denominator * d.numerator;
76          divide.reduction();
77       }
78       else {
79          cout << "Divide by zero error: terminating program" << endl;
80          exit( 1 );    // stdlib function
81       }
82
83       return divide;
84    }
85
86    bool RationalNumber::operator>( const RationalNumber &gr ) const
87    {
88       if ( static_cast<float>( numerator ) / denominator >
89             static_cast<float>( gr.numerator ) / gr.denominator )
90          return true;
```

```
91         else
92            return false;
93     }
94
95     bool RationalNumber::operator<(const RationalNumber &lr) const
96     {
97         if ( static_cast<float>( numerator ) / denominator <
98              static_cast<float>( lr.numerator ) / lr.denominator )
99            return true;
100        else
101           return false;
102    }
103
104    bool RationalNumber::operator>=( const RationalNumber &ger ) const
105       { return *this == ger || *this > ger; }
106
107    bool RationalNumber::operator<=( const RationalNumber &ler ) const
108       { return *this == ler || *this < ler; }
109
110    bool RationalNumber::operator==( const RationalNumber &er ) const
111    {
112        if ( numerator == er.numerator && denominator == er.denominator )
113           return true;
114        else
115           return false;
116    }
117
118    bool RationalNumber::operator!=( const RationalNumber &ner ) const
119       { return !( *this == ner ); }
120
121    void RationalNumber::printRational( void ) const
122    {
123        if ( numerator == 0 )            // print fraction as zero
124           cout << numerator;
125        else if ( denominator == 1 )  // print fraction as integer
126           cout << numerator;
127        else
128           cout << numerator << '/' << denominator;
129    }
130
131    void RationalNumber::reduction( void )
132    {
133        int largest, gcd = 1;  // greatest common divisor;
134
135        largest = ( numerator > denominator ) ? numerator: denominator;
136
137        for ( int loop = 2; loop <= largest; ++loop )
138           if ( numerator % loop == 0 && denominator % loop == 0 )
139              gcd = loop;
140
141        numerator /= gcd;
142        denominator /= gcd;
143    }
```

```
144    // driver for p8_17.cpp
145    #include "p8_17.h"
146
147    int main()
148    {
149        RationalNumber c( 7, 3 ), d( 3, 9 ), x;
150
151        c.printRational();
152        cout << " + " ;
```

```
153      d.printRational();
154      cout << " = ";
155      x = c + d;
156      x.printRational();
157
158      cout << '\n';
159      c.printRational();
160      cout << " - " ;
161      d.printRational();
162      cout << " = ";
163      x = c - d;
164      x.printRational();
165
166      cout << '\n';
167      c.printRational();
168      cout << " * " ;
169      d.printRational();
170      cout << " = ";
171      x = c * d;
172      x.printRational();
173
174      cout << '\n';
175      c.printRational();
176      cout << " / " ;
177      d.printRational();
178      cout << " = ";
179      x = c / d;
180      x.printRational();
181
182      cout << '\n';
183      c.printRational();
184      cout << " is:\n";
185
186      cout << ( ( c > d ) ? "  > " : "  <= " );
187      d.printRational();
188      cout << " according to the overloaded > operator\n";
189
190      cout << ( ( c < d ) ? "  < " : "  >= " );
191      d.printRational();
192      cout << " according to the overloaded < operator\n";
193
194      cout << ( ( c >= d ) ? "  >= " : "  < " );
195      d.printRational();
196      cout << " according to the overloaded >= operator\n";
197
198      cout << ( ( c <= d ) ? "  <= " : "  > " );
199      d.printRational();
200      cout << " according to the overloaded <= operator\n";
201
202      cout << ( ( c == d ) ? "  == " : "  != " );
203      d.printRational();
204      cout << " according to the overloaded == operator\n";
205
206      cout << ( ( c != d ) ? "  != " : "  == " );
207      d.printRational();
208      cout << " according to the overloaded != operator" << endl;
209
210      return 0;
211  }
```

```
7/3 + 1/3 = 8/3
7/3 - 1/3 = 2
7/3 * 1/3 = 7/9
7/3 / 1/3 = 7
7/3 is:
   > 1/3 according to the overloaded > operator
  >= 1/3 according to the overloaded < operator
  >= 1/3 according to the overloaded >= operator
   > 1/3 according to the overloaded <= operator
  != 1/3 according to the overloaded == operator
  != 1/3 according to the overloaded != operator
```

8.18   Study the C string-handling library functions and implement each of the functions as part of the **String** class. Then, use these functions to perform text manipulations.

8.19   Develop class **Polynomial**. The internal representation of a **Polynomial** is an array of terms. Each term contains a coefficient and an exponent. The term

$$2x^4$$

has a coefficient of 2 and an exponent of 4. Develop a full class containing proper constructor and destructor functions as well as *set* and *get* functions. The class should also provide the following overloaded operator capabilities:

   a) Overload the addition operator (**+**) to add two **Polynomials**.
   b) Overload the subtraction operator (**-**) to subtract two **Polynomials**.
   c) Overload the assignment operator to assign one **Polynomial** to another.
   d) Overload the multiplication operator (*****) to multiply two **Polynomials**.
   e) Overload the addition assignment operator (**+=**), the subtraction assignment operator
      (**-=**), and the multiplication assignment operator (***=**).

   ANS: NOTE: This solution does not use a destructor. Also note that get and set methods are not implemented for this solution.

```
1    // P8_19P.H
2    #ifndef P8_19P_H
3    #define P8_19P_H
4
5    #include <iostream.h>
6
7    class Polynomial {
8    public:
9       Polynomial();
10      Polynomial operator+( const Polynomial& ) const;
11      Polynomial operator-( const Polynomial& ) const;
12      Polynomial operator*( const Polynomial& );
13      Polynomial& operator+=( const Polynomial& );
14      Polynomial& operator-=( const Polynomial& );
15      Polynomial& operator*=( const Polynomial& );
16      void enterTerms( void );
17      void printPolynomial( void ) const;
18   private:
19      int exponents[ 100 ];
20      int coefficients[ 100 ];
21      void polynomialCombine( Polynomial& );   // combine common terms
22   };
23
24   #endif
```

```
25   // P8_19M.cpp
26   // member function definitions for p8_19.cpp
27   // NOTE: The assignment operator does not need to be overloaded,
28   // because default member-wise copy can be used
```

```
29   #include <iomanip.h>
30   #include "p8_19p.h"
31
32   Polynomial::Polynomial()
33   {
34      for ( int t = 0; t < 100; ++t ) {
35         coefficients[ t ] = 0;
36         exponents[ t ] = 0;
37      }
38   }
39
40   void Polynomial::printPolynomial( void ) const
41   {
42      int start;
43      bool zero = false;
44
45      if ( coefficients[ 0 ] ) {          // output constants
46         cout << coefficients[ 0 ];
47         start = 1;
48         zero = true;     // at least one term exists
49      }
50      else {
51
52         if ( coefficients[ 1 ] ) {
53            cout << coefficients[ 1 ] << 'x';  // constant does not exist
54                                               // so output first term
55                                               // without a sign
56            if ( ( exponents[ 1 ] != 0 ) && ( exponents[ 1 ] != 1 ) )
57               cout << '^' << exponents[ 1 ];
58
59            zero = true;  // at least one term exists
60         }
61
62         start = 2;
63      }
64
65      // output remaining polynomial terms
66      for ( int x = start; x < 100; ++x ) {
67         if ( coefficients[ x ] != 0 ) {
68            cout << setiosflags( ios::showpos ) << coefficients[ x ]
69                 << resetiosflags( ios::showpos ) << 'x';
70
71            if ( ( exponents[ x ] != 0 ) && ( exponents[ x ] != 1 ) )
72               cout << '^' << exponents[ x ];
73
74            zero = true;  // at least one term exists
75         }
76      }
77
78      if ( !zero )   // no terms exist in the polynomial
79         cout << '0';
80
81      cout << endl;
82   }
83
84   Polynomial Polynomial::operator+( const Polynomial& r ) const
85   {
86      Polynomial temp;
87      bool exponentExists;
88
89      // process element with a zero exponent
90      temp.coefficients[ 0 ] = coefficients[ 0 ] + r.coefficients[ 0 ];
91
```

```
92        // copy right arrays into temp object s will be used to keep
93        // track of first open coefficient element
94        for ( int s = 1; ( s < 100 ) && ( r.exponents[ s ] != 0 ); ++s ) {
95           temp.coefficients[ s ] = r.coefficients[ s ];
96           temp.exponents[ s ] = r.exponents[ s ];
97        }
98
99        for ( int x = 1; x < 100; ++x ) {
100          exponentExists = false; // assume exponent will not be found
101
102          for ( int t = 1; ( t < 100 ) && ( !exponentExists ); ++t )
103             if ( exponents[ x ] == temp.exponents[ t ] ) {
104                temp.coefficients[ t ] += coefficients[ x ];
105                exponentExists = true;   // exponent found
106             }
107
108          // exponent was not found, insert into temp
109          if ( !exponentExists ) {
110             temp.exponents[ s ] = exponents[ x ];
111             temp.coefficients[ s ] += coefficients[ x ];
112             ++s;
113          }
114       }
115
116       return temp;
117   }
118
119   Polynomial &Polynomial::operator+=( const Polynomial &r )
120   {
121      *this = *this + r;
122      return *this;
123   }
124
125   Polynomial Polynomial::operator-( const Polynomial& r ) const
126   {
127      Polynomial temp;
128      bool exponentExists;
129
130      // process element with a zero exponent
131      temp.coefficients[ 0 ] = coefficients[ 0 ] - r.coefficients[ 0 ];
132
133      // copy left arrays into temp object s will be used to keep
134      // track of first open coefficient element
135      for ( int s = 1; ( s < 100 ) && ( exponents[ s ] != 0 ); ++s ) {
136         temp.coefficients[ s ] = coefficients[ s ];
137         temp.exponents[ s ] = exponents[ s ];
138      }
139
140      for ( int x = 1; x < 100; ++x) {
141         exponentExists = false; // assume exponent will not be found
142
143         for ( int t = 1; ( t < 100 ) && !exponentExists ); ++t )
144            if ( r.exponents[ x ] == temp.exponents[ t ] ) {
145               temp.coefficients[ t ] -= r.coefficients[ x ];
146               exponentExists = true;   // exponent found
147            }
148
149         // exponent was not found, insert into temp
150         if ( !exponentExists ) {
151            temp.exponents[ s ] = r.exponents[ x ];
152            temp.coefficients[ s ] -= r.coefficients[ x ];
153            ++s;
154         }
155      }
```

```
156
157        return temp;
158   }
159
160   Polynomial &Polynomial::operator-=( const Polynomial& r )
161   {
162        *this = *this - r;
163        return *this;
164   }
165
166   Polynomial Polynomial::operator*( const Polynomial& r )
167   {
168        Polynomial temp;
169        int s = 1;        // subscript location for temp coefficients and exponents
170
171        for ( int x = 0; ( x < 100 ) && ( x == 0 || coefficients[ x ] != 0 ); ++x )
172          for ( int y = 0; ( y < 100 ) && ( y == 0 || r.coefficients[ y ] != 0 ); ++y )
173             if ( coefficients[ x ] * r.coefficients[ y ] )
174
175                if ( ( exponents[ x ] == 0 ) && ( r.exponents[ y ] == 0 ) )
176                  temp.coefficients[ 0 ] += coefficients[ x ] * r.coefficients[ y ];
177                else {
178                  temp.coefficients[ s ] = coefficients[ x ] * r.coefficients[ y ];
179                   temp.exponents[ s ] = exponents[ x ] + r.exponents[ y ];
180                   ++s;
181                }
182
183        polynomialCombine( temp );    // combine common terms
184        return temp;
185   }
186
187   void Polynomial::polynomialCombine( Polynomial& w )
188   {
189        Polynomial temp = w;
190        int exp;
191
192        // zero out elements of w
193        for ( int x = 0; x < 100; ++x ) {
194           w.coefficients[ x ] = 0;
195           w.exponents[ x ] = 0;
196        }
197
198        for ( x = 1; x < 100; ++x ) {
199           exp = temp.exponents[ x ];
200
201           for ( int y = x + 1; y < 100; ++y )
202             if ( exp == temp.exponents[ y ] ) {
203                temp.coefficients[ x ] += temp.coefficients[ y ];
204                temp.exponents[ y ] = 0;
205                temp.coefficients[ y ] = 0;
206             }
207        }
208
209        w = temp;
210   }
211
212   Polynomial &Polynomial::operator*=( const Polynomial& r )
213   {
214        *this = *this * r;
215        return *this;
216   }
217
```

```
218  void Polynomial::enterTerms( void )
219  {
220     bool found = false;
221     int numberOfTerms, c, e;
222
223     cout << "\nEnter number of polynomial terms: ";
224     cin >> numberOfTerms;
225
226     for ( int n = 1; n <= numberOfTerms; ++n ) {
227        cout << "\nEnter coefficient: ";
228        cin >> c;
229        cout << "Enter exponent: ";
230        cin >> e;
231
232        if ( c != 0 ) {
233           // exponents of zero are forced into first element
234           if ( e == 0 ) {
235              coefficients[ 0 ] += c;
236              continue;
237           }
238
239           for ( int term = 1; ( term < 100 ) &&
240                    ( coefficients[ term ] != 0 ); ++term )
241              if ( e == exponents[ term ] ) {
242                 coefficients[ term ] += c;
243                 exponents[ term ] = e;
244                 found = true;   // existing exponent updated
245              }
246
247           if ( !found ) {                 // add term
248              coefficients[ term ] += c;
249              exponents[ term ] = e;
250           }
251        }
252     }
253  }
```

```
254  // driver for p8_19.cpp
255  #include "p8_19p.h"
256
257  int main()
258  {
259     Polynomial a, b, c, t;
260
261     a.enterTerms();
262     b.enterTerms();
263     cout << "First polynomial is:\n";
264     a.printPolynomial();
265     cout << "Second polynomial is:\n";
266     b.printPolynomial();
267     cout << "\nAdding the polynomials yields:\n";
268     c = a + b;
269     c.printPolynomial();
270     cout << "\n+= the polynomials yields:\n";
271     t = a;  // save value of a
272     a += b;
273     a.printPolynomial();
274     cout << "\nSubtracting the polynomials yields:\n";
275     a = t;  // reset a to original value
276     c = a - b;
277     c.printPolynomial();
278     cout << "\n-= the polynomials yields:\n";
279     a -= b;
```

```
280    a.printPolynomial();
281    cout << "\nMultiplying the polynomials yields:\n";
282    a = t;  // reset a to original value
283    c = a * b;
284    c.printPolynomial();
285    cout << "\n*= the polynomials yields:\n";
286    a *= b;
287    a.printPolynomial();
288    cout << endl;
289    return 0;
290  }
```

```
Enter number of polynomial terms: 2

Enter coefficient: 2
Enter exponent: 2

Enter coefficient: 3
Enter exponent: 3

Enter number of polynomial terms: 3

Enter coefficient: 1
Enter exponent: 1

Enter coefficient: 2
Enter exponent: 2

Enter coefficient: 2
Enter exponent: 3

First polynomial is:
2x^2+3x^3
Second polynomial is:
1x+2x^2+3x^3

Adding the polynomials yields:
1x+4x^2+6x^3

+= the polynomials yields:
1x+4x^2+6x^3

Subtracting the polynomials yields:
-1x

-= the polynomials yields:
-1x

Multiplying the polynomials yields:
2x^3+7x^4+12x^5+9x^6

*= the polynomials yields:
2x^3+7x^4+12x^5+9x^6
```

8.20   The program of Fig. 8.3 contains the comment

```
// Overloaded stream-insertion operator (cannot be
// a member function if we would like to invoke it with
// cout << somePhoneNumber;)
```

Actually, it cannot be a member function of class **ostream**, but it can be a member function of class **PhoneNumber** if we were willing to invoke it in either of the following ways:

```
somePhoneNumber.operator<<( cout );
```

or

```
somePhoneNumber << cout;
```

Rewrite the program of Fig. 8.3 with the overloaded stream-insertion **operator<<** as a member function and try the two preceding statements in the program to prove that they work.

Chapter 9 Solutions

Inheritance

Solutions

9.2 Consider the class **Bicycle**. Given your knowledge of some common components of bicycles, show a class hierarchy in which the class **Bicycle** inherits from other classes, which, in turn, inherit from yet other classes. Discuss the instantiation of various objects of class **Bicycle**. Discuss inheritance from class **Bicycle** for other closely related derived classes.

       ANS: Possible classes are displayed in bold.

       Bicycle composed of:
           HandleBars
           Seat
           Frame
           Wheels composed of:
                Tires
                Rims composed of:
                      Spokes
           Pedals
           Chain composed of:
                Links
           Brakes composed of:
                Wires
                BrakePads
                BrakeHandles

       Classes that can be derived from **Bicycle** are **Unicycle**, **Tricycle**, **TandemBicycle**, etc.

9.3 Briefly define each of the following terms: inheritance, multiple inheritance, base class and derived class.
       ANS:
       inheritance: The process by which a class incorporates the attributes and behaviors of a previously defined class.
       multiple inheritance: The process by which a class incorporates the attributes and behaviors of two or more previously defined classes.
       base class: A class from which other classes inherit attributes and behaviors.
       derived class: A class that has inherited attributes and behaviors from one or more base classes.

9.4 Discuss why converting a base-class pointer to a derived-class pointer is considered dangerous by the compiler.
       ANS: The pointer must "point" to the object of the derived class, before being dereferenced. When the compiler looks at an object through a derived-class pointer, it expects to see the all the pieces of the derived class. However, if the base-class pointer originally pointed to a base-class object, the additional pieces added by the derived class do not exist.

9.5 Distinguish between single inheritance and multiple inheritance.
       ANS: Single inheritance inherits from one class only. Multiple inheritance inherits from two or more classes.

9.6 (True/False) A derived class is often called a subclass because it represents a subset of its base class, i.e., a derived class is generally smaller than its base class.
       ANS: False. Derived classes are often larger than their base classes, because they need specific features in addition to those inherited from the base class. The term subclass means that the derived class is a more specific version of its base class. For example, a cat is a specific type of animal.

9.7 (True/False) A derived-class object is also an object of that derived class's base class.
ANS: True.

9.8 Some programmers prefer not to use **protected** access because it breaks the encapsulation of the base class. Discuss the relative merits of using **protected** access vs. insisting on using **private** access in base classes.
ANS: Inherited **private** data is hidden in the derived class and is accessible only through the **public** or **protected** member functions of the base class. Using **protected** access enables the derived class to manipulate the **protected** members without using the base class access functions. If the base class members are **private**, the **public** or **protected** member functions of the base class must be used to access **private** members. This can result in additional function calls—which can decrease performance.

9.9 Many programs written with inheritance could be solved with composition instead, and vice versa. Discuss the relative merits of these approaches in the context of the **Point**, **Circle**, **Cylinder** class hierarchy in this chapter. Rewrite the program of Fig. 9.10 (and the supporting classes) to use composition rather than inheritance. After you do this, reassess the relative merits of the two approaches both for the **Point**, **Circle**, **Cylinder** problem and for object-oriented programs in general.
ANS:

```
1  // P9_09.H
2  #ifndef P9_09_H
3  #define P9_09_H
4
5  class Point {
6     friend ostream &operator<<( ostream &, const Point & );
7  public:
8     Point( double a = 0, double b = 0 ) { setPoint( a, b ); }
9     void setPoint( double, double );
10    void print( void ) const;
11    double getX( void ) const { return x; }
12    double getY( void ) const { return y; }
13 private:
14    double x, y;
15 };
16
17 #endif
```

```
18 // P9_09PM.cpp
19 // Member functions for class Point
20 #include <iostream.h>
21 #include "p9_09.h"
22
23 void Point::setPoint( double a, double b )
24 {
25    x = a;
26    y = b;
27 }
28
29 ostream &operator<<( ostream &output, const Point &p )
30 {
31    p.print();
32    return output;
33 }
34
35 void Point::print( void ) const
36    { cout << '[' << getX() << ", " << getY() << ']'; }
```

```
37 // P9_09C.H
38 #ifndef P9_09C_H
39 #define P9_09C_H
40 #include "p9_09.h"
41
```

```
42  class Circle {
43      friend ostream &operator<<( ostream &, const Circle & );
44  public:
45      Circle( double = 0.0, double = 0.0, double = 0.0 );
46      void setRadius( double r ) { radius = r; }
47      double getRadius( void ) const { return radius; }
48      double area( void ) const;
49      void print( void ) const;
50  private:
51      double radius;
52      Point pointObject;
53  };
54
55  #endif
```

```
56  // P9_09CM.cpp
57  // Member function definitions for class Circle
58  #include <iostream.h>
59  #include <iomanip.h>
60  #include "p9_09c.h"
61
62  Circle::Circle( double r, double a, double b ) : pointObject( a, b )
63      { setRadius( r ); }
64
65  double Circle::area( void ) const
66      { return 3.14159 * getRadius() * getRadius(); }
67
68  ostream &operator<<( ostream &output, const Circle &c )
69  {
70      c.print();
71      return output;
72  }
73
74  void Circle::print( void ) const
75  {
76      cout << "Center = ";
77      pointObject.print();
78      cout << "; Radius = " << setiosflags( ios::fixed | ios::showpoint )
79          << setprecision( 2 ) << getRadius()
80          << resetiosflags( ios::fixed | ios::showpoint );
81  }
```

```
82   // P9_09CY.H
83   #ifndef P9_09CY_H
84   #define P9_09CY_H
85   #include "p9_09.h"
86   #include "p9_09c.h"
87
88   class Cylinder {
89       friend ostream& operator<<(ostream&, const Cylinder&);
90   public:
91       Cylinder(double = 0.0, double = 0.0, double = 0.0, double = 0.0);
92       void setHeight(double h) { height = h; }
93       double getHeight(void) const { return height; }
94       void print(void) const;
95       double area(void) const;
96       double volume(void) const;
97   private:
98       double height;
99       Circle circleObject;
100  };
101
102  #endif
```

```
103  // P9_09CYM.cpp
104  // Member function definitions for class Cylinder.
105  #include <iostream.h>
106  #include <iomanip.h>
107  #include "p9_09cy.h"
108
109  Cylinder::Cylinder( double h, double r, double x, double y )
110     : circleObject( r, x, y ) { height = h; }
111
112  double Cylinder::area( void ) const
113     { return 2 * circleObject.area() + 2 * 3.14159 *
114       circleObject.getRadius() * getHeight(); }
115
116  ostream& operator<<( ostream &output, const Cylinder& c )
117  {
118     c.print();
119     return output;
120  }
121
122  double Cylinder::volume( void ) const
123     { return circleObject.area() * getHeight(); }
124
125  void Cylinder::print( void ) const
126  {
127     circleObject.print();
128     cout << "; Height = " << getHeight() << '\n';
129  }
```

```
130  // P9_09.cpp
131  #include <iostream.h>
132  #include <iomanip.h>
133  #include "p9_09.h"
134  #include "p9_09c.h"
135  #include "p9_09cy.h"
136
137  int main()
138  {
139     Point p( 1.1, 8.5 );
140     Circle c( 2.0, 6.4, 9.8 );
141     Cylinder cyl( 5.7, 2.5, 1.2, 2.3 );
142
143     cout << "Point: " << p << "\nCircle: " << c
144        << "\nCylinder: " << cyl << endl;
145
146     return 0;
147  }
```

```
Point: [1.1, 8.5]
Circle: Center = [6.4, 9.8]; Radius = 2.00
Cylinder: Center = [1.2, 2.3]; Radius = 2.50; Height = 5.7
```

9.10   Rewrite the **Point**, **Circle**, **Cylinder** program of Fig. 9.10 as a **Point**, **Square**, **Cube** program. Do this two ways—once with inheritance and once with composition.

   ANS:

   Inheritance solution. All relevant files do NOT have a 'b' in the file name.

```
1  // P9_10.H
2  #ifndef P9_10_H
3  #define P9_10_H
4
```

```
5   class Point {
6       friend ostream &operator<<( ostream&, const Point& );
7   public:
8       Point( double = 0, double = 0, double = 0 );
9       void setPoint( double, double, double );
10      double getX( void ) const { return x; }
11      double getY( void ) const { return y; }
12      double getZ( void ) const { return z; }
13  private:
14      double x, y, z;
15  };
16
17  #endif
```

```
18  //P9_10MP.cpp
19  // member function defintions for class Point
20  #include <iostream.h>
21  #include <iomanip.h>
22  #include "p9_10.h"
23
24  Point::Point( double a, double b, double c) { setPoint( a, b, c ); }
25
26  void Point::setPoint( double a, double b, double c )
27  {
28      x = a;
29      y = b;
30      z = c;
31  }
32
33  ostream &operator<<( ostream &output, const Point &p )
34  {
35      output << setiosflags( ios::fixed | ios::showpoint )
36              << "The point is: [" << setprecision( 2 ) << p.x
37              << ", " << setprecision( 2 ) << p.y << setprecision( 2 )
38              << ", " << p.z << "]\n"
39              << resetiosflags( ios::fixed | ios::showpoint );
40      return output;
41  }
```

```
42  //P9_10S.H
43  #ifndef P9_10S_H
44  #define P9_10S_H
45  #include "p9_10.h"
46
47  class Square : public Point {
48      friend ostream &operator<<( ostream &, const Square & );
49  public:
50      Square( double = 0, double = 0, double = 0, double = 1.0 );
51      void setSide( double s) { side = s > 0 && s <= 20.0 ? s : 1.0; }
52      double area( void ) const { return side * side; }
53      double getSide( void ) const { return side; }
54  protected:
55      double side;
56  };
57
58  #endif
```

```
59  //P9_10MS.cpp
60  //member functions for class Square
61  #include <iostream.h>
62  #include <iomanip.h>
63  #include "p9_10s.h"
```

```
64
65  Square::Square( double x, double y, double z, double s ) : Point( x, y, z )
66     { setSide( s ); }
67
68  ostream &operator<<( ostream &output, const Square &s )
69  {
70     output << setiosflags( ios::fixed | ios::showpoint )
71            << "The lower left coordinate of the square is: ["
72            << setprecision( 2 ) << s.getX() << ", " << setprecision( 2 )
73            << s.getY() << ", " << setprecision( 2 ) << s.getZ() << ']'
74            << "\nThe square side is: " << setprecision( 2 ) << s.side
75            << "\nThe area of the square is: " << setprecision( 2 )
76            << s.area() << '\n'
77            << resetiosflags( ios::fixed | ios::showpoint );
78
79     return output;
80  }
```

```
81  // P9_10C.H
82  #ifndef P9_10C_H
83  #define P9_10C_H
84  #include "p9_10s.h"
85
86  class Cube : public Square {
87     friend ostream &operator<<( ostream&, const Cube& );
88  public:
89     Cube( double = 0, double = 0, double = 0, double = 1.0 );
90     double area( void ) const { return 6 * Square::area(); }
91     double volume( void ) const { return Square::area() * getSide(); }
92  };
93
94  #endif
```

```
95  //P9_10MC.cpp
96  //member function definitions for class Cube
97  #include <iostream.h>
98  #include <iomanip.h>
99  #include "p9_10c.h"
100
101 Cube::Cube( double j, double k, double m, double s ) : Square( j, k, m, s ) { }
102
103 ostream &operator<<( ostream &output, const Cube &c )
104 {
105    output << setiosflags( ios::fixed | ios::showpoint )
106           << "The lower left coordinate of the cube is: ["
107           << setprecision( 2 ) << c.getX() << ", " << setprecision( 2 )
108           << c.getY() << ", " << setprecision( 2 ) << c.getZ()
109           << "]\nThe cube side is: " << setprecision( 2 ) << c.side
110           << "\nThe surface area of the cube is: " << setprecision( 2 )
111           << c.area() << "\nThe volume of the cube is: "
112           << setprecision( 2 ) << c.volume()
113           << resetiosflags( ios::showpoint | ios::fixed ) << '\n';
114
115    return output;
116 }
```

```
117 // driver for p9_10.cpp
118 #include <iostream.h>
119 #include <iomanip.h>
120 #include "p9_10.h"
121 #include "p9_10s.h"
122 #include "p9_10c.h"
```

```
123
124  int main()
125  {
126      Point p( 7.9, 12.5, 8.8 );
127      Square s( 0.0, 0.0, 0.0, 5.0 );
128      Cube c( 0.5, 8.3, 12.0, 2.0 );
129
130      cout << p << '\n' << s << '\n' << c << '\n';
131      return 0;
132  }
```

```
The point is: [7.90, 12.50, 8.80]

The lower left coordinate of the square is: [0.00, 0.00,
0.00]
The square side is: 5.00
The area of the square is: 25.00

The lower left coordinate of the cube is: [0.50, 8.30,
12.00]
The cube side is: 2.00
The surface area of the cube is: 24.00
The volume of the cube is: 8.00
```

Composition solution. All relevant files have a 'b' in the file name.

```
1   // P9_10B.H
2   #ifndef P9_10B_H
3   #define P9_10B_H
4
5   class Point {
6       friend ostream &operator<<( ostream&, const Point& );
7   public:
8       Point( double = 0, double = 0, double = 0 );
9       void setPoint( double, double, double );
10      void print( void ) const;
11      double getX( void ) const { return x; }
12      double getY( void ) const { return y; }
13      double getZ( void ) const { return z; }
14  private:
15      double x, y, z;
16  };
17
18  #endif
```

```
19  //P9_10BMP.cpp
20  // member function defintions for class Point
21  #include <iostream.h>
22  #include <iomanip.h>
23  #include "p9_10b.h"
24
25  Point::Point( double a, double b, double c ) { setPoint( a, b, c ); }
26
27  void Point::setPoint( double a, double b, double c )
28  {
29      x = a;
30      y = b;
31      z = c;
32  }
33
```

```
34   ostream &operator<<( ostream &output, const Point &p )
35   {
36       output << "The point is: ";
37       p.print();
38       return output;
39   }
40
41   void Point::print( void ) const
42   {
43       cout << setiosflags( ios::fixed | ios::showpoint )
44           << '[' << setprecision( 2 ) << getX()
45           << ", " << setprecision( 2 ) << getY() << setprecision( 2 )
46           << ", " << getZ() << "]\n"
47           << resetiosflags( ios::fixed | ios::showpoint );
48   }
```

```
49   //P9_10BS.H
50   #ifndef P9_10BS_H
51   #define P9_10BS_H
52   #include "p9_10B.h"
53
54   class Square {
55       friend ostream &operator<<( ostream &, const Square & );
56   public:
57       Square( double = 0, double = 0, double = 0, double = 1.0 );
58       void setSide( double s ) { side = s > 0 && s <= 20.0 ? s : 1.0; }
59       void print( void ) const;
60       double getXCoord() const { return pointObject.getX(); }
61       double getYCoord() const { return pointObject.getY(); }
62       double getZCoord() const { return pointObject.getZ(); }
63       double area( void ) const { return side * side; }
64       double getSide( void ) const { return side; }
65   protected:
66       double side;
67       Point pointObject;
68   };
69
70   #endif
```

```
71   //P9_10BMS.cpp
72   //member functions for class Square
73   #include <iostream.h>
74   #include <iomanip.h>
75   #include "p9_10bs.h"
76   Square::Square( double x, double y, double z, double s )
77          : pointObject( x, y, z )
78      { setSide( s ); }
79
80   ostream &operator<<( ostream &output, const Square &s )
81   {
82       s.print();
83       return output;
84   }
85
86   void Square::print( void ) const
87   {
88       cout << setiosflags( ios::fixed | ios::showpoint )
89           << "The lower left coordinate of the square is: ";
90       pointObject.print();
91       cout << "The square side is: " << setprecision( 2 ) << getSide()
92           << "\nThe area of the square is: " << setprecision( 2 )
93           << area() << '\n';
94   }
```

```
95   // P9_10BC.H
96   #ifndef P9_10BC_H
97   #define P9_10BC_H
98   #include "p9_10bs.h"
99
100  class Cube {
101      friend ostream &operator<<( ostream&, const Cube& );
102  public:
103      Cube( double = 0, double = 0, double = 0, double = 1.0 );
104      void print( void ) const;
105      double area( void ) const;
106      double volume( void ) const;
107  private:
108      Square squareObject;
109  };
110
111  #endif
```

```
112  //P9_10BMC.cpp
113  //member function definitions for class Cube
114  #include <iostream.h>
115  #include <iomanip.h>
116  #include "p9_10bc.h"
117
118  Cube::Cube( double j, double k, double m, double s )
119      : squareObject( j, k, m, s ) { }
120
121  ostream &operator<<( ostream &output, const Cube &c )
122  {
123      c.print();
124      return output;
125  }
126
127  void Cube::print( void ) const
128  {
129      cout << setiosflags( ios::fixed | ios::showpoint )
130          << "The lower left coordinate of the cube is: [" << setprecision( 2 )
131          << squareObject.getXCoord() << ", " << setprecision( 2 )
132          << squareObject.getYCoord() << ", " << setprecision( 2 )
133          << squareObject.getZCoord() << "]\nThe cube side is: "
134          << setprecision( 2 ) << squareObject.getSide()
135          << "\nThe surface area of the cube is: " << setprecision( 2 ) << area()
136          << "\nThe volume of the cube is: " << setprecision( 2 ) << volume() << '\n';
137  }
138
139  double Cube::area( void ) const  { return 6 * squareObject.area(); }
140
141  double Cube::volume( void ) const
142      { return squareObject.area() * squareObject.getSide(); }
```

```
143  // driver for p9_10b.cpp
144  #include <iostream.h>
145  #include <iomanip.h>
146  #include "p9_10b.h"
147  #include "p9_10bs.h"
148  #include "p9_10bc.h"
149
150  int main()
151  {
152      Point p( 7.9, 12.5, 8.8 );
153      Square s( 0.0, 0.0, 0.0, 5.0 );
154      Cube c( 0.5, 8.3, 12.0, 2.0 );
155
```

```
156    cout << p << '\n' << s << '\n' << c << endl;
157    return 0;
158 }
```

```
The point is: [7.90, 12.50, 8.80]

The lower left coordinate of the square is: [0.00, 0.00,
0.00]
The square side is: 5
The area of the square is: 25

The lower left coordinate of the cube is: [0.50, 8.30,
12.00]
The cube side is: 2.00
The surface area of the cube is: 24.00
The volume of the cube is: 8.00
```

9.11 In the chapter, we stated, "When a base-class member is inappropriate for a derived class, that member can be overridden in the derived class with an appropriate implementation." If this is done, does the derived-class-is-a-base-class-object relationship still hold? Explain your answer.

ANS: No. The "is a" relationship assumes that everything that belongs to the base class object belongs to the derived class object and also assumes that all functionality of the base class is present in the derived class object as well.

9.12 Study the inheritance hierarchy of Fig. 9.2. For each class, indicate some common attributes and behaviors consistent with the hierarchy. Add some other classes (e.g., **UndergraduateStudent**, **GraduateStudent**, **Freshman**, **Sophomore**, **Junior**, **Senior**, etc.) to enrich the hierarchy.

ANS:

```
CommunityMember
    Employee
        Staff
            Maintenance
            Janitorial
        Faculty
            Administrator
            Professor
                TenuredProfessor
    Student
        Graduate
            MasterCandidate
            DoctoralCandidate
        Undergraduate
            Freshman
            Sophomore
            Junior
            Senior
```

9.13 Write an inheritance hierarchy for class **Quadrilateral**, **Trapezoid**, **Parallelogram**, **Rectangle** and **Square**. Use **Quadrilateral** as the base class of the hierarchy. Make the hierarchy as deep (i.e., as many levels) as possible. The private data of **Quadrilateral** should be the *(x, y)* coordinate pairs for the four endpoints of the **Quadrilateral**. Write a driver program that instantiates and displays objects of each of these classes.

ANS:

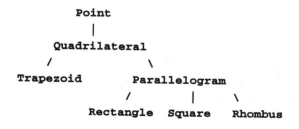

```
1    // P9_13.H
2    #ifndef P9_13_H
3    #define P9_13_H
4    #include <iostream.h>
5
6    class Point {
7        friend ostream &operator<<( ostream&, const Point& );
8    public:
9        Point( double = 0, double = 0 );
10       void setPoint( double, double );
11       void print( void ) const;
12       double getX( void ) const { return x; }
13       double getY( void ) const { return y; }
14   private:
15       double x, y;
16   };
17
18   #endif
```

```
19   //P9_13PM.cpp
20   // member function defintions for class Point
21   #include <iostream.h>
22   #include <iomanip.h>
23   #include "p9_13.h"
24
25   Point::Point( double a, double b ) { setPoint( a, b ); }
26
27   void Point::setPoint( double a, double b )
28   {
29       x = a;
30       y = b;
31   }
32
33   ostream &operator<<( ostream &output, const Point &p )
34   {
35       output << "The point is: ";
36       p.print();
37       return output;
38   }
39
40   void Point::print( void ) const
41   {
42       cout << setiosflags( ios::fixed | ios::showpoint )
43            << '[' << setprecision( 2 ) << getX()
44            << ", " << setprecision( 2 ) << getY() << "]\n"
45            << resetiosflags( ios::fixed | ios::showpoint );
46   }
```

```
47   // P9_13Q.H
48   #ifndef P9_13Q_H
49   #define P9_13Q_H
50   #include "p9_13.h"
51
52   class Quadrilateral {
53       friend ostream &operator<<( ostream&, Quadrilateral& );
54   public:
55       Quadrilateral( double = 0, double = 0, double = 0, double = 0, double = 0,
56                      double = 0, double = 0, double = 0 );
57       void print( void ) const;
58   protected:
59       Point p1;
60       Point p2;
```

```
61      Point p3;
62      Point p4;
63   };
64
65   #endif
```

```
66   // P9_13QM.cpp
67   // member functions for class Quadrilateral
68   #include "p9_13q.h"
69
70   Quadrilateral::Quadrilateral( double x1, double y1, double x2, double y2,
71                                 double x3, double y3, double x4, double y4 )
72      : p1( x1, y1 ), p2( x2, y2 ), p3( x3, y3 ), p4( x4, y4 )  { }
73
74   ostream &operator<<( ostream& output, Quadrilateral& q )
75   {
76      output << "Coordinates of Quadrilateral are:\n";
77      q.print();
78      output << '\n';
79      return output;
80   }
81
82   void Quadrilateral::print( void ) const
83   {
84      cout << '(' << p1.getX()
85           << ", " << p1.getY() << ") , (" << p2.getX() << ", " << p2.getY()
86           << ") , (" << p3.getX() << ", " << p3.getY() << ") , ("
87           << p4.getX() << ", " << p4.getY() << ")\n";
88   }
```

```
89   // P9_13T.H
90   #ifndef P9_13T_H
91   #define P9_13T_H
92   #include "p9_13q.h"
93
94   class Trapazoid : public Quadrilateral {
95      friend ostream& operator<<( ostream&, Trapazoid& );
96   public:
97      Trapazoid( double = 0, double = 0, double = 0, double = 0, double = 0,
98                 double = 0, double = 0, double = 0, double = 0 );
99      void print( void ) const;
100     void setHeight( double h ) { height = h; }
101     double getHeight( void ) const { return height; }
102  private:
103     double height;
104  };
105
106  #endif
```

```
107  // P9_13TM.cpp
108  // member function definitions for class Trapazoid
109  #include "p9_13t.h"
110
111  Trapazoid::Trapazoid( double h, double x1, double y1, double x2, double y2,
112                        double x3, double y3, double x4, double y4 )
113          : Quadrilateral( x1, y1, x2, y2, x3, y3, x4, y4 )
114  { setHeight( h ); }
115
116  ostream& operator<<( ostream& out, Trapazoid& t )
117  {
118     out << "The Coordinates of the Trapazoid are:\n";
119     t.print();
```

```
120      return out;
121  }
122
123  void Trapazoid::print( void ) const
124  {
125      Quadrilateral::print();
126      cout << "Height is : " << getHeight() << "\n\n";
127  }
```

```
128  // P9_13PA_H
129  #ifndef P9_13PA_H
130  #define P9_13PA_H
131  #include "p9_13q.h"
132
133  class Parallelogram : public Quadrilateral {
134      friend ostream& operator<<( ostream&, Parallelogram& );
135  public:
136      Parallelogram( double = 0, double = 0, double = 0, double = 0,
137                     double = 0, double = 0, double = 0, double = 0 );
138      void print( void ) const;
139  private:
140      // no private data members
141  };
142
143  #endif
```

```
144  // P9_13PAM.cpp
145  #include "p9_13q.h"
146  #include "p9_13pa.h"
147
148  Parallelogram::Parallelogram( double x1, double y1, double x2, double y2,
149                                double x3, double y3, double x4, double y4 )
150      : Quadrilateral( x1, y1, x2, y2, x3, y3, x4, y4 ) { }
151
152  ostream& operator<<( ostream& out, Parallelogram& pa )
153  {
154      out << "The coordinates of the Parallelogram are:\n";
155      pa.print();
156      return out;
157  }
158
159  void Parallelogram::print( void ) const
160      {   Quadrilateral::print();    }
```

```
161  // P9_13R.H
162  #ifndef P9_13R_H
163  #define P9_13R_H
164  #include "p9_13pa.h"
165
166  class Rectangle : public Parallelogram {
167      friend ostream& operator<<( ostream&, Rectangle& );
168  public:
169      Rectangle( double = 0, double = 0, double = 0, double = 0,
170                 double = 0, double = 0, double = 0, double = 0 );
171      void print( void ) const;
172  private:
173      // no private data members
174  };
175
176  #endif
```

```
177  // P9_13RM.cpp
178  #include "p9_13r.h"
179  #include "p9_13pa.h"
180
181  Rectangle::Rectangle( double x1, double y1, double x2, double y2,
182                        double x3, double y3, double x4, double y4 )
183     : Parallelogram( x1, y1, x2, y2, x3, y3, x4, y4 ) { }
184
185  ostream& operator<<( ostream& out, Rectangle& r )
186  {
187     out << "\nThe coordinates of the Rectangle are:\n";
188     r.print();
189     return out;
190  }
191
192  void Rectangle::print( void ) const
193     {  Parallelogram::print(); }
```

```
194  // P9_13RH.H
195  #ifndef P9_13RH_H
196  #define P9_13RH_H
197  #include "p9_13pa.h"
198
199  class Rhombus : public Parallelogram {
200     friend ostream& operator<<(ostream&, Rhombus&);
201  public:
202     Rhombus( double = 0, double = 0, double = 0, double = 0, double = 0,
203             double = 0, double = 0, double = 0 );
204     void print( void ) const { Parallelogram::print(); }
205  private:
206     // no private data members
207  };
208
209  #endif
```

```
210  //P9_13HM.cpp
211  #include "p9_13rh.h"
212  #include "p9_13pa.h"
213
214  Rhombus::Rhombus( double x1, double y1, double x2, double y2,
215                    double x3, double y3, double x4, double y4 )
216     : Parallelogram( x1, y1, x2, y2, x3, y3, x4, y4 ) { }
217
218  ostream& operator<<( ostream& out, Rhombus& r )
219  {
220     out << "\nThe coordinates of the Rhombus are:\n";
221     r.print();
222     return out;
223  }
```

```
224  // P9_13S.H
225  #ifndef P9_13S_H
226  #define P9_13S_H
227  #include "p9_13pa.h"
228
229  class Square : public Parallelogram {
230     friend ostream& operator<<( ostream&, Square& );
231  public:
232     Square( double = 0, double = 0, double = 0, double = 0,
233             double = 0, double = 0, double = 0, double = 0 );
234     void print( void ) const { Parallelogram::print(); }
```

```
235  private:
236      // no private data members
237  };
238
239  #endif
```

```
240  // P9_13SM.cpp
241  #include "p9_13s.h"
242  #include "p9_13pa.h"
243
244  Square::Square( double x1, double y1, double x2, double y2,
245                  double x3, double y3, double x4, double y4 )
246      : Parallelogram( x1, y1, x2, y2, x3, y3, x4, y4 ) { }
247
248  ostream& operator<<( ostream& out, Square& s )
249  {
250      out << "\nThe coordinates of the Square are:\n";
251      s.print();
252      return out;
253  }
```

```
254  // P9_13.cpp
255  #include "p9_13.h"
256  #include "p9_13q.h"
257  #include "p9_13t.h"
258  #include "p9_13pa.h"
259  #include "p9_13rh.h"
260  #include "p9_13r.h"
261  #include "p9_13s.h"
262
263  int main()
264  {
265      // NOTE: All coordinates are assumed to form the proper shapes
266
267      // A quadrilateral is a four-sided polygon
268      Quadrilateral q( 1.1, 1.2, 6.6, 2.8, 6.2, 9.9, 2.2, 7.4 );
269      // A trapezoid is a quadrilateral having two and only two parallel sides
270      Trapezoid t( 5.0, 0.0, 0.0, 10.0, 0.0, 8.0, 5.0, 3.3, 5.0 );
271      // A parallelogram is a quadrilateral whose opposite sides are parallel
272      Parallelogram p( 5.0, 5.0, 11.0, 5.0, 12.0, 20.0, 6.0, 20.0 );
273      // A rhombus is an equilateral parallelogram
274      Rhombus rh( 0.0, 0.0, 5.0, 0.0, 8.5, 3.5, 3.5, 3.5 );
275      // A rectangle is an equiangular parallelogram
276      Rectangle r( 17.0, 14.0, 30.0, 14.0, 30.0, 28.0, 17.0, 28.0 );
277      // A square is an equiangular and equilateral parallelogram
278      Square s( 4.0, 0.0, 8.0, 0.0, 8.0, 4.0, 4.0, 4.0 );
279
280      cout << q << t << p << rh << r << s << endl;
281      return 0;
282  }
```

```
Coordinates of Quadrilateral are:
(1.1, 1.2) , (6.6, 2.8) , (6.2, 9.9) , (2.2, 7.4)

The Coordinates of the Trapazoid are:
(0, 0) , (10, 0) , (8, 5) , (3.3, 5)
Height is : 5

The coordinates of the Parallelogram are:
(5, 5) , (11, 5) , (12, 20) , (6, 20)
```

```
The coordinates of the Rhombus are:
(0, 0) , (5, 0) , (8.5, 3.5) , (3.5, 3.5)

The coordinates of the Rectangle are:
(17, 14) , (30, 14) , (30, 28) , (17, 28)

The coordinates of the Square are:
(4, 0) , (8, 0) , (8, 4) , (4, 4)
```

9.14 Write down all the shapes you can think of—both two-dimensional and three-dimensional—and form those shapes into a shape hierarchy. Your hierarchy should have base class **Shape** from which class **TwoDimensionalShape** and class **ThreeDimensionalShape** are derived. Once you have developed the hierarchy, define each of the classes in the hierarchy. We will use this hierarchy in the exercises of Chapter 10 to process all shapes as objects of base-class **Shape**. This is a technique called polymorphism.

```
ANS:
Shape
    TwoDimensionalShape
        Quadrilateral
            Parallelogram
                Rectangle
                    Square
                Rhombus
        Ellipse
            Circle
        Triangle
            RightTriangle
            EquilateralTriangle
            IsocelesTriangle
        Parabola
        Line
        Hyperbola
    ThreeDimensionalShape
        Ellipsoid
            Sphere
        Prism
        Cylinder
        Cone
        Cube
        Tetrahedron
        Hyperboloid
            OneSheetHyperboloid
            TwoSheetHyperboloid
        Plane
```

Chapter 10 Solutions
Virtual Functions and Polymorphism

Solutions

10.2   What are **virtual** functions? Describe a circumstance in which **virtual** functions would be appropriate.

ANS: Virtual functions are functions with the same function prototype that are defined throughout a class hierarchy. At least the base class occurrence of the function is preceded by the keyword **virtual**. Virtual functions are used to enable generic processing of an entire class hierarchy of objects through a base class pointer. For example, in a shape hierarchy, all shapes can be drawn. If all shapes are derived from a base class **Shape** which contains a **virtual** **draw** function, then generic processing of the hierarchy can be performed by calling every shape's **draw** generically through a base class **Shape** pointer.

10.3   Given that constructors cannot be **virtual**, describe a scheme for how you might achieve a similar effect.

ANS: Create a virtual function called **initialize** that the constructor invokes.

10.4   How is it that polymorphism enables you to program "in the general" rather than "in the specific." Discuss the key advantages of programming "in the general."

ANS: Polymorphism enables the programmer to concentrate on the processing of common operations that are applied to all data types in the system without going into the individual details of each data type. The general processing capabilities are separated from the internal details of each type.

10.5   Discuss the problems of programming with **switch** logic. Explain why polymorphism is an effective alternative to using **switch** logic.

ANS: The main problem with programming using the **switch** structure is extensibility and maintainability of the program. A program containing many **switch** structures is difficult to modify. Many, but not necessarily all, **switch** structures will need to add or remove cases for a specified type. Note: switch logic includes if/else structures which are more flexible than the **switch** structure.

10.6   Distinguish between static binding and dynamic binding. Explain the use of **virtual** functions and the *vtable* in dynamic binding.

ANS: Static binding is performed at compile-time when a function is called via a specific object or via a pointer to an object. Dynamic binding is performed at run-time when a **virtual** function is called via a base class pointer to a derived class object (the object can be of any derived class). The **virtual** functions table (vtable) is used at run-time to enable the proper function to be called for the object to which the base class pointer "points". Each class containing **virtual** functions has its own vtable that specifies where the **virtual** functions for that class are located. Every object of a class with **virtual** functions contains a hidden pointer to the class's vtable. When a **virtual** function is called via a base class pointer, the hidden pointer is dereferenced to locate the vtable, then the vtable is searched for the proper function call.

10.7   Distinguish between inheriting interface and inheriting implementation. How do inheritance hierarchies designed for inheriting interface differ from those designed for inheriting implementation?

ANS: When a class inherits implementation, it inherits previously defined functionality from another class. When a class inherits interface, it inherits the definition of what the interface to the new class type should be. The implementation is then provided by the programmer defining the new class type. Inheritance hierarchies designed for inheriting implementation are used to reduce the amont of new code that is being written. Such hierarchies are used to facilitate software reusability. Inheritance hierarchies designed for inheriting interface are used to write programs that perform generic processing of many class types. Such hierarchies are commonly used to facilitate software extensibility (i.e., new types can be added to the hierarchy without changing the generic processing capabilitiesof the program.)

10.8 Distinguish between **virtual** functions and pure **virtual** functions.
ANS: A **virtual** function must have a definition in the class in which it is declared. A pure **virtual** function does not provide a definition. Classes derived directly from the abstract class must provide definitions for the inherited pure **virtual** functions in order to avoid becoming an abstract base class.

10.9 (True/False) All **virtual** functions in an abstract base class must be declared as pure **virtual** functions.
ANS: False.

10.10 Suggest one or more levels of abstract base classes for the **Shape** hierarchy discussed in this chapter (the first level is **Shape** and the second level consists of the classes **TwoDimensionalShape** and **ThreeDimensionalShape**).

10.11 How does polymorphism promote extensibility?
ANS: Polymorphism makes programs more extensible by making all function calls generic. When a new class type with the appropriate **virtual** functions is added to the hierarchy, no changes need to be made to the generic function calls.

10.12 You have been asked to develop a flight simulator that will have elaborate graphical outputs. Explain why polymorphic programming would be especially effective for a problem of this nature.

10.13 Develop a basic graphics package. Use the **Shape** class inheritance hierarchy from Chapter 9. Limit yourself to two-dimensional shapes such as squares, rectangles, triangles and circles. Interact with the user. Let the user specify the position, size, shape and fill characters to be used in drawing each shape. The user can specify many items of the same shape. As you create each shape, place a **Shape *** pointer to each new **Shape** object into an array. Each class has its own **draw** member function. Write a polymorphic screen manager that walks through the array (preferably using an iterator) sending **draw** messages to each object in the array to form a screen image. Redraw the screen image each time the user specifies an additional shape.

10.14 Modify the payroll system of Fig. 10.1 to add private data members **birthDate** (a **Date** object) and **department-Code** (an **int**) to class **Employee**. Assume this payroll is processed once per month. Then, as your program calculates the payroll for each **Employee** (polymorphically), add a $100.00 bonus to the person's payroll amount if this is the month in which the **Employee**'s birthday occurs.
ANS:

```
1   // EMPLOY.H
2   // Abstract base class Employee
3   #ifndef EMPLOY_H
4   #define EMPLOY_H
5
6   #include "date.h"
7
8   class Employee {
9   public:
10     Employee( const char * const, const char * const,
11              int, int, int, int);
12     ~Employee();
13     const char *getFirstName() const;
14     const char *getLastName() const;
15     Date getBirthDate() const;
16     int getDepartmentCode() const;
17
18     // Pure virtual functions make Employee abstract base class.
19     virtual double earnings() const = 0; // pure virtual
20     virtual void print() const = 0;      // pure virtual
21   private:
22     char *firstName;
23     char *lastName;
24     Date birthDate;
25     int departmentCode;
26   };
27
28   #endif
```

```
29  // EMPLOY.CPP
30  // Member function definitions for
31  // abstract base class Employee.
32  //
33  // Note: No definitions given for pure virtual functions.
34  #include <iostream.h>
35  #include <string.h>
36  #include <assert.h>
37  #include "employ.h"
38
39  // Constructor dynamically allocates space for the
40  // first and last name and uses strcpy to copy
41  // the first and last names into the object.
42  Employee::Employee( const char * const first, const char * const last,
43                      int mn, int dy, int yr, int dept )
44  : birthDate( mn, dy, yr ), departmentCode( dept )
45  {
46     firstName = new char[ strlen( first ) + 1 ];
47     assert( firstName != 0 );     // test that new worked
48     strcpy( firstName, first );
49
50     lastName = new char[ strlen( last ) + 1 ];
51     assert( lastName != 0 );      // test that new worked
52     strcpy( lastName, last );
53  }
54
55  // Destructor deallocates dynamically allocated memory
56  Employee::~Employee()
57  {
58     delete [] firstName;
59     delete [] lastName;
60  }
61
62  // Return a pointer to the first name
63  const char *Employee::getFirstName() const
64  {
65     // Const prevents caller from modifying private data.
66     // Caller should copy returned string before destructor
67     // deletes dynamic storage to prevent undefined pointer.
68
69     return firstName;    // caller must delete memory
70  }
71
72  // Return a pointer to the last name
73  const char *Employee::getLastName() const
74  {
75     // Const prevents caller from modifying private data.
76     // Caller should copy returned string before destructor
77     // deletes dynamic storage to prevent undefined pointer.
78
79     return lastName;    // caller must delete memory
80  }
81
82  // Return the employee's birth date
83  Date Employee::getBirthDate() const { return birthDate; }
84
85  // Return the employee's department code
86  int Employee::getDepartmentCode() const { return departmentCode; }
```

```
87  // BOSS.H
88  // Boss class derived from Employee
89  #ifndef BOSS_H
90  #define BOSS_H
```

```
91   #include "employ.h"
92
93   class Boss : public Employee {
94   public:
95      Boss( const char * const, const char * const, int, int, int,
96            double = 0.0, int = 0 );
97      void setWeeklySalary( double );
98      virtual double earnings() const;
99      virtual void print() const;
100  private:
101     double weeklySalary;
102  };
103
104  #endif
```

```
105  // BOSS.CPP
106  // Member function definitions for class Boss
107  #include <iostream.h>
108  #include "boss.h"
109
110  // Constructor function for class Boss
111  Boss::Boss( const char * const first, const char * const last,
112             int mn, int dy, int yr, double s, int dept )
113     : Employee( first, last, mn, dy, yr, dept )
114  { weeklySalary = s > 0 ? s : 0; }
115
116  // Set the Boss's salary
117  void Boss::setWeeklySalary( double s )
118     { weeklySalary = s > 0 ? s : 0; }
119
120  // Get the Boss's pay
121  double Boss::earnings() const { return weeklySalary; }
122
123  // Print the Boss's name
124  void Boss::print() const
125  {
126     cout << "\nBoss: " << getFirstName()
127          << ' ' << getLastName();
128  }
```

```
129  // HOURLY.H
130  // Definition of class HourlyWorker
131  #ifndef HOURLY_H
132  #define HOURLY_H
133  #include "employ.h"
134
135  class HourlyWorker : public Employee {
136  public:
137     HourlyWorker( const char * const, const char * const, int, int, int,
138                  double = 0.0, double = 0.0, int = 0 );
139     void setWage( double );
140     void setHours( double );
141     virtual double earnings() const;
142     virtual void print() const;
143  private:
144     double wage;    // wage per hour
145     double hours;   // hours worked for week
146  };
147
148  #endif
```

```
149  // HOURLY.CPP
150  // Member function definitions for class HourlyWorker
151  #include <iostream.h>
152  #include "hourly.h"
153
154  // Constructor for class HourlyWorker
155  HourlyWorker::HourlyWorker( const char * const first, const char * const last,
156                             int mn, int dy, int yr, double w, double h, int dept )
157  : Employee( first, last, mn, dy, yr, dept )
158  {
159     wage = w > 0 ? w : 0;
160     hours = h >= 0 && h < 168 ? h : 0;
161  }
162
163  // Set the wage
164  void HourlyWorker::setWage( double w ) { wage = w > 0 ? w : 0; }
165
166  // Set the hours worked
167  void HourlyWorker::setHours( double h )
168     { hours = h >= 0 && h < 168 ? h : 0; }
169
170  // Get the HourlyWorker's pay
171  double HourlyWorker::earnings() const { return wage * hours; }
172
173  // Print the HourlyWorker's name
174  void HourlyWorker::print() const
175  {
176     cout << "\nHourly worker: " << getFirstName()
177          << ' ' << getLastName();
178  }
```

```
179  // PIECE.H
180  // PieceWorker class derived from Employee
181  #ifndef PIECE_H
182  #define PIECE_H
183  #include "employ.h"
184
185  class PieceWorker : public Employee {
186  public:
187     PieceWorker( const char * const, const char * const, int, int, int,
188                 double = 0.0, unsigned = 0, int = 0 );
189     void setWage( double );
190     void setQuantity( unsigned );
191     virtual double earnings() const;
192     virtual void print() const;
193  private:
194     double wagePerPiece; // wage for each piece output
195     unsigned quantity;   // output for week
196  };
197
198  #endif
```

```
199  // PIECE.CPP
200  // Member function definitions for class PieceWorker
201  #include <iostream.h>
202  #include "piece.h"
203
204  // Constructor for class PieceWorker
205  PieceWorker::PieceWorker( const char * const first, const char * const last,
206                           int mn, int dy, int yr, double w, unsigned q, int dept )
207     : Employee( first, last, mn, dy, yr, dept )
208  {
209     wagePerPiece = w > 0 ? w : 0;
```

```
210        quantity = q > 0 ? q : 0;
211 }
212
213 // Set the wage
214 void PieceWorker::setWage( double w ) { wagePerPiece = w > 0 ? w : 0; }
215
216 // Set the number of items output
217 void PieceWorker::setQuantity( unsigned q )
218     { quantity = q > 0 ? q : 0; }
219
220 // Determine the PieceWorker's earnings
221 double PieceWorker::earnings() const
222     { return quantity * wagePerPiece; }
223
224 // Print the PieceWorker's name
225 void PieceWorker::print() const
226 {
227     cout << "\nPiece worker: " << getFirstName()
228          << ' ' << getLastName();
229 }
```

```
230 // COMMIS.H
231 // CommissionWorker class derived from Employee
232 #ifndef COMMIS_H
233 #define COMMIS_H
234 #include "employ.h"
235
236 class CommissionWorker : public Employee {
237 public:
238     CommissionWorker(const char * const, const char * const, int, int, int,
239                      double = 0.0, double = 0.0, unsigned = 0, int = 0 );
240     void setSalary( double );
241     void setCommission( double );
242     void setQuantity( unsigned );
243     virtual double earnings() const;
244     virtual void print() const;
245 private:
246     double salary;        // base salary per week
247     double commission;    // amount per item sold
248     unsigned quantity;    // total items sold for week
249 };
250
251 #endif
```

```
252 // COMMIS.CPP
253 // Member function definitions for class CommissionWorker
254 #include <iostream.h>
255 #include "commis.h"
256
257 // Constructor for class CommissionWorker
258 CommissionWorker::CommissionWorker( const char * const first,
259   const char * const last, int mn, int dy, int yr,
260   double s, double c, unsigned q, int dept )
261     : Employee( first, last, mn, dy, yr, dept )
262 {
263     salary = s > 0 ? s : 0;
264     commission = c > 0 ? c : 0;
265     quantity = q > 0 ? q : 0;
266 }
267
268 // Set CommissionWorker's weekly base salary
269 void CommissionWorker::setSalary( double s )
270     { salary = s > 0 ? s : 0; }
```

```
271  // Set CommissionWorker's commission
272  void CommissionWorker::setCommission( double c )
273     { commission = c > 0 ? c : 0; }
274
275  // Set CommissionWorker's quantity sold
276  void CommissionWorker::setQuantity( unsigned q )
277     { quantity = q > 0 ? q : 0; }
278
279  // Determine CommissionWorker's earnings
280  double CommissionWorker::earnings() const
281     { return salary + commission * quantity; }
282
283  // Print the CommissionWorker's name
284  void CommissionWorker::print() const
285  {
286     cout << "\nCommission worker: " << getFirstName()
287          << ' ' << getLastName();
288  }
```

```
289  // DATE.H
290  // Declaration of the Date class.
291  // Member functions defined in DATE1.CPP
292  #ifndef DATE_H
293  #define DATE_H
294
295  class Date {
296  public:
297     Date( int = 1, int = 1, int = 1900 );  // default constructor
298     int getMonth() const; // return the month
299     int getDay() const;   // return the day
300     int getYear()const;   // return the year
301     void print() const;   // print date in month/day/year format
302  private:
303     int month;   // 1-12
304     int day;     // 1-31 based on month
305     int year;    // any year
306
307     // utility function to test proper day for month and year
308     int checkDay( int ) const;
309  };
310
311  #endif
```

```
312  // DATE.CPP
313  // Member function definitions for Date class.
314  #include <iostream.h>
315  #include "date.h"
316
317  // Constructor: Confirm proper value for month;
318  // call utility function checkDay to confirm proper
319  // value for day.
320  Date::Date( int mn, int dy, int yr )
321  {
322     if ( mn > 0 && mn <= 12 )            // validate the month
323        month = mn;
324     else {
325        month = 1;
326        cout << "Month " << mn << " invalid. Set to month 1.\n";
327     }
328
329     year = yr >= 1900 && yr <= 2100 ? yr : 1990;
330     day = checkDay( dy );                // validate the day
331  }
```

```
332
333  // Utility function to confirm proper day value
334  // based on month and year.
335  int Date::checkDay( int testDay ) const
336  {
337     int daysPerMonth[ 13 ] = { 0, 31, 28, 31, 30, 31, 30,
338                                  31, 31, 30, 31, 30, 31 };
339
340     if ( testDay > 0 && testDay <= daysPerMonth[ month ] )
341        return testDay;
342
343     if ( month == 2 &&       // February: Check for possible leap year
344         testDay == 29 &&
345         ( year % 400 == 0 || (year % 4 == 0 && year % 100 != 0 ) ) )
346        return testDay;
347
348     cout << "Day " << testDay << " invalid. Set to day 1.\n";
349
350     return 1;  // leave object in consistent state if bad value
351  }
352
353  // Return the month
354  int Date::getMonth() const { return month; }
355
356  // Return the day
357  int Date::getDay() const { return day; }
358
359  // Return the year
360  int Date::getYear() const { return year; }
361
362  // Print Date object in form  month/day/year
363  void Date::print() const
364     { cout << month << '/' << day << '/' << year; }
```

```
365  // Exercise 10.14 solution
366  // Driver for Employee hierarchy
367  #include <iostream.h>
368  #include <iomanip.h>
369  #include <time.h>
370  #include <stdlib.h>
371  #include "employ.h"
372  #include "boss.h"
373  #include "commis.h"
374  #include "piece.h"
375  #include "hourly.h"
376
377  int determineMonth();
378
379  int main()
380  {
381     // set output formatting
382     cout << setiosflags( ios::fixed | ios::showpoint )
383          << setprecision( 2 );
384
385     Boss b( "John", "Smith", 6, 15, 1944, 800.00, 1 );
386     CommissionWorker c( "Sue", "Jones", 9, 8, 1954, 200.0, 3.0, 150, 1 );
387     PieceWorker p( "Bob", "Lewis", 3, 2, 1965, 2.5, 200, 1 );
388     HourlyWorker h( "Karen", "Price", 12, 29, 1960, 13.75, 40, 1 );
389
390     Employee *ptr[ 4 ] = { &b, &c, &p, &h };
391
392     int month = determineMonth();
393
```

```
394        cout << "The month is " << month << "\nThe payroll is:\n";
395
396        for ( int x = 0; x < 4; ++x ) {
397           ptr[ x ]->print();
398           cout << " of department " << ptr[ x ]->getDepartmentCode()
399                << "\n whose birthday is ";
400           ptr[ x ]->getBirthDate().print();
401           cout << " earned ";
402
403           if ( ptr[ x ]->getBirthDate().getMonth() == month )
404              cout << ptr[ x ]->earnings() + 100.0
405                   << " HAPPY BIRTHDAY!\n";
406           else
407              cout << ptr[x]->earnings() << endl;
408        }
409
410        return 0;
411 }
412
413 // Determine the current month using standard library functions
414 // of time.h.
415 int determineMonth()
416 {
417     time_t currentTime;
418     char monthString[ 3 ];
419
420     time( &currentTime );
421     strftime( monthString, 3, "%m", localtime( &currentTime ) );
422     return atoi( monthString );
423 }
```

```
The month is 12
The payroll is:

Boss: John Smith of department 1
 whose birthday is 6/15/1944 earned 800.00

Commission worker: Sue Jones of department 1
 whose birthday is 9/8/1954 earned 650.00

Piece worker: Bob Lewis of department 1
 whose birthday is 3/2/1965 earned 500.00

Hourly worker: Karen Price of department 1
 whose birthday is 12/29/1960 earned 650.00 HAPPY BIRTHDAY!
```

10.15 In Exercise 9.14, you developed a **Shape** class hierarchy and defined the classes in the hierarchy. Modify the hierarchy so that class **Shape** is an abstract base class containing the interface to the hierarchy. Derive **TwoDimensionalShape** and **ThreeDimensionalShape** from class **Shape**—these classes should also be abstract. Use a **virtual print** function to output the type and dimensions of each class. Also include **virtual area** and **volume** functions so these calculations can be performed for objects of each concrete class in the hierarchy. Write a driver program that tests the **Shape** class hierarchy.

ANS:

```
1  // SHAPE.H
2  // Definition of base-class Shape
3  #ifndef SHAPE_H
4  #define SHAPE_H
5
6  #include <iostream.h>
7
```

```
8    class Shape {
9       friend ostream & operator<<( ostream &, Shape & );
10   public:
11      Shape( double = 0, double = 0 );
12      double getCenterX() const;
13      double getCenterY() const;
14      virtual void print() const = 0;
15   protected:
16      double xCenter;
17      double yCenter;
18   };
19
20   #endif
```

```
21   // SHAPE.CPP
22   // Member and friend definitions for Shape
23   #include "shape.h"
24
25   Shape::Shape( double x, double y )
26   {
27      xCenter = x;
28      yCenter = y;
29   }
30
31   double Shape::getCenterX() const { return xCenter; }
32
33   double Shape::getCenterY() const { return yCenter; }
34
35   ostream & operator<<( ostream &out, Shape &s )
36   {
37      s.print();
38      return out;
39   }
```

```
40   // TWODIM.H
41   // Defnition of class TwoDimensionalShape
42   #ifndef TWODIM_H
43   #define TWODIM_H
44   #include "shape.h"
45
46   class TwoDimensionalShape : public Shape {
47   public:
48      TwoDimensionalShape( double x, double y ) : Shape( x, y ) { }
49      virtual double area() const = 0;
50   };
51
52   #endif
```

```
53   // THREEDIM.H
54   // Defnition of class ThreeDimensionalShape
55   #ifndef THREEDIM_H
56   #define THREEDIM_H
57   #include "shape.h"
58
59   class ThreeDimensionalShape : public Shape {
60   public:
61      ThreeDimensionalShape( double x, double y ) : Shape( x, y ) { }
62      virtual double area() const = 0;
63      virtual double volume() const = 0;
64   };
65
66   #endif
```

```
67   // CIRCLE.H
68   // Definition of class Circle
69   #ifndef CIRCLE_H
70   #define CIRCLE_H
71
72   #include "twodim.h"
73
74   class Circle : public TwoDimensionalShape {
75   public:
76      Circle( double = 0.0, double = 0, double = 0 );
77      double getRadius() const;
78      double area() const;
79      void print() const;
80   private:
81      double radius;
82   };
83
84   #endif
```

```
85    // CIRCLE.CPP
86    // Member function definitions for Circle
87    #include "circle.h"
88
89    Circle::Circle( double r, double x, double y )
90       : TwoDimensionalShape( x, y ) { radius = r > 0 ? r : 0; }
91
92    double Circle::getRadius() const { return radius; }
93
94    double Circle::area() const { return 3.14159 * radius * radius; }
95
96    void Circle::print() const
97    {
98       cout << "Circle with radius " << radius << "; center at ("
99            << xCenter << ", " << yCenter << ");\narea of " << area() << '\n';
100   }
```

```
101  // SQUARE.H
102  // Definition of class Square
103  #ifndef SQUARE_H
104  #define SQUARE_H
105
106  #include "twodim.h"
107
108  class Square : public TwoDimensionalShape {
109  public:
110     Square( double = 0, double = 0, double = 0 );
111     double getSideLength() const;
112     double area() const;
113     void print() const;
114  private:
115     double sideLength;
116  };
117
118  #endif
```

```
119  // SQUARE.CPP
120  // Member function definitions for Square
121  #include "square.h"
122
123  Square::Square( double s, double x, double y )
124     : TwoDimensionalShape( x, y ) { sideLength = s > 0 ? s : 0; }
125
```

```
126  double Square::getSideLength() const { return sideLength; }
127
128  double Square::area() const { return sideLength * sideLength; }
129
130  void Square::print() const
131  {
132     cout << "Square with side length " << sideLength << "; center at ("
133          << xCenter << ", " << yCenter << ");\narea of " << area() << '\n';
134  }
```

```
135  // CUBE.H
136  // Definition of class Cube
137  #ifndef CUBE_H
138  #define CUBE_H
139
140  #include "threedim.h"
141
142  class Cube : public ThreeDimensionalShape {
143  public:
144     Cube( double = 0, double = 0, double = 0 );
145     double area() const;
146     double volume() const;
147     double getSideLength() const;
148     void print() const;
149  private:
150     double sideLength;
151  };
152
153  #endif
```

```
154  // CUBE.CPP
155  // Member function definitions for Cube
156  #include "cube.h"
157
158  Cube::Cube( double s, double x, double y )
159     : ThreeDimensionalShape( x, y ) { sideLength = s > 0 ? s : 0; }
160
161  double Cube::area() const { return sideLength * sideLength; }
162
163  double Cube::volume() const
164     { return sideLength * sideLength * sideLength; }
165
166  double Cube::getSideLength() const { return sideLength; }
167
168  void Cube::print() const
169  {
170     cout << "Cube with side length " << sideLength << "; center at ("
171          << xCenter << ", " << yCenter << ");\narea of "
172          << area() << "; volume of " << volume() << '\n';
173  }
```

```
174  // SPHERE.H
175  // Definition of class Shere
176  #ifndef SPHERE_H
177  #define SPHERE_H
178
179  #include "threedim.h"
180
181  class Sphere : public ThreeDimensionalShape {
182  public:
183     Sphere( double = 0, double = 0, double = 0 );
184     double area() const;
```

```
185      double volume() const;
186      double getRadius() const;
187      void print() const;
188 private:
189      double radius;
190 };
191
192 #endif
```

```
193 // SPHERE.CPP
194 // Member function definitions for Sphere
195 #include "sphere.h"
196
197 Sphere::Sphere( double r, double x, double y )
198      : ThreeDimensionalShape( x, y ) { radius = r > 0 ? r : 0; }
199
200 double Sphere::area() const
201      { return 4.0 * 3.14159 * radius * radius; }
202
203 double Sphere::volume() const
204      { return 4.0/3.0 * 3.14159 * radius * radius * radius; }
205
206 double Sphere::getRadius() const { return radius; }
207
208 void Sphere::print() const
209 {
210     cout << "Sphere with radius " << radius << "; center at ("
211          << xCenter << ", " << yCenter << ");\narea of "
212          << area() << "; volume of " << volume() << '\n';
213 }
```

```
214 // Exercise 10.15 solution
215 // Driver to test Shape hierarchy
216 #include <iostream.h>
217 #include "circle.h"
218 #include "square.h"
219 #include "sphere.h"
220 #include "cube.h"
221
222 int main()
223 {
224     Circle cir( 3.5, 6, 9 );
225     Square sqr( 12, 2, 2 );
226     Sphere sph( 5, 1.5, 4.5 );
227     Cube cub( 2.2 );
228     Shape *ptr[ 4 ] = { &cir, &sqr, &sph, &cub };
229
230     for ( int x = 0; x < 4; ++x )
231         cout << *( ptr[ x ] ) << '\n';
232
233     return 0;
234 }
```

```
Circle with radius 3.5; center at (6, 9);
area of 38.4845

Square with side length 12; center at (2, 2);
area of 144

Sphere with radius 5; center at (1.5, 4.5);
area of 314.159; volume of 523.598

Cube with side length 2.2; center at (0, 0);
area of 4.84; volume of 10.648
```

Chapter 11 Solutions

C++ *Stream Input/Output*

Solutions

11.6   Write a statement for each of the following:

a) Print integer **40000** left-justified in a **15**-digit field.

ANS: `cout << setiosflags( ios::left ) << setw( 15 ) << 40000 << '\n';`

b) Read a string into character array variable **state**.

ANS: `cin >> state;`

c) Print **200** with and without a sign.

ANS:
```
cout << setiosflags( ios::showpos ) << 200 << setw( 4 )
     << resetiosflags( ios::showpos ) << 200 << '\n';
```

d) Print the decimal value **100** in hexadecimal form preceded by **0x**.

ANS: `cout << setiosflags( ios::showbase ) << hex << 100 << '\n';`

e) Read characters into array **s** until the character **'p'** is encountered up to a limit of 10 characters (including the terminating null character). Extract the delimiter from the input stream and discard it.

ANS: `cin.getline( s, 10, 'p' );`

f) Print **1.234** in a **9**-digit field with preceding zeros.

ANS:
```
cout << setiosflags( ios::fixed | ios::showpoint ) << setw( 9 )
     << setfill( '0' ) << setiosflags( ios::internal ) << 1.234 << '\n';
```

g) Read a string of the form **"characters"** from the standard input. Store the string in character array **s**. Eliminate the quotation marks from the input stream. Read a maximum of 50 characters (including the terminating null character).

11.7   Write a program to test inputting integer values in decimal, octal, and hexadecimal format. Output each integer read by the program in all three formats. Test the program with the following input data: 10, 010, 0x10.

ANS:

```
1   // Exercise 11.7 Solution
2   #include <iostream.h>
3   #include <iomanip.h>
4
5   int main()
6   {
7      int integer;
8
9      cout << "Enter an integer: ";
10     cin >> integer;
11
12     cout << setiosflags( ios::showbase ) << "As a decimal number "  << dec
13          << integer << "\nAs an octal number " << oct << integer
14          << "\nAs a hexadecimal number " << hex << integer << endl;
15
16     return 0;
17  }
```

```
Enter an integer: 76
As a decimal number 76
As an octal number 0114
As a hexadecimal number 0x4c
```

11.8   Write a program that prints pointer values using casts to all the integer data types. Which ones print strange values? Which ones cause errors?

ANS:

```
1   // Exercise 11.8 Solution
2   #include <iostream.h>
3
4   int main()
5   {
6      char *string = "test";
7
8      cout << "Value of string is             : " << string << '\n'
9           << "Value of static_cast<void *>(string) is    : "
10          << static_cast<void *>( string ) << '\n'
11
12         // The Following generate errors.
13         // reinterpret_cast will allow this
14         // type of casting. See Chap. 21 for
15         // a discussion of reinterpret_cast.
16
17  /*      << "Value of static_cast<char>(string) is      : "
18          << static_cast<char>( string ) << '\n'
19          << "Value of static_cast<int>(string) is      : "
20          << static_cast<int>( string ) << '\n'
21          << "Value of static_cast<long>(string) is     : "
22          << static_cast<long>( string ) << '\n'
23          << "Value of static_cast<short>(string) is      : "
24          << static_cast<short>( string ) << '\n'
25          << "Value of static_cast<unsigned>(string) is  : "
26          << static_cast<unsigned>( string )
27  */
28          << endl;
29
30      return 0;
31  }
```

```
Value of string is                : test
Value of static_cast<void *>(string) is     : 0x00416D50
```

11.9   Write a program to test the results of printing the integer value **12345** and the floating-point value **1.2345** in various size fields. What happens when the values are printed in fields containing fewer digits than the values?

ANS:

```
1   // Exercise 11.9 Solution
2   #include <iostream.h>
3   #include <iomanip.h>
4
5   int main()
6   {
7      int x = 12345;
8      double y = 1.2345;
9
10     for ( int loop = 0; loop <= 10; ++loop )
11        cout << x << "  printed in a field of size " << loop << " is "
```

```
12          << setw( loop ) << x << '\n' << y << " printed in a field "
13          << "of size " << loop << " is " << setw( loop ) << y << '\n';
14
15      return 0;
16  }
```

```
12345  printed in a field of size 0 is 12345
1.2345 printed in a field of size 0 is 1.2345
12345  printed in a field of size 1 is 12345
1.2345 printed in a field of size 1 is 1.2345
12345  printed in a field of size 2 is 12345
1.2345 printed in a field of size 2 is 1.2345
12345  printed in a field of size 3 is 12345
1.2345 printed in a field of size 3 is 1.2345
12345  printed in a field of size 4 is 12345
1.2345 printed in a field of size 4 is 1.2345
12345  printed in a field of size 5 is 12345
1.2345 printed in a field of size 5 is 1.2345
12345  printed in a field of size 6 is  12345
1.2345 printed in a field of size 6 is 1.2345
12345  printed in a field of size 7 is   12345
1.2345 printed in a field of size 7 is  1.2345
12345  printed in a field of size 8 is    12345
1.2345 printed in a field of size 8 is   1.2345
12345  printed in a field of size 9 is     12345
1.2345 printed in a field of size 9 is    1.2345
12345  printed in a field of size 10 is      12345
1.2345 printed in a field of size 10 is     1.2345
```

11.10 Write a program that prints the value **100.453627** rounded to the nearest digit, tenth, hundredth, thousandth, and ten thousandth.

> ANS:

```
1   // Exercise 11.10 Solution
2   #include <iostream.h>
3   #include <iomanip.h>
4
5   int main()
6   {
7       double x = 100.453627;
8
9       cout << setiosflags( ios::fixed | ios::showpoint );
10      for ( int loop = 0; loop <= 5; ++loop )
11          cout << setprecision( loop ) << "Rounded to " << loop
12              << " digit(s) is " << x << endl;
13
14      return 0;
15  }
```

```
Rounded to 0 digit(s) is 100.
Rounded to 1 digit(s) is 100.5
Rounded to 2 digit(s) is 100.45
Rounded to 3 digit(s) is 100.454
Rounded to 4 digit(s) is 100.4536
Rounded to 5 digit(s) is 100.45363
```

11.11 Write a program that inputs a string from the keyboard and determines the length of the string. Print the string using twice the length as the field width.

> ANS:

```
1   // Exercise 11.11 Solution
2   #include <iostream.h>
3   #include <iomanip.h>
4   #include <string.h>
5
6   const int SIZE = 80;
7
8   int main()
9   {
10      char string[ SIZE ];
11      int stringLength;
12
13      cout << "Enter a string: ";
14      cin >> string;
15
16      stringLength = strlen( string );
17
18      // print string using twice the length as field with
19      cout << setw( 2 * stringLength ) << string << endl;
20
21      return 0;
22  }
```

```
Enter a string: castle
        castle
```

11.12 Write a program that converts integer Fahrenheit temperatures from **0** to **212** degrees to floating-point Celsius temperatures with **3** digits of precision. Use the formula

```
celsius = 5.0 / 9.0 * ( fahrenheit - 32 );
```

to perform the calculation. The output should be printed in two right-justified columns, and the Celsius temperatures should be preceded by a sign for both positive and negative values.

ANS:

```
1   // Exercise 11.12 Solution
2   #include <iostream.h>
3   #include <iomanip.h>
4
5   int main()
6   {
7      double celsius;
8
9      cout << setw( 20 ) << "Fahrenheit " << setw( 20 ) << "Celsius\n"
10         << setiosflags( ios::fixed | ios::showpoint );
11
12      for ( int fahrenheit = 0; fahrenheit <= 212; ++fahrenheit ) {
13         celsius = 5.0 / 9.0 * ( fahrenheit - 32 );
14         cout << setw( 15 ) << resetiosflags( ios::showpos ) << fahrenheit
15              << setw( 23 ) << setprecision( 3 ) << setiosflags( ios::showpos )
16              << celsius << '\n';
17      }
18
19      return 0;
20  }
```

Fahrenheit	Celsius	
0	-17.778	
1	-17.222	
2	-16.667	
3	-16.111	
4	-15.556	*continued...*

```
    ...
                206                    +96.667
                207                    +97.222
                208                    +97.778
                209                    +98.333
                210                    +98.889
                211                    +99.444
                212                   +100.000
```

11.13 In some programming languages, strings are entered surrounded by either single or double quotation marks. Write a program that reads the three strings **suzy**, **"suzy"**, and **'suzy'**. Are the single and double quotes ignored or read as part of the string?

ANS:

```
1   // Exercise 11.13 Solution
2   #include <iostream.h>
3
4   const int SIZE = 80;
5
6   int main()
7   {
8       char string[ SIZE ];
9
10      for ( int k = 0; k < 3; ++k ) {
11          cout << "Enter a string: ";
12          cin >> string;
13          cout << "String is " << string << '\n';
14      }
15
16      return 0;
17  }
```

```
Enter a string: "vacuum"
String is "vacuum"
Enter a string: 'grape'
String is 'grape'
Enter a string: water
String is water
```

11.14 In Fig. 8.3, the stream-extraction and -insertion operators were overloaded for input and output of objects of the **PhoneNumber** class. Rewrite the stream-extraction operator to perform the following error checking on input. The **operator>>** function will need to be entirely recoded.

a) Input the entire phone number into an array. Test that the proper number of characters have been entered. There should be a total of 14 characters read for a phone number of the form **(800) 555-1212**. Use the stream member function **clear** to set **ios::failbit** for improper input.

b) The area code and exchange do not begin with **0** or **1**. Test the first digit of the area code and exchange portions of the phone number to be sure that neither begins with **0** or **1**. Use stream member function **clear** to set **ios::failbit** for improper input.

c) The middle digit of an area code used to always be **0** or **1** (although this has changed recently). Test the middle digit for a value of **0** or **1**. Use the stream member function **clear** to set **ios::failbit** for improper input. If none of the above operations results in **ios::failbit** being set for improper input, copy the three parts of the telephone number into the **areaCode**, **exchange**, and **line** members of the **PhoneNumber** object. In the main program, if **ios::failbit** has been set on the input, have the program print an error message and end rather than print the phone number.

ANS:

```
1    // P11_14.H
2    #ifndef P11_14_H
3    #define P11_14_H
4    #include <iostream.h>
5    #include <iomanip.h>
6    #include <string.h>
7    #include <stdlib.h>
8
9    class PhoneNumber {
10      friend ostream& operator<<( ostream&, PhoneNumber& );
11      friend istream& operator>>( istream&, PhoneNumber& );
12   public:
13      PhoneNumber();
14   private:
15      char phone[ 15 ];
16      char areaCode[ 4 ];
17      char exchange[ 4 ];
18      char line[ 5 ];
19   };
20
21   #endif
```

```
22   // P11_14M.cpp
23   // member function definition definition for p11_14.cpp
24   #include "p11_14.h"
25
26   PhoneNumber::PhoneNumber()
27   {
28      phone[ 0 ] = '\0';
29      areaCode[ 0 ] = '\0';
30      exchange[ 0 ] = '\0';
31      line[ 0 ] = '\0';
32   }
33
34   ostream &operator<<( ostream &output, PhoneNumber &number )
35   {
36      output << "(" << number.areaCode << ") " << number.exchange
37              << "-" << number.line << '\n';
38
39      return output;
40   }
41
42   istream &operator>>( istream &input, PhoneNumber &number )
43   {
44      cin.getline( number.phone, 15 );
45
46      if ( strlen( number.phone ) != 14 )
47         cin.clear( ios::failbit );
48
49      if ( number.phone[ 1 ] == '0' || number.phone[ 6 ] == '0' ||
50           number.phone[ 1 ] == '1' || number.phone[ 6 ] == '1')
51         cin.clear( ios::failbit );
52
53      if ( number.phone[ 2 ] != '0' && number.phone[ 2 ] != '1' )
54         cin.clear( ios::failbit );
55
56      if ( !cin.fail() ) {
57         for ( int loop = 0; loop <= 2; ++loop ) {
58            number.areaCode[ loop ] = number.phone[ loop + 1 ];
59            number.exchange[ loop ] = number.phone[ loop + 6 ];
60         }
61
62         number.areaCode[ loop ] = number.exchange[ loop ] = '\0';
```

```
63
64          for ( loop = 0; loop <= 3; ++loop )
65              number.line[ loop ] = number.phone[ loop + 10 ];
66
67          number.line[ loop ] = '\0';
68       }
69       else {
70          cerr << "Invalid phone number entered.\n";
71          exit( 1 );
72       }
73
74       return input;
75    }
```

```
76    // driver for p11_14.cpp
77    #include "p11_14.h"
78
79    int main()
80    {
81       PhoneNumber telephone;
82
83       cout << "Enter a phone number in the form (123) 456-7890:\n";
84       cin >> telephone;
85
86       cout << "The phone number entered was:  " << telephone << endl;
87       return 0;
88    }
```

```
Enter a phone number in the form (123) 456-7890:
(800) 987-4567
The phone number entered was:   (800) 987-4567
```

11.15 Write a program that accomplishes each of the following:

    a) Create the user-defined class **Point** that contains the private integer data members **xCoordinate** and **yCo-ordinate**, and declares stream-insertion and stream-extraction overloaded operator functions as **friend**s of the class.

    b) Define the stream-insertion and stream-extraction operator functions. The stream-extraction operator function should determine if the data entered is valid data, and if not, it should set the **ios::failbit** to indicate improper input. The stream-insertion operator should not be able to display the point after an input error occurred.

    c) Write a **main** function that tests input and output of user-defined class **Point** using the overloaded stream-extraction and stream-insertion operators.

    ANS:

```
1     // P11_15.H
2     #ifndef P11_15_H
3     #define P11_15_H
4     #include <iostream.h>
5
6     class Point {
7        friend ostream &operator<<( ostream&, Point& );
8        friend istream &operator>>( istream&, Point& );
9     private:
10       int xCoordinate;
11       int yCoordinate;
12    };
13
14    #endif
```

```
15    // P11_15M.cpp
16    // member function definitions for p11_15.cpp
```

```
17   #include "p11_15.h"
18
19   ostream& operator<<( ostream& out, Point& p )
20   {
21      if ( !cin.fail() )
22         cout << "(" << p.xCoordinate << ", " << p.yCoordinate << ")" << '\n';
23      else
24         cout << "\nInvalid data\n";
25
26      return out;
27   }
28
29   istream& operator>>( istream& i, Point& p )
30   {
31      if ( cin.peek() != '(' )
32         cin.clear( ios::failbit );
33      else
34         i.ignore();   // skip (
35
36      cin >> p.xCoordinate;
37
38      if ( cin.peek() != ',' )
39         cin.clear( ios::failbit );
40      else {
41         i.ignore(); // skip ,
42
43         if ( cin.peek() == ' ' )
44            i.ignore(); // skip space
45         else
46            cin.clear( ios::failbit );
47      }
48
49      cin >> p.yCoordinate;
50
51      if ( cin.peek() == ')' )
52            i.ignore();   // skip )
53         else
54            cin.clear( ios::failbit );
55
56      return i;
57   }
```

```
58   // driver for p11_15.cpp
59   #include "p11_15.h"
60
61   int main()
62   {
63      Point pt;
64
65      cout << "Enter a point in the form (x, y):\n";
66      cin >> pt;
67
68      cout << "Point entered was: " << pt << endl;
69      return 0;
70   }
```

```
Enter a point in the form (x, y):
(7, 8)

Point entered was: (7, 8)
```

11.16 Write a program that accomplishes each of the following:
    a) Create the user-defined class **Complex** that contains the private integer data members **real** and **imaginary**,

and declares stream-insertion and stream-extraction overloaded operator functions as **friend**s of the class.

b) Define the stream-insertion and -extraction operator functions. The stream-extraction operator function should determine if the data entered is valid, and if not, it should set **ios::failbit** to indicate improper input. The input should be of the form:

```
3 + 8i
```

c) The values can be negative or positive, and it is possible that one of the two values is not provided. If a value is not provided, the appropriate data member should be set to 0. The stream-insertion operator should not be able to display the point if an input error occurred. The output format should be identical to the input format shown above. For negative imaginary values, a minus sign should be printed rather than a plus sign.

d) Write a **main** function that tests input and output of user-defined class **Complex** using the overloaded stream-extraction and stream-insertion operators.

ANS:

```
1   // P11_16.H
2   #ifndef P11_16_H
3   #define P11_16_H
4   #include <iostream.h>
5   #include <iomanip.h>
6
7   class Complex {
8      friend ostream &operator<<( ostream&, Complex& );
9      friend istream &operator>>( istream&, Complex& );
10  public:
11     Complex( void );      // constructor
12  private:
13     int real;
14     int imaginary;
15  };
16
17  #endif
```

```
18  // P11_16M.cpp
19  // member function definitions for p11_16.cpp
20  #include <iomanip.h>
21  #include "p11_16.h"
22
23  Complex::Complex( void )
24  {
25     real = 0;
26     imaginary = 0;
27  }
28
29  ostream &operator<<( ostream &output, Complex &c )
30  {
31     if ( !cin.fail() )
32        output << c.real
33                << setiosflags( ios::showpos )
34                << c.imaginary << "i\n"
35                << resetiosflags( ios::showpos );
36     else
37        output << "Invalid Data Entered" << '\n';
38
39     return output;
40  }
41
```

```
42  istream &operator>>( istream &input, Complex &c )
43  {
44      int number, multiplier;
45      char temp;
46
47      input >> number;
48
49      if ( cin.peek() == ' ' ) {                    // case a + bi
50          c.real = number;
51          cin >> temp;
52
53          multiplier = ( temp == '+' ) ? 1 : -1;
54
55          if ( cin.peek() != ' ' )
56              cin.clear( ios::failbit );        // set bad bit
57          else {
58
59              if ( cin.peek() == ' ' ) {
60                  input >> c.imaginary;
61                  c.imaginary *= multiplier;
62
63                  cin >> temp;
64                  if ( cin.peek() != '\n' )
65                      cin.clear( ios::failbit ); // set bad bit
66              }
67              else
68                  cin.clear( ios::failbit );     // set bad bit
69          }
70      }
71      else if ( cin.peek() == 'i' ) {           // case bi
72          cin >> temp;
73
74          if ( cin.peek() == '\n' ) {
75              c.real = 0;
76              c.imaginary = number;
77          }
78          else
79              cin.clear( ios::failbit );         // set bad bit
80      }
81
82      else if ( cin.peek() == '\n' ) {          // case a
83          c.real = number;
84          c.imaginary = 0;
85      }
86      else
87          cin.clear( ios::failbit );            // set bad bit
88
89      return input;
90  }
```

```
91  // driver for p11_16.cpp
92  #include "p11_16.h"
93
94  int main()
95  {
96      Complex complex;
97
98      cout << "Input a complex number in the form A + Bi:\n";
99      cin >> complex;
100
101     cout << "Complex number entered was:\n" << complex << endl;
102     return 0;
103 }
```

```
Input a complex number in the form A + Bi:
7 - 7777i
Complex number entered was:
7-7777i
```

11.17 Write a program that uses a **for** structure to print a table of ASCII values for the characters in the ASCII character set from **33** to **126**. The program should print the decimal value, octal value, hexadecimal value, and character value for each character. Use the stream manipulators **dec**, **oct**, and **hex** to print the integer values.

ANS:

```
1   // Exercise 11.17 Solution
2   #include <iostream.h>
3   #include <iomanip.h>
4
5   int main()
6   {
7       cout << setw( 7 ) << "Decimal" << setw( 9 ) << "Octal " << setw( 15 )
8            << "Hexadecimal " << setw( 13 ) << "Character"
9            << setiosflags( ios::showbase ) << '\n';
10
11      for ( int loop = 33; loop <= 126; ++loop )
12          cout << setw( 7 ) << dec << loop << setw( 9 ) << oct << loop
13               << setw( 15 ) << hex << loop << setw(13)
14               << static_cast<char>( loop ) << endl;
15
16      return 0;
17  }
```

```
Decimal    Octal    Hexadecimal    Character
     33     041         0x21           !
     34     042         0x22           "
     35     043         0x23           #
     36     044         0x24           $
     37     045         0x25           %
     38     046         0x26           &
     39     047         0x27           '
...
    120     0170        0x78           x
    121     0171        0x79           y
    122     0172        0x7a           z
    123     0173        0x7b           {
    124     0174        0x7c           |
    125     0175        0x7d           }
    126     0176        0x7e           ~
```

11.18 Write a program to show that the **getline** and three-argument **get** istream member functions each end the input string with a string terminating null character. Also show that **get** leaves the delimiter character on the input stream while **getline** extracts the delimiter character and discards it. What happens to the unread characters in the stream?

ANS:

```
1   // Exercise 11.18 Solution
2   #include <iostream.h>
3   #include <ctype.h>
4
5   const int SIZE = 80;
6
7   int main()
8   {
9       char array[ SIZE ], array2[ SIZE ], c;
```

```
10
11      cout << "Enter a sentence to test getline() and get():\n";
12      cin.getline( array, SIZE, '*' );
13      cout << array << '\n';
14
15      cin >> c;   // read next character in input
16      cout << "The next character in the input is: " << c << '\n';
17
18      cin.get( array2, SIZE, '*' );
19      cout << array2 << '\n';
20
21      cin >> c;   // read next character in input
22      cout << "The next character in the input is: " << c << '\n';
23
24      return 0;
25   }
```

```
Enter a sentence to test getline() and get():
wishing*on*a*star
wishing
The next character in the input is: o
n
The next character in the input is: *
```

11.19 Write a program that creates the user-defined manipulator **skipwhite** to skip leading whitespace characters in the input stream. The manipulator should use the **isspace** function from the **ctype.h** library to test if the character is a whitespace character. Each character should be input using the **istream** member function **get**. When a non-whitespace character is encountered, the **skipwhite** manipulator finishes its job by placing the character back on the input stream and returning an **istream** reference.

Test the manipulator by creating a **main** function in which the **ios::skipws** flag is unset so that the stream-extraction operator does not automatically skip whitespace. Then test the manipulator on the input stream by entering a character preceded by whitespace as input. Print the character that was input to confirm that a whitespace character was not input.

Chapter 12 Solutions

Templates

12.3   Write a function template **bubbleSort** based on the sort program of Fig. 5.15. Write a driver program that inputs, sorts, and outputs an **int** array and a **float** array.

ANS:

```
1   // Exercise 12.3 solution
2   // This program puts values into an array, sorts the values into
3   // ascending order, and prints the resulting array.
4   #include <iostream.h>
5   #include <iomanip.h>
6
7   // Function template for bubbleSort
8   template < class T >
9   void bubbleSort( T * const array, int size )
10  {
11     void swap( T * const, T * const );
12
13     for ( int pass = 1; pass < size; ++pass )
14        for ( int j = 0; j < size - pass; ++j )
15           if ( array[ j ] > array[ j + 1 ] )
16              swap( &array[ j ], &array[ j + 1 ] );
17  }
18
19  template < class T >
20  void swap( T * const element1Ptr, T * const element2Ptr )
21  {
22     temp = *element1Ptr;
23     *element1Ptr = *element2Ptr;
24     *element2Ptr = temp;
25  }
26
27  int main()
28  {
29     const int arraySize = 10;
30     int a[ arraySize ] = { 10, 9, 8, 7, 6, 5, 4, 3, 2, 1 }, i;
31
32     // Process an array of integers
33     cout << "Integer data items in original order\n";
34
35     for ( i = 0; i < arraySize; ++i )
36        cout << setw( 6 ) << a[ i ];
37
38     bubbleSort( a, arraySize );              // sort the array
39     cout << "\nInteger data items in ascending order\n";
40
41     for ( i = 0; i < arraySize; ++i )
42        cout << setw( 6 ) << a[ i ];
43
```

```
44        cout << "\n\n";
45
46        // Process an array of floating point values
47        float b[ arraySize ] = { 10.1, 9.9, 8.8, 7.7, 6.6, 5.5,
48                                  4.4, 3.3, 2.2, 1.1 };
49
50        cout << "Floating point data items in original order\n";
51
52        for ( i = 0; i < arraySize; ++i )
53           cout << setw( 6 ) << b[ i ];
54
55        bubbleSort( b, arraySize );              // sort the array
56        cout << "\nFloating point data items in ascending order\n";
57
58        for ( i = 0; i < arraySize; ++i )
59           cout << setw( 6 ) << b[ i ];
60
61        cout << endl;
62        return 0;
63     }
```

```
Integer data items in original order
    10     9     8     7     6     5     4     3     2     1
Integer data items in ascending order
    10     9     8     7     6     5     4     3     2     1

Floating point data items in original order
  10.1   9.9   8.8   7.7   6.6   5.5   4.4   3.3   2.2   1.1
Floating point data items in ascending order
  10.1   9.9   8.8   7.7   6.6   5.5   4.4   3.3   2.2   1.1
```

12.4   Overload function template **printArray** of Fig. 12.2 so that it takes two-additional integer arguments, namely **int lowSubscript** and **int highSubscript**. A call to this function will print only the designated portion of the array. Validate **lowSubscript** and **highSubscript**; if either is out-of-range or if **highSubscript** is less than or equal to **lowSubscript**, the overloaded **printArray** function should return 0; otherwise, **printArray** should return the number of elements printed. Then modify **main** to exercise both versions of **printArray** on arrays **a**, **b**, and **c**. Be sure to test all capabilities of both versions of **printArray**.

   ANS:

```
1    // Exercise 12.4 solution
2    // Using template functions
3    #include <iostream.h>
4
5    template< class T >
6    int printArray( T const * const array, int size, int lowSubscript,
7                    int highSubscript )
8    {
9       if ( size < 0 || lowSubscript < 0 || highSubscript >= size )
10          return 0;   // negative size or subscript out of range
11
12       for ( int i = lowSubscript, count = 0; i <= highSubscript; ++i ) {
13          ++count;
14          cout << array[ i ] << ' ';
15       }
16
17       cout << '\n';
18
19       return count;   // number or elements output
20    }
21
```

```
22   int main()
23   {
24       const int aCount = 5, bCount = 7, cCount = 6;
25       int a[ aCount ] = { 1, 2, 3, 4, 5 };
26       double b[ bCount ] = { 1.1, 2.2, 3.3, 4.4, 5.5, 6.6, 7.7 };
27       char c[ cCount ] = "HELLO";   // 6th position for null
28       int elements;
29
30       cout << "\nArray a contains:\n";
31       elements = printArray( a, aCount, 0, aCount - 1 );
32       cout << elements << " elements were output\n";
33
34       cout << "Array a from 1 to 3 is:\n";
35       elements = printArray( a, aCount, 1, 3 );
36       cout << elements << " elements were output\n";
37
38       cout << "Array a output with invalid subscripts:\n";
39       elements = printArray( a, aCount, -1, 10 );
40       cout << elements << " elements were output\n\n";
41
42       cout << "Array b contains:\n";
43       elements = printArray( b, bCount, 0, bCount - 1 );
44       cout << elements << " elements were output\n";
45
46       cout << "Array b from 1 to 5 is:\n";
47       elements = printArray( b, bCount, 1, 3 );
48       cout << elements << " elements were output\n";
49
50       cout << "Array b output with invalid subscripts:\n";
51       elements = printArray( b, bCount, -1, 10 );
52       cout << elements << " elements were output\n\n";
53
54       cout << "Array c contains:\n";
55       elements = printArray( c, cCount, 0, cCount - 1 );
56       cout << elements << " elements were output\n";
57
58       cout << "Array c from 1 to 4 is:\n";
59       elements = printArray( c, cCount, 1, 3 );
60       cout << elements << " elements were output\n";
61
62       cout << "Array c output with invalid subscripts:\n";
63       elements = printArray( c, cCount, -1, 10 );
64       cout << elements << " elements were output" << endl;
65
66       return 0;
67   }
```

```
Array a contains:
1 2 3 4 5
5 elements were output
Array a from 1 to 3 is:
2 3 4
3 elements were output
Array a output with invalid subscripts:
0 elements were output

Array b contains:
1.1 2.2 3.3 4.4 5.5 6.6 7.7
7 elements were output
Array b from 1 to 5 is:
2.2 3.3 4.4
3 elements were output                    continued...
```

```
Array b output with invalid subscripts:
0 elements were output

Array c contains:
H E L L O
6 elements were output
Array c from 1 to 4 is:
E L L
3 elements were output
Array c output with invalid subscripts:
0 elements were output
```

12.5   Overload function template `printArray` of Fig. 12.2 with a non-template version that specifically prints an array of character strings in neat, tabular, column format.

ANS:

```cpp
1    // Exercise 12.5 solution
2    // Using template functions
3    #include <iostream.h>
4    #include <iomanip.h>
5
6    template< class T >
7    void printArray( T const * const array, int size )
8    {
9       for ( int i = 0; i < size; ++i )
10         cout << array[ i ] << ' ';
11
12      cout << '\n';
13   }
14
15   void printArray( char const * const stringArray[], int size )
16   {
17      for ( int i = 0; i < size; ++i ) {
18         cout << setw( 10 ) << stringArray[ i ];
19
20         if ( ( i + 1 ) % 4 == 0 )
21            cout << '\n';
22      }
23
24      cout << '\n';
25   }
26
27   int main()
28   {
29      const int aCount = 5, bCount = 7, cCount = 6, sCount = 8;
30      int a[ aCount ] = { 1, 2, 3, 4, 5 };
31      double b[ bCount ] = { 1.1, 2.2, 3.3, 4.4, 5.5, 6.6, 7.7 };
32      char c[ cCount ] = "HELLO";   // 6th position for null
33      char *strings[ sCount ] = { "one", "two", "three", "four",
34                         "five", "six", "seven", "eight" };
35
36      cout << "Array a contains:\n";
37      printArray( a, aCount );  // integer template function
38
39      cout << "\nArray b contains:\n";
40      printArray( b, bCount );  // float template function
41
42      cout << "\nArray c contains:\n";
43      printArray( c, cCount );  // character template function
44
45      cout << "\nArray strings contains:\n";
```

```
46        printArray( strings, sCount );   // function specific to string arrays
47
48        return 0;
49   }
```

```
Array a contains:
1 2 3 4 5

Array b contains:
1.1 2.2 3.3 4.4 5.5 6.6 7.7

Array c contains:
H E L L O

Array strings contains:
one two three four five six seven eight
```

12.6 Write a simple function template for predicate function **isEqualTo** that compares its two arguments with the equality operator (**==**) and returns 1 if they are equal and 0 if they are not equal. Use this function template in a program that calls **isEqualTo** only with a variety of built-in types. Now write a separate version of the program that calls **isEqualTo** with a user-defined class type, but does not overload the equality operator. What happens when you attempt to run this program? Now overload the equality operator (with operator function **operator==**). Now what happens when you attempt to run this program?

ANS:

```
1   // Exercise 12.6 solution
2   // Combined solution to entire problem
3   #include <iostream.h>
4
5   template < class T >
6   bool isEqualTo( const T &arg1, const T &arg2 ) { return arg1 == arg2; }
7
8   class SomeClass {
9      friend ostream &operator<<(ostream &, SomeClass &);
10  public:
11     SomeClass( int s, double t )
12     {
13        x = s;
14        y = t;
15     }
16
17     // Overloaded equality operator. If this is not provided, the
18     // program will not compile.
19     bool operator==( const SomeClass &right ) const
20        { return x == right.x && y == right.y; }
21  private:
22     int x;
23     double y;
24  };
25
26  ostream &operator<<( ostream &out, SomeClass &obj )
27  {
28     out << '(' << obj.x << ", " << obj.y << ')';
29     return out;
30  }
31
32  int main()
33  {
34     int a, b;
35
36     cout << "Enter two integer values: ";
37     cin >> a >> b;
```

```
38      cout << a << " and " << b << " are "
39          << ( isEqualTo( a, b ) ? "equal" : "not equal" ) << '\n';
40
41      char c, d;
42
43      cout << "\nEnter two character values: ";
44      cin >> c >> d;
45      cout << c << " and " << d << " are "
46          << ( isEqualTo( c, d ) ? "equal" : "not equal" ) << '\n';
47
48      double e, f;
49
50      cout << "\nEnter two double values: ";
51      cin >> e >> f;
52      cout << e << " and " << f << " are "
53          << ( isEqualTo( e, f ) ? "equal" : "not equal") << '\n';
54
55      SomeClass g( 1, 1.1 ), h( 1, 1.1 );
56
57      cout << "\nThe class objects " << g << " and " << h << " are "
58          << ( isEqualTo( g, h ) ? "equal" : "not equal" ) << '\n';
59      return 0;
60  }
```

```
Enter two integer values: 8 22
8 and 22 are not equal

Enter two character values: Y Y
Y and Y are equal

Enter two double values: 3.3 8.7
3.3 and 8.7 are not equal

The class objects (1, 1.1) and (1, 1.1) are equal
```

12.7   Use a non-type parameter **numberOfElements** and a type parameter **elementType** to help create a template for the **Array** class we developed in Chapter 8, "Operator Overloading." This template will enable **Array** objects to be instantiated with a specified number of elements of a specified element type at compile time.

ANS:

```
1   #ifndef ARRAY1_H
2   #define ARRAY1_H
3
4   #include <iostream.h>
5   #include <stdlib.h>
6   #include <assert.h>
7
8   template < class elementType, int numberOfElements >
9   class Array {
10  public:
11      Array();                                    // default constructor
12      ~Array();                                   // destructor
13      int getSize() const;                        // return size
14      bool operator==( const Array & ) const;     // compare equal
15      bool operator!=( const Array & ) const;     // compare !equal
16      elementType &operator[]( int );             // subscript operator
17      static int getArrayCount();                 // Return count of
18                                                  // arrays instantiated.
19      void inputArray();                          // input the array elements
20      void outputArray() const;                   // output the array elements
```

```
21  private:
22     elementType ptr[ numberOfElements ]; // pointer to first element of array
23     int size; // size of the array
24     static int arrayCount;   // # of Arrays instantiated
25  };
26
27  // Initialize static data member at file scope
28  template < class elementType, int numberOfElements >
29  int Array< elementType, numberOfElements >::arrayCount = 0;    // no objects yet
30
31  // Default constructor for class Array
32  template < class elementType, int numberOfElements >
33  Array< elementType, numberOfElements >::Array()
34  {
35     ++arrayCount;                    // count one more object
36     size = numberOfElements;
37
38     for ( int i = 0; i < size; ++i )
39        ptr[ i ] = 0;                 // initialize array
40  }
41
42  // Destructor for class Array
43  template < class elementType, int numberOfElements >
44  Array< elementType, numberOfElements >::~Array() { --arrayCount; }
45
46  // Get the size of the array
47  template < class elementType, int numberOfElements >
48  int Array< elementType, numberOfElements >::getSize() const { return size; }
49
50  // Determine if two arrays are equal and
51  // return true or false.
52  template < class elementType, int numberOfElements >
53  bool Array< elementType, numberOfElements >::
54              operator==( const Array &right ) const
55  {
56     if ( size != right.size )
57        return false;     // arrays of different sizes
58
59     for ( int i = 0; i < size; ++i )
60        if ( ptr[ i ] != right.ptr[ i ] )
61           return false; // arrays are not equal
62
63     return true;         // arrays are equal
64  }
65
66  // Determine if two arrays are not equal and
67  // return true or false.
68  template < class elementType, int numberOfElements >
69  bool Array< elementType, numberOfElements >::
70              operator!=( const Array &right ) const
71  {
72     if ( size != right.size )
73        return true;          // arrays of different sizes
74
75     for ( int i = 0; i < size; ++i )
76        if ( ptr[ i ] != right.ptr[ i ] )
77           return true;       // arrays are not equal
78
79     return false;            // arrays are equal
80  }
81
```

```
82   // Overloaded subscript operator
83   template < class elementType, int numberOfElements >
84   elementType &Array< elementType, numberOfElements >::
85                operator[]( int subscript )
86   {
87      // check for subscript out of range error
88      assert( 0 <= subscript && subscript < size );
89
90      return ptr[ subscript ];   // reference return creates lvalue
91   }
92
93   // Return the number of Array objects instantiated
94   template < class elementType, int numberOfElements >
95   int Array< elementType, numberOfElements >::getArrayCount()
96      { return arrayCount; }
97
98   // Input values for entire array.
99   template < class elementType, int numberOfElements >
100  void Array< elementType, numberOfElements >::inputArray()
101  {
102     for ( int i = 0; i < size; ++i )
103        cin >> ptr[ i ];
104  }
105
106  // Output the array values
107  template < class elementType, int numberOfElements >
108  void Array< elementType, numberOfElements >::outputArray() const
109  {
110     for ( int i = 0; i < size; ++i ) {
111        cout << ptr[ i ] << ' ';
112
113        if ( ( i + 1 ) % 10 == 0 )
114           cout << '\n';
115     }
116
117     if ( i % 10 != 0 )
118        cout << '\n';
119  }
120
121  #endif
```

```
122  // Exercise 12.7 solution
123  #include <iostream.h>
124  #include "arraytmp.h"
125
126  int main()
127  {
128     Array< int, 5 > intArray;
129
130     cout << "Enter " << intArray.getSize() << " integer values:\n";
131     intArray.inputArray();
132
133     cout << "\nThe values in intArray are:\n";
134     intArray.outputArray();
135
136     Array< float, 5 > floatArray;
137
138     cout << "\nEnter " << floatArray.getSize()
139          << " floating point values:\n";
140     floatArray.inputArray();
141
142     cout << "\nThe values in the double array are:\n";
143     floatArray.outputArray();
```

```
144
145      return 0;
146  }
```

```
Enter 5 integer values:
99 98 97 96 95

The values in intArray are:
99 98 97 96 95

Enter 5 floating point values:
1.12 1.13 1.45 1.22 9.11

The values in the double array are:
1.12 1.13 1.45 1.22 9.11
```

12.8   Write a program with class template **Array**. The template can instantiate an **Array** of any element type. Override the template with a specific definition for an **Array** of **float** elements (**class Array< float >**). The driver should demonstrate the instantiation of an **Array** of **int** through the template, and should show that an attempt to instantiate an **Array** of **float** uses the definition provided in **class Array< float >**.

12.9   Distinguish between the terms function template and template function.
    ANS: A function template is used to instantiate template functions.

12.10   Which is more like a stencil—a class template or a template class? Explain your answer.
    ANS: A class template can be viewed as a stencil from which a template class can be created. A template class can be viewed as a stencil from which objects of that class can be created. So, in a way, both can be viewed as stencils.

12.11   What is the relationship between function templates and overloading?
    ANS: Function templates create overloaded versions of a function. The main difference is at compile time, where the compiler automatically creates the code for the template functions from the function template rather than the programmer creating the code.

12.12   Why might you choose to use a function template instead of a macro?
    ANS: A macro is a text substitution done by the preprocessor. A function template provides real function definitions with all the type checking to ensure proper function calls.

12.13   What performance problem can result from using function templates and class templates?
    ANS: There can be a tremendous proliferation of code in the program due to many copies of code generated by the compiler.

12.14   The compiler performs a matching process to determine which template function to call when a function is invoked. Under what circumstances does an attempt to make a match result in a compile error?
    ANS: If the compiler cannot match the function call made to a template or if the matching process results in multiple matches at compile time, the compiler generates an error.

12.15   Why is it appropriate to call a class template a parameterized type?
    ANS: When creating template classes from a class template, it is necessary to provide a type (or possibly several types) to complete the definition of the new type being declared. For example, when creating an "array of integers" from an **Array** class template, the type **int** is provided to the class template to complete the definition of an array of integers.

12.16   Explain why you might use the statement

        Array< Employee > workerList(100);

in a C++ program.
    ANS: Declares an **Array** object to store **Employee** objects and passes **100** to the constructor.

12.17   Review your answer to Exercise 12.16. Now, why might you use the statement

        Array< Employee > workerList;

in a C++ program?
    ANS: Declares an **Array** object to store an **Employee**. The default constructor is used.

12.18 Explain the use of the following notation in a C++ program.

```
template< class T > Array< T >::Array( int s )
```

ANS: This notation is used to begin the definition of the **Array(int)** constructor for the class template **Array**.

12.19 Why might you typically use a non-type parameter with a class template for a container such as an array or stack?
ANS: To specify at compile time the size of the container class object being declared.

12.20 Describe how to provide a class for a specific type to override the class template for that type.

12.21 Describe the relationship between class templates and inheritance.

12.22 Suppose a class template has the header

```
template< class T1 > class C1
```

Describe the friendship relationships established by placing each of the following friendship declarations inside this class template header. Identifiers beginning with "**f**" are functions, identifiers beginning with "**C**" are classes, and identifiers beginning with "**T**" can represent any type (i.e., built-in types or class types).

a) **friend void f1();**
ANS: Function **f1** is a **friend** of all template classes instantiated from class template **C1**.
b) **friend void f2(C1< T1 > &);**
ANS: Function **f2** for a specific type of **T1** is a **friend** of the template class of type **T1**. For example, if **T1** is of type **int**, the function with the prototype

```
void f2( C1< int > & );
```

is a **friend** of the class **C1< int >**.
c) **friend void C2::f4();**
ANS: Function **f4** of class **C2** is a **friend** of all template classes instantiated from class template **C1**.
d) **friend void C3< T1 >::f5(C1< T1 > &);**
ANS: Function **f5** of class **C3** for a specific type of **T1** is a **friend** of the template class of type **T1**. For example, if **T1** is **int**, the function with the prototype

```
void c3< int >::f5( C1< int > & );
```

e) **friend class C5;**
ANS: Makes every member function of class **C5** a **friend** of all template classes instantiated from the class template **C1**.
f) **friend class C6< T1 >;**
ANS: For a specific type **T1**, makes every member function of **C6< T1 >** a **friend** of class **C1< T1 >**. For example, if **T1** is **int**, every member function of class **C6< int >** is a **friend** of **C1< int >**.

12.23 Suppose class template **Employee** has a **static** data member **count**. Suppose three template classes are instantiated from the class template. How many copies of the **static** data member will exist? How will the use of each be constrained (if at all)?
ANS: For **static** members of a class template, each template class instantiated receives its own copy of all the **static** members. Then all objects instantiated for a given template class access that particular template class's **static** members.

Chapter 13 Solutions
Exception Handling

Solutions

13.20   List the various exceptional conditions that have occurred in programs throughout this text. List as many additional exceptional conditions as you can. For each of these, describe briefly how a program would typically handle the exception using the exception-handling techniques discussed in this chapter. Some typical exceptions are: Division by zero, arithmetic overflow, array subscript out of bounds, exhaustion of the free store, etc.

13.21   Under what circumstances would the programmer not provide a parameter name when defining the type of the object that will be caught by a handler?
> **ANS:** If there is no information in the object that is required in the handler, a parameter name is not required in the handler.

13.22   A program contains the statement

```
throw;
```

Where would you normally expect to find such a statement? What if that statement appeared in a different part of a program?
> **ANS:** The statement would be found in an exception handler to rethrow an exception. If any **throw** expression occurs outside a **try** block, the function **unexpected** is called.

13.23   Under what circumstances would you use the following statement?

```
catch(...) { throw; }
```

> **ANS:** The preceding statement is used to **catch** any exception and rethrow it for handling by an exception handler in a function within the call stack.

13.24   Compare and contrast exception handling with the various other error-processing schemes discussed in the text.
> **ANS:** Exception handling enables the programmer to build more robust classes with built-in error processing capabilities. Once created, such classes allow clients of classes to concentrate on using the classes rather than defining what should happen if an error occurs while using the class. Exception handling offers the possibility that an error can be processed and that the program can continue execution. Other forms of error checking such as **assert** exit the program immediately without any further processing.

13.25   List the benefits of exception handling over conventional means of error processing.

13.26   Provide reasons why exceptions should not be used as an alternate form of program control.
> **ANS:** Exceptions were designed for "exceptional cases." Exceptions do not follow conventional forms of program control. Therefore, using exceptions for anything other than error processing will not be easily recognized by others reading the code. This may make the program more difficult to modify and maintain.

13.27   Describe a technique for handling related exceptions.
> **ANS:** Create a base class for all related exceptions. In the base class, derive all the related exception classes. Once the exception class hierarchy is created, exceptions from the hierarchy can be caught as the base class exception type or as one of the derived class exception types.

13.28   Until this chapter, we have found that dealing with errors detected by constructors is a bit awkward. Exception handling gives us a much better means of dealing with such errors. Consider a constructor for a **String** class. The constructor uses **new** to obtain space from the free store. Suppose **new** fails. Show how you would deal with this without exception handling. Discuss the key issues. Show how you would deal with such memory exhaustion with exception handling. Explain why the exception handling method is superior.

ANS:

```
1   // Exercise 13.28 Solution
2   #include <iostream.h>
3   #include <iomanip.h>
4   #include <new.h>
5   #include <stdlib.h>
6   void message( void );
7   int main()
8   {
9      long double *d[ 50 ];
10     set_new_handler( message );
11
12     for ( int q = 0; q < 50; ++q ) {
13        d[ q ] = new long double[ 1000000 ];
14        cout << "allocated 1000000 long doubles to d[" << q << "]\n";
15     }
16     cout << "Memory Allocated\n";
17     return 0;
18  }
19  void message( void )
20  {
21     cerr << "Memory Allocation Failed\n";
22     exit( EXIT_FAILURE );
23  }
```

```
allocated 1000000 long doubles to d[0]
allocated 1000000 long doubles to d[1]
allocated 1000000 long doubles to d[2]
allocated 1000000 long doubles to d[3]
allocated 1000000 long doubles to d[4]
allocated 1000000 long doubles to d[5]
allocated 1000000 long doubles to d[6]
allocated 1000000 long doubles to d[7]
allocated 1000000 long doubles to d[8]
allocated 1000000 long doubles to d[9]
allocated 1000000 long doubles to d[10]
allocated 1000000 long doubles to d[11]
allocated 1000000 long doubles to d[12]
allocated 1000000 long doubles to d[13]
allocated 1000000 long doubles to d[14]
allocated 1000000 long doubles to d[15]
allocated 1000000 long doubles to d[16]
Memory Allocation Failed
```

13.29 Suppose a program **throws** an exception and the appropriate exception handler begins executing. Now suppose that the exception handler itself **throws** the same exception. Does this create an infinite recursion? Write a C++ program to check your observation.

ANS:

```
1   // Exercise 13.29 solution
2   #include <iostream.h>
3
4   class TestException {
5   public:
6      TestException( char *mPtr ) : message( mPtr ) {}
7      void print() const { cout << message << '\n'; }
8   private:
9      char *message;
10  };
```

```
11
12   int main()
13   {
14      try {
15         throw TestException( "This is a test" );
16      }
17      catch ( TestException &t ) {
18         t.print();
19         throw TestException( "This is another test" );
20      }
21
22      return 0;
23   }
```

```
This is a test
Abnormal program termination
```

13.30 Use inheritance to create a base exception class and various derived exception classes. Then show that a **catch** handler specifying the base class can **catch** derived-class exceptions.

   ANS:

```
1    // Exercise 13.30 Solution
2    #include <iostream.h>
3    #include <stdlib.h>
4    #include <time.h>
5
6    class BaseException {
7    public:
8       BaseException( char *mPtr ) : message( mPtr ) {}
9       void print() const { cout << message << '\n'; }
10   private:
11      char *message;
12   };
13
14   class DerivedException : public BaseException {
15   public:
16      DerivedException( char *mPtr ) : BaseException( mPtr ) {}
17   };
18
19   class DerivedException2 : public DerivedException {
20   public:
21      DerivedException2( char *mPtr ) : DerivedException( mPtr ) {}
22   };
23
24   int main()
25   {
26      srand( time( 0 ) );
27
28      try {
29         throw ( rand() % 2 ? DerivedException( "DerivedException" ) :
30                              DerivedException2( "DerivedException2" ) );
31      }
32      catch ( BaseException &b ) {
33         b.print();
34      }
35
36      return 0;
37   }
```

```
DerivedException2
```

13.31 Show a conditional expression that returns either a **double** or an **int**. Provide an **int catch** handler and a **double catch** handler. Show that only the **double catch** handler executes regardless of whether the **int** or the **double** is returned.

ANS:

```
1   // Exercise 13.31 Solution
2   #include <iostream.h>
3
4   int main()
5   {
6      try {
7         int a = 7;
8         double b = 9.9;
9
10        throw a < b ? a : b;
11     }
12     catch ( int x ) {
13        cerr << "The int value " << x << " was thrown\n";
14     }
15     catch ( double y ) {
16        cerr << "The double value " << y << " was thrown\n";
17     }
18
19     return 0;
20  }
```

```
The double value 7 was thrown
```

13.32 Write a C++ program designed to generate and handle a memory exhaustion error. Your program should loop on a request to create dynamic storage through operator **new**.

ANS:

```
1   // Exercise 13.32 Solution
2   #include <iostream>
3   #include <iomanip>
4   #include <new>
5   int main()
6   {
7      long double *d[ 50 ];
8
9      for ( int q = 0; q < 50; ++q ) {
10        try{
11           d[ q ] = new long double[ 1000000 ];
12           cout << "allocated 1000000 long doubles to d[" << q << "]\n";
13        }
14        catch( bad_alloc b ) {
15           cout << "allocation failed at element " << q << " of array\n";
16           break;
17        }
18     }
19     return 0;
20  }
```

```
allocated 1000000 long doubles to d[0]
allocated 1000000 long doubles to d[1]
allocated 1000000 long doubles to d[2]
...
allocated 1000000 long doubles to d[13]
allocated 1000000 long doubles to d[14]
allocation failed at element 15 of array
```

13.33 Write a C++ program which shows that all destructors for objects constructed in a block are called before an exception is thrown from that block.
   ANS:

```
1   // Exercise 13.33 Solution
2   #include <iostream.h>
3
4   class Object {
5   public:
6      Object( int val ) : value( val )
7         { cout << "Object " << value << " constructor\n"; }
8      ~Object()
9         { cout << "Object " << value << " destructor\n"; }
10  private:
11     int value;
12  };
13
14  class Error {
15  public:
16     Error( char *s ) : string( s ) {}
17     void print() const { cerr << '\n' << string << '\n'; }
18  private:
19     char *string;
20  };
21
22  int main()
23  {
24     try {
25        Object a( 1 ), b( 2 ), c( 3 );
26        cout << '\n';
27        throw Error( "This is a test exception" );
28     }
29     catch ( Error &e ) {
30        e.print();
31     }
32
33     return 0;
34  }
```

```
Object 1 constructor
Object 2 constructor
Object 3 constructor
Object 3 destructor
Object 2 destructor
Object 1 destructor

This is a test exception
```

13.34 Write a C++ program which shows that member object destructors are called for only those member objects that were constructed before an exception occurred.
   ANS:

```
1   // Exercise 13_34 Solution
2   #include <iostream.h>
3
4   // A sample exception class
5   class ExceptionClass {
6   public:
7      ExceptionClass() : message( "An exception was thrown" ) {}
8      void print() const { cerr << '\n' << message << '\n'; }
```

```
 9   private:
10      char *message;
11   };
12
13   // A class from which to build member objects
14   class Member {
15   public:
16      Member( int val ) : value( val )
17      {
18         cout << "Member object " << value << " constructor called\n";
19
20         // If value is 3, throw an exception for demonstration purposes.
21         if ( value == 3 )
22            throw ExceptionClass();
23      }
24
25      ~Member()
26      { cout << "Member object " << value << " destructor called\n"; }
27   private:
28      int value;
29   };
30
31   // A class to encapsulate objects of class Member
32   class Encapsulate {
33   public:
34      Encapsulate() : m1( 1 ), m2( 2 ), m3( 3 ), m4( 4 ), m5( 5 ) {}
35   private:
36      Member m1, m2, m3, m4, m5;
37   };
38
39   int main()
40   {
41      cout << "Constructing an object of class Encapsulate\n";
42
43      try {
44         Encapsulate e;
45      }
46      catch( ExceptionClass &except ) {
47         except.print();
48      }
49
50      return 0;
51   }
```

```
Constructing an object of class Encapsulate
Member object 1 constructor called
Member object 2 constructor called
Member object 3 constructor called
Member object 2 destructor called
Member object 1 destructor called

An exception was thrown
```

13.35 Write a C++ program that demonstrates how any exception is caught with `catch( ... )`.
       ANS:

```
1   // Exercise 13.35 Solution
2   #include <iostream.h>
3
4   // A sample exception class
5   class ExceptionClass {
6   public:
```

```
7       ExceptionClass() : message( "An exception was thrown" ) {}
8       void print() const { cerr << '\n' << message << '\n'; }
9   private:
10      char *message;
11  };
12
13  void generateException();
14
15  int main()
16  {
17      try {
18          generateException();
19      }
20      catch( ... ) {
21          cerr << "The \"catch all\" exception handler was invoked\n";
22      }
23
24      return 0;
25  }
26
27  void generateException()
28  {
29      throw ExceptionClass();
30  }
```

```
The "catch all" exception handler was invoked
```

13.36   Write a C++ program which shows that the order of exception handlers is important. The first matching handler is the one that executes. Compile and run your program two different ways to show that two different handlers execute with two different effects.

13.37   Write a C++ program that shows a constructor passing information about constructor failure to an exception handler after a **try** block.

ANS:

```
1   // Exercise 13.37 Solution
2   #include <iostream.h>
3
4   class InvalidIDNumberError {
5   public:
6       InvalidIDNumberError( char *s ) : errorMessage( s ) {}
7       void print() const { cerr << errorMessage; }
8   private:
9       char *errorMessage;
10  };
11
12  class TestInvalidIDNumberError {
13  public:
14      TestInvalidIDNumberError( int id ) : idNumber( id )
15      {
16          cout << "Constructor for object " << idNumber << '\n';
17
18          if ( idNumber < 0 )
19              throw InvalidIDNumberError( "ERROR: Negative ID number" );
20      }
21  private:
22      int idNumber;
23  };
24
```

```
25   int main()
26   {
27      try {
28         TestInvalidIDNumberError valid( 10 ), invalid( -1 );
29      }
30      catch ( InvalidIDNumberError &error ) {
31         error.print();
32         cerr << '\n';
33      }
34
35      return 0;
36   }
```

```
Constructor for object 10
Constructor for object -1
ERROR: Negative ID number
```

13.38 Write a C++ program that uses a multiple inheritance hierarchy of exception classes to create a situation in which the order of exception handlers matters.

13.39 Using **setjmp/longjmp**, a program can transfer control immediately to an error routine from a deeply nested function invocation. Unfortunately, as the stack is unwound, destructors are not called for the automatic objects that were created during the sequence of nested function calls. Write a C++ program which demonstrates that these destructors are, in fact, not called.

13.40 Write a C++ program that illustrates rethrowing an exception.
ANS:

```
1    // Exercise 13.40 Solution
2    #include <iostream.h>
3
4    class TestException {
5    public:
6       TestException( char *m ) : message( m ) {}
7       void print() const { cout << message << '\n'; }
8    private:
9       char *message;
10   };
11
12   void f() { throw TestException( "Test exception thrown" ); }
13
14   void g()
15   {
16      try {
17         f();
18      }
19      catch ( ... ) {
20         cerr << "Exception caught in function g(). Rethrowing...\n";
21         throw;
22      }
23   }
24
25   int main()
26   {
27      try {
28         g();   // start function call chain
29      }
30      catch ( ... ) {
31         cerr << "Exception caught in function main()\n";
32      }
33      return 0;
34   }
```

```
Exception caught in function g(). Rethrowing...
Exception caught in function main()
```

13.41 Write a C++ program that uses **set_unexpected** to set a user-defined function for **unexpected**, uses **set_unexpected** again, and then resets **unexpected** back to its previous function. Write a similar program to test **set_terminate** and **terminate**.

13.42 Write a C++ program which shows that a function with its own **try** block does not have to catch every possible error generated within the **try**. Some exceptions can slip through to, and be handled in, outer scopes.

ANS:

```
1   // Exercise 13.42 Solution
2   #include <iostream.h>
3
4   class TestException1 {
5   public:
6      TestException1( char *m ) : message( m ) {}
7      void print() const { cerr << message << '\n'; }
8   private:
9      char *message;
10  };
11
12  class TestException2 {
13  public:
14     TestException2( char *m ) : message( m ) {}
15     void print() const { cout << message << '\n'; }
16  private:
17     char *message;
18  };
19
20  void f()
21  {
22     throw TestException1( "TestException1" );
23  }
24
25  void g()
26  {
27     try {
28        f();
29     }
30     catch ( TestException2 &t2 ) {
31        cerr << "In g: Caught ";
32        t2.print();
33     }
34  }
35
36  int main()
37  {
38     try {
39        g();
40     }
41     catch ( TestException1 &t1 ) {
42        cerr << "In main: Caught ";
43        t1.print();
44     }
45
46     return 0;
47  }
```

```
In main: Caught TestException1
```

13.43 Write a C++ program that **throws** an error from a deeply nested function call and still has the **catch** handler following the **try** block enclosing the call chain catch the exception.

ANS:

```
1    // Exercise 13.43 Solution
2    #include <iostream.h>
3
4    class TestException {
5    public:
6       TestException( char *m ) : message( m ) {}
7       void print() const { cout << message << '\n'; }
8    private:
9       char *message;
10   };
11
12   void f() { throw TestException( "TestException" ); }
13
14   void g() { f(); }
15
16   void h() { g(); }
17
18   int main()
19   {
20      try {
21         h();
22      }
23      catch ( TestException &t ) {
24         cerr << "In main: Caught ";
25         t.print();
26      }
27
28      return 0;
29   }
```

```
In main: Caught TestException
```

Chapter 14 Solutions

File Processing

14.5 Fill in the blanks in each of the following:

a) Computers store large amounts of data on secondary storage devices as _____.
ANS: files.

b) A _____ is composed of several fields.
ANS: record.

c) A field that may contain only digits, letters, and blanks is called an_____ field.
ANS: alphanumeric.

d) To facilitate the retrieval of specific records from a file, one field in each record is chosen as a _____.
ANS: key.

e) The vast majority of information stored in computer systems is stored in _____ files.
ANS: sequential.

f) A group of related characters that conveys meaning is called a _____.
ANS: field.

g) The standard stream objects declared by header file **<iostream.h>** are
_____ , _____ , _____ , and_____ .
ANS: cin, cout, cerr, clog.

h) The **ostream** member function _____ outputs a character to the specified stream.
ANS: put.

i) The **ostream** member function _____ is generally used to write data to a randomly accessed file.
ANS: write.

j) The **istream** member function _____ repositions the file position pointer in a file.
ANS: seekg.

14.6 State which of the following are true and which are false (and for those that are false, explain why):

a) The impressive functions performed by computers essentially involve the manipulation of zeros and ones.
ANS: True.

b) People prefer to manipulate bits instead of characters and fields because bits are more compact.
ANS: False. People prefer to manipulate characters and fields because they are less cumbersome and more understandable.

c) People specify programs and data items as characters; computers then manipulate and process these characters as groups of zeros and ones.
ANS: True.

d) A person's 5-digit zip code is an example of a numeric field.
ANS: True.

e) A person's street address is generally considered to be an alphabetic field in computer applications.
ANS: False. A street address is generally considered to be alphanumeric.

f) Data items represented in computers form a data hierarchy in which data items become larger and more complex as we progress from fields to characters to bits, etc.
ANS: False. Data items processed by a computer form a data hierarchy in which data items become larger and more complex as we progress from bits to characters to fields, etc.

g) A record key identifies a record as belonging to a particular field.
ANS: False. A record key identifies a record as belonging to a particular person or entity.

h) Most organizations store all their information in a single file to facilitate computer processing.
ANS: False. Most organizations have many files in which they store their information.

    i)   Each statement that processes a file in a C++ program explicitly refers to that file by name.
    ANS: False. A pointer to each file is used to refer to the file.
    j)   When a program creates a file, the file is automatically retained by the computer for future reference.
    ANS: True.

14.7   Exercise 14.3 asked the reader to write a series of single statements. Actually, these statements form the core of an important type of file processing program, namely, a file-matching program. In commercial data processing, it is common to have several files in each application system. In an accounts receivable system, for example, there is generally a master file containing detailed information about each customer such as the customer's name, address, telephone number, outstanding balance, credit limit, discount terms, contract arrangements, and possibly a condensed history of recent purchases and cash payments.

    As transactions occur (i.e., sales are made and cash payments arrive in the mail), they are entered into a file. At the end of each business period (i.e., a month for some companies, a week for others, and a day in some cases) the file of transactions (called **"trans.dat"** in Exercise 14.3) is applied to the master file (called **"oldmast.dat"** in Exercise 14.3), thus updating each account's record of purchases and payments. During an updating run, the master file is rewritten as a new file (**"newmast.dat"**), which is then used at the end of the next business period to begin the updating process again.

    File-matching programs must deal with certain problems that do not exist in single-file programs. For example, a match does not always occur. A customer on the master file may not have made any purchases or cash payments in the current business period, and therefore no record for this customer will appear on the transaction file. Similarly, a customer who did make some purchases or cash payments may have just moved to this community, and the company may not have had a chance to create a master record for this customer.

    Use the statements written in Exercise 14.3 as a basis for writing a complete file-matching accounts receivable program. Use the account number on each file as the record key for matching purposes. Assume that each file is a sequential file with records stored in increasing order by account number.

    When a match occurs (i.e., records with the same account number appear on both the master file and the transaction file), add the dollar amount on the transaction file to the current balance on the master file, and write the **"newmast.dat"** record. (Assume that purchases are indicated by positive amounts on the transaction file, and that payments are indicated by negative amounts.) When there is a master record for a particular account but no corresponding transaction record, merely write the master record to **"newmast.dat"**. When there is a transaction record but no corresponding master record, print the message **"Unmatched transaction record for account number ..."** (fill in the account number from the transaction record).
    ANS:

```
1   // Exercise 14.7 Solution
2   #include <iostream.h>
3   #include <iomanip.h>
4   #include <fstream.h>
5   #include <stdlib.h>
6
7   void printOutput( ofstream&, int, const char *, const char *, double );
8
9   int main()
10  {
11      int masterAccount, transactionAccount;
12      double masterBalance, transactionBalance;
13      char masterFirstName[ 20 ], masterLastName[ 20 ];
14
15      ifstream inOldMaster( "oldmast.dat" ),
16              inTransaction( "trans.dat" );
17      ofstream outNewMaster( "newmast.dat" );
18
19      if ( !inOldMaster ) {
20         cerr << "Unable to open oldmast.dat\n";
21         exit( EXIT_FAILURE );
22      }
23
24      if ( !inTransaction ) {
25         cerr << "Unable to open trans.dat\n";
26         exit( EXIT_FAILURE );
27      }
28
```

```
29      if ( !outNewMaster ) {
30          cerr << "Unable to open newmast.dat\n";
31          exit( EXIT_FAILURE );
32      }
33
34      cout << "Processing...\n";
35      inTransaction >> transactionAccount >> transactionBalance;
36
37      while ( !inTransaction.eof() ) {
38          inOldMaster >> masterAccount >> masterFirstName
39                      >> masterLastName >> masterBalance;
40
41          while ( masterAccount < transactionAccount && !inOldMaster.eof() ) {
42              printOutput( outNewMaster, masterAccount, masterFirstName,
43                      masterLastName, masterBalance );
44              inOldMaster >> masterAccount >> masterFirstName
45                      >> masterLastName >> masterBalance;
46          }
47
48          if ( masterAccount > transactionAccount ) {
49              cout << "Unmatched transaction record for account "
50                  << transactionAccount << '\n';
51
52              inTransaction >> transactionAccount >> transactionBalance;
53          }
54
55          if ( masterAccount == transactionAccount ) {
56              masterBalance += transactionBalance;
57              printOutput( outNewMaster, masterAccount, masterFirstName,
58                      masterLastName, masterBalance );
59          }
60
61          inTransaction >> transactionAccount >> transactionBalance;
62      }
63
64      inTransaction.close();
65      inOldMaster.close();
66      outNewMaster.close();
67
68      return 0;
69  }
70
71  void printOutput( ofstream &oRef, int mAccount, const char *mfName,
72                  const char *mlName, double mBalance )
73  {
74      cout.setf( ios::fixed | ios::showpoint );
75      oRef.setf( ios::fixed | ios::showpoint );
76
77      oRef << mAccount << ' ' << mfName << ' ' << mlName << ' '
78          << setprecision( 2 ) << mBalance << '\n';
79      cout << mAccount << ' ' << mfName << ' ' << mlName << ' '
80          << setprecision( 2 ) << mBalance << '\n';
81  }
```

```
Processing...
100 Ajax Guppie 678.06
300 Sue Pirhana 650.07
400 Clint Bass 994.22
Unmatched transaction record for account 445
500 Aias Shark 895.80
700 Tom Mahi-Mahi -23.57
900 Marisal Carp 200.55
```

Contents of "oldmast.dat"

```
100 Ajax Guppie 543.89
300 Sue Pirhana 22.88
400 Clint Bass -6.32
500 Aias Shark 888.71
700 Tom Mahi-Mahi 76.09
900 Marisal Carp 100.55
```

Contents of "trans.dat"

```
100 134.17
300 627.19
400 1000.54
445 55.55
500 7.09
700 -99.66
900 100.00
```

Contents of "newmast.dat"

```
100 Ajax Guppie 678.06
300 Sue Pirhana 650.07
400 Clint Bass 994.22
500 Aias Shark 895.80
700 Tom Mahi-Mahi -23.57
900 Marisal Carp 200.55
```

14.8 After writing the program of Exercise 14.7, write a simple program to create some test data for checking out the program. Use the following sample account data:

Master file Account number	Name	Balance
100	Alan Jones	348.17
300	Mary Smith	27.19
500	Sam Sharp	0.00
700	Suzy Green	-14.22

Transaction file Account number	Transaction amount
100	27.14
300	62.11
400	100.56
900	82.17

ANS: NOTE: We generate our own data in this solution.

```
1  // Exercise 14.8 Solution
2  #include <iostream.h>
3  #include <iomanip.h>
4  #include <fstream.h>
5  #include <stdlib.h>
6  #include <time.h>
```

```
7   int main()
8   {
9       const char *firstNames[] = { "Walter", "Alice", "Alan", "Mary", "Steve",
10                                    "Gina", "Tom", "Cindy", "Ilana", "Pam" },
11                 *lastNames[] = { "Red", "Blue", "Yellow", "Orange", "Purple",
12                                  "Green", "Violet", "White", "Black", "Brown" };
13      ofstream outOldMaster( "oldMast.dat" ), outTransaction( "trans.dat" );
14      int z;
15      srand( time( 0 ) );
16
17      if ( !outOldMaster ) {
18          cerr << "Unable to open oldmast.dat\n";
19          exit( EXIT_SUCCESS );
20      }
21
22      if ( !outTransaction ) {
23          cerr << "Unable to open trans.dat\n";
24          exit( EXIT_SUCCESS );
25      }
26
27      // write data to "oldmast.dat"
28      cout << setiosflags( ios::fixed | ios::showpoint )
29           << "Contents of \"oldmast.dat\":\n";
30      outOldMaster.setf( ios::fixed | ios::showpoint );
31      for ( z = 1; z < 11; ++z ) {
32          int value = rand() % 10, value2 = rand() % 50;
33          outOldMaster << z * 100 << ' ' << firstNames[ z - 1 ] << ' '
34                       << lastNames[ value ] << ' ' << setprecision( 2 )
35                       << ( value * 100 ) / ( value2 / 3 + 4.32 ) << '\n';
36          cout << z * 100 << ' ' << firstNames[ z - 1 ] << ' '
37               << lastNames[ value ] << ' ' << setprecision( 2 )
38               << ( value * 100 ) / ( value2 / 3 + 4.32 ) << '\n';
39      }
40
41      // write data to "trans.dat"
42      cout << "\nContents of \"trans.dat\":\n";
43      outTransaction.setf( ios::fixed | ios::showpoint );
44
45      for ( z = 1; z < 11; ++z ) {
46          int value = 25 - rand() % 50;
47          outTransaction << z * 100 << ' ' << setprecision( 2 )
48                         << ( value * 100 ) / ( 2.667 * ( 1 + rand() % 10 ) ) << '\n';
49          cout << z * 100 << ' ' << setprecision( 2 )
50               << ( value * 100 ) / ( 2.667 * ( 1 + rand() % 10 ) ) << '\n';
51      }
52
53      outTransaction.close();
54      outOldMaster.close();
55
56      ifstream inMaster( "oldmast.dat" ), inTrans( "trans.dat" );
57      ofstream newMaster( "newMast.dat" );
58
59      if ( !inMaster ) {
60          cerr << "Unable to open oldmast.dat\n";
61          exit( EXIT_SUCCESS );
62      }
63
64      if ( !inTrans ) {
65          cerr << "Unable to open trans.dat\n";
66          exit( EXIT_SUCCESS );
67      }
68
69      if ( !newMaster ) {
70          cerr << "Unable to open newmast.dat\n";
```

```
71          exit( EXIT_SUCCESS );
72      }
73
74      int account, mAccount;
75      double balance, mBalance;
76      char mFirst[ 20 ], mLast[ 20 ];
77
78      cout << "Processing...\n";
79      inTrans >> account >> balance;
80
81      while ( !inTrans.eof() ) {
82          inMaster >> mAccount >> mFirst >> mLast >> mBalance;
83
84          while ( mAccount < account && !inMaster.eof() )
85              inMaster >> mAccount >> mFirst >> mLast >> mBalance;
86
87          if ( mAccount > account ) {
88              cout << "Unmatched transaction record: account " << account << '\n';
89              inTrans >> account >> balance;
90          }
91
92          if ( mAccount == account ) {
93              mBalance += balance;
94              newMaster << mAccount << ' ' << mFirst << ' ' << mLast
95                      << ' ' << mBalance << '\n';
96          }
97
98          inTrans >> account >> balance;
99      }
100
101     newMaster.close();
102     inTrans.close();
103     inMaster.close();
104     return 0;
105 }
```

```
Contents of "oldmast.dat":
100 Walter Brown 46.58
200 Alice Orange 47.47
300 Alan Green 28.87
400 Mary Black 49.02
500 Steve White 67.83
600 Gina Orange 56.39
700 Tom White 38.21
800 Cindy Red 0.00
900 Ilana Brown 87.21
1000 Pam Red 0.00

Contents of "trans.dat":
100 -149.98
200 262.47
300 -41.24
400 -412.45
500 23.43
600 318.71
700 -224.97
800 -33.33
900 -249.97
1000 -71.24
```

Contents of oldmast.dat:

```
100 Walter Brown 46.58
200 Alice Orange 47.47
300 Alan Green 28.87
400 Mary Black 49.02
500 Steve White 67.83
600 Gina Orange 56.39
700 Tom White 38.21
800 Cindy Red 0.00
900 Ilana Brown 87.21
1000 Pam Red 0.00
```

Contents of trans.dat:

```
100 -149.98
200 262.47
300 -41.24
400 -412.45
500 23.43
600 318.71
700 -224.97
800 -33.33
900 -249.97
1000 -71.24
```

14.9 Run the program of Exercise 14.7 using the files of test data created in Exercise 14.8. Print the new master file. Check that the accounts have been updated correctly.

ANS: Contents of newmast.dat:

```
100 Walter Brown -103.4
200 Alice Orange 309.94
300 Alan Green -12.37
400 Mary Black -363.43
500 Steve White 91.26
600 Gina Orange 375.1
700 Tom White -186.76
800 Cindy Red -33.33
900 Ilana Brown -162.76
1000 Pam Red -71.24
```

14.10 It is possible (actually common) to have several transaction records with the same record key. This occurs because a particular customer might make several purchases and cash payments during a business period. Rewrite your accounts receivable file-matching program of Exercise 14.7 to provide for the possibility of handling several transaction records with the same record key. Modify the test data of Exercise 14.8 to include the following additional transaction records:

Account number	Dollar amount
300	83.89
700	80.78
700	1.53

ANS:

```
1    // Exercise 14.10 Solution
2    #include <iostream.h>
3    #include <fstream.h>
4    #include <iomanip.h>
5    #include <stdlib.h>
```

```
6
7   void printOutput( ofstream &, int, const char *, const char *, double );
8
9   int main()
10  {
11      int masterAccount, transactionAccount;
12      double masterBalance, transactionBalance;
13      char masterFirstName[ 20 ], masterLastName[ 20 ];
14
15      ifstream inOldmaster( "oldmast.dat" ),
16              inTransaction( "trans.dat" );
17      ofstream outNewmaster( "newmast.dat" );
18
19      if ( !inOldmaster ) {
20          cerr << "Unable to open oldmast.dat\n";
21          exit( EXIT_FAILURE );
22      }
23
24      if ( !inTransaction ) {
25          cerr << "Unable to open trans.dat\n";
26          exit( EXIT_FAILURE );
27      }
28
29      if ( !outNewmaster ) {
30          cerr << "Unable to open newmast.dat\n";
31          exit( EXIT_FAILURE );
32      }
33
34      cout << "Processing....\n";
35      inTransaction >> transactionAccount >> transactionBalance;
36
37      while ( !inTransaction.eof() ) {
38          inOldmaster >> masterAccount >> masterFirstName >> masterLastName
39                      >> masterBalance;
40
41          while ( masterAccount < transactionAccount && !inOldmaster.eof() ) {
42              printOutput( outNewmaster, masterAccount, masterFirstName,
43                          masterLastName, masterBalance );
44              inOldmaster >> masterAccount >> masterFirstName >> masterLastName
45                          >> masterBalance;
46          }
47
48          if ( masterAccount > transactionAccount ) {
49              cout << "Unmatched transaction record for account "
50                   << transactionAccount << '\n';
51              inTransaction >> transactionAccount >> transactionBalance;
52          }
53          else if ( masterAccount < transactionAccount ) {
54              cout << "Unmatched transaction record for account "
55                   << transactionAccount << '\n';
56              inTransaction >> transactionAccount >> transactionBalance;
57          }
58
59          while ( masterAccount == transactionAccount &&
60                  !inTransaction.eof() ) {
61              masterBalance += transactionBalance;
62              inTransaction >> transactionAccount >> transactionBalance;
63          }
64
65          printOutput( outNewmaster, masterAccount, masterFirstName,
66                      masterLastName, masterBalance );
67      }
```

```
68
69      inTransaction.close();
70      outNewmaster.close();
71      inOldmaster.close();
72
73      return 0;
74   }
75
76   void printOutput( ofstream &oRef, int mAccount, const char *mfName,
77                     const char *mlName, double mBalance )
78   {
79      cout.setf( ios::showpoint | ios::fixed );
80      oRef.setf( ios::showpoint | ios::fixed );
81      oRef << mAccount << ' ' << mfName << ' ' << mlName << ' '
82           << setprecision( 2 ) << mBalance << '\n';
83      cout << mAccount << ' ' << mfName << ' ' << mlName << ' '
84           << setprecision( 2 ) << mBalance << '\n';
85      cout.unsetf( ios::showpoint | ios::fixed );
86   }
```

```
Processing....
100 Walter Brown -103.40
200 Alice Orange 309.94
300 Alan Green 71.52
400 Mary Black -363.43
500 Steve White 91.26
600 Gina Orange 375.10
700 Tom White -104.45
800 Cindy Red -33.33
900 Ilana Brown -162.76
1000 Pam Red -71.24
```

Contents of "oldmast.dat":

```
100 Walter Brown 46.58
200 Alice Orange 47.47
300 Alan Green 28.87
400 Mary Black 49.02
500 Steve White 67.83
600 Gina Orange 56.39
700 Tom White 38.21
800 Cindy Red 0.00
900 Ilana Brown 87.21
1000 Pam Red 0.00
```

Contents of trans.dat:

```
100 -149.98
200 262.47
300 -41.24
300 83.89
400 -412.45
500 23.43
600 318.71
700 -224.97
700 80.78
700 1.53
800 -33.33
900 -249.97
1000 -71.24
```

Contents of newmast.dat:

```
100 Walter Brown -103.40
200 Alice Orange 309.94
300 Alan Green 71.52
400 Mary Black -363.43
500 Steve White 91.26
600 Gina Orange 375.10
700 Tom White -104.45
800 Cindy Red -33.33
900 Ilana Brown -162.76
1000 Pam Red -71.24
```

14.11 Write a series of statements that accomplish each of the following. Assume the structure

```
struct Person {
    char lastName[ 15 ];
    char firstName[ 15 ];
    char age[ 2 ];
};
```

has been defined, and that the random access file has been opened properly.

a) Initialize the file **"nameage.dat"** with 100 records containing **lastName = "unassigned"**, **firstName = ""**, and **age = "0"**.

ANS:

```
// fstream object "fileObject" corresponds to file "nameage.dat"
Person personInfo = { "unassigned", "", 0 };
for ( int r = 0; r < 100; ++r )
    fileObject.write( reinterpret_cast< char * >( &personInfo,
                      sizeof( personInfo ) );
```

b) Input 10 last names, first names, and ages, and write them to the file.

ANS:

```
fileObject.seekp( 0 );
for ( int x = 1; x <= 10; ++x ) {
    cout << "Enter last name, first name, and age: ";
    cin >> personInfo.lastName >> personInfo.firstName >> personInfo.age;
    fileObject.write( reinterpret_cast< char * > &personInfo,
                      sizeof( personInfo ) );
}
```

c) Update a record that has information in it, and if there is none tell the user "No info".

d) Delete a record that has information by reinitializing that particular record.

14.12 You are the owner of a hardware store and need to keep an inventory that can tell you what different tools you have, how many of each you have on hand, and the cost of each one. Write a program that initializes the random access file **"hardware.dat"** to one hundred empty records, lets you input the data concerning each tool, enables you to list all your tools, lets you delete a record for a tool that you no longer have, and lets you update *any* information in the file. The tool identification number should be the record number. Use the following information to start your file:

Record #	Tool name	Quantity	Cost
3	Electric sander	7	57.98
17	Hammer	76	11.99
24	Jig saw	21	11.00
39	Lawn mower	3	79.50
56	Power saw	18	99.99
68	Screwdriver	106	6.99
77	Sledge hammer	11	21.50
83	Wrench	34	7.50

ANS:

```
1    // Exercise 14.12 Solution
2    #include <iostream.h>
3    #include <fstream.h>
4    #include <iomanip.h>
5    #include <string.h>
6    #include <ctype.h>
7    #include <stdlib.h>
8
9    void initializeFile( fstream & );
10   void inputData( fstream & );
11   void listTools( fstream & );
12   void updateRecord( fstream & );
13   void insertRecord( fstream & );
14   void deleteRecord( fstream & );
15   int instructions( void );
16
17   const int LENGTH = 30;
18
19   struct Data {
20      int partNumber;
21      char toolName[ LENGTH ];
22      int inStock;
23      double unitPrice;
24   };
25
26   int main()
27   {
28      int choice;
29      char response;
30      fstream file( "hardware.dat", ios::in | ios::out );
31      void ( *f[] )( fstream & ) = { listTools, updateRecord, insertRecord,
32                                     deleteRecord };
33
34      if ( !file ) {
35         cerr << "File could not be opened.\n";
36         exit( EXIT_FAILURE );
37      }
38
39      cout << "Should the file be initialized (Y or N): ";
40      cin >> response;
41
42      while ( toupper( response ) != 'Y' && toupper( response ) != 'N' ) {
43         cout << "Invalid response. Enter Y or N: ";
44         cin >> response;
45      }
46
47      if ( toupper( response ) == 'Y' ) {
48         initializeFile( file );
49         inputData( file );
50      }
51
52      while ( ( choice = instructions() ) != 5 ) {
53         ( *f[ choice - 1 ] )( file );
54         file.clear();    // reset eof indicator
55      }
56
57      file.close();
58      return 0;
59   }
60
```

```
61  void initializeFile( fstream &fRef )
62  {
63     Data blankItem = { -1, "", 0, 0.0 };
64     // See Chapter 21 for a discussion of reinterpret_cast
65     for ( int i = 0; i < 100; ++i )
66        fRef.write( reinterpret_cast< char * >( &blankItem ), sizeof( Data ) );
67  }
68
69  void inputData( fstream &fRef )
70  {
71     Data temp;
72
73     cout << "Enter the partnumber (0 - 99, -1 to end input): ";
74     cin >> temp.partNumber;
75
76     while ( temp.partNumber != -1 ) {
77        cout << "Enter the tool name: ";
78        cin.ignore();   // ignore the newline on the input stream
79        cin.get( temp.toolName, LENGTH );
80        cout << "Enter quantity and price: ";
81        cin >> temp.inStock >> temp.unitPrice;
82        fRef.seekp( ( temp.partNumber ) * sizeof( Data ) );
83        fRef.write( reinterpret_cast< char * >( &temp ), sizeof( Data ) );
84        cout << "Enter the partnumber (0 - 99, -1 to end input): ";
85        cin >> temp.partNumber;
86     }
87  }
88
89  int instructions( void )
90  {
91     int choice;
92
93     cout << "\nEnter a choice:\n1  List all tools."
94          << "\n2  Update record.\n3  Insert record."
95          << "\n4  Delete record.\n5  End program.\n";
96
97     do {
98        cout << "? ";
99        cin >> choice;
100    } while ( choice < 1 || choice > 5 );
101
102    return choice;
103 }
104
105 void listTools( fstream &fRef )
106 {
107    Data temp;
108    cout << setw( 7 ) << "Record#" << "     " << setiosflags( ios::left )
109         << setw( 30 ) << "Tool name" << resetiosflags( ios::left )
110         << setw( 13 ) << "Quantity" << setw( 10 ) << "Cost\n";
111
112    for ( int count = 0; count < 100 && !fRef.eof(); ++count ) {
113       fRef.seekg( count * sizeof( Data ) );
114       fRef.read( reinterpret_cast< char * >( &temp ), sizeof( Data ) );
115
116       if ( temp.partNumber >= 0 && temp.partNumber < 100 ) {
117          cout.setf( ios::fixed | ios::showpoint );
118          cout << setw( 7 ) << temp.partNumber << "     "
119               << setiosflags( ios::left ) << setw( 30 ) << temp.toolName
120               << resetiosflags( ios::left ) << setw( 13 ) << temp.inStock
121               << setprecision( 2 ) << setw( 10 ) << temp.unitPrice << '\n';
122       }
123    }
124 }
```

```
125
126  void updateRecord( fstream &fRef )
127  {
128     Data temp;
129     int part;
130
131     cout << "Enter the part number for update: ";
132     cin >> part;
133     fRef.seekg( part * sizeof( Data ) );
134     fRef.read( reinterpret_cast< char * >( &temp ), sizeof( Data ) );
135
136     if ( temp.partNumber != -1 ) {
137        cout << setw( 7 ) << "Record#" << "      " << setiosflags( ios::left )
138             << setw( 30 ) << "Tool name" << resetiosflags( ios::left )
139             << setw( 13 ) << "Quantity" << setw( 10 ) << "Cost\n";
140
141        cout.setf( ios::fixed | ios::showpoint );
142        cout << setw( 7 ) << temp.partNumber << "      "
143             << setiosflags( ios::left ) << setw( 30 ) << temp.toolName
144             << resetiosflags( ios::left ) << setw( 13 ) << temp.inStock
145             << setprecision( 2 ) << setw( 10 ) << temp.unitPrice << '\n'
146             << "Enter the tool name: ";
147
148        cin.ignore();  // ignore the newline on the input stream
149        cin.get( temp.toolName, LENGTH );
150        cout << "Enter quantity and price: ";
151        cin >> temp.inStock >> temp.unitPrice;
152
153        fRef.seekp( ( temp.partNumber ) * sizeof( Data ) );
154        fRef.write( reinterpret_cast< char * > ( &temp ), sizeof( Data ) );
155     }
156     else
157        cerr << "Cannot update. The record is empty.\n";
158  }
159
160  void insertRecord( fstream &fRef )
161  {
162     Data temp;
163     int part;
164
165     cout << "Enter the partnumber for insertion: ";
166     cin >> part;
167     fRef.seekg( ( part ) * sizeof( Data ) );
168     fRef.read( reinterpret_cast< char * > ( &temp ), sizeof( Data ) );
169
170     if ( temp.partNumber == -1 ) {
171        temp.partNumber = part;
172        cout << "Enter the tool name: ";
173        cin.ignore();  // ignore the newline on the input stream
174        cin.get( temp.toolName, LENGTH );
175        cout << "Enter quantity and price: ";
176        cin >> temp.inStock >> temp.unitPrice;
177
178        fRef.seekp( ( temp.partNumber ) * sizeof( Data ) );
179        fRef.write( reinterpret_cast< char * >( &temp ), sizeof( Data ) );
180     }
181     else
182        cerr << "Cannot insert. The record contains information.\n";
183  }
184
185  void deleteRecord( fstream &fRef )
186  {
187     Data blankItem = { -1, "", 0, 0.0 }, temp;
188     int part;
```

```
189
190     cout << "Enter the partnumber for deletion: ";
191     cin >> part;
192
193     fRef.seekg( part * sizeof( Data ) );
194     fRef.read( reinterpret_cast< char * >( &temp ), sizeof( Data ) );
195
196     if ( temp.partNumber != -1 ) {
197         fRef.seekp( part * sizeof( Data ) );
198         fRef.write( reinterpret_cast< char * >( &blankItem ), sizeof( Data ) );
199         cout << "Record deleted.\n";
200     }
201     else
202         cerr << "Cannot delete. The record is empty.\n";
203  }
```

```
Should the file be initialized (Y or N): Y
Enter the partnumber (0 - 99, -1 to end input): 77
Enter the tool name: Sledge hammer

Enter quantity and price: 11 21.50
Enter the partnumber (0 - 99, -1 to end input): -1

Enter a choice:
1  List all tools.
2  Update record.
3  Insert record.
4  Delete record.
5  End program.
? 1
Record#     Tool name                              Quantity     Cost
    77      Sledge hammer                                11     21.50

Enter a choice:
1  List all tools.
2  Update record.
3  Insert record.
4  Delete record.
5  End program.
? 3

Enter the partnumber for insertion: 44
Enter the tool name: Pipe wrench
Enter quantity and price: 1 19.99

Enter a choice:
1  List all tools.
2  Update record.
3  Insert record.
4  Delete record.
5  End program.
? 2
Enter the part number for update: 44
Record#     Tool name                              Quantity     Cost
    44      Pipe wrench                                  1     19.99

Enter the tool name: Pipe wrench
Enter quantity and price: 1 14.99                      continued...
```

```
Enter a choice:
1  List all tools.
2  Update record.
3  Insert record.
4  Delete record.
5  End program.
? 1

Record#      Tool name                        Quantity      Cost
      44     Pipe wrench                            1      14.99
      77     Sledge hammer                         11      21.50

Enter a choice:
1  List all tools.
2  Update record.
3  Insert record.
4  Delete record.
5  End program.
? 4
Enter the partnumber for deletion: 44
Record deleted.
...
```

14.13 Modify the telephone number word generating program you wrote in Chapter 4 so that it writes its output to a file. This allows you to read the file at your convenience. If you have a computerized dictionary available, modify your program to look up the thousands of seven-letter words in the dictionary. Some of the interesting seven-letter combinations created by this program may consist of two or more words. For example, the phone number 8432677 produces "THEBOSS." Modify your program to use the computerized dictionary to check each possible seven-letter word to see if it is a valid one-letter word followed by a valid six-letter word, a valid two-letter word followed by a valid five-letter word, etc.

ANS:

```
1   // Exercise 14.13 Solution
2   #include <iostream.h>
3   #include <iomanip.h>
4   #include <fstream.h>
5   #include <stdlib.h>
6   #include <ctype.h>
7
8   void wordGenerator( const int * const );
9
10  int main()
11  {
12     int phoneNumber[ 7 ] = { 0 };
13
14     cout << "Enter a phone number (digits 2 through 9) "
15          << "in the form: xxx-xxxx\n";
16
17     // loop 8 times: 7 digits plus hyphen
18     // hyphen is is not placed in phoneNumber
19     for ( int u = 0, v = 0; u < 8; ++u ) {
20        int i = cin.get();
21
22        // See chapter 16 for a discussion of isdigit
23        if ( isdigit( i ) )  // ctype library
24           phoneNumber[ v++ ] = i - '0';
25     }
26
27     wordGenerator( phoneNumber );
28     return 0;
29  }
30
```

```
31    void wordGenerator( const int * const n )
32    {
33       ofstream outFile( "phone.dat" );
34       const char *phoneLetters[ 10 ] = { "", "", "ABC", "DEF", "GHI", "JKL",
35                                          "MNO", "PRS", "TUV", "WXY" };
36
37       if ( !outFile ) {
38          cerr << "\"phone.dat\" could not be opened.\n";
39          exit( EXIT_FAILURE );
40       }
41
42       int count = 0;
43
44       // output all possible combinations
45       for ( int i1 = 0; i1 <= 2; ++i1 )
46          for ( int i2 = 0; i2 <= 2; ++i2 )
47             for ( int i3 = 0; i3 <= 2; ++i3 )
48                for ( int i4 = 0; i4 <= 2; ++i4 )
49                   for ( int i5 = 0; i5 <= 2; ++i5 )
50                      for ( int i6 = 0; i6 <= 2; ++i6 )
51                         for ( int i7 = 0; i7 <= 2; ++i7 ) {
52                            outFile << phoneLetters[ n[ 0 ] ][ i1 ]
53                                    << phoneLetters[ n[ 1 ] ][ i2 ]
54                                    << phoneLetters[ n[ 2 ] ][ i3 ]
55                                    << phoneLetters[ n[ 3 ] ][ i4 ]
56                                    << phoneLetters[ n[ 4 ] ][ i5 ]
57                                    << phoneLetters[ n[ 5 ] ][ i6 ]
58                                    << phoneLetters[ n[ 6 ] ][ i7 ] << ' ';
59
60                            if ( ++count % 9 == 0 )
61                               outFile << '\n';
62                         }
63
64       outFile << "\nPhone number is ";
65
66       for ( int i = 0; i < 7; ++i ) {
67          if ( i == 3 )
68             outFile << '-';
69
70          outFile << n[ i ];
71       }
72
73       outFile.close();
74    }
```

Contents of phone.dat:

```
TMPJDPW  TMPJDPX  TMPJDPY  TMPJDRW  TMPJDRX  TMPJDRY  TMPJDSW  TMPJDSX  TMPJDSY
TMPJEPW  TMPJEPX  TMPJEPY  TMPJERW  TMPJERX  TMPJERY  TMPJESW  TMPJESX  TMPJESY
TMPJFPW  TMPJFPX  TMPJFPY  TMPJFRW  TMPJFRX  TMPJFRY  TMPJFSW  TMPJFSX  TMPJFSY
TMPKDPW  TMPKDPX  TMPKDPY  TMPKDRW  TMPKDRX  TMPKDRY  TMPKDSW  TMPKDSX  TMPKDSY
TMPKEPW  TMPKEPX  TMPKEPY  TMPKERW  TMPKERX  TMPKERY  TMPKESW  TMPKESX  TMPKESY
...
VOSLDPW  VOSLDPX  VOSLDPY  VOSLDRW  VOSLDRX  VOSLDRY  VOSLDSW  VOSLDSX  VOSLDSY
VOSLEPW  VOSLEPX  VOSLEPY  VOSLERW  VOSLERX  VOSLERY  VOSLESW  VOSLESX  VOSLESY
VOSLFPW  VOSLFPX  VOSLFPY  VOSLFRW  VOSLFRX  VOSLFRY  VOSLFSW  VOSLFSX  VOSLFSY

Phone number is 867-5379
```

14.14 Write a program that uses the **sizeof** operator to determine the sizes in bytes of the various data types on your computer system. Write the results to the file **"datasize.dat"** so you may print the results later. The format for the results in the file should be:

```
           Data type                Size
           char                      1
           unsigned char             1
           short int                 2
           unsigned short int        2
           int                       4
           unsigned int              4
           long int                  4
           unsigned long int         4
           float                     4
           double                    8
           long double              16
```

Note: The sizes of the built-in data types on your computer may differ from those listed above.

ANS:

```
1    // Exercise 14.14 Solution
2    #include <iostream.h>
3    #include <iomanip.h>
4    #include <fstream.h>
5    #include <stdlib.h>
6
7    int main()
8    {
9        ofstream outFile( "datasize.dat" );
10
11       if ( !outFile ) {
12          cerr << "Unable to open \"datasize.dat\".\n";
13          exit( EXIT_FAILURE );
14       }
15
16       outFile << "Data type" << setw( 20 ) << "Size\nchar"
17               << setw( 21 ) << sizeof( char )
18               << "\nunsigned char" << setw( 12 ) << sizeof( unsigned char )
19               << "\nshort int" << setw(16) << sizeof( short int )
20               << "\nunsigned short int" << setw( 7 ) << sizeof( unsigned short )
21               << "\nint" << setw( 22 ) << sizeof( int ) << '\n';
22
23       outFile << "unsigned int" << setw( 13 ) << sizeof( unsigned )
24               << "\nlong int" << setw( 17 ) << sizeof( long )
25               << "\nunsigned long int" << setw( 8 ) << sizeof( unsigned long )
26               << "\nfloat" << setw( 20 ) << sizeof( float )
27               << "\ndouble" << setw( 19 ) << sizeof( double )
28               << "\nlong double" << setw( 14 ) << sizeof( long double ) << endl;
29
30       outFile.close();
31       return 0;
32   }
```

Contents of datasize.dat:

```
           Data type                Size
           char                      1
           unsigned char             1
           short int                 2
           unsigned short int        2
           int                       4
           unsigned int              4
           long int                  4
           unsigned long int         4
           float                     4
           double                    8
           long double               8
```

Chapter 15 Solutions

Data Structures

Solutions

NOTE: THE SOLUTIONS PRESENTED DO NOT USE THE ANSI/ISO DRAFT STANDARD EXCEPTION HAN-DLING FOR OPERATOR new. AT THE TIME OF THIS WRITING, NOT ALL COMPILERS SUPPORT ANSI/ ISO DRAFT STANDARD EXCEPTION HANDLING FOR OPERATOR new.

15.6 Write a program that concatenates two linked list objects of characters. The program should include function **con-catenate** that takes references to both list objects as arguments and concatenates the second list to the first list.

   ANS:

```
1   // LIST.H
2   // Template List class definition
3   // Added copy constructor to member functions (not included in chapter).
4   #ifndef LIST_H
5   #define LIST_H
6
7   #include <iostream.h>
8   #include <assert.h>
9   #include "listnd.h"
10
11  template< class NODETYPE >
12  class List {
13  public:
14     List();                              // default constructor
15     List( const List< NODETYPE > & );    // copy constructor
16     ~List();                             // destructor
17     void insertAtFront( const NODETYPE & );
18     void insertAtBack( const NODETYPE & );
19     bool removeFromFront( NODETYPE & );
20     bool removeFromBack( NODETYPE & );
21     bool isEmpty() const;
22     void print() const;
23  protected:
24     ListNode< NODETYPE > *firstPtr;  // pointer to first node
25     ListNode< NODETYPE > *lastPtr;   // pointer to last node
26
27     // Utility function to allocate a new node
28     ListNode< NODETYPE > *getNewNode( const NODETYPE & );
29  };
30
31  // Default constructor
32  template< class NODETYPE >
33  List< NODETYPE >::List() { firstPtr = lastPtr = 0; }
34
```

```
35   // Copy constructor
36   template< class NODETYPE >
37   List< NODETYPE >::List( const List<NODETYPE> &copy )
38   {
39      firstPtr = lastPtr = 0;   // initialize pointers
40
41      ListNode< NODETYPE > *currentPtr = copy.firstPtr;
42
43      while ( currentPtr != 0 ) {
44         insertAtBack( currentPtr -> data );
45         currentPtr = currentPtr -> nextPtr;
46      }
47   }
48
49   // Destructor
50   template< class NODETYPE >
51   List< NODETYPE >::~List()
52   {
53      if ( !isEmpty() ) {      // List is not empty
54         cout << "Destroying nodes ...\n";
55
56         ListNode< NODETYPE > *currentPtr = firstPtr, *tempPtr;
57
58         while ( currentPtr != 0 ) {  // delete remaining nodes
59            tempPtr = currentPtr;
60            cout << tempPtr -> data << ' ';
61            currentPtr = currentPtr -> nextPtr;
62            delete tempPtr;
63         }
64      }
65
66      cout << "\nAll nodes destroyed\n\n";
67   }
68
69   // Insert a node at the front of the list
70   template< class NODETYPE >
71   void List< NODETYPE >::insertAtFront( const NODETYPE &value )
72   {
73      ListNode<NODETYPE> *newPtr = getNewNode( value );
74
75      if ( isEmpty() )  // List is empty
76         firstPtr = lastPtr = newPtr;
77      else {            // List is not empty
78         newPtr -> nextPtr = firstPtr;
79         firstPtr = newPtr;
80      }
81   }
82
83   // Insert a node at the back of the list
84   template< class NODETYPE >
85   void List< NODETYPE >::insertAtBack( const NODETYPE &value )
86   {
87      ListNode< NODETYPE > *newPtr = getNewNode( value );
88
89      if ( isEmpty() )  // List is empty
90         firstPtr = lastPtr = newPtr;
91      else {            // List is not empty
92         lastPtr -> nextPtr = newPtr;
93         lastPtr = newPtr;
94      }
95   }
96
```

```
97   // Delete a node from the front of the list
98   template< class NODETYPE >
99   bool List< NODETYPE >::removeFromFront( NODETYPE &value )
100  {
101     if ( isEmpty() )                // List is empty
102        return false;               // delete unsuccessful
103     else {
104        ListNode< NODETYPE > *tempPtr = firstPtr;
105
106        if ( firstPtr == lastPtr )
107           firstPtr = lastPtr = 0;
108        else
109           firstPtr = firstPtr -> nextPtr;
110
111        value = tempPtr -> data;   // data being removed
112        delete tempPtr;
113        return true;                // delete successful
114     }
115  }
116
117  // Delete a node from the back of the list
118  template< class NODETYPE >
119  bool List< NODETYPE >::removeFromBack( NODETYPE &value )
120  {
121     if ( isEmpty() )
122        return false;    // delete unsuccessful
123     else {
124        ListNode< NODETYPE > *tempPtr = lastPtr;
125
126        if ( firstPtr == lastPtr )
127           firstPtr = lastPtr = 0;
128        else {
129           ListNode< NODETYPE > *currentPtr = firstPtr;
130
131           while ( currentPtr -> nextPtr != lastPtr )
132              currentPtr = currentPtr -> nextPtr;
133
134           lastPtr = currentPtr;
135           currentPtr -> nextPtr = 0;
136        }
137
138        value = tempPtr -> data;
139        delete tempPtr;
140        return true;    // delete successful
141     }
142  }
143
144  // Is the List empty?
145  template< class NODETYPE >
146  bool List< NODETYPE >::isEmpty() const { return firstPtr == 0; }
147
148  // Return a pointer to a newly allocated node
149  template< class NODETYPE >
150  ListNode< NODETYPE > *List< NODETYPE >::getNewNode( const NODETYPE &value )
151  {
152     ListNode< NODETYPE > *ptr = new ListNode< NODETYPE >( value );
153     assert( ptr != 0 );
154     return ptr;
155  }
156
157  // Display the contents of the List
158  template< class NODETYPE >
159  void List< NODETYPE >::print() const
160  {
```

```
161     if ( isEmpty() ) {
162         cout << "The list is empty\n\n";
163         return;
164     }
165
166     ListNode< NODETYPE > *currentPtr = firstPtr;
167
168     cout << "The list is: ";
169
170     while ( currentPtr != 0 ) {
171         cout << currentPtr -> data << ' ';
172         currentPtr = currentPtr -> nextPtr;
173     }
174
175     cout << "\n\n";
176 }
177
178 #endif
```

```
179 // LISTND.H
180 // ListNode template definition
181 #ifndef LISTND_H
182 #define LISTND_H
183
184 template< class T > class List;  // forward declaration
185
186 template< class NODETYPE >
187 class ListNode {
188     friend class List< NODETYPE >; // make List a friend
189 public:
190     ListNode( const NODETYPE & );  // constructor
191     NODETYPE getData() const;      // return the data in the node
192     void setNextPtr( ListNode *nPtr ) { nextPtr = nPtr; }
193     ListNode *getNextPtr() const { return nextPtr; }
194 private:
195     NODETYPE data;                 // data
196     ListNode *nextPtr;             // next node in the list
197 };
198
199 // Constructor
200 template< class NODETYPE >
201 ListNode< NODETYPE >::ListNode( const NODETYPE &info )
202 {
203     data = info;
204     nextPtr = 0;
205 }
206
207 // Return a copy of the data in the node
208 template< class NODETYPE >
209 NODETYPE ListNode< NODETYPE >::getData() const { return data; }
210
211 #endif
```

```
212 // Exercise 15.6 solution
213 #include <iostream.h>
214 #include "list.h"
215
216 template< class T >
217 void concatenate( List< T > &first, List< T > &second )
218 {
219     List< T > temp( second ); // create a copy of second
220     T value;                  // variable to store removed item from temp
221
```

```
222      while ( !temp.isEmpty() ) {
223          temp.removeFromFront( value );   // remove value from temp list
224          first.insertAtBack( value );     // insert at end of first list
225      }
226  }
227
228  int main()
229  {
230      List< char > list1, list2;
231      char c;
232
233      for ( c = 'a'; c <= 'e'; ++c )
234          list1.insertAtBack( c );
235
236      list1.print();
237
238      for ( c = 'f'; c <= 'j'; ++c )
239          list2.insertAtBack( c );
240
241      list2.print();
242
243      concatenate( list1, list2 );
244      cout << "The new list1 after concatenation is:\n";
245      list1.print();
246
247      return 0;
248  }
```

```
The list is: a b c d e

The list is: f g h i j


All nodes destroyed

The new list1 after concatenation is:
The list is: a b c d e f g h i j

Destroying nodes ...
f g h i j
All nodes destroyed

Destroying nodes ...
a b c d e f g h i j
All nodes destroyed
```

15.7   Write a program that merges two ordered list objects of integers into a single ordered list object of integers. Function **merge** should receive references to each of the list objects to be merged, and should return a reference to the merged list object.

ANS:

```
1  // LIST.H
2  // Template List class definition
3  #ifndef LIST_H
4  #define LIST_H
5
6  #include <iostream.h>
7  #include <assert.h>
8  #include "listnd.h"
9
```

```
10   template< class NODETYPE >
11   class List {
12   public:
13      List();                                  // default constructor
14      List( const List< NODETYPE > & );   // copy constructor
15      ~List();                                 // destructor
16      void insertAtFront( const NODETYPE & );
17      void insertAtBack( const NODETYPE & );
18      bool removeFromFront( NODETYPE & );
19      bool removeFromBack( NODETYPE & );
20      bool isEmpty() const;
21      void print() const;
22   protected:
23      ListNode< NODETYPE > *firstPtr;   // pointer to first node
24      ListNode< NODETYPE > *lastPtr;    // pointer to last node
25
26      // Utility function to allocate a new node
27      ListNode< NODETYPE > *getNewNode( const NODETYPE & );
28   };
29
30   // Default constructor
31   template< class NODETYPE >
32   List< NODETYPE >::List() { firstPtr = lastPtr = 0; }
33
34   // Copy constructor
35   template< class NODETYPE >
36   List< NODETYPE >::List( const List<NODETYPE> &copy )
37   {
38      firstPtr = lastPtr = 0;   // initialize pointers
39
40      ListNode< NODETYPE > *currentPtr = copy.firstPtr;
41
42      while ( currentPtr != 0 ) {
43         insertAtBack( currentPtr -> data );
44         currentPtr = currentPtr -> nextPtr;
45      }
46   }
47
48   // Destructor
49   template< class NODETYPE >
50   List< NODETYPE >::~List()
51   {
52      if ( !isEmpty() ) {      // List is not empty
53         cout << "Destroying nodes ...\n";
54
55         ListNode< NODETYPE > *currentPtr = firstPtr, *tempPtr;
56
57         while ( currentPtr != 0 ) {   // delete remaining nodes
58            tempPtr = currentPtr;
59            cout << tempPtr -> data << ' ';
60            currentPtr = currentPtr -> nextPtr;
61            delete tempPtr;
62         }
63      }
64
65      cout << "\nAll nodes destroyed\n\n";
66   }
67
68   // Insert a node at the front of the list
69   template< class NODETYPE >
70   void List< NODETYPE >::insertAtFront( const NODETYPE &value )
71   {
72      ListNode<NODETYPE> *newPtr = getNewNode( value );
73
```

```
74      if ( isEmpty() )   // List is empty
75         firstPtr = lastPtr = newPtr;
76      else {            // List is not empty
77         newPtr -> nextPtr = firstPtr;
78         firstPtr = newPtr;
79      }
80   }
81
82   // Insert a node at the back of the list
83   template< class NODETYPE >
84   void List< NODETYPE >::insertAtBack( const NODETYPE &value )
85   {
86      ListNode< NODETYPE > *newPtr = getNewNode( value );
87
88      if ( isEmpty() )   // List is empty
89         firstPtr = lastPtr = newPtr;
90      else {            // List is not empty
91         lastPtr -> nextPtr = newPtr;
92         lastPtr = newPtr;
93      }
94   }
95
96   // Delete a node from the front of the list
97   template< class NODETYPE >
98   bool List< NODETYPE >::removeFromFront( NODETYPE &value )
99   {
100     if ( isEmpty() )              // List is empty
101        return false;             // delete unsuccessful
102     else {
103        ListNode< NODETYPE > *tempPtr = firstPtr;
104
105        if ( firstPtr == lastPtr )
106           firstPtr = lastPtr = 0;
107        else
108           firstPtr = firstPtr -> nextPtr;
109
110        value = tempPtr -> data;   // data being removed
111        delete tempPtr;
112        return true;              // delete successful
113     }
114  }
115
116  // Delete a node from the back of the list
117  template< class NODETYPE >
118  bool List< NODETYPE >::removeFromBack( NODETYPE &value )
119  {
120     if ( isEmpty() )
121        return false;    // delete unsuccessful
122     else {
123        ListNode< NODETYPE > *tempPtr = lastPtr;
124
125        if ( firstPtr == lastPtr )
126           firstPtr = lastPtr = 0;
127        else {
128           ListNode< NODETYPE > *currentPtr = firstPtr;
129
130           while ( currentPtr -> nextPtr != lastPtr )
131              currentPtr = currentPtr -> nextPtr;
132
133           lastPtr = currentPtr;
134           currentPtr -> nextPtr = 0;
135        }
136
```

```
137          value = tempPtr -> data;
138          delete tempPtr;
139          return true;     // delete successful
140     }
141  }
142
143  // Is the List empty?
144  template< class NODETYPE >
145  bool List< NODETYPE >::isEmpty() const { return firstPtr == 0; }
146
147  // Return a pointer to a newly allocated node
148  template< class NODETYPE >
149  ListNode< NODETYPE > *List< NODETYPE >::getNewNode( const NODETYPE &value )
150  {
151     ListNode< NODETYPE > *ptr = new ListNode< NODETYPE >( value );
152     assert( ptr != 0 );
153     return ptr;
154  }
155
156  // Display the contents of the List
157  template< class NODETYPE >
158  void List< NODETYPE >::print() const
159  {
160     if ( isEmpty() ) {
161        cout << "The list is empty\n\n";
162        return;
163     }
164
165     ListNode< NODETYPE > *currentPtr = firstPtr;
166
167     cout << "The list is: ";
168
169     while ( currentPtr != 0 ) {
170        cout << currentPtr -> data << ' ';
171        currentPtr = currentPtr -> nextPtr;
172     }
173
174     cout << "\n\n";
175  }
176
177  #endif
```

```
178  // LISTND.H
179  // ListNode template definition
180  #ifndef LISTND_H
181  #define LISTND_H
182
183  template< class T > class List;   // forward declaration
184
185  template< class NODETYPE >
186  class ListNode {
187     friend class List< NODETYPE >; // make List a friend
188  public:
189     ListNode( const NODETYPE & );   // constructor
190     NODETYPE getData() const;       // return the data in the node
191     void setNextPtr( ListNode *nPtr ) { nextPtr = nPtr; }
192     ListNode *getNextPtr() const { return nextPtr; }
193  private:
194     NODETYPE data;                  // data
195     ListNode *nextPtr;              // next node in the list
196  };
197
```

```
198  // Constructor
199  template< class NODETYPE >
200  ListNode< NODETYPE >::ListNode( const NODETYPE &info )
201  {
202     data = info;
203     nextPtr = 0;
204  }
205
206  // Return a copy of the data in the node
207  template< class NODETYPE >
208  NODETYPE ListNode< NODETYPE >::getData() const { return data; }
209
210  #endif
```

```
211  // Exercise 15.7 solution
212  #include <iostream.h>
213  #include "list.h"
214
215  template< class T >
216  List< T > &merge( List< T > &first, List< T > &second )
217  {
218     // If both lists are empty, return an empty result
219     if ( first.isEmpty() && second.isEmpty() ) {
220        List< T > *ptr = new List< T >;          // dynamically allocated
221        return *ptr;
222     }
223
224     // If first list is empty, return result containing second list
225     if ( first.isEmpty() ) {
226        List< T > *ptr = new List< T >( second ); // dynamically allocated
227        return *ptr;
228     }
229
230     // If second list is empty, return result containing first list
231     if ( second.isEmpty() ) {
232        List< T > *ptr = new List< T >( first ); // dynamically allocated
233        return *ptr;
234     }
235
236     List< T > tempFirst( first ),    // create a copy of first
237              tempSecond( second ); // create a copy of second
238     List< T > *ptr = new List< T >; // dynamically allocated result object
239     T value1, value2;
240
241     tempFirst.removeFromFront( value1 );
242     tempSecond.removeFromFront( value2 );
243
244     while ( !tempFirst.isEmpty() && !tempSecond.isEmpty() ) {
245        if ( value1 <= value2 ) {
246           ptr -> insertAtBack( value1 );
247           tempFirst.removeFromFront( value1 );
248        }
249        else {
250           ptr -> insertAtBack( value2 );
251           tempSecond.removeFromFront( value2 );
252        }
253     }
254
255     // Insert the values currently in value1 and value2
256     if ( value1 < value2 ) {
257        ptr -> insertAtBack( value1 );
258        ptr -> insertAtBack( value2 );
259     }
```

```
260        else {
261           ptr -> insertAtBack( value2 );
262           ptr -> insertAtBack( value1 );
263        }
264
265        // Complete the insertion of the list that is not empty.
266        // NOTE: Only one of the following 2 while structures will execute
267        // because one of the lists must be empty to exit the preceding while.
268        if ( !tempFirst.isEmpty() )  // Items left in tempFirst? Insert in result.
269           do {
270              tempFirst.removeFromFront( value1 );
271              ptr -> insertAtBack( value2 );
272           } while ( !tempFirst.isEmpty() );
273        else                         // Items left in tempSecond? Insert in result.
274           do {
275              tempSecond.removeFromFront( value2 );
276              ptr -> insertAtBack( value2 );
277           } while ( !tempSecond.isEmpty() );
278
279        return *ptr;
280  }
281
282  int main()
283  {
284     List< int > list1, list2;
285     int i;
286
287     for ( i = 1; i <= 9; i += 2 )
288        list1.insertAtBack( i );
289
290     list1.print();
291
292     for ( i = 2; i <= 10; i += 2 )
293        list2.insertAtBack( i );
294
295     list2.print();
296
297     List< int > &listRef = merge( list1, list2 );
298
299     cout <<  "The merged list is:\n";
300     listRef.print();
301
302     delete &listRef;    // delete the dynamically allocated list
303
304     return 0;
305  }
```

```
 The list is: a b c d e

 The list is: f g h i j


 All nodes destroyed

 The new list1 after concatenation is:
 The list is: a b c d e f g h i j

 Destroying nodes ...
 f g h i j
 All nodes destroyed

 Destroying nodes ...
 a b c d e f g h i j
 All nodes destroyed
```

15.8   Write a program that inserts 25 random integers from 0 to 100 in order in a linked list object. The program should calculate the sum of the elements, and the floating-point average of the elements.

   ANS:

```
1   // LIST.H
2   // Template List class definition
3   // Added copy constructor to member functions (not included in chapter).
4   #ifndef LIST_H
5   #define LIST_H
6
7   #include <iostream.h>
8   #include <assert.h>
9   #include "listnd.h"
10
11  template< class NODETYPE >
12  class List {
13  public:
14     List();                                 // default constructor
15     List( const List< NODETYPE > & );       // copy constructor
16     ~List();                                // destructor
17     void insertAtFront( const NODETYPE & );
18     void insertAtBack( const NODETYPE & );
19     bool removeFromFront( NODETYPE & );
20     bool removeFromBack( NODETYPE & );
21     bool isEmpty() const;
22     void print() const;
23  protected:
24     ListNode< NODETYPE > *firstPtr;  // pointer to first node
25     ListNode< NODETYPE > *lastPtr;   // pointer to last node
26
27     // Utility function to allocate a new node
28     ListNode< NODETYPE > *getNewNode( const NODETYPE & );
29  };
30
31  // Default constructor
32  template< class NODETYPE >
33  List< NODETYPE >::List() { firstPtr = lastPtr = 0; }
34
35  // Copy constructor
36  template< class NODETYPE >
37  List< NODETYPE >::List( const List<NODETYPE> &copy )
38  {
39     firstPtr = lastPtr = 0;   // initialize pointers
40
41     ListNode< NODETYPE > *currentPtr = copy.firstPtr;
42
43     while ( currentPtr != 0 ) {
44        insertAtBack( currentPtr -> data );
45        currentPtr = currentPtr -> nextPtr;
46     }
47  }
48
49  // Destructor
50  template< class NODETYPE >
51  List< NODETYPE >::~List()
52  {
53     if ( !isEmpty() ) {      // List is not empty
54        cout << "Destroying nodes ...\n";
55
56        ListNode< NODETYPE > *currentPtr = firstPtr, *tempPtr;
57
58        while ( currentPtr != 0 ) {  // delete remaining nodes
59           tempPtr = currentPtr;
```

```
60              cout << tempPtr -> data << ' ';
61              currentPtr = currentPtr -> nextPtr;
62              delete tempPtr;
63          }
64      }
65
66      cout << "\nAll nodes destroyed\n\n";
67  }
68
69  // Insert a node at the front of the list
70  template< class NODETYPE >
71  void List< NODETYPE >::insertAtFront( const NODETYPE &value )
72  {
73      ListNode<NODETYPE> *newPtr = getNewNode( value );
74
75      if ( isEmpty() )  // List is empty
76          firstPtr = lastPtr = newPtr;
77      else {            // List is not empty
78          newPtr -> nextPtr = firstPtr;
79          firstPtr = newPtr;
80      }
81  }
82
83  // Insert a node at the back of the list
84  template< class NODETYPE >
85  void List< NODETYPE >::insertAtBack( const NODETYPE &value )
86  {
87      ListNode< NODETYPE > *newPtr = getNewNode( value );
88
89      if ( isEmpty() )  // List is empty
90          firstPtr = lastPtr = newPtr;
91      else {            // List is not empty
92          lastPtr -> nextPtr = newPtr;
93          lastPtr = newPtr;
94      }
95  }
96
97  // Delete a node from the front of the list
98  template< class NODETYPE >
99  bool List< NODETYPE >::removeFromFront( NODETYPE &value )
100 {
101     if ( isEmpty() )                  // List is empty
102         return false;                // delete unsuccessful
103     else {
104         ListNode< NODETYPE > *tempPtr = firstPtr;
105
106         if ( firstPtr == lastPtr )
107             firstPtr = lastPtr = 0;
108         else
109             firstPtr = firstPtr -> nextPtr;
110
111         value = tempPtr -> data;  // data being removed
112         delete tempPtr;
113         return true;                 // delete successful
114     }
115 }
116
117 // Delete a node from the back of the list
118 template< class NODETYPE >
119 bool List< NODETYPE >::removeFromBack( NODETYPE &value )
120 {
121     if ( isEmpty() )
122         return false;     // delete unsuccessful
```

```
123      else {
124         ListNode< NODETYPE > *tempPtr = lastPtr;
125
126         if ( firstPtr == lastPtr )
127            firstPtr = lastPtr = 0;
128         else {
129            ListNode< NODETYPE > *currentPtr = firstPtr;
130
131            while ( currentPtr -> nextPtr != lastPtr )
132               currentPtr = currentPtr -> nextPtr;
133
134            lastPtr = currentPtr;
135            currentPtr -> nextPtr = 0;
136         }
137
138         value = tempPtr -> data;
139         delete tempPtr;
140         return true;    // delete successful
141      }
142   }
143
144   // Is the List empty?
145   template< class NODETYPE >
146   bool List< NODETYPE >::isEmpty() const { return firstPtr == 0; }
147
148   // Return a pointer to a newly allocated node
149   template< class NODETYPE >
150   ListNode< NODETYPE > *List< NODETYPE >::getNewNode( const NODETYPE &value )
151   {
152      ListNode< NODETYPE > *ptr = new ListNode< NODETYPE >( value );
153      assert( ptr != 0 );
154      return ptr;
155   }
156
157   // Display the contents of the List
158   template< class NODETYPE >
159   void List< NODETYPE >::print() const
160   {
161      if ( isEmpty() ) {
162         cout << "The list is empty\n\n";
163         return;
164      }
165
166      ListNode< NODETYPE > *currentPtr = firstPtr;
167
168      cout << "The list is: ";
169
170      while ( currentPtr != 0 ) {
171         cout << currentPtr -> data << ' ';
172         currentPtr = currentPtr -> nextPtr;
173      }
174
175      cout << "\n\n";
176   }
177
178   #endif
```

```
179   // LISTND.H
180   // ListNode template definition
181   #ifndef LISTND_H
182   #define LISTND_H
183
```

```
184  template< class T > class List;  // forward declaration
185
186  template< class NODETYPE >
187  class ListNode {
188     friend class List< NODETYPE >; // make List a friend
189  public:
190     ListNode( const NODETYPE & );  // constructor
191     NODETYPE getData() const;     // return the data in the node
192     void setNextPtr( ListNode *nPtr ) { nextPtr = nPtr; }
193     ListNode *getNextPtr() const { return nextPtr; }
194  private:
195     NODETYPE data;                // data
196     ListNode *nextPtr;            // next node in the list
197  };
198
199  // Constructor
200  template< class NODETYPE >
201  ListNode< NODETYPE >::ListNode( const NODETYPE &info )
202  {
203     data = info;
204     nextPtr = 0;
205  }
206
207  // Return a copy of the data in the node
208  template< class NODETYPE >
209  NODETYPE ListNode< NODETYPE >::getData() const { return data; }
210
211  #endif
```

```
212  // LIST2.H
213  // Template List2 class definition
214  // Enhances List by adding insertInOrder
215  #ifndef LIST2_H
216  #define LIST2_H
217
218  #include <iostream.h>
219  #include <assert.h>
220  #include "listnd.h"
221  #include "list.h"
222
223  template< class NODETYPE >
224  class List2 : public List< NODETYPE > {
225  public:
226     void insertInOrder( const NODETYPE & );
227  };
228
229  // Insert a node in order
230  template< class NODETYPE >
231  void List2< NODETYPE >::insertInOrder( const NODETYPE &value )
232  {
233     if ( isEmpty() ) { // List is empty
234        ListNode< NODETYPE > *newPtr = getNewNode( value );
235        firstPtr = lastPtr = newPtr;
236     }
237     else {              // List is not empty
238        if ( firstPtr -> getData() > value )
239           insertAtFront( value );
240        else if ( lastPtr -> getData() < value )
241           insertAtBack( value );
242        else {
243           ListNode< NODETYPE > *currentPtr = firstPtr -> getNextPtr(),
244                               *previousPtr = firstPtr,
245                               *newPtr = getNewNode( value );
```

```
246
247         while ( currentPtr != lastPtr && currentPtr -> getData() < value ) {
248            previousPtr = currentPtr;
249            currentPtr = currentPtr -> getNextPtr();
250         }
251
252         previousPtr -> setNextPtr( newPtr );
253         newPtr -> setNextPtr( currentPtr );
254      }
255   }
256 }
257
258 #endif
```

```
259 // Exercise 15.8 solution
260 #include <iostream.h>
261 #include <stdlib.h>
262 #include <time.h>
263 #include "list2.h"
264
265 // Integer specific list sum
266 int sumList( List2< int > &listRef )
267 {
268    List2< int > temp( listRef );
269    int sum = 0, value;
270
271    while ( !temp.isEmpty() ) {
272       temp.removeFromFront( value );
273       sum += value;
274    }
275
276    return sum;
277 }
278
279 // Integer specific list average
280 double aveList( List2< int > &listRef )
281 {
282    List2< int > temp( listRef );
283    int sum = 0, value, count = 0;
284
285    while ( !temp.isEmpty() ) {
286       temp.removeFromFront( value );
287       ++count;
288       sum += value;
289    }
290
291    return static_cast< double >( sum ) / count;
292 }
293
294 int main()
295 {
296    srand( time( 0 ) );   // randomize the random number generator
297
298    List2< int > intList;
299
300    for ( int i = 1; i <= 25; ++i )
301       intList.insertInOrder( rand() % 101 );
302
303    intList.print();
304    cout << "The sum of the elements is: " << sumList( intList ) << '\n';
305    cout << "The average of the elements is: " << aveList( intList ) << '\n';
306    return 0;
307 }
```

```
The list is: 0 2 4 19 21 28 35 36 39 45 49 50 50 53 53 58 63 79 79 84 88
90 91 94 100


All nodes destroyed

The sum of the elements is: 1310

All nodes destroyed

The average of the elements is: 52.4
Destroying nodes ...
0 2 4 19 21 28 35 36 39 45 49 50 50 53 53 58 63 79 79 84 88 90 91 94 100
All nodes destroyed
```

15.9 Write a program that creates a linked list object of 10 characters, then creates a second list object containing a copy of the first list, but in reverse order.

ANS:

```
1   // LIST.H
2   // Template List class definition
3   // Added copy constructor to member functions (not included in chapter).
4   #ifndef LIST_H
5   #define LIST_H
6
7   #include <iostream.h>
8   #include <assert.h>
9   #include "listnd.h"
10
11  template< class NODETYPE >
12  class List {
13  public:
14     List();                                // default constructor
15     List( const List< NODETYPE > & );   // copy constructor
16     ~List();                               // destructor
17     void insertAtFront( const NODETYPE & );
18     void insertAtBack( const NODETYPE & );
19     bool removeFromFront( NODETYPE & );
20     bool removeFromBack( NODETYPE & );
21     bool isEmpty() const;
22     void print() const;
23  protected:
24     ListNode< NODETYPE > *firstPtr;  // pointer to first node
25     ListNode< NODETYPE > *lastPtr;   // pointer to last node
26
27     // Utility function to allocate a new node
28     ListNode< NODETYPE > *getNewNode( const NODETYPE & );
29  };
30
31  // Default constructor
32  template< class NODETYPE >
33  List< NODETYPE >::List() { firstPtr = lastPtr = 0; }
34
35  // Copy constructor
36  template< class NODETYPE >
37  List< NODETYPE >::List( const List<NODETYPE> &copy )
38  {
39     firstPtr = lastPtr = 0;  // initialize pointers
40
41     ListNode< NODETYPE > *currentPtr = copy.firstPtr;
42
```

```
43      while ( currentPtr != 0 ) {
44          insertAtBack( currentPtr -> data );
45          currentPtr = currentPtr -> nextPtr;
46      }
47  }
48
49  // Destructor
50  template< class NODETYPE >
51  List< NODETYPE >::~List()
52  {
53      if ( !isEmpty() ) {       // List is not empty
54          cout << "Destroying nodes ...\n";
55
56          ListNode< NODETYPE > *currentPtr = firstPtr, *tempPtr;
57
58          while ( currentPtr != 0 ) {  // delete remaining nodes
59              tempPtr = currentPtr;
60              cout << tempPtr -> data << ' ';
61              currentPtr = currentPtr -> nextPtr;
62              delete tempPtr;
63          }
64      }
65
66      cout << "\nAll nodes destroyed\n\n";
67  }
68
69  // Insert a node at the front of the list
70  template< class NODETYPE >
71  void List< NODETYPE >::insertAtFront( const NODETYPE &value )
72  {
73      ListNode<NODETYPE> *newPtr = getNewNode( value );
74
75      if ( isEmpty() )  // List is empty
76          firstPtr = lastPtr = newPtr;
77      else {            // List is not empty
78          newPtr -> nextPtr = firstPtr;
79          firstPtr = newPtr;
80      }
81  }
82
83  // Insert a node at the back of the list
84  template< class NODETYPE >
85  void List< NODETYPE >::insertAtBack( const NODETYPE &value )
86  {
87      ListNode< NODETYPE > *newPtr = getNewNode( value );
88
89      if ( isEmpty() )  // List is empty
90          firstPtr = lastPtr = newPtr;
91      else {            // List is not empty
92          lastPtr -> nextPtr = newPtr;
93          lastPtr = newPtr;
94      }
95  }
96
97  // Delete a node from the front of the list
98  template< class NODETYPE >
99  bool List< NODETYPE >::removeFromFront( NODETYPE &value )
100 {
101     if ( isEmpty() )              // List is empty
102         return false;            // delete unsuccessful
103     else {
104         ListNode< NODETYPE > *tempPtr = firstPtr;
105
```

```
106          if ( firstPtr == lastPtr )
107             firstPtr = lastPtr = 0;
108          else
109             firstPtr = firstPtr -> nextPtr;
110
111          value = tempPtr -> data;   // data being removed
112          delete tempPtr;
113          return true;                  // delete successful
114       }
115    }
116
117    // Delete a node from the back of the list
118    template< class NODETYPE >
119    bool List< NODETYPE >::removeFromBack( NODETYPE &value )
120    {
121       if ( isEmpty() )
122          return false;    // delete unsuccessful
123       else {
124          ListNode< NODETYPE > *tempPtr = lastPtr;
125
126          if ( firstPtr == lastPtr )
127             firstPtr = lastPtr = 0;
128          else {
129             ListNode< NODETYPE > *currentPtr = firstPtr;
130
131             while ( currentPtr -> nextPtr != lastPtr )
132                currentPtr = currentPtr -> nextPtr;
133
134             lastPtr = currentPtr;
135             currentPtr -> nextPtr = 0;
136          }
137
138          value = tempPtr -> data;
139          delete tempPtr;
140          return true;    // delete successful
141       }
142    }
143
144    // Is the List empty?
145    template< class NODETYPE >
146    bool List< NODETYPE >::isEmpty() const { return firstPtr == 0; }
147
148    // Return a pointer to a newly allocated node
149    template< class NODETYPE >
150    ListNode< NODETYPE > *List< NODETYPE >::getNewNode( const NODETYPE &value )
151    {
152       ListNode< NODETYPE > *ptr = new ListNode< NODETYPE >( value );
153       assert( ptr != 0 );
154       return ptr;
155    }
156
157    // Display the contents of the List
158    template< class NODETYPE >
159    void List< NODETYPE >::print() const
160    {
161       if ( isEmpty() ) {
162          cout << "The list is empty\n\n";
163          return;
164       }
165
166       ListNode< NODETYPE > *currentPtr = firstPtr;
167
168       cout << "The list is: ";
169
```

```
170      while ( currentPtr != 0 ) {
171         cout << currentPtr -> data << ' ';
172         currentPtr = currentPtr -> nextPtr;
173      }
174
175      cout << "\n\n";
176   }
177
178   #endif
```

```
179   // LISTND.H
180   // ListNode template definition
181   #ifndef LISTND_H
182   #define LISTND_H
183
184   template< class T > class List;   // forward declaration
185
186   template< class NODETYPE >
187   class ListNode {
188      friend class List< NODETYPE >; // make List a friend
189   public:
190      ListNode( const NODETYPE & );   // constructor
191      NODETYPE getData() const;       // return the data in the node
192      void setNextPtr( ListNode *nPtr ) { nextPtr = nPtr; }
193      ListNode *getNextPtr() const { return nextPtr; }
194   private:
195      NODETYPE data;                  // data
196      ListNode *nextPtr;              // next node in the list
197   };
198
199   // Constructor
200   template< class NODETYPE >
201   ListNode< NODETYPE >::ListNode( const NODETYPE &info )
202   {
203      data = info;
204      nextPtr = 0;
205   }
206
207   // Return a copy of the data in the node
208   template< class NODETYPE >
209   NODETYPE ListNode< NODETYPE >::getData() const { return data; }
210
211   #endif
```

```
212   // Exercise 15.9 solution
213   #include <iostream.h>
214   #include "list.h"
215
216   // Function template that takes two List objects as arguments
217   // and makes a copy of the second argument reversed in the first argument.
218   template< class T >
219   void reverseList( List< T > &first, List< T > &second )
220   {
221      List< T > temp( second ); // create a copy of second
222      T value;                  // variable to store removed item from temp
223
224      while ( !temp.isEmpty() ) {
225         temp.removeFromFront( value );  // remove value from temp list
226         first.insertAtFront( value );   // insert at beginning of first list
227      }
228   }
229
```

```
230  int main()
231  {
232     List< char > list1, list2;
233
234     for ( char c = 'a'; c <= 'g'; ++c )
235        list1.insertAtBack( c );
236
237     list1.print();
238
239     reverseList( list2, list1 );
240     cout << "After reversing:\n";
241     list2.print();
242
243     return 0;
244  }
```

```
The list is: a b c d e f g


All nodes destroyed

After reversing:
The list is: g f e d c b a

Destroying nodes ...
g f e d c b a
All nodes destroyed

Destroying nodes ...
a b c d e f g
All nodes destroyed
```

15.10   Write a program that inputs a line of text and uses a stack object to print the line reversed.
ANS:

```
1   // STACK.H
2   // Definition of class Stack
3   // NOTE: This Stack class is a standalone Stack class template.
4   #ifndef STACK_H
5   #define STACK_H
6
7   #include <iostream.h>
8   #include <assert.h>
9   #include "stacknd.h"
10
11  template < class T >
12  class Stack {
13  public:
14     Stack();                // default constructor
15     ~Stack();               // destructor
16     void push( T & );       // insert item in stack
17     T pop();                // remove item from stack
18     bool isEmpty() const;   // is the stack empty?
19     void print() const;     // output the stack
20     StackNode< T > *getTopPtr() const { return topPtr; }
21  private:
22     StackNode< T > *topPtr;     // pointer to fist StackNode
23  };
24
25  // Member function definitions for class Stack
26  template < class T >
27  Stack< T >::Stack() { topPtr = 0; }
```

```
28   template < class T >
29   Stack< T >::~Stack()
30   {
31      StackNode< T > *tempPtr, *currentPtr = topPtr;
32
33      while ( currentPtr != 0 ) {
34         tempPtr = currentPtr;
35         currentPtr = currentPtr -> getNextPtr();
36         delete tempPtr;
37      }
38   }
39
40   template < class T >
41   void Stack< T >::push( T &d )
42   {
43      StackNode< T > *newPtr = new StackNode< T >( d, topPtr );
44      assert( newPtr != 0 );   // was memory allocated?
45      topPtr = newPtr;
46   }
47
48   template < class T >
49   T Stack< T >::pop()
50   {
51      assert( !isEmpty() );
52      StackNode< T > *tempPtr = topPtr;
53
54      topPtr = topPtr -> nextPtr;
55      T poppedValue = tempPtr -> data;
56      delete tempPtr;
57      return poppedValue;
58   }
59
60   template < class T >
61   bool Stack< T >::isEmpty() const { return topPtr == 0; }
62
63   template < class T >
64   void Stack< T >::print() const
65   {
66      StackNode< T > *currentPtr = topPtr;
67
68      if ( isEmpty() )               // Stack is empty
69         cout << "Stack is empty\n";
70      else {                         // Stack is not empty
71         cout << "The stack is:\n";
72
73         while ( currentPtr != 0 ) {
74            cout << currentPtr -> data << ' ';
75            currentPtr = currentPtr -> nextPtr;
76         }
77
78         cout << '\n';
79      }
80   }
81
82   #endif
```

```
83   // STACKND.H
84   // Definition of template class StackNode
85   #ifndef STACKND_H
86   #define STACKND_H
87
88   template< class T > class Stack;   // forward declaration
89
```

```
90   template < class T >
91   class StackNode {
92      friend class Stack< T >;
93   public:
94      StackNode( const T & = 0, StackNode * = 0 );
95      T getData() const;
96      void setNextPtr( StackNode *nPtr ) { nextPtr = nPtr; }
97      StackNode *getNextPtr() const { return nextPtr; }
98   private:
99      T data;
100     StackNode *nextPtr;
101  };
102
103  // Member function definitions for class StackNode
104  template < class T >
105  StackNode< T >::StackNode( const T &d, StackNode< T > *ptr )
106  {
107     data = d;
108     nextPtr = ptr;
109  }
110
111  template < class T >
112  T StackNode< T >::getData() const { return data; }
113
114  #endif
```

```
115  // Exercise 15.10 solution
116  #include <iostream.h>
117  #include "stack.h"
118
119  int main()
120  {
121     Stack< char > charStack;
122     char c;
123
124     cout << "Enter a sentence:\n";
125     while ( ( c = static_cast< char >( cin.get() ) ) != '\n' )
126        charStack.push( c );
127
128     cout << "\nThe sentence in reverse is:\n";
129     while ( !charStack.isEmpty() )
130        cout << charStack.pop();
131
132     cout << '\n';
133     return 0;
134  }
```

```
The list is: a b c d e f g

All nodes destroyed

After reversing:
The list is: g f e d c b a

Destroying nodes ...
g f e d c b a
All nodes destroyed

Destroying nodes ...
a b c d e f g
All nodes destroyed
```

15.11   Write a program that uses a stack object to determine if a string is a palindrome (i.e., the string is spelled identically backwards and forwards). The program should ignore spaces and punctuation.

ANS:

```
1    // STACK.H
2    // Definition of class Stack
3    // NOTE: This Stack class is a standalone Stack class template.
4    #ifndef STACK_H
5    #define STACK_H
6
7    #include <iostream.h>
8    #include <assert.h>
9    #include "stacknd.h"
10
11   template < class T >
12   class Stack {
13   public:
14      Stack();              // default constructor
15      ~Stack();             // destructor
16      void push( T & );     // insert item in stack
17      T pop();              // remove item from stack
18      bool isEmpty() const; // is the stack empty?
19      void print() const;   // output the stack
20      StackNode< T > *getTopPtr() const { return topPtr; }
21   private:
22      StackNode< T > *topPtr;    // pointer to fist StackNode
23   };
24
25   // Member function definitions for class Stack
26   template < class T >
27   Stack< T >::Stack() { topPtr = 0; }
28
29   template < class T >
30   Stack< T >::~Stack()
31   {
32      StackNode< T > *tempPtr, *currentPtr = topPtr;
33
34      while ( currentPtr != 0 ) {
35         tempPtr = currentPtr;
36         currentPtr = currentPtr -> getNextPtr();
37         delete tempPtr;
38      }
39   }
40
41   template < class T >
42   void Stack< T >::push( T &d )
43   {
44      StackNode< T > *newPtr = new StackNode< T >( d, topPtr );
45      assert( newPtr != 0 );  // was memory allocated?
46      topPtr = newPtr;
47   }
48
49   template < class T >
50   T Stack< T >::pop()
51   {
52      assert( !isEmpty() );
53      StackNode< T > *tempPtr = topPtr;
54
55      topPtr = topPtr -> nextPtr;
56      T poppedValue = tempPtr -> data;
57      delete tempPtr;
58      return poppedValue;
59   }
```

```
60
61   template < class T >
62   bool Stack< T >::isEmpty() const { return topPtr == 0; }
63
64   template < class T >
65   void Stack< T >::print() const
66   {
67      StackNode< T > *currentPtr = topPtr;
68
69      if ( isEmpty() )            // Stack is empty
70         cout << "Stack is empty\n";
71      else {                      // Stack is not empty
72         cout << "The stack is:\n";
73
74         while ( currentPtr != 0 ) {
75            cout << currentPtr -> data << ' ';
76            currentPtr = currentPtr -> nextPtr;
77         }
78
79         cout << '\n';
80      }
81   }
82
83   #endif
```

```
84   // STACKND.H
85   // Definition of template class StackNode
86   #ifndef STACKND_H
87   #define STACKND_H
88
89   template< class T > class Stack;   // forward declaration
90
91   template < class T >
92   class StackNode {
93      friend class Stack< T >;
94   public:
95      StackNode( const T & = 0, StackNode * = 0 );
96      T getData() const;
97      void setNextPtr( StackNode *nPtr ) { nextPtr = nPtr; }
98      StackNode *getNextPtr() const { return nextPtr; }
99   private:
100     T data;
101     StackNode *nextPtr;
102  };
103
104  // Member function definitions for class StackNode
105  template < class T >
106  StackNode< T >::StackNode( const T &d, StackNode< T > *ptr )
107  {
108     data = d;
109     nextPtr = ptr;
110  }
111
112  template < class T >
113  T StackNode< T >::getData() const { return data; }
114
115  #endif
```

```
116  // Exercise 15.11 solution
117  #include <iostream.h>
118  #include <ctype.h>
119  #include <string.h>
120  #include "stack.h"
```

```
121
122  int main()
123  {
124     Stack< char > charStack;
125     char c, string1[ 80 ], string2[ 80 ];
126     int i = 0;
127
128     cout << "Enter a sentence:\n";
129
130     while ( ( c = static_cast< char >( cin.get() ) ) != '\n' )
131        if ( isalpha( c ) ) {
132           string1[ i++ ] = c;
133           charStack.push( c );
134        }
135
136     string1[ i ] = '\0';
137
138     i = 0;
139
140     while ( !charStack.isEmpty() )
141        string2[ i++ ] = charStack.pop();
142
143     string2[ i ] = '\0';
144
145     if ( strcmp( string1, string2 ) == 0 )
146        cout << "\nThe sentence is a palindrome\n";
147     else
148        cout << "\nThe sentence is not a palindrome\n";
149
150     return 0;
151  }
```

```
Enter a sentence:
oat y tao

The sentence is a palindrome
```

15.12 Stacks are used by compilers to help in the process of evaluating expressions and generating machine language code. In this and the next exercise, we investigate how compilers evaluate arithmetic expressions consisting only of constants, operators, and parentheses.

Humans generally write expressions like **3 + 4** and **7 / 9** in which the operator (**+** or **/** here) is written between its operands—this is called *infix notation*. Computers "prefer" *postfix notation* in which the operator is written to the right of its two operands. The preceding infix expressions would appear in postfix notation as **3 4 +** and **7 9 /**, respectively.

To evaluate a complex infix expression, a compiler would first convert the expression to postfix notation, and then evaluate the postfix version of the expression. Each of these algorithms requires only a single left-to-right pass of the expression. Each algorithm uses a stack object in support of its operation, and in each algorithm the stack is used for a different purpose.

In this exercise, you will write a C++ version of the infix-to-postfix conversion algorithm. In the next exercise, you will write a C++ version of the postfix expression evaluation algorithm. Later in the chapter, you will discover that code you write in this exercise can help you implement a complete working compiler.

Write a program that converts an ordinary infix arithmetic expression (assume a valid expression is entered) with single digit integers such as

> **(6 + 2) * 5 - 8 / 4**

to a postfix expression. The postfix version of the preceding infix expression is

> **6 2 + 5 * 8 4 / -**

The program should read the expression into character array **infix**, and use modified versions of the stack functions implemented in this chapter to help create the postfix expression in character array **postfix**. The algorithm for creating a postfix expression is as follows:

  a) Push a left parenthesis **' ('** onto the stack.

    b) Append a right parenthesis ')' to the end of **infix**.

    c) While the stack is not empty, read **infix** from left to right and do the following:

        If the current character in **infix** is a digit, copy it to the next element of **postfix**.

        If the current character in **infix** is a left parenthesis, push it onto the stack.

        If the current character in **infix** is an operator,

            Pop operators (if there are any) at the top of the stack while they have equal or higher precedence than the current operator, and insert the popped operators in **postfix**.

        Push the current character in **infix** onto the stack.

        If the current character in **infix** is a right parenthesis

            Pop operators from the top of the stack and insert them in **postfix** until a left parenthesis is at the top of the stack.

        Pop (and discard) the left parenthesis from the stack.

The following arithmetic operations are allowed in an expression:

    +   addition

    –   subtraction

    *   multiplication

    /   division

    ^   exponentiation

    %   modulus

The stack should be maintained with stack nodes that each contain a data member and a pointer to the next stack node.

    Some of the functional capabilities you may want to provide are:

    a) Function **convertToPostfix** that converts the infix expression to postfix notation.

    b) Function **isOperator** that determines if **c** is an operator.

    c) Function **precedence** that determines if the precedence of **operator1** is less than, equal to, or greater than the precedence of **operator2**. The function returns -1, 0, and 1, respectively.

    d) Function **push** that pushes a value onto the stack.

    e) Function **pop** that pops a value off the stack.

    f) Function **stackTop** that returns the top value of the stack without popping the stack.

    g) Function **isEmpty** that determines if the stack is empty.

    h) Function **printStack** that prints the stack.

    ANS: NOTE: although not stated in the problem the solution uses a **Stack** class template.

```
1   // STACK.H
2   // Definition of class Stack
3   // NOTE: This Stack class is a standalone Stack class template.
4   #ifndef STACK_H
5   #define STACK_H
6   #include <iostream.h>
7   #include <assert.h>
8   #include "stacknd.h"
9
10  template < class T >
11  class Stack {
12  public:
13     Stack();              // default constructor
14     ~Stack();             // destructor
15     void push( T & );     // insert item in stack
16     T pop();              // remove item from stack
17     bool isEmpty() const; // is the stack empty?
18     void print() const;   // output the stack
19     StackNode< T > *getTopPtr() const { return topPtr; }
20  private:
21     StackNode< T > *topPtr;     // pointer to fist StackNode
22  };
23
24  // Member function definitions for class Stack
25  template < class T >
26  Stack< T >::Stack() { topPtr = 0; }
```

```
27
28   template < class T >
29   Stack< T >::~Stack()
30   {
31       StackNode< T > *tempPtr, *currentPtr = topPtr;
32
33       while ( currentPtr != 0 ) {
34          tempPtr = currentPtr;
35          currentPtr = currentPtr -> getNextPtr();
36          delete tempPtr;
37       }
38   }
39
40   template < class T >
41   void Stack< T >::push( T &d )
42   {
43       StackNode< T > *newPtr = new StackNode< T >( d, topPtr );
44
45       assert( newPtr != 0 );   // was memory allocated?
46       topPtr = newPtr;
47   }
48
49   template < class T >
50   T Stack< T >::pop()
51   {
52       assert( !isEmpty() );
53       StackNode< T > *tempPtr = topPtr;
54       topPtr = topPtr -> nextPtr;
55       T poppedValue = tempPtr -> data;
56       delete tempPtr;
57       return poppedValue;
58   }
59
60   template < class T >
61   bool Stack< T >::isEmpty() const { return topPtr == 0; }
62
63   template < class T >
64   void Stack< T >::print() const
65   {
66       StackNode< T > *currentPtr = topPtr;
67
68       if ( isEmpty() )              // Stack is empty
69          cout << "Stack is empty\n";
70       else {                       // Stack is not empty
71          cout << "The stack is:\n";
72
73          while ( currentPtr != 0 ) {
74             cout << currentPtr -> data << ' ';
75             currentPtr = currentPtr -> nextPtr;
76          }
77
78          cout << '\n';
79       }
80   }
81
82   #endif
```

```
83   // STACKND.H
84   // Definition of template class StackNode
85   #ifndef STACKND_H
86   #define STACKND_H
87
88   template< class T > class Stack;   // forward declaration
```

```
89
90   template < class T >
91   class StackNode {
92      friend class Stack< T >;
93   public:
94      StackNode( const T & = 0, StackNode * = 0 );
95      T getData() const;
96      void setNextPtr( StackNode *nPtr ) { nextPtr = nPtr; }
97      StackNode *getNextPtr() const { return nextPtr; }
98   private:
99      T data;
100     StackNode *nextPtr;
101  };
102
103  // Member function definitions for class StackNode
104  template < class T >
105  StackNode< T >::StackNode( const T &d, StackNode< T > *ptr )
106  {
107     data = d;
108     nextPtr = ptr;
109  }
110
111  template < class T >
112  T StackNode< T >::getData() const { return data; }
113
114  #endif
```

```
115  // STACK2.H
116  // Definition of class Stack2
117  #ifndef STACK2_H
118  #define STACK2_H
119
120  #include <iostream.h>
121  #include <assert.h>
122  #include "stacknd.h"
123  #include "stack.h"
124
125  template < class T >
126  class Stack2 : public Stack< T > {
127  public:
128     T stackTop() const;   // check the top value
129  };
130
131  template < class T >
132  T Stack2< T >::stackTop() const
133  { return !isEmpty() ? getTopPtr() -> getData() : static_cast< T >( 0 ); }
134
135  #endif
```

```
136  // Exercise 15.12 Solution
137  // Infix to postfix conversion
138  #include <iostream.h>
139  #include <ctype.h>
140  #include <string.h>
141  #include "stack2.h"
142
143  void convertToPostfix( char * const, char * const );
144  bool isOperator( char );
145  bool precedence( char, char );
146
```

```
147  int main()
148  {
149     const int MAXSIZE = 100;
150     char c, inFix[ MAXSIZE ], postFix[ MAXSIZE ];
151     int pos = 0;
152
153     cout << "Enter the infix expression.\n";
154
155     while ( ( c = static_cast< char >( cin.get() ) ) != '\n' )
156        if ( c != ' ' )
157           inFix[ pos++ ] = c;
158
159     inFix[ pos ] = '\0';
160
161     cout << "The original infix expression is:\n" << inFix << '\n';
162     convertToPostfix( inFix, postFix );
163     cout << "The expression in postfix notation is:\n" << postFix << endl;
164     return 0;
165  }
166
167  void convertToPostfix( char * const infix, char * const postfix )
168  {
169     Stack2< char > charStack;
170     int infixCount, postfixCount;
171     bool higher;
172     char popValue, leftParen = '(';
173
174     // push a left paren onto the stack and add a right paren to infix
175     charStack.push( leftParen );
176     charStack.print();
177     strcat( infix, ")" );
178
179     // convert the infix expression to postfix
180     for ( infixCount = 0, postfixCount = 0; charStack.stackTop();
181           ++infixCount ) {
182
183        if ( isdigit( infix[ infixCount ] ) )
184           postfix[ postfixCount++ ] = infix[ infixCount ];
185        else if ( infix[ infixCount ] == '(' ) {
186           charStack.push( leftParen );
187           charStack.print();
188        }
189        else if ( isOperator( infix[ infixCount ] ) ) {
190           higher = true;    // used to store value of precedence test
191
192           while ( higher ) {
193              if ( isOperator( charStack.stackTop() ) )
194                 if ( precedence( charStack.stackTop(), infix[ infixCount ] ) ) {
195                    postfix[ postfixCount++ ] = charStack.pop();
196                    charStack.print();
197                 }
198                 else
199                    higher = false;
200              else
201                 higher = false;
202           }
203
204           charStack.push( infix[ infixCount ] );
205           charStack.print();
206        }
```

```
207            else if ( infix[ infixCount ] == ')' ) {
208               while ( ( popValue = charStack.pop() ) != '(' ) {
209                  charStack.print();
210                  postfix[ postfixCount++ ] = popValue;
211               }
212               charStack.print();
213            }
214         }
215         postfix[ postfixCount ] = '\0';
216      }
217
218      // check if c is an operator
219      bool isOperator( char c )
220      {
221         if ( c == '+' || c == '-' || c == '*' || c == '/' || c == '^' )
222            return true;
223         else
224            return false;
225      }
226
227      bool precedence( char operator1, char operator2 )
228      {
229         if ( operator1 == '^' )
230            return true;
231         else if ( operator2 == '^' )
232            return false;
233         else if ( operator1 == '*' || operator1 == '/' )
234            return true;
235         else if ( operator1 == '+' || operator1 == '-' )
236            if ( operator2 == '*' || operator2 == '/' )
237               return false;
238            else
239               return true;
240         return false;
241      }
```

```
Enter the infix expression.
(6 + 2) * 5 - 8 / 4

The original infix expression is:
(6+2)*5-8/4
The stack is:
(
The stack is:
( (
The stack is:
+ ( (
The stack is:
( (
The stack is:
(
The stack is:
* (
The stack is:
(
The stack is:
- (
The stack is:
/ - (
The stack is:
- (
The stack is:
(
Stack is empty
The expression in postfix notation is:
62+5*84/-
```

15.13 Write a program that evaluates a postfix expression (assume it is valid) such as

> 6 2 + 5 * 8 4 / -

The program should read a postfix expression consisting of digits and operators into a character array. Using modified versions of the stack functions implemented earlier in this chapter, the program should scan the expression and evaluate it. The algorithm is as follows:

a) Append the null character ('\0') to the end of the postfix expression. When the null character is encountered, no further processing is necessary.

b) While '\0' has not been encountered, read the expression from left to right.

> If the current character is a digit,
>> Push its integer value onto the stack (the integer value of a digit character is its value in the computer's character set minus the value of '0' in the computer's character set).
>
> Otherwise, if the current character is an *operator*,
>> Pop the two top elements of the stack into variables **x** and **y**.
>> Calculate **y** *operator* **x**.
>> Push the result of the calculation onto the stack.

c) When the null character is encountered in the expression, pop the top value of the stack. This is the result of the postfix expression.

Note: In 2) above, if the operator is '/', the top of the stack is **2**, and the next element in the stack is **8**, then pop **2** into **x**, pop **8** into **y**, evaluate **8 / 2**, and push the result, **4**, back onto the stack. This note also applies to operator '-'. The arithmetic operations allowed in an expression are:

+   addition
–   subtraction
*   multiplication
/   division
^   exponentiation
%   modulus

The stack should be maintained with stack nodes that contain an **int** data member and a pointer to the next stack node. You may want to provide the following functional capabilities:

a) Function **evaluatePostfixExpression** that evaluates the postfix expression.

b) Function **calculate** that evaluates the expression **op1 operator op2**.

c) Function **push** that pushes a value onto the stack.

d) Function **pop** that pops a value off the stack.

e) Function **isEmpty** that determines if the stack is empty.

f) Function **printStack** that prints the stack.

ANS: NOTE: although not stated in the problem the solution uses a **Stack** class template.

```
1   // STACK.H
2   // Definition of class Stack
3   // NOTE: This Stack class is a standalone Stack class template.
4   #ifndef STACK_H
5   #define STACK_H
6
7   #include <iostream.h>
8   #include <assert.h>
9   #include "stacknd.h"
10
11  template < class T >
12  class Stack {
13  public:
14     Stack();                // default constructor
15     ~Stack();               // destructor
16     void push( T & );       // insert item in stack
17     T pop();                // remove item from stack
18     bool isEmpty() const;   // is the stack empty?
19     void print() const;     // output the stack
20     StackNode< T > *getTopPtr() const { return topPtr; }
```

```
21   private:
22       StackNode< T > *topPtr;      // pointer to fist StackNode
23   };
24
25   // Member function definitions for class Stack
26   template < class T >
27   Stack< T >::Stack() { topPtr = 0; }
28
29   template < class T >
30   Stack< T >::~Stack()
31   {
32       StackNode< T > *tempPtr, *currentPtr = topPtr;
33
34       while ( currentPtr != 0 ) {
35          tempPtr = currentPtr;
36          currentPtr = currentPtr -> getNextPtr();
37          delete tempPtr;
38       }
39   }
40
41   template < class T >
42   void Stack< T >::push( T &d )
43   {
44       StackNode< T > *newPtr = new StackNode< T >( d, topPtr );
45       assert( newPtr != 0 );  // was memory allocated?
46       topPtr = newPtr;
47   }
48
49   template < class T >
50   T Stack< T >::pop()
51   {
52       assert( !isEmpty() );
53
54       StackNode< T > *tempPtr = topPtr;
55
56       topPtr = topPtr -> nextPtr;
57       T poppedValue = tempPtr -> data;
58       delete tempPtr;
59       return poppedValue;
60   }
61
62   template < class T >
63   bool Stack< T >::isEmpty() const { return topPtr == 0; }
64
65   template < class T >
66   void Stack< T >::print() const
67   {
68       StackNode< T > *currentPtr = topPtr;
69
70       if ( isEmpty() )             // Stack is empty
71          cout << "Stack is empty\n";
72       else {                       // Stack is not empty
73          cout << "The stack is:\n";
74
75          while ( currentPtr != 0 ) {
76             cout << currentPtr -> data << ' ';
77             currentPtr = currentPtr -> nextPtr;
78          }
79
80          cout << '\n';
81       }
82   }
83
84   #endif
```

```
85   // STACKND.H
86   // Definition of template class StackNode
87   #ifndef STACKND_H
88   #define STACKND_H
89
90   template< class T > class Stack;   // forward declaration
91
92   template < class T >
93   class StackNode {
94      friend class Stack< T >;
95   public:
96      StackNode( const T & = 0, StackNode * = 0 );
97      T getData() const;
98      void setNextPtr( StackNode *nPtr ) { nextPtr = nPtr; }
99      StackNode *getNextPtr() const { return nextPtr; }
100  private:
101     T data;
102     StackNode *nextPtr;
103  };
104
105  // Member function definitions for class StackNode
106  template < class T >
107  StackNode< T >::StackNode( const T &d, StackNode< T > *ptr )
108  {
109     data = d;
110     nextPtr = ptr;
111  }
112
113  template < class T >
114  T StackNode< T >::getData() const { return data; }
115
116  #endif
```

```
117  // Exercise 15.13 Solution
118  // Using a stack to evaluate an expression in postfix notation
119  #include <iostream.h>
120  #include <string.h>
121  #include <ctype.h>
122  #include <math.h>
123  #include "stack.h"
124
125  int evaluatePostfixExpression( char * const );
126  int calculate( int, int, char );
127
128  int main()
129  {
130     char expression[ 100 ], c;
131     int answer, i = 0;
132
133     cout << "Enter a postfix expression:\n";
134
135     while ( ( c = static_cast< char >( cin.get() ) ) != '\n')
136        if ( c != ' ' )
137           expression[ i++ ] = c;
138
139     expression[ i ] = '\0';
140
141     answer = evaluatePostfixExpression( expression );
142     cout << "The value of the expression is: " << answer << endl;
143
144     return 0;
145  }
146
```

```
147  int evaluatePostfixExpression( char * const expr )
148  {
149      int i, popVal1, popVal2, pushVal;
150      Stack< int > intStack;
151      char c;
152
153      strcat( expr, ")" );
154
155      for ( i = 0; ( c = expr[ i ] ) != ')'; ++i )
156         if ( isdigit( expr[ i ] ) ) {
157            pushVal = c - '0';
158            intStack.push( pushVal );
159            intStack.print();
160         }
161         else {
162            popVal2 = intStack.pop();
163            intStack.print();
164            popVal1 = intStack.pop();
165            intStack.print();
166            pushVal = calculate( popVal1, popVal2, expr[ i ] );
167            intStack.push( pushVal );
168            intStack.print();
169         }
170
171      return intStack.pop();
172  }
173
174  int calculate( int op1, int op2, char oper )
175  {
176      switch( oper ) {
177         case '+':
178            return op1 + op2;
179         case '-':
180            return op1 - op2;
181         case '*':
182            return op1 * op2;
183         case '/':
184            return op1 / op2;
185         case '^':    // exponentiation
186            return static_cast< int >( pow( op1, op2 ) );
187      }
188
189      return 0;
190  }
```

```
Enter a postfix expression:
6 2 + 5 * 8 4 / -

The stack is:
6
The stack is:
2 6
The stack is:
6
Stack is empty
The stack is:
8
The stack is:
5 8
The stack is:
8
Stack is empty
```

```
The stack is:
40
The stack is:
8 40
The stack is:
4 8 40
The stack is:
8 40
The stack is:
40
The stack is:
2 40
The stack is:
40
Stack is empty
The stack is:
38
The value of the expression is: 38
```

15.14 Modify the postfix evaluator program of Exercise 15.13 so that it can process integer operands larger than 9.

15.15 *(Supermarket simulation)* Write a program that simulates a check-out line at a supermarket. The line is a queue object. Customers (i.e., customer objects) arrive in random integer intervals of 1 to 4 minutes. Also, each customer is serviced in random integer intervals of 1 to 4 minutes. Obviously, the rates need to be balanced. If the average arrival rate is larger than the average service rate, the queue will grow infinitely. Even with "balanced" rates, randomness can still cause long lines. Run the supermarket simulation for a 12-hour day (720 minutes) using the following algorithm:

   a) Choose a random integer between 1 and 4 to determine the minute at which the first customer arrives.

   b) At the first customer's arrival time:
   Determine customer's service time (random integer from 1 to 4);
   Begin servicing the customer;
   Schedule arrival time of next customer (random integer 1 to 4 added to the current time).

   c) For each minute of the day:
   If the next customer arrives,
   Say so,
   Enqueue the customer;
   Schedule the arrival time of the next customer;
   If service was completed for the last customer;
   Say so
   Dequeue next customer to be serviced
   Determine customer's service completion time (random integer from 1 to 4 added to the current time).

Now run your simulation for 720 minutes and answer each of the following:

   a) What is the maximum number of customers in the queue at any time?

   b) What is the longest wait any one customer experiences?

   c) What happens if the arrival interval is changed from 1-to-4 minutes to 1-to-3 minutes?

15.16 Modify the program of Fig. 15.16 to allow the binary tree object to contain duplicates.
   ANS:

```
1   // TREE.H
2   // Definition of template class Tree
3   #ifndef TREE_H
4   #define TREE_H
5
6   #include <iostream.h>
7   #include <assert.h>
8   #include "treenode.h"
9
```

```
10    template< class NODETYPE >
11    class Tree {
12    public:
13       Tree();
14       void insertNode( const NODETYPE & );
15       void preOrderTraversal() const;
16       void inOrderTraversal() const;
17       void postOrderTraversal() const;
18    protected:
19       TreeNode<NODETYPE> *rootPtr;
20
21       // utility functions
22       void insertNodeHelper( TreeNode< NODETYPE > **, const NODETYPE & );
23       void preOrderHelper( TreeNode< NODETYPE > * ) const;
24       void inOrderHelper( TreeNode< NODETYPE > * ) const;
25       void postOrderHelper( TreeNode< NODETYPE > * ) const;
26    };
27
28    template< class NODETYPE >
29    Tree< NODETYPE >::Tree() { rootPtr = 0; }
30
31    template< class NODETYPE >
32    void Tree< NODETYPE >::insertNode( const NODETYPE &value )
33       { insertNodeHelper( &rootPtr, value ); }
34
35    // This function receives a pointer to a pointer so the
36    // pointer can be modified.
37    // NOTE: THIS FUNCTION WAS MODIFIED TO ALLOW DUPLICATES.
38    template< class NODETYPE >
39    void Tree< NODETYPE >::insertNodeHelper( TreeNode< NODETYPE > **ptr,
40                                             const NODETYPE &value )
41    {
42       if ( *ptr == 0 ) {                        // tree is empty
43          *ptr = new TreeNode< NODETYPE >( value );
44          assert( *ptr != 0 );
45       }
46       else                                      // tree is not empty
47          if ( value <= ( *ptr ) -> data )
48             insertNodeHelper( &( ( *ptr ) -> leftPtr ), value );
49          else
50             insertNodeHelper( &( ( *ptr ) -> rightPtr ), value );
51    }
52
53    template< class NODETYPE >
54    void Tree< NODETYPE >::preOrderTraversal() const { preOrderHelper( rootPtr ); }
55
56    template< class NODETYPE >
57    void Tree< NODETYPE >::preOrderHelper( TreeNode< NODETYPE > *ptr ) const
58    {
59       if ( ptr != 0 ) {
60          cout << ptr -> data << ' ';
61          preOrderHelper( ptr -> leftPtr );
62          preOrderHelper( ptr -> rightPtr );
63       }
64    }
65
66    template< class NODETYPE >
67    void Tree< NODETYPE >::inOrderTraversal() const { inOrderHelper( rootPtr ); }
68
69    template< class NODETYPE >
70    void Tree< NODETYPE >::inOrderHelper( TreeNode< NODETYPE > *ptr ) const
71    {
72       if ( ptr != 0 ) {
73          inOrderHelper( ptr -> leftPtr );
```

```
74         cout << ptr -> data << ' ';
75         inOrderHelper( ptr -> rightPtr );
76     }
77  }
78
79  template< class NODETYPE >
80  void Tree< NODETYPE >::postOrderTraversal() const { postOrderHelper( rootPtr ); }
81
82  template< class NODETYPE >
83  void Tree< NODETYPE >::postOrderHelper( TreeNode< NODETYPE > *ptr ) const
84  {
85     if ( ptr != 0 ) {
86         postOrderHelper( ptr -> leftPtr );
87         postOrderHelper( ptr -> rightPtr );
88         cout << ptr -> data << ' ';
89     }
90  }
91
92  #endif
```

```
93  // TREENODE.H
94  // Definition of class TreeNode
95  #ifndef TREENODE_H
96  #define TREENODE_H
97
98  template< class T > class Tree;      // forward declaration
99
100 template< class NODETYPE >
101 class TreeNode {
102    friend class Tree< NODETYPE >;
103 public:
104    TreeNode( const NODETYPE & );  // constructor
105    NODETYPE getData() const;         // return data
106    TreeNode *getLeftPtr() const { return leftPtr; }
107    TreeNode *getRightPtr() const { return rightPtr; }
108    void setLeftPtr( TreeNode *ptr ) { leftPtr = ptr; }
109    void setRightPtr( TreeNode *ptr ) { rightPtr = ptr; }
110 private:
111    TreeNode *leftPtr;   // pointer to left subtree
112    NODETYPE data;
113    TreeNode *rightPtr;  // pointer to right subtree
114 };
115
116 // Constructor
117 template< class NODETYPE >
118 TreeNode< NODETYPE >::TreeNode( const NODETYPE &d )
119 {
120    data = d;
121    leftPtr = rightPtr = 0;
122 }
123
124 //Return a copy of the data value
125 template< class NODETYPE >
126 NODETYPE TreeNode< NODETYPE >::getData() const { return data; }
127
128 #endif
```

```
129 // Exercise 15.16 solution
130 // Driver to test class Tree
131 #include <iostream.h>
132 #include <iomanip.h>
133 #include "tree.h"
134
```

```
135  int main()
136  {
137      Tree< int > intTree;
138      int intVal, i;
139
140      cout << "Enter 10 integer values:\n";
141      for ( i = 0; i < 10; ++i ) {
142         cin >> intVal;
143         intTree.insertNode( intVal );
144      }
145
146      cout << "\nPreorder traversal\n";
147      intTree.preOrderTraversal();
148
149      cout << "\nInorder traversal\n";
150      intTree.inOrderTraversal();
151
152      cout << "\nPostorder traversal\n";
153      intTree.postOrderTraversal();
154
155      Tree< float > floatTree;
156      float floatVal;
157
158      cout << "\n\n\nEnter 10 float values:\n"
159           << setiosflags( ios::fixed | ios::showpoint )
160           << setprecision( 1 );
161      for ( i = 0; i < 10; ++i ) {
162         cin >> floatVal;
163         floatTree.insertNode( floatVal );
164      }
165
166      cout << "\nPreorder traversal\n";
167      floatTree.preOrderTraversal();
168
169      cout << "\nInorder traversal\n";
170      floatTree.inOrderTraversal();
171
172      cout << "\nPostorder traversal\n";
173      floatTree.postOrderTraversal();
174
175      return 0;
176  }
```

```
Enter 10 integer values:
22 8 88 73 83 78 79 89 86 21

Preorder traversal
22 8 21 88 73 83 78 79 86 89
Inorder traversal
8 21 22 73 78 79 83 86 88 89
Postorder traversal
21 8 79 78 86 83 73 89 88 22


Enter 10 float values:
9.9 8.8 0.0 4.4 5.5 6.6 1.1 7.7 2.2 3.3

Preorder traversal
9.9 8.8 0.0 4.4 1.1 2.2 3.3 5.5 6.6 7.7
Inorder traversal
0.0 1.1 2.2 3.3 4.4 5.5 6.6 7.7 8.8 9.9
Postorder traversal
3.3 2.2 1.1 7.7 6.6 5.5 4.4 0.0 8.8 9.9
```

15.17   Write a program based on the program of Fig. 15.16 that inputs a line of text, tokenizes the sentence into separate words (you may want to use the **strtok** library function), inserts the words in a binary search tree, and prints the inorder, preorder, and postorder traversals of the tree. Use an OOP approach.

   ANS:

```
1    // TREE.H
2    // Definition of template class Tree
3    #ifndef TREE_H
4    #define TREE_H
5
6    #include <iostream.h>
7    #include <assert.h>
8    #include "treenode.h"
9
10   template< class NODETYPE >
11   class Tree {
12   public:
13      Tree();
14      void insertNode( const NODETYPE & );
15      void preOrderTraversal() const;
16      void inOrderTraversal() const;
17      void postOrderTraversal() const;
18   protected:
19      TreeNode<NODETYPE> *rootPtr;
20
21      // utility functions
22      void insertNodeHelper( TreeNode< NODETYPE > **, const NODETYPE & );
23      void preOrderHelper( TreeNode< NODETYPE > * ) const;
24      void inOrderHelper( TreeNode< NODETYPE > * ) const;
25      void postOrderHelper( TreeNode< NODETYPE > * ) const;
26   };
27
28   template< class NODETYPE >
29   Tree< NODETYPE >::Tree() { rootPtr = 0; }
30
31   template< class NODETYPE >
32   void Tree< NODETYPE >::insertNode( const NODETYPE &value )
33      { insertNodeHelper( &rootPtr, value ); }
34
35   // This function receives a pointer to a pointer so the
36   // pointer can be modified.
37   // NOTE: THIS FUNCTION WAS MODIFIED TO ALLOW DUPLICATES.
38   template< class NODETYPE >
39   void Tree< NODETYPE >::insertNodeHelper( TreeNode< NODETYPE > **ptr,
40                                            const NODETYPE &value )
41   {
42      if ( *ptr == 0 ) {                        // tree is empty
43         *ptr = new TreeNode< NODETYPE >( value );
44         assert( *ptr != 0 );
45      }
46      else                                      // tree is not empty
47         if ( value <= ( *ptr ) -> data )
48            insertNodeHelper( &( ( *ptr ) -> leftPtr ), value );
49         else
50            insertNodeHelper( &( ( *ptr ) -> rightPtr ), value );
51   }
52
53   template< class NODETYPE >
54   void Tree< NODETYPE >::preOrderTraversal() const { preOrderHelper( rootPtr ); }
55
```

```
56   template< class NODETYPE >
57   void Tree< NODETYPE >::preOrderHelper( TreeNode< NODETYPE > *ptr ) const
58   {
59      if ( ptr != 0 ) {
60         cout << ptr -> data << ' ';
61         preOrderHelper( ptr -> leftPtr );
62         preOrderHelper( ptr -> rightPtr );
63      }
64   }
65
66   template< class NODETYPE >
67   void Tree< NODETYPE >::inOrderTraversal() const { inOrderHelper( rootPtr ); }
68
69   template< class NODETYPE >
70   void Tree< NODETYPE >::inOrderHelper( TreeNode< NODETYPE > *ptr ) const
71   {
72      if ( ptr != 0 ) {
73         inOrderHelper( ptr -> leftPtr );
74         cout << ptr -> data << ' ';
75         inOrderHelper( ptr -> rightPtr );
76      }
77   }
78
79   template< class NODETYPE >
80   void Tree< NODETYPE >::postOrderTraversal() const { postOrderHelper( rootPtr ); }
81
82   template< class NODETYPE >
83   void Tree< NODETYPE >::postOrderHelper( TreeNode< NODETYPE > *ptr ) const
84   {
85      if ( ptr != 0 ) {
86         postOrderHelper( ptr -> leftPtr );
87         postOrderHelper( ptr -> rightPtr );
88         cout << ptr -> data << ' ';
89      }
90   }
91
92   #endif
```

```
93   // TREENODE.H
94   // Definition of class TreeNode
95   #ifndef TREENODE_H
96   #define TREENODE_H
97
98   template< class T > class Tree;     // forward declaration
99
100  template< class NODETYPE >
101  class TreeNode {
102     friend class Tree< NODETYPE >;
103  public:
104     TreeNode( const NODETYPE & );   // constructor
105     NODETYPE getData() const;        // return data
106     TreeNode *getLeftPtr() const { return leftPtr; }
107     TreeNode *getRightPtr() const { return rightPtr; }
108     void setLeftPtr( TreeNode *ptr ) { leftPtr = ptr; }
109     void setRightPtr( TreeNode *ptr ) { rightPtr = ptr; }
110  private:
111     TreeNode *leftPtr;    // pointer to left subtree
112     NODETYPE data;
113     TreeNode *rightPtr;   // pointer to right subtree
114  };
115
```

```
116  // Constructor
117  template< class NODETYPE >
118  TreeNode< NODETYPE >::TreeNode( const NODETYPE &d )
119  {
120      data = d;
121      leftPtr = rightPtr = 0;
122  }
123
124  //Return a copy of the data value
125  template< class NODETYPE >
126  NODETYPE TreeNode< NODETYPE >::getData() const { return data; }
127
128  #endif
```

```
129  // STRING2.H
130  // Definition of a String class
131  #ifndef STRING1_H
132  #define STRING1_H
133
134  #include <iostream.h>
135
136  class String {
137      friend ostream &operator<<( ostream &, const String & );
138      friend istream &operator>>( istream &, String & );
139  public:
140      String( const char * = "" ); // conversion constructor
141      String( const String & );     // copy constructor
142      ~String();                    // destructor
143      const String &operator=( const String & );  // assignment
144      String &operator+=( const String & );       // concatenation
145      bool operator!() const;                      // is String empty?
146      bool operator==( const String & ) const;  // test s1 == s2
147      bool operator!=( const String & ) const;  // test s1 != s2
148      bool operator<( const String & )  const;  // test s1 < s2
149      bool operator>( const String & )  const;  // test s1 > s2
150      bool operator>=( const String & ) const;  // test s1 >= s2
151      bool operator<=( const String & ) const;  // test s1 <= s2
152      char &operator[]( int );         // return char reference
153      String &operator()( int, int ); // return a substring
154      int getLength() const;           // return string length
155  private:
156      char *sPtr;                      // pointer to start of string
157      int length;                      // string length
158  };
159
160  #endif
```

```
161  // STRING2.CPP
162  // Member function definitions for class String.
163  // NOTE: The printing capabilities have been removed
164  // from the constructor and destructor functions.
165  #include <iostream.h>
166  #include <iomanip.h>
167  #include <string.h>
168  #include <assert.h>
169  #include "string2.h"
170
171  // Conversion constructor: Convert char * to String
172  String::String( const char *ptr )
173  {
174      length = strlen( ptr );          // compute length
175      sPtr = new char[ length + 1 ];   // allocate storage
176      assert( sPtr != 0 );             // terminate if memory not allocated
```

```
177       strcpy( sPtr, ptr );                    // copy literal to object
178  }
179
180  // Copy constructor
181  String::String( const String &copy )
182  {
183      length = copy.length;           // copy length
184      sPtr = new char[ length + 1 ]; // allocate storage
185      assert( sPtr != 0 );            // ensure memory allocated
186      strcpy( sPtr, copy.sPtr );      // copy string
187  }
188
189  // Destructor
190  String::~String()
191  {
192      delete [] sPtr;                 // reclaim string
193  }
194
195  // Overloaded = operator; avoids self assignment
196  const String &String::operator=( const String &right )
197  {
198      if ( &right != this ) {         // avoid self assignment
199          delete [] sPtr;             // prevents memory leak
200          length = right.length;      // new String length
201          sPtr = new char[ length + 1 ]; // allocate memory
202          assert( sPtr != 0 );        // ensure memory allocated
203          strcpy( sPtr, right.sPtr ); // copy string
204      }
205      else
206          cout << "Attempted assignment of a String to itself\n";
207
208      return *this;    // enables concatenated assignments
209  }
210
211  // Concatenate right operand to this object and
212  // store in this object.
213  String &String::operator+=( const String &right )
214  {
215      char *tempPtr = sPtr;           // hold to be able to delete
216      length += right.length;         // new String length
217      sPtr = new char[ length + 1 ]; // create space
218      assert( sPtr != 0 );            // terminate if memory not allocated
219      strcpy( sPtr, tempPtr );        // left part of new String
220      strcat( sPtr, right.sPtr );     // right part of new String
221      delete [] tempPtr;              // reclaim old space
222      return *this;                   // enables concatenated calls
223  }
224
225  // Is this String empty?
226  bool String::operator!() const { return length == 0; }
227
228  // Is this String equal to right String?
229  bool String::operator==( const String &right ) const
230      { return strcmp( sPtr, right.sPtr ) == 0; }
231
232  // Is this String not equal to right String?
233  bool String::operator!=( const String &right ) const
234      { return strcmp( sPtr, right.sPtr ) != 0; }
235
236  // Is this String less than right String?
237  bool String::operator<( const String &right ) const
238      { return strcmp( sPtr, right.sPtr ) < 0; }
239
```

```
240  // Is this String greater than right String?
241  bool String::operator>( const String &right ) const
242     { return strcmp( sPtr, right.sPtr ) > 0; }
243
244  // Is this String greater than or equal to right String?
245  bool String::operator>=( const String &right ) const
246     { return strcmp( sPtr, right.sPtr ) >= 0; }
247
248  // Is this String less than or equal to right String?
249  bool String::operator<=( const String &right ) const
250     { return strcmp( sPtr, right.sPtr ) <= 0; }
251
252  // Return a reference to a character in a String.
253  char &String::operator[]( int subscript )
254  {
255     // First test for subscript out of range
256     assert( subscript >= 0 && subscript < length );
257
258     return sPtr[ subscript ];   // creates lvalue
259  }
260
261  // Return a substring beginning at index and
262  // of length subLength as a reference to a String object.
263  String &String::operator()( int index, int subLength )
264  {
265     // ensure index is in range and substring length >= 0
266     assert( index >= 0 && index < length && subLength >= 0 );
267
268     String *subPtr = new String;   // empty String
269     assert( subPtr != 0 );      // ensure new String allocated
270
271     // determine length of substring
272     if ( ( subLength == 0 ) || ( index + subLength > length ) )
273        subPtr -> length = length - index + 1;
274     else
275        subPtr -> length = subLength + 1;
276
277     // allocate memory for substring
278     delete subPtr -> sPtr;          // delete character from object
279     subPtr -> sPtr = new char[ subPtr -> length ];
280     assert( subPtr -> sPtr != 0 ); // ensure space allocated
281
282     // copy substring into new String
283     strncpy( subPtr -> sPtr, &sPtr[ index ], subPtr -> length );
284     subPtr -> sPtr[ subPtr -> length ] = '\0'; // terminate new String
285
286     return *subPtr;             // return new String
287  }
288
289  // Return string length
290  int String::getLength() const { return length; }
291
292  // Overloaded output operator
293  ostream &operator<<( ostream &output, const String &s )
294  {
295     output << s.sPtr;
296     return output;   // enables concatenation
297  }
298
299  // Overloaded input operator
300  istream &operator>>( istream &input, String &s )
301  {
302     char temp[ 100 ];   // buffer to store input
303
```

```
304     input >> setw( 100 ) >> temp;
305     s = temp;          // use String class assignment operator
306     return input;      // enables concatenation
307 }
```

```
308 // Exercise 15.17 solution
309 #include <iostream.h>
310 #include <iomanip.h>
311 #include <string.h>
312 #include "tree.h"
313 #include "string2.h"
314
315 int main()
316 {
317     Tree< String > stringTree;
318     char sentence[ 80 ], *tokenPtr;
319
320     cout << "Enter a sentence:\n";
321     cin.getline( sentence, 80 );
322     tokenPtr = strtok( sentence, " " );
323
324     while ( tokenPtr != 0 ) {
325         String *newString = new String( tokenPtr );
326         stringTree.insertNode( *newString );
327         tokenPtr = strtok( 0, " " );
328     }
329
330     cout << "\nPreorder traversal\n";
331     stringTree.preOrderTraversal();
332
333     cout << "\nInorder traversal\n";
334     stringTree.inOrderTraversal();
335
336     cout << "\nPostorder traversal\n";
337     stringTree.postOrderTraversal();
338
339     cout << endl;
340     return 0;
341 }
```

```
Enter a sentence:
ANSI/ISO C++ How to Program

Preorder traversal
ANSI/ISO C++ How to Program
Inorder traversal
ANSI/ISO C++ How Program to
Postorder traversal
Program to How C++ ANSI/ISO
```

15.18   In this chapter, we saw that duplicate elimination is straightforward when creating a binary search tree. Describe how you would perform duplicate elimination using only a single-subscripted array. Compare the performance of array-based duplicate elimination with the performance of binary-search-tree-based duplicate elimination.

15.19   Write a function **depth** that receives a binary tree and determines how many levels it has.
     ANS:

```
1  // TREE.H
2  // Definition of template class Tree
3  #ifndef TREE_H
4  #define TREE_H
```

```
5
6    #include <iostream.h>
7    #include <assert.h>
8    #include "treenode.h"
9
10   template< class NODETYPE >
11   class Tree {
12   public:
13      Tree();
14      void insertNode( const NODETYPE & );
15      void preOrderTraversal() const;
16      void inOrderTraversal() const;
17      void postOrderTraversal() const;
18   protected:
19      TreeNode<NODETYPE> *rootPtr;
20
21      // utility functions
22      void insertNodeHelper( TreeNode< NODETYPE > **, const NODETYPE & );
23      void preOrderHelper( TreeNode< NODETYPE > * ) const;
24      void inOrderHelper( TreeNode< NODETYPE > * ) const;
25      void postOrderHelper( TreeNode< NODETYPE > * ) const;
26   };
27
28   template< class NODETYPE >
29   Tree< NODETYPE >::Tree() { rootPtr = 0; }
30
31   template< class NODETYPE >
32   void Tree< NODETYPE >::insertNode( const NODETYPE &value )
33      { insertNodeHelper( &rootPtr, value ); }
34
35   // This function receives a pointer to a pointer so the
36   // pointer can be modified.
37   // NOTE: THIS FUNCTION WAS MODIFIED TO ALLOW DUPLICATES.
38   template< class NODETYPE >
39   void Tree< NODETYPE >::insertNodeHelper( TreeNode< NODETYPE > **ptr,
40                                            const NODETYPE &value )
41   {
42      if ( *ptr == 0 ) {                        // tree is empty
43         *ptr = new TreeNode< NODETYPE >( value );
44         assert( *ptr != 0 );
45      }
46      else                                      // tree is not empty
47         if ( value <= ( *ptr ) -> data )
48            insertNodeHelper( &( ( *ptr ) -> leftPtr ), value );
49         else
50            insertNodeHelper( &( ( *ptr ) -> rightPtr ), value );
51   }
52
53   template< class NODETYPE >
54   void Tree< NODETYPE >::preOrderTraversal() const { preOrderHelper( rootPtr ); }
55
56   template< class NODETYPE >
57   void Tree< NODETYPE >::preOrderHelper( TreeNode< NODETYPE > *ptr ) const
58   {
59      if ( ptr != 0 ) {
60         cout << ptr -> data << ' ';
61         preOrderHelper( ptr -> leftPtr );
62         preOrderHelper( ptr -> rightPtr );
63      }
64   }
65
66   template< class NODETYPE >
67   void Tree< NODETYPE >::inOrderTraversal() const { inOrderHelper( rootPtr ); }
68
```

```
69  template< class NODETYPE >
70  void Tree< NODETYPE >::inOrderHelper( TreeNode< NODETYPE > *ptr ) const
71  {
72     if ( ptr != 0 ) {
73        inOrderHelper( ptr -> leftPtr );
74        cout << ptr -> data << ' ';
75        inOrderHelper( ptr -> rightPtr );
76     }
77  }
78
79  template< class NODETYPE >
80  void Tree< NODETYPE >::postOrderTraversal() const { postOrderHelper( rootPtr ); }
81
82  template< class NODETYPE >
83  void Tree< NODETYPE >::postOrderHelper( TreeNode< NODETYPE > *ptr ) const
84  {
85     if ( ptr != 0 ) {
86        postOrderHelper( ptr -> leftPtr );
87        postOrderHelper( ptr -> rightPtr );
88        cout << ptr -> data << ' ';
89     }
90  }
91
92  #endif
```

```
1   // TREENODE.H
2   // Definition of class TreeNode
3   #ifndef TREENODE_H
4   #define TREENODE_H
5
6   template< class T > class Tree;     // forward declaration
7
8   template< class NODETYPE >
9   class TreeNode {
10     friend class Tree< NODETYPE >;
11  public:
12     TreeNode( const NODETYPE & );  // constructor
13     NODETYPE getData() const;       // return data
14     TreeNode *getLeftPtr() const { return leftPtr; }
15     TreeNode *getRightPtr() const { return rightPtr; }
16     void setLeftPtr( TreeNode *ptr ) { leftPtr = ptr; }
17     void setRightPtr( TreeNode *ptr ) { rightPtr = ptr; }
18  private:
19     TreeNode *leftPtr;    // pointer to left subtree
20     NODETYPE data;
21     TreeNode *rightPtr;   // pointer to right subtree
22  };
23
24  // Constructor
25  template< class NODETYPE >
26  TreeNode< NODETYPE >::TreeNode( const NODETYPE &d )
27  {
28     data = d;
29     leftPtr = rightPtr = 0;
30  }
31
32  //Return a copy of the data value
33  template< class NODETYPE >
34  NODETYPE TreeNode< NODETYPE >::getData() const { return data; }
35
36  #endif
```

```
37   // TREE2.H
38   // Definition of template class Tree
39   // Modified to include getDepth and determineDepth member functions.
40   #ifndef TREE2_H
41   #define TREE2_H
42
43   #include <iostream.h>
44   #include <assert.h>
45   #include "treenode.h"
46   #include "tree.h"
47
48   template< class NODETYPE >
49   class Tree2 : public Tree< NODETYPE > {
50   public:
51      int getDepth() const;
52   private:
53      void determineDepth( TreeNode< NODETYPE > *, int *, int * ) const;
54   };
55
56   template< class NODETYPE >
57   int Tree2< NODETYPE >::getDepth() const
58   {
59      int totalDepth = 0, currentDepth = 0;
60
61      determineDepth( rootPtr, &totalDepth, &currentDepth );
62
63      return totalDepth;
64   }
65
66   template< class NODETYPE >
67   void Tree2< NODETYPE >::determineDepth( TreeNode< NODETYPE > *ptr,
68                                           int *totPtr, int *currPtr ) const
69   {
70      if ( ptr != 0 ) {
71         ++( *currPtr );
72
73         if ( *currPtr > *totPtr )
74            *totPtr = *currPtr;
75
76         determineDepth( ptr -> getLeftPtr(), totPtr, currPtr );
77         determineDepth( ptr -> getRightPtr(), totPtr, currPtr );
78         --( *currPtr );
79      }
80   }
81
82   #endif
```

```
83   // Exercise 15.19 solution
84   #include <iostream.h>
85   #include "tree2.h"
86
87   int main()
88   {
89      Tree2< int > intTree;
90      int intVal;
91
92      cout << "Enter 10 integer values:\n";
93
94      for ( int i = 0; i < 10; ++i ) {
95         cin >> intVal;
96         intTree.insertNode( intVal );
97      }
98
```

```
99      cout << "\nPreorder traversal\n";
100     intTree.preOrderTraversal();
101
102     cout << "\nInorder traversal\n";
103     intTree.inOrderTraversal();
104
105     cout << "\nPostorder traversal\n";
106     intTree.postOrderTraversal();
107
108     cout << "\n\nThere are " << intTree.getDepth()
109         << " levels in this binary tree\n";
110
111     return 0;
112 }
```

```
Enter 10 integer values:
1 2 3 88 4 6 0 22 21 10

Preorder traversal
1 0 2 3 88 4 6 22 21 10
Inorder traversal
0 1 2 3 4 6 10 21 22 88
Postorder traversal
0 10 21 22 6 4 88 3 2 1

There are 9 levels in this binary tree
```

15.20 (*Recursively print a list backwards*) Write a member function **printListBackwards** that recursively outputs the items in a linked list object in reverse order. Write a test program that creates a sorted list of integers and prints the list in reverse order.

ANS:

```
1   // LIST.H
2   // Template List class definition
3   // Added copy constructor to member functions (not included in chapter).
4   #ifndef LIST_H
5   #define LIST_H
6
7   #include <iostream.h>
8   #include <assert.h>
9   #include "listnd.h"
10
11  template< class NODETYPE >
12  class List {
13  public:
14      List();                                 // default constructor
15      List( const List< NODETYPE > & );  // copy constructor
16      ~List();                                // destructor
17      void insertAtFront( const NODETYPE & );
18      void insertAtBack( const NODETYPE & );
19      bool removeFromFront( NODETYPE & );
20      bool removeFromBack( NODETYPE & );
21      bool isEmpty() const;
22      void print() const;
23  protected:
24      ListNode< NODETYPE > *firstPtr;  // pointer to first node
25      ListNode< NODETYPE > *lastPtr;   // pointer to last node
26
27      // Utility function to allocate a new node
28      ListNode< NODETYPE > *getNewNode( const NODETYPE & );
29  };
30
```

```
31   // Default constructor
32   template< class NODETYPE >
33   List< NODETYPE >::List() { firstPtr = lastPtr = 0; }
34
35   // Copy constructor
36   template< class NODETYPE >
37   List< NODETYPE >::List( const List<NODETYPE> &copy )
38   {
39      firstPtr = lastPtr = 0;   // initialize pointers
40      ListNode< NODETYPE > *currentPtr = copy.firstPtr;
41
42      while ( currentPtr != 0 ) {
43         insertAtBack( currentPtr -> data );
44         currentPtr = currentPtr -> nextPtr;
45      }
46   }
47
48   // Destructor
49   template< class NODETYPE >
50   List< NODETYPE >::~List()
51   {
52      if ( !isEmpty() ) {       // List is not empty
53         cout << "Destroying nodes ...\n";
54
55         ListNode< NODETYPE > *currentPtr = firstPtr, *tempPtr;
56
57         while ( currentPtr != 0 ) {   // delete remaining nodes
58            tempPtr = currentPtr;
59            cout << tempPtr -> data << ' ';
60            currentPtr = currentPtr -> nextPtr;
61            delete tempPtr;
62         }
63      }
64
65      cout << "\nAll nodes destroyed\n\n";
66   }
67
68   // Insert a node at the front of the list
69   template< class NODETYPE >
70   void List< NODETYPE >::insertAtFront( const NODETYPE &value )
71   {
72      ListNode<NODETYPE> *newPtr = getNewNode( value );
73
74      if ( isEmpty() )  // List is empty
75         firstPtr = lastPtr = newPtr;
76      else {            // List is not empty
77         newPtr -> nextPtr = firstPtr;
78         firstPtr = newPtr;
79      }
80   }
81
82   // Insert a node at the back of the list
83   template< class NODETYPE >
84   void List< NODETYPE >::insertAtBack( const NODETYPE &value )
85   {
86      ListNode< NODETYPE > *newPtr = getNewNode( value );
87
88      if ( isEmpty() )  // List is empty
89         firstPtr = lastPtr = newPtr;
90      else {            // List is not empty
91         lastPtr -> nextPtr = newPtr;
92         lastPtr = newPtr;
93      }
94   }
```

```
95
96   // Delete a node from the front of the list
97   template< class NODETYPE >
98   bool List< NODETYPE >::removeFromFront( NODETYPE &value )
99   {
100     if ( isEmpty() )                    // List is empty
101       return false;                     // delete unsuccessful
102     else {
103       ListNode< NODETYPE > *tempPtr = firstPtr;
104
105       if ( firstPtr == lastPtr )
106         firstPtr = lastPtr = 0;
107       else
108         firstPtr = firstPtr -> nextPtr;
109
110       value = tempPtr -> data;   // data being removed
111       delete tempPtr;
112       return true;                      // delete successful
113     }
114   }
115
116   // Delete a node from the back of the list
117   template< class NODETYPE >
118   bool List< NODETYPE >::removeFromBack( NODETYPE &value )
119   {
120     if ( isEmpty() )
121       return false;      // delete unsuccessful
122     else {
123       ListNode< NODETYPE > *tempPtr = lastPtr;
124
125       if ( firstPtr == lastPtr )
126         firstPtr = lastPtr = 0;
127       else {
128         ListNode< NODETYPE > *currentPtr = firstPtr;
129
130         while ( currentPtr -> nextPtr != lastPtr )
131           currentPtr = currentPtr -> nextPtr;
132
133         lastPtr = currentPtr;
134         currentPtr -> nextPtr = 0;
135       }
136
137       value = tempPtr -> data;
138       delete tempPtr;
139       return true;      // delete successful
140     }
141   }
142
143   // Is the List empty?
144   template< class NODETYPE >
145   bool List< NODETYPE >::isEmpty() const { return firstPtr == 0; }
146
147   // Return a pointer to a newly allocated node
148   template< class NODETYPE >
149   ListNode< NODETYPE > *List< NODETYPE >::getNewNode( const NODETYPE &value )
150   {
151     ListNode< NODETYPE > *ptr = new ListNode< NODETYPE >( value );
152     assert( ptr != 0 );
153     return ptr;
154   }
155
```

```
156  // Display the contents of the List
157  template< class NODETYPE >
158  void List< NODETYPE >::print() const
159  {
160     if ( isEmpty() ) {
161        cout << "The list is empty\n\n";
162        return;
163     }
164
165     ListNode< NODETYPE > *currentPtr = firstPtr;
166
167     cout << "The list is: ";
168
169     while ( currentPtr != 0 ) {
170        cout << currentPtr -> data << ' ';
171        currentPtr = currentPtr -> nextPtr;
172     }
173
174     cout << "\n\n";
175  }
176
177  #endif
```

```
178  // LISTND.H
179  // ListNode template definition
180  #ifndef LISTND_H
181  #define LISTND_H
182
183  template< class T > class List;   // forward declaration
184
185  template< class NODETYPE >
186  class ListNode {
187     friend class List< NODETYPE >; // make List a friend
188  public:
189     ListNode( const NODETYPE & );  // constructor
190     NODETYPE getData() const;      // return the data in the node
191     void setNextPtr( ListNode *nPtr ) { nextPtr = nPtr; }
192     ListNode *getNextPtr() const { return nextPtr; }
193  private:
194     NODETYPE data;                 // data
195     ListNode *nextPtr;             // next node in the list
196  };
197
198  // Constructor
199  template< class NODETYPE >
200  ListNode< NODETYPE >::ListNode( const NODETYPE &info )
201  {
202     data = info;
203     nextPtr = 0;
204  }
205
206  // Return a copy of the data in the node
207  template< class NODETYPE >
208  NODETYPE ListNode< NODETYPE >::getData() const { return data; }
209
210  #endif
```

```
211  // LIST2.H
212  // Template List class definition
213  #ifndef LIST2_H
214  #define LIST2_H
215
216  #include <iostream.h>
```

```
217  #include <assert.h>
218  #include "listnd.h"
219  #include "list.h"
220
221  template< class NODETYPE >
222  class List2 : public List< NODETYPE > {
223  public:
224     void recursivePrintReverse() const;
225  private:
226     void recursivePrintReverseHelper( ListNode< NODETYPE > * ) const;
227  };
228
229  // Print a List backwards recursively.
230  template< class NODETYPE >
231  void List2< NODETYPE >::recursivePrintReverse() const
232  {
233     cout << "The list printed recursively backwards is:\n";
234     recursivePrintReverseHelper( firstPtr );
235     cout << '\n';
236  }
237
238  // Helper for printing a list backwards recursively.
239  template< class NODETYPE >
240  void List2< NODETYPE >::recursivePrintReverseHelper(
241                         ListNode< NODETYPE > *currentPtr ) const
242  {
243     if ( currentPtr == 0 )
244        return;
245
246     recursivePrintReverseHelper( currentPtr -> getNextPtr() );
247     cout << currentPtr -> getData() << ' ';
248  }
249
250  #endif
```

```
251  // Exercise 15.20 solution
252  #include <iostream.h>
253  #include "list2.h"
254
255  int main()
256  {
257     List2< int > intList;
258
259     for ( int i = 1; i <= 10; ++i )
260        intList.insertAtBack( i );
261
262     intList.print();
263     intList.recursivePrintReverse();
264
265     return 0;
266  }
```

```
The list is: 1 2 3 4 5 6 7 8 9 10

The list printed recursively backwards is:
10 9 8 7 6 5 4 3 2 1
Destroying nodes ...
1 2 3 4 5 6 7 8 9 10
All nodes destroyed
```

15.21 (*Recursively search a list*) Write a member function **searchList** that recursively searches a linked list object for a specified value. The function should return a pointer to the value if it is found; otherwise, null should be returned. Use your function in a test program that creates a list of integers. The program should prompt the user for a value to locate in the list.

ANS:

```
1    // LIST.H
2    // Template List class definition
3    // Added copy constructor to member functions (not included in chapter).
4    #ifndef LIST_H
5    #define LIST_H
6
7    #include <iostream.h>
8    #include <assert.h>
9    #include "listnd.h"
10
11   template< class NODETYPE >
12   class List {
13   public:
14      List();                                 // default constructor
15      List( const List< NODETYPE > & );  // copy constructor
16      ~List();                                // destructor
17      void insertAtFront( const NODETYPE & );
18      void insertAtBack( const NODETYPE & );
19      bool removeFromFront( NODETYPE & );
20      bool removeFromBack( NODETYPE & );
21      bool isEmpty() const;
22      void print() const;
23   protected:
24      ListNode< NODETYPE > *firstPtr;  // pointer to first node
25      ListNode< NODETYPE > *lastPtr;   // pointer to last node
26
27      // Utility function to allocate a new node
28      ListNode< NODETYPE > *getNewNode( const NODETYPE & );
29   };
30
31   // Default constructor
32   template< class NODETYPE >
33   List< NODETYPE >::List() { firstPtr = lastPtr = 0; }
34
35   // Copy constructor
36   template< class NODETYPE >
37   List< NODETYPE >::List( const List<NODETYPE> &copy )
38   {
39      firstPtr = lastPtr = 0;   // initialize pointers
40
41      ListNode< NODETYPE > *currentPtr = copy.firstPtr;
42
43      while ( currentPtr != 0 ) {
44         insertAtBack( currentPtr -> data );
45         currentPtr = currentPtr -> nextPtr;
46      }
47   }
48
49   // Destructor
50   template< class NODETYPE >
51   List< NODETYPE >::~List()
52   {
53      if ( !isEmpty() ) {      // List is not empty
54         cout << "Destroying nodes ...\n";
55
56         ListNode< NODETYPE > *currentPtr = firstPtr, *tempPtr;
57
58         while ( currentPtr != 0 ) {  // delete remaining nodes
59            tempPtr = currentPtr;
60            cout << tempPtr -> data << ' ';
61            currentPtr = currentPtr -> nextPtr;
```

```
62          delete tempPtr;
63        }
64      }
65
66      cout << "\nAll nodes destroyed\n\n";
67   }
68
69   // Insert a node at the front of the list
70   template< class NODETYPE >
71   void List< NODETYPE >::insertAtFront( const NODETYPE &value )
72   {
73      ListNode<NODETYPE> *newPtr = getNewNode( value );
74
75      if ( isEmpty() )  // List is empty
76         firstPtr = lastPtr = newPtr;
77      else {            // List is not empty
78         newPtr -> nextPtr = firstPtr;
79         firstPtr = newPtr;
80      }
81   }
82
83   // Insert a node at the back of the list
84   template< class NODETYPE >
85   void List< NODETYPE >::insertAtBack( const NODETYPE &value )
86   {
87      ListNode< NODETYPE > *newPtr = getNewNode( value );
88
89      if ( isEmpty() )  // List is empty
90         firstPtr = lastPtr = newPtr;
91      else {            // List is not empty
92         lastPtr -> nextPtr = newPtr;
93         lastPtr = newPtr;
94      }
95   }
96
97   // Delete a node from the front of the list
98   template< class NODETYPE >
99   bool List< NODETYPE >::removeFromFront( NODETYPE &value )
100  {
101     if ( isEmpty() )              // List is empty
102        return false;             // delete unsuccessful
103     else {
104        ListNode< NODETYPE > *tempPtr = firstPtr;
105
106        if ( firstPtr == lastPtr )
107           firstPtr = lastPtr = 0;
108        else
109           firstPtr = firstPtr -> nextPtr;
110
111        value = tempPtr -> data;  // data being removed
112        delete tempPtr;
113        return true;              // delete successful
114     }
115  }
116
117  // Delete a node from the back of the list
118  template< class NODETYPE >
119  bool List< NODETYPE >::removeFromBack( NODETYPE &value )
120  {
121     if ( isEmpty() )
122        return false;   // delete unsuccessful
123     else {
124        ListNode< NODETYPE > *tempPtr = lastPtr;
125
```

```
126          if ( firstPtr == lastPtr )
127             firstPtr = lastPtr = 0;
128          else {
129             ListNode< NODETYPE > *currentPtr = firstPtr;
130
131             while ( currentPtr -> nextPtr != lastPtr )
132                currentPtr = currentPtr -> nextPtr;
133
134             lastPtr = currentPtr;
135             currentPtr -> nextPtr = 0;
136          }
137
138          value = tempPtr -> data;
139          delete tempPtr;
140          return true;    // delete successful
141       }
142    }
143
144    // Is the List empty?
145    template< class NODETYPE >
146    bool List< NODETYPE >::isEmpty() const { return firstPtr == 0; }
147
148    // Return a pointer to a newly allocated node
149    template< class NODETYPE >
150    ListNode< NODETYPE > *List< NODETYPE >::getNewNode( const NODETYPE &value )
151    {
152       ListNode< NODETYPE > *ptr = new ListNode< NODETYPE >( value );
153       assert( ptr != 0 );
154       return ptr;
155    }
156
157    // Display the contents of the List
158    template< class NODETYPE >
159    void List< NODETYPE >::print() const
160    {
161       if ( isEmpty() ) {
162          cout << "The list is empty\n\n";
163          return;
164       }
165
166       ListNode< NODETYPE > *currentPtr = firstPtr;
167
168       cout << "The list is: ";
169
170       while ( currentPtr != 0 ) {
171          cout << currentPtr -> data << ' ';
172          currentPtr = currentPtr -> nextPtr;
173       }
174
175       cout << "\n\n";
176    }
177
178    #endif
```

```
179    // LISTND.H
180    // ListNode template definition
181    #ifndef LISTND_H
182    #define LISTND_H
183
184    template< class T > class List;  // forward declaration
185
```

```
186  template< class NODETYPE >
187  class ListNode {
188     friend class List< NODETYPE >; // make List a friend
189  public:
190     ListNode( const NODETYPE & );  // constructor
191     NODETYPE getData() const;      // return the data in the node
192     void setNextPtr( ListNode *nPtr ) { nextPtr = nPtr; }
193     ListNode *getNextPtr() const { return nextPtr; }
194     NODETYPE *getAddress() { return &data; }
195  private:
196     NODETYPE data;                 // data
197     ListNode *nextPtr;             // next node in the list
198  };
199
200  // Constructor
201  template< class NODETYPE >
202  ListNode< NODETYPE >::ListNode( const NODETYPE &info )
203  {
204     data = info;
205     nextPtr = 0;
206  }
207
208  // Return a copy of the data in the node
209  template< class NODETYPE >
210  NODETYPE ListNode< NODETYPE >::getData() const { return data; }
211
212  #endif
```

```
213  // LIST2.H
214  // Template List class definition
215  #ifndef LIST2_H
216  #define LIST2_H
217
218  #include <iostream.h>
219  #include <assert.h>
220  #include "listnd.h"
221  #include "list.h"
222
223  template< class NODETYPE >
224  class List2 : public List< NODETYPE > {
225  public:
226     void recursivePrintReverse() const;
227     NODETYPE *recursiveSearch( NODETYPE & ) const;
228  private:
229     // Utility functions
230     void recursivePrintReverseHelper( ListNode< NODETYPE > * ) const;
231     NODETYPE *recursiveSearchHelper( ListNode< NODETYPE > *, NODETYPE & ) const;
232  };
233
234  // Print a List backwards recursively.
235  template< class NODETYPE >
236  void List2< NODETYPE >::recursivePrintReverse() const
237  {
238     cout << "The list printed recursively backwards is:\n";
239     recursivePrintReverseHelper( firstPtr );
240     cout << '\n';
241  }
242
```

```
243  // Helper for printing a list backwards recursively.
244  template< class NODETYPE >
245  void List2< NODETYPE >::recursivePrintReverseHelper(
246                             ListNode< NODETYPE > *currentPtr ) const
247  {
248     if ( currentPtr == 0 )
249        return;
250
251     recursivePrintReverseHelper( currentPtr -> nextPtr );
252     cout << currentPtr -> data << ' ';
253  }
254
255  // Search a List recursively.
256  template< class NODETYPE >
257  NODETYPE *List2< NODETYPE >::recursiveSearch( NODETYPE &val ) const
258     { return recursiveSearchHelper( firstPtr, val ); }
259
260  // Helper for searching a list recursively.
261  template< class NODETYPE >
262  NODETYPE *List2< NODETYPE >::recursiveSearchHelper(
263                  ListNode< NODETYPE > *currentPtr, NODETYPE &value ) const
264  {
265     if ( currentPtr == 0 )
266        return 0;
267
268     if ( currentPtr -> getData() == value )
269        return currentPtr -> getAddress();
270
271     return recursiveSearchHelper( currentPtr -> getNextPtr(), value );
272  }
273
274  #endif
```

```
275  // Exercise 15.21 solution
276  #include <iostream.h>
277  #include "list2.h"
278
279  int main()
280  {
281     List2< int > intList;
282
283     for ( int i = 2; i <= 20; i += 2 )
284        intList.insertAtBack( i );
285
286     intList.print();
287
288     int value, *ptr;
289
290     cout << "Enter a value to search for: ";
291     cin >> value;
292     ptr = intList.recursiveSearch( value );
293
294     if ( ptr != 0 )
295        cout << *ptr << " was found\n";
296     else
297        cout << "Element not found\n";
298
299     return 0;
300  }
```

```
The list is: 2 4 6 8 10 12 14 16 18 20

Enter a value t\o search for: 14
14 was found

Destroying nodes ...
2 4 6 8 10 12 14 16 18 20
All nodes destroyed
```

15.22 (*Binary tree delete*) In this exercise, we discuss deleting items from binary search trees. The deletion algorithm is not as straightforward as the insertion algorithm. There are three cases that are encountered when deleting an item—the item is contained in a leaf node (i.e., it has no children), the item is contained in a node that has one child, or the item is contained in a node that has two children.

If the item to be deleted is contained in a leaf node, the node is deleted and the pointer in the parent node is set to null.

If the item to be deleted is contained in a node with one child, the pointer in the parent node is set to point to the child node and the node containing the data item is deleted. This causes the child node to take the place of the deleted node in the tree.

The last case is the most difficult. When a node with two children is deleted, another node in the tree must take its place. However, the pointer in the parent node cannot simply be assigned to point to one of the children of the node to be deleted. In most cases, the resulting binary search tree would not adhere to the following characteristic of binary search trees (with no duplicate values): *The values in any left subtree are less than the value in the parent node, and the values in any right subtree are greater than the value in the parent node.*

Which node is used as a *replacement node* to maintain this characteristic? Either the node containing the largest value in the tree less than the value in the node being deleted, or the node containing the smallest value in the tree greater than the value in the node being deleted. Let us consider the node with the smaller value. In a binary search tree, the largest value less than a parent's value is located in the left subtree of the parent node and is guaranteed to be contained in the rightmost node of the subtree. This node is located by walking down the left subtree to the right until the pointer to the right child of the current node is null. We are now pointing to the replacement node which is either a leaf node or a node with one child to its left. If the replacement node is a leaf node, the steps to perform the deletion are as follows:

a) Store the pointer to the node to be deleted in a temporary pointer variable (this pointer is used to delete the dynamically allocated memory)
b) Set the pointer in the parent of the node being deleted to point to the replacement node
c) Set the pointer in the parent of the replacement node to null
d) Set the pointer to the right subtree in the replacement node to point to the right subtree of the node to be deleted
e) Delete the node to which the temporary pointer variable points.

The deletion steps for a replacement node with a left child are similar to those for a replacement node with no children, but the algorithm also must move the child in to the replacement node's position in the tree. If the replacement node is a node with a left child, the steps to perform the deletion are as follows:

a) Store the pointer to the node to be deleted in a temporary pointer variable
b) Set the pointer in the parent of the node being deleted to point to the replacement node
c) Set the pointer in the parent of the replacement node to point to the left child of the replacement node
d) Set the pointer to the right subtree in the replacement node to point to the right subtree of the node to be deleted
e) Delete the node to which the temporary pointer variable points.

Write member function **deleteNode** which takes as its arguments a pointer to the root node of the tree object and the value to be deleted. The function should locate in the tree the node containing the value to be deleted and use the algorithms discussed here to delete the node. If the value is not found in the tree, the function should print a message that indicates whether or not the value is deleted. Modify the program of Fig. 15.16 to use this function. After deleting an item, call the **inOrder**, **preOrder**, and **postOrder** traversal functions to confirm that the delete operation was performed correctly.

15.23 (*Binary tree search*) Write member function **binaryTreeSearch** that attempts to locate a specified value in a binary search tree object. The function should take as arguments a pointer to the root node of the binary tree and a search key to be located. If the node containing the search key is found, the function should return a pointer to that node; otherwise, the function should return a null pointer.

ANS:

```
1    // TREE.H
2    // Definition of template class Tree
3    #ifndef TREE_H
4    #define TREE_H
5
6    #include <iostream.h>
7    #include <assert.h>
8    #include "treenode.h"
9
10   template< class NODETYPE >
11   class Tree {
12   public:
13      Tree();
14      void insertNode( const NODETYPE & );
15      void preOrderTraversal() const;
16      void inOrderTraversal() const;
17      void postOrderTraversal() const;
18   protected:
19      TreeNode<NODETYPE> *rootPtr;
20
21      // utility functions
22      void insertNodeHelper( TreeNode< NODETYPE > **, const NODETYPE & );
23      void preOrderHelper( TreeNode< NODETYPE > * ) const;
24      void inOrderHelper( TreeNode< NODETYPE > * ) const;
25      void postOrderHelper( TreeNode< NODETYPE > * ) const;
26   };
27
28   template< class NODETYPE >
29   Tree< NODETYPE >::Tree() { rootPtr = 0; }
30
31   template< class NODETYPE >
32   void Tree< NODETYPE >::insertNode( const NODETYPE &value )
33      { insertNodeHelper( &rootPtr, value ); }
34
35   // This function receives a pointer to a pointer so the
36   // pointer can be modified.
37   // NOTE: THIS FUNCTION WAS MODIFIED TO ALLOW DUPLICATES.
38   template< class NODETYPE >
39   void Tree< NODETYPE >::insertNodeHelper( TreeNode< NODETYPE > **ptr,
40                                            const NODETYPE &value )
41   {
42      if ( *ptr == 0 ) {                    // tree is empty
43         *ptr = new TreeNode< NODETYPE >( value );
44         assert( *ptr != 0 );
45      }
46      else                                  // tree is not empty
47         if ( value <= ( *ptr ) -> data )
48            insertNodeHelper( &( ( *ptr ) -> leftPtr ), value );
49         else
50            insertNodeHelper( &( ( *ptr ) -> rightPtr ), value );
51   }
52
53   template< class NODETYPE >
54   void Tree< NODETYPE >::preOrderTraversal() const { preOrderHelper( rootPtr ); }
55
56   template< class NODETYPE >
57   void Tree< NODETYPE >::preOrderHelper( TreeNode< NODETYPE > *ptr ) const
58   {
59      if ( ptr != 0 ) {
60         cout << ptr -> data << ' ';
61         preOrderHelper( ptr -> leftPtr );
```

```
62          preOrderHelper( ptr -> rightPtr );
63       }
64    }
65
66    template< class NODETYPE >
67    void Tree< NODETYPE >::inOrderTraversal() const { inOrderHelper( rootPtr ); }
68
69    template< class NODETYPE >
70    void Tree< NODETYPE >::inOrderHelper( TreeNode< NODETYPE > *ptr ) const
71    {
72       if ( ptr != 0 ) {
73          inOrderHelper( ptr -> leftPtr );
74          cout << ptr -> data << ' ';
75          inOrderHelper( ptr -> rightPtr );
76       }
77    }
78
79    template< class NODETYPE >
80    void Tree< NODETYPE >::postOrderTraversal() const { postOrderHelper( rootPtr ); }
81
82    template< class NODETYPE >
83    void Tree< NODETYPE >::postOrderHelper( TreeNode< NODETYPE > *ptr ) const
84    {
85       if ( ptr != 0 ) {
86          postOrderHelper( ptr -> leftPtr );
87          postOrderHelper( ptr -> rightPtr );
88          cout << ptr -> data << ' ';
89       }
90    }
91
92    #endif
```

```
93    // TREENODE.H
94    // Definition of class TreeNode
95    #ifndef TREENODE_H
96    #define TREENODE_H
97
98    template< class T > class Tree;      // forward declaration
99
100   template< class NODETYPE >
101   class TreeNode {
102      friend class Tree< NODETYPE >;
103   public:
104      TreeNode( const NODETYPE & );  // constructor
105      NODETYPE getData() const;        // return data
106      TreeNode *getLeftPtr() const { return leftPtr; }
107      TreeNode *getRightPtr() const { return rightPtr; }
108      void setLeftPtr( TreeNode *ptr ) { leftPtr = ptr; }
109      void setRightPtr( TreeNode *ptr ) { rightPtr = ptr; }
110   private:
111      TreeNode *leftPtr;    // pointer to left subtree
112      NODETYPE data;
113      TreeNode *rightPtr;   // pointer to right subtree
114   };
115
116   // Constructor
117   template< class NODETYPE >
118   TreeNode< NODETYPE >::TreeNode( const NODETYPE &d )
119   {
120      data = d;
121      leftPtr = rightPtr = 0;
122   }
123
```

```
124  //Return a copy of the data value
125  template< class NODETYPE >
126  NODETYPE TreeNode< NODETYPE >::getData() const { return data; }
127
128  #endif
```

```
129  // TREE2.H
130  // Definition of template class Tree
131  #ifndef TREE2_H
132  #define TREE2_H
133
134  #include <iostream.h>
135  #include <assert.h>
136  #include "treenode.h"
137  #include "tree.h"
138
139  template< class NODETYPE >
140  class Tree2 : public Tree< NODETYPE > {
141  public:
142     TreeNode< NODETYPE > *binarySearch( int ) const;
143  private:
144     TreeNode< NODETYPE > *binarySearchHelper( TreeNode< NODETYPE > *,
145                                               int ) const;
146  };
147
148  template< class NODETYPE >
149  TreeNode< NODETYPE > *Tree2< NODETYPE >::binarySearch( int val ) const
150     { return binarySearchHelper( rootPtr, val ); }
151
152  template< class NODETYPE >
153  TreeNode< NODETYPE > *Tree2< NODETYPE >::binarySearchHelper(
154                          TreeNode< NODETYPE > *ptr, int value ) const
155  {
156     if ( ptr == 0 )
157        return 0;
158
159     cout << "Comparing " << value << " to " << ptr -> getData();
160
161     if ( value == ptr -> getData() ) {     // match
162        cout << "; search complete\n";
163        return ptr;
164     }
165     else if ( value < ptr -> getData() ) { // search val less than current data
166        cout << "; smaller, walk left\n";
167        return binarySearchHelper( ptr -> getLeftPtr(), value );
168     }
169     else {                           // search val greater than current data
170        cout << "; larger, walk right\n";
171        return binarySearchHelper( ptr -> getRightPtr(), value );
172     }
173  }
174
175  #endif
```

```
176  // Exercise 15.23 solution
177  #include <iostream.h>
178  #include <stdlib.h>
179  #include <time.h>
180  #include "tree2.h"
181
182  int main()
183  {
184     srand( time( 0 ) );  // randomize the random number generator
```

```
185    Tree2< int > intTree;
186    int intVal;
187
188    cout << "The values being placed in the tree are:\n";
189
190    for ( int i = 1; i <= 15; ++i ) {
191       intVal = rand() % 100;
192       cout << intVal << ' ';
193       intTree.insertNode( intVal );
194    }
195
196    cout << "\n\nEnter a value to search for: ";
197    cin >> intVal;
198
199    TreeNode< int > *ptr = intTree.binarySearch( intVal );
200
201    if ( ptr != 0 )
202       cout << ptr -> getData() << " was found\n";
203    else
204       cout << "Element was not found\n";
205
206    cout << endl;
207    return 0;
208 }
```

```
The values being placed in the tree are:
69 48 27 78 42 18 70 58 6 9 16 23 50 74 39

Enter a value to search for: 72
Comparing 72 to 69; larger, walk right
Comparing 72 to 78; smaller, walk left
Comparing 72 to 70; larger, walk right
Comparing 72 to 74; smaller, walk left
Element was not found
```

15.24 *(Level-order binary tree traversal)* The program of Fig. 15.16 illustrated three recursive methods of traversing a binary tree—inorder, preorder, and postorder traversals. This exercise presents the *level-order traversal* of a binary tree in which the node values are printed level-by-level starting at the root node level. The nodes on each level are printed from left to right. The level-order traversal is not a recursive algorithm. It uses a queue object to control the output of the nodes. The algorithm is as follows:

a) Insert the root node in the queue
b) While there are nodes left in the queue,
    Get the next node in the queue
    Print the node's value
    If the pointer to the left child of the node is not null
        Insert the left child node in the queue
    If the pointer to the right child of the node is not null
        Insert the right child node in the queue.

Write member function **levelOrder** to perform a level-order traversal of a binary tree object. Modify the program of Fig 15.16 to use this function. (Note: You will also need to modify and incorporate the queue processing functions of Fig. 15.12 in this program.)

ANS:

```
1  // TREE.H
2  // Definition of template class Tree
3  #ifndef TREE_H
4  #define TREE_H
5
6  #include <iostream.h>
7  #include <assert.h>
8  #include "treenode.h"
```

```
 9
10   template< class NODETYPE >
11   class Tree {
12   public:
13      Tree();
14      void insertNode( const NODETYPE & );
15      void preOrderTraversal() const;
16      void inOrderTraversal() const;
17      void postOrderTraversal() const;
18   protected:
19      TreeNode< NODETYPE > *rootPtr;
20
21      // utility functions
22      void insertNodeHelper( TreeNode< NODETYPE > **, const NODETYPE & );
23      void preOrderHelper( TreeNode< NODETYPE > * ) const;
24      void inOrderHelper( TreeNode< NODETYPE > * ) const;
25      void postOrderHelper( TreeNode< NODETYPE > * ) const;
26   };
27
28   template< class NODETYPE >
29   Tree< NODETYPE >::Tree() { rootPtr = 0; }
30
31   template< class NODETYPE >
32   void Tree< NODETYPE >::insertNode( const NODETYPE &value )
33      { insertNodeHelper( &rootPtr, value ); }
34
35   // This function receives a pointer to a pointer so the
36   // pointer can be modified.
37   // NOTE: THIS FUNCTION WAS MODIFIED TO ALLOW DUPLICATES.
38   template< class NODETYPE >
39   void Tree< NODETYPE >::insertNodeHelper( TreeNode< NODETYPE > **ptr,
40                                            const NODETYPE &value )
41   {
42      if ( *ptr == 0 ) {                        // tree is empty
43         *ptr = new TreeNode< NODETYPE >( value );
44         assert( *ptr != 0 );
45      }
46      else                                      // tree is not empty
47         if ( value <= ( *ptr ) -> data )
48            insertNodeHelper( &( ( *ptr ) -> leftPtr ), value );
49         else
50            insertNodeHelper( &( ( *ptr ) -> rightPtr ), value );
51   }
52
53   template< class NODETYPE >
54   void Tree< NODETYPE >::preOrderTraversal() const { preOrderHelper( rootPtr ); }
55
56   template< class NODETYPE >
57   void Tree< NODETYPE >::preOrderHelper( TreeNode< NODETYPE > *ptr ) const
58   {
59      if ( ptr != 0 ) {
60         cout << ptr -> data << ' ';
61         preOrderHelper( ptr -> leftPtr );
62         preOrderHelper( ptr -> rightPtr );
63      }
64   }
65
66   template< class NODETYPE >
67   void Tree< NODETYPE >::inOrderTraversal() const { inOrderHelper( rootPtr ); }
68
```

```
69   template< class NODETYPE >
70   void Tree< NODETYPE >::inOrderHelper( TreeNode< NODETYPE > *ptr ) const
71   {
72      if ( ptr != 0 ) {
73         inOrderHelper( ptr -> leftPtr );
74         cout << ptr -> data << ' ';
75         inOrderHelper( ptr -> rightPtr );
76      }
77   }
78
79   template< class NODETYPE >
80   void Tree< NODETYPE >::postOrderTraversal() const
81   { postOrderHelper( rootPtr ); }
82
83   template< class NODETYPE >
84   void Tree< NODETYPE >::postOrderHelper( TreeNode< NODETYPE > *ptr ) const
85   {
86      if ( ptr != 0 ) {
87         postOrderHelper( ptr -> leftPtr );
88         postOrderHelper( ptr -> rightPtr );
89         cout << ptr -> data << ' ';
90      }
91   }
92
93   #endif
```

```
94   // TREENODE.H
95   // Definition of class TreeNode
96   #ifndef TREENODE_H
97   #define TREENODE_H
98
99   template< class T > class Tree;     // forward declaration
100
101  template< class NODETYPE >
102  class TreeNode {
103     friend class Tree< NODETYPE >;
104  public:
105     TreeNode( const NODETYPE & );  // constructor
106     NODETYPE getData() const;       // return data
107     TreeNode *getLeftPtr() const { return leftPtr; }
108     TreeNode *getRightPtr() const { return rightPtr; }
109     void setLeftPtr( TreeNode *ptr ) { leftPtr = ptr; }
110     void setRightPtr( TreeNode *ptr ) { rightPtr = ptr; }
111  private:
112     TreeNode *leftPtr;    // pointer to left subtree
113     NODETYPE data;
114     TreeNode *rightPtr;   // pointer to right subtree
115  };
116
117  // Constructor
118  template< class NODETYPE >
119  TreeNode< NODETYPE >::TreeNode( const NODETYPE &d )
120  {
121     data = d;
122     leftPtr = rightPtr = 0;
123  }
124
125  //Return a copy of the data value
126  template< class NODETYPE >
127  NODETYPE TreeNode< NODETYPE >::getData() const { return data; }
128
129  #endif
```

```
130  // TREE2.H
131  // Definition of template class Tree
132  #ifndef TREE2_H
133  #define TREE2_H
134
135  #include <iostream.h>
136  #include <assert.h>
137  #include "treenode.h"
138  #include "queue.h"
139  #include "tree.h"
140
141  template< class NODETYPE >
142  class Tree2 : public Tree< NODETYPE > {
143  public:
144     void levelOrderTraversal();
145  };
146
147  template< class NODETYPE >
148  void Tree2< NODETYPE >::levelOrderTraversal()
149  {
150     Queue< TreeNode< NODETYPE > * > queue;
151     TreeNode< NODETYPE > *nodePtr;
152
153     if ( rootPtr != 0 )
154        queue.enqueue( rootPtr );
155
156     while ( !queue.isEmpty() ) {
157        nodePtr = queue.dequeue();
158        cout << nodePtr -> getData() << ' ';
159
160        if ( nodePtr -> getLeftPtr() != 0 )
161           queue.enqueue( nodePtr -> getLeftPtr() );
162
163        if ( nodePtr -> getRightPtr() != 0 )
164           queue.enqueue( nodePtr -> getRightPtr() );
165     }
166  }
167
168  #endif
```

```
169  // QUEUE.H
170  // Definition of class Queue
171  #ifndef QUEUE_H
172  #define QUEUE_H
173
174  #include <iostream.h>
175  #include <new>
176  #include <cstdlib>
177  #include "queuend.h"
178
179  template < class T >
180  class Queue {
181  public:
182     Queue();              // default constructor
183     ~Queue();             // destructor
184     void enqueue( T );    // insert item in queue
185     T dequeue();          // remove item from queue
186     bool isEmpty() const; // is the queue empty?
187     void print() const;   // output the queue
188  private:
189     QueueNode< T > *headPtr;  // pointer to first QueueNode
190     QueueNode< T > *tailPtr;  // pointer to last QueueNode
191  };
```

```
192
193   // Member function definitions for class Queue
194   template < class T >
195   Queue< T >::Queue() { headPtr = tailPtr = 0; }
196
197   template < class T >
198   Queue< T >::~Queue()
199   {
200      QueueNode< T > *tempPtr, *currentPtr = headPtr;
201
202      while ( currentPtr != 0 ) {
203         tempPtr = currentPtr;
204         currentPtr = currentPtr -> nextPtr;
205         delete tempPtr;
206      }
207   }
208
209   template < class T >
210   void Queue< T >::enqueue( T d )
211   {
212      QueueNode< T > *newPtr = new QueueNode< T >( d );
213      assert( newPtr != 0 );
214
215      if ( isEmpty() )
216         headPtr = tailPtr = newPtr;
217      else {
218         tailPtr -> nextPtr = newPtr;
219         tailPtr = newPtr;
220      }
221   }
222
223   template < class T >
224   T Queue< T >::dequeue()
225   {
226      assert( !isEmpty() );
227      QueueNode< T > *tempPtr = headPtr;
228
229      headPtr = headPtr -> nextPtr;
230      T value = tempPtr -> data;
231      delete tempPtr;
232
233      if ( headPtr == 0 )
234         tailPtr = 0;
235
236      return value;
237   }
238
239   template < class T >
240   bool Queue< T >::isEmpty() const { return headPtr == 0; }
241
242   template < class T >
243   void Queue< T >::print() const
244   {
245      QueueNode< T > *currentPtr = headPtr;
246
247      if ( isEmpty() )              // Queue is empty
248         cout << "Queue is empty\n";
249      else {                       // Queue is not empty
250         cout << "The queue is:\n";
251
252         while ( currentPtr != 0 ) {
253            cout << currentPtr -> data << ' ';
254            currentPtr = currentPtr -> nextPtr;
255         }
```

```
256
257            cout << endl;
258        }
259   }
260
261   #endif
```

```
262   // QUEUEND.H
263   // Definition of template class QueueNode
264   #ifndef QUEUEND_H
265   #define QUEUEND_H
266
267   template< class T > class Queue;   // forward declaration
268
269   template < class T >
270   class QueueNode {
271      friend class Queue< T >;
272   public:
273      QueueNode( const T & = 0 );
274      T getData() const;
275   private:
276      T data;
277      QueueNode *nextPtr;
278   };
279
280   // Member function definitions for class QueueNode
281   template < class T >
282   QueueNode< T >::QueueNode( const T &d )
283   {
284      data = d;
285      nextPtr = 0;
286   }
287
288   template < class T >
289   T QueueNode< T >::getData() const { return data; }
290
291   #endif
```

```
292   // Exercise 15.24 solution
293   #include <iostream.h>
294   #include <stdlib.h>
295   #include <time.h>
296   #include "tree2.h"
297
298   int main()
299   {
300      srand( time( 0 ) );   // randomize the random number generator
301      Tree2< int > intTree;
302      int intVal;
303
304      cout << "The values being placed in the tree are:\n";
305
306      for ( int i = 1; i <= 15; ++i ) {
307         intVal = rand() % 100;
308         cout << intVal << ' ';
309         intTree.insertNode( intVal );
310      }
311
312      cout << "\n\nThe level order traversal is:\n";
313      intTree.levelOrderTraversal();
314      cout << endl;
315      return 0;
316   }
```

```
The values being placed in the tree are:
98 37 49 15 70 65 85 5 83 14 54 50 72 20 81

The level order traversal is:
98 37 15 49 5 20 70 14 65 85 54 83 50 72 81
```

15.25 (*Printing trees*) Write a recursive member function **outputTree** to display a binary tree object on the screen. The function should output the tree row-by-row with the top of the tree at the left of the screen and the bottom of the tree toward the right of the screen. Each row is output vertically. For example, the binary tree illustrated in Fig. 15.19 is output as follows:

```
                              99
                        97
                              92
                  83
                              72
                        71
                              69
            49
                              44
                        40
                              32
                  28
                              19
                        18
                              11
```

Note the rightmost leaf node appears at the top of the output in the rightmost column and the root node appears at the left of the output. Each column of output starts five spaces to the right of the previous column. Function **outputTree** should receive an argument **totalSpaces** representing the number of spaces preceding the value to be output (this variable should start at zero so the root node is output at the left of the screen). The function uses a modified inorder traversal to output the tree—it starts at the rightmost node in the tree and works back to the left. The algorithm is as follows:

While the pointer to the current node is not null

Recursively call **outputTree** with the right subtree of the current node and
    totalSpaces + 5

Use a **for** structure to count from 1 to **totalSpaces** and output spaces
Output the value in the current node
Set the pointer to the current node to point to the left subtree of the current node
Increment **totalSpaces** by 5.

ANS:

```
1   // TREE.H
2   // Definition of template class Tree
3   #ifndef TREE_H
4   #define TREE_H
5
6   #include <iostream.h>
7   #include <assert.h>
8   #include "treenode.h"
9
10  template< class NODETYPE >
11  class Tree {
12  public:
13     Tree();
14     void insertNode( const NODETYPE & );
15     void preOrderTraversal() const;
16     void inOrderTraversal() const;
17     void postOrderTraversal() const;
18  protected:
19     TreeNode<NODETYPE> *rootPtr;
```

```
20
21       // utility functions
22       void insertNodeHelper( TreeNode< NODETYPE > **, const NODETYPE & );
23       void preOrderHelper( TreeNode< NODETYPE > * ) const;
24       void inOrderHelper( TreeNode< NODETYPE > * ) const;
25       void postOrderHelper( TreeNode< NODETYPE > * ) const;
26   };
27
28   template< class NODETYPE >
29   Tree< NODETYPE >::Tree() { rootPtr = 0; }
30
31   template< class NODETYPE >
32   void Tree< NODETYPE >::insertNode( const NODETYPE &value )
33      { insertNodeHelper( &rootPtr, value ); }
34
35   // This function receives a pointer to a pointer so the
36   // pointer can be modified.
37   // NOTE: THIS FUNCTION WAS MODIFIED TO ALLOW DUPLICATES.
38   template< class NODETYPE >
39   void Tree< NODETYPE >::insertNodeHelper( TreeNode< NODETYPE > **ptr,
40                                            const NODETYPE &value )
41   {
42      if ( *ptr == 0 ) {                       // tree is empty
43         *ptr = new TreeNode< NODETYPE >( value );
44         assert( *ptr != 0 );
45      }
46      else                                     // tree is not empty
47         if ( value <= ( *ptr ) -> data )
48            insertNodeHelper( &( ( *ptr ) -> leftPtr ), value );
49         else
50            insertNodeHelper( &( ( *ptr ) -> rightPtr ), value );
51   }
52
53   template< class NODETYPE >
54   void Tree< NODETYPE >::preOrderTraversal() const { preOrderHelper( rootPtr ); }
55
56   template< class NODETYPE >
57   void Tree< NODETYPE >::preOrderHelper( TreeNode< NODETYPE > *ptr ) const
58   {
59      if ( ptr != 0 ) {
60         cout << ptr -> data << ' ';
61         preOrderHelper( ptr -> leftPtr );
62         preOrderHelper( ptr -> rightPtr );
63      }
64   }
65
66   template< class NODETYPE >
67   void Tree< NODETYPE >::inOrderTraversal() const { inOrderHelper( rootPtr ); }
68
69   template< class NODETYPE >
70   void Tree< NODETYPE >::inOrderHelper( TreeNode< NODETYPE > *ptr ) const
71   {
72      if ( ptr != 0 ) {
73         inOrderHelper( ptr -> leftPtr );
74         cout << ptr -> data << ' ';
75         inOrderHelper( ptr -> rightPtr );
76      }
77   }
78
79   template< class NODETYPE >
80   void Tree< NODETYPE >::postOrderTraversal() const { postOrderHelper( rootPtr ); }
81
```

```
82  template< class NODETYPE >
83  void Tree< NODETYPE >::postOrderHelper( TreeNode< NODETYPE > *ptr ) const
84  {
85     if ( ptr != 0 ) {
86        postOrderHelper( ptr -> leftPtr );
87        postOrderHelper( ptr -> rightPtr );
88        cout << ptr -> data << ' ';
89     }
90  }
91
92  #endif
```

```
93   // TREENODE.H
94   // Definition of class TreeNode
95   #ifndef TREENODE_H
96   #define TREENODE_H
97
98   template< class T > class Tree;    // forward declaration
99
100  template< class NODETYPE >
101  class TreeNode {
102     friend class Tree< NODETYPE >;
103  public:
104     TreeNode( const NODETYPE & );  // constructor
105     NODETYPE getData() const;        // return data
106     TreeNode *getLeftPtr() const { return leftPtr; }
107     TreeNode *getRightPtr() const { return rightPtr; }
108     void setLeftPtr( TreeNode *ptr ) { leftPtr = ptr; }
109     void setRightPtr( TreeNode *ptr ) { rightPtr = ptr; }
110  private:
111     TreeNode *leftPtr;   // pointer to left subtree
112     NODETYPE data;
113     TreeNode *rightPtr;  // pointer to right subtree
114  };
115
116  // Constructor
117  template< class NODETYPE >
118  TreeNode< NODETYPE >::TreeNode( const NODETYPE &d )
119  {
120     data = d;
121     leftPtr = rightPtr = 0;
122  }
123
124  //Return a copy of the data value
125  template< class NODETYPE >
126  NODETYPE TreeNode< NODETYPE >::getData() const { return data; }
127
128  #endif
```

```
129  // TREE2.H
130  // Definition of template class Tree
131  #ifndef TREE2_H
132  #define TREE2_H
133
134  #include <iostream.h>
135  #include <assert.h>
136  #include "treenode.h"
137  #include "tree.h"
138
```

```
139  template< class NODETYPE >
140  class Tree2 : public Tree< NODETYPE > {
141  public:
142     void outputTree() const;
143  private:
144     void outputTreeHelper( TreeNode< NODETYPE > *, int ) const;
145  };
146
147  template< class NODETYPE >
148  void Tree2< NODETYPE >::outputTree() const { outputTreeHelper( rootPtr, 0 ); }
149
150  template< class NODETYPE >
151  void Tree2< NODETYPE >::outputTreeHelper( TreeNode< NODETYPE > *ptr,
152                                            int totalSpaces ) const
153  {
154     if ( ptr != 0 ) {
155        outputTreeHelper( ptr -> getRightPtr(), totalSpaces + 5 );
156
157        for ( int i = 1; i <= totalSpaces; ++i )
158           cout << ' ';
159
160        cout << ptr -> getData() << '\n';
161        outputTreeHelper( ptr -> getLeftPtr(), totalSpaces + 5 );
162     }
163  }
164
165  #endif
```

```
166  // Exercise 15.25 solution
167  #include <iostream.h>
168  #include <stdlib.h>
169  #include <time.h>
170  #include "tree2.h"
171
172  int main()
173  {
174     srand( time( 0 ) );   // randomize the random number generator
175
176     Tree2< int > intTree;
177     int intVal;
178
179     cout << "The values being placed in the tree are:\n";
180
181     for ( int i = 1; i <= 15; ++i ) {
182        intVal = rand() % 100;
183        cout << intVal << ' ';
184        intTree.insertNode( intVal );
185     }
186
187     cout << "\n\nThe tree is:\n";
188     intTree.outputTree();
189
190     return 0;
191  }
```

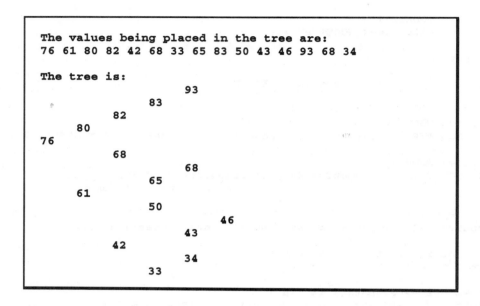

Special Section: Building Your Own Compiler

In Exercises 5.18 and 5.19, we introduced Simpletron Machine Language (SML) and you implemented a Simpletron computer simulator to execute programs written in SML. In this section, we build a compiler that converts programs written in a high-level programming language to SML. This section "ties" together the entire programming process. You will write programs in this new high-level language, compile these programs on the compiler you build, and run the programs on the simulator you built in Exercise 7.19. You should make every effort to implement your compiler in an object-oriented manner.

15.26 *(The Simple Language)* Before we begin building the compiler, we discuss a simple, yet powerful, high-level language similar to early versions of the popular language BASIC. We call the language *Simple*. Every Simple *statement* consists of a *line number* and a Simple *instruction*. Line numbers must appear in ascending order. Each instruction begins with one of the following Simple *commands*: **rem**, **input**, **let**, **print**, **goto**, **if/goto**, or **end** (see Fig. 15.20). All commands except **end** can be used repeatedly. Simple evaluates only integer expressions using the **+**, **-**, *****, and **/** operators. These operators have the same precedence as in C. Parentheses can be used to change the order of evaluation of an expression

Command	Example statement	Description
rem	50 rem this is a remark	Any text following the command **rem** is for documentation purposes only and is ignored by the compiler.
input	30 input x	Display a question mark to prompt the user to enter an integer. Read that integer from the keyboard and store the integer in **x**.
let	80 let u = 4 * (j - 56)	Assign **u** the value of **4 * (j - 56)**. Note that an arbitrarily complex expression can appear to the right of the equal sign.
print	10 print w	Display the value of **w**.
goto	70 goto 45	Transfer program control to line **45**.
if/goto	35 if i == z goto 80	Compare **i** and **z** for equality and transfer program control to line **80** if the condition is true; otherwise, continue execution with the next statement.
end	99 end	Terminate program execution.

Fig. 15.20 Simple commands.

Our Simple compiler recognizes only lowercase letters. All characters in a Simple file should be lowercase (uppercase letters result in a syntax error unless they appear in a **rem** statement in which case they are ignored). A *variable name* is a single letter. Simple does not allow descriptive variable names, so variables should be explained in remarks to indicate their use in a program. Simple uses only integer variables. Simple does not have variable declarations—merely mentioning a variable name in a program causes the variable to be declared and initialized to zero automatically. The syntax of Simple does not allow string manipulation (reading a string, writing a string, comparing strings, etc.). If a string is encountered in a Simple program (after a command other than **rem**), the compiler generates a syntax error. The first version of our compiler will assume that Simple programs are entered correctly. Exercise 15.29 asks the student to modify the compiler to perform syntax error checking.

Simple uses the conditional **if/goto** statement and the unconditional **goto** statement to alter the flow of control during program execution. If the condition in the **if/goto** statement is true, control is transferred to a specific line of the program. The following relational and equality operators are valid in an **if/goto** statement: **<, >, <=, >=, ==,** or **!=**. The precedence of these operators is the same as in C++.

Let us now consider several programs that demonstrate Simple's features. The first program (Fig. 15.21) reads two integers from the keyboard, stores the values in variables **a** and **b**, and computes and prints their sum (stored in variable **c**).

```
 1    10 rem    determine and print the sum of two integers
 2    15 rem
 3    20 rem    input the two integers
 4    30 input a
 5    40 input b
 6    45 rem
 7    50 rem    add integers and store result in c
 8    60 let c = a + b
 9    65 rem
10    70 rem    print the result
11    80 print c
12    90 rem    terminate program execution
13    99 end
```

Fig. 15.21 Simple program that determines the sum of two integers.

The program of Fig. 15.22 determines and prints the larger of two integers. The integers are input from the keyboard and stored in **s** and **t**. The **if/goto** statement tests the condition **s >= t**. If the condition is true, control is transferred to line **90** and **s** is output; otherwise, **t** is output and control is transferred to the **end** statement in line **99** where the program terminates.

Simple does not provide a repetition structure (such as C++'s **for**, **while**, or **do/while**). However, Simple can simulate each of C++'s repetition structures using the **if/goto** and **goto** statements. Figure 15.23 uses a sentinel-controlled loop to calculate the squares of several integers. Each integer is input from the keyboard and stored in variable **j**. If the value entered is the sentinel **-9999**, control is transferred to line **99** where the program terminates. Otherwise, **k** is assigned the square of **j**, **k** is output to the screen, and control is passed to line **20** where the next integer is input.

```
 1    10 rem    determine the larger of two integers
 2    20 input s
 3    30 input t
 4    32 rem
 5    35 rem    test if s >= t
 6    40 if s >= t goto 90
 7    45 rem
 8    50 rem    t is greater than s, so print t
 9    60 print t
10    70 goto 99
11    75 rem
12    80 rem    s is greater than or equal to t, so print s
13    90 print s
14    99 end
```

Fig. 15.22 Simple program that finds the larger of two integers.

```
1   10 rem    calculate the squares of several integers
2   20 input j
3   23 rem
4   25 rem    test for sentinel value
5   30 if j == -9999 goto 99
6   33 rem
7   35 rem    calculate square of j and assign result to k
8   40 let k = j * j
9   50 print k
10  53 rem
11  55 rem    loop to get next j
12  60 goto 20
13  99 end
```

Fig. 15.23 Calculate the squares of several integers.

Using the sample programs of Fig. 15.21, Fig. 15.22, and Fig. 15.23 as your guide, write a Simple program to accomplish each of the following:

a) Input three integers, determine their average, and print the result.

b) Use a sentinel-controlled loop to input 10 integers and compute and print their sum.

c) Use a counter-controlled loop to input 7 integers, some positive and some negative, and compute and print their average.

d) Input a series of integers and determine and print the largest. The first integer input indicates how many numbers should be processed.

e) Input 10 integers and print the smallest.

f) Calculate and print the sum of the even integers from 2 to 30.

g) Calculate and print the product of the odd integers from 1 to 9.

15.27 (*Building A Compiler; Prerequisite: Complete Exercises 5.18, 5.19, 15.12, 15.13, and 15.26*) Now that the Simple language has been presented (Exercise 15.26), we discuss how to build a Simple compiler. First, we consider the process by which a Simple program is converted to SML and executed by the Simpletron simulator (see Fig. 15.24). A file containing a Simple program is read by the compiler and converted to SML code. The SML code is output to a file on disk, in which SML instructions appear one per line. The SML file is then loaded into the Simpletron simulator, and the results are sent to a file on disk and to the screen. Note that the Simpletron program developed in Exercise 5.19 took its input from the keyboard. It must be modified to read from a file so it can run the programs produced by our compiler.

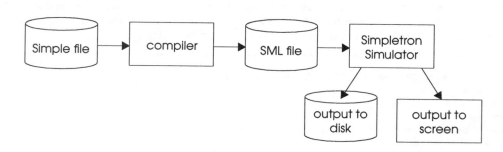

Fig. 15.24 Writing, compiling, and executing a Simple language program.

The Simple compiler performs two *passes* of the Simple program to convert it to SML. The first pass constructs a *symbol table* (object) in which every *line number* (object), *variable name* (object) and *constant* (object) of the Simple program is stored with its type and corresponding location in the final SML code (the symbol table is discussed in detail below). The first pass also produces the corresponding SML instruction object(s) for each of the Simple statements (object, etc.). As we will see, if the Simple program contains statements that transfer control to a line later in the program, the first pass results in an SML program containing some "unfinished" instructions. The second pass of the compiler locates and completes the unfinished instructions, and outputs the SML program to a file.

First Pass

The compiler begins by reading one statement of the Simple program into memory. The line must be separated into its individual *tokens* (i.e., "pieces" of a statement) for processing and compilation (standard library function **strtok** can be used to facilitate this task). Recall that every statement begins with a line number followed by a command. As the compiler breaks a statement into tokens, if the token is a line number, a variable, or a constant, it is placed in the symbol table. A line number is placed in the symbol table only if it is the first token in a statement. The **symbolTable** object is an array of **tableEntry** objects representing each symbol in the program. There is no restriction on the number of symbols that can appear in the program. Therefore, the **symbolTable** for a particular program could be large. Make the **symbolTable** a 100-element array for now. You can increase or decrease its size once the program is working.

Each **tableEntry** object contains three members. Member **symbol** is an integer containing the ASCII representation of a variable (remember that variable names are single characters), a line number, or a constant. Member **type** is one of the following characters indicating the symbol's type: **'C'** for constant, **'L'** for line number, or **'V'** for variable. Member **location** contains the Simpletron memory location (**00** to **99**) to which the symbol refers. Simpletron memory is an array of 100 integers in which SML instructions and data are stored. For a line number, the location is the element in the Simpletron memory array at which the SML instructions for the Simple statement begin. For a variable or constant, the location is the element in the Simpletron memory array in which the variable or constant is stored. Variables and constants are allocated from the end of Simpletron's memory backwards. The first variable or constant is stored in location at **99**, the next in location at **98**, etc.

The symbol table plays an integral part in converting Simple programs to SML. We learned in Chapter 5 that an SML instruction is a four-digit integer comprised of two parts—the *operation code* and the *operand*. The operation code is determined by commands in Simple. For example, the simple command **input** corresponds to SML operation code **10** (read), and the Simple command **print** corresponds to SML operation code **11** (write). The operand is a memory location containing the data on which the operation code performs its task (e.g., operation code **10** reads a value from the keyboard and stores it in the memory location specified by the operand). The compiler searches **symbolTable** to determine the Simpletron memory location for each symbol so the corresponding location can be used to complete the SML instructions.

The compilation of each Simple statement is based on its command. For example, after the line number in a **rem** statement is inserted in the symbol table, the remainder of the statement is ignored by the compiler because a remark is for documentation purposes only. The **input**, **print**, **goto** and **end** statements correspond to the SML *read*, *write*, *branch* (to a specific location) and *halt* instructions. Statements containing these Simple commands are converted directly to SML (note that a **goto** statement may contain an unresolved reference if the specified line number refers to a statement further into the Simple program file; this is sometimes called a forward reference).

When a **goto** statement is compiled with an unresolved reference, the SML instruction must be *flagged* to indicate that the second pass of the compiler must complete the instruction. The flags are stored in 100-element array **flags** of type **int** in which each element is initialized to **-1**. If the memory location to which a line number in the Simple program refers is not yet known (i.e., it is not in the symbol table), the line number is stored in array **flags** in the element with the same subscript as the incomplete instruction. The operand of the incomplete instruction is set to **00** temporarily. For example, an unconditional branch instruction (making a forward reference) is left as **+4000** until the second pass of the compiler. The second pass of the compiler will be described shortly.

Compilation of **if/goto** and **let** statements is more complicated than other statements—they are the only statements that produce more than one SML instruction. For an **if/goto** statement, the compiler produces code to test the condition and to branch to another line if necessary. The result of the branch could be an unresolved reference. Each of the relational and equality operators can be simulated using SML's *branch zero* and *branch negative* instructions (or possibly a combination of both).

For a **let** statement, the compiler produces code to evaluate an arbitrarily complex arithmetic expression consisting of integer variables and/or constants. Expressions should separate each operand and operator with spaces. Exercises 15.12 and 15.13 presented the infix-to-postfix conversion algorithm and the postfix evaluation algorithm used by compilers to evaluate expressions. Before proceeding with your compiler, you should complete each of these exercises. When a compiler encounters an expression, it converts the expression from infix notation to postfix notation, then evaluates the postfix expression.

How is it that the compiler produces the machine language to evaluate an expression containing variables? The postfix evaluation algorithm contains a "hook" where the compiler can generate SML instructions rather than actually evaluating the expression. To enable this "hook" in the compiler, the postfix evaluation algorithm must be modified to search the symbol table for each symbol it encounters (and possibly insert it), determine the symbol's corresponding memory location, and *push the memory location onto the stack (instead of the symbol)*. When an operator is encountered in the postfix expression, the two memory locations at the top of the stack are popped and machine language for effecting the operation is produced using the memory locations as operands. The result of each subexpression is stored in a temporary location in memory and pushed back onto the stack so the evaluation of the postfix expression can continue. When postfix evaluation is complete, the memory location containing the result is the only location left on the stack. This is popped and SML instructions are generated to assign the result to the variable at the left of the **let** statement.

Second Pass

The second pass of the compiler performs two tasks: resolve any unresolved references and output the SML code to a file. Resolution of references occurs as follows:

a) Search the **flags** array for an unresolved reference (i.e., an element with a value other than **-1**).

b) Locate the object in array **symbolTable** containing the symbol stored in the **flags** array (be sure that the type of the symbol is **'L'** for line number).

c) Insert the memory location from member **location** into the instruction with the unresolved reference (remember that an instruction containing an unresolved reference has operand **00**).

d) Repeat steps 1, 2, and 3 until the end of the **flags** array is reached.

After the resolution process is complete, the entire array containing the SML code is output to a disk file with one SML instruction per line. This file can be read by the Simpletron for execution (after the simulator is modified to read its input from a file). Compiling your first Simple program into an SML file and then executing that file should give you a real sense of personal accomplishment.

A Complete Example

The following example illustrates a complete conversion of a Simple program to SML as it will be performed by the Simple compiler. Consider a Simple program that inputs an integer and sums the values from 1 to that integer. The program and the SML instructions produced by the first pass of the Simple compiler are illustrated in Fig. 15.25. The symbol table constructed by the first pass is shown in Fig. 15.26.

Simple program	SML location and instruction	Description
`5 rem sum 1 to x`	*none*	**rem** ignored
`10 input x`	00 +1099	read **x** into location **99**
`15 rem check y == x`	*none*	**rem** ignored
`20 if y == x goto 60`	01 +2098	load **y** (**98**) into accumulator
	02 +3199	sub **x** (**99**) from accumulator
	03 +4200	branch zero to unresolved location
`25 rem    increment y`	*none*	**rem** ignored
`30 let y = y + 1`	04 +2098	load **y** into accumulator
	05 +3097	add **1** (**97**) to accumulator
	06 +2196	store in temporary location **96**
	07 +2096	load from temporary location **96**
	08 +2198	store accumulator in **y**
`35 rem    add y to total`	*none*	**rem** ignored
`40 let t = t + y`	09 +2095	load **t** (**95**) into accumulator
	10 +3098	add **y** to accumulator
	11 +2194	store in temporary location **94**
	12 +2094	load from temporary location **94**
	13 +2195	store accumulator in **t**
`45 rem    loop y`	*none*	**rem** ignored
`50 goto 20`	14 +4001	branch to location **01**
`55 rem    output result`	*none*	**rem** ignored
`60 print t`	15 +1195	output **t** to screen
`99 end`	16 +4300	terminate execution

Fig. 15.25 SML instructions produced after the compiler's first pass.

Symbol	Type	Location
5	L	00
10	L	00
'x'	V	99
15	L	01
20	L	01
'y'	V	98
25	L	04
30	L	04
1	C	97
35	L	09
40	L	09
't'	V	95
45	L	14
50	L	14
55	L	15
60	L	15
99	L	16

Fig. 15.26 Symbol table for program of Fig. 15.25.

Most Simple statements convert directly to single SML instructions. The exceptions in this program are remarks, the **if/goto** statement in line **20**, and the **let** statements. Remarks do not translate into machine language. However, the line number for a remark is placed in the symbol table in case the line number is referenced in a **goto** statement or an **if/goto** statement. Line **20** of the program specifies that if the condition **y == x** is true, program control is transferred to line **60**. Because line **60** appears later in the program, the first pass of the compiler has not as yet placed **60** in the symbol table (statement line numbers are placed in the symbol table only when they appear as the first token in a statement). Therefore, it is not possible at this time to determine the operand of the SML *branch zero* instruction at location **03** in the array of SML instructions. The compiler places **60** in location **03** of the **flags** array to indicate that the second pass completes this instruction.

We must keep track of the next instruction location in the SML array because there is not a one-to-one correspondence between Simple statements and SML instructions. For example, the **if/goto** statement of line **20** compiles into three SML instructions. Each time an instruction is produced, we must increment the *instruction counter* to the next location in the SML array. Note that the size of Simpletron's memory could present a problem for Simple programs with many statements, variables and constants. It is conceivable that the compiler will run out of memory. To test for this case, your program should contain a *data counter* to keep track of the location at which the next variable or constant will be stored in the SML array. If the value of the instruction counter is larger than the value of the data counter, the SML array is full. In this case, the compilation process should terminate and the compiler should print an error message indicating that it ran out of memory during compilation. This serves to emphasize that although the programmer is freed from the burdens of managing memory by the compiler, the compiler itself must carefully determine the placement of instructions and data in memory, and must check for such errors as memory being exhausted during the compilation process.

A Step-by-Step View of the Compilation Process

Let us now walk through the compilation process for the Simple program in Fig. 15.25. The compiler reads the first line of the program

```
5 rem sum 1 to x
```

into memory. The first token in the statement (the line number) is determined using **strtok** (see Chapters 5 and 16 for a discussion of C++'s string manipulation functions). The token returned by **strtok** is converted to an integer using **atoi** so the symbol **5** can be located in the symbol table. If the symbol is not found, it is inserted in the symbol table. Since we are at the beginning of the program and this is the first line, no symbols are in the table yet. So, **5** is inserted into the symbol table as type **L** (line number) and assigned the first location in SML array (**00**). Although this line is a remark, a space in the symbol table is still allocated for the line number (in case it is referenced by a **goto** or an **if/goto**). No SML instruction is generated for a **rem** statement, so the instruction counter is not incremented.

The statement

> **10 input x**

is tokenized next. The line number **10** is placed in the symbol table as type **L** and assigned the first location in the SML array (**00** because a remark began the program so the instruction counter is currently **00**). The command **input** indicates that the next token is a variable (only a variable can appear in an **input** statement). Because **input** corresponds directly to an SML operation code, the compiler simply has to determine the location of **x** in the SML array. Symbol **x** is not found in the symbol table. So, it is inserted into the symbol table as the ASCII representation of **x**, given type **V**, and assigned location **99** in the SML array (data storage begins at **99** and is allocated backwards). SML code can now be generated for this statement. Operation code **10** (the SML read operation code) is multiplied by 100, and the location of **x** (as determined in the symbol table) is added to complete the instruction. The instruction is then stored in the SML array at location **00**. The instruction counter is incremented by 1 because a single SML instruction was produced.

The statement

> **15 rem   check y == x**

is tokenized next. The symbol table is searched for line number **15** (which is not found). The line number is inserted as type **L** and assigned the next location in the array, **01** (remember that **rem** statements do not produce code, so the instruction counter is not incremented).

The statement

> **20 if y == x goto 60**

is tokenized next. Line number **20** is inserted in the symbol table and given type **L** with the next location in the SML array **01**. The command **if** indicates that a condition is to be evaluated. The variable **y** is not found in the symbol table, so it is inserted and given the type **V** and the SML location **98**. Next, SML instructions are generated to evaluate the condition. Since there is no direct equivalent in SML for the **if/goto**, it must be simulated by performing a calculation using **x** and **y** and branching based on the result. If **y** is equal to **x**, the result of subtracting **x** from **y** is zero, so the *branch zero* instruction can be used with the result of the calculation to simulate the **if/goto** statement. The first step requires that **y** be loaded (from SML location **98**) into the accumulator. This produces the instruction **01 +2098**. Next, **x** is subtracted from the accumulator. This produces the instruction **02 +3199**. The value in the accumulator may be zero, positive, or negative. Since the operator is **==**, we want to *branch zero*. First, the symbol table is searched for the branch location (**60** in this case), which is not found. So, **60** is placed in the **flags** array at location **03**, and the instruction **03 +4200** is generated (we cannot add the branch location because we have not assigned a location to line **60** in the SML array yet). The instruction counter is incremented to **04**.

The compiler proceeds to the statement

> **25 rem   increment y**

The line number **25** is inserted in the symbol table as type **L** and assigned SML location **04**. The instruction counter is not incremented.

When the statement

> **30 let y = y + 1**

is tokenized, the line number **30** is inserted in the symbol table as type **L** and assigned SML location **04**. Command **let** indicates that the line is an assignment statement. First, all the symbols on the line are inserted in the symbol table (if they are not already there). The integer **1** is added to the symbol table as type **C** and assigned SML location **97**. Next, the right side of the assignment is converted from infix to postfix notation. Then the postfix expression (**y 1 +**) is evaluated. Symbol **y** is located in the symbol table and its corresponding memory location is pushed onto the stack. Symbol **1** is also located in the symbol table and its corresponding memory location is pushed onto the stack. When the operator **+** is encountered, the postfix evaluator pops the stack into the right operand of the operator and pops the stack again into the left operand of the operator, then produces the SML instructions

> **04 +2098**   *(load **y**)*
> **05 +3097**   *(add **1**)*

The result of the expression is stored in a temporary location in memory (**96**) with instruction

> **06 +2196**   *(store temporary)*

and the temporary location is pushed on the stack. Now that the expression has been evaluated, the result must be stored in **y** (i.e., the variable on the left side of **=**). So, the temporary location is loaded into the accumulator and the accumulator is stored in **y** with the instructions

```
07  +2096    (load temporary)
08  +2198    (store y)
```

The reader will immediately notice that SML instructions appear to be redundant. We will discuss this issue shortly.

When the statement

```
35 rem    add y to total
```

is tokenized, line number **35** is inserted in the symbol table as type **L** and assigned location **09**.

The statement

```
40 let t = t + y
```

is similar to line **30**. The variable **t** is inserted in the symbol table as type **V** and assigned SML location **95**. The instructions follow the same logic and format as line **30**, and the instructions **09 +2095, 10 +3098, 11 +2194, 12 +2094**, and **13 +2195** are generated. Note that the result of **t + y** is assigned to temporary location **94** before being assigned to **t** (**95**). Once again, the reader will note that the instructions in memory locations **11** and **12** appear to be redundant. Again, we will discuss this shortly.

The statement

```
45 rem    loop y
```

is a remark, so line **45** is added to the symbol table as type **L** and assigned SML location **14**.

The statement

```
50 goto 20
```

transfers control to line **20**. Line number **50** is inserted in the symbol table as type **L** and assigned SML location **14**. The equivalent of **goto** in SML is the *unconditional branch* (**40**) instruction that transfers control to a specific SML location. The compiler searches the symbol table for line **20** and finds that it corresponds to SML location **01**. The operation code (**40**) is multiplied by 100 and location **01** is added to it to produce the instruction **14 +4001**.

The statement

```
55 rem    output result
```

is a remark, so line **55** is inserted in the symbol table as type **L** and assigned SML location **15**.

The statement

```
60 print t
```

is an output statement. Line number **60** is inserted in the symbol table as type **L** and assigned SML location **15**. The equivalent of **print** in SML is operation code **11** (*write*). The location of **t** is determined from the symbol table and added to the result of the operation code multiplied by 100.

The statement

```
99 end
```

is the final line of the program. Line number **99** is stored in the symbol table as type **L** and assigned SML location **16**. The **end** command produces the SML instruction **+4300** (**43** is *halt* in SML) which is written as the final instruction in the SML memory array.

This completes the first pass of the compiler. We now consider the second pass. The **flags** array is searched for values other than **−1**. Location **03** contains **60**, so the compiler knows that instruction **03** is incomplete. The compiler completes the instruction by searching the symbol table for **60**, determining its location, and adding the location to the incomplete instruction. In this case, the search determines that line **60** corresponds to SML location **15**, so the completed instruction **03 +4215** is produced replacing **03 +4200**. The Simple program has now been compiled successfully.

To build the compiler, you will have to perform each of the following tasks:

a) Modify the Simpletron simulator program you wrote in Exercise 5.19 to take its input from a file specified by the user (see Chapter 14). The simulator should output its results to a disk file in the same format as the screen output. Convert the simulator to be an object-oriented program. In particular, make each part of the hardware an object. Arrange the instruction types into a class hierarchy using inheritance. Then execute the program polymorphically simply by telling each instruction to execute itself with an **executeInstruction** message.

b) Modify the infix-to-postfix conversion algorithm of Exercise 15.12 to process multi-digit integer operands and single-letter variable name operands. Hint: Standard library function **strtok** can be used to locate each constant and variable in an expression, and constants can be converted from strings to integers using standard library function **atoi**. (Note: The data representation of the postfix expression must be altered to support variable names and integer constants.)

c) Modify the postfix evaluation algorithm to process multi-digit integer operands and variable name operands. Also, the algorithm should now implement the "hook" discussed above so that SML instructions are produced rather than directly evaluating the expression. Hint: Standard library function **strtok** can be used to locate each constant and variable in an expression, and constants can be converted from strings to integers using standard library function **atoi**. (Note: The data representation of the postfix expression must be altered to support variable names and integer constants.)

d) Build the compiler. Incorporate parts (b) and (c) for evaluating expressions in **let** statements. Your program should contain a function that performs the first pass of the compiler and a function that performs the second pass of the compiler. Both functions can call other functions to accomplish their tasks. Make your compiler as object oriented as possible.

ANS: Note: the program listing begins with class **StackNode** and class **Stack** followed by the compiler code.

```
1   // STACKND.H
2   // Definition of template class StackNode
3   #ifndef STACKND_H
4   #define STACKND_H
5   template < class T > class Stack;
6
7   template < class T >
8   class StackNode {
9      friend class Stack< T >;
10  public:
11     StackNode( const T & = 0, StackNode * = 0 );
12     T getData() const;
13  private:
14     T data;
15     StackNode *nextPtr;
16  };
17
18  // Member function definitions for class StackNode
19  template < class T >
20  StackNode< T >::StackNode( const T &d, StackNode< T > *ptr )
21  {
22     data = d;
23     nextPtr = ptr;
24  }
25
26  template < class T >
27  T StackNode< T >::getData() const { return data; }
28
29  #endif
```

```
30  // STACK.H
31  // Definition of class Stack
32  #ifndef STACK_H
33  #define STACK_H
34
35  #include <iostream.h>
36  #include <assert.h>
37  #include "stacknd.h"
38
39  template < class T >
40  class Stack {
41  public:
42     Stack();              // default constructor
43     ~Stack();             // destructor
44     void push( T & );     // insert item in stack
45     T pop();              // remove item from stack
46     bool isEmpty() const; // is the stack empty?
47     T stackTop() const;   // return the top element of stack
48     void print() const;   // output the stack
```

```
 49   private:
 50      StackNode< T > *topPtr;        // pointer to fist StackNode
 51   };
 52
 53   // Member function definitions for class Stack
 54   template < class T >
 55   Stack< T >::Stack() { topPtr = 0; }
 56
 57   template < class T >
 58   Stack< T >::~Stack()
 59   {
 60      StackNode< T > *tempPtr, *currentPtr = topPtr;
 61
 62      while ( currentPtr != 0 ) {
 63         tempPtr = currentPtr;
 64         currentPtr = currentPtr -> nextPtr;
 65         delete tempPtr;
 66      }
 67   }
 68
 69   template < class T >
 70   void Stack< T >::push( T &d )
 71   {
 72      StackNode< T > *newPtr = new StackNode< T >( d, topPtr );
 73
 74      assert( newPtr != 0 );   // was memory allocated?
 75      topPtr = newPtr;
 76   }
 77
 78   template < class T >
 79   T Stack< T >::pop()
 80   {
 81      assert( !isEmpty() );
 82
 83      StackNode< T > *tempPtr = topPtr;
 84
 85      topPtr = topPtr -> nextPtr;
 86      T poppedValue = tempPtr -> data;
 87      delete tempPtr;
 88      return poppedValue;
 89   }
 90
 91   template < class T >
 92   bool Stack< T >::isEmpty() const { return topPtr == 0; }
 93
 94   template < class T >
 95   T Stack< T >::stackTop() const
 96   { return !isEmpty() ? topPtr -> data : 0; }
 97
 98   template < class T >
 99   void Stack< T >::print() const
100   {
101      StackNode< T > *currentPtr = topPtr;
102
103      if ( isEmpty() )          // Stack is empty
104         cout << "Stack is empty\n";
105      else {                    // Stack is not empty
106         cout << "The stack is:\n";
107
108         while ( currentPtr != 0 ) {
109            cout << currentPtr -> data << ' ';
110            currentPtr = currentPtr -> nextPtr;
111         }
112
```

```
113            cout << '\n';
114      }
115 }
116
117 #endif
```

```
118 // compiler.h
119 #include <iostream.h>
120 #include <iomanip.h>
121 #include <fstream.h>
122 #include <string.h>
123 #include <ctype.h>
124 #include <stdlib.h>
125 #include "stack.h"
126
127 const int MAXIMUM = 81;                    // maximum length for lines
128 const int SYMBOLTABLESIZE = 100;           // maximum size of symbol table
129 const int MEMORYSIZE = 100;                // maximum Simpletron memory
130
131 // Definition of structure for symbol table entries
132 struct TableEntry {
133    int location;                   // SML memory location 00 to 99
134    char type;                      // 'C' = constant, 'V' = variable,
135    int symbol;                     // or 'L' = line number
136 };
137
138 // Function prototypes for compiler functions
139 int checkSymbolTable( TableEntry *, int, char );
140 int checkOperand( TableEntry *, char *, int *, int *, int * );
141 void addToSymbolTable( char, int, int, TableEntry *, int );
142 void addLineToFlags( int, int, int *, int *, const int * );
143 void compile( ifstream &, char * );
144 void printOutput( const int [], char * );
145 void lineNumber( char *, TableEntry *, int, int );
146 void initArrays( int *, int *, TableEntry * );
147 void firstPass( int *, int *, TableEntry *, ifstream & );
148 void secondPass( int *, int *, TableEntry * );
149 void separateToken( char *, int *, int *, TableEntry *, int *, int * );
150 void keyWord( char *, int *, int *, TableEntry *, int *, int * );
151 void keyLet( char *, int *, int *, TableEntry *, int *, int * );
152 void keyInput( char *, int *, int *, TableEntry *, int *, int * );
153 void keyPrint( char *, int *, int *, TableEntry *, int *, int * );
154 void keyGoto( char *, int *, int *, TableEntry *, int * );
155 void keyIfGoto( char *, int *, int *, TableEntry *, int *, int * );
156 void evaluateExpression( int, int, char *, int *,
157                          TableEntry *, int *, int *, char * );
158 int createLetSML( int, int, int *, int *, int *, char );
159 void infixToPostfix( char *, char *, int, TableEntry *, int *, int *, int * );
160 void evaluatePostfix( char *, int *, int *, int *, int, TableEntry * );
161 bool isOperator( char );
162 bool precedence( char, char );
163
164 // Simpletron Machine Language (SML) Operation Codes
165 enum SMLOperationCodes { READ = 10, WRITE = 11, LOAD = 20, STORE = 21, ADD = 30,
166                         SUBTRACT = 31, DIVIDE = 32, MULTIPLY = 33, BRANCH = 40,
167                         BRANCHNEG = 41, BRANCHZERO = 42, HALT = 43 };
168
```

```
169 // Exercise 15.27 Solution
170 // Non-optimized version.
171 #include "compiler.h"
172
```

```
173  int main()
174  {
175      char inFileName[ 15 ] = "", outFileName[ 15 ] = "";
176      int last = 0;
177
178      cout << "Enter Simple file to be compiled: ";
179      cin >> setw( 15 ) >> inFileName;
180
181      while ( isalnum( inFileName[ last ] ) != 0 ) {
182         outFileName[ last ] = inFileName[ last ];
183         last++;                    // note the last occurance
184      }
185
186      outFileName[ last ] = '\0';        // append a NULL character
187      strcat( outFileName, ".sml" );  // add .sml to name
188
189      ifstream inFile( inFileName, ios::in );
190
191      if ( inFile )
192         compile( inFile, outFileName );
193      else
194         cerr << "File not opened. Program execution terminating.\n";
195
196      return 0;
197  }
198
199  // compile function calls the first pass and the second pass
200  void compile( ifstream &input, char *outFileName )
201  {
202      TableEntry symbolTable[ SYMBOLTABLESIZE ]; // symbol table
203      int flags[ MEMORYSIZE ];              // array for forward references
204      int machineArray[ MEMORYSIZE ];     // array for SML instructions
205
206      initArrays( flags, machineArray, symbolTable );
207
208      firstPass( flags, machineArray, symbolTable, input );
209      secondPass( flags, machineArray, symbolTable );
210      printOutput( machineArray, outFileName );
211  }
212
213  // firstPass constructs the symbol table, creates SML, and flags unresolved
214  // references for goto and if/goto statements.
215  void firstPass( int flags[], int machineArray[], TableEntry symbolTable[],
216                  ifstream &input )
217  {
218      char array[ MAXIMUM ];                    // array to copy a Simple line
219      int n = MAXIMUM;                          // required for fgets()
220      int dataCounter = MEMORYSIZE - 1; // 1st data location in machineArray
221      int instCounter = 0;                     // 1st instruction location in machineArray
222
223      input.getline( array, n );
224
225      while ( !input.eof() ) {
226         separateToken( array, flags, machineArray, symbolTable, &dataCounter,
227                        &instCounter );
228         input.getline( array, n );
229      }
230  }
231
232  // Separate Tokens tokenizes a Simple statement, process the line number,
233  // and passes the next token to keyWord for processing.
234  void separateToken( char array[], int flags[], int machineArray[],
235                      TableEntry symbolTable[], int *dataCounterPtr,
236                      int *instCounterPtr )
```

```
237  {
238     char *tokenPtr = strtok( array, " " );       // tokenize line
239     lineNumber( tokenPtr, symbolTable, *instCounterPtr, *dataCounterPtr );
240     tokenPtr = strtok( 0, " \n" );          // get next token
241     keyWord( tokenPtr, flags, machineArray, symbolTable, dataCounterPtr,
242             instCounterPtr );
243  }
244
245  // checkSymbolTable searches the symbol table and returns
246  // the symbols SML location or a -1 if not found.
247  int checkSymbolTable( TableEntry symbolTable[], int symbol, char type )
248  {
249     for ( int loop = 0; loop < SYMBOLTABLESIZE; ++loop )
250        if ( ( symbol == symbolTable[ loop ].symbol ) &&
251             ( type == symbolTable[ loop ].type ) )
252           return symbolTable[ loop ].location;  // return SML location
253
254     return -1;                                  // symbol not found
255  }
256
257  // lineNumber processes line numbers
258  void lineNumber( char *tokenPtr, TableEntry symbolTable[],
259                   int instCounter, int dataCounter )
260  {
261     const char type = 'L';
262     int symbol;
263
264     if ( isdigit( tokenPtr[ 0 ] ) ) {
265        symbol = atoi( tokenPtr );
266
267        if ( -1 == checkSymbolTable( symbolTable, symbol, type ) )
268           addToSymbolTable( type, symbol, dataCounter, symbolTable,
269                             instCounter );
270     }
271  }
272
273  // keyWord determines the key word type and calls the appropriate function
274  void keyWord( char *tokenPtr, int flags[], int machineArray[],
275                TableEntry symbolTable[], int *dataCounterPtr,
276                int *instCounterPtr )
277  {
278     if ( strcmp( tokenPtr, "rem" ) == 0 )
279        ; // no instructions are generated by comments
280     else if ( strcmp( tokenPtr, "input" ) == 0 ) {
281        tokenPtr = strtok( 0, " " );  // assign pointer to next token
282        keyInput( tokenPtr, machineArray, symbolTable, dataCounterPtr,
283                  instCounterPtr );
284     }
285     else if ( strcmp( tokenPtr, "print" ) == 0 ) {
286        tokenPtr = strtok( 0, " " );  // assign pointer to next token
287        keyPrint( tokenPtr, machineArray, symbolTable, dataCounterPtr,
288                  instCounterPtr );
289     }
290     else if ( strcmp( tokenPtr, "goto" ) == 0 ) {
291        tokenPtr = strtok( 0, " " );  // assign pointer to next token
292        keyGoto( tokenPtr, flags, machineArray, symbolTable, instCounterPtr );
293     }
294     else if ( strcmp( tokenPtr, "if" ) == 0 ) {
295        tokenPtr = strtok( 0, " " );  // assign pointer to next token
296        keyIfGoto( tokenPtr, flags, machineArray, symbolTable, dataCounterPtr,
297                   instCounterPtr );
298     }
```

```
299      else if ( strcmp( tokenPtr, "end" ) == 0 ) {
300         machineArray[ *instCounterPtr ] = HALT * 100;
301         ++( *instCounterPtr );
302         tokenPtr = 0;          // assign tokenPtr to 0
303      }
304      else if ( strcmp( tokenPtr, "let" ) == 0 ) {
305         tokenPtr = strtok( 0, " " );  // assign pointer to next token
306         keyLet( tokenPtr, machineArray, symbolTable, dataCounterPtr,
307                 instCounterPtr );
308      }
309  }
310
311  // keyInput process input keywords
312  void keyInput( char *tokenPtr, int machineArray[], TableEntry symbolTable[],
313                 int *dataCounterPtr, int *instCounterPtr )
314  {
315      const char type = 'V';
316
317      machineArray[ *instCounterPtr ] = READ * 100;
318      int symbol = tokenPtr[ 0 ];
319      int tableTest = checkSymbolTable( symbolTable, symbol, type );
320
321      if ( -1 == tableTest ) {
322         addToSymbolTable( type, symbol, *dataCounterPtr, symbolTable,
323                           *instCounterPtr );
324         machineArray[ *instCounterPtr ] += *dataCounterPtr;
325         --( *dataCounterPtr );
326      }
327      else
328         machineArray[ *instCounterPtr ] += tableTest;
329
330      ++( *instCounterPtr );
331  }
332
333  // keyPrint process print keywords
334  void keyPrint( char *tokenPtr, int machineArray[], TableEntry symbolTable[],
335                 int *dataCounterPtr, int *instCounterPtr )
336  {
337      const char type = 'V';
338
339      machineArray[ *instCounterPtr ] = WRITE * 100;
340      int symbol = tokenPtr[ 0 ];
341      int tableTest = checkSymbolTable( symbolTable, symbol, type );
342
343      if ( -1 == tableTest ) {
344         addToSymbolTable( type, symbol, *dataCounterPtr, symbolTable,
345                           *instCounterPtr );
346         machineArray[*instCounterPtr] += *dataCounterPtr;
347         --( *dataCounterPtr );
348      }
349      else
350         machineArray[ *instCounterPtr ] += tableTest;
351
352      ++( *instCounterPtr );
353  }
354
355  // keyGoto process goto keywords
356  void keyGoto( char *tokenPtr, int flags[], int machineArray[],
357                TableEntry symbolTable[], int *instCounterPtr )
358  {
359      const char type = 'L';
360
361      machineArray[*instCounterPtr] = BRANCH * 100;
362      int symbol = atoi( tokenPtr );
```

```
363         int tableTest = checkSymbolTable( symbolTable, symbol, type );
364         addLineToFlags( tableTest, symbol, flags, machineArray, instCounterPtr );
365         ++( *instCounterPtr );
366 }
367
368 // keyIfGoto process if/goto commands
369 void keyIfGoto( char *tokenPtr, int flags[], int machineArray[],
370                 TableEntry symbolTable[], int *dataCounterPtr,
371                 int *instCounterPtr )
372 {
373     int operand1Loc = checkOperand( symbolTable, tokenPtr, dataCounterPtr,
374                                     instCounterPtr, machineArray );
375
376     char *operatorPtr = strtok( 0, " " );    // get the operator
377
378     tokenPtr = strtok( 0, " " );  // get the right operand of comparison operator
379
380     int operand2Loc = checkOperand( symbolTable, tokenPtr, dataCounterPtr,
381                                     instCounterPtr, machineArray );
382
383     tokenPtr = strtok( 0, " " );  // read in the goto keyword
384
385     char *gotoLinePtr = strtok( 0, " " );  // read in the goto line number
386
387     evaluateExpression( operand1Loc, operand2Loc, operatorPtr, machineArray,
388                         symbolTable, instCounterPtr, flags, gotoLinePtr );
389 }
390
391 // checkOperand ensures that the operands of an if/goto statement are
392 // in the symbol table.
393 int checkOperand( TableEntry symbolTable[], char *symPtr, int *dataCounterPtr,
394                   int *instCounterPtr, int machineArray[] )
395 {
396     char type;
397     int tableTest, operand, temp;
398
399     if ( isalpha( symPtr[ 0 ] ) ) {
400         type = 'V';
401         operand = symPtr[ 0 ];
402         tableTest = checkSymbolTable( symbolTable, operand, type );
403
404         if ( tableTest == -1 ) {
405             addToSymbolTable( type, operand, *dataCounterPtr, symbolTable,
406                               *instCounterPtr );
407             temp = *dataCounterPtr;
408             --( *dataCounterPtr );
409             return temp;
410         }
411         else
412             return tableTest;
413     }
414     // if the symbol is a digit or a signed digit
415     else if ( isdigit( symPtr[ 0 ] ) ||
416              ( ( symPtr[ 0 ] == '-' || symPtr[ 0 ] == '+' ) &&
417              isdigit( symPtr[ 1 ] ) != 0 ) ) {
418         type = 'C';
419         operand = atoi( symPtr );
420         tableTest = checkSymbolTable( symbolTable, operand, type );
421
422         if ( tableTest == -1 ) {
423             addToSymbolTable( type, operand, *dataCounterPtr, symbolTable,
424                               *instCounterPtr );
425             machineArray[ *dataCounterPtr ] = operand;
426             temp = *dataCounterPtr;
```

```
427              --( *dataCounterPtr );
428              return temp ;
429          }
430          else
431              return tableTest;
432      }
433
434      return 0;           // default return for compilation purposes
435  }
436
437  // evaluateExpression creates SML for conditional operators
438  void evaluateExpression( int operator1Loc, int operator2Loc, char *operandPtr,
439                           int machineArray[], TableEntry symbolTable[],
440                           int *instCounterPtr, int flags[], char *gotoLinePtr )
441  {
442      const char type = 'L';
443      int tableTest, symbol;
444
445      if ( strcmp( operandPtr, "==" ) == 0 ) {
446          machineArray[ *instCounterPtr ] = LOAD * 100;
447          machineArray[ *instCounterPtr ] += operator1Loc;
448          ++( *instCounterPtr );
449
450          machineArray[ *instCounterPtr ] = SUBTRACT * 100;
451          machineArray[ *instCounterPtr ] += operator2Loc;
452          ++( *instCounterPtr );
453
454          machineArray[ *instCounterPtr ] = BRANCHZERO * 100;
455
456          symbol = atoi( gotoLinePtr );
457          tableTest = checkSymbolTable( symbolTable, symbol, type );
458          addLineToFlags( tableTest, symbol, flags, machineArray, instCounterPtr );
459          ++( *instCounterPtr );
460      }
461      else if ( strcmp( operandPtr, "!=" ) == 0 ) {
462          machineArray[ *instCounterPtr ] = LOAD * 100;
463          machineArray[ *instCounterPtr ] += operator2Loc;
464          ++( *instCounterPtr );
465
466          machineArray[ *instCounterPtr ] = SUBTRACT * 100;
467          machineArray[ *instCounterPtr ] += operator1Loc;
468          ++( *instCounterPtr );
469
470          machineArray[ *instCounterPtr ] = BRANCHNEG * 100;
471
472          symbol = atoi( gotoLinePtr );
473          tableTest = checkSymbolTable( symbolTable, symbol, type );
474
475          addLineToFlags( tableTest, symbol, flags, machineArray, instCounterPtr );
476
477          ++( *instCounterPtr );
478
479          machineArray[ *instCounterPtr ] = LOAD * 100;
480          machineArray[ *instCounterPtr ] += operator1Loc;
481          ++( *instCounterPtr );
482
483          machineArray[ *instCounterPtr ] = SUBTRACT * 100;
484          machineArray[ *instCounterPtr ] += operator2Loc;
485          ++( *instCounterPtr );
486
487          machineArray[ *instCounterPtr ] = BRANCHNEG * 100;
488
489          symbol = atoi( gotoLinePtr );
490          tableTest = checkSymbolTable( symbolTable, symbol, type );
```

```
491
492         addLineToFlags( tableTest, symbol, flags, machineArray, instCounterPtr );
493
494         ++( *instCounterPtr );
495     }
496     else if ( strcmp( operandPtr, ">" ) == 0 ) {
497         machineArray[ *instCounterPtr ] = LOAD * 100;
498         machineArray[ *instCounterPtr ] += operator2Loc;
499         ++( *instCounterPtr );
500
501         machineArray[ *instCounterPtr ] = SUBTRACT * 100;
502         machineArray[ *instCounterPtr ] += operator1Loc;
503         ++( *instCounterPtr );
504
505         machineArray[ *instCounterPtr ] = BRANCHNEG * 100;
506
507         symbol = atoi( gotoLinePtr );
508         tableTest = checkSymbolTable( symbolTable, symbol, type );
509
510         addLineToFlags( tableTest, symbol, flags, machineArray, instCounterPtr );
511         ++( *instCounterPtr );
512     }
513     else if ( strcmp( operandPtr, "<" ) == 0 ) {
514         machineArray[ *instCounterPtr ] = LOAD * 100;
515         machineArray[ *instCounterPtr ] += operator1Loc;
516         ++( *instCounterPtr );
517
518         machineArray[ *instCounterPtr ] = SUBTRACT * 100;
519         machineArray[ *instCounterPtr ] += operator2Loc;
520         ++( *instCounterPtr );
521
522         machineArray[ *instCounterPtr ] = BRANCHNEG * 100;
523
524         symbol = atoi( gotoLinePtr );
525         tableTest = checkSymbolTable( symbolTable, symbol, type );
526
527         addLineToFlags( tableTest, symbol, flags, machineArray, instCounterPtr );
528         ++( *instCounterPtr );
529     }
530     else if ( strcmp( operandPtr, ">=" ) == 0 ) {
531         machineArray[ *instCounterPtr ] = LOAD * 100;
532         machineArray[ *instCounterPtr ] += operator2Loc;
533         ++( *instCounterPtr );
534
535         machineArray[ *instCounterPtr ] = SUBTRACT * 100;
536         machineArray[ *instCounterPtr ] += operator1Loc;
537         ++( *instCounterPtr );
538
539         machineArray[ *instCounterPtr ] = BRANCHNEG * 100;
540         symbol = atoi( gotoLinePtr );
541         tableTest = checkSymbolTable( symbolTable, symbol, type );
542
543         addLineToFlags( tableTest, symbol, flags, machineArray, instCounterPtr );
544         ++( *instCounterPtr );
545
546         machineArray[ *instCounterPtr ] = BRANCHZERO * 100;
547
548         addLineToFlags( tableTest, symbol, flags, machineArray, instCounterPtr );
549         ++( *instCounterPtr );
550     }
551     else if ( strcmp( operandPtr, "<=" ) == 0 ) {
552         machineArray[ *instCounterPtr ] = LOAD * 100;
553         machineArray[ *instCounterPtr ] += operator1Loc;
554         ++( *instCounterPtr );
```

```
555         machineArray[ *instCounterPtr ] = SUBTRACT * 100;
556         machineArray[ *instCounterPtr ] += operator2Loc;
557         ++( *instCounterPtr );
558
559         machineArray[ *instCounterPtr ] = BRANCHNEG * 100;
560
561         symbol = atoi( gotoLinePtr );
562         tableTest = checkSymbolTable( symbolTable, symbol, type );
563
564         addLineToFlags( tableTest, symbol, flags, machineArray, instCounterPtr );
565         ++( *instCounterPtr );
566
567         machineArray[ *instCounterPtr ] = BRANCHZERO * 100;
568
569         addLineToFlags( tableTest, symbol, flags, machineArray, instCounterPtr );
570         ++( *instCounterPtr );
571      }
572  }
573
574  // secondPass resolves incomplete SML instructions for forward references
575  void secondPass( int flags[], int machineArray[], TableEntry symbolTable[] )
576  {
577      const char type = 'L';
578
579      for ( int loop = 0; loop < MEMORYSIZE; ++loop ) {
580         if ( flags[ loop ] != -1 ) {
581            int symbol = flags[ loop ];
582            int flagLocation = checkSymbolTable( symbolTable, symbol, type );
583            machineArray[ loop ] += flagLocation;
584         }
585      }
586  }
587
588  // keyLet processes the keyword let
589  void keyLet( char *tokenPtr, int machineArray[], TableEntry symbolTable[],
590               int *dataCounterPtr, int *instCounterPtr )
591  {
592      const char type = 'V';
593      char infixArray[ MAXIMUM ] = "", postfixArray[ MAXIMUM ] = "";
594      int tableTest, symbol, location;
595      static int subscript = 0;
596
597      symbol = tokenPtr[ 0 ];
598      tableTest = checkSymbolTable( symbolTable, symbol, type );
599
600      if ( -1 == tableTest ) {
601         addToSymbolTable( type, symbol, *dataCounterPtr, symbolTable,
602                           *instCounterPtr );
603         location = *dataCounterPtr;
604         --( *dataCounterPtr );
605      }
606      else
607         location = tableTest;
608
609      tokenPtr = strtok( 0, " " );      // grab equal sign
610      tokenPtr = strtok( 0, " " );      // get next token
611
612      while ( tokenPtr != 0 ) {
613         checkOperand( symbolTable, tokenPtr, dataCounterPtr,
614                       instCounterPtr, machineArray );
615         infixArray[ subscript ] = tokenPtr[ 0 ];
616         ++subscript;
617         tokenPtr = strtok( 0, " " );  // get next token
618      }
```

```
619
620       infixArray[ subscript ] = '\0';
621
622       infixToPostfix( infixArray, postfixArray, location, symbolTable,
623                       instCounterPtr, dataCounterPtr, machineArray );
624
625       subscript = 0;      // reset static subscript when done
626    }
627
628    void addToSymbolTable( char type, int symbol, int dataCounter,
629                           TableEntry symbolTable[], int instCounter )
630    {
631       static int symbolCounter = 0;
632
633       symbolTable[ symbolCounter ].type = type;
634       symbolTable[ symbolCounter ].symbol = symbol;
635
636       if ( type == 'V' || type == 'C' )
637          symbolTable[ symbolCounter ].location = dataCounter;
638       else
639          symbolTable[ symbolCounter ].location = instCounter;
640
641       ++symbolCounter;
642    }
643
644    void addLineToFlags( int tableTest, int symbol, int flags[],
645                         int machineArray[], const int *instCounterPtr )
646    {
647       if ( tableTest == -1 )
648          flags[ *instCounterPtr ] = symbol;
649       else
650          machineArray[ *instCounterPtr ] += tableTest;
651    }
652
653    void printOutput( const int machineArray[], char *outFileName )
654    {
655       ofstream output( outFileName, ios::out );
656
657       if ( !output )
658          cerr << "File was not opened.\n";
659       else                     // output every memory cell
660          for ( int loop = 0; loop <= MEMORYSIZE - 1; ++loop )
661             output << machineArray[ loop ] << '\n';
662    }
663
664    void initArrays( int flags[], int machineArray[], TableEntry symbolTable[] )
665    {
666       TableEntry initEntry = { 0, 0, -1 };
667
668       for ( int loop = 0; loop < MEMORYSIZE; ++loop ) {
669          flags[ loop ] = -1;
670          machineArray[ loop ] = 0;
671          symbolTable[ loop ] = initEntry;
672       }
673    }
674
675    /////////////////////////////////////////////////////////////////////////////
676    // INFIX TO POSTFIX CONVERSION and POSTFIX EVALUATION FOR THE LET STATEMENT //
677    /////////////////////////////////////////////////////////////////////////////
678
679    // infixToPostfix converts an infix expression to a postfix expression
680    void infixToPostfix( char infix[], char postfix[], int getsVariable,
681                         TableEntry symbolTable[], int *instCounterPtr,
682                         int *dataCounterPtr, int machineArray[] )
```

```
683  {
684      Stack< int > intStack;
685      int infixCount, postfixCount, popValue;
686      bool higher;
687      int leftParen = '(';    /// made int
688
689      // push a left paren onto the stack and add a right paren to infix
690      intStack.push( leftParen );
691      strcat( infix, ")" );
692
693      // convert the infix expression to postfix
694      for ( infixCount = 0, postfixCount = 0; intStack.stackTop();
695            ++infixCount ) {
696
697          if ( isalnum( infix[ infixCount ] ) )
698              postfix[ postfixCount++ ] = infix[ infixCount ];
699          else if ( infix[ infixCount ] == '(' )
700              intStack.push( leftParen );
701          else if ( isOperator( infix[ infixCount ] ) ) {
702              higher = true;    // used to store value of precedence test
703
704              while ( higher ) {
705                  if ( isOperator( static_cast< char >( intStack.stackTop() ) ) )
706                      if ( precedence( static_cast< char >( intStack.stackTop() ),
707                               infix[ infixCount ] ) )
708
709                          postfix[ postfixCount++ ] =
710                                          static_cast< char >( intStack.pop() );
711                      else
712                          higher = false;
713                  else
714                      higher = false;
715              }
716
717              // See chapter 21 for a discussion of reinterpret_cast
718              intStack.push( reinterpret_cast< int & > ( infix[ infixCount ] ) );
719          }
720          else if ( infix[ infixCount ] == ')' )
721              while ( ( popValue = intStack.pop() ) != '(' )
722                  postfix[ postfixCount++ ] = static_cast< char >( popValue );
723      }
724
725      postfix[ postfixCount ] = '\0';
726
727      evaluatePostfix( postfix, dataCounterPtr, instCounterPtr,
728                  machineArray, getsVariable, symbolTable );
729  }
730
731  // check if c is an operator
732  bool isOperator( char c )
733  {
734      if ( c == '+' || c == '-' || c == '*' || c == '/' || c == '^' )
735          return true;
736      else
737          return false;
738  }
739
740  // If the precedence of operator1 is >= operator2,
741  bool precedence( char operator1, char operator2 )
742  {
743      if ( operator1 == '^' )
744          return true;
745      else if ( operator2 == '^' )
746          return false;
```

```
747        else if ( operator1 == '*' || operator1 == '/' )
748           return true;
749        else if ( operator1 == '+' || operator1 == '-' )
750           if ( operator2 == '*' || operator2 == '/' )
751              return false;
752           else
753              return true;
754
755        return false;
756     }
757
758     // evaluate postfix expression and produce code
759     void evaluatePostfix( char *expr, int *dataCounterPtr,
760                           int *instCounterPtr, int machineArray[],
761                           int getsVariable, TableEntry symbolTable[] )
762     {
763        Stack< int > intStack;
764        int popRightValue, popLeftValue, accumResult, symbolLocation, symbol;
765        char type, array[ 2 ] = "";
766        int i;
767
768        strcat( expr, ")" );
769
770        for ( i = 0; expr[ i ] != ')'; ++i )
771           if ( isdigit( expr[ i ] ) ) {
772              type = 'C';
773              array[ 0 ] = expr[ i ];
774              symbol = atoi( array );
775
776              symbolLocation = checkSymbolTable( symbolTable, symbol, type );
777              intStack.push( symbolLocation );
778           }
779           else if ( isalpha( expr[ i ] ) ) {
780              type = 'V';
781              symbol = expr[ i ];
782              symbolLocation = checkSymbolTable( symbolTable, symbol, type );
783              intStack.push( symbolLocation );
784           }
785           else {
786              popRightValue = intStack.pop();
787              popLeftValue = intStack.pop();
788              accumResult = createLetSML( popRightValue, popLeftValue, machineArray,
789                                          instCounterPtr, dataCounterPtr,
790                                          expr[ i ] );
791              intStack.push( accumResult );
792           }
793
794        machineArray[ *instCounterPtr ] = LOAD * 100;
795        machineArray[ *instCounterPtr ] += intStack.pop();
796        ++( *instCounterPtr );
797        machineArray[ *instCounterPtr ] = STORE * 100;
798        machineArray[ *instCounterPtr ] += getsVariable;
799        ++( *instCounterPtr );
800     }
801
802     int createLetSML( int right, int left, int machineArray[],
803                       int *instCounterPtr, int *dataCounterPtr, char oper )
804     {
805        int location;
806
807        switch( oper ) {
808           case '+':
809              machineArray[ *instCounterPtr ] = LOAD * 100;
810              machineArray[ *instCounterPtr ] += left;
```

```
811              ++( *instCounterPtr );
812              machineArray[ *instCounterPtr ] = ADD * 100;
813              machineArray[ *instCounterPtr ] += right;
814              ++( *instCounterPtr );
815              machineArray[ *instCounterPtr ] = STORE * 100;
816              machineArray[ *instCounterPtr ] += *dataCounterPtr;
817              location = *dataCounterPtr;
818              --( *dataCounterPtr );
819              ++( *instCounterPtr );
820              return location;
821           case '-':
822              machineArray[ *instCounterPtr ] = LOAD * 100;
823              machineArray[ *instCounterPtr ] += left;
824              ++( *instCounterPtr );
825              machineArray[ *instCounterPtr ] = SUBTRACT * 100;
826              machineArray[ *instCounterPtr ] += right;
827              ++( *instCounterPtr );
828              machineArray[ *instCounterPtr ] = STORE * 100;
829              machineArray[ *instCounterPtr ] += *dataCounterPtr;
830              location = *dataCounterPtr;
831              --( *dataCounterPtr );
832              ++( *instCounterPtr );
833              return location;
834           case '/':
835              machineArray[ *instCounterPtr ] = LOAD * 100;
836              machineArray[ *instCounterPtr ] += left;
837              ++( *instCounterPtr );
838              machineArray[ *instCounterPtr ] = DIVIDE * 100;
839              machineArray[ *instCounterPtr ] += right;
840              ++( *instCounterPtr );
841              machineArray[ *instCounterPtr ] = STORE * 100;
842              machineArray[ *instCounterPtr ] += *dataCounterPtr;
843              location = *dataCounterPtr;
844              --( *dataCounterPtr );
845              ++( *instCounterPtr );
846              return location;
847           case '*':
848              machineArray[ *instCounterPtr ] = LOAD * 100;
849              machineArray[ *instCounterPtr ] += left;
850              ++( *instCounterPtr );
851              machineArray[ *instCounterPtr ] = MULTIPLY * 100;
852              machineArray[ *instCounterPtr ] += right;
853              ++( *instCounterPtr );
854              machineArray[ *instCounterPtr ] = STORE * 100;
855              machineArray[ *instCounterPtr ] += *dataCounterPtr;
856              location = *dataCounterPtr;
857              --( *dataCounterPtr );
858              ++( *instCounterPtr );
859              return location;
860           default:
861              cerr << "ERROR: operator not recognized.\n";
862              break;
863        }
864
865     return 0;     // default return
866  }
```

15.28 (*Optimizing the Simple Compiler*) When a program is compiled and converted into SML, a set of instructions is generated. Certain combinations of instructions often repeat themselves, usually in triplets called *productions*. A production normally consists of three instructions such as *load*, *add*, and *store*. For example, Fig. 15.27 illustrates five of the SML instructions that were produced in the compilation of the program in Fig. 15.25 The first three instructions are the production that adds **1** to **y**. Note that instructions **06** and **07** store the accumulator value in temporary location **96**, then load the value back into the accumulator so instruction **08** can store the value in location **98**. Often a production is followed by a load instruction for the same location that was just stored. This code can be *optimized* by eliminating the store instruction and the subsequent load instruction that operate on the same memory location, thus enabling the Simpletron to execute the program faster. Figure 15.28 illustrates the optimized SML for the program of Fig. 15.25. Note that there are four fewer instructions in the optimized code—a memory-space savings of 25%.

```
867  04   +2098   (load)
868  05   +3097   (add)
869  06   +2196   (store)
870  07   +2096   (load)
871  08   +2198   (store)
```

Fig. 15.27 Unoptimized code from the program of Fig. 15.25.

Simple program	SML location and instruction	Description
5 rem sum 1 to x	*none*	**rem** ignored
10 input x	00 +1099	read **x** into location **99**
15 rem check y == x	*none*	**rem** ignored
20 if y == x goto 60	01 +2098	load **y** (**98**) into accumulator
	02 +3199	sub **x** (**99**) from accumulator
	03 +4211	branch to location **11** if zero
25 rem increment y	*none*	**rem** ignored
30 let y = y + 1	04 +2098	load **y** into accumulator
	05 +3097	add **1** (**97**) to accumulator
	06 +2198	store accumulator in **y** (**98**)
35 rem add y to total	*none*	**rem** ignored
40 let t = t + y	07 +2096	load **t** from location (**96**)
	08 +3098	add **y** (**98**) accumulator
	09 +2196	store accumulator in **t** (**96**)
45 rem loop y	*none*	**rem** ignored
50 goto 20	10 +4001	branch to location **01**
55 rem output result	*none*	**rem** ignored
60 print t	11 +1196	output **t** (**96**) to screen
99 end	12 +4300	terminate execution

Fig. 15.28 Optimized code for the program of Fig. 15.25.

Modify the compiler to provide an option for optimizing the Simpletron Machine Language code it produces. Manually compare the non-optimized code with the optimized code, and calculate the percentage reduction.

15.29 (*Modifications to the Simple compiler*) Perform the following modifications to the Simple compiler. Some of these modifications may also require modifications to the Simpletron Simulator program written in Exercise 5.19.

    a) Allow the modulus operator (**%**) to be used in **let** statements. Simpletron Machine Language must be modified to include a modulus instruction.

    b) Allow exponentiation in a **let** statement using **^** as the exponentiation operator. Simpletron Machine Language must be modified to include an exponentiation instruction.

    c) Allow the compiler to recognize uppercase and lowercase letters in Simple statements (e.g., **'A'** is equivalent to **'a'**). No modifications to the Simpletron Simulator are required.

    d) Allow **input** statements to read values for multiple variables such as **input x, y**. No modifications to the Simpletron Simulator are required.

    e) Allow the compiler to output multiple values in a single **print** statement such as **print a, b, c**. No modifications to the Simpletron Simulator are required.

f) Add syntax-checking capabilities to the compiler so error messages are output when syntax errors are encountered in a Simple program. No modifications to the Simpletron Simulator are required.

g) Allow arrays of integers. No modifications to the Simpletron Simulator are required.

h) Allow subroutines specified by the Simple commands **gosub** and **return**. Command **gosub** passes program control to a subroutine and command **return** passes control back to the statement after the **gosub**. This is similar to a function call in C++. The same subroutine can be called from many **gosub** commands distributed throughout a program. No modifications to the Simpletron Simulator are required.

i) Allow repetition structures of the form

```
for x = 2 to 10 step 2
    Simple statements
next
```

This **for** statement loops from **2** to **10** with an increment of **2**. The **next** line marks the end of the body of the **for** line. No modifications to the Simpletron Simulator are required.

j) Allow repetition structures of the form

```
for x = 2 to 10
    Simple statements
next
```

This **for** statement loops from **2** to **10** with a default increment of **1**. No modifications to the Simpletron Simulator are required.

k) Allow the compiler to process string input and output. This requires the Simpletron Simulator to be modified to process and store string values. Hint: Each Simpletron word can be divided into two groups, each holding a two-digit integer. Each two-digit integer represents the ASCII decimal equivalent of a character. Add a machine language instruction that will print a string beginning at a certain Simpletron memory location. The first half of the word at that location is a count of the number of characters in the string (i.e., the length of the string). Each succeeding half word contains one ASCII character expressed as two decimal digits. The machine language instruction checks the length and prints the string by translating each two-digit number into its equivalent character.

l) Allow the compiler to process floating-point values in addition to integers. The Simpletron Simulator must also be modified to process floating-point values.

15.30 (*A Simple interpreter*) An interpreter is a program that reads a high-level language program statement, determines the operation to be performed by the statement, and executes the operation immediately. The high-level language program is not converted into machine language first. Interpreters execute slowly because each statement encountered in the program must first be deciphered. If statements are contained in a loop, the statements are deciphered each time they are encountered in the loop. Early versions of the BASIC programming language were implemented as interpreters.

Write an interpreter for the Simple language discussed in Exercise 15.26. The program should use the infix-to-postfix converter developed in Exercise 15.12 and the postfix evaluator developed in Exercise 15.13 to evaluate expressions in a **let** statement. The same restrictions placed on the Simple language in Exercise 15.26 should be adhered to in this program. Test the interpreter with the Simple programs written in Exercise 15.26. Compare the results of running these programs in the interpreter with the results of compiling the Simple programs and running them in the Simpletron Simulator built in Exercise 5.19.

15.31 (*Insert/Delete Anywhere in a Linked List*) Our linked list class template allowed insertions and deletions at only the front and the back of the linked list. These capabilities were convenient for us when we used private inheritance and composition to produce a stack class template and a queue class template with a minimal amount of code simply by reusing the list class template. Actually linked lists are more general that those we provided. Modify the linked list class template we developed in this chapter to handle insertions and deletions anywhere in the list.

ANS:

```
1   // LIST.H
2   // Template List class definition
3   // Added copy constructor to member functions (not included in chapter).
4   #ifndef LIST_H
5   #define LIST_H
6
7   #include <iostream.h>
8   #include <assert.h>
9   #include "listnd.h"
10
```

```
11   template< class NODETYPE >
12   class List {
13   public:
14      List();                                  // default constructor
15      List( const List< NODETYPE > & );  // copy constructor
16      ~List();                                 // destructor
17      void insertAtFront( const NODETYPE & );
18      void insertAtBack( const NODETYPE & );
19      bool removeFromFront( NODETYPE & );
20      bool removeFromBack( NODETYPE & );
21      void insertInOrder( const NODETYPE & );
22      bool isEmpty() const;
23      void print() const;
24   protected:
25      ListNode< NODETYPE > *firstPtr;  // pointer to first node
26      ListNode< NODETYPE > *lastPtr;   // pointer to last node
27
28      // Utility function to allocate a new node
29      ListNode< NODETYPE > *getNewNode( const NODETYPE & );
30   };
31
32   // Default constructor
33   template< class NODETYPE >
34   List< NODETYPE >::List() { firstPtr = lastPtr = 0; }
35
36   // Copy constructor
37   template< class NODETYPE >
38   List< NODETYPE >::List( const List<NODETYPE> &copy )
39   {
40      firstPtr = lastPtr = 0;  // initialize pointers
41
42      ListNode< NODETYPE > *currentPtr = copy.firstPtr;
43
44      while ( currentPtr != 0 ) {
45         insertAtBack( currentPtr -> data );
46         currentPtr = currentPtr -> nextPtr;
47      }
48   }
49
50   // Destructor
51   template< class NODETYPE >
52   List< NODETYPE >::~List()
53   {
54      if ( !isEmpty() ) {      // List is not empty
55         cout << "Destroying nodes ...\n";
56
57         ListNode< NODETYPE > *currentPtr = firstPtr, *tempPtr;
58
59         while ( currentPtr != 0 ) {  // delete remaining nodes
60            tempPtr = currentPtr;
61            cout << tempPtr -> data << ' ';
62            currentPtr = currentPtr -> nextPtr;
63            delete tempPtr;
64         }
65      }
66
67      cout << "\nAll nodes destroyed\n\n";
68   }
69
70   // Insert a node at the front of the list
71   template< class NODETYPE >
72   void List< NODETYPE >::insertAtFront( const NODETYPE &value )
73   {
74      ListNode<NODETYPE> *newPtr = getNewNode( value );
```

```
75
76     if ( isEmpty() )   // List is empty
77        firstPtr = lastPtr = newPtr;
78     else {              // List is not empty
79        newPtr -> nextPtr = firstPtr;
80        firstPtr = newPtr;
81     }
82  }
83
84  // Insert a node at the back of the list
85  template< class NODETYPE >
86  void List< NODETYPE >::insertAtBack( const NODETYPE &value )
87  {
88     ListNode< NODETYPE > *newPtr = getNewNode( value );
89
90     if ( isEmpty() )   // List is empty
91        firstPtr = lastPtr = newPtr;
92     else {              // List is not empty
93        lastPtr -> nextPtr = newPtr;
94        lastPtr = newPtr;
95     }
96  }
97
98  // Delete a node from the front of the list
99  template< class NODETYPE >
100 bool List< NODETYPE >::removeFromFront( NODETYPE &value )
101 {
102    if ( isEmpty() )                 // List is empty
103       return false;                 // delete unsuccessful
104    else {
105       ListNode< NODETYPE > *tempPtr = firstPtr;
106
107       if ( firstPtr == lastPtr )
108          firstPtr = lastPtr = 0;
109       else
110          firstPtr = firstPtr -> nextPtr;
111
112       value = tempPtr -> data;   // data being removed
113       delete tempPtr;
114       return true;                  // delete successful
115    }
116 }
117
118 // Delete a node from the back of the list
119 template< class NODETYPE >
120 bool List< NODETYPE >::removeFromBack( NODETYPE &value )
121 {
122    if ( isEmpty() )
123       return false;    // delete unsuccessful
124    else {
125       ListNode< NODETYPE > *tempPtr = lastPtr;
126
127       if ( firstPtr == lastPtr )
128          firstPtr = lastPtr = 0;
129       else {
130          ListNode< NODETYPE > *currentPtr = firstPtr;
131
132          while ( currentPtr -> nextPtr != lastPtr )
133             currentPtr = currentPtr -> nextPtr;
134
135          lastPtr = currentPtr;
136          currentPtr -> nextPtr = 0;
137       }
138
```

```
139          value = tempPtr -> data;
140          delete tempPtr;
141          return true;    // delete successful
142       }
143    }
144
145    // Is the List empty?
146    template< class NODETYPE >
147    bool List< NODETYPE >::isEmpty() const { return firstPtr == 0; }
148
149    // Return a pointer to a newly allocated node
150    template< class NODETYPE >
151    ListNode< NODETYPE > *List< NODETYPE >::getNewNode( const NODETYPE &value )
152    {
153       ListNode< NODETYPE > *ptr = new ListNode< NODETYPE >( value );
154       assert( ptr != 0 );
155       return ptr;
156    }
157
158    // Display the contents of the List
159    template< class NODETYPE >
160    void List< NODETYPE >::print() const
161    {
162       if ( isEmpty() ) {
163          cout << "The list is empty\n\n";
164          return;
165       }
166
167       ListNode< NODETYPE > *currentPtr = firstPtr;
168
169       cout << "The list is: ";
170
171       while ( currentPtr != 0 ) {
172          cout << currentPtr -> data << ' ';
173          currentPtr = currentPtr -> nextPtr;
174       }
175
176       cout << "\n\n";
177    }
178
179    template< class NODETYPE >
180    void List< NODETYPE >::insertInOrder( const NODETYPE &value )
181    {
182       if ( isEmpty() ) {
183          ListNode< NODETYPE > *newPtr = getNewNode( value );
184          firstPtr = lastPtr = newPtr;
185       }
186       else {
187          if ( firstPtr -> data > value )
188             insertAtFront( value );
189          else if ( lastPtr -> data < value )
190             insertAtBack( value );
191          else {
192             ListNode< NODETYPE > *currentPtr = firstPtr -> nextPtr,
193                                  *previousPtr = firstPtr,
194                                  *newPtr = getNewNode( value );
195
196             while ( currentPtr != lastPtr && currentPtr -> data < value ) {
197                previousPtr = currentPtr;
198                currentPtr = currentPtr -> nextPtr;
199             }
200
201             previousPtr -> nextPtr = newPtr;
202             newPtr -> nextPtr = currentPtr;
```

```
203            }
204         }
205    }
206
207    #endif
```

```
208    // LISTND.H
209    // ListNode template definition
210    #ifndef LISTND_H
211    #define LISTND_H
212
213    template< class T > class List;   // forward declaration
214
215    template< class NODETYPE >
216    class ListNode {
217       friend class List< NODETYPE >; // make List a friend
218    public:
219       ListNode( const NODETYPE & );   // constructor
220       NODETYPE getData() const;       // return the data in the node
221       void setNextPtr( ListNode *nPtr ) { nextPtr = nPtr; }
222       ListNode *getNextPtr() const { return nextPtr; }
223    private:
224       NODETYPE data;                  // data
225       ListNode *nextPtr;              // next node in the list
226    };
227
228    // Constructor
229    template< class NODETYPE >
230    ListNode< NODETYPE >::ListNode( const NODETYPE &info )
231    {
232       data = info;
233       nextPtr = 0;
234    }
235
236    // Return a copy of the data in the node
237    template< class NODETYPE >
238    NODETYPE ListNode< NODETYPE >::getData() const { return data; }
239
240    #endif
```

```
241    // LIST2.H
242    // Template List class definition
243    // NOTE: This solution only provides the delete anywhere operation.
244    #ifndef LIST2_H
245    #define LIST2_H
246
247    #include <iostream.h>
248    #include <assert.h>
249    #include "listnd.h"
250    #include "list.h"
251
252    template< class NODETYPE >
253    class List2 : public List< NODETYPE > {
254    public:
255       bool deleteNode( const NODETYPE &, NODETYPE & );
256    };
257
258    // Delete a node from anywhere in the list
259    template< class NODETYPE >
260    bool List2< NODETYPE >::deleteNode( const NODETYPE &val, NODETYPE &deletedVal )
261    {
262       if ( isEmpty() )
263          return false;    // delete unsuccessful
```

```
264       else {
265          if ( firstPtr -> getData() == val ) {
266             removeFromFront( deletedVal );
267             return true;   // delete successful
268          }
269          else if ( lastPtr -> getData() == val ) {
270             removeFromBack( deletedVal );
271             return true;   // delete successful
272          }
273          else {
274             ListNode< NODETYPE > *currentPtr = firstPtr -> getNextPtr(),
275                                 *previousPtr = firstPtr;
276
277             while ( currentPtr != lastPtr && currentPtr -> getData() < val ) {
278                previousPtr = currentPtr;
279                currentPtr = currentPtr -> getNextPtr();
280             }
281
282             if ( currentPtr -> getData() == val ) {
283                ListNode< NODETYPE > *tempPtr = currentPtr;
284                deletedVal = currentPtr -> getData();
285                previousPtr -> setNextPtr( currentPtr -> getNextPtr() );
286                delete tempPtr;
287                return true;   // delete successful
288             }
289             else
290                return false;   // delete unsuccessful
291          }
292       }
293    }
294
295    #endif
```

```
296    // Exercise 15.31 solution
297    #include <iostream.h>
298    #include <stdlib.h>
299    #include <time.h>
300    #include "list2.h"
301
302    int main()
303    {
304       srand( time( 0 ) );   // randomize the random number generator
305
306       List2< int > intList;
307
308       for ( int i = 1; i <= 10; ++i )
309          intList.insertInOrder( rand() % 101 );
310
311       intList.print();
312
313       int value, deletedValue;
314
315       cout << "Enter an integer to delete (-1 to end): ";
316       cin >> value;
317
318       while ( value != -1 ) {
319          if ( intList.deleteNode( value, deletedValue ) ) {
320             cout << deletedValue << " was deleted from the list\n";
321             intList.print();
322          }
323          else
324             cout << "Element was not found";
325
```

CHAPTER 15 SOLUTIONS   DATA STRUCTURES 447

```
326            cout << "Enter an integer to delete (-1 to end): ";
327            cin >> value;
328        }
329
330        return 0;
331    }
```

```
The list is:
8 20 51 55 71 76 77 86 92 93

Enter an integer to delete (-1 to end): 8
8 was deleted from the list
The list is:
20 51 55 71 76 77 86 92 93

Enter an integer to delete (-1 to end): 86
86 was deleted from the list
The list is:
20 51 55 71 76 77 92 93
...
```

15.32 *(List and Queues without Tail Pointers)* Our implementation of a linked list (Fig. 15.3) used both a **firstPtr** and a **lastPtr**. The **lastPtr** was useful for the **insertAtBack** and **removeFromBack** member functions of the **List** class. The **insertAtBack** function corresponds to the **enqueue** member function of the **Queue** class. Rewrite the **List** class so that it does not use a **lastPtr**. Thus, any operations on the tail of a list must begin searching the list from the front. Does this affect our implementation of the **Queue** class (Fig. 15.12)?

15.33 Use the composition version of the stack program (Fig. 15.11) to form a complete working stack program. Modify this program to **inline** the member functions. Compare the two approaches. Summarize the advantages and disadvantages of inlining member functions.

15.34 *(Performance of Binary Tree Sorting and Searching)* One problem with the binary tree sort is that the order in which the data is inserted affects the shape of the tree—for the same collection of data, different orderings can yield binary trees of dramatically different shapes. The performance of the binary tree sorting and searching algorithms is sensitive to the shape of the binary tree. What shape would a binary tree have if its data were inserted in increasing order? in decreasing order? What shape should the tree have to achieve maximal searching performance?

15.35 *(Indexed Lists)* As presented in the text, linked lists must be searched sequentially. For large lists, this can result in poor performance. A common technique for improving list searching performance is to create and maintain an index to the list. An index is a set of pointers to various key places in the list. For example, an application that searches a large list of names could improve performance by creating an index with 26 entries—one for each letter of the alphabet. A search operation for a last name beginning with 'Y' would then first search the index to determine where the 'Y' entries begin, and then "jump into" the list at that point and search linearly until the desired name is found. This would be much faster than searching the linked list from the beginning. Use the **List** class of Fig. 15.3 as the basis of an **IndexedList** class. Write a program that demonstrates the operation of indexed lists. Be sure to include member functions **insertInIndexedList**, **searchIndexedList**, and **deleteFromIndexedList**.

Chapter 16 Solutions
Bits, Characters, Strings, and Structures

Solutions

16.6 Provide the definition for each of the following structures and unions:

a) Structure **Inventory** containing character array **partName[30]**, integer **partNumber**, floating-point **price**, integer **stock**, and integer **reorder**.

ANS:
```
struct Inventory {
   char partName[ 30 ];
   int partNumber;
   double price;
   int stock;
   int reorder;
};
```

b) A structure called **Address** that contains character arrays **streetAddress[25]**, **city[20]**, **state[3]**, and **zipCode[6]**.

ANS:
```
struct Address {
   char streetAddress[ 25 ];
   char city[ 20 ];
   char state[ 3 ];
   char zipCode[ 6 ];
};
```

c) Structure **Student** that contains arrays **firstName[15]** and **lastName[15]**, and variable **homeAddress** of type **struct Address** from part (b).

ANS:
```
struct Student {
   char firstName[ 15 ];
   char lastName[ 15 ];
   struct Address homeAddress;
};
```

d) Structure **Test** containing 16 bit fields with widths of 1 bit. The names of the bit fields are the letters **a** to **p**.

ANS:
```
struct Test {
   unsigned a:1, b:1, c:1, d:1, e:1, f:1, g:1, h:1,
            i:1, j:1, k:1, l:1, m:1, n:1, o:1, p:1;
};
```

16.7   Given the following structure definitions and variable declarations,

```
struct Customer {
    char lastName[ 15 ];
    char firstName[ 15 ];
    int customerNumber;

    struct {
        char phoneNumber[ 11 ];
        char address[ 50 ];
        char city[ 15 ];
        char state[ 3 ];
        char zipCode[ 6 ];
    } personal;
} customerRecord, *customerPtr;

customerPtr = &customerRecord;
```

write a separate expression that can be used to access the structure members in each of the following parts.

    a) Member `lastName` of structure `customerRecord`.
ANS: `customerRecord.lastName`
    b) Member `lastName` of the structure pointed to by `customerPtr`.
ANS: `customerPtr->lastName`
    c) Member `firstName` of structure `customerRecord`.
ANS: `customerRecord.firstName`
    d) Member `firstName` of the structure pointed to by `customerPtr`.
ANS: `customerPtr->firstName`
    e) Member `customerNumber` of structure `customerRecord`.
ANS: `customerRecord.customerNumber`
    f) Member `customerNumber` of the structure pointed to by `customerPtr`.
ANS: `customerPtr->customerNumber`
    g) Member `phoneNumber` of member `personal` of structure `customerRecord`.
ANS: `customerRecord.personal.phoneNumber`
    h) Member `phoneNumber` of member `personal` of the structure pointed to by `customerPtr`.
ANS: `customerPtr->personal.phoneNumber`
    i) Member `address` of member `personal` of structure `customerRecord`.
ANS: `customerRecord.personal.address`
    j) Member `address` of member `personal` of the structure pointed to by `customerPtr`.
ANS: `customerPtr->personal.address`
    k) Member `city` of member `personal` of structure `customerRecord`.
ANS: `customerRecord.personal.city`
    l) Member `city` of member `personal` of the structure pointed to by `customerPtr`.
ANS: `customerPtr->personal.city`
    m) Member `state` of member `personal` of structure `customerRecord`.
ANS: `customerRecord.personal.state`
    n) Member `state` of member `personal` of the structure pointed to by `customerPtr`.
ANS: `customerPtr->personal.state`
    o) Member `zipCode` of member `personal` of structure `customerRecord`.
ANS: `customerRecord.personal.zipCode`
    p) Member `zipCode` of member `personal` of the structure pointed to by `customerPtr`.
ANS: `customerPtr->personal.zipCode`

16.8   Modify the program of Fig. 16.14 to shuffle the cards using a high-performance shuffle (as shown in Fig. 16.2). Print the resulting deck in two column format as in Fig. 16.3. Precede each card with its color.
    ANS:

```
1   // Exercise 16.8 Solution
2   #include <iostream.h>
3   #include <iomanip.h>
4   #include <stdlib.h>
5   #include <time.h>
```

```
6
7    struct bitCard {
8       unsigned face : 4;
9       unsigned suit : 2;
10      unsigned color : 1;
11   };
12
13   typedef struct bitCard Card;
14
15   void fillDeck( Card * const );
16   void shuffle( Card * const );
17   void deal( const Card * const );
18
19   int main()
20   {
21      Card deck[ 52 ];
22
23      srand( 0 );
24
25      fillDeck( deck );
26      shuffle( deck );
27      deal( deck );
28      return 0;
29   }
30
31   void fillDeck( Card * const wDeck )
32   {
33      for ( int i = 0; i < 52; ++i ) {
34         wDeck[ i ].face = i % 13;
35         wDeck[ i ].suit = i / 13;
36         wDeck[ i ].color = i / 26;
37      }
38   }
39
40   void shuffle( Card * const wDeck )
41   {
42      int j;
43      Card temp;
44
45      for ( int i = 0; i < 52; ++i ) {
46         j = rand() % 52;
47
48         temp = wDeck[ i ];
49         wDeck[ i ] = wDeck[ j ];
50         wDeck[ j ] = temp;
51      }
52   }
53
54   void deal( const Card * const wDeck2 )
55   {
56      char *face[] = { "Ace", "Deuce", "Three", "Four", "Five", "Six", "Seven",
57                       "Eight", "Nine", "Ten", "Jack", "Queen", "King" },
58          *suit[] = { "Hearts", "Diamonds", "Clubs", "Spades" },
59          *color[] = { "Red", "Black" };
60
61      for ( int i = 0; i < 52; ++i ) {
62         cout << setw( 5 ) << color[ wDeck2[ i ].color ] << ": "
63              << setw( 8 ) << face[ wDeck2[ i ].face ] << " of "
64              << setiosflags( ios::left ) << setw( 8 )
65              << suit[ wDeck2[ i ].suit ] << resetiosflags( ios::left );
66
67         cout.put( ( i + 1 ) % 2 ? '\t' : '\n' );
68      }
69   }
```

```
Black:     King of Clubs    Black:    Three of Clubs
Black:     Five of Clubs    Red:        Ten of Hearts
Black:    Deuce of Clubs    Red:       Four of Hearts
  Red:      Six of Hearts   Black:     Nine of Clubs
Black:    Seven of Clubs    Red:       Five of Hearts
Black:    Deuce of Spades   Red:      Eight of Diamonds
  Red:     Nine of Hearts   Red:       Nine of Diamonds
Black:    Three of Spades   Black:     Nine of Spades
  Red:    Seven of Diamonds Red:       King of Diamonds
Black:      Six of Clubs    Red:       Jack of Diamonds
  Red:    Queen of Hearts   Black:      Ten of Clubs
  Red:    Deuce of Hearts   Red:        Six of Diamonds
Black:     Five of Spades   Black:     Four of Clubs
Black:     Jack of Clubs    Red:      Three of Diamonds
  Red:     Jack of Hearts   Red:        Ace of Hearts
  Red:      Ten of DiamondsBlack:    Eight of Clubs
Black:    Queen of Spades   Black:      Six of Spades
  Red:    Seven of Hearts   Black:      Ace of Spades
Black:    Seven of Spades   Red:       King of Hearts
Black:      Ten of Spades   Black:     Four of Spades
  Red:    Queen of DiamondsBlack:     Jack of Spades
Black:      Ace of Clubs    Black:     King of Spades
Black:    Eight of Spades   Black:    Queen of Clubs
  Red:    Eight of Hearts   Red:        Ace of Diamonds
  Red:     Four of Diamonds Red:      Three of Hearts
  Red:     Five of Diamonds Red:      Deuce of Diamonds
```

16.9 Write a program that right shifts an integer variable 4 bits. The program should print the integer in bits before and after the shift operation. Does your system place 0s or 1s in the vacated bits?

ANS:

```
1   // Exercise 16.9 Solution
2   #include <iostream.h>
3   #include <iomanip.h>
4
5   void displayBits( unsigned );
6
7   int main()
8   {
9      unsigned val;
10
11     cout << "Enter an integer: ";
12     cin >> val;
13
14     cout << "Before right shifting 4 bits is:\n";
15     displayBits( val );
16     cout << "After right shifting 4 bits is:\n";
17     displayBits( val >> 4 );
18     return 0;
19  }
20
21  void displayBits( unsigned value )
22  {
23     unsigned displayMask = 1 << 15;
24
25     cout << setw( 7 ) << value << " = ";
26
27     for ( unsigned c = 1; c <= 16; ++c ) {
28        cout.put( value & displayMask ? '1' : '0' );
29        value <<= 1;
30
```

```
31            if ( c % 8 == 0 )
32               cout.put( ' ' );
33         }
34
35      cout.put( '\n' );
36   }
```

```
Enter an integer: 888
Before right shifting 4 bits is:
    888 = 00000011 01111000
After right shifting 4 bits is:
     55 = 00000000 00110111
```

16.10 If your computer uses 4-byte integers, modify the program of Fig. 16.5 so that it works with 4-byte integers.

16.11 Left shifting an **unsigned** integer by 1 bit is equivalent to multiplying the value by 2. Write function **power2** that takes two integer arguments **number** and **pow**, and calculates

number * 2^pow

Use the shift operator to calculate the result. The program should print the values as integers and as bits.

ANS:

```
1   // Exercise 16.11 Solution
2   #include <iostream.h>
3   #include <iomanip.h>
4
5   void displayBits( unsigned );
6   unsigned power2( unsigned, unsigned );
7
8   int main()
9   {
10     unsigned number, pow, result;
11
12     cout << "Enter two integers: ";
13     cin >> number >> pow;
14     cout << "number:\n";
15     displayBits( number );
16     cout << "\npower:\n";
17     displayBits( pow );
18     result = power2( number, pow );
19     cout << '\n' << number << " * 2^" << pow << " = " << result << '\n';
20     displayBits( result );
21     return 0;
22   }
23
24   unsigned power2( unsigned n, unsigned p )  { return n << p; }
25
26   void displayBits( unsigned value )
27   {
28      unsigned displayMask = 1 << 15;
29
30      cout << setw( 7 ) << value << " = ";
31
32      for ( unsigned c = 1; c <= 16; ++c ) {
33         cout.put( value & displayMask ? '1' : '0' );
34         value <<= 1;
35
36         if ( c % 8 == 0 )
37            cout.put( ' ' );
38      }
39
40      cout << '\n';
41   }
```

```
Enter two integers: number:
        3 = 00000000 00000011

power:
        4 = 00000000 00000100

3 * 2^4 = 48
       48 = 00000000 00110000
```

16.12   The left shift operator can be used to pack two character values into a 2-byte unsigned integer variable. Write a program that inputs two characters from the keyboard and passes them to function **packCharacters**. To pack two characters into an **unsigned** integer variable, assign the first character to the **unsigned** variable, shift the **unsigned** variable left by 8 bit positions, and combine the **unsigned** variable with the second character using the bitwise inclusive OR operator. The program should output the characters in their bit format before and after they are packed into the **unsigned** integer to prove that the characters are in fact packed correctly in the **unsigned** variable.

ANS:

```
1   // Exercise 16.12 Solution
2   #include <iostream.h>
3   #include <iomanip.h>
4
5   unsigned packCharacters( char, char );
6   void displayBits( unsigned );
7
8   int main()
9   {
10     char a, b;
11     unsigned result;
12
13     cout << "Enter two characters: ";
14     cin.setf( ios::skipws );
15     cin >> a >> b;
16
17     cout << '\'' << a << '\'' << " in bits as an unsigned integers is:\n";
18     displayBits( a );
19
20     cout << '\'' << b << '\'' << " in bits as an unsigned integers is:\n";
21     displayBits( b );
22
23     result = packCharacters( a, b );
24
25     cout << "\n\'" << a << '\'' << " and " << '\'' << b << '\''
26          << " packed in an unsigned integer:\n";
27     displayBits( result );
28     return 0;
29   }
30
31   unsigned packCharacters( char x, char y )
32   {
33     unsigned pack = x;
34
35     pack <<= 8;
36     pack |= y;
37     return pack;
38   }
39
40   void displayBits( unsigned value )
41   {
42     unsigned displayMask = 1 << 15;
43
44     cout << setw( 7 ) << value << " = ";
```

```
45
46        for ( unsigned c = 1; c <= 16; ++c ) {
47           cout.put( value & displayMask ? '1' : '0' );
48           value <<= 1;
49
50           if ( c % 8 == 0 )
51              cout.put(' ');
52        }
53
54        cout << '\n';
55     }
```

```
Enter two characters: T N
'T' in bits as an unsigned integers is:
    84 = 00000000 01010100
'N' in bits as an unsigned integers is:
    78 = 00000000 01001110

'T' and 'N' packed in an unsigned integer:
  21582 = 01010100 01001110
```

16.13   Using the right shift operator, the bitwise AND operator, and a mask, write function **unpackCharacters** that takes the **unsigned** integer from Exercise 16.12 and unpacks it into two characters. To unpack two characters from an **unsigned** 2-byte integer, combine the unsigned integer with the mask **65280** (**11111111 00000000**) and right shift the result 8 bits. Assign the resulting value to a **char** variable. Then combine the **unsigned** integer with the mask **255** (**00000000 11111111**). Assign the result to another **char** variable. The program should print the **unsigned** integer in bits before it is unpacked, then print the characters in bits to confirm that they were unpacked correctly.

ANS:

```
1   // Exercise 16.13 Solution
2   #include <iostream.h>
3   #include <iomanip.h>
4
5   void unpackCharacters( char * const, char * const, unsigned );
6   void displayBits( unsigned );
7
8   int main()
9   {
10     char a, b;
11     unsigned packed = 16706;
12
13     cout << "The packed character representation is:\n";
14     displayBits( packed );
15     unpackCharacters( &a, &b, packed );
16     cout << "\nThe unpacked characters are \'" << a << "\' and \'" << b
17          << "\'\n";
18     displayBits( a );
19     displayBits( b );
20     return 0;
21   }
22
23   void unpackCharacters( char * const aPtr, char * const bPtr, unsigned pack )
24   {
25     unsigned mask1 = 65280, mask2 = 255;
26
27     *aPtr = static_cast< char >( ( pack & mask1 ) >> 8 );
28     *bPtr = static_cast< char >( pack & mask2 );
29   }
30
31   void displayBits( unsigned value )
32   {
33     unsigned displayMask = 1 << 15;
```

```
34
35        cout << setw( 7 ) << value << " = ";
36
37        for ( unsigned c = 1; c <= 16; ++c ) {
38           cout.put( value & displayMask ? '1' : '0' );
39           value <<= 1;
40
41           if ( c % 8 == 0 )
42              cout.put(' ');
43        }
44
45        cout << '\n';
46    }
```

```
    The packed character representation is:
      16706 = 01000001 01000010

    The unpacked characters are 'A' and 'B'
         65 = 00000000 01000001
         66 = 00000000 01000010
```

16.14   If your system uses 4-byte integers, rewrite the program of Exercise 16.12 to pack 4 characters.

16.15   If your system uses 4-byte integers, rewrite the function **unpackCharacters** of Exercise 16.13 to unpack 4 characters. Create the masks you need to unpack the 4 characters by left shifting the value 255 in the mask variable by 8 bits 0, 1, 2, or 3 times (depending on the byte you are unpacking).

16.16   Write a program that reverses the order of the bits in an unsigned integer value. The program should input the value from the user and call function **reverseBits** to print the bits in reverse order. Print the value in bits both before and after the bits are reversed to confirm that the bits are reversed properly.

   ANS:

```
 1    // Exercise 16.16 Solution
 2    #include <iostream.h>
 3    #include <iomanip.h>
 4
 5    void reverseBits( unsigned * const );
 6    void displayBits( unsigned );
 7
 8    int main()
 9    {
10       unsigned a;
11
12       cout << "Enter an unsigned integer: ";
13       cin >> a;
14
15       cout << "\nBefore bits are reversed:\n";
16       displayBits( a );
17       reverseBits( &a );
18       cout << "\nAfter bits are reversed:\n";
19       displayBits( a );
20       return 0;
21    }
22
23    void reverseBits( unsigned * const vPtr )
24    {
25       unsigned mask = 1, temp = 0, value = *vPtr;
26
27       for ( int i = 0; i <= 15; ++i ) {
28          *vPtr <<= 1;
29          *vPtr |= ( value & mask );
30          value >>= 1;
```

```
31        }
32   }
33
34   void displayBits( unsigned value )
35   {
36      unsigned displayMask = 1 << 15;
37
38      cout << setw( 7 ) << value << " = ";
39
40      for ( unsigned c = 1; c <= 16; ++c ) {
41         cout.put( value & displayMask ? '1' : '0' );
42         value <<= 1;
43
44         if ( c % 8 == 0 )
45            cout.put( ' ' );
46      }
47
48      cout << '\n';
49   }
```

```
Enter an unsigned integer: 330

Before bits are reversed:
   330 = 00000001 01001010

After bits are reversed:
21648000 = 01010010 10000000
```

16.17   Modify the **displayBits** function of Fig. 16.5 so it is portable between systems using 2-byte integers and systems using 4-byte integers. Hint: Use the **sizeof** operator to determine the size of an integer on a particular machine.

   ANS:

```
1   // Exercise 16.17 Solution
2   #include <iostream.h>
3   #include <iomanip.h>
4
5   void displayBits( unsigned );
6
7   int main()
8   {
9      unsigned x;
10
11     cout << "Enter an unsigned integer: ";
12     cin >> x;
13     displayBits( x );
14     return 0;
15  }
16
17  void displayBits( unsigned value )
18  {
19     unsigned displayMask = 1 << ( sizeof( unsigned ) * 8 - 1 );
20
21     for ( unsigned c = 1; c <= sizeof( int ) * 8; ++c ) {
22        cout.put( value & displayMask ? '1' : '0' );
23        value <<= 1;
24
25        if ( c % 8 == 0 )
26           cout.put( ' ' );
27     }
28
29     cout << '\n';
30  }
```

```
Enter an unsigned integer: 1999
00000000 00000000 00000111 11001111
```

16.18   Write a program that inputs a character from the keyboard, and tests the character with each of the functions in the character handling library. The program should print the value returned by each function.

   ANS:

```
1   // Exercise 16.18 Solution
2   #include <iostream.h>
3   #include <ctype.h>
4
5   int main()
6   {
7      char c;
8
9      cout << "Enter a character: ";
10     c = static_cast< char >( cin.get() );
11
12     cout << "isdigit(\'" << c << "\') = " << isdigit( c )
13          << "\nisalpha(\'" << c << "\') = " << isalpha( c )
14          << "\nisalnum(\'" << c << "\') = " << isalnum( c );
15
16     cout << "\nisxdigit(\'" << c << "\') = " << isxdigit( c )
17          << "\nislower(\'" << c << "\') = " << islower( c )
18          << "\nisupper(\'" << c << "\') = " << isupper( c )
19          << "\ntolower(\'" << c << "\') = " << tolower( c )
20          << "\ntoupper(\'" << c << "\') = " << toupper( c )
21          << "\nisspace(\'" << c << "\') = " << isspace( c );
22
23     cout << "\niscntrl(\'" << c << "\') = " << iscntrl( c )
24          << "\nispunct(\'" << c << "\') = " << ispunct( c )
25          << "\nisprint(\'" << c << "\') = " << isprint( c )
26          << "\nisgraph(\'" << c << "\') = " << isgraph( c ) << endl;
27
28     return 0;
29  }
```

```
Enter a character: ~
isdigit('~')   = 0
isalpha('~')   = 0
isalnum('~')   = 0
isxdigit('~') = 0
islower('~')   = 0
isupper('~')   = 0
tolower('~')   = 126
toupper('~')   = 126
isspace('~')   = 0
iscntrl('~')   = 0
ispunct('~')   = 16
isprint('~')   = 16
isgraph('~')   = 16
```

16.19   The following program uses function **multiple** to determine if the integer entered from the keyboard is a multiple of some integer **X**. Examine the function **multiple**, then determine the value of **X**.

```
1   // This program determines if a value is a multiple of X
2   #include <iostream.h>
3
4   int multiple( int );
5
```

```
6   int main()
7   {
8      int y;
9
10     cout << "Enter an integer between 1 and 32000: ";
11     cin >> y;
12
13     if ( multiple( y ) )
14        cout << y << " is a multiple of X" << endl;
15     else
16        cout << y << " is not a multiple of X" << endl;
17
18     return 0;
19  }
20
21  int multiple( int num )
22  {
23     int mask = 1, mult = 1;
24
25     for ( int i = 0; i < 10; i++, mask <<= 1 )
26        if ( ( num & mask ) != 0 ) {
27           mult = 0;
28           break;
29        }
30
31     return mult;
32  }
```

ANS: Determines if the number input is a multiple of X. The value of X is 1024.

16.20 What does the following program do?

```
1   #include <iostream.h>
2
3   int mystery( unsigned );
4
5   int main()
6   {
7      unsigned x;
8
9      cout << "Enter an integer: ";
10     cin >> x;
11     cout << "The result is " << mystery( x ) << endl;
12     return 0;
13  }
14
15  int mystery( unsigned bits )
16  {
17     unsigned mask = 1 << 15, total = 0;
18
19     for ( int i = 0; i < 16; i++, bits <<= 1 )
20        if ( ( bits & mask ) == mask )
21           ++total;
22
23     return total % 2 == 0 ? 1 : 0;
24  }
```

ANS: The program prints 0 if the total number of 1s in the bit representation is odd, and prints a 1 if the number of bits is even.

16.21 Write a program that inputs a line of text with **istream** member function **getline** (see Chapter 11) into character array **s[100]**. Output the line in uppercase letters and lowercase letters.

ANS:

```
1   // Exercise 16.21 Solution
2   #include <iostream.h>
3   #include <ctype.h>
4
5   const int SIZE = 100;
6
7   int main()
8   {
9      char s[ SIZE ];
10     int i;
11
12     cout << "Enter a line of text:\n";
13     cin.getline( s, SIZE );
14     cout << "\nThe line in uppercase is:\n";
15
16     for ( i = 0; s[ i ] != '\0'; ++i )
17        cout.put( static_cast< char >( toupper( s[ i ] ) ) );
18
19     cout << "\n\nThe line in lowercase is:\n";
20
21     for ( i = 0; s[ i ] != '\0'; ++i )
22        cout.put( static_cast< char >( tolower( s[ i ] ) ) );
23
24     return 0;
25  }
```

```
Enter a line of text:
CPPTHP2 Instructor's Manual

The line in uppercase is:
CPPTHP2 INSTRUCTOR'S MANUAL

The line in lowercase is:
cppthp2 instructor's manual
```

16.22 Write a program that inputs 4 strings that represent integers, converts the strings to integers, sums the values, and prints the total of the 4 values.

ANS:

```
1   // Exercise 16.22 Solution
2   #include <iostream.h>
3   #include <stdlib.h>
4
5   const int SIZE = 6;
6
7   int main()
8   {
9      char stringValue[ SIZE ];
10     int sum = 0;
11
12     for ( int i = 1; i <= 4; ++i ) {
13        cout << "Enter an integer string: ";
14        cin >> stringValue;
15        sum += atoi( stringValue );
16     }
17
18     cout << "The total of the values is " << sum << endl;
19     return 0;
20  }
```

```
Enter an integer string: 11
Enter an integer string: 22
Enter an integer string: 44
Enter an integer string: 88

The total of the values is 165
```

16.23 Write a program that inputs 4 strings that represent floating-point values, converts the strings to double values, sums the values, and prints the total of the 4 values.

ANS:

```cpp
// Exercise 16.23 Solution
#include <iostream.h>
#include <iomanip.h>
#include <stdlib.h>

const int SIZE = 15;

int main()
{
   char stringValue[ SIZE ];
   double sum = 0.0;

   for ( int i = 1; i <= 4; ++i ) {
      cout << "Enter a floating point string: ";
      cin >> stringValue;
      sum += atof( stringValue );
   }

   cout.setf( ios::fixed | ios::showpoint );
   cout << "\nThe total of the values is " << setprecision( 3 ) << sum
        << endl;
   return 0;
}
```

```
Enter a floating point string: 1.1
Enter a floating point string: 1.2
Enter a floating point string: 1.3
Enter a floating point string: 1.4

The total of the values is 5.000
```

16.24 Write a program that inputs a line of text and a search string from the keyboard. Using function **strstr**, locate the first occurrence of the search string in the line of text, and assign the location to variable **searchPtr** of type **char ***. If the search string is found, print the remainder of the line of text beginning with the search string. Then, use **strstr** again to locate the next occurrence of the search string in the line of text. If a second occurrence is found, print the remainder of the line of text beginning with the second occurrence. Hint: The second call to **strstr** should contain **searchPtr + 1** as its first argument.

ANS:

```cpp
// Exercise 16.24 Solution
#include <iostream.h>
#include <string.h>

const int SIZE1 = 80, SIZE2 = 15;

int main()
{
   char text[ SIZE1 ], search[ SIZE2 ], *searchPtr;
```

```
10        cout << "Enter a line of text:\n";
11        cin.get( text, SIZE1 );
12        cout << "Enter a search string: ";
13        cin >> search;
14        searchPtr = strstr( text, search );
15
16        if ( searchPtr ) {
17           cout << "\nThe remainder of the line beginning with\n"
18                << "the first occurrence of\n\"" << search << "\":\n"
19                << searchPtr << '\n';
20           searchPtr = strstr( searchPtr + 1, search );
21
22           if ( searchPtr )
23              cout << "\nThe remainder of the line beginning with"
24                   << "\nthe second occurrence of\n\"" << search << "\":\n"
25                   << searchPtr << '\n';
26           else
27              cout << "The search string appeared only once.\n";
28        }
29        else
30           cout << "\"" << search << "\" not found.\n";
31
32        return 0;
33  }
```

```
Enter a line of text:
alphabet soup tastes good
Enter a search string: be
The remainder of the line beginning with
the first occurrence of
"as":
astes good
The search string appeared only once.
```

16.25 Write a program based on the program of Exercise 16.24 that inputs several lines of text and a search string, and uses function **strstr** to determine the total number of occurrences of the string in the lines of text. Print the result.

ANS:

```
1   // Exercise 16.25 Solution
2   #include <iostream.h>
3   #include <iomanip.h>
4   #include <string.h>
5   #include <ctype.h>
6
7   const int SIZE1 = 80, SIZE2 = 20;
8
9   int main()
10  {
11     char text[ 3 ][ SIZE1 ], search[ SIZE2 ], *searchPtr;
12     int count = 0, i;
13
14     cout << "Enter three lines of text:\n";
15
16     for ( i = 0; i <= 2; ++i )
17        cin.getline( &text[ i ][ 0 ], SIZE1 );
18
19     // make all characters lowercase
20     for ( i = 0; i <= 2; ++i )
21        for ( int j = 0; text[ i ][ j ] != '\0'; ++j ) {
22           char c = static_cast< char >( tolower( text[ i ][ j ] ) );
23           text[ i ][ j ] = c;
24        }
```

```
25
26       cout << "\nEnter a search string: ";
27       cin >> search;
28
29       for ( i = 0; i <= 2; ++i ) {
30          searchPtr = &text[ i ][ 0 ];
31
32          while ( searchPtr = strstr( searchPtr, search ) ) {
33             ++count;
34             ++searchPtr;
35          }
36       }
37
38       cout << "\nThe total occurrences of \"" << search
39            << "\" in the text is:" << setw( 3 ) << count << endl;
40
41       return 0;
42    }
```

```
Enter three lines of text:
first line of text
second line of text
third line of text

Enter a search string: in

The total occurrences of "in" in the text is:   3
```

16.26   Write a program that inputs several lines of text and a search character, and uses function **strchr** to determine the total number of occurrences of the character in the lines of text.

   ANS:

```
1    // Exercise 16.26 Solution
2    #include <iostream.h>
3    #include <iomanip.h>
4    #include <string.h>
5    #include <ctype.h>
6
7    const int SIZE = 80;
8
9    int main()
10   {
11      char text[ 3 ][ SIZE ], search, *searchPtr;
12      int count = 0, i;
13
14      cout << "Enter three lines of text:\n";
15
16      for ( i = 0; i <= 2; ++i )
17         cin.getline( &text[ i ][ 0 ], SIZE );
18
19      // convert all letters to lowercase
20      for ( i = 0; i <= 2; ++i )
21         for ( int j = 0; text[ i ][ j ] != '\0'; ++j ) {
22            char c = static_cast< char >( tolower( text[ i ][ j ] ) );
23            text[ i ][ j ] = c;
24         }
25
26      cout << "\nEnter a search character: ";
27      cin >> search;
28
29      for ( i = 0; i <= 2; ++i ) {
30         searchPtr = &text[ i ][ 0 ];
```

```
31          while ( searchPtr = strchr( searchPtr, search ) ) {
32             ++count;
33             ++searchPtr;
34          }
35       }
36
37       cout << "The total occurrences of \'" << search << "\' in the text is:"
38          << setw( 3 ) << count << endl;
39
40       return 0;
41    }
```

```
Enter three lines of text:
one line of text
two lines of text
three lines of text

Enter a search character: e
The total occurrences of 'e' in the text is:  9
```

16.27   Write a program based on the program of Exercise 16.26 that inputs several lines of text and uses function **strchr** to determine the total number of occurrences of each letter of the alphabet in the text. Uppercase and lowercase letters should be counted together. Store the totals for each letter in an array, and print the values in tabular format after the totals have been determined.

ANS:

```
1   // Exercise 16.27 Solution
2   #include <iostream.h>
3   #include <iomanip.h>
4   #include <string.h>
5   #include <ctype.h>
6
7   const int SIZE1 = 80, SIZE2 = 26;
8
9   int main()
10  {
11     char text[ 3 ][ SIZE1 ], *searchPtr;
12     int characters[ SIZE2 ] = { 0 }, count = 0;
13
14     cout << "Enter three lines of text:\n";
15
16     for ( int i = 0; i <= 2; ++i )
17        cin.getline( &text[ i ][ 0 ], SIZE1 );
18
19     // convert letters to lowercase
20     for ( int k = 0; k <= 2; ++k )
21        for ( int j = 0; text[ k ][ j ] != '\0'; ++j ) {
22           char c = static_cast< char >( tolower( text[ k ][ j ] ) );
23           text[ k ][ j ] = c;
24        }
25
26     for ( int q = 0; q < SIZE2; ++q ) {
27        count = 0;
28
29        for ( int j = 0; j <= 2; ++j ) {
30           searchPtr = &text[ j ][ 0 ];
31
32           while ( searchPtr = strchr( searchPtr, 'a' + q ) ) {
33              ++count;
34              ++searchPtr;
35           }
36        }
```

```
37
38          characters[ q ] = count;
39       }
40
41       cout << "\nThe total occurrences of each character:\n";
42
43       for ( int w = 0; w < SIZE2; ++w )
44          cout << setw( 3 ) << static_cast< char >( 'a' + w ) << ':' << setw( 3 )
45             << characters[ w ] << '\n';
46
47       return 0;
48    }
```

```
    Enter three lines of text:
    The yak ran away
    A giant parrot flew by
    The cat pounced on the rat

    The total occurrences of each character:
      a:   9
      b:   1
      c:   2
      d:   1
      e:   5
      f:   1
      g:   1
      h:   3
      i:   1
      j:   0
      k:   1
      l:   1
      m:   0
      n:   4
      o:   3
      p:   2
      q:   0
      r:   4
      s:   0
      t:   7
      u:   1
      v:   0
      w:   2
      x:   0
      y:   3
      z:   0
```

16.28   The chart in Appendix D shows the numeric code representations for the characters in the ASCII character set. Study this chart and then state whether each of the following is true or false.

a)   The letter "**A**" comes before the letter "**B**."

b)   The digit "**9**" comes before the digit "**0**."

c)   The commonly used symbols for addition, subtraction, multiplication, and division all come before any of the digits.

d)   The digits come before the letters.

e)   If a sort program sorts strings into ascending sequence, then the program will place the symbol for a right parenthesis before the symbol for a left parenthesis.

16.29   Write a program that reads a series of strings and prints only those strings beginning with the letter "**b**."
        ANS:

```
1    // Exercise 16.29 Solution
2    #include <iostream.h>
3    const int SIZE = 20;
```

```
4
5   int main()
6   {
7      char array[ 5 ][ SIZE ];
8      int i;
9
10     for ( i = 0; i <= 4; ++i ) {
11        cout << "Enter a string: ";
12        cin.getline( &array[ i ][ 0 ], SIZE );
13     }
14
15     cout << "The strings starting with 'b' are:\n";
16
17     for ( i = 0; i <= 4; ++i )
18        if ( array[ i ][ 0 ] == 'b' )
19           cout << &array[ i ][ 0 ] << '\n';
20
21     return 0;
22  }
```

```
Enter a string: c++
Enter a string: apple
Enter a string: burger
Enter a string: band
Enter a string: bag

The strings starting with 'b' are:
burger
band
bag
```

16.30   Write a program that reads a series of strings and prints only those strings that end with the letters "**ED**."
ANS:

```
1   // Exercise 16.30 Solution
2   #include <iostream.h>
3   #include <string.h>
4
5   const int SIZE = 20;
6
7   int main()
8   {
9      int length, i;
10     char array[ 5 ][ SIZE ];
11
12     for ( i = 0; i <= 4; ++i ) {
13        cout << "Enter a string: ";
14        cin.getline( &array[ i ][ 0 ], SIZE );
15     }
16
17     cout << "\nThe strings ending with \"ED\" are:\n";
18
19     for ( i = 0; i <= 4; ++i ) {
20        length = strlen( &array[ i ][ 0 ] );
21
22        if ( strcmp( &array[ i ][ length - 2 ], "ED" ) == 0 )
23           cout << &array[ i ][ 0 ] << '\n';
24     }
25
26     return 0;
27  }
```

```
Enter a string: MOVED
Enter a string: SAW
Enter a string: RAN
Enter a string: CARVED
Enter a string: PROVED

The strings ending with "ED" are:
MOVED
CARVED
PROVED
```

16.31   Write a program that inputs an ASCII code and prints the corresponding character. Modify this program so that it generates all possible three-digit codes in the range 000 to 255 and attempts to print the corresponding characters. What happens when this program is run?

ANS:

```
1   // Exercise 16.31 Solution
2   // NOTE: This solution is easily modified to print all
3   // possible three digit codes.
4   #include <iostream.h>
5
6   int main()
7   {
8      int c;
9
10      cout << "Enter an ASCII character code (EOF to end): ";
11      cin >> c;
12
13      while ( c != EOF ) {
14         if ( c >= 0 && c <= 255 )
15            cout << "The corresponding character is '"
16                 << static_cast< char > ( c ) << "\'\n";
17         else
18            cout << "Invalid character code\n";
19
20         cout << "\nEnter an ASCII character code (EOF to end): ";
21         cin >> c;
22      }
23
24      return 0;
25   }
```

```
Enter an ASCII character code (EOF to end): 44
The corresponding character is ','

Enter an ASCII character code (EOF to end): 77
The corresponding character is 'M'

Enter an ASCII character code (EOF to end): 26
The corresponding character is '
...
```

16.32   Using the ASCII character chart in Appendix D as a guide, write your own versions of the character handling functions in Fig. 16.16.

ANS:

```
1   // Exercise 16.32 Solution
2   #include <iostream.h>
3
```

```cpp
 4   int isDigit( int );
 5   int isAlpha( int );
 6   int isAlNum( int );
 7   int isLower( int );
 8   int isUpper( int );
 9   int isSpace( int );
10   int isPunct( int );
11   int isPrint( int );
12   int isGraph( int );
13   int toLower( int );
14   int toUpper( int );
15
16   int main()
17   {
18      int v;
19      char a, header[] = "According to",
20              *names[] = { "isDigit ", "isAlpha ", "isAlNum ",
21                           "isLower ", "isUpper ", "isSpace ",
22                           "isPunct ", "isPrint ", "isGraph ",
23                           "toLower ", "toUpper " },
24              *names2[] = { "digit", "letter", "letter/digit", "lowercase",
25                            "uppercase", "space", "punctuation", "print", "graph",
26                            "converted lowercase", "converted uppercase" };
27      int ( *f[] )( int ) = { isDigit, isAlpha, isAlNum, isLower,
28                              isUpper, isSpace, isPunct, isPrint,
29                              isGraph, toLower, toUpper };
30
31      cout << "Enter a character: ";
32      cin >> a;
33
34      for ( int k = 0; k < 11; ++k ) {
35         v = ( *f[ k ] )( static_cast< int >( a ) );
36         cout.write( header, 13 );
37         cout << names[ k ] << a << ( !v ? " is not a " : " is a " )
38              << names2[ k ] << " character\n";
39      }
40
41      return 0;
42   }
43
44   // Normally these would return bool, but int return type
45   // is consistent with the ctype library.
46   int isDigit( int c )
47   {
48      return ( c >= 48 && c <= 57 ) ? 1 : 0;
49   }
50
51   int isAlpha( int c )
52   {
53      return ( ( c >= 65 && c <= 90 ) || ( c >= 97 && c <= 122 ) ) ? 1 : 0;
54   }
55
56   int isAlNum( int c )
57   {
58      return ( isDigit( c ) == 1 || isAlpha( c ) == 1 ) ? 1 : 0;
59   }
60
61   int isLower( int c )
62   {
63      return ( c >= 97 && c <= 122 ) ? 1 : 0;
64   }
65
```

```
66   int isUpper( int c )
67   {
68      return ( c >= 65 && c <= 90 ) ? 1 : 0;
69   }
70
71   int isSpace( int c )
72   {
73      return ( ( c == 32 ) || ( c >= 9 && c <= 13 ) ) ? 1 : 0;
74   }
75
76   int isPunct( int c )
77   {
78      return ( isAlNum( c ) == 0 && isSpace( c ) == 0 ) ? 1 : 0;
79   }
80
81   int isPrint( int c )
82   {
83      return ( c >= 32 && c <= 126 ) ? 1 : 0;
84   }
85
86   int isGraph( int c )
87   {
88      return ( c >= 33 && c <= 126 ) ? 1 : 0;
89   }
90
91   int toLower( int c )
92   {
93      return ( isUpper( c ) == 1 ) ? c + 32 : c;
94   }
95
96   int toUpper( int c )
97   {
98      return ( isLower( c ) == 1 ) ? c - 32 : c;
99   }
```

```
Enter a character: U
According to isDigit U is not a digit character
According to isAlpha U is a letter character
According to isAlNum U is a letter/digit character
According to isLower U is not a lowercase character
According to isUpper U is a uppercase character
According to isSpace U is not a space character
According to isPunct U is not a punctuation character
According to isPrint U is a print character
According to isGraph U is a graph character
According to toLower U is a converted lowercase character
According to toUpper U is a converted uppercase character
```

16.33   Write your own versions of the functions in Fig. 16.20 for converting strings to numbers.

16.34   Write your own versions of the functions in Fig. 16.27 for searching strings.

16.35   Write your own versions of the functions in Fig. 16.34 for manipulating blocks of memory.

16.36   *(Project: A Spelling Checker)* Many popular word processing software packages have built-in spell checkers. We used the spell-checking capabilities of Microsoft Word 5.0 in preparing this book and discovered that no matter how careful we thought we were in writing a chapter, Word was always able to find a few more spelling errors than we were able to catch manually.

In this project, you are asked to develop your own spell-checker utility. We make suggestions to help get you started. You should then consider adding more capabilities. You may find it helpful to use a computerized dictionary as a source of words.

Why do we type so many words with incorrect spellings? In some cases, it is because we simply do not know the correct spelling, so we make a "best guess." In some cases, it is because we transpose two letters (e.g., "defualt" instead of "default"). Sometimes we double-type a letter accidentally (e.g., "hanndy" instead of "handy"). Sometimes we type a nearby key instead of the one we intended (e.g., "biryhday" instead of "birthday"). And so on.

Design and implement a spell-checker program in C++. Your program maintains an array **wordList** of character strings. You can either enter these strings or obtain them from a computerized dictionary.

Your program asks a user to enter a word. The program then looks up that word in the **wordList** array. If the word is present in the array, your program should print "**Word is spelled correctly**."

If the word is not present in the array, your program should print "**word is not spelled correctly**." Then your program should try to locate other words in **wordList** that might be the word the user intended to type. For example, you can try all possible single transpositions of adjacent letters to discover that the word "default" is a direct match to a word in **wordList**. Of course, this implies that your program will check all other single transpositions such as "edfault," "dfeault," "deafult," "defalut," and "defautl." When you find a new word that matches one in **wordList**, print that word in a message such as, "**Did you mean "default?"**."

Implement other tests such as replacing each double letter with a single letter and any other tests you can develop to improve the value of your spell checker.

Chapter 17 Solutions

The Preprocessor

Solutions

17.4   Write a program that defines a macro with one argument to compute the volume of a sphere. The program should compute the volume for spheres of radius 1 to 10, and print the results in tabular format. The formula for the volume of a sphere is:

$$(4 / 3) * \pi * r^3$$

where π is **3.14159**.
   ANS:

```
1   // Exercise 17.4 Solution
2   #include <iostream.h>
3   #include <iomanip.h>
4   #define PI 3.14159
5
6   // define macro for sphere volume
7   #define SPHEREVOLUME( r ) ( 4.0 / 3.0 * PI * ( r ) * ( r ) * ( r ) )
8
9   int main()
10  {
11      // print header
12      cout << setw( 10 ) << "Radius" << setw( 10 ) << "Volume\n";
13
14      cout.setf( ios::fixed | ios::showpoint );
15      for ( int i = 1; i <= 10; ++i )
16          cout << setw( 10 ) << i << setw( 10 ) << setprecision( 3 )
17              << SPHEREVOLUME( i ) << '\n';
18
19      return 0;
20  }
```

```
Radius    Volume
     1      4.189
     2     33.510
     3    113.097
     4    268.082
     5    523.598
     6    904.778
     7   1436.754
     8   2144.659
     9   3053.625
    10   4188.787
```

17.5   Write a program that produces the following output:

```
The sum of x and y is 13
```

The program should define macro **SUM** with two arguments, **x** and **y**, and use **SUM** to produce the output.

ANS:

```
1   // Exercise 17.5 Solution
2   #include <iostream.h>
3
4   #define SUM( x, y ) ( ( x ) + ( y ) )
5
6   int main()
7   {
8      cout << "The sum of 6 and 7 is " << SUM( 6, 7 ) << endl;
9      return 0;
10  }
```

17.6   Write a program that uses macro **MINIMUM2** to determine the smallest of two numeric values. Input the values from the keyboard.

ANS:

```
1   // Exercise 17.6 Solution
2   #include <iostream.h>
3   #include <iomanip.h>
4
5   #define MINIMUM2( X, Y ) ( ( X ) < ( Y ) ? ( X ) : ( Y ) )
6
7   int main()
8   {
9      int a, b;
10     double c, d;
11
12     cout << "Enter two integers: ";
13     cin >> a >> b;
14     cout << "The minimum of " << a << " and " << b << " is " << MINIMUM2( a, b )
15          << "\n\n";
16
17     cout << "Enter two doubles: ";
18     cin >> c >> d;
19
20     cout.setf( ios::fixed | ios::showpoint );
21     cout << "The minimum of " << setprecision( 2 ) << c << " and " << d
22          << " is " << MINIMUM2( c, d ) << '\n';
23
24     return 0;
25  }
```

```
Enter two integers: 8 22
The minimum of 8 and 22 is 8

Enter two doubles: 73.46 22.22
The minimum of 73.46 and 22.22 is 22.22
```

17.7   Write a program that uses macro **MINIMUM3** to determine the smallest of three numeric values. Macro **MINIMUM3** should use macro **MINIMUM2** defined in Exercise 17.6 to determine the smallest number. Input the values from the keyboard.

ANS:

```
1   // Exercise 17.7 Solution
2   #include <iostream.h>
3   #include <iomanip.h>
4
5   #define MINIMUM2( X, Y ) ( ( X ) < ( Y ) ? ( X ) : ( Y ) )
6   #define MINIMUM3( U, V, W ) ( MINIMUM2( W, MINIMUM2( U, V ) ) )
```

```
 7  int main()
 8  {
 9     int a, b, c;
10     double d, e, f;
11
12     cout << "Enter three integers: ";
13     cin >> a >> b >> c;
14     cout << "The minimum of " << a << ", " << b << ", and " << c
15          << " is " << MINIMUM3( a, b, c ) << "\n\nEnter three doubles: ";
16
17     cin >> d >> e >> f;
18     cout.setf( ios::fixed | ios::showpoint );
19     cout << "The minimum of " << setprecision( 2 ) << d << ", "
20          << e << ", and " << f << " is " << MINIMUM3( d, e, f ) << '\n';
21
22     return 0;
23  }
```

```
Enter three integers: 44 22 55
The minimum of 44, 22, and 55 is 22

Enter three doubles: 9.5 7.3 3.22
The minimum of 9.50, 7.30, and 3.22 is 3.22
```

17.8 Write a program that uses macro **PRINT** to print a string value.

ANS:

```
 1  // Exercise 17.8 Solution
 2  #include <iostream.h>
 3
 4  #define PRINT( s ) cout << ( s )
 5  #define SIZE 20
 6
 7  int main()
 8  {
 9     char text[ SIZE ];
10
11     PRINT( "Enter a string: " );
12     cin >> text;
13
14     PRINT( "The string entered was: " );
15     PRINT( text );
16     PRINT( endl );
17
18     return 0;
19  }
```

```
Enter a string: HELLO
The string entered was: HELLO
```

17.9 Write a program that uses macro **PRINTARRAY** to print an array of integers. The macro should receive the array and the number of elements in the array as arguments.

ANS:

```
 1  // Exercise 17.9 Solution
 2  #include <iostream.h>
 3  #include <iomanip.h>
 4
 5  #define PRINTARRAY( A, N )  for ( int i = 0; i < ( N ); ++i ) \
 6                                 cout << setw( 3 ) << A[ i ]
```

```
7
8    #define SIZE 10
9
10   int main()
11   {
12      int b[ SIZE ] = { 2, 4, 6, 8, 10, 12, 14, 16, 18, 20 };
13
14      cout << "The array values are:\n";
15      PRINTARRAY( b, SIZE );
16      cout << endl;
17      return 0;
18   }
```

```
The array values are:
   2   4   6   8  10  12  14  16  18  20
```

17.10 Write a program that uses macro **SUMARRAY** to sum the values in a numeric array. The macro should receive the array and the number of elements in the array as arguments.

ANS:

```
1    // Exercise 17.10 Solution
2    #include <iostream.h>
3
4    #define SUMMARRAY( A, S )  for ( int c = 0; c < S; ++c )    \
5                                  sum += A[ c ];
6    #define SIZE 10
7
8    int main()
9    {
10      int array[ SIZE ] = { 1, 2, 3, 4, 5, 6, 7, 8, 9, 10 }, sum = 0;
11
12      SUMMARRAY( array, SIZE );
13      cout << "Sum is " << sum << endl;
14      return 0;
15   }
```

```
Sum is 55
```

17.11 Rewrite the solutions to 17.4 to 17.10 as **inline** functions.

ANS:

```
1    // Exercise 17.11 Solution
2    // NOTE: Exercises 17.9 and 17.10 cannot be
3    // expanded inline because they require the
4    // use of for repitition structures
5    #include <iostream.h>
6    #include <iomanip.h>
7    #define PI 3.14159
8
9    inline double sphereVolume( int r )
10      { return 4.0 / 3.0 * PI * ( r ) * ( r ) * ( r ); }
11   inline int sum( int x, int y ) { return x + y; }
12   inline int minimum2( int x, int y ) { return x < y ? x : y; }
13   inline int minimum3( int x, int y, int z )
14      { return minimum2( z, minimum2( x, y ) ); }
15   inline void print( char const * const cPtr ) { cout << cPtr; }
16
```

```
17  int main()
18  {
19     // print header
20     cout << "Function sphereVolume as an inline function:\n"
21         << setw( 10 ) << "Radius" << setw( 10 ) << "Volume\n";
22
23     cout.setf( ios::fixed | ios::showpoint );
24     for ( int i = 1; i <= 10; ++i )
25        cout << setw( 10 ) << i << setw( 10 ) << setprecision( 3 )
26            << sphereVolume( i ) << '\n';
27
28     int x = 6, y = 7;
29     cout << "\nFunction sum as an inline function:\n"
30         << "The sum of " << x << " and " << y << " is "
31         << sum( 6, 7 ) << '\n';
32
33     cout << "\nFunction minimum2 as an inline function:\n"
34         << "The minimum of " << x << " and " << y << " is "
35         << minimum2( x, y ) << '\n';
36
37     int z = 4;
38     cout << "\nFunction minimum3 as an inline function:\n"
39         << "The minimum of " << x << ", " << y << " and " << z << " is "
40         << minimum3( x, y, z ) << '\n';
41
42     char s[] = "string...";
43     cout << "\nFunction print as an inline function:\n"
44         << "The output of print is: ";
45     print( s );
46     cout << endl;
47     return 0;
48  }
```

```
Function sphereVolume as an inline function:
    Radius    Volume
         1     4.189
         2    33.510
         3   113.097
         4   268.082
         5   523.598
         6   904.778
         7  1436.754
         8  2144.659
         9  3053.625
        10  4188.787

Function sum as an inline function:
The sum of 6 and 7 is 13

Function minimum2 as an inline function:
The minimum of 6 and 7 is 6

Function minimum3 as an inline function:
The minimum of 6, 7 and 4 is 4

Function print as an inline function:
The output of print is: string...
```

17.12 For each of the following macros, identify the possible problems (if any) when the preprocessor expands the macros.

a) `#define SQR( x ) x * x`

ANS: When **x** is an expression, such as **z - y**.

b) `#define SQR( x ) ( x * x )`

ANS: When **x** is an expression, such as **z - y**.

c) `#define SQR( x ) ( x ) * ( x )`

ANS: When `SQR( x )` is used in an expression such as `12 / SQR( 2 )`.

d) `#define SQR( x ) ( ( x ) * ( x ) )`

ANS: No problems.

Chapter 18 Solutions

C Legacy Code Topics

18.2   Write a program that calculates the product of a series of integers that are passed to function **product** using a variable-length argument list. Test your function with several calls each with a different number of arguments.

   ANS:

```
1   // Exercise 18.2 Solution
2   #include <iostream.h>
3   #include <stdarg.h>
4
5   int sum( int, ... );
6
7   int main()
8   {
9      int a = 1, b = 2, c = 3, d = 4, e = 5;
10
11     cout << "a = " << a << ", b = " << b << ", c = " << c << ", d = " << d
12         << ", e = " << e << "\n\n";
13     cout << "The sum of a and b is: " << sum( 2, a, b )
14         << "\nThe sum of a, b, and c is: " << sum( 3, a, b, c )
15         << "\nThe sum of a, b, c, and d is: " << sum( 4, a, b, c, d )
16         << "\nThe sum of a, b, c, d, and e is: " << sum( 5, a, b, c, d, e )
17         << endl;
18     return 0;
19  }
20
21  int sum( int i, ... )
22  {
23     int total = 0;
24     va_list ap;
25
26     va_start( ap, i );
27
28     // calculate total
29     for ( int j = 1; j <= i; ++j )
30        total += va_arg( ap, int );
31
32     va_end( ap );
33     return total;
34  }
```

```
   a = 1, b = 2, c = 3, d = 4, e = 5

   The sum of a and b is: 3
   The sum of a, b, and c is: 6
   The sum of a, b, c, and d is: 10
   The sum of a, b, c, d, and e is: 15
```

18.3   Write a program that prints the command-line arguments of the program.
           ANS:

```
1  // Exercise 18.3 Solution
2  #include <iostream.h>
3
4  int main( int argc, char *argv[] )
5  {
6     cout << "The command line arguments are:\n";
7
8     for ( int i = 0; i < argc; ++i )
9        cout << argv[ i ] << ' ';
10
11    return 0;
12 }
```

```
c:\>p18_03.exe arg1 arg2 arg3
The command line arguments are:
p18_03.exe arg1 arg2 arg3
```

18.4   Write a program that sorts an integer array into ascending order or descending order. The program should use command-line arguments to pass either argument **-a** for ascending order or **-d** for descending order. (Note: This is the standard format for passing options to a program in UNIX.)
           ANS:

```
1  // Exercise 18.4 Solution
2  #include <iostream.h>
3  #include <iomanip.h>
4
5  const int SIZE = 100;
6
7  void swap( int * const, int * const );
8
9  int main( int argc, char *argv[] )
10 {
11    int a[ SIZE ];
12    bool order;
13
14    if ( argc != 2 )
15       cout << "Usage: p18_4 -option\n";
16    else {
17       cout << "Enter up to " << SIZE << " integers (EOF to end input): ";
18
19       for ( int count = 0; !( cin.eof() ) && count < SIZE; ++count )
20          cin >> a[ count ];
21
22       // count is incremented before for loop continuation fails
23       --count;
24       order = ( argv[ 1 ][ 1 ] == 'd' ) ? true : false;
25
26       for ( int i = 1; i < count; ++i )
27          for ( int j = 0; j < count - 1; ++j )
28             if ( order ) {
29                if ( a[ i ] > a[ j ] )
30                   swap( &a[ i ], &a[ j ] );
31             }
32             else if ( a[ i ] < a[ j ] )
33                swap( &a[ j ], &a[ i ] );
34
35       cout << "\n\nThe sorted array is:\n";
36
```

```
37              for ( int j = 0; j < count; ++j )
38                  cout << setw( 3 ) << a[ j ];
39
40              cout << '\n';
41          }
42
43      return 0;
44  }
45
46  void swap( int * const xPtr, int * const yPtr )
47  {
48      int temp;
49
50      temp = *xPtr;
51      *xPtr = *yPtr;
52      *yPtr = temp;
53  }
```

```
c:\>p18_04.exe -d
Enter up to 100 integers (EOF to end input): 77 2 -8 9 44 8 76 41 99
The sorted array is:
 99 77 76 44 41  9  8  2 -8
```

18.5   Read the manuals for your system to determine what signals are supported by the signal handling library (**signal.h**). Write a program with signal handlers for the signals **SIGABRT** and **SIGINT**. The program should test the trapping of these signals by calling function **abort** to generate a signal of type **SIGABRT**, and by typing **<ctrl> c** to generate a signal of type **SIGINT**.

18.6   Write a program that dynamically allocates an array of integers. The size of the array should be input from the keyboard. The elements of the array should be assigned values input from the keyboard. Print the values of the array. Next, reallocate the memory for the array to half of the current number of elements. Print the values remaining in the array to confirm that they match the first half of the values in the original array.

ANS:

```
1   // Exercise 18.6 Solution
2   #include <iostream.h>
3   #include <iomanip.h>
4   #include <stdlib.h>
5
6   int main()
7   {
8       int count, *array;
9
10      cout << "This program dynamically allocates an array of integers."
11           << "\nEnter the number of elements in the array: ";
12      cin >> count;
13
14      // allocate memory
15      array = static_cast< int * >( calloc( count, sizeof( int ) ) );
16
17      for ( int i = 0; i < count; ++i ) {
18          cout << "Enter an integer: ";
19          cin >> array[ i ];
20      }
21
22      cout << "\nThe elements of the array are:\n";
23
24      for ( int j = 0; j < count; ++j )
25          cout << setw( 3 ) << array[ j ];
26
```

```
27      // reallocate to half the original size
28      realloc( array, count / 2 * sizeof( int ) );
29      cout << "\n\nThe elements of the array after reallocation are:\n";
30
31      for ( int k = 0; k < count / 2; ++k )
32         cout << setw( 3 ) << array[ k ];
33
34      cout << '\n';
35      return 0;
36   }
```

```
This program dynamically allocates an array of integers.
Enter the number of elements in the array: 5
Enter an integer: 1
Enter an integer: 2
Enter an integer: 3
Enter an integer: 4
Enter an integer: 5

The elements of the array are:
   1  2  3  4  5

The elements of the array after reallocation are:
   1  2
```

18.7   Write a program that takes two file name command-line arguments, reads the characters from the first file one at a time, and writes the characters in reverse order to the second file.

ANS:

```
1   // Exercise 18.7 Solution
2   #include <iostream.h>
3   #include <fstream.h>
4
5   void reverseFile( istream&, ostream& );
6
7   int main( int argc, char *argv[] )
8   {
9      ifstream inFile( argv[ 1 ], ios::in );
10     ofstream outFile( argv[ 2 ], ios::out );
11
12     if ( argc != 3 )
13        cout << "Usage: copy infile outfile\n";
14     else
15        if ( inFile )
16           if ( outFile )
17              reverseFile( inFile, outFile );
18           else
19              cerr << "File \"" << argv[ 2 ] << "\" could not be opened\n";
20        else
21           cerr << "File \"" << argv[ 1 ] << "\" could not be opened\n";
22
23     return 0;
24   }
25
26   void reverseFile( istream &in, ostream &out )
27   {
28      int c;
29
30      if ( ( c = in.get() ) != EOF )
31         reverseFile( in, out );
32      else
33         return;  // do not write EOF character
```

```
34      out.put( static_cast< char > ( c ) );
35  }
```

```
c:\>p18_07.exe test.txt copy.txt
```

18.8   Write a program that uses **goto** statements to simulate a nested looping structure that prints a square of asterisks, as follows:

```
*****
*   *
*   *
*   *
*****
```

The program should use only the following three output statements:

```
cout << '*';
cout << ' ';
cout << endl;
```

ANS:

```
1   // Exercise 18.8 Solution
2   #include <iostream.h>
3
4   int main()
5   {
6      int size, row = 0, col;
7
8      cout << "Enter the side length of the square: ";
9      cin >> size;
10
11     start:              // label
12        ++row;
13        cout << '\n';
14
15        if ( row > size )
16           goto end;
17
18        col = 1;
19
20        innerLoop:        // label
21           if ( col > size )
22              goto start;
23
24           cout << ( row == 1 || row == size || col == 1 ||
25                     col == size ? '*' : ' ' );
26           ++col;
27           goto innerLoop;
28
29     end:                // label
30
31     return 0;
32  }
```

```
Enter the side length of the square: 5
*****
*   *
*   *
*   *\
*****
```

18.9 Provide the definition for **union Data** containing **char c**, **short s**, **long l**, **float f**, and **double d**.
ANS:

```
union Data {
   char c;
   short s;
   long l;
   float f;
   double d;
};
```

18.10 Create **union Integer** with members **char c**, **short s**, **int i**, and **long l**. Write a program that inputs values of type **char**, **short**, **int** and **long**, and stores the values in **union** variables of type **union Integer**. Each union variable should be printed as a **char**, a **short**, an **int**, and a **long**. Do the values always print correctly?

ANS:

```
1   // Exercise 18.10 Solution
2   #include <iostream.h>
3
4   union Integer {
5      char c;
6      short s;
7      int i;
8      long l;
9   };
10
11  void printUnion( Integer );
12
13  int main()
14  {
15     Integer value;
16
17     cout << "Enter a character: ";
18     value.c = static_cast< char >( cin.get() );
19     printUnion( value );
20
21     cout << "Enter a short: ";
22     cin >> value.s;
23     printUnion( value );
24
25     cout << "Enter an int: ";
26     cin >> value.i;
27     printUnion( value );
28
29     cout << "Enter a long: ";
30     cin >> value.l;
31     printUnion( value );
32
33     return 0;
34  }
35
36  void printUnion( Integer x )
37  {
38      cout << "Current values in union Integer are:\n"
39           << "char c  = " << x.c
40           << "\nshort s = " << x.s
41           << "\nint i   = " << x.i
42           << "\nlong l  = " << x.l << "\n\n";
43  }
```

```
      Enter a character: w
      Current values in union Integer are:
      char c  = w
      short s = 119
      int i   = 119
      long l  = 119

      Enter a short: 5
      Current values in union Integer are:
      char c  = ?
      short s = 5
      int i   = 5
      long l  = 5

      Enter an int: 9999
      Current values in union Integer are:
      char c  = ¤
      short s = 9999
      int i   = 9999
      long l  = 9999

      Enter a long: 1000000
      Current values in union Integer are:
      char c  = @
      short s = 16960
      int i   = 1000000
      long l  = 1000000
```

18.11 Create **union FloatingPoint** with members **float f**, **double d**, and **long double l**. Write a program that inputs value of type **float**, **double**, and **long double**, and stores the values in **union** variables of type **union FloatingPoint**. Each **union** variable should be printed as a **float**, a **double**, and a **long double**. Do the values always print correctly?

　　　　ANS:

```cpp
1   // Exercise 18.11 Solution
2   #include <iostream.h>
3
4   union FloatingPoint {
5      float f;
6      double d;
7      long double l;
8   };
9
10  void printUnion( FloatingPoint );
11
12  int main()
13  {
14     FloatingPoint value;
15
16     cout << "Enter a float: ";
17     cin >> value.f;
18     printUnion( value );
19
20     cout << "Enter a double: ";
21     cin >> value.d;
22     printUnion( value );
23
24     cout << "Enter a long double: ";
25     cin >> value.l;
26     printUnion( value );
27
```

```
28      return 0;
29  }
30
31  void printUnion( FloatingPoint x )
32  {
33      cout << "Current values in union Integer are:\n"
34           << "float f  = " << x.f
35           << "\ndouble d = " << x.d
36           << "\nlong double l  = " << x.l << "\n\n";
37  }
```

```
Enter a float: 4.567
Current values in union Integer are:
float f  = 4.567
double d = 9.78688e-307
long double l  = 9.78688e-307

Enter a double: 9998888.765
Current values in union Integer are:
float f  = 3.24255e-024
double d = 9.99889e+006
long double l  = 9.99889e+006

Enter a long double: 5e306
Current values in union Integer are:
float f  = 0.0210515
double d = 5e+306
long double l  = 5e+306
```

18.12 Given the **union**

```
union A {
    float y;
    char *z;
};
```

which of the following are correct statements for initializing the **union**?

a) `A p = B;  // B is of same type as A`
ANS: Correct.
b) `A q = x; // x is a float`
ANS: Incorrect.
c) `A r = 3.14159;`
ANS: Incorrect.
d) `A s = { 79.63 };`
ANS: Correct.
e) `A t = { "Hi There!" };`
ANS: Incorrect.
f) `A u = { 3.14159, "Pi" };`
ANS: Incorrect.

Chapter 19 Solutions

Class *string* and String Stream Processing

Solutions

19.4 Fill in the blanks in each of the following:

    a) Functions _____, _____, and _____ convert **string**s to C-style strings.
    ANS: data, c_str, copy

    b) Function _____ is used for assignment.
    ANS: assign

    c) _____ is the return type of function **rbegin**.
    ANS: string::reverse_iterator

    d) Function _____ is used to retrieve a substring.
    ANS: substr

19.5 State which of the following statements are true and which are false. If a statement is false, explain why.

    a) **string**s are null terminated.
    ANS: False. **string**s are not necessarily null terminated.

    b) Function **max_size** returns the maximum size for a **string**.
    ANS: True.

    c) Function **at** is capable of throwing an **out_of_range** exception.
    ANS: True.

    d) Function **begin** returns an **iterator**.
    ANS: True (**string::iterator** is more precise).

    e) **string**s are passed by reference by default.
    ANS: False. By default, **string**s are passed by value.

19.6 Find any error(s) in each of the following and explain how to correct it (them).

    a) **std::cout << s.data() << std::endl;   // s is "hello"**
    ANS: The array returned by **data** is not null terminated.

    b) **erase(s.rfind("x"), 1);   // s is "xenon"**
    ANS: Function **erase** is a **string** class member function (i.e., **erase** must be called by an object of type **string**).

    c)
```
string& foo( void )
{
   string s( "Hello" );
   ...   // other statements of function
   return;
}
```
    ANS: A value is not being returned from the function (i.e., the **return** statement should be **return s;**). The **return** type should be **string** not **string&**.

19.7 (*Simple Encryption*) Some information on the Internet may be encrypted with a simple algorithm known as "rot13"—which rotates each character by 13 positions in the alphabet. Thus, **'a'** corresponds to **'n'**, **'x'** corresponds to **'k'**. rot13 is an example of *symmetric key encryption*. With symmetric key encryption, both the encrypter and decrypter use the same key.

    a) Write a program that encrypts a message using rot13.

    b) Write a program that decrypts the scrambled message using 13 as the key.

    c) After writing the programs of part (a) and part (b) briefly answer the following question: If you did not know the key for part (b), how difficult do you think it would be to break the code using any resources available? What if you had access to substantial computing power (e.g., Cray supercomputers)? In Exercise 19.27 we ask you to write a program to accomplish this.

ANS:

```
1   // Execise 19.07 Part A Solution
2   // When solving Part B of this exercise, you
3   // might find it more convenient to only use
4   // uppercase letters for your input.
5   #include <iostream>
6   #include <string>
7   using namespace std;
8
9   int main()
10  {
11     string m;
12     int key = 13;   // Our key for encryption
13
14     cout << "Enter a string:";
15     getline( cin, m );
16
17     string::iterator mi = m.begin();
18
19     while ( mi != m.end() ) {
20        *mi += key;
21        ++mi;
22     }
23
24     cout << "\nEncypted string is:" << m << endl;
25
26     return 0;
27  }
```

```
Enter a string:JAMES BOND IS 007
Encypted string is:WNZR`-O\[Q-V`-==D
```

```
1   // Execise 19.07 Part B Solution
2   #include <iostream>
3   #include <string>
4   using namespace std;
5
6   int main()
7   {
8      string m;
9      int key = 13;   // Our key for decryption
10
11     cout << "Enter encrypted string:";
12     getline( cin, m );
13
14     string::iterator mi = m.begin();
15
16     while ( mi != m.end() ) {
17        *mi -= key;
18        ++mi;
19     }
20
21     cout << "\nDecypted string is:" << m << endl;
22
23     return 0;
24  }
```

```
Enter encrypted string:WNZR`-O\[Q-V`-==D
Decypted string is:JAMES BOND IS 007
```

19.8   Write a program using iterators that demonstrates the use of functions **rbegin** and **rend**.

```
1   // Exercise 19.8 Solution
2   // Program demonstrates rend and rbegin.
3   #include <iostream>
4   #include <string>
5   using namespace std;
6
7   int main()
8   {
9      string s( "abcdefghijklmnopqrstuvwxyz" );
10     string::reverse_iterator re = s.rend(), rb = s.rbegin();
11
12     cout << "Using rend() string is: ";
13     while ( re >= s.rbegin() ) {
14        cout << *re;
15        --re;
16     }
17
18     cout << "\nUsing rbegin() string is: ";
19     while ( rb != s.rend() ) {
20        cout << *rb;
21        ++rb;
22     }
23
24     cout << endl;
25     return 0;
26  }
```

```
Using rend() string is: _abcdefghijklmnopqrstuvwxyz
Using rbegin() string is: zyxwvutsrqponmlkjihgfedcba
```

19.9   Write your own versions of functions **data** and **c_str**.

19.10   Write a program that reads in several **string**s and prints only those ending in "**r**" or "**ay**". Only lowercase letters should be considered.

```
1   // Exercise 19.10 Solution
2   // Program determines if string ends in 'r'
3   // or "ay".
4   #include <iostream>
5   #include <string>
6   using namespace std;
7
8   int main()
9   {
10     string s[ 5 ];
11
12     for ( int i = 0; i < 5; ++i ) {
13        cout << "Enter a word: ";
14        cin >> s[ i ];
15     }
16
```

```
17      for ( int j = 0; j < 5; ++j ) {
18         if ( ( ( s[ j ].rfind( "ay" ) == s[ j ].length() - 2 ) )
19              || ( s[ j ].rfind( "r" ) == s[ j ].length() - 1 ) )
20            cout << s[ j ] << endl;
21      }
22
23      return 0;
24   }
```

```
Enter a word: bicycle
Enter a word: car
Enter a word: tree
Enter a word: canary
Enter a word: iron
car
```

19.11   Write a program that demonstrates passing a **string** both by reference and by value.

```
1    // Exercise 19.11 Solution
2    // Program passes a string by value and
3    // passes a string by reference.
4    #include <iostream>
5    #include <string>
6    using namespace std;
7
8    void byValue( string );
9    void byReference( string& );
10
11   int main()
12   {
13      string s = "ANSI C++ draft standard";
14
15      cout << "Original string: " << s;
16
17      byValue( s );
18      cout << "\nAfter calling byValue: " << s;
19
20      byReference( s );
21      cout << "\nAfter calling byReference: " << s << endl;
22
23      return 0;
24   }
25
26   void byValue( string s )
27   {
28      s.erase( 0, 4 );
29   }
30
31   void byReference( string& sRef )
32   {
33      sRef.erase( 0, 9 );
34   }
```

```
Original string: ANSI C++ draft standard
After calling byValue: ANSI C++ draft standard
After calling byReference: draft standard
```

19.12   Write a program that separately inputs a first name and a last name and then concatenates the two into a new **string**.

```
1   // Exercise 19.12 Solution
2   // Program reads a first name and
3   // last name and concatenates the two.
4   #include <iostream>
5   #include <string>
6   #include <iomanip>
7   using namespace std;
8
9   int main()
10  {
11     string first, last;
12
13     cout << "Enter first name: ";
14     cin >> first;
15
16     cout << "Enter last name: ";
17     cin >> last;
18
19     first.append( " " ).append( last );
20     cout << "The full name is: " << first << endl;
21
22     return 0;
23  }
```

```
Enter first name: Hans
Enter last name: Gruber
The full name is: Hans Gruber
```

19.13   Write a program that plays the game of hangman. The program should pick a word (which is either coded directly into the program or read from a text file) and displays the following:

> **Guess the word: XXXXXX**

Each **X** represents a letter. If the user guesses correctly, the program should display:

> **Congratulations!!! You guessed my word. Play again? yes/no**

The appropriate response **yes** or **no** should be input. If the user guesses incorrectly, display the

appropriate body part.

After seven incorrect guesses, the user should be hung. The display should look like:

```
     o
    /|\
     |
    / \
```

After each guess you want to display all their guesses.

```
1   // Exercise 19.13 Solution
2   #include <iostream>
3   #include <string>
4   #include <ctype.h>
5   #include <iomanip>
6   #include <stdlib.h>
7   using namespace std;
8
9   int main()
10  {
11     string response;   // "yes"/"no" input from user
12     int w = 0;         // index for current word
13     const int WORDS = 4;   // total number of words
14
```

```
15      do {
16         const char body[] = " o/|\\|/\\"; // body parts
17         string words[ WORDS ] = { "MACAW", "SADDLE", "TOASTER", "XENOCIDE" };
18         string xword( words[ w ].length(), '?' ); // masked display
19         string::iterator i, ix = xword.begin();
20         char letters[ 26 ] = { '\0' };  // letters guessed
21         int n = 0, xcount = xword.length();
22         bool found = false, solved = false;
23         int offset = 0, bodyCount = 0;
24         bool hung = false;
25
26         // clear window; system is a stdlib function
27         system( "cls" );  // "cls" for DOS; "clear" for unix
28
29         do {
30            cout << "\n\nGuess a letter (case does"
31                 << " not matter):  " << xword << "\n?";
32            char temp;
33            cin >> temp;  // letter guessed
34
35            if ( !isalpha( temp ) ) {  // validate for letters
36               cout << "\nLETTERS ONLY PLEASE\n";
37               continue; // next iteration of do/while
38            }
39
40            letters[ n ] = toupper( temp ); // convert to uppercase
41            system( "cls" );  // "cls" for DOS; "clear" for unix
42
43            // seach word for letters
44            i = words[ w ].begin(); // initialize iterator to beginning
45            found = false;          // assume letter is not found in word
46            offset = 0;             // initial position set to 0
47
48            // replace letter in mask string in all the necessary
49            // places. decrement count of characters masked such
50            // that we know when word is solved.
51            while ( i != words[ w ].end() ) {
52               if ( *i == letters[ n ] ) {
53                  *( ix + offset ) = *i;
54                  found = true;
55
56                  if ( --xcount == 0 )
57                     solved = true;
58               }
59
60               ++i;
61               ++offset;
62            }
63
64            if ( !found )   // if the letter was not found
65               ++bodyCount; // increment our count of incorrect guesses.
66
67            // graphically draw the pieces of the body
68            // based upon the number of incorrect answers.
69            bool newline = false;
70            for ( int q = 1; q <= bodyCount; ++q ) {
71               if ( q == 1 || q == 5 || q == 7 ) {
72                  newline = true;
73                  cout << body[ 0 ];   // output space
74               }
75               else if ( q == 4 )
76                  newline = true;
77               else
78                  newline = false;
```

```
79
80              cout << body[ q ];
81
82          if ( newline )
83              cout << '\n';
84       }
85
86       // test to see if guesses were exceeded.
87       if ( bodyCount == 7 ) {
88          cout << "\n\n...GAME OVER...\n";
89          hung = true;
90          break;
91       }
92
93       // display all guesses. note we did not provide
94       // the code that would politely refuse duplicates.
95       cout << "\n\n\nYour guesses:\n";
96       for ( int k = 0; k <= n; ++k )
97          cout << setw( 2 ) << letters[ k ];
98
99       ++n;
100    } while ( !solved );
101
102    cout << "\n\nWord: " << words[ w ] << "\n\n";
103
104    if ( !hung )
105       cout << "\nCongratulations!!! You guessed "
106            << "my word.\n";
107
108    // if we are out of words, then time to exit loop
109    if ( ++w >= WORDS )
110       break;
111
112    cout << "Play again (yes/no)? ";
113    cin >> response;
114
115    } while ( !response.compare( "yes" ) );
116
117    cout << "\nThank you for playing hangman." << endl;
118    return 0;
119 }
```

```
...
 o
/|\
 |
/ \
...GAME OVER...

Word: MACAW

Play again (yes/no)? yes
...
Guess a letter (case does not matter):  ??????
? R
...
 o
Your guesses:
 R
Guess a letter (case does not matter):  ??????
? M
...
```

```
    o
   /|
```

```
Your guesses:
R A T S U D L E

Word: SADDLE

Congratulations!!! You guessed my word.
Play again (yes/no)? no

Thank you for playing hangman.
```

19.14 Write a program that inputs a **string** and prints the **string** backwards. Convert all uppercase characters to lower-case and all lowercase characters to uppercase.

```cpp
// Exercise 19.14 Solution
#include <iostream>
#include <string>
#include <ctype.h>
using namespace std;

int main()
{
   string s;

   cout << "Enter a string: ";
   getline( cin, s, '\n' );

   string::reverse_iterator r = s.rbegin();

   while ( r != s.rend() ) {
      *r = ( isupper( *r ) ? tolower( *r ): toupper( *r ) );
      cout << *( r++ );
   }

   cout << endl;
   return 0;
}
```

```
Enter a string: The sinking of HMS Titanic
CINATIt smh FO GNIKNIS EHt
```

19.15 Write a program that uses the comparison capabilities introduced in this chapter to alphabetize a series of animal names. Only uppercase letters should be used for the comparisons.

```cpp
// Exercise 19.15 Solution
// NOTE: The problem description should have asked
// the programmer to use a quicksort.
#include <iostream>
#include <string>
using namespace std;

void output( const string const *, const int );
void quickSort( string [], int, int );

```

```
11  int main()
12  {
13      string animals[] = { "Macaw", "Lion", "Tiger",
14                           "Bear", "Toucan", "Zebra",
15                           "Puma", "Cat", "Yak", "Boar",
16                           "Fox", "Ferret", "Crocodile",
17                           "Alligator", "Elk", "Ox",
18                           "Horse", "Eagle", "Hawk" };
19
20      cout << "before:";
21      output( animals, 19 );
22
23      quickSort( animals, 0, 19 );
24
25      cout << "\nafter:";
26      output( animals, 19 );
27
28      return 0;
29  }
30
31  void output( const string * const ani, const int length )
32  {
33      for ( int j = 0; j < length; ++j )
34          cout << ( j % 10 ? ' ': '\n' ) << ani[ j ];
35
36      cout << endl;
37  }
38
39  void quickSort( string a[], int first, int last )
40  {
41      int partition( string [], int, int );
42      int currentLocation;
43
44      if ( first >= last )
45          return;
46
47      currentLocation = partition( a, first, last );
48      quickSort( a, first, currentLocation - 1 );
49      quickSort( a, currentLocation + 1, last );
50  }
51
52  int partition( string b[], int left, int right )
53  {
54      int pos = left;
55
56      while ( true ) {
57
58          while ( b[ pos ] <= b[ right ] && pos != right )
59              --right;
60
61          if ( pos == right )
62              return pos;
63
64          if ( b[ pos ] > b[ right ] ) {
65              b[ pos ].swap( b[ right ] );
66              pos = right;
67          }
68
69          while ( b[ left ] <= b[ pos ] && pos != left )
70              ++left;
71
72          if ( pos == left )
73              return pos;
74
```

```
75          if ( b[ left ] > b[ pos ] ) {
76              b[ pos ].swap( b[ left ] );
77              pos = left;
78          }
79      }
80  }
```

```
before:
Macaw Lion Tiger Bear Toucan Zebra Puma Cat Yak Boar
Fox Ferret Crocodile Alligator Elk Ox Horse Eagle Hawk
after:
Alligator Bear Boar Cat Crocodile Eagle Elk Ferret Fox Hawk
Horse Lion Macaw Ox Puma Tiger Toucan Yak Zebra
```

19.16   Write a program that creates a cryptogram out of a **string**. A cryptogram is a message or word, where each letter is replaced with another letter. For example the **string**

> **The birds name was squawk**

might be scrambled to form

> **xms kbypo zhqs fho obrhfu**

Note that spaces are not scrambled. In this particular case, **'T'** was replaced with **'x'**, each **'a'** was replaced with **'h'**, etc. Uppercase letters and lowercase letters should be treated the same. Use techniques similar to those in Exercise 19.7.

```
1   // Exercise 19.16 Solution
2   // Program creates a cryptogram from a string.
3   #include <iostream>
4   #include <string>
5   #include <stdlib.h>
6   #include <time.h>
7   #include <ctype.h>
8   using namespace std;
9
10  void convertToLower( string::iterator, string::iterator );
11
12  int main()
13  {
14      string s, alpha = "ABCDEFGHIJKLMNOPQRSTUVWXYZ";
15      string::iterator is, is2, is3;
16
17      srand( time( 0 ) );
18      cout << "Enter a string: ";
19      getline( cin, s, '\n' ); // allow white space to be read
20
21      is = s.begin();
22      convertToLower( is, s.end() );
23      string s2( s ); // instantiate s2
24
25      is3 = s2.begin();
26
27      do {
28          is2 = is3;  // position location on string s2
29
30          // do not change spaces
31          if ( *is == ' ' ) {
32              is++;
33              continue;
34          }
35
36          int x = rand() % alpha.length(); // pick letter
37          char c = alpha.at( x );  // get letter
38          alpha.erase( x, 1 );     // remove picked letter
```

```
39
40            // iterate along s2 doing replacement
41            while ( is2 != s2.end() ) {
42               if ( *is2 == *is )
43                  *is2 = c;
44
45               ++is2;
46            }
47
48            ++is3;  // position to next element
49            ++is;   // position to next element
50         } while ( is != s.end() );
51
52         // change s2 to lowercase
53         is3 = s2.begin();
54         convertToLower( is3, s2.end() );
55
56         // output strings
57         cout << "Original string:        " << s
58              << "\nCryptogram of string: " << s2 << endl;
59
60         return 0;
61     }
62
63     void convertToLower( string::iterator i,
64                          string::iterator e )
65     {
66         while ( i != e ) {
67            *i = tolower( *i );
68            ++i;
69         }
70     } .
```

```
Enter a string: a cold hard rain fell
Original string:        a cold hard rain fell
Cryptogram of string: u clfj muoj ouyv drff
```

19.17 Modify the previous exercise to allow a user to solve the cryptogram by inputting two characters. The first character specifies the letter in the cryptogram and the second letter specifies the user's guess. For example, if the user inputs **r g**, then the user is guessing that the letter **r** is really a **g**.

19.18 Write a program that inputs a sentence and counts the number of palindromes in the sentence. A palindrome is a word that reads the same backwards and forwards. For example, **"tree"** is not a palindrome but **"noon"** is.

19.19 Write a program that counts the total number of vowels in a sentence. Output the frequency of each vowel.

19.20 rite a program that inserts the characters **"*******"** in the exact middle of a **string**.

19.21 Write a program that erases the sequences **"by"** and **"BY"** from a **string**.

```
 1    // Exercise 19.21 Solution
 2    // Program erases "by" or "BY" from strings.
 3    #include <iostream>
 4    #include <string>
 5    using namespace std;
 6
 7    void deleteBy( string&, string );
 8
 9    int main()
10    {
11        string s;
12        cout << "Enter a word:";
```

```
13        cin >> s;
14
15        deleteBy( s, "by" );
16        deleteBy( s, "BY" );
17
18        cout << s << endl;
19        return 0;
20  }
21
22  void deleteBy( string& sRef, string z )
23  {
24     int x = sRef.find( z );
25     while ( x <= sRef.length() ) {
26        sRef.erase( x, 2 );
27        x = sRef.find( z );
28     }
29  }
```

```
Enter a word:DERBY
DER
```

19.22   Write a program that inputs a line of text, replaces all punctuation marks with spaces then uses the C-string library function **strtok** to tokenize the **string** into individual words.

19.23   Write a program that inputs a line of text and prints the text backwards. Use iterators in your solution.

```
1   // Exercise 19.23 Solution
2   // Program prints a string backwards.
3   #include <iostream>
4   #include <string>
5   using namespace std;
6
7   int main()
8   {
9      string s;
10
11     cout << "Enter a string: ";
12     getline( cin, s, '\n' );
13     string::reverse_iterator rb = s.rbegin();
14
15     while ( rb != s.rend() ) {
16        cout << *rb;
17        ++rb;
18     }
19
20     cout << endl;
21     return 0;
22  }
```

```
Enter a string: PRINT THIS BACKWARDS
SDRAWKCAB SIHT TNIRP
```

19.24   Write a recursive version of Exercise 19.23.

```
1   // Exercise 19.23 Solution
2   // Program recursively prints a string backwards.
3   #include <iostream>
4   #include <string>
5   using namespace std;
6
```

```
7   void printBackwards( const string::reverse_iterator,
8                        string::reverse_iterator );
9
10  int main()
11  {
12     string s;
13
14     cout << "Enter a string: ";
15     getline( cin, s );
16     string::reverse_iterator r = s.rend();
17
18     printBackwards( s.rbegin(), r - 1 );
19     cout << endl;
20     return 0;
21  }
22
23  void printBackwards( const string::reverse_iterator s,
24                       string::reverse_iterator rb )
25  {
26     if ( rb == s - 1 )
27        return;
28
29     printBackwards( s, rb - 1 );
30     cout << *rb;
31  }
```

```
Enter a string: automobile
elibomotua
```

19.25 Write a program that demonstrates the use of the **erase** functions that take **iterator** arguments.

19.26 Write a program that generates from the **string "abcdefghijklmnopqrstuvwxyz{"** the following:

```
              a
             bcb
            cdedc
           defgfed
          efghihgfe
         fghijkjihgf
        ghijklmlkjihg
       hijklmnonmlkjih
      ijklmnopqponmlkji
     jklmnopqrsrqponmlkj
    klmnopqrstutsrqponmlk
   lmnopqrstuvwvutsrqponml
  mnopqrstuvwxyxwvutsrqponm
 nopqrstuvwxyz{zyxwvutsrqpon
```

```
1   // Exercise 19.26 Solution
2   // Program prints a pyramid from a string.
3   #include <iostream>
4   using namespace std;
5
6   int main()
7   {
8      string alpha = "abcdefghijklmnopqrstuvwxyz{";
9      string::const_iterator x = alpha.begin(), x2;
10
11     for ( int p = 1; p <= 14; ++p ) {
12        int w, count = 0;  // set to 0 each iteration
13
```

```
14           // output spaces
15           for ( int k = 13; k >= p; --k )
16              cout << ' ';
17
18           x2 = x;   // set starting point
19
20           // output first half of characters
21           for ( int c = 1; c <= p; ++c ) {
22              cout << *x2;
23              x2++;        // move forwards one letter
24              count++;     // keep count of iterations
25           }
26
27           // output back half of characters
28           for ( w = 1, x2 -= 2; w < count; ++w ) {
29              cout << *x2;
30              --x2;    // move backwards one letter
31           }
32
33           x++;    // next letter
34           cout << '\n';
35        }
36
37        return 0;
38     }
```

19.27 In Exercise 19.7 we asked you to write a simple encryption algorithm. Write a program that will attempt to decrypt a "rot13" message using simple frequency substitution (assume you do not know the key). The most frequent letters in the encrypted phrase should be substituted with the most commonly used English letters (a, e, i, o, u, s, t, r, etc.). Write the possibilities to a file. What made the code breaking easy? How can the encryption mechanism be improved?

19.28 Write a version of the bubble sort routine that sorts **string**s. Use function **swap** in your solution.

```
1   // Exercise 19.28 Solution
2   #include <iostream>
3   #include <string>
4   using namespace std;
5
6   void output( const string const *, const int );
7   void bubbleSort( string [], const int );
8
9   int main()
10  {
11     string animals[] = { "Macaw", "Lion", "Tiger",
12                          "Bear", "Toucan", "Zebra",
13                          "Puma", "Cat", "Yak", "Boar",
14                          "Fox", "Ferret", "Crocodile",
15                          "Alligator", "Elk", "Ox",
16                          "Horse", "Eagle", "Hawk" };
17
18     cout << "before:";
19     output( animals, 19 );
20
21     bubbleSort( animals, 19 );
22
23     cout << "\nafter:";
24     output( animals, 19 );
25
26     return 0;
27  }
28
```

```
29   void output( const string * const ani, const int length )
30   {
31      for ( int j = 0; j < length; ++j )
32         cout << ( j % 10 ? ' ': '\n' ) << ani[ j ];
33
34      cout << endl;
35   }
36
37   void bubbleSort( string mals[], const int length )
38   {
39      for ( int pass = 1; pass < length; ++pass )
40         for ( int comp = 0; comp < length - pass; ++comp )
41            if ( mals[ comp ] > mals[ comp + 1 ] )
42               mals[ comp ].swap( mals[ comp + 1 ] );
43   }
```

```
before:
Macaw Lion Tiger Bear Toucan Zebra Puma Cat Yak Boar
Fox Ferret Crocodile Alligator Elk Ox Horse Eagle Hawk
after:
Alligator Bear Boar Cat Crocodile Eagle Elk Ferret Fox Hawk
Horse Lion Macaw Ox Puma Tiger Toucan Yak Zebra
```

Chapter 20 Solutions

Standard Template Library (STL)

Solutions

20.14 Write a function template **palindrome** that takes as a parameter a **const vector** and returns **true** or **false** depending upon whether the **vector** does or does not read the same forwards as backwards (e.g., a **vector** containing 1, 2, 3, 2, 1 is a palindrome and a **vector** containing 1, 2, 3, 4 is not).

ANS:

```
1   // Exercise 20.14 Solution
2   #include <iostream>
3   #include <vector>
4   using namespace std;
5
6   template < class X >
7   bool palindrome( const vector< X > &vec )
8   {
9       vector< X >::const_reverse_iterator r = vec.rbegin();
10      vector< X >::const_iterator i = vec.begin();
11
12      while ( r != vec.rend() && i != vec.end() )  {
13          if ( *r != *i )
14              return false;
15
16          ++r;
17          ++i;
18      }
19
20      return true;
21  }
22
23  template < class Y >
24  void printVector( const vector< Y > &vec )
25  {
26      vector< Y >::const_iterator i;
27
28      for ( i = vec.begin(); i != vec.end(); ++i )
29          cout << *i << ' ';
30  }
31
32  int main()
33  {
34      vector< int > iv;
35      vector< char > ic;
36      int x = 0;
37
38      for ( int i = 75; i >= 65; --i ) {
39          iv.push_back( i );
40          ic.push_back( static_cast< char > ( i + x ) );
41
```

```
42          if ( i <= 70 )
43              x += 2;
44       }
45
46       printVector( iv );
47       cout << ( palindrome( iv ) ? " is " : " is not " )
48            << "a palindrome\n";
49
50       printVector( ic );
51       cout << ( palindrome( ic ) ? " is " : " is not " )
52            << "a palindrome" << endl;
53       return 0;
54    }
```

```
75 74 73 72 71 70 69 68 67 66 65  is not a palindrome
K J I H G F G H I J K  is a palindrome
```

20.15 Modify the program of Fig. 20.29, the Sieve of Eratosthenes, so that if the number the user inputs into the program is not prime, the program displays the prime factors of the number. Remember that a prime number's factors are only 1 and the prime number itself. Every number that is not prime has a unique prime factorization. For example, consider the number 54. The factors of 54 are 2, 3, 3 and 3. When these values are multiplied together, the result is 54. For the number 54, the prime factors output should be 2 and 3.

ANS:

```
1   // Exercise 20.15 Solution
2   #include <iostream>
3   #include <iomanip>
4   #include <bitset>
5   #include <cmath>
6   using namespace std;
7
8   int main()
9   {
10      const int size = 1024;
11      int i, value, counter;
12      bitset< size > sieve;
13
14      sieve.flip();
15
16      // perform Sieve of Eratosthenes
17      int finalBit = sqrt( sieve.size() ) + 1;
18
19      for ( i = 2; i < finalBit; ++i )
20         if ( sieve.test( i ) )
21            for ( int j = 2 * i; j < size; j += i )
22               sieve.reset( j );
23
24      cout << "The prime numbers in the range 2 to 1023 are:\n";
25
26      for ( i = 2, counter = 0; i < size; ++i )
27         if ( sieve.test( i ) ) {
28            cout << setw( 5 ) << i;
29
30            if ( ++counter % 12 == 0 )
31               cout << '\n';
32         }
33
34      cout << endl;
35
36      // get a value from the user to determine if it is prime
37      cout << "\nEnter a value from 1 to 1023 (-1 to end): ";
38      cin >> value;
```

```
39
40      while ( value != -1 ) {
41         if ( sieve[ value ] )
42            cout << value << " is a prime number\n";
43         else {
44            cout << value << " is not a prime number\n"
45                 << "prime factor(s): ";
46
47            bool print = true;
48
49            for ( int f = 2; f < size; )
50               if ( sieve.test( f ) && value % f == 0 ) {
51                  if ( print )
52                     cout << f << ' '; // output factor
53
54                  value /= f;          // modify value
55
56                  if ( value <= 1 ) // time to stop
57                     break;
58
59                  print = false;
60               }
61               else {
62                  ++f;   // move to next prime
63                  print = true;
64               }
65
66            cout << '\n';
67         }
68
69         cout << "\nEnter a value from 2 to 1023 (-1 to end): ";
70         cin >> value;
71      }
72
73      return 0;
74   }
```

```
The prime numbers in the range 2 to 1023 are:
   2    3    5    7   11   13   17   19   23   29   31   37
  41   43   47   53   59   61   67   71   73   79   83   89
  97  101  103  107  109  113  127  131  137  139  149  151
 157  163  167  173  179  181  191  193  197  199  211  223
 227  229  233  239  241  251  257  263  269  271  277  281
 283  293  307  311  313  317  331  337  347  349  353  359
 367  373  379  383  389  397  401  409  419  421  431  433
 439  443  449  457  461  463  467  479  487  491  499  503
 509  521  523  541  547  557  563  569  571  577  587  593
 599  601  607  613  617  619  631  641  643  647  653  659
 661  673  677  683  691  701  709  719  727  733  739  743
 751  757  761  769  773  787  797  809  811  821  823  827
 829  839  853  857  859  863  877  881  883  887  907  911
 919  929  937  941  947  953  967  971  977  983  991  997
1009 1013 1019 1021

Enter a value from 1 to 1023 (-1 to end): 8
8 is not a prime number
prime factor(s): 2

Enter a value from 2 to 1023 (-1 to end): 444
444 is not a prime number
prime factor(s): 2 3 37

Enter a value from 2 to 1023 (-1 to end): -1
```

20.16   Modify Exercise 20.15 so that if the number the user inputs into the program is not prime, the program displays the prime factors of the number and the number of times that prime factor appears in the unique prime factorization. For example, the output for the number 54 should be

```
The unique prime factorization of 54 is: 2 * 3 * 3 * 3
```

ANS:

```cpp
1   // Exercise 20.16 Solution
2   #include <iostream>
3   #include <iomanip>
4   #include <bitset>
5   #include <cmath>
6   using namespace std;
7
8   int main()
9   {
10      const int size = 1024;
11      int i, value, counter;
12      bitset< size > sieve;
13
14      sieve.flip();
15
16      // perform Sieve of Eratosthenes
17      int finalBit = sqrt( sieve.size() ) + 1;
18
19      for ( i = 2; i < finalBit; ++i )
20         if ( sieve.test( i ) )
21            for ( int j = 2 * i; j < size; j += i )
22               sieve.reset( j );
23
24      cout << "The prime numbers in the range 2 to 1023 are:\n";
25
26      for ( i = 2, counter = 0; i < size; ++i )
27         if ( sieve.test( i ) ) {
28            cout << setw( 5 ) << i;
29
30            if ( ++counter % 12 == 0 )
31               cout << '\n';
32         }
33
34      cout << endl;
35
36      // get a value from the user to determine if it is prime
37      cout << "\nEnter a value from 1 to 1023 (-1 to end): ";
38      cin >> value;
39
40      while ( value != -1 ) {
41         if ( sieve[ value ] )
42            cout << value << " is a prime number\n";
43         else {
44            cout << value << " is not a prime number\n"
45                 << "prime factor(s): ";
46
47            for ( int f = 2; f < size; )
48               if ( sieve.test( f ) && value % f == 0 ) {
49                  cout << f << ' '; // output factor
50                  value /= f;       // modify value
51
52                  if ( value <= 1 ) // time to stop
53                     break;
54               }
55               else
56                  ++f;  // move to next prime
```

```
57
58          cout << '\n';
59      }
60
61      cout << "\nEnter a value from 2 to 1023 (-1 to end): ";
62      cin >> value;
63   }
64
65   return 0;
66 }
```

```
The prime numbers in the range 2 to 1023 are:
    2    3    5    7   11   13   17   19   23   29   31   37
   41   43   47   53   59   61   67   71   73   79   83   89
   97  101  103  107  109  113  127  131  137  139  149  151
  157  163  167  173  179  181  191  193  197  199  211  223
  227  229  233  239  241  251  257  263  269  271  277  281
  283  293  307  311  313  317  331  337  347  349  353  359
  367  373  379  383  389  397  401  409  419  421  431  433
  439  443  449  457  461  463  467  479  487  491  499  503
  509  521  523  541  547  557  563  569  571  577  587  593
  599  601  607  613  617  619  631  641  643  647  653  659
  661  673  677  683  691  701  709  719  727  733  739  743
  751  757  761  769  773  787  797  809  811  821  823  827
  829  839  853  857  859  863  877  881  883  887  907  911
  919  929  937  941  947  953  967  971  977  983  991  997
 1009 1013 1019 1021

Enter a value from 1 to 1023 (-1 to end): 99
99 is not a prime number
prime factor(s): 3 3 11

Enter a value from 2 to 1023 (-1 to end): 888
888 is not a prime number
prime factor(s): 2 2 2 3 37

Enter a value from 2 to 1023 (-1 to end): -1
```

Chapter 21 Solutions
ANSI/ISO C++ Standard Language Additions

Solutions

21.3   Fill in the blanks for each of the following.

a) The _____ operator is used to determine an object's type at run-time.

ANS: typeid or **dynamic_cast**

b) The _____ keyword specifies that a **namespace** or namespace member is being used.

ANS: using

c) The operator _____ is the operator keyword for logical OR.

ANS: or

d) Storage specifier _____ allows a member of a **const** object to be modified.

ANS: mutable

21.4   State which of the following are true and which are false. If a statement is false, explain why.

a) The validity of a **static_cast** operation is checked at compile-time.

ANS: True.

b) The validity of a **dynamic_cast** operation is checked at run-time.

ANS: True.

c) The name **typeid** is a keyword.

ANS: True.

d) The **explicit** keyword may be applied to constructors, member functions, and data members.

ANS: False. Keyword **explicit** can only be used with constructors.

21.5   What does each expression evaluate to? (Note: some expressions may generate errors; if so, say what the cause of the error is.)

a) `cout << false;`

ANS: 0 is output.

b) `cout << ( bool b = 8 );`

ANS: Error. Most compilers will not allow a variable to be declared in this manner. If the compiler permits the expression, 1 is output.

c) `cout << ( a = true );    // a is of type int`

ANS: 1 is output.

d) `cout << ( *ptr + true && p );    // *ptr is 10 and p is 8.88`

ANS: 1 is output.

e) `// *ptr is 0 and m is false`
    `bool k = ( *ptr * 2 || ( true + 24 ) );`

ANS: k is assigned 1.

f) `bool s = true + false;`

ANS: true is assigned to **s**.

g) `cout << boolalpha << false << setw( 3 ) << true;`

ANS: falsetrue is output.

21.6   Write a **namespace Currency** which defines constant members **ONE**, **TWO**, **FIVE**, **TEN**, **TWENTY**, **FIFTY**, and **HUNDRED**. Write two short programs that use **Currency**. One program should make all constants available and the other program should only make **FIVE** available.

ANS:

```
1   // Exercise 21.6 Part A Solution
2   // Program makes namespace members accessible.
3   #include <iostream>
4   using namespace std;
5
6   namespace Currency {
7      enum Money { ONE = 1, TWO, FIVE = 5, TEN = 10,
8                   TWENTY = 20, FIFTY = 50,
9                   HUNDRED = 100 };
10  }
11
12  int main()
13  {
14     using namespace Currency;
15
16     cout << "TWO's value is: " << TWO
17         << "\nTEN's value is: " << TEN << endl;
18
19     return 0;
20  }
```

```
TWO's value is: 2
TEN's value is: 10
```

```
1   // Exercise 21.6 Part B Solution
2   // Program makes one namespace member accessible.
3   #include <iostream>
4   using namespace std;
5
6   namespace Currency {
7      enum Money { ONE = 1, TWO, FIVE = 5, TEN = 10,
8                   TWENTY = 20, FIFTY = 50,
9                   HUNDRED = 100 };
10  }
11
12  int main()
13  {
14     using Currency::FIVE;
15
16     cout << "FIVE's value is: " << FIVE << endl;
17     return 0;
18  }
```

```
FIVE's value is: 5
```

21.7 Write a program that uses the **reinterpret_cast** operator to cast different pointer types to **int**. Do any conversions result in syntax errors?

ANS:

```
1   // Exercise 21.7 Solution
2   // Program exercises reinterpret cast
3   #include <iostream>
4   #include <string>
5   using namespace std;
6
```

```
7   int main()
8   {
9       // declare variables
10      int x;
11      double d;
12      float f;
13      long l;
14      short s;
15      string z;
16      char c;
17
18      // declare and initialize pointers
19      int *xPtr = &x;
20      double *dPtr = &d;
21      float *fPtr = &f;
22      long *lPtr = &l;
23      short *sPtr = &s;
24      string *zPtr = &z;
25      char *cPtr = &c;
26      void *vPtr = &z;
27
28      // test reinterpret_cast
29      cout << "reinterpret_cast< int > ( xPtr ) = "
30          << reinterpret_cast< int > ( xPtr )
31          << "\nreinterpret_cast< int > ( dPtr ) = "
32          << reinterpret_cast< int > ( dPtr )
33          << "\nreinterpret_cast< int > ( fPtr ) = "
34          << reinterpret_cast< int > ( fPtr ) ;
35
36      cout << "\nreinterpret_cast< int > ( lPtr ) = "
37          << reinterpret_cast< int > ( lPtr )
38          << "\nreinterpret_cast< int > ( sPtr ) = "
39          << reinterpret_cast< int > ( sPtr )
40          << "\nreinterpret_cast< int > ( zPtr ) = "
41          << reinterpret_cast< int > ( zPtr )
42          << "\nreinterpret_cast< int > ( cPtr ) = "
43          << reinterpret_cast< int > ( cPtr )
44          << "\nreinterpret_cast< int > ( vPtr ) = "
45          << reinterpret_cast< int > ( vPtr ) << endl;
46
47      return 0;
48  }
```

```
reinterpret_cast< int > ( xPtr ) = 6880716
reinterpret_cast< int > ( dPtr ) = 6880732
reinterpret_cast< int > ( fPtr ) = 6880724
reinterpret_cast< int > ( lPtr ) = 6880680
reinterpret_cast< int > ( sPtr ) = 6880740
reinterpret_cast< int > ( zPtr ) = 6880700
reinterpret_cast< int > ( cPtr ) = 6880744
reinterpret_cast< int > ( vPtr ) = 6880700
```

21.8   Write a program that uses the **static_cast** operator to cast some fundamental data types to **int**. Does the compiler allow the casts to **int**?

   ANS:

```
1   // Exercise 21.8 Solution
2   // Program exercises static casting.
3   #include <iostream>
4   using namespace std;
5
```

```
6   int main()
7   {
8       // declare variables
9       int x = 8;
10      double d = 22.22;
11      float f = 33.33f;   // floating point representation
12      long l = 888888;
13      short s = 32000;
14      unsigned u = 65000;
15      char c = 'U';    // ascii of 85
16      long double ld = 999999999.00;
17      unsigned char uc = 250;
18      unsigned long ul = 777777;
19      unsigned short us = 55555;
20
21      // test static_cast
22      cout << "static_cast< int > ( x ) = "
23          << static_cast< int > ( x )
24          << "\nstatic_cast< int > ( d ) = "
25          << static_cast< int > ( d )
26          << "\nstatic_cast< int > ( f ) = "
27          << static_cast< int > ( f );
28
29      cout << "\nstatic_cast< int > ( l ) = "
30          << static_cast< int > ( l )
31          << "\nstatic_cast< int > ( s ) = "
32          << static_cast< int > ( s )
33          << "\nstatic_cast< int > ( u ) = "
34          << static_cast< int > ( u );
35
36      cout << "\nstatic_cast< int > ( c ) = "
37          << static_cast< int > ( c )
38          << "\nstatic_cast< int > ( ld ) = "
39          << static_cast< int > ( ld )
40          << "\nstatic_cast< int > ( uc ) = "
41          << static_cast< int > ( uc );
42
43      cout << "\nstatic_cast< int > ( ul ) = "
44          << static_cast< int > ( ul )
45          << "\nstatic_cast< int > ( us ) = "
46          << static_cast< int > ( us ) << endl;
47
48      return 0;
49  }
```

```
static_cast< int > ( x ) = 8
static_cast< int > ( d ) = 22
static_cast< int > ( f ) = 33
static_cast< int > ( l ) = 888888
static_cast< int > ( s ) = 32000
static_cast< int > ( u ) = 65000
static_cast< int > ( c ) = 85
static_cast< int > ( ld ) = 999999999
static_cast< int > ( uc ) = 250
static_cast< int > ( ul ) = 777777
static_cast< int > ( us ) = 55555
```

21.9   Write a program that demonstrates upcasting from a derived class to a base class. Use the **static_cast** operator to perform the upcast.

ANS:

```
1   // Exercise 21.9 Solution
2   // Program upcasts with static_cast.
3   #include <iostream>
4   using namespace std;
5
6   class Base {
7   public:
8      void print() const { cout << "BASE"; }
9   };
10
11  class Derived : public Base {
12  public:
13     void print() const { cout << "DERIVED"; }
14  };
15
16  int main()
17  {
18     Base *bPtr;      // base class pointer
19     Derived d, *dPtr;
20
21     dPtr = &d;  // point to d
22
23     // upcast from Derived * to Base *
24     bPtr = static_cast< Base * > ( dPtr );
25     bPtr -> print();  // invoke function print
26
27     cout << endl;
28     return 0;
29  }
```

```
BASE
```

21.10 Write a program that creates an **explicit** constructor that takes two arguments. Does the compiler permit this? Remove **explicit** and attempt an implicit conversion. Does the compiler permit this?

21.11 What is the benefit of an **explicit** constructor?
ANS: An **explicit** constructor prevents arguments from being implicitly converted.

21.12 Write a program that creates a class containing two constructors. One constructor should take a single **int** argument. The second constructor should take one **char *** argument. Write a driver program that constructs several different objects; each object having a different type passed into the constructor. Do not use **explicit**. What happens? Now use **explicit** only for the constructor that takes one **int**. What happens?

21.13 Given the following **namespace**s, answer whether or not each statement is true or false. Explain any false answers.

```
1   #include <string>
2   namespace Misc {
3      using namespace std;
4      enum Countries { POLAND, SWITZERLAND, GERMANY,
5                       AUSTRIA, CZECH_REPUBLIC };
6      int kilometers;
7      string s;
8
9      namespace Temp {
10         short y = 77;
11         Car car;   // assume definition exists
12      }
13  }
14
```

```
15   namespace ABC {
16      using namespace Misc::Temp;
17      void *function( void *, int );
18   }
```

a) Variable **y** is accessible within **namespace ABC**.
ANS: true
b) Object **s** is accessible within **namespace Temp**.
ANS: true
c) Constant **POLAND** is not accessible within **namespace Temp**.
ANS: false
d) Constant **GERMANY** is accessible within **namespace ABC**.
ANS: false
e) Function **function** is accessible to **namespace Temp**.
ANS: false
f) Namespace **ABC** is accessible to **Misc**.
ANS: false
g) Object **car** is accessible to **Misc**.
ANS: true

21.14   Compare and contrast **mutable** and **const_cast**. Give at least one example of when one might be preferred over the other. Note: this exercise does not require any code to be written.

ANS: Operator **const_cast** is used to cast away **const** or **volatile** qualifications. Users of a class usually will not be aware of **const_cast** operations, because this implementation is typically hidden. Storage class specifier **mutable** allows a variable to be modified even if the object is **const**. Users of the class are not likely to be aware of a **mutable** member. Members that are **mutable** usually correspond to some "secret" implementation. **mutable** members are always modifiable, whereas **const_cast** operations are confined to the line where the cast is performed.

21.15   Write a program that uses **const_cast** to modify a **const** variable. (Hint: use a pointer in your solution to point to the **const** identifier.)

ANS:

```
1    // Exercise 21.15 Solution
2    #include <iostream>
3    using namespace std;
4
5    int main()
6    {
7       const char c = 'A';
8       const char *ptr = &c;
9
10      cout << "c is " << *ptr;
11
12      *const_cast< char * > ( ptr ) = 'Z';
13
14      cout << "\nc is " << *ptr << endl;
15      return 0;
16   }
```

```
c is A
c is Z
```

21.16   What problem does **virtual** base classes solve?

ANS: **virtual** base classes solve the problem of "diamond inheritance" where a derived class recieves duplicate subobjects from its base classes. With **virtual** base classes, only one copy of the subobject is inherited into the derived class (at the bottom of the diamond).

21.17 Write a program that use **virtual** base classes. The class at the top of the hierarchy should provide constructor that takes at least one argument (i.e., do not provide a default constructor). What challenges does this present for the inheritance hierarchy.

ANS:

```
1   // Exercise 21.17 Solution
2   #include <iostream>
3   using namespace std;
4
5   class Base {
6   public:
7      Base( int n ) { num = n; }
8      void print() const { cout << num; }
9   private:
10      int num;
11   };
12
13   class D1 : virtual public Base {
14   public:
15      D1(): Base( 3 ) {}
16   };
17
18   class D2 : virtual public Base {
19   public:
20      D2(): Base( 5 ) {}
21   };
22
23   class Multi : public D1, D2 {
24   public:
25      Multi( int a ): Base( a ) {}
26   };
27
28   int main()
29   {
30      Multi m( 9 );
31
32      m.print();
33
34      cout << endl;
35      return 0;
36   }
```

```
9
```

21.18 Find the error(s) in each of the following. When possible, explain how to correct each error.

a) ```
namespace Name {
    int x, y;
    mutable int z;
};
```
ANS: A **mutable** member can only belong to a class.

b) `int integer = const_cast< int >( float );`
ANS: Operator **const_cast** cannot be used to convert a **float** to an **int**. Either **static_cast** or **reinterpret_cast** should be used. Note: The keyword **float** in parentheses should be a floating-point value.

c) `namespace PCM( 111, "hello" );    // construct namespace`
ANS: A **namespace** cannot be constructed, because it only defines a scope.

d) `explicit int x = 99;`
ANS: Keyword **explicit** can only be applied to a constructor definition.
```

Appendix C Solutions

Number Systems

C.20 Some people argue that many of our calculations would be easier in the base **12** number system because **12** is divisible by so many more numbers than **10** (for base **10**). What is the lowest digit in base **12**? What might the highest symbol for the digit in base **12** be? What are the positional values of the rightmost four positions of any number in the base **12** number system?

> **ANS:** The lowest digit is 1. The highest symbol is C. 1728, 144, 12, 1.

C.21 How is the highest symbol value in the number systems we discussed related to the positional value of the first digit to the left of the rightmost digit of any number in these number systems?

C.22 Complete the following chart of positional values for the rightmost four positions in each of the indicated number systems:

```
decimal1000100 10   1
base 6 ......   6...
base 13 ... 169... ...
base 3   27.........
```

> **ANS:**
>
> ```
> decimal1000100 10   1
> base 6 21636   61
> base 13 219716913 1
> base 3   27931
> ```

C.23 Convert binary **100101111010** to octal and to hexadecimal.
ANS: 4572, 97A.

C.24 Convert hexadecimal **3A7D** to binary.
ANS: 11101001111101

C.25 Convert hexadecimal **765F** to octal. (Hint: First convert **765F** to binary, then convert that binary number to octal.)
ANS: 73137

C.26 Convert binary **1011110** to decimal.
ANS: 94

C.27 Convert octal **426** to decimal.
ANS: 278

C.28 Convert hexadecimal **FFFF** to decimal.
ANS: 65535

C.29 Convert decimal **299** to binary, to octal, and to hexadecimal.
ANS: 100101011, 453, 12B.

C.30 Show the binary representation of decimal **779**. Then show the one's complement of **779**, and the two's complement of **779**.
> **ANS:** 110000101. One's complement: 001111010. Two's complement: 001111011.

C.31 What is the result when the two's complement of a number is added to itself?

C.32 Show the two's complement of integer value **-1** on a machine with 32-bit integers.

Appendix

Elevator Simulator

Section 2.22: Elevator Laboratory Assignment 1

In this and the next few assignments, you will perform the separate steps of an object-oriented design. The first step is to *identify the objects* in your problem. You will eventually describe these objects in a formal way and implement them in C++. For this assignment, all you should do is

1. Identify the objects in this elevator simulation problem. The problem statement specifies many objects working together to simulate the elevator and its interactions with the various people, floors of the building, buttons, etc. Locate the *nouns* from the problem statement; with high likelihood, these represent most of the objects necessary to implement the elevator simulation.

    ANS: building, elevator, people, floors, doors, clock, scheduler, buttons, light, bell.

2. For each object you identify, write one precisely worded paragraph that captures all the facts about that object from the problem statement.

    ANS:
    Building: The building contains two floors and an elevator.

    Elevator: The elevator begins the day on Floor 1 with its door closed. The elevator takes 5 clock ticks to travel between floors and has a capacity of one person. The elevator has an up button and a down button. Upon arriving at a floor, the floor light is turned on, the bell sounds, and the elevator door opens. The elevator always knows what floor it is on and the destination floor.

    People: People are created at randomly generated times to ride the elevator. When created, people arrive at either Floor 1 or Floor 2 and depart upon arriving at the opposite floor. People are not permanent floor fixtures or elevator fixtures.

    Door: Each floor as well as the elevator have a door. A door opens when an elevator arrives at a floor and closes when the elevator departs the floor. The floor doors and elevator door are closed when the elevator is in transit.

    Floor: Each floor has a call button that summons the elevator. A person presses the call button. A person randomly arrives on a floor and departs a floor by entering the elevator.

    Clock: The clock will keep track of the elapsed time during the simulation. The elevator takes five clock ticks to move from floor to floor.

    Scheduler: The scheduler creates people arrival times. In this simulation, the scheduler will also create the people.

    Button: Each floor has one call button and the elevator has two buttons. People press floor call buttons to summon the elevator. Floor call buttons are reset when the elevator arrives. People press either the up or down button in the elevator to indicate their destination floor. The elevator button resets upon arrival at the destination floor.

Questions

1. How might you decide if the elevator is able to handle the anticipated traffic volume?

    ANS: The ability to handle the anticipated traffic can be measured by the number of people that are rescheduled immediately after arriving in the simulation. If the total rescheduled time is greater than 0, it means that there are line of people waiting for the elevator at given times. The larger the total rescheduled time, the more people are waiting.

2. Why is it so much more complicated to implement a three-story (or larger) building?

   ANS: Efficiency and logic make this problem more difficult for 3 or more floors. The elevator has more decisions to make as the number of floors increases.

3. We will see later that once we have created one elevator object, it is easy to create as many as we want. What problems do you foresee in having several elevators, each of which may pick up and discharge passengers at every floor in the building?

   ANS: Once a building contains multiple elevators, the elevators must be coordinated for maximum efficiency. For example, in a building with 2 idle elevators on floor 1, when a person presses the call button on floor 2, both elevators should not respond. Thus, there must be another set of controls that coordinates multiple elevators.

4. For simplicity, we have given our elevator and each floor a capacity of one passenger. What problems do you foresee in being able to increase these capacities?

   ANS: Larger capacities on the floor and in the elevator increase the possibility of queues (waiting lines) on each floor. If the floor's queue is larger than the elevator capacity, some people will remain on the floor when the elevator is at capacity. These people will have to wait for the elevator to depart, to discharge its passengers, to arrive back at the floor, and to possibly discharge passengers. However, if the elevator has a large capacity, it is possible that people will not have to wait at all—particularly if multiple elevators exist. Larger capacity elevators are inefficient if they do not transport a minimum number of people.

Section 3.22: Elevator Laboratory Assignment 2

1. To get the process started, type into a word processor or editor program the text of the problem statement for the elevator simulation (from Section 2.22).

   ANS:

A company intends to build a two-story office building and equip it with the "latest" elevator technology. The company wants you to develop an object-oriented software simulator that models the operation of the elevator to determine if this elevator will meet their needs.

The elevator, which has a capacity of one person, is designed to conserve energy, so it only moves when necessary. The elevator starts the day waiting with its door shut on floor 1 of the building. The elevator, of course, alternates directions—first up, then down.

Your simulator includes a clock that begins the day set to time 0 and that "ticks" once per second. The "scheduler" component of the simulator randomly schedules the arrival of the first person on each floor (you will learn how to schedule random arrivals in Chapter 3). When the clock's time becomes equal to the time of the first arrival, the simulator "creates" a new person for the specified floor, and places the person on that floor. The person then presses the button on that floor to summon the elevator. The person's destination floor is never equal to the floor on which that person arrives.

If the first person of the day arrives at floor 1, the person can immediately get on the elevator (after pressing the button and waiting for the elevator's door to open, of course!). If the first person arrives at floor 2, the elevator proceeds to floor 2 to pick up that person. The elevator requires five ticks of the clock to travel between floors.

The elevator signals its arrival at a floor by turning on a light above the elevator door on that floor and by sounding a bell inside the elevator. The button on the floor and the button in the elevator for that floor are reset, the elevator opens its door, the passenger—if there is one whose destination is that floor—gets out of the elevator, another passenger—if there is one waiting on that floor—gets into the elevator and presses a destination button, and the elevator closes its door. If the elevator needs to begin moving, it determines in which direction it should go (a simple decision on a two-story elevator!), and begins moving to the next floor. For simplicity, assume that all of the events that happen once the elevator reaches a floor, and until the elevator closes its doors on that floor, take zero time. The elevator always knows what floor it is on and what floor it is going to.

At most, one person can be waiting on each floor at any time, so if a floor is occupied when a new person (i.e., not a person already on the elevator) is due to arrive at that floor, the new arrival is rescheduled for one second later. Assume that people arrive at random on each floor every 5 to 20 seconds.

2. Extract all the facts from the problem. Eliminate all irrelevant text and place each fact on a separate line of your text file (there are approximately 60 facts in the problem statement).

   ANS:

   • two-story building

- elevator
- elevator capacity of one person
- person
- elevator only moves when necessary
- elevator starts the day waiting on floor one with door closed
- elevator door
- each floor has a door
- floor 1
- floor 2
- elevator alternates direction—up and down
- clock
- clock begins the day set to time 0
- clock "ticks" once per second
- scheduler
- scheduler randomly schedules the arrival of the first person for each floor
- when the clock's time equals the time of the first arrival, a new person is created on a floor
- person walks onto a floor
- person presses floor call button
- destination floor
- arrival floor
- destination floor is never equal to the arrival floor
- elevator requires 5 ticks to move between floors
- bell
- light
- floor button
- elevator buttons
- the first person of the day can immediately enter the elevator if they arrive on floor 1
- the first person of the day presses the floor call button to summon the elevator if they arrive on floor 2
- elevator signals its arrival by ringing the bell and flashing the floor light
- upon arrival, the floor call button and the elevator button are reset
- elevator opens its door
- passenger exits the elevator
- another passenger enters the elevator
- passenger presses either the elevator's up or down button
- elevator closes its door
- if elevator needs to move, it determines which direction it needs to go
- elevator begins moving to the opposite floor
- all events that happen once an elevator reaches a floor, and until the elevator closes its doors on that floor, take zero time
- elevator always knows its arrival floor and its destination floor
- at most, one person can be waiting on a floor at any given time

- if the floor is already occupied when a new person is due to be created (i.e., not an elevator passenger) on that floor, the new arrival is rescheduled for one second later

- only one person can be created in the simulation at any given time, so there is never a duplicate arrival time for the next person

- people arrive at random on each floor every 5 to 20 seconds

3. Group all your facts by class. This will help confirm that you properly identified the classes in the laboratory exercises in Chapter 2. Use an outline form in which the class is listed at the left margin of the page and the facts related to a class are listed below that class and indented one tab. Some facts mention only one class while other facts mention several classes. Each fact should initially be listed under every class the fact mentions. Note that some facts like "directions—up and down" do not explicitly mention a class, but should nevertheless be grouped with a class (in this case, the direction is clearly the direction in which the elevator is moving). This outline file will be used in this assignment and in the next several assignments.

ANS:

<u>Building</u>

- elevator

- floor 1

- floor 2

- clock

- scheduler

<u>Elevator</u>

- elevator capacity of one person

- elevator only moves when necessary

- elevator starts the day waiting on floor one with door closed

- elevator door

- elevator alternates direction—up and down

- elevator requires 5 ticks to move between floors

- if elevator needs to move, it determines which direction it needs to go

- elevator begins moving to the opposite floor

- all events that happen once an elevator reaches a floor, and until the elevator closes its doors on that floor, take zero time

- elevator always knows its arrival floor and its destination floor

- elevator signals its arrival by ringing the bell and flashing the floor light

- destination floor

- arrival floor

- destination floor is never equal to the arrival floor

- bell

- elevator buttons

- upon arrival, the floor call button and the elevator button are reset

- elevator opens its door

- elevator closes its door

- passenger exits the elevator

- another passenger enters the elevator

Floor

- each floor has a door
- floor button
- at most, one person can be waiting on a floor at any given time
- light

Person

- person walks onto a floor
- person presses floor call button
- the first person of the day can immediately enter the elevator if they arrive on floor 1
- the first person of the day presses the floor call button to summon the elevator if they arrive on floor 2
- passenger presses either the elevator's up or down button

Light

- light turns on
- light turns off

Door

- door opened
- door closed

Button

- button pressed
- button reset

Bell

- bell rings
- bell stops ringing

Clock

- clock begins the day set to time 0
- clock "ticks" once per second
- when the clock's time equals the time of the first arrival, a new person is created on a floor

Scheduler

- scheduler randomly schedules the arrival of the first person for each floor
- if the floor is already occupied when a new person is due to be created (i.e., not an elevator passenger) on that floor, the new arrival is rescheduled for one second later
- only one person can be created in the simulation at any given time, so there is never a duplicate arrival time for the next person
- people arrive at random on each floor every 5 to 20 seconds

4. Now separate the facts for each class into two groups. Label the first group *Attributes* and the second group *Other Facts*. For now, actions (behaviors) should be grouped under *Other Facts*. As you place an action under *Other Facts* consider creating an additional entry under *Attributes,* if appropriate. For example, the fact "elevator closes its doors" is an action that for now is grouped under *Other Facts*, but it indicates that an attribute of doors is that they are either open or shut. The fact, "floor is occupied" is an attribute of floor; more specifically, floor is either occupied (by one person) or unoccupied at any time. Some attributes of the elevator are: whether it is moving or stopped, whether it does or does not have a passenger, and if it is moving—whether it is moving up or down. An attribute of a button is whether it is "on" or "off." An attribute of a person is the person's destination floor. And so on.

ANS:

Building

Attributes:

- elevator
- floor 1
- floor 2
- clock
- scheduler

Elevator

Attributes:

- elevator door
- current floor
- bell
- elevator buttons

Other Facts:

- elevator capacity of one person
- elevator only moves when necessary
- destination floor is never equal to the arrival floor
- elevator starts the day waiting on floor one with door closed
- elevator alternates direction—up and down
- elevator requires 5 ticks to move between floors
- if elevator needs to move, it determines which direction it needs to go
- elevator begins moving to the opposite floor
- elevator signals its arrival by ringing the bell and flashing the floor light
- upon arrival, the floor call button and the elevator button are reset
- elevator opens its door
- elevator closes its door
- passenger exits the elevator
- another passenger enters the elevator
- all events that happen once an elevator reaches a floor, and until the elevator closes its doors on that floor, take zero time
- elevator always knows its arrival floor and its destination floor

Floor

Attributes:

- floor door
- floor button
- light

Other Facts:

- at most, one person can be waiting on a floor at any given time

Person

Attributes:

- arrival floor

- destination floor

- sequence number in simulation

Other Facts:

- person walks onto a floor

- person presses floor call button

- the first person of the day can immediately enter the elevator if they arrive on floor 1

- the first person of the day presses the floor call button to summon the elevator if they arrive on floor 2

- passenger presses either the elevator's up or down button

Light
Attributes:

- on/off

Other Facts:

- light turns on

- light turns off

Door
Attributes:

- open/closed

Other Facts:

- door opened

- door closed

Button
Attributes:

- on/off

Other Facts:

- button pressed

- button reset

Bell
Attributes:

- ringing/silent

Other Facts:

- bell rings

- bell stops ringing

Clock
Attributes:

- time

Other Facts:

- clock begins the day set to time 0

- clock "ticks" once per second

- when the clock's time equals the time of the first arrival, a new person is created on a floor

Scheduler
Attributes:

- arrival time for each floor

Other Facts:

- scheduler randomly schedules the arrival of the first person for each floor

- if the floor is already occupied when a new person is due to be created (i.e., not an elevator passenger) on that floor, the new arrival is rescheduled for one second later

- only one person can be created in the simulation at any given time, so there is never a duplicate arrival time for the next person

- people arrive at random on each floor every 5 to 20 seconds

Section 4.10: Elevator Laboratory Assignment 3

1. Continue working with the facts file you created in Chapter 3. You had separated the facts related to each class into two groups. You labeled the first group *Attributes* and the second group *Other Facts*.

2. For each class, add a third group called *Behaviors*. Place in this group every behavior of a class that can be invoked by telling an object of that class to do something, i.e., by sending the object a message. For example, a button can be pushed (by a person), so list *pushButton* as a behavior of class button. Function *pushButton* and the other behaviors of class button are called *member functions* (or *methods*) of class button. The class's attributes (such as whether a button is "on" or "off") are called *data members* of class button. A class's member functions typically manipulate the class's data members (such as *pushButton* changing one of the button's attributes to "on"). Member functions also typically send messages to objects of other classes (such as a button object sending a *comeGetMe* message to summon the elevator). Assume that the elevator will have a button that is illuminated when someone presses it. When the elevator arrives at a floor, the elevator will want to send a *resetButton* message to turn the button's light off. The elevator may want to determine if a particular button has been pressed, so we can provide another behavior called *getButton* which simply examines a button and returns 1 or 0 to indicate that the button is currently "on" or "off." You will probably want the elevator's door to respond to messages *openDoor* and *closeDoor*. And so on.

3. For each behavior you assign to a class, provide a brief description of what the behavior does. List any attribute changes the behavior causes, and list any messages the behavior sends to objects of other classes.

ANS:

Building
Attributes:

- **elevator**:elevator

- **floorOne**:floor 1

- **floorTwo**:floor 2

- **clock**:clock

- **scheduler**:scheduler

Elevator
Attributes:

- **elevatorDoor**:elevator door

- **currentFloor**: current floor

- **direction**: direction up or down

- **bell**:bell

- **destinationButtons**:elevator buttons

- **passengerPtr**:elevator capacity of one person

- **timeOfArrivalAtNextFloor**:time to arrive at next floor

Behaviors:

- **isMoving**:elevator only moves when necessary
- **determineDirection**:if elevator needs to move, it determines which direction it needs to go
- **shouldElevatorMove**:elevator begins moving to the opposite floor
- **stopElevator**:elevator signals its arrival by ringing the bell and flashing the floor light
- **resetButton**:upon arrival, the elevator button is reset
- **passengerExits**:passenger exits the elevator
- **passengerEnters**:another passenger enters the elevator
- **getCurrentFloor**:elevator always knows its arrival floor and its destination floor

Other Facts:

- elevator opens its door
- elevator closes its door
- destination floor is never equal to the arrival floor
- elevator starts the day waiting on floor one with door closed
- elevator alternates direction—up and down
- elevator requires 5 ticks to move between floors
- all events that happen once an elevator reaches a floor, and until the elevator closes its doors on that floor, take zero time

Floor
Attributes:

- **floorDoor**:floor door
- **callButton**:floor button
- **light**:light
- **floorNumber**:floor number
- **personPtr**:person occupying floor

Behaviors:

- **openDoor**: open floor door
- **closeDoor**: close floor door
- **turnLightOn**: turn on floor light
- **turnLightOff**: turn off floor light
- **isLightOn**: check status of light
- **pressCallButton**: call elevator
- **resetCallButton**: reset call button
- **personArriving**: handle person arriving on floor
- **personDeparting**: handle person leaving floor
- **isOccupied**:at most, one person can be waiting on a floor at any given time
- **getFloorNumber**: get the current floor number

Person
Attributes:

- **startFloor**:arrival floor
- **endFloor**:destination floor
- **sequenceNumber**:sequence number in simulation

Behaviors:

- **walkOntoFloor**:person walks onto a floor
- **enterElevator**:person enters elevator
- **exitElevator**:person exits elevator
- **getSequenceNumber**:get the sequence number of the person

Other Facts:

- person presses floor call button
- the first person of the day can immediately enter the elevator if they arrive on floor 1
- the first person of the day presses the floor call button to summon the elevator if they arrive on floor 2
- passenger presses either the elevator's up or down button

Light

Attributes:

- **on**:on/off

Behaviors:

- **setOn**:turn light on/off
- **isOn**:get state of light

Door

Attributes:

- **open**:open/closed

Behaviors:

- **setOpen**:open/close door
- **isOpen**:get state of door

Button

Attributes:

- **pressed**:on/off

Behaviors:

- **setPressed**:reset/press button
- **isPressed**:get state of button

Bell

Attributes:

- **ringing**:ringing/silent

Behaviors:

- **setRinging**:ring/silence bell
- **isRinging**:get state of bell
- **ding**:notify person in elevator to exit

Clock

Attributes:

- **time**:time in simulation

Behaviors:

- **tick**:clock "ticks" once per second
- **getTime**:when the clock's time equals the time of the first arrival, a new person is created on a floor

Other Facts:

- clock begins the day set to time 0

Scheduler

Attributes:

- **arrivalTimes**:arrival time for each floor

Behaviors:

- **scheduleNextRandomArrival**:scheduler randomly schedules the arrival of the first person for each floor

- **rescheduleNextRandomArrival**:if the floor is already occupied when a new person is due to be created (i.e., not an elevator passenger) on that floor, the new arrival is rescheduled for one second later

- **checkIfPersonArriving**:only one person can be created in the simulation at any given time, so there is never a duplicate arrival time for the next person

- **createPerson**:people arrive at random on each floor every 5 to 20 seconds

Section 5.13

Let us consider several of the interactions among classes in the elevator simulation. The problem statement says, "Person presses the button on that floor." The "subject" of that clause is person and the object is button. This is an example of an interaction between classes. An object of the person class sends a message to an object of the button object. We call that message *pushButton*. In the last chapter we made the message a member function of the button class.

At this point, under *Other Facts* for each of the classes in your simulation, about all you should have left are interactions between classes. Some of these explicitly show the interactions among class objects. But consider the statement

"person waits for elevator door to open"

In the last chapter, we listed two behaviors of the elevator's door, namely *openDoor* and *closeDoor*. But now we want to determine which class objects send these messages. It is not explicitly stated in the preceding quoted statement. So we think about this a bit and we realize that the elevator itself sends these messages to the door. These interactions between class objects are implicit in the problem statement.

Now continue refining the *Other Facts* sections for each of the classes in your elevator simulator. These sections should now contain mostly interactions among classes. View each of these as

1. a particular sending class object

2. sending a particular message

3. to a particular receiving class object

Under each class, add the section *Messages Sent to Objects of Other Classes* (such messages are also called *Collaborations*; we will use this term from now on) and list the remaining interactions between classes, i.e., under class person, include the entry

person sends pushButton message to the button on that floor

Under the button class under *Collaborations* place the message

button sends comeGetMe message to elevator

As you make these entries, you may add attributes and behaviors to your objects. This is perfectly natural.

As you complete this laboratory exercise, you will have a reasonably complete listing of the classes you will need to implement your elevator simulator. And for each class you will have a reasonably complete listing of that class's attributes and behaviors, and the messages that objects of that class send to objects of other classes.

In the next chapter, we begin our study of object-oriented programming in C++. You will learn how to create new classes. Once you have read Chapter 6, you will be ready to write a substantial portion of the elevator simulation in C++. After completing Chapters 7 and 8, you will have learned enough to implement a working elevator simulator. In Chapters 9 and 10 you will learn to use inheritance to exploit commonality among classes to minimize the amount of software you will need to write to solve a problem.

Let us summarize the object-oriented design process we have presented in Chapters 2 through 5.

1. Type the problem statement into a text file.

2. Discard unimportant text.

3. Extract all the facts. Arrange the facts one per line in a facts file.

4. Scan the facts looking for nouns; these are with high likelihood many of the classes you will need. Make one top-level outline item per class.

5. For each fact, place that fact as a second-level outline item below the appropriate class. If a fact mentions several classes (as many facts will), place it below each of the classes it mentions.

6. Now refine the set of facts below each of the classes. List three subheads below each class, namely *Attributes, Behaviors,* and *Collaborations.*

7. Under *Attributes,* list the data associated with each class.

8. Under *Behaviors*, list the actions that objects of that class can perform in response to receiving a message. Each behavior is a member function of the class.

9. Under *Collaborations*, list the messages that objects of this class send to objects of other classes and the classes that receive these messages.

10. At this point your design probably still has a few missing pieces. These will probably become apparent as you proceed with implementing your elevator simulator in C++ after reading Chapter 6.

Attributes and behaviors are often called *responsibilities* of a class. The design methodology we have been outlining here is sometimes called *classes, responsibilities and collaborators* or simply *CRC.*

ANS:

Building

Attributes:

- `elevator`:elevator
- `floorOne`:floor 1
- `floorTwo`:floor 2
- `clock`:clock
- `scheduler`:scheduler

Messages Sent to Other Objects:

- `getTime`:sent to clock
- `isMoving`:sent to elevator
- `shouldElevatorStop`:sent to elevator
- `stopElevator`:sent to elevator
- `checkIfPersonArriving`:sent to scheduler
- `shouldElevatorMove`:sent to elevator
- `tick`:sent to clock

Elevator

Attributes:

- `elevatorDoor`:elevator door
- `currentFloor`: current floor
- `direction`: direction up or down
- `bell`:bell
- `destinationButtons`:elevator buttons
- `passengerPtr`:elevator capacity of one person
- `timeOfArrivalAtNextFloor`:time to arrive at next floor

Behaviors:

- **isMoving**:elevator only moves when necessary
- **determineDirection**:if elevator needs to move, it determines which direction it needs to go
- **shouldElevatorMove**:elevator begins moving to the opposite floor
- **stopElevator**:elevator signals its arrival by ringing the bell and flashing the floor light
- **resetButton**:upon arrival, the elevator button is reset
- **passengerExits**:passenger exits the elevator
- **passengerEnters**:another passenger enters the elevator
- **getCurrentFloor**:elevator always knows its arrival floor and its destination floor

Messages Sent to Other Objects:

- **setPressed**:sent to buttons
- **setOpen**:sent to door
- **isOpen**:sent to door
- **getFloorNumber**:sent to floor
- **ding**:sent to bell
- **turnLightOn**:sent to floor
- **isCallButtonPressed**:sent to floor
- **resetCallButton** sent to floor
- **turnLightOff**:sent to floor
- **setRinging**:sent to bell
- **closeDoor**:sent to floor

Other Facts:

- destination floor is never equal to the arrival floor
- elevator starts the day waiting on floor one with door closed
- elevator alternates direction—up and down
- elevator requires 5 ticks to move between floors
- all events that happen once an elevator reaches a floor, and until the elevator closes its doors on that floor, take zero time

Floor
Attributes:

- **floorDoor**:floor door
- **callButton**:floor button
- **light**:light
- **floorNumber**:floor number
- **personPtr**:person occupying floor

Behaviors:

- **openDoor**: open floor door
- **closeDoor**: close floor door
- **turnLightOn**: turn on floor light
- **turnLightOff**: turn off floor light
- **isLightOn**: check status of light

- **pressCallButton**: call elevator
- **resetCallButton**: reset call button
- **personArriving**: handle person arriving on floor
- **personDeparting**: handle person leaving floor
- **isOccupied**:at most, one person can be waiting on a floor at any given time
- **getFloorNumber**: get the current floor number

Messages Sent to Other Objects:

- **setOn**:sent to light
- **isOn**:sent to light
- **setPressed**:sent to button
- **elevatorCalled**:sent to elevator
- **enterElevator**:sent to person
- **setOpen**:sent to door

<u>Person</u>
Attributes:

- **startFloor**:arrival floor
- **endFloor**:destination floor
- **sequenceNumber**:sequence number in simulation

Behaviors:

- **walkOntoFloor**:person walks onto a floor
- **enterElevator**:person enters elevator
- **exitElevator**:person exits elevator
- **getSequenceNumber**:get the sequence number of the person

Messages Sent to Other Objects:

- **getFloorNumber**:sent to floor
- **personArriving**:sent to floor
- **pressCallButton**:sent to floor
- **personDeparting**:sent to floor
- **passengerEnters**:sent to elevator
- **pressButton**:sent to elevator
- **passengerExits**:sent to elevator

Other Facts:

- the first person of the day can immediately enter the elevator if they arrive on floor 1
- the first person of the day presses the floor call button to summon the elevator if they arrive on floor 2

<u>Light</u>
Attributes:

- **on**:on/off

Behaviors:

- **setOn**:turn light on/off
- **isOn**:get state of light

Door

Attributes:

- **open**:open/closed

Behaviors:

- **setOpen**:open/close door

- **isOpen**:get state of door

Button

Attributes:

- **pressed**:on/off

Behaviors:

- **setPressed**:reset/press button

- **isPressed**:get state of button

Bell

Attributes:

- **ringing**:ringing/silent

Behaviors:

- **setRinging**:ring/silence bell

- **isRinging**:get state of bell

- **ding**:notify person in elevator to exit

Messages Sent to Other Objects:

- **exitElevator**:sent to person

Clock

Attributes:

- **time**:time in simulation

Behaviors:

- **tick**:clock "ticks" once per second

- **getTime**:when the clock's time equals the time of the first arrival, a new person is created on a floor

Other Facts:

- clock begins the day set to time 0

Scheduler

Attributes:

- **arrivalTimes**:arrival time for each floor

Behaviors:

- **scheduleNextRandomArrival**:scheduler randomly schedules the arrival of the first person for each floor

- **rescheduleNextRandomArrival**:if the floor is already occupied when a new person is due to be created (i.e., not an elevator passenger) on that floor, the new arrival is rescheduled for one second later

- **checkIfPersonArriving**:only one person can be created in the simulation at any given time, so there is never a duplicate arrival time for the next person

- **createPerson**:people arrive at random on each floor every 5 to 20 seconds

Messages Sent to Other Objects:

- **isOccupied**:sent to floor

- message sent to **Person** constructor to construct a **new Person**

Section 6.18: Elevator Laboratory Assignment 5

1. For each of the classes you identified in the "Thinking About Objects" sections of Chapters 2 through 5, write an appropriate C++ class definition. For each class, include both a header file and a member function definition source file.

2. Write a driver program that tests each of these classes, and that attempts to run the complete elevator simulation. CAUTION: You will probably need to wait until you have studied Chapter 7, "Classes: Part II," before you will be able to complete a reasonable working version of your simulator—so be patient and implement only those portions of the elevator simulator that you can with the knowledge you have gained in Chapter 6. In Chapter 7 you will learn about composition, i.e., creating classes that contain other classes as members; this technique might help you represent the button, bell and door objects inside the elevator as members of the elevator, for example. Also in Chapter 7, you will learn how to create and destroy objects dynamically with **new** and **delete**; this will help you create new person objects as new people arrive in the simulation and destroy these person objects as people leave the simulation (after getting off the elevator).

3. For the first version of your simulator, design only a simple, text-oriented output that displays a message for each significant event that occurs. Your messages might include strings such as: "Person 1 arrives on Floor 1," "Person 1 presses Button on Floor 1," "Elevator arrives on Floor 1," "Person 1 enters Elevator," etc. Note that we suggest you capitalize the words of each message that represent objects in your simulation. Note also that you may choose to defer this portion of the lab assignment until you have read Chapter 7.

4. The more ambitious students will want to use an animated graphical output that shows the elevator moving up and down on the screen.

   ANS: See solution for Assignment 6.

Section 7.11: Elevator Laboratory Assignment 6

1. Each time another person enters the simulator, use operator **new** to create a **Person** object to represent that person. Note that **new** invokes the constructor for the object being created, and, of course, the constructor should properly initialize the object. Each time a person leaves the simulator (after getting off the elevator) use operator **delete** to destroy the **Person** object and reclaim the storage occupied by that object; **delete** invokes the destructor for the object being destroyed.

2. Enumerate the composition relationships among the classes you have implemented for your elevator simulator. Modify the class definitions you created in the "Thinking About Objects" section in Chapter 6 to reflect these composition relationships.

3. Complete the implementation of a working simulator program. We will suggest enhancements to the elevator simulator in subsequent chapters.

   ANS:

```
1   // simulate.cpp
2   // Driver for the elevator simulation
3   #include <iostream.h>
4   #include <stdlib.h>
5   #include <time.h>
6   #include "building.h"
7
8   int main()
9   {
10      int length;
11      Building building;
12
13      srand( time( 0 ) );
14      cout << "Enter length of elevator simulation: ";
15      cin >> length;
16      building.runSimulation( length );
17      return 0;
18  }
```

```
19    // bell.h
20    // Definition of class Bell
21    #ifndef BELL_H
22    #define BELL_H
23
24    class Elevator;   // forward reference
25    class Person;     // forward reference
26
27    class Bell {
28    public:
29       Bell();                                      // constructor
30       void ding( Person * const, Elevator * const ); // ring the bell
31       void setRinging( bool );                     // set bell ringing
32       bool isRinging() const;                      // get state of bell
33    private:
34       bool ringing;                                // state of bell
35    };
36
37    #endif
```

```
38    // bell.cpp
39    // Member function definitions for class Bell
40    #include <iostream.h>
41    #include "bell.h"
42    #include "person.h"
43    #include "elevator.h"
44
45    // Constructor
46    Bell::Bell() : ringing( false ) {}
47
48    // ring the bell
49    void Bell::ding( Person * const personPtr, Elevator * const elevatorPtr )
50    {
51       setRinging( true );
52
53       if ( personPtr != 0 )
54          personPtr -> exitElevator( elevatorPtr );
55    }
56
57    // ring the bell
58    void Bell::setRinging( bool b )
59    {
60       if ( ( ringing = b ) )
61          cout << "\aBell sounded\n";
62       else
63          cout << "Bell reset\n";
64    }
65
66    // determine if bell sounded
67    bool Bell::isRinging() const { return ringing; }
```

```
68    // building.h
69    // Definition of class Building
70    #ifndef BUILDING_H
71    #define BUILDING_H
72
73    #include "floor.h"
74    #include "elevator.h"
75    #include "clock.h"
76    #include "schedule.h"
77
```

```
78    class Building {
79    public:
80       Building();                 // constructor
81       void runSimulation( int ); // start the simulation
82    private:
83       Elevator elevator;          // the elevator
84       Floor floorOne;             // first floor
85       Floor floorTwo;             // second floor
86       Scheduler scheduler;        // scheduler to create random arrivals
87       Clock clock;                // Clock to time the simulation
88    };
89
90    #endif
```

```
91    // building.cpp
92    // Member function definitions for class Building
93    #include <iostream.h>
94    #include <iomanip.h>
95    #include "building.h"
96    #include "constants.h"
97
98    // constructor
99    Building::Building()
100          : elevator( "Elevator" ), floorOne( FLOOR1, &elevator ),
101          floorTwo( FLOOR2, &elevator ) {}
102
103   // start the simulation
104   void Building::runSimulation( int simulationLength )
105   {
106      cout << "STARTING ELEVATOR SIMULATION\n";
107
108      while ( clock.getTime() < simulationLength ) {
109         cout << "Elapsed time:" << setw( 5 ) << clock.getTime() << '\n';
110
111         if ( elevator.isMoving() ) {
112            int result = elevator.shouldElevatorStop( clock.getTime() );
113
114            if ( result != NOARRIVAL )
115               elevator.stopElevator( result == FLOOR1 ? &floorOne : &floorTwo );
116         }
117
118         scheduler.checkIfPersonArriving( clock.getTime(), floorOne, floorTwo );
119
120         if ( !elevator.isMoving() )
121            elevator.shouldElevatorMove( clock.getTime(),
122                                         ( elevator.getCurrentFloor() == FLOOR1 ?
123                                         &floorOne : &floorTwo ) );
124         clock.tick();
125      }
126   }
```

```
127   // button.h
128   // Definition of class Button
129   #ifndef BUTTON_H
130   #define BUTTON_H
131
132   class Button {
133   public:
134      Button();                    // constructor
135      void setPressed( bool );     // set/reset button
136      bool isPressed() const;      // determine if button is on
```

```
137  private:
138     bool pressed;
139  };
140
141  #endif
```

```
142  // button.cpp
143  // Member function definitions for class Button
144  #include <iostream.h>
145  #include "button.h"
146
147  // constructor
148  Button::Button() : pressed( false ) {}
149
150  // turn button on/off
151  void Button::setPressed( bool b )
152  {
153     if ( ( pressed = b ) )
154        cout << " Call button pressed.\n";
155     else
156        cout << " Call button reset.\n";
157  }
158
159  // determine if button is on
160  bool Button::isPressed() const { return pressed; }
```

```
161  // clock.h
162  // Definition of class clock
163  #ifndef CLOCK_H
164  #define CLOCK_H
165
166  class Clock {
167  public:
168     Clock();              // constructor
169     void tick();          // increment time
170     int getTime() const;  // return time
171  private:
172     int time;             // current time
173  };
174
175  #endif
```

```
176  // clock.cpp
177  // Member function definitions for class Clock
178  #include "clock.h"
179
180  // Constructor
181  Clock::Clock() : time( 0 ) {}
182
183  // Increment the time by 1
184  void Clock::tick() { ++time; }
185
186  // Return the current time
187  int Clock::getTime() const { return time; }
```

```
188  // constants.h
189  // header file containing common constants
190  #ifndef CONSTANTS_H
191  #define CONSTANTS_H
192
```

```
193  const int FLOOR1 = 0;
194  const int FLOOR2 = 1;
195  const int DOWN = 0;
196  const int UP = 1;
197  const int NOARRIVAL = -1;
198
199  #endif
```

```
200  // door.h
201  // Definition of class Door
202  #ifndef DOOR_H
203  #define DOOR_H
204
205  class Door {
206  public:
207     Door( char * const );       // constructor
208     void setOpen( bool );        // open/close doors
209     bool isOpen() const;         // determine if the door is open
210  private:
211     bool open;                   // state of the door
212     char *doorName;              // name of the door
213  };
214
215  #endif
```

```
216  // door.cpp
217  // Member function definitions for class Door
218  #include <iostream.h>
219  #include "door.h"
220
221  // constructor
222  Door::Door( char * const name ) : doorName( name ), open( false ) { }
223
224  // open/close door
225  void Door::setOpen( bool b )
226  {
227     if ( ( open = b ) )
228        cout << doorName << " Door Opened.\n";
229     else
230        cout << doorName << " Door Closed.\n";
231  }
232
233  // determine if the door is open
234  bool Door::isOpen() const { return open; }
```

```
235  // elevator.h
236  // Definition of class Elevator
237  #ifndef ELEVATOR_H
238  #define ELEVATOR_H
239
240  #include "door.h"
241  #include "bell.h"
242  #include "button.h"
243  #include "floor.h"
244
245  class Person;
246  class Floor;
247  class Bell;
248
```

```
249  class Elevator {
250  public:
251     Elevator( char * const );                 // constructor
252     void pressButton( int );                  // press a destination button
253     void resetButton( int );                  // reset a destination button
254     int determineDirection() const;           // get elevator's direction
255     void passengerEnters( Person * const );   // passenger entering elevator
256     void passengerExits();                    // passenger exiting elevator
257     void shouldElevatorMove( int, Floor * const ); // should elevator move
258     bool isMoving() const;                    // is elevator moving
259     int shouldElevatorStop( int ) const;      // should elevator stop
260     void stopElevator( Floor * const );       // stop the elevator
261     void elevatorCalled( Floor * const );     // set the callState to true
262     void prepareToLeaveFloor( Floor * const ); // close door, turn off light,etc
263     int getCurrentFloor() const;              // determine the current floor
264  private:
265     Door elevatorDoor;                        // door to the elevator
266     Person *passengerPtr;                     // passenger (if there is one)
267     int currentFloor;                         // elevator's current floor
268     int direction;                            // elevator's direction
269     bool moving;                              // moving state
270     int timeOfArrivalAtNextFloor;             // when elevator will arrive
271     Bell bell;                                // bell
272     Button destinationButtons[ 2 ];           // destination buttons
273     bool callState[ 2 ];                      // has elevator been called
274     char *elevatorName;                       // name of the elevator
275  };
276
277  #endif
```

```
278  // elevator.cpp
279  // Member function definitions for class Elevator
280  #include <iostream.h>
281  #include "elevator.h"
282  #include "floor.h"
283  #include "person.h"
284  #include "constants.h"
285
286  // constructor
287  Elevator::Elevator( char * const name )
288     : elevatorDoor( name ), passengerPtr( 0 ), currentFloor( FLOOR1 ),
289       direction( UP ), moving( false ), timeOfArrivalAtNextFloor( 0 ),
290       elevatorName( name )
291  { callState[ FLOOR1 ] = callState[ FLOOR2 ] = false; }
292
293  // press the button for a specific floor
294  void Elevator::pressButton( int floorNum )
295  {
296    cout << elevatorName << "'s " << ( direction == UP ? "Down" : "Up" );
297    destinationButtons[ floorNum ].setPressed( true );
298  }
299
300  // reset the button for a specific floor
301  void Elevator::resetButton( int floorNum )
302  {
303     // reset only if a passenger is in the elevator
304     if ( passengerPtr != 0 ) {
305        cout << elevatorName << "'s " << ( direction == UP ? "Up" : "Down" );
306        destinationButtons[ floorNum ].setPressed( false );
307     }
308  }
309
```

```
310  // determine the direction of the elevator
311  int Elevator::determineDirection() const { return direction; }
312
313  // indicate that a passenger has entered the elevator; store the
314  // pointer to the person in passengerPtr.
315  void Elevator::passengerEnters( Person * const ptr ) { passengerPtr = ptr; }
316
317  // indicate that a passenger has exited the elevator; store 0 (null)
318  // in passengerPtr.
319  void Elevator::passengerExits() { passengerPtr = 0; }
320
321  // close door to elevator, close door on floor, turn off light
322  // above elevator, reset bell.
323  void Elevator::prepareToLeaveFloor( Floor * const floorPtr )
324  {
325     // reset only if the bell is ringing.
326     if ( bell.isRinging() ) {
327        bell.setRinging( false );
328        floorPtr -> turnLightOff();
329        elevatorDoor.setOpen( false );
330        floorPtr -> closeDoor();
331     }
332  }
333
334  // determine if elevator should move
335  void Elevator::shouldElevatorMove( int time, Floor * const floorPtr )
336  {
337     if ( callState[ ( currentFloor == FLOOR1 ? FLOOR2 : FLOOR1 ) ] == true ||
338          destinationButtons[ ( currentFloor ==
339                               FLOOR1 ? FLOOR2 : FLOOR1 ) ].isPressed() ) {
340        prepareToLeaveFloor( floorPtr );
341        moving = true;
342        direction = ( currentFloor == FLOOR1 ? UP : DOWN );
343        timeOfArrivalAtNextFloor = time + 5;
344
345        cout << elevatorName << " starting to move "
346             << ( direction == UP ? "Up.\n" : "Down.\n" );
347        return;
348     }
349
350     if ( elevatorDoor.isOpen() )     // if not moving, close the doors, etc.
351        prepareToLeaveFloor( floorPtr );
352
353     cout << elevatorName << " waiting on Floor "
354          << ( currentFloor + 1 ) << " for passengers.\n";
355  }
356
357  // determine if elevator is moving
358  bool Elevator::isMoving() const { return moving; }
359
360  // determine if elevator should stop
361  int Elevator::shouldElevatorStop( int time ) const
362  {
363     if ( timeOfArrivalAtNextFloor == time )
364        return currentFloor == FLOOR1 ? FLOOR2 : FLOOR1;
365     else {
366        cout << elevatorName << " moving "
367             << ( direction == UP ? " Up.\n" : " Down.\n" );
368        return NOARRIVAL;
369     }
370  }
371
```

```
372   // stop the elevator
373   void Elevator::stopElevator( Floor * const floorPtr )
374   {
375       currentFloor = floorPtr -> getFloorNumber();
376       cout << elevatorName << " Stopped on Floor "
377            << ( currentFloor + 1 ) << '\n';
378       moving = false;
379       callState[ currentFloor ] = false;
380       floorPtr -> openDoor();
381
382       // opposite floor call button should only
383       // be reset if a person pressed it
384       if ( floorPtr -> isCallButtonPressed() )
385           floorPtr -> resetCallButton();
386
387       resetButton( currentFloor );
388       elevatorDoor.setOpen( true );
389       bell.ding( passengerPtr, this );
390       floorPtr -> turnLightOn();
391   }
392
393   // set the callState to true to indicate that a call button was
394   // pressed on a floor.
395   void Elevator::elevatorCalled( Floor * const floorPtr )
396   {
397       int floor = floorPtr -> getFloorNumber();
398
399       cout << elevatorName << " called from floor " <<  ( floor + 1 ) << '\n';
400
401       // if elevator is waiting when person arrives
402       if ( !moving && currentFloor == floor ) {
403           floorPtr -> openDoor();
404           floorPtr -> resetCallButton();
405           elevatorDoor.setOpen( true );
406           floorPtr -> turnLightOn();
407       }
408       else
409           callState[ floor ] = true;
410   }
411
412   // determine the current floor
413   int Elevator::getCurrentFloor() const { return currentFloor; }
```

```
414   // floor.h
415   // Definition of class Floor
416   #ifndef FLOOR_H
417   #define FLOOR_H
418   #include "door.h"
419   #include "light.h"
420   #include "button.h"
421
422   class Person;     // forward reference
423   class Elevator;   // forward reference
424
425   class Floor {
426   public:
427       Floor( int, Elevator * const );    // constructor
428       void openDoor();                   // open the floor door
429       void closeDoor();                  // close the floor door
430       void turnLightOn();                // turn light on
431       void turnLightOff();               // turn light off
432       bool isLightOn() const;            // determine if light is on
433       void pressCallButton();            // press the button to call elevator
```

```
434       void resetCallButton();              // reset the button
435       void personArriving( Person * const ); // person arriving on floor
436       void personDeparting();              // person departing from floor
437       bool isOccupied() const;             // is there a person here
438       int getFloorNumber() const;          // retrieve the floor number
439       bool isCallButtonPressed() const; // is the floor call button pressed
440    private:
441       Person *personPtr;                   // possible person on floor
442       Door floorDoor;                      // door to elevator from floor
443       Light light;                         // light to indicate elevator arrival
444       Button callButton;                   // button to call elevator
445       int floorNumber;                     // number of the floor
446       Elevator *elevatorPtr;               // knowledge of elevator built into floor
447    };
448
449    #endif
```

```
450    // floor.cpp
451    // Member function definition for class Floor
452    #include <iostream.h>
453    #include "floor.h"
454    #include "elevator.h"
455    #include "person.h"
456    #include "constants.h"
457
458    // constructor
459    Floor::Floor( int num, Elevator * const ePtr )
460         : personPtr( 0 ), floorDoor( !num ? "Floor 1" : "Floor 2" ),
461           floorNumber( num ), elevatorPtr( ePtr ) {}
462
463    // open the floor door
464    void Floor::openDoor() { floorDoor.setOpen( true ); }
465
466    // close the floor door
467    void Floor::closeDoor() { floorDoor.setOpen( false ); }
468
469    // turn light on
470    void Floor::turnLightOn()
471    {
472       light.setOn( true );
473
474       if ( personPtr != 0 )
475          personPtr -> enterElevator( this, elevatorPtr );
476    }
477
478    // turn light off
479    void Floor::turnLightOff() { light.setOn( false ); }
480
481    // determine if light is on
482    bool Floor::isLightOn() const { return light.isOn(); }
483
484    // press the button to call elevator
485    void Floor::pressCallButton()
486    {
487       cout << "Floor " << ( floorNumber + 1 );
488       callButton.setPressed( true );         // turn on the call button
489       elevatorPtr -> elevatorCalled( this ); // elevator called
490    }
491
492    // reset the button
493    void Floor::resetCallButton()
494    {
495       cout << "Floor " << ( floorNumber + 1 );
```

```
496        callButton.setPressed( false );
497  }
498
499  // person arriving on floor
500  void Floor::personArriving( Person * const ptr ) { personPtr = ptr; }
501
502  // person departing from floor
503  void Floor::personDeparting()
504  {
505     cout << "Person " << personPtr -> getSequenceNumber()
506          << " leaving Floor " << ( floorNumber + 1 ) << '\n';
507     personPtr = 0;    // remove person
508  }
509
510  // is there a person here
511  bool Floor::isOccupied() const { return personPtr != 0; }
512
513  // retrieve the floor number
514  int Floor::getFloorNumber() const { return floorNumber; }
515
516  // get status of call button
517  bool Floor::isCallButtonPressed() const { return callButton.isPressed(); }
```

```
518  // light.h
519  // Definition of class Light
520  #ifndef LIGHT_H
521  #define LIGHT_H
522
523  class Light {
524  public:
525     Light();               // constructor
526     void setOn( bool );    // set state
527     bool isOn() const;     // determine if the light is on
528  private:
529     bool on;               // state of the light
530  };
531
532  #endif
```

```
533  // light.cpp
534  // Member function definitions for class Light
535  #include <iostream.h>
536  #include "light.h"
537
538  // constructor
539  Light::Light() : on( false ) {}
540
541  // set light to on/off
542  void Light::setOn( bool b )
543  {
544     if ( ( on = b ) )
545        cout << "Light turned on.\n";
546     else
547        cout << "Light turned off.\n";
548  }
549
550  // determine if the light is on
551  bool Light::isOn() const { return on; }
```

```
552  // person.h
553  // Definition of class Person
554  #ifndef PERSON_H
```

```
555  #define PERSON_H
556
557  #include "floor.h"
558  #include "elevator.h"
559
560  class Person {
561  public:
562     Person( Floor & );                              // constructor
563     void walkOntoFloor( Floor & );                  // walk into simulation
564     void enterElevator( Floor * const, Elevator * const ); // enter elevator
565     void exitElevator( Elevator * const );          // walk out of elevator
566     int getSequenceNumber() const;                  // get sequence number of person
567  private:
568     int startFloor;                                 // starting location
569     int endFloor;                                   // ending location
570     int sequenceNumber;                             // person number in simulation
571     static int totalPeople;                         // total # of people processed
572  };
573
574  #endif
```

```
575  // person.cpp
576  // Member function definitions for class Person
577  #include <iostream.h>
578  #include "person.h"
579  #include "constants.h"
580
581  // initialize static data member for class Person
582  int Person::totalPeople = 0;
583
584  // constructor
585  Person::Person( Floor &floor ) : sequenceNumber( ++totalPeople )
586  {
587     startFloor = floor.getFloorNumber();
588     endFloor = ( startFloor ? FLOOR1 : FLOOR2 );
589     cout << "Person " << sequenceNumber << " created\n";
590     walkOntoFloor( floor );
591  }
592
593  // walk into simulation
594  void Person::walkOntoFloor( Floor &floor )
595  {
596     floor.personArriving( this );
597     cout << "Person " << sequenceNumber << " walked onto floor "
598         << ( startFloor + 1 ) << '\n';
599     floor.pressCallButton();
600  }
601
602  // walk into elevator from floor
603  void Person::enterElevator( Floor * const floorPtr,
604                              Elevator * const elevatorPtr )
605  {
606     cout << "Person " << sequenceNumber << " entered the elevator\n";
607     floorPtr -> personDeparting();
608     elevatorPtr -> passengerEnters( this );
609     elevatorPtr -> pressButton( endFloor );
610  }
611
612  // walk out of elevator
613  void Person::exitElevator( Elevator * const elevatorPtr )
614  {
615     cout << "Person " << sequenceNumber << " exited the elevator.\n";
616     delete this;
```

```
617       elevatorPtr -> passengerExits();
618  }
619
620  // get the sequence number of person
621  int Person::getSequenceNumber() const { return sequenceNumber; }
```

```
622  // schedule.h
623  // Definition of class Scheduler
624  #ifndef SCHEDULE_H
625  #define SCHEDULE_H
626
627  #include "floor.h"
628  #include "person.h"
629
630  class Scheduler {
631  public:
632     Scheduler();                                        // constructor
633     void checkIfPersonArriving( int, Floor &, Floor & );  // determine if
634                                                         // person is arriving
635  private:
636     int arrivalTimes[ 2 ];                    // array of two arrival times
637     void createPerson( Floor & );             // create a Person
638     void scheduleNextRandomArrival( int );    // schedule next arrival
639     void rescheduleConflictingArrival( int ); // reschedule an arrival
640     int getRandom() const;                    // get random val in interval
641  };
642
643  #endif
```

```
644  // schedule.cpp
645  // Member function definitions for class Scheduler
646  #include <iostream.h>
647  #include <stdlib.h>
648  #include "schedule.h"
649  #include "person.h"
650  #include "floor.h"
651  #include "constants.h"
652
653  // constructor
654  Scheduler::Scheduler()
655  {
656     arrivalTimes[ FLOOR1 ] = getRandom();
657     arrivalTimes[ FLOOR2 ] = getRandom();
658
659     while ( arrivalTimes[ FLOOR1 ] == arrivalTimes[ FLOOR2 ] )
660        arrivalTimes[ FLOOR2 ] = getRandom();
661
662     cout << "The first person is scheduled to arrive on Floor 1 at time "
663          << arrivalTimes[ FLOOR1 ]
664          << "\nThe first person is scheduled to arrive on Floor 2 at time "
665          << arrivalTimes[ FLOOR2 ] << '\n';
666  }
667
668  // create a Person
669  void Scheduler::createPerson( Floor &floor )
670     { new Person( floor ); }
671
672  // schedule next arrival
673  void Scheduler::scheduleNextRandomArrival( int floor )
674  {
675     arrivalTimes[ floor ] += getRandom();
676
```

```
677        // If new arrival time is same as next arrival time on other floor,
678        // add one to the new arrival time.
679        if ( arrivalTimes[ floor ] == arrivalTimes[ !floor ? FLOOR2 : FLOOR1 ] )
680           ++arrivalTimes[ floor ];
681
682        cout << "Next person scheduled to arrive on floor " << ( floor + 1 )
683           << " at time " << arrivalTimes[ floor ] << '\n';
684    }
685
686    // reschedule an arrival
687    void Scheduler::rescheduleConflictingArrival( int floor )
688    {
689        while ( ++arrivalTimes[ floor ] == arrivalTimes[ !floor ? FLOOR2 : FLOOR1 ])
690           ;  // empty body
691
692        cout << "Next person to arrive on floor " << ( floor + 1 )
693           << " rescheduled for time " << arrivalTimes[ floor ] << '\n';
694    }
695
696    // get a random number in the specified interval
697    int Scheduler::getRandom() const { return ( 5 + rand() % 16 ); }
698
699    // determine if person is arriving
700    void Scheduler::checkIfPersonArriving( int time, Floor &floor1, Floor &floor2 )
701    {
702        int arrivalFloor = NOARRIVAL;
703
704        if ( arrivalTimes[ FLOOR1 ] == time )
705           arrivalFloor = FLOOR1;          // arrival on floor 1
706        else if ( arrivalTimes[ FLOOR2 ] == time )
707           arrivalFloor = FLOOR2;          // arrival on floor 2
708
709        if ( arrivalFloor == NOARRIVAL )
710           return;                         // no arrival scheduled for this time
711
712        if ( arrivalFloor == FLOOR1 )
713           if ( !floor1.isOccupied() ) {
714              createPerson( floor1 );                   // arrive at 1, go to 2
715              scheduleNextRandomArrival( FLOOR1 );      // schedule next arrival
716           }
717           else
718              rescheduleConflictingArrival( FLOOR1 );   // reschedule arrival
719
720        if ( arrivalFloor == FLOOR2 )
721           if( !floor2.isOccupied() ) {
722              createPerson( floor2 );                   // arrive at 2, go to 1
723              scheduleNextRandomArrival( FLOOR2 );      // schedule next arrival
724           }
725           else
726              rescheduleConflictingArrival( FLOOR2 );   // reschedule arrival
727    }
```

OUTPUT

```
The first person is scheduled to arrive on Floor 1 at time 14
The first person is scheduled to arrive on Floor 2 at time 8
Enter length of elevator simulation: 100
STARTING ELEVATOR SIMULATION
Elapsed time:    0
Elevator waiting on Floor 1 for passengers.
Elapsed time:    1
Elevator waiting on Floor 1 for passengers.
Elapsed time:    2
Elevator waiting on Floor 1 for passengers.
Elapsed time:    3
```

```
Elevator waiting on Floor 1 for passengers.
Elapsed time:    4
Elevator waiting on Floor 1 for passengers.
Elapsed time:    5
Elevator waiting on Floor 1 for passengers.
Elapsed time:    6
Elevator waiting on Floor 1 for passengers.
Elapsed time:    7
Elevator waiting on Floor 1 for passengers.
Elapsed time:    8
Person 1 created
Person 1 walked onto floor 2
Floor 2 Call button pressed.
Elevator called from floor 2
Next person scheduled to arrive on floor 2 at time 17
Elevator starting to move Up.
Elapsed time:     9
Elevator moving  Up.
Elapsed time:    10
Elevator moving  Up.
Elapsed time:    11
Elevator moving  Up.
Elapsed time:    12
Elevator moving  Up.
Elapsed time:    13
Elevator Stopped on Floor 2
Floor 2 Door Opened.
Floor 2 Call button reset.
Elevator Door Opened.
Bell sounded
Light turned on.
Person 1 entered the elevator
Person 1 leaving Floor 2
Elevator's Down Call button pressed.
Bell reset
Light turned off.
Elevator Door Closed.
Floor 2 Door Closed.
Elevator starting to move Down.
Elapsed time:    14
Elevator moving  Down.
Person 2 created
Person 2 walked onto floor 1
Floor 1 Call button pressed.
Elevator called from floor 1
Next person scheduled to arrive on floor 1 at time 25
Elapsed time:    15
Elevator moving  Down.
Elapsed time:    16
Elevator moving  Down.
Elapsed time:    17
Elevator moving  Down.
Person 3 created
Person 3 walked onto floor 2
Floor 2 Call button pressed.
Elevator called from floor 2
Next person scheduled to arrive on floor 2 at time 37
Elapsed time:    18
Elevator Stopped on Floor 1
Floor 1 Door Opened.
Floor 1 Call button reset.
Elevator's Down Call button reset.
Elevator Door Opened.
Bell sounded
```

```
Person 1 exited the elevator.
Light turned on.
Person 2 entered the elevator
Person 2 leaving Floor 1
Elevator's Up Call button pressed.
Bell reset
Light turned off.
Elevator Door Closed.
Floor 1 Door Closed.
Elevator starting to move Up.
Elapsed time:    19
Elevator moving  Up.
Elapsed time:    20
Elevator moving  Up.
Elapsed time:    21
Elevator moving  Up.
Elapsed time:    22
Elevator moving  Up.
Elapsed time:    23
Elevator Stopped on Floor 2
Floor 2 Door Opened.
Floor 2 Call button reset.
Elevator's Up Call button reset.
Elevator Door Opened.
Bell sounded
Person 2 exited the elevator.
Light turned on.
Person 3 entered the elevator
Person 3 leaving Floor 2
Elevator's Down Call button pressed.
Bell reset
Light turned off.
Elevator Door Closed.
Floor 2 Door Closed.
Elevator starting to move Down.
Elapsed time:    24
Elevator moving  Down.
Elapsed time:    25
Elevator moving  Down.
Person 4 created
Person 4 walked onto floor 1
Floor 1 Call button pressed.
Elevator called from floor 1
Next person scheduled to arrive on floor 1 at time 38
Elapsed time:    26
Elevator moving  Down.
Elapsed time:    27
Elevator moving  Down.
Elapsed time:    28
Elevator Stopped on Floor 1
Floor 1 Door Opened.
Floor 1 Call button reset.
Elevator's Down Call button reset.
Elevator Door Opened.
Bell sounded
Person 3 exited the elevator.
Light turned on.
Person 4 entered the elevator
Person 4 leaving Floor 1
Elevator's Up Call button pressed.
Bell reset
Light turned off.
Elevator Door Closed.
Floor 1 Door Closed.
```

```
Elevator starting to move Up.
Elapsed time:    29
Elevator moving  Up.
Elapsed time:    30
Elevator moving  Up.
Elapsed time:    31
Elevator moving  Up.
Elapsed time:    32
Elevator moving  Up.
Elapsed time:    33
Elevator Stopped on Floor 2
Floor 2 Door Opened.
Elevator's Up Call button reset.
Elevator Door Opened.
Bell sounded
Person 4 exited the elevator.
Light turned on.
Bell reset
Light turned off.
Elevator Door Closed.
Floor 2 Door Closed.
Elevator waiting on Floor 2 for passengers.
Elapsed time:    34
Elevator waiting on Floor 2 for passengers.
Elapsed time:    35
Elevator waiting on Floor 2 for passengers.
Elapsed time:    36
Elevator waiting on Floor 2 for passengers.
Elapsed time:    37
Person 5 created
Person 5 walked onto floor 2
Floor 2 Call button pressed.
Elevator called from floor 2
Floor 2 Door Opened.
Floor 2 Call button reset.
Elevator Door Opened.
Light turned on.
Person 5 entered the elevator
Person 5 leaving Floor 2
Elevator's Down Call button pressed.
Next person scheduled to arrive on floor 2 at time 48
Elevator starting to move Down.
Elapsed time:    38
Elevator moving  Down.
Person 6 created
Person 6 walked onto floor 1
Floor 1 Call button pressed.
Elevator called from floor 1
Next person scheduled to arrive on floor 1 at time 54
Elapsed time:    39
Elevator moving  Down.
Elapsed time:    40
Elevator moving  Down.
Elapsed time:    41
Elevator moving  Down.
Elapsed time:    42
Elevator Stopped on Floor 1
Floor 1 Door Opened.
Floor 1 Call button reset.
Elevator's Down Call button reset.
Elevator Door Opened.
Bell sounded
Person 5 exited the elevator.
Light turned on.
```

```
Person 6 entered the elevator
Person 6 leaving Floor 1
Elevator's Up Call button pressed.
Bell reset
Light turned off.
Elevator Door Closed.
Floor 1 Door Closed.
Elevator starting to move Up.
Elapsed time:   43
Elevator moving  Up.
Elapsed time:   44
Elevator moving  Up.
Elapsed time:   45
Elevator moving  Up.
Elapsed time:   46
Elevator moving  Up.
Elapsed time:   47
Elevator Stopped on Floor 2
Floor 2 Door Opened.
Elevator's Up Call button reset.
Elevator Door Opened.
Bell sounded
Person 6 exited the elevator.
Light turned on.
Bell reset
Light turned off.
Elevator Door Closed.
Floor 2 Door Closed.
Elevator waiting on Floor 2 for passengers.
Elapsed time:   48
Person 7 created
Person 7 walked onto floor 2
Floor 2 Call button pressed.
Elevator called from floor 2
Floor 2 Door Opened.
Floor 2 Call button reset.
Elevator Door Opened.
Light turned on.
Person 7 entered the elevator
Person 7 leaving Floor 2
Elevator's Down Call button pressed.
Next person scheduled to arrive on floor 2 at time 57
Elevator starting to move Down.
Elapsed time:   49
Elevator moving  Down.
Elapsed time:   50
Elevator moving  Down.
Elapsed time:   51
Elevator moving  Down.
Elapsed time:   52
Elevator moving  Down.
Elapsed time:   53
Elevator Stopped on Floor 1
Floor 1 Door Opened.
Elevator's Down Call button reset.
Elevator Door Opened.
Bell sounded
Person 7 exited the elevator.
Light turned on.
Bell reset
Light turned off.
Elevator Door Closed.
Floor 1 Door Closed.
Elevator waiting on Floor 1 for passengers.
```

```
Elapsed time:    54
Person 8 created
Person 8 walked onto floor 1
Floor 1 Call button pressed.
Elevator called from floor 1
Floor 1 Door Opened.
Floor 1 Call button reset.
Elevator Door Opened.
Light turned on.
Person 8 entered the elevator
Person 8 leaving Floor 1
Elevator's Up Call button pressed.
Next person scheduled to arrive on floor 1 at time 70
Elevator starting to move Up.
Elapsed time:    55
Elevator moving  Up.
Elapsed time:    56
Elevator moving  Up.
Elapsed time:    57
Elevator moving  Up.
Person 9 created
Person 9 walked onto floor 2
Floor 2 Call button pressed.
Elevator called from floor 2
Next person scheduled to arrive on floor 2 at time 74
Elapsed time:    58
Elevator moving  Up.
Elapsed time:    59
Elevator Stopped on Floor 2
Floor 2 Door Opened.
Floor 2 Call button reset.
Elevator's Up Call button reset.
Elevator Door Opened.
Bell sounded
Person 8 exited the elevator.
Light turned on.
Person 9 entered the elevator
Person 9 leaving Floor 2
Elevator's Down Call button pressed.
Bell reset
Light turned off.
Elevator Door Closed.
Floor 2 Door Closed.
Elevator starting to move Down.
Elapsed time:    60
Elevator moving  Down.
Elapsed time:    61
Elevator moving  Down.
Elapsed time:    62
Elevator moving  Down.
Elapsed time:    63
Elevator moving  Down.
Elapsed time:    64
Elevator Stopped on Floor 1
Floor 1 Door Opened.
Elevator's Down Call button reset.
Elevator Door Opened.
Bell sounded
Person 9 exited the elevator.
Light turned on.
Bell reset
Light turned off.
Elevator Door Closed.
Floor 1 Door Closed.
```

```
Elevator waiting on Floor 1 for passengers.
Elapsed time:    65
Elevator waiting on Floor 1 for passengers.
Elapsed time:    66
Elevator waiting on Floor 1 for passengers.
Elapsed time:    67
Elevator waiting on Floor 1 for passengers.
Elapsed time:    68
Elevator waiting on Floor 1 for passengers.
Elapsed time:    69
Elevator waiting on Floor 1 for passengers.
Elapsed time:    70
Person 10 created
Person 10 walked onto floor 1
Floor 1 Call button pressed.
Elevator called from floor 1
Floor 1 Door Opened.
Floor 1 Call button reset.
Elevator Door Opened.
Light turned on.
Person 10 entered the elevator
Person 10 leaving Floor 1
Elevator's Up Call button pressed.
Next person scheduled to arrive on floor 1 at time 86
Elevator starting to move Up.
Elapsed time:    71
Elevator moving  Up.
Elapsed time:    72
Elevator moving  Up.
Elapsed time:    73
Elevator moving  Up.
Elapsed time:    74
Elevator moving  Up.
Person 11 created
Person 11 walked onto floor 2
Floor 2 Call button pressed.
Elevator called from floor 2
Next person scheduled to arrive on floor 2 at time 92
Elapsed time:    75
Elevator Stopped on Floor 2
Floor 2 Door Opened.
Floor 2 Call button reset.
Elevator's Up Call button reset.
Elevator Door Opened.
Bell sounded
Person 10 exited the elevator.
Light turned on.
Person 11 entered the elevator
Person 11 leaving Floor 2
Elevator's Down Call button pressed.
Bell reset
Light turned off.
Elevator Door Closed.
Floor 2 Door Closed.
Elevator starting to move Down.
Elapsed time:    76
Elevator moving  Down.
Elapsed time:    77
Elevator moving  Down.
Elapsed time:    78
Elevator moving  Down.
Elapsed time:    79
Elevator moving  Down.
Elapsed time:    80
```

```
Elevator Stopped on Floor 1
Floor 1 Door Opened.
Elevator's Down Call button reset.
Elevator Door Opened.
Bell sounded
Person 11 exited the elevator.
Light turned on.
Bell reset
Light turned off.
Elevator Door Closed.
Floor 1 Door Closed.
Elevator waiting on Floor 1 for passengers.
Elapsed time:    81
Elevator waiting on Floor 1 for passengers.
Elapsed time:    82
Elevator waiting on Floor 1 for passengers.
Elapsed time:    83
Elevator waiting on Floor 1 for passengers.
Elapsed time:    84
Elevator waiting on Floor 1 for passengers.
Elapsed time:    85
Elevator waiting on Floor 1 for passengers.
Elapsed time:    86
Person 12 created
Person 12 walked onto floor 1
Floor 1 Call button pressed.
Elevator called from floor 1
Floor 1 Door Opened.
Floor 1 Call button reset.
Elevator Door Opened.
Light turned on.
Person 12 entered the elevator
Person 12 leaving Floor 1
Elevator's Up Call button pressed.
Next person scheduled to arrive on floor 1 at time 97
Elevator starting to move Up.
Elapsed time:    87
Elevator moving  Up.
Elapsed time:    88
Elevator moving  Up.
Elapsed time:    89
Elevator moving  Up.
Elapsed time:    90
Elevator moving  Up.
Elapsed time:    91
Elevator Stopped on Floor 2
Floor 2 Door Opened.
Elevator's Up Call button reset.
Elevator Door Opened.
Bell sounded
Person 12 exited the elevator.
Light turned on.
Bell reset
Light turned off.
Elevator Door Closed.
Floor 2 Door Closed.
Elevator waiting on Floor 2 for passengers.
Elapsed time:    92
Person 13 created
Person 13 walked onto floor 2
Floor 2 Call button pressed.
Elevator called from floor 2
Floor 2 Door Opened.
Floor 2 Call button reset.
```

```
Elevator Door Opened.
Light turned on.
Person 13 entered the elevator
Person 13 leaving Floor 2
Elevator's Down Call button pressed.
Next person scheduled to arrive on floor 2 at time 111
Elevator starting to move Down.
Elapsed time:   93
Elevator moving  Down.
Elapsed time:   94
Elevator moving  Down.
Elapsed time:   95
Elevator moving  Down.
Elapsed time:   96
Elevator moving  Down.
Elapsed time:   97
Elevator Stopped on Floor 1
Floor 1 Door Opened.
Elevator's Down Call button reset.
Elevator Door Opened.
Bell sounded
Person 13 exited the elevator.
Light turned on.
Person 14 created
Person 14 walked onto floor 1
Floor 1 Call button pressed.
Elevator called from floor 1
Floor 1 Door Opened.
Floor 1 Call button reset.
Elevator Door Opened.
Light turned on.
Person 14 entered the elevator
Person 14 leaving Floor 1
Elevator's Up Call button pressed.
Next person scheduled to arrive on floor 1 at time 116
Bell reset
Light turned off.
Elevator Door Closed.
Floor 1 Door Closed.
Elevator starting to move Up.
Elapsed time:   98
Elevator moving  Up.
Elapsed time:   99
Elevator moving  Up.
```

Appendix

C & C++ Multimedia Cyber Classroom: Solutions Provided on CD

This appendix contains the complete list of solutions provided on the *C & C++ Multimedia Cyber Classroom* CD-ROM. This will help instructors avoid the exercises for which students have solutions if they purchase the Cyber Classroom product. Note that key exercises like the Simpletron Simulator (Chapter 5), the compiler (Chapter 15) and the object-oriented elevator simulator (Chapters 1–7) are not provided on the CD.

Chapter 1:   1.11, 1.13, 1.16, 1.19, 1.21, 1.24, 1.25, 1.30, 1.31, 1.34, 1.37

Chapter 2:   2.14, 2.16, 2.18, 2.20, 2.24, 2.26, 2.29, 2.31, 2.33, 2.37a/b, 2.40, 2.43, 2.45, 2.48, 2.49, 2.54, 2.58, 2.60, 2.63

Chapter 3:   3.12, 3.13, 3.16, 3.18, 3.20, 3.22, 3.27, 3.29, 3.33, 3.35, 3.38, 3.40, 3.44, 3.48, 3.53, 3.56, 3.58

Chapter 4:   4.10, 4.12, 4.15, 4.20, 4.23, 4.29, 4.30, 4.33, 4.36, 4.38

Chapter 5:   5.9, 5.12, 5.22, 5.25, 5.26, 5.27, 5.30, 5.31, 5.33, 5.37, 5.42a/b/c, 5.46

Chapter 6:   6.5, 6.7, 6.8, 6.12, 6.16

Chapter 7:   7.7, 7.8

Chapter 8:   8.12, 8.15, 8.19

Chapter 9:   9.10, 9.12

Chapter 10: 10.6, 10.7, 10.14

Chapter 11: 11.7, 11.9, 11.10, 11.12, 11.15, 11.18

Chapter 12: 12.3, 12.7, 12.9, 12.14, 12.15, 12.19, 12.23

Chapter 13: 13.21, 13.27, 13.29, 13.31, 13.34, 13.42, 13.42

Chapter 14: 14.7, 14.12, 14.14

Chapter 15: 15.6, 15.8, 15.10, 15.11, 15.17, 15.20, 15.24

Chapter 16: 16.9, 16.12, 16.17, 16.21, 16.22, 16.26, 16.30

Chapter 17: 17.4, 17.6, 17.8 ,17.10

Chapter 18: 18.3, 18.8, 18.10

Chapter 19: 19.4, 19.5, 19.8, 19.11, 19.12, 19.21, 19.23

Chapter 20: 20.15

Chapter 21: 21.3, 21.4, 21.7, 21.8, 21.13, 21.15

Program Disk
C++ How to Program, Second Edition
Deitel/Deitel/Nieto

YOU SHOULD CAREFULLY READ THE FOLLOWING TERMS AND CONDITIONS BEFORE USING THIS DISKETTE PACKAGE. USING THIS DISKETTE PACKAGE INDICATES YOUR ACCEPTANCE OF THESE TERMS AND CONDITIONS.

Prentice-Hall, Inc. provides this program and licenses its use. You assume responsibility for the selection of the program to achieve your intended results, and for the installation, use, and results obtained from the program.

LICENSE GRANT

You hereby accept a nonexclusive, nontransferable, permanent license to install and use the program ON A SINGLE COMPUTER at any given time. You may copy the program solely for backup or archival purposes in support of your use of the program on the single computer. You may not modify, translate, disassemble, decompile, or reverse engineer the program, in whole or in part.

LIMITED WARRANTY

THE PROGRAM IS PROVIDED "AS IS" WITHOUT WARRANTY OF ANY KIND, EITHER EXPRESSED OR IMPLIED, INCLUDING, BUT NOT LIMITED TO, THE IMPLIED WARRANTIES OF MERCHANTABILITY AND FITNESS FOR A PARTICULAR PURPOSE. THE ENTIRE RISK AS TO THE QUALITY AND PERFORMANCE OF THE PROGRAM IS WITH YOU. SHOULD THE PROGRAM PROVE DEFECTIVE, YOU (AND NOT PRENTICE HALL, INC. OR ANY AUTHORIZED DISTRIBUTOR) ASSUME THE ENTIRE COST OF ALL NECESSARY SERVICING, REPAIR, OR CORRECTION. NO ORAL OR WRITTEN INFORMATION OR ADVICE GIVEN BY PRENTICE-HALL, INC., ITS DEALERS, DISTRIBUTORS, OR AGENTS SHALL CREATE A WARRANTY OR INCREASE THE SCOPE OF THIS WARRANTY.

SOME STATES DO NOT ALLOW THE EXCLUSION OF IMPLIED WARRANTIES, SO THE ABOVE EXCLUSION MAY NOT APPLY TO YOU. THIS WARRANTY GIVE YOU SPECIFIC LEGAL RIGHTS AND YOU MAY ALSO HAVE OTHER RIGHTS THAT VARY FROM STATE TO STATE.

Prentice-Hall, Inc. does not warrant that the function contained in the program with meet your requirements or that the operation of the program will be uninterrupted or error free.

However, Prentice-Hall, Inc. warrants the diskette(s) on which the program is furnished to be free from defects in materials and workmanship under normal use for a period of ninety (90) days from the date of delivery to you as evidenced by a copy of your receipt.

The program should not be relied on as the sole basis to solve a problem whose incorrect solution could result in injury to person or property. If the program is employed in such a manner, it is at the user's own risk and Prentice-Hall, Inc. explicitly disclaims all liability for such misuse.

LIMITATION OF REMEDIES

Prentice-Hall's entire liability and your exclusive remedy shall be:

1.   the replacement of any diskette not meeting Prentice-Hall, Inc.'s "Limited Warranty" and that is returned to Prentice-Hall, or
2.   if Prentice-Hall is unable to deliver a replacement diskette or cassette that is free of defects in materials or workmanship, you may terminate this Agreement by returning the program.

IN NO EVENT WILL PRENTICE-HALL BE LIABLE TO YOU FOR ANY DAMAGES, INCLUDING ANY LOST PROFITS, LOST SAVINGS, OR OTHER INCIDENTAL OR CONSEQUENTIAL DAMAGES ARISING OUT OF THE USE OR INABILITY TO USE SUCH PROGRAM EVEN IF PRENTICE-HALL OR AN AUTHORIZED DISTRIBUTOR HAS BEEN ADVISED OF THE POSSIBILITY OF SUCH DAMAGES, OR FOR ANY CLAIM BY ANY OTHER PARTY.

SOME STATES DO NOT ALLOW THE LIMITATION OR EXCLUSION OF LIABILITY FOR INCIDENTAL OR CONSEQUENTIAL DAMAGES, SO THE ABOVE LIMITATION MAY NOT APPLY TO YOU.

GENERAL

You may not sublicense, assign, or transfer the license or the program except as expressly provided in this Agreement. Any attempt otherwise to sublicense, assign, or transfer any of the rights, duties, or obligations hereunder is void.

This Agreement will be governed by the laws of the State of New York.

Should you have any questions concerning this Agreement, you may contact Prentice-Hall, Inc. by writing to:

Prentice Hall
Engineering, Science, and Math Division
One Lake Street
Upper Saddle River, NJ 07458

YOU ACKNOWLEDGE THAT YOU HAVE READ THIS AGREEMENT, UNDERSTAND IT, AND AGREE TO BE BOUND BY ITS TERMS AND CONDITIONS. YOU FURTHER AGREE THAT IT IS THE COMPLETE AND EXCLUSIVE STATEMENT OF THE AGREEMENT BETWEEN US THAT SUPERSEDES ANY PROPOSAL OR PRIOR AGREEMENT, ORAL OR WRITTEN, AND ANY OTHER COMMUNICATIONS BETWEEN US RELATING TO THE SUBJECT MATTER OF THIS AGREEMENT.

NOTICE TO GOVERNMENT END USERS

The program is provided with RESTRICTED RIGHTS. Use, duplication or disclosure by the government is subject to restrictions set forth in subdivision (b)(3)(iii) of the Rights in Technical Data and Computer Software clause 252.227-7013.

ISBN 0-13-565912-4